HISTORY IN DISPUTE

ADVISORY BOARD

HISTORY IN DISPUTE

Volume 1

The Cold War:
First Series

Edited by Benjamin Frankel

A MANLY, INC. BOOK

ST. JAMES PRESS

AN IMPRINT OF THE GALE GROUP

DETROIT • SAN FRANCISCO • LONDON
BOSTON • WOODBRIDGE, CT

HISTORY IN DISPUTE

 ## Volume 1 ▪ The Cold War: First Series

Matthew J. Bruccoli and Richard Layman, *Editorial Directors*

Karen L. Rood, *Senior Editor*

Copyright ©2000
St. James Press
27500 Drake Road
Farmington Hills, MI 48331

ISBN 1-55862-395-7

St. James Press is an imprint of The Gale Group

Printed in the United States of America

10 9 8 7

CONTENTS

CONTENTS

CONTENTS

CONTENTS

CONTENTS

FOREWORD

Almost as soon as the Second World War ended in 1945, the Soviet Union and the Western powers became embroiled in conflict. The cold war, as that conflict soon came to be called, ended up dominating international politics for nearly half a century.

It was not just that the cold war, for most of the recent past, lay at the heart of international political life. It had a profound impact on many other aspects of life as well. Domestic politics and culture were deeply affected, and the cold war had a massive and far-reaching influence on economic development and on social change in general, not just within the two great blocs that were directly involved but in other areas of the world as well.

The impact was profound in large part because what was at stake was absolutely unprecedented. It was clear to everyone at the time that matters might conceivably get out of hand and that, if they did, the result might well be a third world war. What made this threat so important was the simple fact that world war for most of this period meant general nuclear war.

The specter of all-out war was not just a theoretical possibility. The threat of a thermonuclear holocaust was at times quite real. This was, of course, the only period in human history when international politics was conducted against such a horrifying backdrop—the only time when nations had to face up to the possibility that the policies their governments pursued might actually lead to a war that might wipe out whole societies, indeed whole civilizations, if not the human race itself.

The cold war, then, was certainly an extraordinary episode in human history, but is it now just history? Is there any real point to studying it today? Scholars, of course, might be interested in trying to understand what the cold war was about—what was generating the conflict and why it ran its course the way it did—but given that the

cold war is over, are these now issues of purely historical interest?

The answer is no: in grappling with these issues of historical interpretation we are also trying to understand something more general. We are trying to get some insight into how international politics works and into what makes for good foreign and military policy.

Historical debates often turn on issues of judgment. Is a given policy good or bad? Were the particular choices made in a crisis right or wrong? What is to be made, for example, of President John F. Kennedy's handling of the Cuban Missile Crisis in 1962? Would alternative policies have been any better? What about the policy President Franklin Delano Roosevelt pursued at the Yalta Conference in early 1945? Is the Yalta Agreement to be condemned as a "death warrant for Poland"? Was it a reasonable accommodation to Soviet power in Europe? Or was it something else?

The great debate among scholars about the origins of the cold war is, at least traditionally, an argument about blame—not just about whether the Soviet Union or the United States was primarily responsible for the conflict but, perhaps even more, about how specific American policies are to be judged. Were the Americans too ready to condemn Soviet policy? Should they have been more understanding? Or was the U.S. government, at least at the start, too indulgent, too ready to "appease" Russia—above all at Yalta? If American policy was ill-advised—in either sense, or, indeed, in both senses, albeit at different times—was this a cause of the cold war? Those who say it was are, in effect, saying that other policies would have been better. Those claims about better alternatives both reflect and, if they are well reasoned, support more-basic claims about what policy should be—about the principles that allow us to distinguish good policy from bad policy in general.

To be sure, historical interpretation is not always essentially about judgment. Sometimes the goal is simply to understand what is going on. Sometimes this search for meaning yields an interpretation where neither side is blamed as an aggressor or as a bungler—where conflict is seen as rooted in the clash of essentially defensive policies. Even in such cases, however, the historical analysis sets the stage for thinking about basic issues of policy: were any alternatives possible at all, any courses of action that could have led to better outcomes?

Of course, the assumption here is still that the cold war, like conflict in general, was a bad thing. One can go yet deeper: even that assumption can be challenged. Perhaps the cold-war system was actually better than any alternatives that could realistically have been constructed. To take the alternative most commonly cited: maybe the cold-war system in Europe was actually better than a system based on a reunified, but demilitarized and neutralized, Germany. Maybe a system based on a certain degree of tension—not too much, but not too little either—locked everyone into the status quo and thus provided greater stability than any realistically conceivable alternative. Once again, the fundamental issue here has to do with the assessment of alternatives, and thus with the basic issue of whether anything can be said of a general nature about why certain kinds of policies are better than others.

Even if, in this sense, a favorable judgment is passed on the cold war as a whole, there is plenty of room for disagreement about secondary issues. Even if, in other words, the conclusion is reached that with regard to the core of the system at least—the part of it that had to do with relations among the major powers—the cold-war structure was essentially the best the world could do, one can still argue at length about aspects of the cold war that had more to do with the periphery than with the core. Thus, there are questions about whether the United States overdid it in its policies toward the Third World—questions about whether the United States overdid it with the Central Intelligence Agency (CIA) and covert operations. There are questions about whether the involvement in Vietnam, for example, was more or less inevitable given the basic premises of U.S. policy, or

whether the Vietnam War could have been avoided if certain less basic things had been different—if, for example, President Kennedy had lived to serve a second term.

Finally, there is one major set of issues somewhat different from the ones already mentioned and also having to do with understanding how the system worked. The issues here relate to the military side of the story and its relation to the political core. What role, for example, did the strategic balance play in influencing each side's behavior at key points during the cold war? In what sense, in the nuclear age, can "strategic superiority" even be said to exist? Was either side ever really serious about strategies of nuclear escalation? Was "massive retaliation," for example, simply a gigantic bluff? The basic issue here is fundamental: how does international politics work in the nuclear age? Given that nuclear weapons cannot be uninvented, this question also is bound to have a certain continuing importance.

Such issues can actually be studied. The basic technique is to focus on particular episodes and analyze them in some depth. Did nuclear threats, for example, play a decisive role in 1953 in ending the Korean War? Was the Eisenhower administration serious about nuclear escalation at that time—or, indeed, in any of the crises the world went through in this period, crises over Indochina, over the Taiwan Straits, and over Berlin? What did policy during each of these episodes have to do with the administration's understanding of the strategic balance at those points?

Historical analysis thus provides us with a kind of laboratory for thinking about basic issues of international politics. The historical issues are, of course, quite interesting in their own right. In grappling with them, however, we are also working out our thinking on the most fundamental issues of policy. In assessing the policies of the past and in considering what policy should have been at key points during the cold war, we are also trying to work out the basic principles that should govern our thinking about the most central issues of policy, principles that might help guide us through the present and into the future.

–MARC TRACHTENBERG, UNIVERSITY OF PENNSYLVANIA

FOREWORD

PREFACE

William Faulkner said that, "here in the South, the past is not dead; it is not even past." So it is with the cold war; it ended nearly a decade ago, but the debates over its underlying themes and dramatic events continue unabated. One reason for this ongoing intellectual campaign is the opening to Western scholars of the archives in Russia and other former Eastern-bloc countries. With more information comes more knowledge (if not always more wisdom). Another reason is the growing distance from the events themselves; with added distance come more informed views on and more accurate assessments of both major and mundane occurrences that dominated international life for more than four decades.

The greater availability of information has not dulled the debates, however. In fact, these debates appear to have intensified, and additional forums—at least two new journals dedicated to cold-war studies—have been created to accommodate them. It is not difficult to understand why interest in the cold war should continue. The cold war dominated not only international politics but domestic issues as well. Since early on it was perceived as more than traditional competition between two states jostling with one another over power and influence. Many took the rivalry between the United States and the Soviet Union to be a struggle between two ways of life, two governing philosophies, two political cultures. This belief colored the debates about the cold war as it was unfolding, infusing the different positions people took with intensity and passion not normally found in discussion of international politics. These passions found their way into domestic debates as well, giving rise, in the late 1940s, to a climate of suspicion and hostility which, some claim, threatened the civil liberties of Americans.

The format of this volume reflects the nature of its subject. A hotly debated topic may best be presented through a series of disciplined and focused debates. One important purpose is to use comparative analysis as a tool to examine the validity of scholarly and historical arguments. With the greater availability of information, the field of cold-war stud-

ies has become even more dynamic, with almost every issue becoming the subject of a charged and energetic debate continually fueled by the discovery of new documents, the release of new memoirs, the reevaluation of older materials, and their synthesis into new works of scholarship.

In these circumstances it is often difficult, and perhaps even ill-advised, to accept any one interpretation as truth or any one work as authoritative. This cautionary approach is problematic because the ideological battles that characterized the cold war in the realm of foreign affairs—but not less so domestically—undeniably contribute to the way in which policy is formed today. Without a clear understanding of how the world of the present came to exist, and how that of yesterday ceased to be, it is difficult to see how people who think about foreign policy in the future will approach their subject with clarity and insight. We hope that the chapters of this volume, addressing some of the most contentious issues in cold-war studies, will be instructive. We believe that the clash of ideas is a healthy exercise, and that scholarship is advanced by engaging in scholarly warfare: let writers make the best cases they can for their points of view; when the dust settles and the smoke clears, all may be wiser. The essays collected in this volume thus do not represent the historical "truth," but rather approaches to such truth. The more we discuss these issues; the more we debate them and argue about them; the more we bring new materials to bear on such discussion, the closer we get to this elusive goal. By examining the competing arguments (not all of which have only two sides) directly and evaluating their relative merits, we thus hope to reveal the path to truth.

The essays in this volume do not necessarily represent the personal views of the authors who wrote them. In the spirit of scholarly argumentation and inquiry, we have, at times, asked authors to present points of view with which they may personally disagree. In the best tradition of scholarship, many agreed.

—BENJAMIN FRANKEL, with
PAUL DU QUENOY

CHRONOLOGY

Boldface type refers to a pertaining chapter title.

1939

23 AUGUST: The Soviet Union and Nazi Germany sign a nonaggression pact, the Molotov-Ribbentrop Agreement. (See **Hitler and Stalin**)

1 SEPTEMBER: Germany invades Poland. The Second World War begins.

30 NOVEMBER 1939 – 12 MARCH 1940: The Soviet Union and Finland fight the Winter War. (See **Finlandization**)

1940

27 SEPTEMBER: Germany, Italy, and Japan sign the Tripartite Pact, creating the Axis alliance.

1941

7 DECEMBER: Japanese planes attack U.S. forces at Pearl Harbor, Hawaii.

8 DECEMBER: The United States enters the Second World War.

11 DECEMBER: Germany and Italy declare war on the United States; the United States reciprocates.

1942

1 JANUARY: Twenty-six nations, led by the United States, Great Britain, and the Soviet Union, affirm the Atlantic Charter, issued by the United States and Great Britain in August 1941, pledging military and economic action against the Axis powers.

1943

30 OCTOBER: Allied foreign ministers meeting in Moscow call for an international organization to foster the principle of "sovereign equality of all peace-loving states." (See **Universalism**)

1944

21 AUGUST – 7 OCTOBER: The Dumbarton Oaks Conference lays the foundation for the United Nations. (See **Universalism**)

1945

4–11 FEBRUARY: U.S. president Franklin Delano Roosevelt, British prime minister Winston Churchill, and Soviet premier Joseph Stalin meet at **Yalta**.

6 MARCH: Petru Groza forms a communist-dominated government in Romania. (See **Finlandization, Origins, Yalta Agreement**)

25 APRIL – 26 JUNE: At the San Francisco Conference delegates from fifty nations create the United Nations Organization (UN). (See **Universalism**)

7 MAY: Germany surrenders unconditionally to the Allies.

16 JULY: The United States successfully explodes the first atomic bomb at the Alamogordo test site in New Mexico.

17 JULY: U.S. president Harry S Truman, Churchill, and Stalin arrive at Potsdam. (See **Origins**)

6 & 9 AUGUST: The United States drops the first two atomic bombs on Hiroshima and Nagasaki, Japan.

14 AUGUST: Japan announces its unconditional surrender. The Second World War ends.

2 SEPTEMBER: Ho Chi Minh proclaims the independence of **Vietnam** from France.

18 NOVEMBER: The Communist Party wins communist-controlled elections in Bulgaria. (See **Finlandization, Origins, Yalta Agreement**)

29 NOVEMBER: The Yugoslav assembly, elected on 11 November, proclaims the Federal People's Republic of Yugoslavia and

declares Marshal Josip Broz Tito prime minister.

1946

JANUARY–APRIL: The Soviet Union prompts a crisis in Iran by attempting to create an "autonomous" Azerbaijani republic that includes part of Iran. A military confrontation between the Americans and the Soviets is threatened. (See **Origins**)

9 FEBRUARY: Stalin makes his "Two Camps" speech, declaring the impossibility of Soviet coexistence with the West. (See **Ideology**)

22 FEBRUARY: George F. Kennan transmits his "Long Telegram" from Moscow to Truman. (See **Ideology, Origins, Universalism**)

5 MARCH: Churchill gives his "iron curtain" speech at Westminster College in Fulton, Missouri. (See **Ideology, Origins**)

28 MARCH: The Acheson-Lilienthal Plan, calling for international control of nuclear energy, is released. (See **Baruch Plan, Nonproliferation**)

14 JUNE: Bernard Baruch presents the **Baruch Plan** for international control of nuclear materials and destruction of nuclear arsenals to the first meeting of the UN Atomic Energy Commission.

8 SEPTEMBER: The Republic of Bulgaria is declared, and the Bulgarian monarchy is abolished. (See **Finlandization, Origins, Yalta Agreement**)

19 NOVEMBER: The Communist Party wins communist-controlled elections in Romania. (See **Finlandization, Origins, Yalta Agreement**)

23 NOVEMBER: France bombs Haiphong as the first military move to retain control of its colonies in Indochina. (See **Vietnam War**)

2 DECEMBER: The Americans and British agree to an economic merger of their zones of occupations in Germany. (See **Berlin Crises, Marshall Plan**)

1947

19 JANUARY: The Communist Party wins communist-controlled elections in Poland. (See **Origins**)

FEBRUARY: Hungarians abolish their monarchy and declare their country a republic. (See **Origins**)

12 MARCH: Truman announces his Truman Doctrine, declaring that Americans will support "free peoples who are resisting subjugation by armed minorities or by outside pressures," and requests $400 million in economic and military aid for Greece and Turkey. (See **Containment, Militarizing Containment, Origins**)

22 MARCH: Truman bans communists from serving in the U.S. government. (See **Civil Liberties**)

22 MAY: Truman signs a Greek-Turkish aid bill. (See **Containment, Militarizing Containment**)

5 JUNE: In a commencement address at Harvard University, Secretary of State George C. Marshall proposes the **Marshall Plan** for economic assistance to democracies of Europe.

JULY: "The Sources of Soviet Conduct," by "X" (Kennan), appears in *Foreign Affairs*, recommending U.S. **containment** of the Soviet Union. (See **Ideology, Militarizing Containment, Universalism**)

12 JULY: The **Marshall Plan** conference opens in Paris and is boycotted by the Soviet Union and eastern European countries.

26 JULY: Congress passes the National Security Act, creating the Central Intelligence Agency (CIA) and the National Security Council (NSC). (See **CIA Operations, Containment, Militarizing Containment**)

31 AUGUST: A Communist-led coalition wins a majority in Hungarian elections. (See **Finlandization, Origins, Yalta Agreement**)

2 SEPTEMBER: The United States and Latin American countries sign the Inter-American Treaty of Reciprocal Assistance in Rio de Janeiro, Brazil.

23 OCTOBER: Actor Ronald Reagan testifies before the House Un-American Activities Committee (HUAC) on communist influence in Hollywood. (See **Civil Liberties**)

30 OCTOBER: Brigadier General Leslie Groves, director of the Manhattan Project, testifies that the Soviet Union needs twenty years to develop its own atomic bomb. (See **Nuclear Preemption, Nuclear Spying**)

4 DECEMBER: Bulgaria alters its name to People's Republic of Bulgaria. (See **Origins**)

30 DECEMBER: King Michael of Romania abdicates, and the People's Republic of Romania is established. (See **Finlandization, Origins, Yalta Agreement**)

1948

16 FEBRUARY: A People's Republic is declared in North Korea.

25 FEBRUARY: A bloodless communist coup succeeds in Czechoslovakia. (See **Finlandization, Origins, Yalta Agreement**)

17 MARCH: Great Britain, France, Belgium, the Netherlands, and Luxembourg sign the Brussels Treaty, the precursor of the West-

ern European Union (WEU) and the North Atlantic Treaty Organization (**NATO**).

30 MARCH – 2 MAY: The Organization of American States is created during the Bogotá Conference.

6 APRIL: Finland signs a nonaggression treaty with the Soviet Union. (See **Finlandization**)

14 MAY: **Israel** proclaims its statehood and is invaded by seven Arab states the next day.

18 JUNE: Currency reforms are implemented in the American, British, and French occupation zones of Germany. (See **Berlin Crises**)

24 JUNE: The Soviet Union blockades land access to Berlin, and the United States responds by airlifting supplies to the city. (See **Berlin Crises, Nuclear Preemption**)

28 JUNE: Yugoslavia is expelled from the Cominform.

30 JUNE: British forces leave Palestine.

3 AUGUST: Whittaker Chambers testifies before the House Un-American Activities Committee (HUAC) and names Alger Hiss as a Soviet spy. (See **Civil Liberties**)

15 AUGUST: The Republic of Korea (South Korea) is established.

9 SEPTEMBER: The Democratic People's Republic of Korea (North Korea) is established.

15 DECEMBER: Hiss is indicted by a U.S. grand jury on two counts of perjury. He is eventually found guilty on 21 January 1950. (See **Civil Liberties**)

1949

7 JANUARY: Secretary of State Marshall resigns after disagreements with Truman over U.S. interests in regard to **Israel** and its Arab neighbors.

8 FEBRUARY: Congressmen Karl E. Mundt (R-South Dakota) and Richard M. Nixon (R-California) introduce a bill to register communists in the United States. (See **Civil Liberties**)

15 FEBRUARY: Secreary of State Dean Acheson refuses new aid to Chinese Nationalists. (See **China Hands**)

23 FEBRUARY: The National Security Council announces plans to study domestic communist subversion. (See **Civil Liberties**)

4 APRIL: Belgium, Canada, Denmark, France, Great Britain, Iceland, Italy, Luxembourg, the Netherlands, Norway, Portugal, and the United States form the North Atlantic Treaty Organization (**NATO**).

23 APRIL: The Truman administration cancels plans to build the supercarrier *United States,*

sparking the **Admirals' Revolt** among top naval officers.

2 MAY: Chinese Nationalist leader Chiang Kai-shek flees to Formosa (Taiwan). (See **China Hands**)

5 MAY: The Chinese communists and the North Koreans sign a mutual-defense treaty. The Federal Republic of Germany (West Germany) is established.

12 MAY: The Berlin Blockade ends; the U.S. airlift continues until 30 September. (See **Berlin Crises**)

30 MAY: The Soviet ambassador to the UN, Andrey Y. Vyshinsky, rejects a Western proposal for German reunification. The German Democratic Republic (East Germany) declares its statehood.

19 JUNE: Communist leader Mao Tse-tung declares victory in China. (See **China Hands**)

5 AUGUST: The State Department issues a white paper explaining the loss of China. (See **China Hands**)

29 AUGUST: The Soviet Union explodes its first atomic bomb. (See **Nuclear Deterrence, Nuclear Preemption, Nuclear Spying, Nuclear Weapons**)

1 OCTOBER: The People's Republic of China is established. (See **China Hands**)

8 DECEMBER: Chinese Nationalists abandon the mainland and flee to Formosa (Taiwan). (See **China Hands, Quemoy and Matsu**)

30 DECEMBER: Truman decides not to use American troops to defend Taiwan. (See **Containment**)

1950

JANUARY: The United States releases $1 billion in military aid to Western Europe. (See **Marshall Plan**)

11 JANUARY: The United States approves a plan to aid Tito if Yugoslavia is attacked by pro-Soviet eastern European armies.

3 FEBRUARY: Physicist Klaus Fuchs is arrested in London for spying for the Soviet Union. (See **Nuclear Spying**)

9 FEBRUARY: Senator Joseph R. McCarthy (R-Wisconsin) charges that communists have infiltrated the State Department. (See **China Hands, Civil Liberties**)

14 FEBRUARY: The Soviet Union and the People's Republic of China sign a friendship treaty.

1 MARCH: Chiang establishes the Republic of China on Taiwan. Fuchs is sentenced to prison.

7 APRIL: An interagency committee guided by Paul H. Nitze produces National Security Council memorandum 68 (NSC-68). (See **Containment, Ideology, Militarizing Containment, Universalism**)

15 JUNE: West Germany enters the Council of Europe.

25 JUNE: The North Koreans invade South Korea.

27 JUNE: The UN Security Council approves military aid to South Korea and establishes a fifteen-nation UN force.

30 JUNE: U.S. troops enter the Korean War.

17 JULY: Julius Rosenberg is arrested for spying for the Soviets. His wife, Ethel, is arrested on 11 August. (See **Civil Liberties, Nuclear Spying**)

9 SEPTEMBER: Truman announces a plan to increase the number of U.S. troops in Europe. (See **NATO**)

1 NOVEMBER: The People's Republic of China enters the war on the side of North Korea, and by 4 November UN troops are forced to retreat.

1951

6 MARCH: The Rosenberg spy trial starts. They are convicted on 29 March and condemned to death on 5 April.

21 JUNE: UN troops push communist forces out of South Korea.

8 JULY: Truce talks start in Korea.

9 AUGUST: McCarthy charges twenty-nine State Department employees with disloyalty.

1 SEPTEMBER: The United States, Australia, and New Zealand sign the ANZUS treaty.

8 SEPTEMBER: The United States and Japan sign a mutual security pact.

27 OCTOBER: A cease-fire line is established in Korea.

1952

10 MARCH: Fulgencio Batista y Zaldívar seizes power in Cuba. (See **Cuba Policy**)

30 APRIL: Tito says Yugoslavia will not join **NATO**.

27 MAY: The European Defense Community (EDC) is proposed. (See **NATO**)

2 OCTOBER: Great Britain tests its first atomic weapon. (See **Nonproliferation, Nuclear Deterrence, Nuclear Weapons**)

1953

7 APRIL: The Big Four foreign ministers meet in Berlin to discuss the status of Germany.

10 JUNE: President Dwight D. Eisenhower rejects the isolationist "Fortress America" doctrine. (See **New Look, Universalism**)

18 JUNE: Soviet troops suppress anticommunist rioting in East Germany. (See **Rollback**)

19 JUNE: The Rosenbergs are executed. (See **Civil Liberties, Nuclear Spying**)

27 JULY: The P'anmunjon armistice ends the Korean War.

12 AUGUST: The Soviet Union announces the test of its first hydrogen bomb. (See **Limited Nuclear War, Nuclear Deterrence, Nuclear Weapons**)

19–22 AUGUST: A U.S.-sponsored coup in Iran topples Prime Minister Mohammad Mosaddeq and his government and installs Mohammad Reza Shah Pahlevi on the throne. (See **CIA Operations**)

1954

12 JANUARY: Secretary of State John Foster Dulles calls for a policy of massive retaliation against Soviet expansion. (See **Flexible Response, New Look, Nuclear Deterrence, Nuclear Weapons**)

10 FEBRUARY: Eisenhower opposes U.S. involvement in French Indochina. (See **Vietnam War**)

18 FEBRUARY: McCarthy attacks the U.S. Army for promoting communists. (See **Civil Liberties**)

1–28 MARCH: Delegates to the Caracas Conference discuss policies to stop communism in Latin America. (See **Alliance for Progress, Cuba Policy, Guatemala and Chile**)

5 APRIL: Eisenhower declares that the United States will not be the first nation to use the hydrogen bomb. (See **New Look**)

7 APRIL: Eisenhower says a communist victory in Indochina would set off a chain reaction of disaster for the free world, a view that becomes known as the "domino theory." (See **Vietnam War**)

23 APRIL: McCarthy accuses Secretary of the Army Robert Stevens of communist sympathies; Army-McCarthy hearings open and continue until 17 June. (See **Civil Liberties**)

7 MAY: Vietnamese forces defeat French troops at Dien Bien Phu. (See **Vietnam War**)

27 JUNE: A U.S.-sponsored coup topples leftist Guatemalan president Jacobo Arbenz Guzmán. (See **CIA Operations, Guatemala and Chile**)

20 JULY: The Geneva Accords divide Vietnam at the seventeenth parallel, creating North and South Vietnam. (See **Vietnam War**)

2 AUGUST: The U.S. Senate votes to study possible censure of McCarthy. (See **Civil Liberties**)

6–8 SEPTEMBER: The Southeast Asia Treaty Organization (SEATO) is established by the Manila Pact.

2 DECEMBER: The U.S. Senate condemns McCarthy. (See **Civil Liberties.**) Responding to the Chinese shelling of the Nationalist Chinese islands of **Quemoy and Matsu,** the United States signs a mutual-defense treaty with Taiwan.

1955

17 FEBRUARY: The British announce their plan to build a hydrogen bomb. (See **Nonproliferation**)

18–24 FEBRUARY: The Middle East Treaty Organization (Baghdad Pact) is created.

17–24 APRIL: In Bandung, Indonesia, twenty-nine underdeveloped nations create the Non-Aligned Movement.

29 APRIL: Military clashes begin between North and South Vietnam. (See **Vietnam War**)

5 MAY: The Allied occupation of West Germany formally ends as the Federal Republic of Germany becomes a sovereign nation.

9 MAY: West Germany formally joins **NATO.**

14 MAY: Responding to West German **NATO** membership, the Soviet Union, Albania, Bulgaria, Czechoslovakia, East Germany, Hungary, Poland, and Romania create the Warsaw Pact.

15 MAY: Representatives from the United States, the Soviet Union, Great Britain, France, and Austria sign the Austrian State Treaty, which results in Soviet troops being withdrawn from Austria. (See **Finlandization**)

20 SEPTEMBER: The Soviet Union grants East Germany sovereignty and membership in the Warsaw Pact.

26 OCTOBER: Ngo Dinh Diem declares South Vietnam a republic and himself premier. (See **Vietnam War**)

29 DECEMBER: First Secretary Nikita Khrushchev of the Soviet Union rejects Eisenhower's Open Skies proposal. (See **Détente**)

1956

26 JANUARY: The Soviet Union returns Porkkala Peninsula to Finland. (See **Finlandization**)

14 FEBRUARY: Khrushchev denounces Stalin in a speech to the Twentieth Congress of the Communist Party. (See **Hitler and Stalin**)

4 JUNE: The Voice of America broadcasts Khrushchev's "secret speech" of 14 February.

28–30 JUNE: More than one hundred people die during riots in Poznan, Poland. (See **Rollback**)

26 JULY: Gamal Abdel Nasser nationalizes the Suez Canal. (See **Suez War**)

21 OCTOBER: The "Spring in October" revolution takes place in Poland.

23 OCTOBER: The Hungarian revolt begins. (See **Rollback**)

29 OCTOBER: Israel attacks Egyptian forces in the Sinai. (See **Israel, Suez War**)

31 OCTOBER: Premier Imre Nagy asks the Soviet Union to leave Hungary. British and French troops land in the Suez Canal zone. (See **Rollback, Suez War**)

1 NOVEMBER: Hungary proclaims its neutrality and leaves the Warsaw Pact.

4 NOVEMBER: The Soviet Union invades Hungary. János Kádár is installed as premier. (See **Rollback**)

7 NOVEMBER: A cease-fire takes effect in the **Suez War.**

8 NOVEMBER: Anti-Soviet fighting ends in Hungary.

15 NOVEMBER: A UN peacekeeping force arrives in Egypt. (See **Suez War**)

1957

13 FEBRUARY: The Senate Foreign Relations and Armed Services Committees refuse Eisenhower's request to send American troops to the Middle East. (See **Israel, Suez War**)

7 MARCH: The Eisenhower Doctrine, pledging U.S. aid to Middle Eastern countries resisting communism, is endorsed by a joint resolution of Congress. (See **Israel, Suez War**)

25 MARCH: The Treaty of Rome establishes the European Economic Community (EEC), to become effective 1 January 1958.

22 APRIL: John Foster Dulles announces his policy to "**roll back**" communism in Europe. (See **Nuclear Weapons**)

2 JULY: The United States proposes a ten-month nuclear weapons test ban.

5 OCTOBER: The Soviet Union launches its Sputnik satellite into orbit around the Earth.

1958

31 MARCH: The Soviet Union proclaims a unilateral halt to nuclear-weapons testing.

15 JULY: Eisenhower orders U.S. Marines into Lebanon. (See **Israel, Suez War**)

AUGUST: The Chinese resume the shelling of **Quemoy and Matsu.**

3 OCTOBER: The Soviet Union resumes nuclear tests after Americans and British refuse the proposed ban. (See **Nuclear Deterrence, Nuclear Weapons**)

1959

1 JANUARY: Batista flees Cuba as rebel forces led by Fidel Castro Ruz advance on Havana. (See **Cuba Policy**)

15 & 25–27 JANUARY: Eisenhower and Khrushchev hold summit conferences in Washington, D.C., and at Camp David. (See **Détente**)

19 AUGUST: The Baghdad Pact becomes the Central Treaty Organization (CENTO).

15–19 SEPTEMBER: Khrushchev visits the United States. (See **Détente**)

3 NOVEMBER: Charles De Gaulle declares that France will withdraw from the **NATO** military command.

1960

1 JANUARY: Khrushchev announces the Soviet Union will cut the number of its conventional troops even if arms-limitation talks fail.

19 JANUARY: Secretary of Defense Thomas Gates tells the House Defense Appropriations Committee that there are no bomber or missile gaps favoring the Soviet Union; in fact, correct estimates showed "a clear balance in our favor." (See **Military "Gaps"**)

13 FEBRUARY: France explodes a nuclear device. (See **Nonproliferation, Nuclear Deterrence, Nuclear Weapons**)

1 MAY: An American U-2 reconnaissance plane is shot down over the Soviet Union.

16 MAY: Summit talks in Paris break off after Khrushchev demands a U.S. apology for the U-2 affair.

SEPTEMBER: The Organization of Petroleum Exporting Countries (OPEC) is established.

11 NOVEMBER: President-elect John F. Kennedy disavows the "two-China" policy.

1961

3 JANUARY: Eisenhower cuts off diplomatic relations with Cuba.

1 MARCH: The Peace Corps is founded.

3 MARCH: President Kennedy proposes the **Alliance for Progress.**

15 APRIL: U.S.-trained Cuban exiles launch the Bay of Pigs Invasion of Cuba. They are defeated by Cuban forces on 20 April. (See **CIA Operations, Cuba Policy**)

30 MAY: Dominican Republic ruler Rafael Leonidas Trujillo Molina is assassinated.

3 JUNE: Kennedy meets Khrushchev at a summit meeting in Vienna to discuss the American arms buildup and demilitarization of West Berlin. (See **Berlin Crises**)

13 AUGUST: East Germany forbids its citizens to cross into West Germany. (See **Berlin Crises**)

15 AUGUST: Construction of the Berlin Wall begins. (See **Berlin Crises**)

10 DECEMBER: The Soviet Union and Albania sever diplomatic relations.

1962

2 MARCH: The United States resumes atmospheric nuclear testing. (See **Flexible Response, Nuclear Weapons**)

22 OCTOBER: Kennedy announces a blockade of Cuba until the Soviet Union removes the missiles it has installed there. (See **Cuba Policy, Nuclear Deterrence**)

24 OCTOBER – 20 NOVEMBER: The U.S. Navy blockades Cuba. (See **Cuba Policy**)

27–28 OCTOBER: The United States accepts the Soviet offer to withdraw its missiles in exchange for an American guarantee that the United States will not invade Cuba, and the Soviets begin removing their missiles from the island. (See **Cuba Policy**)

1963

1 JANUARY: The Chinese Communist Party attacks Khrushchev's doctrine of peaceful coexistence with the West. (See **Ideology**)

26 JUNE: Kennedy makes his "Ich bin ein Berliner" speech at the Berlin Wall. (See **Berlin Crises**)

5 AUGUST: The United States, the Soviet Union, and Great Britain sign the Limited Test-Ban Treaty in Moscow. China has denounced the treaty, and France has refused to sign it. (See **Nonproliferation, Nuclear Deterrence, Nuclear Weapons**)

30 AUGUST: A "hot line" goes into service between Washington, D.C., and Moscow. (See **Détente**)

22 NOVEMBER: President Kennedy is assassinated in Dallas and is succeeded by Vice-President Lyndon B. Johnson.

1964

28 MAY: The Palestine Liberation Organization (PLO) is founded. (See **Israel**)

2–4 AUGUST: The USS *Maddox* and USS *C. Turner Joy* are attacked by the North Vietnamese in the Gulf of Tonkin. (See **Vietnam War**)

7 AUGUST: The U.S. Senate passes the Tonkin Gulf Resolution. (See **Vietnam War**)

16 OCTOBER: China detonates an atomic bomb. (See **Nonproliferation**)

1965

7 FEBRUARY: U.S. forces attack North Vietnam for the first time, following an attack on a U.S. base at Pleiku. (See **Vietnam War**)

8 MARCH: U.S. combat troops land in Vietnam. (See **Vietnam War**)

28 APRIL: Johnson sends marines to the Dominican Republic to quell unrest.

1966

3 FEBRUARY: An unmanned Soviet spacecraft lands on the moon.

7 MARCH: France formally announces that it will withdraw from the integrated military structure of **NATO.**

1967

27 JANUARY: Sixty-two nations sign a treaty prohibiting the military use of outer space.

21 APRIL: A coup topples the Greek government of Stephanos Stephanopoulos, preventing leftist Georgios Papandreou from coming back to power.

15 MAY: Egyptian forces move into the Sinai.

23 MAY: Egypt blocks the Strait of Tiran to Israeli shipping.

5 JUNE: The Six Day War begins.

7 JUNE: Defeated Egypt accepts a cease-fire.

9 JUNE: Defeated Syria accepts a cease-fire.

23 JUNE: Johnson and Soviet premier Aleksey Kosygin meet in Glassboro, New Jersey. (See **Détente**)

8 AUGUST: Indonesia, Malaysia, Thailand, the Philippines, and Singapore establish the Association of South East Asian Nations (ASEAN).

10 OCTOBER: Bolivia confirms the death of Latin American guerrilla Ernesto "Che" Guevara de la Serna. (See **Cuba Policy**)

1968

23 JANUARY: The USS *Pueblo* is seized by North Korea, which holds the crew for eleven months.

30 JANUARY: The Vietcong launch the Tet Offensive. (See **Vietnam War**)

31 MARCH: Johnson announces a bombing halt in Vietnam and offers to open negotiations with the North Vietnamese; he also announces that he is dropping out of the presidential race. (See **Vietnam War**)

10 MAY: Paris peace talks open between the United States and North Vietnam. (See **Vietnam War**)

1 JULY: The Nuclear Non-Proliferation Treaty (NPT) is signed. (See **Nonproliferation**)

15 JULY: General Secretary Leonid I. Brezhnev announces the Brezhnev Doctrine. (See **Afghanistan, Ideology**)

20 AUGUST: Warsaw Pact forces invade Czechoslovakia.

24 AUGUST: France explodes a thermonuclear bomb. (See **Nonproliferation, Nuclear Deterrence, Nuclear Weapons**)

1969

18 MARCH: The United States begins secretly bombing **Cambodia.**

8 JUNE: President Richard M. Nixon announces his "Vietnamization" plan. (See **Vietnam War**)

25 JULY: In a speech in Guam, Nixon enunciates the Nixon Doctrine, a plan to reduce the U.S. military presence abroad by helping small nations to defend themselves.

1 SEPTEMBER: Mu'ammar al-Gadhafi stages a military coup, proclaiming the socialist Arab Republic of Libya.

24 NOVEMBER: The United States and the Soviet Union sign the NPT.

1970

30 APRIL: Nixon announces the invasion of **Cambodia** by U.S. troops.

4 MAY: Ohio National Guardsmen kill four students during an antiwar protest at Kent State University. (See **Cambodia, Vietnam War**)

29 JUNE: U.S. ground troops leave Cambodia.

1 OCTOBER: The Senate approves the building of antiballistic missiles. (See **Missile Defense**)

7 OCTOBER: Nixon announces a new Vietnam peace plan.

15–19 DECEMBER: Rioting occurs in Polish cities.

1971

8 FEBRUARY: U.S. forces invade Laos. (See **Vietnam War**)

25 OCTOBER: The UN admits China to membership and expels Taiwan.

16 DECEMBER: Nationalists rebel in East Pakistan and establish Bangladesh.

1972

20 FEBRUARY: Nixon arrives in China, the first American president to visit that country.

22–30 MAY: Pursuing a policy of **détente** with the Soviet Union, Nixon meets Brezhnev for a summit meeting in Moscow. They sign the Strategic Arms Limitations Talks (SALT I) interim agreement on 26 May.

5 SEPTEMBER: Members of the Black September faction of the PLO seize Israeli athletes at the Munich Olympics, killing eleven.

3 OCTOBER: SALT I and the ABM Treaty are signed in Washington. (See **Missile Defense, Nuclear Deterrence**)

1973

1 JANUARY: Great Britain joins the EEC.

27 JANUARY: The Vietnam peace accords are signed.

17–24 JUNE: A summit conference in Washington occurs between Nixon and Brezhnev. (See **Détente**)

15 JULY: Congress imposes a halt on continued U.S. bombing of Cambodia.

11 SEPTEMBER: President Salvador Allende Gossens of Chile is ousted in a coup. (See **CIA Operations, Guatemala and Chile**)

6 OCTOBER: The **Yom Kippur War** starts. (See **Israel**)

30 OCTOBER: Mutual Balanced Force Reductions (MBFR) Talks open in Vienna.

1974

9 MAY: The U.S. House Judiciary Committee votes to impeach Nixon.

18 MAY: India explodes a nuclear device, which it describes as a "peaceful nuclear explosion" (PNE). (See **Nonproliferation, Nuclear Weapons**)

27 JUNE – 3 JULY: The Moscow summit conference between Nixon and Brezhnev takes place.

20 JULY: Turkey invades Cyprus.

9 AUGUST: Nixon resigns because of Watergate scandal. Gerald R. Ford becomes president.

14 AUGUST: Greece cuts **NATO** ties because of Turkish invasion of Cyprus.

4 SEPTEMBER: The United States establishes diplomatic relations with East Germany.

12 SEPTEMBER: Ethiopian emperor Haile Selassie is ousted in a military coup, whose leaders later declare the country a socialist state.

23–24 NOVEMBER: The Vladivostok summit conference between Ford and Brezhnev takes place. (See **Détente**)

26 DECEMBER: CIA director William Colby admits the agency spied on U.S. citizens. (See **CIA Operations**)

1975

16 APRIL: The Khmer Rouge takes over **Cambodia.**

30 APRIL: Saigon falls to North Vietnamese forces. The **Vietnam War** is over.

1 AUGUST: The Helsinki Final Act is signed. (See **Détente, Human Rights**)

23 AUGUST: The Vietnamese-backed Pathet Lao takes over Laos.

1976

20 FEBRUARY: SEATO disbands.

2 JULY: Vietnam formally unites as one nation.

1977

27 JANUARY: President Jimmy Carter orders SALT II negotiations to proceed. (See **Détente**)

30 JULY: The U.S. government announces plan to deploy cruise missiles. (See **Limited Nuclear War**)

7 SEPTEMBER: Panama Canal treaties are signed in Washington, D.C.

23 SEPTEMBER: Secretary of State Cyrus Vance says the United States will abide by the expiring 1972 SALT I treaty.

25 DECEMBER: Israeli prime minister Menachem Begin and Egyptian president Anwar Sadat start peace negotiations in Egypt.

1978

10 MARCH: Congress adopts the Nuclear Non-Proliferation Act of 1978. Carter signs Nuclear Non-Proliferation Treaty. (See **Nonproliferation**)

17 MARCH: Carter warns the Soviet Union against involvement in the domestic affairs of other countries.

7 APRIL: The United States defers production of the neutron bomb. (See **Nonproliferation**)

12 JUNE: Vance announces that the United States will not use nuclear weapons against nonnuclear powers that pledge nuclear abstinence. (See **Limited Nuclear War, Nonproliferation**)

5–17 SEPTEMBER: Sadat and Begin meet with Carter at Camp David and agree on an Egyptian-Israeli peace accord. (See **Israel**)

1979

7 JANUARY: Vietnam invades **Cambodia,** replacing the regime of Pol Pot with a pro-Hanoi communist regime under Heng Samrin.

16 JANUARY: Reza Shah Pahlavi flees Iran.

1 FEBRUARY

Ayatollah Ruhollah Khomeini arrives in Iran.

26 MARCH: Sadat and Begin sign an Egyptian-Israeli peace treaty.

6 APRIL: U.S. aid to Pakistan is cut because of its nuclear-weapons program. (See **Nonproliferation**)

2 MAY: Undersecretary of State Warren Christopher says U.S. foreign policy will link aid with **human rights.**

18 JUNE: Carter and Brezhnev sign the SALT II agreement in Vienna.

19 JULY: Sandinista rebels take Managua and seize power in Nicaragua; President Anastasio Somoza Debayle flees.

1 OCTOBER: The U.S. Panama Canal Zone accords from 1977 go into effect.

4 NOVEMBER: The U.S. embassy in Tehran is seized, and diplomats are taken hostage.

21 NOVEMBER: Muslim fundamentalists burn the U.S. embassy in Pakistan.

12 DECEMBER: **NATO** adopts the "two track" policy, uncoupling Europe, especially Germany, from U.S. protection. (See **Limited Nuclear War**)

25 DECEMBER: Soviet troops invade **Afghanistan.**

1980

24 APRIL: "Desert I" rescue raid by U.S. forces fails to free Iranian-held hostages.

21–27 MAY: About one thousand South Koreans die in political unrest following arrest of opposition leader Kim Dae Jung.

14 AUGUST: Massive strikes occur in Poland, led by Lech Walesa, at Lenin shipyards in Gdansk.

11 NOVEMBER: The Conference on Security and Cooperation in Europe meeting opens in Madrid.

1981

20 JANUARY: The Iranians release the U.S. embassy hostages.

6 OCTOBER: Sadat is assassinated in Cairo; he is succeeded by Muhammad Hosni Mubarak.

30 NOVEMBER: Intermediate-range Nuclear Forces (INF) talks open in Geneva. (See **Limited Nuclear War**)

10 DECEMBER: Spain joins **NATO** (effective 30 May 1982).

13 DECEMBER: Martial law is imposed in Poland, continuing until 21 July 1983.

1982

2 APRIL: Argentina seizes the Falkland Islands.

9 MAY – 14 JUNE: British forces retake the Falkland Islands.

6 JUNE: Israeli forces invade Lebanon.

30 JUNE: The Strategic Arms Reduction Talks (START) in Geneva opens.

AUGUST – SEPTEMBER: U.S. Marines arrive in Lebanon.

1983

23 MARCH: Reagan outlines the Strategic Defense Initiative (SDI). (See **Missile Defense**)

18 APRIL: The U.S. embassy in Beirut is bombed, killing more than fifty people.

1 SEPTEMBER: The Soviet Union shoots down Korean Airlines flight 007.

23 OCTOBER: U.S. barracks are destroyed by car bomb in Lebanon; 241 Marines are killed.

25 OCTOBER: U.S. troops invade Grenada.

23 NOVEMBER: Soviet delegation walks out of the INF talks in Geneva.

30 DECEMBER: The first nine Pershing II missiles in West Germany become operational. (See **Limited Nuclear War**)

1984

1 JANUARY: The first new U.S. cruise missiles are deployed in Great Britain.

26 FEBRUARY: U.S. troops withdraw from Lebanon.

29 JUNE: Soviets offer to negotiate with Americans about nuclear weapons in space. (See **Missile Defense**)

1 AUGUST: Great Britain announces its plan to give up control of Hong Kong in 1997.

20 SEPTEMBER: The new U.S. embassy in Beirut is bombed.

20 OCTOBER: The Chinese Communist Party approves Deng's liberalization program.

1985

21 FEBRUARY: The Soviet Union agrees to international inspection of its civilian nuclear-power plants. (See **Nonproliferation**)

26 APRIL: Member states sign a twenty-year extension of Warsaw Pact.

10 JUNE: The United States announces it will bide by unratified SALT II treaty.

6 OCTOBER: The United States says SDI does not violate the 1972 ABM treaty. (See **Missile Defense**)

19–21 OCTOBER: Reagan and General Secretary Mikhail Gorbachev of the Soviet Union meet at the Geneva summit conference. (See **Détente**)

1986

1 JANUARY: Spain and Portugal join the EEC.

15 APRIL: American planes attack targets in Libya in response to Libyan-sponsored terrorism.

5 OCTOBER: The *Sunday Times* (London) reports that **Israel** has been building nuclear weapons for twenty years. (See **Israel, Nonproliferation**)

11–12 OCTOBER: The Reykjavík Summit between Reagan and Gorbachev proposes a 50 percent cut in long-range missiles. (See **Détente**)

17 OCTOBER: Congress approves aid to the contras in Nicaragua. (See **Central America**)

3 NOVEMBER: The U.S. press breaks the Iran-Contra Affair. (See **Central America**)

28 NOVEMBER: The United States exceeds the weapon limits of the unratified SALT II treaty by deploying the B-52 bomber.

1987

26 FEBRUARY: The Soviet Union ends an eighteen-month unilateral moratorium on nuclear testing with an underground nuclear test. (See **Nuclear Deterrence, Nuclear Weapons**)

17 MAY: Iraqi planes attack the U.S. frigate *Stark* in the Persian Gulf.

8–10 DECEMBER: Reagan and Gorbachev meet in Washington.

8 DECEMBER: The INF Treaty is signed, mandating the removal of 2,611 intermediate-range nuclear missiles from Europe.

9 DECEMBER: The Palestinian *intifada* against **Israel** begins.

1988

14 APRIL: The Geneva Accords on **Afghanistan** are signed; the Soviets agree to withdraw half their forces by 15 August 1988 and the remainder by 15 February 1989.

27 MAY: The Senate approves the INF Treaty.

29 MAY – 2 JUNE: A summit between Reagan and Gorbachev is held in Moscow.

3 JULY: The U.S. cruiser *Vincennes* downs an Iranian commercial jet over the Persian Gulf.

20 AUGUST: A cease-fire is reached in the Iran-Iraq war.

6 DECEMBER: Gorbachev announces to the UN a plan to reduce the Soviet military by five hundred thousand men.

14 DECEMBER: The U.S. government opens talks with the Palestinian Liberation Organization (PLO).

1989

15 JANUARY: Demonstrations in Prague commemorate the twentieth anniversary of the protest-suicides by students after the 1968 Soviet invasion.

23 JANUARY: East German leader Erich Honecker announces a 10 percent cut in military spending by 1990.

20–21 FEBRUARY: The Hungarian Central Committee approves a new constitution, omitting mention of the leading role of the Communist Party.

21 FEBRUARY: Václav Havel is sentenced to nine months in prison for inciting protests against the Czech government. He is released on 17 May.

26 MARCH: Elections are held for a new Soviet Congress of People's Deputies. Many party and military officials lose to independent candidates. Boris Yeltsin wins an at-large seat for Moscow with 89 percent of the vote.

17 APRIL: The Solidarity trade union is legalized in Poland.

25 APRIL: One thousand Soviet tanks leave Hungary.

11 MAY: Gorbachev announces that the Soviet Union will unilaterally reduce its nuclear forces in eastern Europe by five hundred warheads.

25 MAY: The Soviet Congress of People's Deputies elects Gorbachev as president.

3–4 JUNE: The Chinese government orders suppression of a prodemocracy demonstration by students in Tiananmen Square.

4 JUNE: Solidarity wins a decisive majority in the first free parliamentary elections in Poland for almost half a century.

19 JUNE: START negotiations resume in Geneva.

25 JULY: President Wojciech W. Jaruzelski of Poland invites Solidarity to join a coalition government.

17 AUGUST: The Soviet Politburo endorses a plan for limited economic autonomy for the fifteen Soviet republics.

7 OCTOBER: The Hungarian Communist Party formally disbands.

23 OCTOBER: Hungary adopts a new constitution, becoming the Republic of Hungary.

9 NOVEMBER: East Germany opens its borders, including the Berlin Wall.

20 NOVEMBER: Mass demonstrations are held in Prague.

1–3 DECEMBER: At the Malta summit between Gorbachev and President George Bush, Gorbachev says that "the characteristics of the Cold War should be abandoned." (See **Détente**)

CHRONOLOGY

7 DECEMBER: East Germany announces multiparty elections for 6 May 1990.

22 DECEMBER: Nicolae Ceausescu is toppled after leading Romania for twenty-four years. He and his wife, Elena, are executed on 25 December.

1990

1 JANUARY: Poland enacts sweeping economic reforms.

11–13 FEBRUARY: At the Ottawa Conference foreign ministers of Warsaw Pact and **NATO** countries discuss Bush's "open skies" proposal and agree to formal talks on German reunification.

26 FEBRUARY: The Soviet Union agrees to a phased withdrawal of Soviet troops from Czechoslovakia, to be completed by July 1991.

11 MARCH: Lithuania declares its independence from the Soviet Union. Soviet troops begin withdrawal from Hungary.

3 MAY: **NATO** foreign ministers agree to allow full membership to a reunified Germany.

30 MAY – 3 JUNE: The Washington summit between Gorbachev and Bush is held.

8–9 JUNE: Havel's party captures a majority in parliamentary elections in Czechoslovakia.

12 SEPTEMBER: Meeting in Moscow, foreign ministers of the two Germanies and the Big Four powers agree to set 1994 as the date of withdrawal of Soviet troops from East Germany.

3 OCTOBER: West and East Germany unite as the Federal Republic of Germany.

22 DECEMBER: Walesa is sworn in as president of Poland. Slovenians vote for independence from Yugoslavia.

1991

2 JANUARY: Soviet elite forces capture buildings in Latvia and Lithuania and kill fifteen protesters in Vilnius on 13 January.

20 JANUARY: Hundreds of thousands march on the Kremlin to protest Soviet crackdown in the Baltic states.

21 JANUARY: The EEC suspends $1 billion in economic aid to the Soviet Union.

16 MARCH: Serbian president Slobodan Milosevic announces Serbia will no longer recognize the authority of the Yugoslavian federal government.

27 MARCH: The United States withdraws its medium-range missiles from Europe.

APRIL–SEPTEMBER: The Soviet Union disintegrates as its constituent republics declare independence.

12 JUNE: Boris Yeltsin is elected president of the Russian Federation.

19 JUNE: Soviet troops complete their withdrawal from Hungary.

21 JUNE: Soviet troops complete their withdrawal from Czechoslovakia.

25 JUNE: Slovenia and Croatia declare independence from Yugoslavia.

1 JULY: The Warsaw Pact is formally dissolved. The Supreme Soviet permits the sale of state-owned enterprises.

19 AUGUST: In a coup attempt Gorbachev is held at his vacation dacha and replaced by Gennadi Yanayev. Yeltsin denounces coup leaders as traitors.

21 AUGUST: The Soviet coup collapses; Gorbachev is released from house arrest.

24 AUGUST: Gorbachev resigns, disbands the Central Committee, and places Communist Party property under control of the Soviet parliament.

29 AUGUST: The Supreme Soviet bans the activities of the Communist Party. The Russian republics sign political and economic treaties with Ukraine and Kazakhstan.

2 SEPTEMBER: The European Community recognizes the independence of the Baltic states, and the United States establishes diplomatic relations with them.

7 SEPTEMBER: Croatia and Slovenia declare immediate secession from Yugoslavia.

8 SEPTEMBER: Macedonia votes to declare independence from Yugoslavia.

27 SEPTEMBER: Bush announces unilateral dismantling of 2,400 U.S. nuclear warheads.

19 OCTOBER: Ethnic Albanian legislators declare Kosovo independent from Yugoslavia.

23 OCTOBER: Yugoslav forces attack Dubrovnik in Croatia.

8 NOVEMBER: The EEC imposes economic sanctions on Yugoslavia.

25 NOVEMBER: Soviet republics reject a union treaty proposed by Gorbachev.

8 DECEMBER: The leaders of Russia, Ukraine, and Belorussia proclaim that the Soviet Union has ceased to exist and declare the creation of the Commonwealth of Independent States.

19 DECEMBER: The EEC announces it will recognize Slovenia and Croatia by 15 January 1992.

20 DECEMBER: Bosnia-Herzegovina applies to the EEC for recognition as an independent state.

21 DECEMBER: Eleven former Soviet republics announce they constitute the Commonwealth of Independent States, to begin operations by 15 January 1992. Russia retains the permanent seat held by the Soviets at the UN Security Council.

25 DECEMBER: Gorbachev resigns as president of the Soviet Union.

ADMIRALS' REVOLT

Were U.S. Navy admirals right to challenge publicly the 1949 cancellation of the supercarrier project?

Viewpoint: Yes, the admirals were right to challenge the decision because it diminished the postwar role of the navy.

Viewpoint: No, the admirals were not right to challenge the civilian leadership.

Tension, competition, and conflict among its branches have always been an integral part of the U.S. military establishment—as if the pluralism that characterizes American political life also found expression in U.S. military practices. Even against this background of bickering and rivalry, the 1949 "revolt of the admirals" stands out in its intensity. Traditional interservice rivalry boiled over, revealing its existence to the public as never before. Moreover, some found in the admirals' behavior discomforting echoes of a military challenge to civilian authority.

In the background of this episode were the emergence of the Soviet Union as the major adversary of the United States in the post–Second World War era and the introduction of nuclear weapons. After the war ended, it became clear that the Soviet Union would replace the old powers as a prime mover in world affairs. Not only was it the largest country on Earth, but it was also equipped with an alien, messianic ideology that challenged the foundations of the Western way of life. What would be the best military strategy against this new adversary? The services fell back on their experience in the war that had just ended: the navy argued that control of the seas and the projection of power by aircraft carriers had been decisive in the war; the air force (which, during the Second World War, was still part of the army) believed that its campaign of strategic bombing—the methodical destruction of the enemy's military-industrial capacity and the demoralizing destruction of cities—had tipped the scales; and the army pointed out that the campaign on the ground to push back the Nazi and Japanese armies, then the occupation of Italy and Germany and the threat of occupying Japan, had finally forced the Axis powers to surrender. The lessons for each service were clear: the navy wanted more and bigger carriers; the air force, having become an independent service, wanted more bombers; and the army wanted more divisions. The introduction of nuclear weapons complicated this rivalry. The air force saw itself as the natural home for these new weapons—bombs, after all, were delivered by bombers. The navy, afraid that more and more resources would flow to the air force, insisted on having a role in delivering nuclear weapons.

The rivalry exploded to the surface in 1949, as the navy and the air force publicly debated the relative merits of the supercarrier and the B-36 bomber. Secretary of Defense Louis Johnson's decision to support the B-36 created a firestorm among navy supporters, who launched an open challenge to Johnson's decision. In the end the navy lost, but not before rancorous and bitter public debate. The outbreak of the Korean War in June 1950 diverted attention from this particular controversy, but interservice rivalry continued, erupting every so often in debates over roles and missions, strategies and weapon systems.

Viewpoint:
Yes, the admirals were right to challenge the decision because it diminished the postwar role of the navy.

The onset of the cold war and the introduction of nuclear weapons forced the United States and its armed services to engage in a comprehensive reappraisal of U.S. strategy and the roles and missions of the armed forces. The Soviet Union was a massive land power, straddling the Eurasian land mass, threatening American allies in both Europe and Asia. Moreover, the USSR was largely autarkic, unengaged in global commerce and trade. This situation meant that the traditional U.S. reliance on a large navy might not be the most effective means of contending with Soviet power. In addition, the experience using bombers for massive strategic bombing during the Second World War, coupled with the introduction of the atomic bomb, led many to believe that a more effective strategy to cope with the Soviet threat would be to increase considerably the role of air power (especially bombers carrying nuclear weapons). This increase would also be accompanied by an augmentation of U.S. ground forces. The navy, however, was unwilling to accept this reorientation in strategy and the implied diminution in its role, especially with regard to nuclear weapons. When Secretary of Defense Louis Johnson sided with the air force on the issue of the B-36 bomber, leading admirals in the navy decided to oppose his decision. The result was the Revolt of the Admirals, a tense episode in the history of civil-military relations in the United States.

The tensions that gave rise to the revolt were particularly strong because there were many reasons, not just one, for the need to adjust military organizations and doctrines to the new reality. The rise of the United States to a position of global responsibility meant that its armed forces would now be called on to defend not only their homeland but also far-flung interests and to pursue policy objectives for which previous generations of military planners did not have to prepare. The introduction of new weapons also necessitated rethinking roles and missions. Among these technologies were nuclear weapons, which were used against Japan at the end of the Second World War, and air power, which was used for the first time in a systematic fashion as a strategic weapon during the war. Rather than just an instrument to provide close support for ground troops, air power became a means to inflict damage on the enemy's society and economy. The theory behind strategic bombing was

that massive and repeated attacks on industrial and manufacturing facilities and transportation and communication links would paralyze the adversary and cut off its military force. Furthermore, a systematic campaign of bombing large urban centers, killing hundreds of thousands of civilians, would disrupt the enemy's society and economy and weaken the morale and resolve of its people. The development of nuclear weapons, and the ability to deliver them by long-range planes or rockets, made the promise of strategic bombing especially appealing.

Early discussions between the navy and the army led nowhere—the services could not agree on a redefinition of their role and mission and on a delineation of their responsibilities. (The air force was then still part of the army and was called the U.S. Army Air Force.) The services drew different lessons from the Second World War. The army pointed to the performance of its units in the field as the key to victory, suggesting that the budgetary constraints that prevented the maintenance of a large army in the years before the war probably delayed victory unnecessarily. The army was thus uncomfortable with the role of the Marine Corps, which is part of the navy, believing that budgets allocated to the Marines should go to the army. Supporters of army air power believed that land-based air power, especially in its strategic role, was decisive for victory in the war. They favored creating a separate air force, especially for the role of strategic bombing. Because strategic bombing required heavy planes capable of carrying large nuclear payloads, army strategists argued that this new air force must be land-based rather than sea-based. The navy believed that its large aircraft carriers had made the major contribution to winning the war and wanted more of them.

Two philosophies concerning air power thus emerged during these early negotiations among the services and their civilian superiors. The army and army air force wanted missions defined by their weapons and the medium in which these weapons operated. On this definition, all ground forces would be under army command, all sea forces under the navy command, and all air forces under air force command. The navy feared that with such a definition of missions it would lose its naval aviation and Marines Corps. According to Steven L. Rearden, the navy offered an alternative definition of role and mission, based on function and objective rather than on weapons and medium. To break the impasse, Secretary of the Navy James V. Forrestal appointed General Lauris Norstad and Admiral Forrest P. Sherman to draft a paper on roles and missions that the administration and Congress could use as they tried to solve the interservice rivalry. The Norstad-

Artist's rendition of the supercarrier *United States,* whose construction was canceled by the Truman administration in 1949

Sherman proposal divided the responsibility among the services according to the environment in which they operated: the army was given responsibilities for land warfare and the navy for sea warfare (but also for controlling the air above the sea). A proposed air force was given the responsibility for air combat, strategic bombing, and airlifts, as well as for providing close support to army and naval units. The Marine Corps was left with the navy, and its tasks were described as "seizure and defense of advanced naval bases," but also assistance to army and air force units. The report was given to President Harry S Truman in January 1947, and on 26 July 1947 he issued the Norstad-Sherman paper as Executive Order 9877. On that same day Congress passed the National Security Act, which made the army air force a separate branch of the services, and established the cabinet post of secretary of defense to oversee all branches.

The Norstad-Sherman paper did not resolve the debate. In fact, three debates were running concurrently and damaging the relations among the services: Which service should control nuclear weapons? Should the supercarrier be built? What should be the size of the Marine Corps? Forrestal, who had become the first secretary of defense, grew frustrated with the marathon negotiation sessions and endless meetings that served only to entrench the services in their antagonistic positions. On 11 March 1948 he took the Joint Chiefs of Staff (without Admiral William D. Leahy) for a three-day retreat in Key West, Florida. The group met again in Washington, D.C., on 20 March. Forrestal was able to narrow the differences between the navy and the

air force about their respective aviation roles. Progress was also made on defining the role and responsibilities of the Marine Corps in a way that was acceptable to the army. On 21 April 1948, on Forrestal's recommendation, Truman revoked Executive Order 9877 and replaced it with what came to be known as the Key West "Functions" paper (also called the Key West Agreement).

The interservice peace engendered by the Key West Agreement, and subsequent clarifications made at a conference in Newport, Rhode Island, on 20 August, was short lived. Some differences were resolved, but the two main protagonists, the navy and the air force, were unable to reach an agreement concerning the role of nuclear weapons and strategic bombing. These issues, and disagreements over budget allocation, came to a head in 1949 in the debate between the two services over the relative merits of the B-36 bomber and the supercarrier. The navy estimated the cost of the carrier at $190 million, but this figure did not include the thirty-nine ships that would be required for the carrier task force or the aircraft on the carrier. Including these brought the price tag to $1.265 billion (in 1949 prices). Louis A. Johnson, who had become secretary of defense in March 1949, asked the Joint Chiefs of Staff for their views. With the exception of Admiral Louis E. Denfield, they recommended cancellation of the project. Johnson acted quickly. On Saturday, 23 April, after clearing his decision with Truman but without informing or consulting with Secretary of the Navy John L. Sullivan or Admiral Denfield, Johnson issued instructions to cancel the project. Three days later, Sullivan resigned.

The decision—and the manner in which it was made—outraged the navy and its supporters. They accused Johnson of being antinavy, of trying to relegate the navy to a secondary force, if not do away with its separate existence altogether. Johnson's decision to cancel the supercarrier in favor of more B-36s created at least the appearance of conflict of interest because he was once a member of the board of Consolidated-Vultee, the manufacturer of the B-36. The case for the air-force position was not helped by a finding by the Joint Intelligence Committee of the Joint Chiefs of Staff that General Hoyt Vandenberg, the air force chief of staff, had oversimplified and underestimated the size of the Soviet bomber fleet by some four hundred planes. It appeared that, contrary to Vandenberg's optimistic scenarios, the air force would not be able to bomb the Soviet Union unimpeded and without fear of retaliation. The navy decided to strike back, launching an all-out campaign not only against the decision to cancel the supercarrier but also aimed at denying funds for the air force's prized B-36. The navy gave Op-23, a research unit under the deputy secretary of defense, the task of collecting information to assist in the campaign. Headed by Captain Arleigh A. Burke, Op-23 not only compiled background and technical information on the value of the supercarrier; it also researched and documented technical flaws in the B-36. The navy then found ways to share much of that information with the press, which described the B-36 as a "billion dollar blunder" and a plane with "mediocre capabilities." Navy supporters in Congress launched an investigation, and in the hearings before the House Armed Services Committee, held in August and October 1949, a series of witnesses—including Vice Admiral Arthur W. Radford, Admiral Denfield, and Captain Burke, as well as technical specialists—questioned the secretary's decision, its motives, and its wisdom. Admiral Denfield raised three issues, in the process reopening the Key West Agreement to which he had earlier agreed: first, the B-36 was not a good plane because it was afflicted with technical flaws and could be easily intercepted; second, strategic bombing—especially if it relied on nuclear weapons—was not a sound theory on which to base the country's military doctrine; and third, the supercarrier was a more versatile and effective fighting machine. Admiral Radford was especially effective in his presentation, although some would say that his criticism of the B-36 and its vulnerabilities was not always factually based. He presented the navy's national-security strategy for the United States—an idea markedly different from that offered by the air force. The air force believed the best way to defeat the Soviet Union was to attack its territory and population from the air, especially with

nuclear weapons. This approach was an extension of the strategic-bombing concept. The navy said that the air force did not have the planes that could penetrate Soviet air space in large enough numbers to carry out this mission. Instead, the goal should be to provide support for the American troops in Europe so they could withstand a Soviet ground assault. For that goal the United States needed to control the seas, and to do so it needed large carriers.

The air force presented impressive witnesses too, including General Omar N. Bradley, chairman of the Joint Chiefs of Staff; W. Stuart Symington, secretary of the air force; and General J. Lawton Collins, the army chief of staff. General Bradley's testimony was especially effective, convincing many that the issue at stake was not the merits of the supercarrier relative to those of the B-36. Rather, Bradley hinted that the issue was the navy's refusal to cooperate more closely with the other services in order to avoid redundancy, reduce waste, and increase efficiency. He warned against challenging the authority of the president and the secretary of defense over defense matters, arguing that this was nothing short of an "open rebellion against civilian control." He urged the navy to be more amenable to cooperation with the other services.

The hearing helped Johnson, and the committee expressed its confidence in and support for his decision. Admiral Denfield, who publicly criticized Francis P. Matthews, Sullivan's successor as secretary of the navy—and who had also angered his navy comrades by accepting the Key West Agreement—was removed from his post as chief of naval operations and transferred to "other duties." (He is still considered the only member of the Joint Chiefs of Staff to have been fired.) Admiral Burke's name was temporarily removed from the list of officers due for promotion. Another navy officer, Captain John G. Crommelin, was placed on furlough and took early retirement. Admiral Sherman, who replaced Denfield, abolished Op-23. The Revolt of the Admirals was over. The navy lost the battle.

It is not a pretty sight to see the chief commander of one of the military branches openly questioning the decisions made by his civilian superior and organize a public campaign to overturn that decision. Some of the criticism—especially that offered by Admiral Denfield—went too far. The episode, however, was not completely out of line with the tradition of civil-military relations in the United States. The leaders of one of the military branches have often formed a coalition with members of Congress in whose districts the service has important installations in order to advance legislation or budgetary allocations favored by that particular service. The admirals' pleading in 1949 was more public; they

ADMIRALS' REVOLT

openly questioned the wisdom of their civilian superior's decision. The hearings did have beneficial effects. They showed the public the degree of animosity and mistrust that existed among the services, leading to greater interest in Congress in correcting the situation. The hearings also put to rest the accusation that the B-36 decision was not made on the merits of the airplane itself. The hearings, however, did not resolve the issues of redefined roles and missions for the services, the merit of strategic bombing as a strategy, or the role of nuclear weapons. On these, like on so many other issues, the services continued to muddle through.

—BENJAMIN FRANKEL, SECURITY STUDIES

Viewpoint:
No, the admirals were not right to challenge the civilian leadership.

The period between the end of the Second World War in 1945 and the outbreak of the Korean War in 1950 was a time of virtually unprecedented change in the priorities, organization, technology, and politics of U.S. foreign and defense policy. Given the tumult of the times, it is not surprising that members of one service, the U.S. Navy, believed that their organizational interests and those of the United States were being compromised by the strategic choices and procurement priorities embraced by the Truman administration. In the opinion of many naval officers, these administration decisions favored the new U.S. Air Force, separated from the U.S. Army by the National Security Act of 1947, at the expense of carrier aviation. These naval officers decided to take their complaints about the Truman administration decision to cancel the construction of the supercarrier *United States* (CVA–58) in favor of the air force B-36 bomber directly to Congress. This so-called Revolt of the Admirals culminated in hearings before the House Armed Services Committee in August and October 1949.

The Revolt of the Admirals was set in motion by a series of events that started with the draw down in U.S. military forces at the end of the Second World War. The Truman administration was committed to reducing defense spending to a peacetime level of about $15 billion annually, an amount that would be shared more or less evenly among the army, navy, and air force. This new austerity forced the services to make some difficult choices. The navy chose to abandon its diversified wartime ship-construction program in favor of devoting scarce

resources to its next generation of aircraft carrier, which would allow it to deploy larger aircraft capable of delivering nuclear weapons. The air force chose to reduce the number of fighter and transport aircraft in its programs to build greater numbers of its first intercontinental nuclear bomber, the B-36.

Several developments complicated this inevitable and appropriate draw down in U.S. defense spending and force structure. The National Security Act of 1947 created the Department of Defense, along with the air force. Often referred to at the time as "service unification," this reorganization of the U.S. defense establishment had an extraordinarily disruptive effect on interservice and civil-military relations within the U.S. government. Naval aviators feared that the nascent air force

ADMIRALS' REVOLT

would gain control of naval aviation, just as it had gained control of army aircraft.

Service unification created a host of unresolved issues that required negotiation. For example, the 1947 Key West Agreement, which divided roles and missions among the services, seemed to create confusion about the role the newly established Joint Chiefs of Staff would play in setting defense budgets and priorities. The new institutions and procedures created by the National Security Act seemed to leave important actors, such as the Joint Chiefs of Staff, unsure about whether they were being consulted or informed by Truman administration officials. These organizational reforms, however, occurred as the postwar strategic landscape was evolving. The emerging cold war suggested that the United States might again face a hostile land power in the heart of Europe just as the marriage of nuclear weapons and long-range aviation seemed to promise a relatively inexpensive way to deter Soviet adventurism. The American public also became enamored with the image of air power depicted by a sophisticated air-force public-relations campaign, which highlighted the capabilities of the long-range aircraft that were beginning to enter the U.S. inventory.

All of these events coalesced in the spring of 1949 as Louis A. Johnson, Truman's new secretary of defense, asked the Joint Chiefs of Staff to help prepare the fiscal year 1951 defense budget. The air-force and army chiefs voted against the navy on the construction of the supercarrier, advising Johnson that the capability provided by the supercarrier would duplicate the Air Force strategic-bombing mission, that the Soviet Union was not a naval power, that the British and U.S. fleets already dominated the oceans, and that existing naval capabilities to project power about seven-hundred miles inland were sufficient.

On Saturday, 23 April 1949, just as the keel of the new carrier was about to be laid, Johnson canceled the navy's most important program. Immediately, Secretary of the Navy John L. Sullivan submitted his resignation to Johnson. Sullivan stated that neither he nor the chief of naval operations, Admiral Louis E. Denfield, was informed in advance about Johnson's decision, and he reiterated how the navy had sacrificed other programs to finance the supercarrier. Sullivan also described the long list of budgetary, congressional, and presidential actions that approved construction of the supercarrier. Although naval officers were horrified by Johnson's action, public and congressional reactions to the decision were generally favorable. The powerful chairman of the House Armed Services Committee, Representative Carl Vinson (D-Georgia), supported Johnson and lauded his decision to eliminate an expensive navy weapon that apparently just duplicated an air-force program (the B-36) and mission (strategic bombardment).

The first round in the Admirals' Revolt was actually fired by Captain John G. Crommelin on 9 September 1949, after the navy learned that it faced a $353 million reduction in its fiscal year 1949 budget. Crommelin told reporters that service unification had been a catastrophic mistake and that the navy was gradually being eliminated by the secretary of defense and the Joint Chiefs of Staff. Crommelin was immediately backed by many naval officers, much to the horror of Francis P. Matthews, who had succeeded Sullivan as secretary of the navy and was trying to contain dissension within navy ranks. When Undersecretary of the Navy Dan A. Kimball addressed a meeting of senior naval officers in Monterey, California, on 21–23 September 1949, he encouraged them to voice their concerns through their chain of command and not to go directly to the press with their complaints. Vice Admiral Gerald F. Bogan, commander of the First Task Force of the Pacific Fleet, followed Kimball's advice and forwarded a letter to the secretary of the navy. Endorsed by Admiral Arthur W. Radford, commander in chief of the U.S. Pacific Fleet and the chief of naval operations, Bogan's letter and attached endorsements criticized defense unification, called attention to deteriorating morale within the navy, and noted the important role of the navy in defending America. Crommelin, following a 1 October appearance on *Meet the Press,* during which he stated that he had been ordered not to talk about interservice differences, provided copies of the Bogan correspondence to the press. After meeting with Matthews, Denfield, and Radford on 3 October, Vinson decided he could no longer postpone hearings about service unification and should give the navy an opportunity to express its views.

The hearings were a strange affair. Navy representatives called into question the destructive power of nuclear weapons, the efficacy of strategic bombardment, and the survivability of the B-36 if attacked by the navy's best carrier-based fighters. Navy witnesses sometimes contradicted each other, and their testimony failed to make a coherent attack against the air force or a compelling case for their supercarrier. Naval officers spoke of the important role played by carrier aviation in defeating the Japanese navy in the Pacific island-hopping campaign during the Second World War, but they failed to respond to questions about how this capability was relevant to meeting a Soviet land threat in the heart of Europe. By contrast, air-force spokesmen made a moderate case for how strategic bombing, especially by the B-36, addressed the primary security threat to the United States by supplying a nuclear deterrent against an emerging Soviet nuclear arsenal.

Although the weak case offered by the navy may be attributed partly to the secrecy required as officers prepared to make their case to Congress, the navy's position suffered from a more fundamental flaw embedded in its organizational culture. When challenged, the navy turns to tradition—in this case the dominant role played by carrier aviation during the last war—as a guide to policy and strategy. Yet, in the changing strategic environment of the late 1940s, no one except naval officers seemed to understand how the navy's experience in the Pacific would be relevant to the emerging cold war with the Soviet Union. Instead, most observers believed that the supercarrier was just a navy gambit to steal the strategic-bombing mission allocated to the air force.

Naval officers were wrong to revolt—to go outside their chain of command to inform members of Congress that they disagreed with an administration's policies—not because this sort of activity is categorically wrong but because they failed to justify the revolt by clearly and convincingly linking their concerns to national interests. Cancellation of the supercarrier in 1949 threatened naval officers because many of them viewed the ship as representing the navy's future. The ship was so obviously important to them and the future of the navy that they saw no need to articulate its role in fulfilling national-security requirements. Instead, they asserted the importance of carrier aviation and the folly of strategic bombing. In a sense naval leaders were forced to revolt because they never really attempted to explain how the supercarrier represented more than just a bureaucratic priority for the navy. Carrying their case to Congress failed to advance the admirals' cause because it simply highlighted the weakness of the navy's position to a larger and more influential audience.

–JAMES J. WIRTZ, U.S. NAVAL POSTGRADUATE
SCHOOL

References

George W. Baer, *One Hundred Years of Sea Power: The U.S. Navy, 1890–1990* (Stanford, Cal.: Stanford University Press, 1994);

Carl H. Builder, *The Masks of War: American Military Styles in Strategy and Analysis* (Baltimore: Johns Hopkins University Press, 1989);

Demetrios Caraley, *The Politics of Military Unification: A Study of Conflict and the Military Process* (New York: Columbia University Press, 1966);

Paolo E. Coletta, *The United States Navy and Defense Unification, 1947–1953* (Newark: University of Delaware Press, 1981);

Vincent Davis, *The Admirals Lobby* (Chapel Hill: University of North Carolina Press, 1967);

Paul Y. Hammond, "Supercarriers and B–36 Bombers: Appropriations, Strategy and Politics," in *American Civil-Military Decisions: A Book of Case Studies*, edited by Harold Stein (Birmingham: University of Alabama Press, 1963), pp. 465–567;

Michael A. Palmer, *Origins of the Maritime Strategy: American Naval Strategy in the First Postwar Decade* (Washington, D.C.: Naval Historical Center, Department of the Navy, 1988);

Mark Perry, *Four Stars: The Inside Story of the Forty-Year Battle Between the Joint Chiefs of Staff and America's Civilian Leaders* (Boston: Houghton Mifflin, 1989);

Steven L. Rearden, *The Formative Years, 1947–1950*, volume 1 of *History of the Office of the Secretary of Defense*, edited by Alfred Goldberg (Washington, D.C.: Office of the Secretary of Defense, 1984);

David Alan Rosenberg, "American Postwar Air Doctrine and Organization: The Navy Experience," in *Air Power and Warfare: Proceedings of the 8th Military History Symposium*, edited by Alfred F. Hurley and Robert C. Erhart (Washington, D.C.: Office of Air Force History, 1979), pp. 245–278.

AFGHANISTAN

Was U.S. opposition to the Soviet-supported government in Afghanistan the right policy?

Viewpoint: Yes, U.S. policy toward the Soviet-supported government in Afghanistan was successful in blocking communist expansion.

Viewpoint: No, U.S. policy toward Soviet-supported government in Afghanistan sacrificed important foreign-policy goals for marginal ones and left greater problems in its wake.

In December 1979 the Soviet Union invaded Afghanistan. Much of the available evidence suggests that the deterioration of Hafizullah Amin's Marxist regime in that country during the later months of that year presented what the Soviets believed to be challenges to their security interests. The loss of the American influence in neighboring Iran, beginning in January 1979 with the increasing success of the fundamentalist Islamic revolutionary movement, presented the Soviets with an opportunity to expand their influence in the Middle East. Shoring up a tottering socialist regime also promised to fulfill the Brezhnev doctrine's commitment not to allow socialist states to "lapse" into capitalism.

Regardless of Soviet motivations, the United States strongly opposed Moscow's intervention in Afghanistan and the puppet government it established under Babrak Karmal. President Jimmy Carter immediately withdrew the SALT II arms-limitation treaty, an agreement favorable to the Soviets, from Senate consideration for ratification. He also stepped up the defense spending that was already under way and announced that U.S. athletes would boycott the Summer 1980 Moscow Olympic Games.

The administration of his successor, Ronald W. Reagan, went further. Over the course of the 1980s, it supplied the Afghan resistance, the mujahidin, with large amounts of military hardware. Agreements with bordering Pakistan, and other Muslim countries in the Middle East, increased the flow of armaments to the Afghan guerrillas. Although the Soviets expected a quick campaign to install and stabilize a strong pro-Soviet government, the resistance of the mujahidin caused them to remain for nearly ten years and sustain significant casualties. In 1989 the last Soviet troops were withdrawn, without having achieved their goal.

**Viewpoint:
Yes, U.S. policy toward the Soviet-supported government in Afghanistan was successful in blocking communist expansion.**

The Soviet involvement and eventual intervention in the domestic politics of Afghanistan in the late 1970s led to the installation of a pro-Soviet government whose continued existence relied on Soviet military operations within its national borders. Under Presidents Jimmy Carter and Ronald W. Reagan, the

United States opposed the satellite government in Kabul and the Soviet military presence that supported it. The catalyst of the Soviet invasion and the threats it posed to American security interests moved the United States and much of the rest of the Western world away from their previous inclinations toward détente, an attempt to reduce superpower tensions through improved commercial and diplomatic relations. Instead, the United States and many of its allies returned to a confrontational relationship with the Soviet Union. Although Carter responded to the invasion with a return to many of the containment policies of his predecessors, it was during the Reagan presidency that the policy toward Afghanistan was prominently coordinated with other attempts to "roll back" Soviet power and influence on a global scale. In the long run American opposition to the pro-Soviet Afghan regime tied Moscow down in a long, destructive war and contributed to the ultimate collapse of the USSR.

Given the disastrous military and diplomatic consequences of the Soviet invasion of Afghanistan, it is difficult to understand why the Soviet leadership decided to do it. The Politburo's chief military advisers opposed it from the beginning. The decision seems to have been made by a relatively small working group of the leadership, whose resolve was based partly on ideology. The so-called Brezhnev Doctrine, best exemplified by the invasion of Czechoslovakia in 1968, brought upon Moscow the responsibility to support and maintain existing socialist regimes. Claiming to have history on its side, the Soviet Union could not tolerate setbacks, and the factionalism of the Afghan leadership seemed to threaten the country's stability. Soviet intelligence believed that the recently installed Afghan prime minister, Hafizullah Amin, was inclined toward rapprochement with the West or even a Western agent.

Doubts about Amin's reliability fueled the strategic rationale behind the invasion. The Soviets had for decades regarded Afghanistan as within their sphere of influence. Even before its monarchy was overthrown by Mohammad Daud Kahn's broadly based revolutionary movement in 1973, the connection between Moscow and Kabul had been close. Daud's regime maintained those close relations with the Soviets at first. When they began to deteriorate, Moscow intervened to unify the Afghan communist movement under the leader of one of its factions, Nur Mohammad Taraki. By April 1978 Taraki had become strong enough to depose Daud and resume close contact with the Soviet Union. Marxist reforms undertaken by the new government enjoyed little popularity, however, and even less practical success in the underdeveloped country. As Taraki became less and less effective, the Soviets promoted his replacement by

Amin, whose followers murdered Taraki and took power in the fall of 1979.

As Afghanistan was sinking into domestic crisis, the Islamic revolution in neighboring Iran began to attract Soviet attention. From the strategic viewpoint of the United States, losing its close relationship with Iran, a country President Richard M. Nixon had described as one of the "twin pillars of stability" in the Middle East only a few years before, was a terrible prospect. Although one aspect of détente was its emphasis on retracting overseas American military commitments, the mismanagement of that process in Iran had created a dangerous situation. While the Ayatollah Ruholla Khomeini was no friend of communism, from the outset it was no secret that he despised the United States and would distance his country from Washington in the future.

Much analysis of the problem of U.S. relations with Iran loses track of the connection between it and Soviet influence in Afghanistan, even though its geographic position gave the Soviet Union a means of exerting geopolitical influence on Iran. Examining the American loss of Iran in the context of the decline of détente is also revealing. In the months that followed Mohammad Reza Shah Pahlavi's departure from Iran in January 1979, provocative Soviet and Soviet-sponsored military activity elsewhere in the Third World continued without cessation. Violations of the Helsinki agreements on human rights worsened bilateral superpower relations in the final Brezhnev years. Even though the second round of Strategic Arms Limitation Talks (SALT II) was signed after long and difficult negotiations in the summer of 1979, the atmosphere surrounding the agreement was poisoned. These events, together with the Iranian revolution and its threat to American interests in the Middle East, elicited the beginning of increases in American rearmament.

Some Soviet apologists have argued that it was actually Carter's increases in American military power, particularly his administration's agreements with Western European countries to deploy the Pershing II cruise missile, that accentuated Soviet insecurity and led Moscow to invade Afghanistan. They cannot say why the Soviets chose to respond to this "provocation" in Afghanistan and not in a more direct and meaningful area, nor do they take into account the nature of Soviet behavior, which included improvements in strategic-nuclear forces, in the years leading up to the invasion. It is clear, however, that Soviet designs on Afghanistan increased in direct proportion to Carter's reinforcement of the American military. In July 1979 a "military mission" that happened to include eleven prominent Soviet field commanders (one of whom, General Pavlovsky, had commanded the Soviet invasion of Czechoslovakia in 1968) was sent to take up residence in Kabul, a

AFGHANISTAN

few months before Taraki was replaced with Soviet support by the seemingly more reliable Amin. The deployment of five American aircraft-carrier battle groups to the Persian Gulf and Eastern Mediterranean after radical Iranians took hostage the staff of the American embassy in Tehran in November and the unsuccessful covert attempt to rescue them left the impression that the United States might try to restore its position in Iran through a massive military operation.

However seriously Carter considered that option, the Soviets could not have ignored a major deployment of American military power in an area where they had the opportunity to alter the balance of forces. Strategically, they faced a choice. They could either do nothing and allow the United States to restore its influence in Iran, or they could make their own deployment nearby in the region to deter that possibility, and even have the chance of influencing events in Iran to their own benefit. The Senate's refusal to ratify SALT II, largely because of Soviet transgressions of human-rights issues and Moscow's continuing lack of geopolitical restraint, could hardly have created the impression that the USSR had something to lose by defying the West more directly. The Soviets' questions raised about Amin's reliability following his recent ascendency to power increased the urgency of the matter.

On 25 December 1979 Soviet troops entered Afghanistan. Two days later crack KGB combat troops seized the presidential residence in Kabul, promptly murdered Amin, and installed a puppet regime under Babrak Karmal. More than 80,000 Soviet troops entered the country, forming a presence that rose to 100,000 by the end of January 1980. World reaction was a disaster for Moscow. A censure vote in the United Nations resoundingly criticized the Soviet Union for its unprovoked attack. President Carter withdrew SALT II from Senate consideration and announced an American boycott of the 1980 Moscow Olympic Games. The American military buildup that had started in mid 1979 increased dramatically. Western European governments that had been inclined toward improved relations with the Soviet Union veered sharply toward Washington. Even communist parties in Western Europe, once slavishly loyal to Moscow, criticized the invasion.

Militarily, the course of the invasion indicated an important strain in Soviet strategic thought and illustrated its potential as a liability. Although most of the resistance was to be found in the southeastern part of Afghanistan, more than half of the Soviet troops were sent to the western part of the country, bordering on Iran, where there was comparatively little opposition. While American military action against Iran never occurred, however, the potential Soviet influence over the development of the Islamic revolution did not conciliate Tehran with Moscow, despite some initial success. Perhaps it was enough that Iran's departure from the American orbit was permanent.

A more serious issue was the future of the Soviet role in Afghanistan. As far as the pacification of the country was concerned, Moscow believed that the installation of a firmly pro-Soviet regime would be a brief operation, on the model of its effective interventions in Hungary in 1956 and Czechoslovakia in 1968. The existing instability in Afghanistan, however, made it much more difficult to keep Karmal in power. What had been accomplished in days in 1956 and 1968 could not be accomplished by ten years of Soviet involvement in Afghanistan. Resistance to the new government, led by the mujahidin, enjoyed tremendous popular support and was sanctioned by Islamic religious leaders. In these circumstances Soviet troops had to remain.

In that resistance the Reagan administration, committed to a strategy of "rolling back" Soviet forward positions and disrupting the USSR's domestic economy, saw a tremendous opportunity. Washington's favorable relationship with Pakistan enabled it to supply the mujahidin with a high volume of the latest and most sophisticated conventional weaponry. Energized by firm American support, the Afghan resistance carried out a guerrilla campaign that put the Soviets in the same position in which the United States had found itself in Vietnam. The mujahidin were so successful in

AFGHANISTAN

fighting the Soviets that they actually devoted some of their resources to serving as a conduit for trafficking destabilizing and subversive materials to the Soviet Central Asian republics. For most of the rest of its existence, the Soviet Union had to contend with what amounted to an open wound on its southern frontier.

For Moscow the consequences of American opposition to the pro-Soviet government in Kabul were legion. The resolve and success of the mujahidin completely demoralized the Soviet military and had substantial consequences for Soviet society. The continuing drain on the USSR's resources exacerbated its anemic economic growth and its geopolitical overextension. Commitments in Afghanistan undermined the reform policies of Yuri Andropov and Mikhail Gorbachev, reforms to which reductions in military expenditure and diplomatic tension were unmistakably prerequisite. Even though Gorbachev suggested the withdrawal of Soviet forces from Afghanistan as early as October 1985, that essential step in reducing the drain on Soviet resources was not accomplished until February 1989.

Escalations of American aid to the mujahidin continued to bog down the Soviets and caused dangerously high levels of disillusionment in the ranks of their army. After the initial attack, Soviet military policy was directed toward sparing the USSR's best resources, and the consequences for the campaign were horrendous. Troops deployed to Afghanistan were generally sent there as punishment for criminal behavior or poor discipline records, or out of ethnic prejudice. While the first policy brought the worst elements of the Soviet military into its only major combat situation, the second mainly involved Muslim recruits from Central Asia, who had many cultural commonalities with the people they were supposed to fight and no great love for Moscow or their ethnic Russian comrades. A recent study suggests that as many as 50 percent of the Soviet troops in Afghanistan used narcotics derived from the large and easily accessible poppy crop. Sanitation and hygiene were extremely problematic. While about thirteen thousand Soviet troops were killed in Afghanistan, more than four hundred thousand contracted serious diseases. Domestically, Soviet citizens were becoming frustrated over a pointless war that continued even while Gorbachev talked about peace. The reformist policy of glasnost, or public openness, gave them limited freedoms to express their dissatisfaction. The ethnic component of Soviet military policy and the infiltration of subversive materials into Central Asia through the mujahidin contributed to the political destabilization of the region in the late 1980s. These problems, it must be remembered, were catalyzed by tepid responses to American policies broadly designed to drain Soviet power.

American opposition to the Soviet-backed regime in Afghanistan was a crucial element in the victory of the United States in the cold war. Most important, the Soviet intervention and support for Karmal's government galvanized the return to containment under Carter and set the stage for Reagan's ultimately victorious policies of rolling back Soviet influence. The American policy was important psychologically because it represented fresh successful resistance to communist expansion in the Third World. The politics of the entire cold war were influenced by Afghanistan because continued Soviet involvement frustrated the reformist Andropov-Gorbachev strategy of renewing détente with the West and focusing resources on domestic economic reform. At a time in its history when the Soviet Union could least afford prolonged military operations, its Afghan war was instrumental in precipitating the collapse of the Soviet military. The Russian army is less effective today than it was when it left Afghanistan in 1989. Even though the human costs for the people of Afghanistan were enormous, they never wavered in fighting for their freedom. The United States employed the right policy.

–PAUL DU QUENOY,
GEORGE WASHINGTON UNIVERSITY

Viewpoint:
No, U.S. policy toward Soviet-supported government in Afghanistan sacrificed important foreign-policy goals for marginal ones and left greater problems in its wake.

A policy should be embedded in a clear strategy that defines goals to be achieved, means to achieve them, and the priority in which they should be pursued. The ranking of priorities is especially important because countries have many goals and only limited means to pursue them. It is difficult to see what, precisely, were the criteria by which the Reagan administration decided a friendly government in Afghanistan was so important to the United States that other significant goals should be compromised or neglected in its favor.

During the cold war the main justification given for U.S. military interventions, or support for proxies, in other countries was that such direct or indirect actions prevented the balance of power from tipping toward the Soviets or pro-

**Soviet soldiers removing
a land mine from a road in
Afghanistan**

*(Collection of Oleg Sarin
and Lev Dvoretsky)*

them carefully in places and on issues that count. Leaders in a democracy face additional hurdles: their policies are subject to public scrutiny, and unwise policies have repercussions beyond the personal careers of these officials. The unwise U.S. intervention in Vietnam is a good example. The United States paid a heavy price in blood and treasure for its venture into the jungles of southeast Asia. One of the casualties of the Vietnam War was the freedom of action of postwar American decisionmakers, who were hobbled by the Vietnam Syndrome; that is, the wasteful excesses of Vietnam heightened American sensitivity to casualties in foreign wars to such a degree that the United States has found it difficult to contemplate the sacrifices that, at times, have been necessary to advance important national-security interests. Wasteful ventures are thus doubly harmful. They squander resources on unimportant objectives, and they make it more difficult to use these resources for securing important objectives.

The preoccupation of the Reagan and Bush administrations with Afghanistan was not as costly to the United States as Vietnam, but it did compromise important U.S. interests, and it is not clear how it advanced U.S. national goals. As was the case with Reagan's activist anticommunist crusade in Latin America, the administration's "stand" against the Soviet Union in Afghanistan came at a time when the Soviet system was already failing on its own. Russia was reeling under the weight and cost of maintaining an empire while trying to provide for itself with a stagnant and unwieldy economic system. This recognition led the Politburo to choose the reform-oriented Mikhail Gorbachev to succeed Konstantin Chernenko in 1985, and it led Gorbachev to launch his policies of perestroika and glasnost.

The December 1979 invasion of Afghanistan by the Soviet Union did not—and could not—change the balance of power between the two superpowers. In fact, most of the countries in the Third World do not matter strategically to the United States. They do not have the resources or military potential to enhance the strength of either superpower. According to figures published by Stephen Van Evera in 1992, the Gross National Product (GNP) of all Latin America is less than half that of Japan; the aggregate GNP of all the countries of Africa is smaller than that of Italy or Britain; and the combined GNP of all the countries of the Third World is smaller than the aggregate GNP of Western Europe. Therefore, Van Evera writes, "Because the Third World has little industrial power, it has little military potential, and correspondingly little strategic importance. . . . [With the exception of the

moted democracy and human rights. By these criteria, it was a mistake for the United States to back the Afghan mujahidin in their resistance to the Soviet invasion of their country. U.S. support for the mujahidin was ill advised because Afghanistan did not matter to the superpowers' relative power and because the mujahidin and their successors, the Taliban, did not fight to make Afghanistan a liberal democracy but rather a backward, oppressive theocracy that instituted reactionary measures such as not allowing girls to go to school. The Reagan administration's preoccupation with the question of who should rule a remote and marginal state such as Afghanistan led it to ignore the more important issue of Pakistan's nuclear-weapons program while devoting its attention to training and equipping Muslim fanatics who, after helping to push the USSR out of Afghanistan, turned against the United States and its interests.

Even rich and powerful countries such as the United States do not have limitless power. They have to husband their resources and spend

Persian Gulf] realignments in . . . the Third World would have little effect on the global distribution of industrial strength, and thus would have little effect on the global balance of power."

Even in comparison to other Third World countries, Afghanistan is an especially poor and destitute country, devoid of any assets or resources that would be of interest to outside powers. Assuming that the Soviet Union were interested in creating an empire and augmenting it, even assuming that in the late 1970s and early 1980s the USSR was in a position to stave off its secular decline or that the Soviets saw the invasion of Afghanistan as an element in a campaign to forestall their decline, it is not clear how the "addition" of Afghanistan to the Soviet sphere of influence would have strengthened the USSR in its competition with the United States. Adding Afghanistan to an already declining Soviet empire was not adding an asset, but a liability. When Gorbachev came to power, he recognized the burdens imposed on the Soviet Union by Afghanistan and other possessions and moved to disengage the USSR from them.

There was thus no strategic reason for the United States to intervene in Afghanistan, even through proxy. There was nothing in Afghanistan that would have added to Soviet power. There was nothing there that, if denied to the United States, would have weakened America.

Nor was U.S. intervention by proxy helpful, perhaps, in fostering democratic practices and human rights in Afghanistan. It is doubtful whether any U.S. interventions in the Third World during the cold war were genuinely motivated by the desire to spread democratic practices, or, if so motivated, truly effective in doing so. In light of the professed adherence of the United States to the goal of spreading democracy in the Third World, it is striking to note how many of the states in which the United States intervened had democratically elected governments whose policies the United States found disagreeable: Iran (1953), Guatemala (1954), British Guiana (1953–1964), Indonesia (1957), Ecuador (1960–1963), Brazil (1964), the Dominican Republic (1965), Costa Rica (mid 1950s), and Chile (1973). The role the United States played in Greece (1967) and Jamaica (1976–1980) has also come under suspicion. Some of America's clients in the Third World—in El Salvador and Guatemala, for example—or movements it has supported—such as the Khmer Rouge in Cambodia—were implicated in mass killing of civilians (tens of thousands in El Salvador, hundreds of thousands in Guatemala, millions in Cambodia).

Aid to the mujahidin, who were fighting the Soviet-supported regime in Kabul and the Soviet troops sustaining it, could not have possibly been construed as aid for democracy or human rights. The mujahidin were an eclectic group dominated by Islamic fundamentalists such as Gulbuddin Hekmatyar (the "Afghan Khomeini"), eager to impose a theocratic rule on Afghanistan, and drug traffickers such as Nasin Akhunzada (the "heroin king"), upset with the measures the pro-Soviet regime of Hafizullah Amin took to restrict their trade. On 27 December 1979, two days after the Soviet invasion, Amin was killed in a Soviet-orchestrated coup and was replaced by Babrak Karmal. The mujahidin did not fight only the Russians; they engaged in a widespread terror campaign against their political and religious opponents in Afghanistan and Pakistan while continuing to export opium to support their activities. (Afghanistan is the second largest opium producer in the world, after Burma.) After the Soviets withdrew from Afghanistan, the mujahidin, by then under the leadership of the fundamentalist Taliban movement, plunged Afghanistan into a bitter and costly civil war. They have been able to take over most of Afghanistan, imposing harsh Islamic laws in the areas under their control. They have also engaged in periodic massacres of Sh'ite Muslims, leading to rising tensions with neighboring Iran.

Using American taxpayers' money to help impose a medieval, punitive theocracy, whose leaders are dedicated to increasing Afghanistan's sale of opium to Western criminal organizations, was not a wise decision. There are, however, more-dangerous consequences of Reagan's policies in Afghanistan.

First, Pakistan has become a nuclear-weapon state. The Carter administration had cut U.S. economic and military aid to Pakistan after that nation violated U.S. wishes by pursuing the development of nuclear weapons. Yet, when the Soviets invaded Afghanistan, the United States needed Pakistan as a conduit for aid to the mujahidin, and Pakistan would allow such aid to flow through it only if American sanctions were lifted. U.S. law allows the president to "certify" that a country under suspicion of developing nuclear weapons is not, in fact, doing so, thus permitting aid to that country to continue. Carter made such a "certification" in 1980, and Reagan and Bush continued to issue these bogus documents until the Soviets withdrew from Afghanistan. This ten-year grace period allowed Pakistan to build its bombs unmolested and to test several of them openly in May 1998. It is not clear whether sustained American pressure would have persuaded Pakistan to end its nuclear-weapons program. It is also not clear whether the Reagan administration, always lax on the issue of the proliferation of nuclear weapons, would have pressured Pakistan to do so even if there had been no need to use that country as a conduit of

AFGHANISTAN

aid to Afghanistan. The fact is, because of its pre-occupation with Afghanistan, the United States did not apply such pressure during the crucial years of weapons development in Pakistan. By any measure, the addition of one more state to the nuclear club is a far more important issue than who rules Afghanistan. If a state such as Pakistan were to share its nuclear knowledge with yet other states, the consequences for the United States could be dire. Yet, the Reagan administration appeared to have cared more about who ruled the dusty streets of Kabul than about the next nuclear upstart.

Second, American security was compromised in yet another, more immediate, way by the Reagan administration's policies in Afghanistan. The United States helped to train and equip thousands of Muslim fanatics who fought the Soviet occupiers with daring and dedication. These fanatics, however, have no more warm feeling toward the United States and the West than they did toward the USSR. Once they helped to push the Soviets out of Afghanistan, they turned their attention to the hated "infidel" West and its "satanic" leader, the United States. Many of the terrorist activities against the United States in the last decade have been perpetrated by former mujahidin. From the Khobar Tower in Saudi Arabia to the World Trade Center in New York City to the U.S. embassies in East Africa, the trail unmistakably leads to former mujahidin and their leaders. Afghanistan also happens to be the home base of Osama bin Laden, the Saudi master-terrorist who relies on the hospitality and support of erstwhile U.S. allies in Afghanistan to pursue his goals of bringing down the United States and everything with which it is associated.

Some commentators have argued that the costly involvement in Afghanistan may have helped to hasten the demise of the Soviet Union. Yet, the Soviet Union was already declining, and the inner contradictions of its economy and society would likely have caused it to disintegrate with or without the involvement in Afghanistan. Even assuming that Soviet military presence in Afghanistan hastened the Soviet decline, in the long run the U.S. policy toward that involve-ment was costly for the United States. The Reagan administration ignored the nuclear program in Pakistan—thus contributing to the nucle-arization of the subcontinent—while helping a theocratic, fundamentalist movement that is now an egregious human-rights violator in its own country and the major actor in a terrorist campaign against the United States. It is not often that the costs of a policy and its aims are so mismatched. Reagan's Afghanistan policy is such a case.

–BENJAMIN FRANKEL, SECURITY STUDIES

References

Robert H. Johnson, "Exaggerating America's Stakes in Third World Conflict," *International Security,* 10 (Winter 1985/1986): 32–68;

William E. Odom, *The Collapse of the Soviet Military* (New Haven: Yale University Press, 1998);

Peter Schweizer, *Victory: The Reagan Administration's Secret Strategy that Hastened the Collapse of the Soviet Union* (New York: Atlantic Monthly Press, 1994);

Jerome Slater, "Dominos in Central America: Will They Fall? Does It Matter?" *International Security,* 12 (Fall 1987): 105–134;

Stephen Van Evera, "The United States and the Third World: When to Intervene?" in *Eagle in a New World: American Grand Strategy in the Post–Cold War Era,* edited by Kenneth A. Oye, Robert J. Lieber, and Donald Rothchild (New York: HarperCollins, 1992), pp. 105–150;

Stephen M. Walt, "The Case for Finite Containment: Analyzing U.S. Grand Strategy," *International Security,* 14 (Summer 1989): 5–49;

Bob Woodward, *Veil: The Secret Wars of the CIA, 1981–1987* (New York: Simon & Schuster, 1987).

AFGHANISTAN

ALLIANCE FOR PROGRESS

Did the Alliance for Progress achieve its goals?

Viewpoint: Yes, the Alliance for Progress contributed to economic and social development in Latin America and laid the groundwork for later reforms.

Viewpoint: No, the Alliance for Progress fell far short of achieving the reforms it promised.

On 10 September 1960, while campaigning for the presidency in Tampa, Florida, the Democratic candidate, Senator John F. Kennedy of Massachusetts, declared that, if elected, his administration would engage in "a great common effort to develop the resources of the entire hemisphere, strengthen the forces of democracy, and widen the vocational and educational opportunities of every person in all of the Americas."

The impetus behind what was dubbed a "Marshall Plan for Latin America" was the increasing fear among American policymakers that, unless something was done to improve living conditions for people of the western hemisphere, more and more countries in the region would become vulnerable to communist subversion and takeover similar to the one led by Fidel Castro in Cuba in 1959–1960. On assuming office, Kennedy asked Adolph Berle, an old New Dealer, to head a task force on Latin America to recommend strategies for dealing with the poverty, social ills, and political instability in the southern half of the hemisphere. On 13 March 1961 Kennedy proposed a ten-point, ten-year program based on the recommendations of the task force and asked Congress for $500 million to support the new initiative. On 17 August 1961 twenty countries from the hemisphere met at Punta del Este, Uruguay, to sign the Alliance for Progress Charter and the Declaration of Punta del Este.

The charter called for a ten-year, $20 billion American aid package to Latin American states for economic and social development. It was expected that this money, accompanied by $80 billion of internal investment, would generate a real annual economic growth rate of 2.5 percent. In addition to real economic growth the authors of the charter envisioned improvements in health, education, and housing; reforms in land ownership and taxation; strengthening of democratic institutions; and the economic integration of the countries of Latin America.

Viewpoint:
Yes, the Alliance for Progress contributed to economic and social development in Latin America and laid the groundwork for later reforms.

Few U.S. foreign-policy initiatives have attracted as much controversy and scholarly attention as the Alliance for Progress, the multibillion-dollar program designed to promote economic, social, and political development in Latin America during the 1960s. For a brief period the Alliance for Progress ranked next to the Good Neighbor Policy of the pre–Second World War era as the most successful U.S. policy toward Latin America. In the context of an often unhappy, even bloody, history of relations between the United States and the region, the Alliance for Progress was hailed in all the Americas as a milestone. It called for nothing less than the complete transformation of Latin American society, economy, and politics—a far more ambitious undertaking than the Marshall Plan, as some scholars have pointed out. It captivated the public and their leaders for what it promised, for the breadth of its vision and scale of its initiatives. Until the hemispheric free-trade and economic-integration schemes of the 1990s, never in inter-American relations had there been such a collective, institutionalized undertaking. Nor had there been such concerted political commitment to social and economic reform. Never before or since had the United States committed itself to a progressive, redistributive agenda in Latin America.

The Alliance for Progress also aroused opposition, criticism, and condemnation from all over the region and from opposite ends of the political spectrum, both for what it achieved and for what it failed to accomplish. There is even debate as to when the Alliance for Progress ended: some point to President John F. Kennedy's death or to the end of the Lyndon B. Johnson administration, and still others point to the "benign neglect" days of President Richard M. Nixon. By and large, the received wisdom has been that the Alliance for Progress was a failure, flawed in design and pitiful in outcome. It has been widely criticized for having brought about neither progress nor alliance, for not only having "lost its way" but even for bringing about the harsh military dictatorships that swept across the region in the mid 1960s.

The Alliance for Progress, however, was not a failure. The indiscriminate arguments to the contrary neglect the tangible and intangible achievements of the program. The Alliance for Progress did not, and could not, bring about the transformation of Latin American society, but it is wrong to assess its contributions by this criterion.

Given the lofty rhetoric and overly ambitious goals of the framers of the Alliance for Progress, "failure" was the only possible outcome. There is no scale—no conceivable standard—to measure the success or failure of any program that seeks to arrest and reverse two centuries of social inequities and economic underdevelopment and to induce stable politics on soil where stable institutions have been scarce since the time of the Spanish conquistadors Hernán Cortés and Francisco Pizarro. Claims that the program failed to achieve peaceful revolution in Latin America overlook some important concrete, smaller-scale achievements—such as increased primary-school enrollments or the establishment of a hemispheric institutional framework and coordination. Likewise, such claims neglect the less quantifiable, intangible, and indirect, but equally important, successes that can be attributed to the alliance. It may not have achieved all its ambitious educational goals, but aggregate numbers in the area of education, for example, reveal little about the inestimable social value of the program to the portion of society that received benefits from it. Indiscriminate claims that the Alliance for Progress failed also do not take into consideration that many of its initiatives were geared toward long-term social investments, and, therefore, the results would not have registered until long after the program had faded and was abandoned altogether.

In view of the inherent difficulties and limitations involved in evaluating the results of any policy initiative, assessments of the success or failure of the Alliance for Progress must ultimately rest on shaky grounds. In this case measurement problems are aggravated because many specific policies included broad, abstract goals such as social justice, improved human rights, and the not-too-hidden U.S. goal of "preventing another Cuba" from emerging in the hemisphere. Moreover, an accurate judgment of the Alliance for Progress is ultimately impossible because there is no way to address the counterfactual, what the economic, social, and political situation would have become in the absence of the alliance. Because Latin America is a region whose economies and societies are buffeted by international forces and trends, it is impossible to identify a baseline by which to evaluate macro indicators. Likewise, there is also no way to know how many "other Cubas" were prevented, assuming the highly unlikely scenario that there would have been others in the first place.

Critics of the Alliance for Progress fall into two categories. In the first are those who point to its inability to improve a host of specifically targeted areas, such as higher economic growth or land reform. The second group criticizes the program for even trying, for believing that such fundamental structural transformations were possible or that one program could bring them about. Specifically, the second group argues that the program had contradictory objectives, conflicting means, and not just flawed and ethnocentric presumptions about political and social change. Unlike the claims of the first group, which are overstated because there were real accomplishments, the arguments of the second have some resonance. True, the Alliance for Progress embodied some quintessentially North American presumptions, which must be recognized because they illuminate underlying features of U.S. foreign policy as well as the

limitations to U.S. power. Even while the alliance had distinct cold-war objectives (from the U.S. standpoint), it also embodied deep philosophical and historic proclivities, a long-standing self-image, and ethnocentric beliefs about the nature of political change, the capacity of the United States to effect such change, and the exportability of the U.S. social and political model. The Alliance for Progress, however, was not an exercise in Wilsonian idealism. At the heart of the alliance philosophically was the peculiarly North American faith in the relationship of economic prosperity, stability, and democracy dating back to the early Republic. Not only did it have cold-war objectives, but it was accompanied by a hard-nosed, elaborate counterinsurgency program. (The Kennedy administration initiated a 50 percent increase in U.S. military aid to Latin America.) Indeed, any assessment of the program must take into account the inherent inconsistencies and ambivalence in U.S. policy from the start. Kennedy supported democracies in Latin America but also acquiesced to military takeovers. Yet, neither the counterinsurgency policy nor the cold-war objectives of the alliance made the U.S. commitment to social justice and political reform any less genuine or real, the alliance simply broadened the

range of means by which the United States hoped to achieve its traditional goals in the hemisphere (strategic denial and stability). Critics are right to point out that these conflicting objectives and means led to the undoing of the alliance, but there was nothing inherently contradictory in them. In practice, the two-track policy toward Latin America meant that the United States was unwilling to abandon traditional means fully or to downgrade strategic interests. It meant that in context of the cold war conflicting goals and methods would pull at policy, that the long-term, but probabilistic, payoffs of the alliance would frequently be sacrificed for short-term certainties and exigencies. On the whole, such criticisms are equally applicable to nearly all U.S. foreign-policy initiatives, and they say much more about underlying themes in U.S. foreign policy than about the Alliance for Progress itself.

In general terms the Alliance for Progress must be judged along three interrelated, but distinct, dimensions: first, by the guiding principles and overarching ideas with which the program was imbued; second, by the various policy instruments and means chosen to implement specific policy ideas and measures; and third, by the outcomes of the program. One must be sensitive to the distinctions in these criteria. In some

President John F. Kennedy meeting the residents of a housing development in San Jose, Costa Rica, that was funded by the Alliance for Progress, 22 March 1963

(CORBIS-Bettmann)

ALLIANCE FOR PROGRESS

instances policy failures or successes may not be products of the underlying idea or design but of implementation methods or other intervening factors. In a deeper sense, looking solely at outcomes, be they good or bad, reveals nothing about the equally important learning and contagion effects of the program in other areas or future policies. Successes and failures are often valuable learning experiences in themselves. It should also be noted that the Alliance for Progress was not solely a U.S. policy initiative, or originally a U.S. idea. It was a collective undertaking, and however significant American participation may have been, this collective responsibility means that it would be rash to frame the issue as a success or failure of U.S. policy. Scholars frequently overlook the regional political context of the alliance. Resistance and opposition of the elite classes and landed oligarchy to the redistributive agendas of the alliance is widely noted, but one should also note that the alliance also appeared in the region at a time of growing polarization that left a weak, eroded center and little political base for the program. It was criticized by the Left for doing too little and by the Right for doing too much. The Left saw the only alternative for Latin America as revolution and socialism. The Right was simply bewildered that anyone believed change was needed.

The $20 billion for the Alliance for Progress was to come from the United States, other creditor nations, and international financial institutions such as the World Bank. The idea for the alliance is often attributed to Kennedy, who announced the initiative in March 1961, but its origins date to the late 1950s, and the core concepts of the program were first advanced by several reformist Latin American leaders. The Alliance for Progress was a Latin American idea, even though many of the resources needed to realize it invariably had to come from the richest and largest nation in the hemisphere. By the late 1950s a cadre of popular, reformist leaders had emerged in the region. Prominent among them were Juscelino Kubitschek of Brazil, Alberto Lleras Camargo of Colombia, and Rómulo Betancourt of Venezuela. Kubitschek, already engaged in his gargantuan project to transform Brazil with the construction of Brasília, a new capital city in the Amazon hinterlands, had called for a hemisphere-wide "operation Pan-America" in 1958. By the end of that year the Eisenhower administration—eager to improve relations following the U.S. covert intervention in Guatemala—was putting in place core features of what became the Alliance for Progress. A key part of Eisenhower's initiatives was the establishment of the Social Progress Trust Fund, devoted to promoting social development in Latin America.

With the Cuban Revolution of 1959 and national-liberation movements all over the developing world lending a sense of urgency and inevitable change, the Kennedy administration explicitly intended the program to forestall revolutions and communism in the region. Although core ideas of the Alliance were already in place before Fidel Castro's march into Havana, the underlying motives for both U.S. and Latin American leaders were not divorced from the larger intellectual and political currents that swept the global political arena. Important on the Latin American side was the intellectual influence and development thinking of Raúl Prebisch, head of the United Nations Economic Commission for Latin America (ECLA), who advocated large-scale, state-led industrialization and socioeconomic reform. For the United States, of course, the cold war was at its peak, as were U.S. concerns with how to prevent "communist subversion" in the region. By the late 1950s there was a general sense in U.S. academic and policy worlds that Latin America had entered the "twilight of the tyrants," a time of democratic change, social mobilization, and upheaval. Another intellectual context also found expression in the Alliance for Process: a belief in both Americas that large-scale structural change was not only needed, but also possible. Whether framed in terms of Walt W. Rostow's "take off" thesis or ECLA's structuralism, two distinct intellectual traditions converged to present the same prescriptions and guiding policy.

The Alliance for Progress outlined more than ninety specific targets and initiatives. In general, the program focused on social and economic issues, even though the ultimate goal was political: promoting stability and democracy in the region. Specific objectives ranged from improved life expectancy, tax reform, and lower infant mortality rates to higher per capita income growth. The essence of the alliance was a progressive agenda for socioeconomic reforms and redistribution aimed at improving the lot of the overwhelming majority of people in the region. Its overemphasis on specific campaigns and conspicuous short-term development projects turned the overall program into a target for critics since failure in any of these narrow, high-profile areas would necessarily be associated with failure of the overall program.

Based on numerical data alone, the success rate of alliance programs was mixed at best, but it is impossible to isolate the precise contribution made by the alliance to regional economic and social trends. First, during the period from the 1950s to 1970s Latin America achieved its highest rates of economic growth, industrialization, and social progress in modern history. Progress attributed to the alliance may have reflected an extension of trends already under way since the early 1950s, when the Korean War raised world demand for Latin American exports and thus provided new stimulus for growth. Second, with or without the alliance, there was tremendous intraregional variation, especially with regard to aggregates such as per capita income and economic-growth rates. Given the regional sensitivity to external economic shocks and trends, it would be a tenuous correlation at best to posit the effects of the alliance on economic-growth rates or other macroeconomic indicators.

This essay seeks to highlight a few of the overlooked "successes" of the Alliance for Progress. Pledged to promote the transfer of $20 billion in resources over ten years, the program not only met its annual average but by 1971 had actually delivered more than $22 billion. There is enough inferential evidence to support a thesis that the alliance helped to stimulate new sources of external private and domestic investments. A central goal of the alliance was to achieve per capita income growth of more than 2.5 percent annually. The region-wide performance between 1961 and 1970 was an unspectacular 2.4 percent, but clusters of countries performed far above the targeted rate. Intraregional variation was to be expected, given that some countries had the technical, institutional, and economic bases to absorb and profit from resource transfers and stimuli provided by the alliance. On the whole, the social and economic advances made by the program were largely offset by soaring population growth.

The one area in which the Alliance for Progress can be said to have failed, both politically and in terms of numbers, was the agrarian sector. Agricultural output declined precipitously during the years of the alliance, but as a result of systematic, long-term discrimination against this sector rather than the program itself. By the early 1950s the region had entered its second stage of import-substitution industrialization, a development strategy that was highly discriminatory against the agricultural sector. Resources were squeezed from and diverted to industry, and traditional export sectors were neglected. (The debt crisis and economic rupture of the 1980s had been in the making since the 1950s.)

Land reform was the centerpiece of the Alliance for Progress. In a region where the bulk of the population still lived in rural areas, where less than 10 percent of the population owned 70 to 80 percent of the land, and where poverty rates were staggering, no socioeconomic reform was possible without some form of land redistribution. The immediate goal was poverty reduction; the broader aim was political democracy

and stability. High concentrations of land and income formed the basis of oligarchic political power and rule, in addition to the rural and political violence such inequalities bred. As for land distribution, although accurate data are scarce, few can argue that any meaningful progress was made in the area of land reform except in Mexico and Bolivia, which were driven by their own revolutionary commitments. Ultimately, it was never really a question about numbers of landless families resettled or acreage of uncultivated *latifundias* expropriated. It was a question of political and economic power. No feature of the Alliance for Progress sparked more fear and was more resisted by Latin American elites than its call for land redistribution. Claims that the alliance threatened to provoke class warfare, rural violence, and political instability cannot be so easily dismissed.

The Alliance for Progress did promote advances in the areas of health, education, and other social services, though once again the scarcity of reliable data (especially on rural conditions) must temper any overall assessment. Life expectancy improved, reaching levels comparable to those in the industrialized world. Through the combined efforts of the International Development Bank (IDB) and the U.S. Agency for International Development (USAID), important progress was made in the provision of potable water for the urban population. Education was also improved, even if the overall alliance goal of eradicating illiteracy was not achieved. The major impetus of the alliance was to prompt regional governments to spend greater resources on education, especially higher education. Some of these smaller-scale achievements, even if they fell short of the target figures outlined by the program, had multiplier and spillover effects. The broader social payoffs of better-educated and trained people, even if small in number, cannot be easily calculated. Runaway population-growth rates and urban migration meant that in aggregate terms little inroad was made in these areas.

Often overlooked, the three major accomplishments of the Alliance for Progress were hemispheric institutionalization, national planning and state building, and improved U.S. foreign policy toward the region. In view of the growing trend toward institutionalization of hemispheric political and economic relations in the 1990s one area in which the alliance attained important successes was the establishment and consolidation of a hemisphere-wide institutional network. Alliance programs made tremendous institutional and infrastructural demands, domestically and regionally, sparking the growth of coordinating organs and arrangements within and among countries. First, the Alliance for Progress gave new life and purpose to the Organization of American States (OAS), which at first had appeared to be little more than an instrument of U.S. anticommunist policy. Though never immune to U.S. manipulation, the OAS was given new administrative, supervisory, and coordinating functions. The Inter-American Economic and Social Council, attached to the OAS, was responsible for reviewing development plans and submitting annual reports on the progress of the alliance, as well as annual country reviews. The council evolved into the principal intergovernmental body for coordinating and overseeing alliance programs. An important, if at times highly political, function was its annual estimates of external financing needs. The council not only put the OAS in position to carry out tasks that its Latin American proponents had originally intended, but it also became a coordinating forum that united the activities of the IDB, the World Bank, the International Monetary Fund (IMF), various United Nations agencies, and USAID. Given that the regional-development functions of several international and intergovernmental organizations overlapped in terms of their functions and purposes, such institutionalized coordination proved critical. Much of the hemispheric agenda of the 1990s, including summitry and economic-integration issues, rests on the institutional foundations created under the Alliance of Progress.

The second important accomplishment of the Alliance for Progress was the legitimation and institutionalization of central planning and calling attention to sustained efforts at building state capacity. The domestic-organizational requirements needed to achieve alliance goals spurred state building, especially in the areas of social services and the extension of administrative capacity beyond the principal urban areas. In no small way the alliance stimulated the growth of national and hemisphere-wide technocracy, a dense network of experts and technically trained professionals responsible for implementing and supervising the program. One interesting and often overlooked aspect of the alliance was that it unintentionally provided ECLA with a regional forum and instrument to carry out its structuralist ideas. Likewise, the alliance represented a philosophical and ideological departure on the part of the United States, because it endorsed ideas and practices (such as central planning and redistribution) that were regarded as anathema by most American policymakers throughout much of the cold war.

The Alliance for Progress marked an important phase in U.S. policy toward Latin America, if only for a brief span of years until the program and its guiding principles were consumed by cold-war events and clashes elsewhere. From the standpoint of U.S. policy, the program was sig-

nificant for several reasons. For the first time in its long history of relations with Latin America, the United States threw its weight behind a progressive, redistributive agenda. There is reason to believe that the United States viewed the alliance in technocratic, rather than political, terms, which helped to explain the Americans' effortless embrace of policies and ideas otherwise deemed subversive. Moreover, support for this progressive agenda hid practical, less lofty objectives: immunizing the region against communism by removing underlying socioeconomic, political, and psychological grounds for its appeal and spread. (In this regard the alliance drew inspiration from the Marshall Plan and early containment policy as enunciated by George F. Kennan.) Geopolitical objectives did not make the other commitments, such as the promotion of political reforms and income redistribution, any less genuine or remarkable. The Alliance for Progress embodied a new approach to the region and the emerging developing world. The United States would "side with the forces of change," as Kennedy often remarked. The change in policy and attitude made an indelible impression on a generation of Latin Americans, who continue to hold the alliance in high regard despite its shortcomings.

The Alliance for Progress embraced an ambitious agenda for hemispheric change. That it did not achieve everything it set out to accomplish does not mean that it failed. Its record is uneven, but impressive. The alliance contributed to many tangible, measurable successes, but, just as important, it can be credited with helping to build the institutional and political infrastructure that provided a firm basis for hemispheric reforms and progress in the decades that followed.

–JOÃO RESENDE-SANTOS, UNIVERSITY OF PENNSYLVANIA

Viewpoint:
No, the Alliance for Progress fell far short of achieving the reforms it promised.

The Alliance for Progress represents President John F. Kennedy's social-economic approach to the question of U.S. relations with the Third World. The United States had three basic foreign-policy approaches to the Third World. The cold-war approach emphasized the need to support almost any noncommunist regime, regardless of its character, in order to bolster the U.S. military and political position vis-à-vis the Soviet

KENNEDY'S VISION

At his inauguration on 20 January 1961, President John F. Kennedy proposed a new foreign policy that paid special attention to newly independent nations and Latin American countries.

The world is very different now. For man holds in his mortal hands the power to abolish all forms of human poverty and all forms of human life. And yet the same revolutionary beliefs for which our forebears fought are still at issue around the globe—the belief that the rights of man come not from the generosity of the state, but from the hand of God.

We dare not forget today that we are the heirs of that first revolution. Let the word go forth from this time and place, to friend and foe alike, that the torch has been passed to a new generation of Americans—born in this century, tempered by war, disciplined by a hard and bitter peace, proud of our ancient heritage—and unwilling to witness or permit the slow undoing of those human rights to which this Nation has already been committed, and to which we are committed today at home and around the world.

Let every nation know, whether it wishes us well or ill, that we shall pay any price, bear any burden, meet any hardship, support any friend, oppose any foe, in order to assure the survival and the success of liberty.

This much we pledge—and more.

To those old allies whose cultural and spiritual origins we share, we pledge the loyalty of faithful friends. United, there is little we cannot do in a host of cooperative ventures. Divided, there is little we can do—for we dare not meet a powerful challenge at odds and split asunder.

To those new States whom we welcome to the ranks of the free, we pledge our word that one form of colonial control shall not have passed merely to be replaced by a far more iron tyranny. We shall not always expect to find them supporting our view. But we shall always hope to find them strongly supporting their own freedom—and to remember that, in the past, those who foolishly sought power by riding the back of the tiger ended up inside.

To those people in the huts and villages across the globe struggling to break the bonds of misery, we pledge our best efforts to help them help themselves, for whatever period is required—not because the Communists may be doing it, not because we seek their votes, but because it is right. If a free society cannot help the many that are poor, it cannot save the few that are rich.

To our sister republics south of our border, we offer a special pledge—to convert our good words into good deeds—in a new alliance for progress—to assist free men and free governments in casting off the chains of poverty. But this peaceful revolution of hope cannot become the prey of hostile powers. Let all our neighbors know that we shall join with them to oppose aggression or subversion anywhere in the Americas. And let every other power know that this hemisphere intends to remain the master of its own house.

Source: *Janet Podell and Steven Anzovin, eds.,* Speeches of the American Presidents *(New York: H. W. Wilson, 1988), p. 604.*

Union. Rather than fostering social or economic reform, this approach stressed the need to provide military and political aid to regimes willing to stand with the United States against the communist bloc. The economic approach was based on the idea that political stability and pro-Western foreign policy would likely flow from economic development. This approach suggested that the United States should invest foreign-aid money in economic development and reform because they would create a prosperous and democratically oriented middle class and improve the standard of living of the masses—thus lessening the appeal of revolutionary communist movements, as well as creating markets for U.S. prod-

ucts. The democratic approach asserted that support for and promotion of democratic institutions and practices was the best way to guarantee domestic stability and a climate hospitable to U.S. values and interests. Kennedy's policies in Latin America, including the Alliance for Progress, combined the democratic and economic approaches. According to Robert Packenham, these policies were "probably the most sustained explicit attempt since the late forties to foster democracy in the Third World."

During the 1960s the United States provided $18 billion in aid to Latin American countries, with an additional $3 billion in commercial investment. Yet, there was less to this sum than meets the eye. Latin America's foreign borrowing was high ($10 billion in 1960, $13 billion in 1966), and 90 percent of the new aid went to debt servicing. According to J. P. D. Dunbabin, much of the alliance program amounted to not much more than a refinancing scheme; in addition the commercial investment was surpassed by repatriated capital, money that went back to the United States rather than remaining in Latin America.

The Alliance of Progress was more than a program of economic aid, however. It was an expression of the democratic approach to foreign policy, declaring the goal of bringing the benefits of democracy to the peoples of the Americas. The fact that the alliance fell well short of its aims was largely the result of its failure to reform political institutions and practices. One manifestation of this failure was the fact that during the Kennedy administration, six democratically elected governments in the region were toppled by military coups: Argentina, Peru, Guatemala, Honduras, Ecuador, and the Dominican Republic. The Kennedy administration reacted by breaking off diplomatic relations with, and cutting off economic aid to, some of these countries, but it soon realized that these measures made little difference. Moreover, they were not applied consistently. When the military took over in Peru in 1962, Kennedy used diplomatic and economic leverage to persuade the armed forces to allow elections in 1963; but, when the military in Guatemala took over in 1963 to prevent the possibility that Juan José Arévalo, Jacobo Arbenz Guzmán's leftist predecessor, might win the elections, the administration welcomed the move and suspended aid for only three weeks. In addition to this inconsistent application, the Kennedy administration also intervened covertly to subvert popular rulers when it thought they were not serving American interests. It followed this policy not only in the persistent campaign to topple Fidel Castro but in other instances as well. In 1963 the administration became worried that the Marxist-leaning Cheddi Berret Jagan would be head of government in British Guiana (now Guyana) when the British gave independence to the small Latin American nation in 1966. The CIA helped to finance and organize a general strike, which convinced the British administration to change the electoral system, allowing a coalition of Jagan's opponents, led by Forbes Burnham, to win the 1964 elections.

Any pretense for fostering democracy in the hemisphere was abandoned by the time Lyndon B. Johnson became president. In what became known as the Mann Doctrine (after Thomas C. Mann, Johnson's assistant secretary of state for inter-American affairs), the United States made it known that its only concerns in regard to the hemisphere were economic growth, the protection of $9 billion in U.S. investments, nonintervention in the internal affairs of other countries, and opposition to communism. The Johnson administration was, however, willing to violate the third provision in the interest of the fourth, as the 1965 U.S. invasion of the Dominican Republic shows. President Juan Bosch, who was elected in December 1962, initially won U.S. support, but Washington soon came to believe that Bosch was too weak to prevent a communist takeover of the government. The Kennedy administration looked the other way when the military toppled Bosch in September 1963, assuring the United States that it would hold free elections in 1965. In April 1965, following unrest and rumors of another military coup, twenty-three thousand Marines landed in the Dominican Republic. In the elections held in summer 1966 Joaquín Balaguer, who had held the position of president for a short time in the early 1960s, was returned to power. In another instance of intervention in internal affairs, the Johnson administration became alarmed by the populist policies of President João Goulart of Brazil in 1964 and tacitly approved his removal.

The political inconsistency of the Kennedy and Johnson administrations undermined much of what the Alliance for Progress was trying to achieve. The failure of the alliance to meet many of its goals is not the main criticism that may be leveled at it. More damning than specific instances where the alliance fell short is the criticism that its approach to solving problems was flawed. As Joseph Sheahan has argued, "Official aid programs can in principle favor more equitable societies as well as economic growth. In practice, it is doubtful that they do more good than harm." There is no doubt that the Alliance for Progress made some positive gains: public-health programs, agricultural research, and public education gained from better financing and technical assistance; the tax systems in many countries were improved and made more effective; thousands of rural families benefited from modest land reforms; young people gained more access to better education; national and local governments became more efficient and effective; productive capacities in the private sector were enhanced; and Peace Corps volunteers, who arrived in Latin America in the wake of the launching of the alliance, reached neglected villages in remote areas, improving education and health in many of them.

An argument can be made, however, that despite the best of intentions, Alliance for Progress programs did more harm than good to the societies they were aiming to help. Land reforms soon slowed down or were stopped altogether. Improvements in agricultural productivity had negative effects on the landless poor, who became more and more redundant as more and more farms improved their productivity through the introduction of efficiency and machinery. Educational reforms, heralded with such fanfare, ended up benefiting the middle and upper classes, not the poor, thereby increasing the gap in educational attainment. Tax systems became more efficient, but no more progressive or equitable. Above all, the institutional structures of the societies receiving alliance aid did not change.

Indeed, the emphasis the Alliance for Progress placed on achieving reforms through reliance on the free market promised that the poor and less educated would suffer the most onerous burden of many of the alliance-inspired reforms. First, the creation of a net of social benefits (such as unemployment benefits and retraining), if it was initiated at all, lagged far behind some of the market reforms. Second, many of the reforms tended to strengthen further the already rich and powerful segments in society, who saw to it that reforms benefiting them were implemented sooner and faster than the second wave of reforms, meant to blunt effects first. Third, as Albert Fishlow has noted, the alliance "lacked any definition of what to do about the many possible conflicts between the concerns of private investors and the goal of structural reform." It was reasonable to expect the powerful economic and political segments in the societies targeted by the Alliance for Progress to cooperate with it as long as the suggested reforms enhanced their political and economic power. It was not reasonable to expect the same level of cooperation from them when structural reforms were involved—reforms that would have weakened their grip on the economy and society.

Thus, when efficiency was introduced into the farming sector, the owners of large farms benefited enormously, while the many uneducated peasants who became redundant joined the ranks of the unemployed. When loans became available for import promotion, the natural result was to increase imports at the expense of domestic production while decreasing the interest of domestic producers in looking for ways to promote exports. Many of the programs aimed at opening up markets were specifically tied to the promotion of sales of

capital goods from the United States. The fact that such goods became cheaper and more readily available meant that domestic producers of capital goods found it more difficult to earn the money necessary for further diversification of their product lines. When governments tried to address the social and economic dislocation created by alliance-inspired reforms, they were told to stop.

The case of Brazil is instructive. During the first two years of the alliance, the Brazilian government, under President Jânio Quadros, was pushing land and tax reforms but also relaxing fiscal controls in order to address the mounting social unrest in the country. The reforms were opposed by conservative elements in the Brazilian parliament, and, after a tense tug of war, Quadros resigned, claiming that the Brazilian political system was beyond correction. His successor, João Goulart, appealed to peasants and labor to support him against pressures from the military and the conservative elements in parliament. In the meantime, the relaxed fiscal policy led to inflation, as measured by the GDF deflator, which climbed from 26 percent in 1960 to 72 percent in 1963. In response the United States cut off aid to Brazil, and foreign investment there dropped sharply. With no solution to Brazil's political and economic crisis in sight, the United States signaled its growing displeasure with Goulart and made clear its desire for him to leave the presidency.

In March 1964 Army Chief of Staff Humberto de Alencar Castelo Branco staged a coup to topple Goulart, with the tacit blessing of the United States. Fearing that if the coup failed, leftist sentiment in Brazil would become even stronger, the Johnson administration dispatched a naval force to Brazil with oil and arms for the rebels, in case they needed help. (They did not. The Goulart government collapsed quickly.) Three years of anticommunist terror ensued and was only somewhat eased after Artur da Costa e Silva took office in 1967. (The military took over again in 1969.) After the 1964 coup the United States resumed its aid to Brazil, as Castelo Branco's regime instituted harsh economic measures, tightening fiscal control, deeply cutting real wages, and curbing labor activism. The message to Brazil was clear: to avoid the dire consequences of losing foreign aid and foreign investment, go more slowly on reforms so as not to arouse expectations among the people or scare the oligarchs, and do not engage in ameliorative fiscal measures to blunt the egregious social and economic consequences of reforms. The U.S.-approved military takeover in Brazil was soon followed by similar coups in Chile, Uruguay, and Argentina.

All the governments in the hemisphere received increased assistance—including training, equipment, and intelligence sharing—for the fight against communist subversion. The United States provided this support whether the governments were moderately reform oriented, as in Chile and Colombia, or harshly repressive, as in Guatemala and Nicaragua. It later became clear that the U.S. intelligence and covert-action training provided to the police forces and militaries of already repressive regimes enabled them to become much more effective (that is, brutal and murderous) in their campaigns not only against communist guerrillas but also against the political opposition in their countries. March 1999 articles in *The New York Times* revealed that a "truth commission" came to highly critical conclusions regarding U.S. involvement in training paramilitaries from Guatemala and El Salvador, noting that 1982 was a peak period for a program of genocide directed at Mayan Indians.

An argument can be made that the Alliance for Progress, while achieving some modest gains, also ushered in the brutal decades of the 1970s and 1980s. It did so because it aroused popular expectations that could not be met and because its reformist language—as well as a string of leftist-leaning leaders such as Goulart in Brazil and Salvador Allende in Chile—scared the old power structure, which joined with the military to reimpose repressive rule in Argentina, Brazil, Chile, Bolivia, El Salvador, Uruguay, and Paraguay.

The verdict on the Alliance for Progress is thus mixed. Some of its programs contributed to modest improvements in health care, education, and government services. Four elements, however, may have undermined the alliance and prevented it from achieving even more: the inconsistency of the U.S. approach to political reforms in the hemisphere, the lack of sufficient attention to the need for a social safety net to accompany economic reforms, the timidity in challenging the stranglehold of the old oligarchies on the society and economy of the region, and the insistence on the rigid introduction of a free-market approach to situations in which it might not have been appropriate yet. The question is not whether or not the Alliance for Progress had some achievements—it certainly had. The questions that should be asked are: Did it achieve the goals it had set for itself? Was the program designed and implemented in the most efficacious way? Did it tackle the structural problems besetting many countries in the region? Were its politi-cal and economic aspects always in harmony with each other? The answer to each of these questions must be "no."

It is true that, in general, Latin America is now more pacific, stable, democratic, and prosperous. It is not accurate to attribute these gains to the Alliance for Progress. In fact, during the 1970s and 1980s a bloody backlash against the alliance and its goals—and against the fact that the United States appeared to be meddling in the internal affairs of the region—took place in many countries in the hemisphere. The general openness and stability in Latin America may also be attributed to factors such as the general global relaxation following the end of the cold war, the diminished appeal of leftist movements and ideas, the growing tensions between the requirements of the modern economy and repressive military regimes, and the growing interdependence of the global economy. All these developments have nothing to do with the Alliance for Progress, and it is difficult to disentangle their influence from the contributions of the alliance.

—BENJAMIN FRANKEL, SECURITY STUDIES

References

J. P. D. Dunbabin, *International Relations Since 1945,* volume 2: *The Post Imperial Age: The Great Powers and the Wider World* (London & New York: Longman, 1994);

Albert Fishlow, *The Mature Neighbor Policy: A New United States Economic Policy for Latin America* (Berkeley: Institute of International Studies, University of California, 1977);

Jerome Levinson and Juan de Onis, *The Alliance That Lost Its Way: A Critical Report on the Alliance for Progress* (Chicago: Quadrangle, 1970);

Robert A. Packenham, *Liberal America and the Third World: Political Development Ideas in Foreign Aid and Social Science* (Princeton, N.J.: Princeton University Press, 1973);

L. Ronald Scheman, ed., *The Alliance for Progress: A Retrospective* (New York: Praeger, 1988);

Joseph Sheahan, *Patterns of Development in Latin America: Poverty, Repression, and Economic Strategy* (Princeton, N.J.: Princeton University Press, 1987);

Joseph S. Tulchin, "The United States and Latin America in the 1960s," *Journal of Inter-American Studies and World Affairs,* 30 (Spring 1988): 1–36.

Was the Baruch Plan a genuine effort to achieve global cooperation on nuclear control?

Viewpoint: Yes, the Baruch Plan attempted to establish international control over nuclear development.

Viewpoint: No, the Baruch Plan was not a sincere attempt to achieve global cooperation because it included provisions that the United States knew the Soviet Union would find unacceptable.

In 1946 President Harry S Truman appointed financier Bernard Baruch to head the U.S. delegation to the United Nations Atomic Energy Commission. Baruch was given the task of presenting to the commission the U.S. plan for the international control of nuclear energy. The plan was based on an earlier report, prepared by a committee headed by Undersecretary of State Dean Acheson and David E. Lilienthal, the head of the Tennessee Valley Authority (TVA). Baruch took the Acheson-Lilienthal Report and strengthened the language about enforcing its various provisions. Among the changes he introduced were the elimination of the great powers' veto rights (meaning that these nations would not be able to block UN decisions against them in the event they violated the proposed treaty), and the addition of language about "swift and condine [*sic*] punishment" for violators. Probably the most controversial of Baruch's suggestions was that the United States be allowed to maintain its nuclear-weapons monopoly until it made sure that no other nation was building its own nuclear weapons. Speaking to the UN commission, Baruch declared that the acceptance or rejection of his plan was a choice between the "quick and the dead." Negotiations in the commission led nowhere. In a vote taken on 31 December 1946, the USSR and Poland abstained from voting on the plan, thus killing it since the commission could adopt decisions only by a unanimous vote.

Viewpoint:
Yes, the Baruch Plan attempted to establish international control over nuclear development.

The Baruch Plan was a genuine effort on the part of U.S. policymakers to achieve a measure of international control over the nuclear activities of states—including the building of nuclear weapons. That the effort failed is not an indication that it was not genuine. Rather, it can be argued that the climate was not right for such a bold departure: the state of international institutions, the limitations of verification technology, and mutual suspicions and fears were more important than tactical mistakes of either side in dooming the plan.

For U.S. policymakers during the first years of the nuclear age there was a natural urge to hold on to the U.S. monopoly in nuclear weapons, a monopoly that would give the United States a preponderance over any adversary for a long time to come. Yet, at the same time they recognized that it was only a matter of time before nuclear

Andrey Gromyko of the
Soviet Union, Sir
Alexander Cadogan of
Great Britain, and
Bernard Baruch of the
United States at a
meeting of the United
Nations Atomic Energy
Commission, 1946

know-how spread to more countries, making them capable of producing nuclear weapons. These two perceptions gave rise to two different policy preferences. The first, more traditional, approach saw nuclear weapons as just another weapon system that the United States should exploit for its own benefit. Proponents of this approach called for jealously guarding U.S. nuclear secrets, incorporating nuclear weapons quickly into the U.S. military arsenal, and relying on the nuclear monopoly to shore up the U.S. position vis-à-vis the Soviet Union. The second school saw nuclear weapons as a completely new kind of weapon, which, if allowed to spread to other countries, might bring about a situation in which the existence of mankind would be put in danger. This group called for giving up the U.S. nuclear monopoly, halting the building of more nuclear weapons, and establishing an international monitoring system to verify that no country would ever build these weapons. As is often the case with such complicated matters, some policymakers moved back and forth between the two positions.

The first serious discussions on the future of the bomb began in Washington in September 1945 between representatives of the United States, Britain, and Canada, the three countries that collaborated in the Manhattan Project. Vannevar Bush, a leading scientific adviser to Presidents Franklin Delano Roosevelt and Harry S Truman, had already urged Secretary of State James F. Byrnes to consider setting up an inspection system under the newly formed United Nations to deal with the

technical details of verification. This early push for some kind of an international monitoring mechanism was accompanied by skepticism about the political feasibility of the project. At the end of October a group of British officials prepared a report on the topic for British prime minister Clement Attlee. The report echoed thoughts already expressed by Secretary of War Henry L. Stimson and Undersecretary of State Dean Acheson. First, they said, the American monopoly on nuclear weapons could not be maintained for long, perhaps five years. Second, they noted, no monitoring and verification plan that would be technically reliable would be politically feasible. Because of the nature of the Soviet regime, little could be expected of it other than evasion, obstruction, and cheating. Thus, powers observing any international agreement to limit the building of nuclear weapons would find themselves at a grave disadvantage because while they would be limited by the terms of the treaty, other powers (such as the Soviet Union) would likely cheat, resulting in an inspection system that would be "a highly dangerous sham, productive of endless suspicion and friction."

To deal with these conflicting pressures, Stimson appointed a committee to formulate the U.S. position on the issue of international control of atomic energy. The committee was chaired by Acheson, and its members included Bush, James B. Conant, General Leslie Groves, and John J. McCloy. The committee relied on a board of experts chaired by David E. Lilienthal, the chairman of the Tennessee Valley Authority (TVA). Among the experts was J. Robert Oppenheimer, whose contributions to the committee's recommendations were considerable. The committee began its deliberations on 23 January 1946 and submitted its report in March. The central recommendation of the report, which became known as the Acheson-Lilienthal Report, was to create an international "Atomic Development Authority" with worldwide monopoly over the dangerous elements of the entire nuclear cycle–from mining through manufacturing. The report also stated that this authority should be the leader in nuclear research and development. Led on this issue by Oppenheimer, the committee did not believe that nuclear research and development could, or should, be outlawed or banned. There were many possible benefits to nuclear research, and mankind should not deny itself these benefits. "So long as intrinsically dangerous activities may be carried on by nations," the report noted, "rivalries are inevitable and fears are engendered that place so great a pressure upon a system of international enforcement by police methods that no degree of ingenuity or technical competence could possibly hope to cope with them."

Members of the committee differed about whether they should recommend that their proposal be implemented immediately or in stages. Yet, as McGeorge Bundy writes, these disagreements "were differences within an agreement": "For Acheson, Bush, Conant, and McCloy this was the best plan they had seen for doing a job they strongly believed in."

On 17 March 1946, the day the committee reached its agreement on the report, President Truman appointed Bernard Baruch to be the chief U.S. negotiator at the United Nations. Baruch accepted the Acheson-Lilienthal Report as the basis for his negotiations, but he insisted on strengthening the means of enforcing it. For him, any agreement that did not promise its violators an "immediate and certain punishment" that could not be blocked by a veto would be open to fraud and evasion. The Truman administration accepted Baruch's view, if not his precise language, and on 14 June 1946 he presented the Baruch Plan for the control of nuclear activities to the Atomic Energy Commission of the United Nations, which met in the gymnasium of Hunter College in New York City. He opened his presentation with the words: "We are here to make a choice between the quick and the dead."

The plan ran into immediate Soviet opposition. The Soviets objected both to the idea of an international atomic agency and to the notion that no country would have a veto right in atomic matters. There were hardly any negotiations between the United States and the Soviet Union; by December the committee took a vote, endorsing the U.S.

position ten to zero, with the USSR and Poland abstaining. Since votes on commission decisions had to be unanimous, the Baruch Plan was effectively killed. There are indications that the United States would have been willing to compromise if the Soviets had accepted these two fundamental principles, but the rigid Soviet position prevented a reciprocal American flexibility. The debate was thus between those who believed that the Soviet Union was the major danger against which the United States and the West must arm themselves with whatever technology afforded (a view shared by most U.S. government officials) and those who believed that, in the long run, there would be no winners or losers in a nuclear-arms race (the belief of most atomic scientists). The government officials were willing to contemplate giving up the bomb but only against an ironclad and verifiable agreement that made it impossible for the Soviets to build their own nuclear weapons. The atomic scientists stressed that the inherent dangers to mankind resulting from large nuclear arsenals in the hands of countries far outweigh the short-term challenge posed by the USSR and that the prime interest of the United States was to bring atomic activities under control, especially the atomic activities of an adversary such as the USSR. The Acheson-Lilienthal report agreed with the scientists on this point, and the committee's suggestions largely followed this view.

It is possible, in hindsight, to think of ways in which Baruch might have been more successful. One would have been to change the American proposal so that it reflected more-traditional politics: rather than insist on zero nuclear weapons, perhaps it would have been easier to negotiate an agreement that would allow each of the great powers to possess a small arsenal of nuclear weapons, and draw the line there. In keeping with this line of thought, which emphasizes the traditional prerogatives of the great powers, perhaps the United States should not have insisted on denying the great powers' veto rights with regard to nuclear activities. The American approach, however, appeared incapable of accommodating such a nuanced, realistic view. High officials as well as public opinion appeared more comfortable with an either-or view of the issue: either ban the bomb completely, or strive to maintain U.S. superiority. This view was a typical post–Second World War American attitude: it combined a crusading spirit that sought to improve the world and transform traditional international politics, a belief in the superiority of American science and technology, and a dismissive attitude toward Soviet scientific attainments. To say all that, however, is not to say that the Baruch Plan was not a genuine effort to bring atomic activities under control. It is only to say that the plan was a product of its time, reflecting prevailing attitudes and manifesting accepted wisdom.

–BENJAMIN FRANKEL, SECURITY STUDIES

NUCLEAR SHARING

On 15 November 1945 the United States, Great Britain, and Canada announced a proposal for sharing information on atomic energy for peaceful purposes, under the supervision of the United Nations and with sufficient safeguards against military use of this new technology. Their declaration included the following provisions:

The military exploitation of atomic energy depends, in large part, upon the same methods and processes as would be required for industrial uses.

We are not convinced that the spreading of the specialized information regarding the practical application of atomic energy, before it is possible to devise effective, reciprocal, and enforceable safeguards acceptable to all nations, would contribute to a constructive solution of the problem of the atomic bomb.

On the contrary we think it might have the opposite effect. We are, however, prepared to share, on a reciprocal basis with others of the United Nations, detailed information concerning the practical industrial application of atomic energy just as soon as effective enforceable safeguards against its use for destructive purposes can be devised. . . .

Faced with the terrible realities of the application of science to destruction, every nation will realize more urgently than before the overwhelming need to maintain the rule of law among nations and to banish the scourge of war from the earth. This can only be brought about by giving wholehearted support to the United Nations Organization and by consolidating and extending its authority, thus creating conditions of mutual trust in which all peoples will be free to devote themselves to the arts of peace. It is our firm resolve to work without reservation to achieve these ends.

Source: *"Three-Nation Declaration on Atomic Energy,"* New York Times, *16 November 1945, p. A3.*

Viewpoint:
No, the Baruch Plan was not a sincere attempt to achieve global cooperation because it included provisions that the United States knew the Soviet Union would find unacceptable.

In 1945–1946 the United States developed a proposal to transfer their know-how and technology regarding atomic weaponry to the United Nations. The impetus for the American proposal was the common fear among Ameri-

cans and many worldwide that without international control over this weaponry nations would eventually go to atomic war. The original plan was a serious, complicated proposal to establish gradual international control. By the summer of 1946, however, Harry S Truman's administration, along with Bernard Baruch, the Democratic Party contributor and statesman named to submit the plan to the UN, modified the plan significantly. The new Baruch Plan included provisions that the United States understood would never be acceptable to the Soviet Union. It was not a serious offer.

In 1945 many American atomic scientists, government officials, and other public figures believed that the new atomic bomb, two of which were used to demolish the cities of Hiroshima and Nagasaki in Japan and end the Second World War, needed to be placed under some form of international control. The prospect of an international order dominated by hostile nations deploying atomic weaponry terrified many Americans, who had just witnessed the ruthlessness and absolute destruction of the Second World War. Many Americans, not only idealists, retained a strong conviction that the United Nations could be made to quell international rivalries and establish a form of international security that its predecessor, the League of Nations, was wholly unable to achieve. Furthermore, many government officials and industrialists believed that the United States could both prosper and do good for the global economy by transferring atomic energy know-how to the UN, and in particular to its Atomic Energy Commission (AEC). Nations rich and poor could then partake of this inexhaustible energy source, purchasing necessary materials and industrial plants from American companies.

Immediately after the war Truman, who subscribed to all three of these convictions, commissioned a top-level panel to study the technical and political possibilities of transferring atomic information to the UN. Undersecretary of State Dean Acheson, former director of the Tennessee Valley Authority (TVA) David E. Lilienthal, and a host of atomic scientists, including J. Robert Oppenheimer, went to work in the fall and winter of 1945. By early 1946 the panel had completed the Acheson-Lilienthal Report, which recommended that the United States make as a primary political objective the eventual, gradual transfer of atomic energy and weaponry expertise and technology to the UNAEC. To avoid the serious possibility of another nation, in particular the Soviet Union, perfidiously stealing this information for its own purposes, the report argued for a step-by-step process, whereby the United States would transfer only basic technology at first and more-sensitive plans and materials after the satisfactory establishment of inspection programs in all nations.

The Acheson-Lilienthal plan was a complex, arduous, and painstaking proposal to comply with Truman's request. Acheson and Lilienthal believed that with an adequate regime of inspection no nation would be able to develop atomic weaponry surreptitiously. As with any such plan, it was impossible to rule out absolutely the possibility that a nation might be able to develop its own bomb away from UN supervision. In late 1945 and early 1946 many Americans viewed the prospect of international atomic control as something worth the risk. This attitude, however, was about to change.

In March 1946 Truman and Secretary of State James F. Byrnes agreed to appoint Baruch as the U.S. delegate to the UNAEC, thus giving him the assignment of presenting the American plan to the world organization. With quiet support from Truman and other more-hard-line administration officials, Baruch set about to toughen the report in two fundamental ways. First, he added a conspicuous and severe penalty provision to the American plan. Any nation caught violating UN inspections, the new proposal stated, would be subject to a "swift, terrible" military reprisal at the hands of the UN Security Council. Second, the Security Council veto, which allows any one of the five permanent members to negate any UN action, would not apply on matters of atomic inspection.

By changing the plan in these two respects Baruch was able to assure himself and the Truman administration that no other nation could possibly take advantage of American generosity and evade the UN inspection regime. Baruch hoped to make his plan "airtight": no plan with his name on it could be used by a cynical regime to steal atomic secrets and build weaponry even as the United States was turning over its own bombs.

As many in the Truman administration understood, however, by adding these strict provisions the United States was eliminating any possibility that the Soviet Union would accept the plan and vote for it in the UNAEC. From the Soviet point of view, the American plan seemed like a scheme to invade their nation with atomic inspectors, contrive a Soviet violation of UNAEC regulations, and then embark on a punitive war waged by the other three members of the Security Council, all of which in 1946 were allies of the United States. It would have been difficult to invent a scenario more repulsive to the Soviet Union, a nation cynical about international agreements, historically averse to penetration by outsiders, suspicious about capitalist plotting and encirclement, and exhausted by four years of brutal warfare.

The chances of their accepting the Baruch Plan as written were zero.

American proponents of the internationalization of atomic energy, including Oppenheimer, Lilienthal, and Secretary of Commerce Henry A. Wallace, recognized that the Soviet Union would veto the Baruch Plan and put an end to their hopes. Together they urged Baruch and supporters of his plan in the Truman administration (including the president himself) to modify the proposal so as to allow for some chance that the Soviet Union might not turn it down flat. Stubbornly, Baruch refused to budge on the issue, and in late 1946 he presented the plan as it was to the UNAEC. As expected, both the Soviet Union and Poland abstained from the vote, thus killing the proposal and with it any likelihood of establishing international control over atomic technology and weaponry for the foreseeable future.

Why did the Truman administration accede to Baruch's transformation of the Acheson-Lilienthal Report from a serious, complex proposal for atomic-energy transfer into a threatening plan that no one believed had a chance of acceptance? The answer to this question lies in the changing climate of international politics. In 1945 many Americans believed quite genuinely that it would be possible to establish some kind of international accord with the Soviet Union. Truman quite likely agreed in general with this point of view, as did a large part of the Democratic Party. In early 1946, however, just as the Acheson-Lilienthal Report was being completed, U.S.-Soviet relations began to chill. Revelations that a Canadian spy ring passed atomic secrets to the Russians gave ammunition to advocates of a stricter plan, as did the "long telegram" that George F. Kennan sent in February from Moscow, warning Washington of Russia's traditional paranoia, cynicism, and contempt for international treaties. During that month as well, Stalin gave a well-publicized speech predicting the inevitable conflict of capitalist and socialist forces, rhetoric that was returned in kind the following month by former British prime minister Winston Churchill, who charged that an "iron curtain" had fallen across central Europe.

These events and arguments led Truman, Byrnes, and others in the administration to cast away any ideas about postwar accord with the Soviet Union and develop an antagonistic position toward their erstwhile allies. Naturally, one of the first casualties of this new attitude was the plan to transfer atomic energy, which seemed to many in the administration a blueprint for naively shifting the monopoly over atomic weaponry to the Soviet Union. Baruch realized that the only way to salvage the plan was to toughen it beyond reproach, even though this strategy meant sure Soviet rejection. By the time Baruch submitted the plan to the AEC, it was a dead letter.

The politics of the Baruch Plan epitomize the "security dilemma" of international politics. The United States, increasingly insecure about the dark possibility of the Soviet Union cynically exploiting American generosity and stealing the atomic monopoly, found itself unable in the end to offer a proposal that risked anything at all. The Soviet Union, increasingly suspicious about American motivations and the nightmarish prospect of being attacked by the Security Council in the name of international inspection, saw in the Baruch Plan a blueprint for American penetration and domination. Neither side was animated by offensive motivations in their increasingly cynical approach to international control of atomic energy, but both perceived offensiveness in the other's insecurity.

–CAMPBELL CRAIG, UNIVERSITY OF CANTERBURY, NEW ZEALAND

References

Dean Acheson, *Present at the Creation: My Years at the State Department* (New York: Norton, 1969);

McGeorge Bundy, *Danger and Survival* (New York: Random House, 1988);

Gregg Herken, *The Winning Weapon: The Atomic Bomb in the Cold War, 1945–1950* (Princeton, N.J.: Princeton University Press, 1988);

David E. Lilienthal, *The Journals of David E. Lilienthal* (New York: Harper & Row, 1964).

BARUCH PLAN

BERLIN CRISES

Why did the Berlin crises occur?

Viewpoint: The Berlin crises occurred not because the city had any intrinsic strategic value, but because it was a powerful symbol of the cold-war conflict between capitalism and communism.

Viewpoint: The Berlin crises took place because of the vital strategic importance of the city to both the West and the Soviet Union.

Allied agreements about the occupation of Germany after the Second World War created an unusual status for the city of Berlin. Like Germany itself, Berlin was divided into four separate occupation zones. As the cold war became the dominant factor in international relations, the British, French, and Americans combined their zones of the country and the city into one economic and administrative unit to form what became the Federal Republic of Germany, leaving West Berlin in an especially precarious situation one hundred miles within the separate Soviet occupation zone, which soon became East Germany.

The exposed position left the population of West Berlin dangerously dependent on Soviet willingness to allow supplies through. In 1948–1949 the Soviet Union blockaded West Berlin in response to the introduction of currency reform in the Western sectors without Moscow's consent. Although an American airlift that lasted for more than a year saved the city and persuaded the Soviets to relent without a military confrontation, the city remained in a delicate situation for the rest of the cold war.

In 1958 Soviet leader Nikita S. Khrushchev, who described West Berlin as "the testicles of the West," demanded that the West withdraw its military presence from the city within six months. If the Western powers failed to comply, he threatened to conclude a separate peace treaty with the Soviets' East German satellite and give it control of access routes to the city. The West resisted Khrushchev's demands. In August 1961—in the face of this defiance and a continuing problem of mass emigration from East Germany to the West—the Soviets and East Germans constructed one of the most evocative symbols of the cold war, the Berlin Wall, which remained standing until 1989, when East Germany announced the opening of its borders with the West.

**Viewpoint:
The Berlin crises occurred not because the city had any intrinsic strategic value, but because it was a powerful symbol of the cold-war conflict between capitalism and communism.**

The Prussian city of Berlin, the capital city of Germany during the Third Reich, was one of the most profound symbols of the cold war. The occupation of Berlin by American, French, British, and Soviet troops for four decades after the Second World War reminded the world of the military and political foundations of the cold war. Berlin was the only place in Europe where American and Russian forces faced one another directly,

Children in West Berlin waiting for a U.S. supply plane to land during the Berlin airlift of 1948–1949

(CORBIS/Bettmann)

for they were separated elsewhere on the continent by the buffer of central Europe. While troops confronted one another at the Checkpoint Charlie and Friedrichstrasse border crossings, Berlin was also the center of high-level intrigue and espionage and of competing claims for the German political soul, with the imported glitz and prosperity of West Berlin contending with the grim and ostensibly egalitarian East Berlin. It was also the home of the infamous Berlin Wall. Its erection in 1961 demonstrated like nothing else an admission by the Soviet Union that their working-class paradise was failing–while its destruction in 1989 symbolized like nothing else the final collapse of the myth.

The significance of Berlin in the history of the cold war, however, lies not in its historical and ideological symbolism, as important as these were. Rather, Berlin's central role was as a direct stake in the military and political rivalry between the United States and the Soviet Union over central Europe. On three separate occasions–in 1948–1949, 1958–1959, and 1961–the superpowers pushed their squabble over control of the western sectors of Berlin into bona fide cold-war crises. The evolving status of Berlin from 1948 to 1961 represents quite accurately the growth of Soviet military power to the point of effective thermonuclear parity with the United States. This fact makes Premier Nikita Khrushchev's decision to build the wall in 1961 a great irony of recent history.

At the end of the Second World War, the four allies–Great Britain, France, the United States, and the Soviet Union–each occupied sectors of Berlin, as victorious nations often divide a vanquished nation's capital. Once the Second World War was over, the formal purposes of occupation were becoming distant memories, subsumed by the cold-war division of Germany into East and West. Berlin, in the eastern German region of Prussia, rested well inside the Soviet-held portion of Germany, which had also been divided into occupied regions. The cold war turned these three former allies into enemies of the Soviets, and there arose the peculiar situation of having American, British, and French soldiers and diplomats ranging about a large city in the middle of the Soviet bloc. Naturally, the Soviet Union was eager to see the three Western nations leave Berlin. During meetings of the Allied Control Council in 1947–1948, the Soviet delegates demanded with increasing impatience that the Western powers pack up and leave.

Nevertheless, many in the West, particularly Americans stationed in Berlin, as well as non- or anticommunist West Berliners, argued that the Soviet demand should be rebuffed. Secretary of State George C. Marshall emphasized that the Western powers still had a legal right to remain in Berlin, since a formal peace treaty ending the Second World War had never been completed.

Berliners such as Willy Brandt, mayor of Berlin (1957–1966) and later chancellor of West Germany (1969–1974), called attention to the plight of two million West Berliners who would be consigned to the Soviet bloc should the Western powers depart. Robert D. Murphy, a State Department expert on Germany, and General Lucius D. Clay, U.S. Army commander in Berlin, provided the most compelling argument: a departure by the West would demoralize Western Europeans, making them feel that the Americans would abandon them at the first sign of trouble. So after Soviet premier Joseph Stalin decided to raise the stakes by establishing a formal ground blockade around Berlin in the summer of 1948, President Harry S Truman decided to contest it by airlifting supplies to the isolated citizens during the winter of 1948–1949. The heroic efforts of American and British airmen and the endurance of the citizens of West Berlin made the airlift a success. In early 1949 the Soviet Union gave up, abandoned its blockade, and reconciled itself, for the time being, to a divided Berlin.

Though the moral obligation to the West Berliners and the fear of a "bandwagon effect" certainly influenced the American decision to stay, the basic reason the United States chose to remain in Berlin was because it could. At that moment the United States held a monopoly over the atomic bomb, making the Soviet Union extremely averse to pushing matters toward war over a stake such as Berlin. The Americans could afford to take a hard-line position on Berlin. They exploited this accident of history because the Soviets were not prepared to go to war. Even with the American "occupation" as aggravating as it was, the massive Red Army could not stop planes from dropping atomic bombs on Russian cities. The Americans perceived the Soviets' unwillingness and exploited the U.S. advantage.

As with so many other events and trends of the cold war, the gradual Soviet attainment of a thermonuclear arsenal in the late 1950s changed the dynamics of the debate over Berlin substantially. In November 1958, having put up with the Western occupation of West Berlin for thirteen years, Khrushchev issued an ultimatum: the Western powers would have to leave in six months. The continued occupation, he said aptly, was like "a bone in my throat." Now that the Soviet Union had thermonuclear bombs, Khrushchev believed, the determination of the West to stand tough over its Second World War occupation rights in Berlin would falter.

Despite the official North Atlantic Treaty Organization (NATO) policy of refusing to negotiate while under an ultimatum and treating any Soviet move against West Berlin as an act of general war, the Western powers, led by

President Dwight D. Eisenhower, scrambled to find some kind of compromise. The British in particular were aghast at the idea of initiating a thermonuclear world war over the political status of West Berlin. Eisenhower deftly played on these British fears, quietly going along with Prime Minister Harold Macmillan's plea for a four-power summit (despite the no-negotiation policy) and put off contingency plans for a war to defend Berlin. Khrushchev, despite his tough rhetoric, gladly seized the opportunity to negotiate. Delegates from all four powers met in Geneva in the spring of 1959. Khrushchev even visited the United States that fall and was prepared to finalize a compromise over Berlin with Eisenhower at the Paris summit in 1960 when the downing of an American U-2 spy plane in Soviet territory derailed the talks, leaving the Berlin question unresolved.

As many in the West predicted, Khrushchev revived his ultimatum once a new American president, John F. Kennedy, assumed office in January 1961. The failure of the U.S.-sponsored invasion of Cuba in April 1961 persuaded Khrushchev that Kennedy was weak, and at a June 1961 summit meeting in Vienna the Soviet leader delivered his ultimatum to Kennedy. The Kennedy administration thus had to confront the same issue that Eisenhower had: whether or not the United States should go to war to protect West Berlin.

Despite Kennedy's campaign rhetoric about waging a virile and dynamic cold war, the new administration, like the previous one, declined to take a hard line on Berlin. Realizing that the military policy left to them by Eisenhower allowed for little choice in a war over Berlin—street skirmishes or global thermonuclear exchange—Kennedy administration officials began to consider how to avoid actual conflict while at the same time appearing to give in to the ultimatum. Khrushchev, equally nervous about going to war over the issue, provided the answer: a wall around West Berlin. The wall would allow the Western powers to retain their formal occupying status, while stopping the exodus of East Germans and eliminating the temptation to East Germans of Western capitalist prosperity and glamour. Best of all, it would allow Khrushchev to cancel his ultimatum. In August of 1961 East German leader Walter Ulbricht, with Khrushchev's approval, ordered his soldiers to begin erecting a large wall around the western sectors of Berlin. This wall gradually developed into a formal cold-war boundary, replete with watchtowers, guard dogs, and barbed wire: a sad, unmistakable symbol of the unpopularity of Soviet communism.

BERLIN CRISES

While publicly expressing outrage, Kennedy and his advisers privately breathed a sigh of relief. Not one major official in the White House advocated a military challenge to the wall. When Lucius Clay, the newly appointed ambassador to the enclosed city of West Berlin, tried to start a war anyway in October, the White House was forced to reel him in. The wall put an end to the struggle between the United States and the Soviet Union over the status of Berlin: it remained an artificially divided city, a cold-war peculiarity (not unlike Korea) until the Soviet empire began to collapse in the late 1980s and Berliners knocked the structure down.

—CAMPBELL CRAIG, UNIVERSITY OF
CANTERBURY, NEW ZEALAND

Viewpoint:
The Berlin crises took place because of the vital strategic importance of the city to both the West and the Soviet Union.

One provision of the wartime agreements among the four Allied powers provided for their joint post–Second World War occupation of Germany with a sharing of administrative authority. Although the city of Berlin was located well within the Soviet zone of occupation, it, too, was divided among the four allies. The onset of the cold war and loss of the wartime strategic partnership of the three Western allies with the Soviet Union meant that the future of Germany stood little chance of being decided by its mutually hostile occupiers. The future of Berlin was even more clouded.

The crisis atmosphere that surrounded the city must be understood in the context of the developing cold war. By 1946 Soviet premier Joseph Stalin, while trying to maintain a conciliatory relationship with the West, also followed his obsession with Soviet security and attempted to expand Soviet influence as far and wide as possible without drawing the West into a general war that the Soviet Union was in no condition to fight. As a result, in July 1946 Soviet foreign minister Vyacheslav Molotov demanded that the industrial Ruhr region, well inside the Western zones, be shared with the Soviet Union. There were no provisions for Soviet occupation there in the four allies' occupation agreement, and the attempt to justify the demand by saying that the USSR was not getting enough reparation from Germany was ill founded. Indeed, accounts of the Soviet military administration's transfer to

Russia of almost all the heavy industrial base in its zone and its use of large numbers of the population for slave labor did not suggest to anyone that reparations were lacking. Rejecting the Soviet demand out of hand, the Western allies were becoming increasingly convinced that the USSR was an unreliable partner in joint occupation. Shortly thereafter, the three Western allies made plans to combine their zones politically and economically.

Further afield, Soviet attempts to extract military-base rights and territorial concessions from Turkey and Iran, two other places where no wartime agreement guaranteed the Soviets a future role, met with firm Western resistance. Although we now know that Stalin pressured Josip Tito, the leader of the Communist Party in Yugoslavia, not to arm or support the communist rebellion in Greece lest it provoke a Western military response, the West perceived that Moscow was behind the Greek uprising, and, in March 1947, President Harry S Truman elaborated the Truman Doctrine of U.S. resistance to communist expansion anywhere in the world. Irregularities in Soviet promises to allow democratic governments in eastern Europe also caused concern in the West.

When the announcement of the Marshall Plan in June 1947 caused Stalin to believe that the United States was trying to marginalize extreme ideologies, such as his own, throughout Europe, he used coercion to force the otherwise enthusiastic governments of eastern Europe to reject participation in the plan. Realizing that he had perhaps miscalculated what the West would tolerate, he moved to consolidate what already lay within his grasp. In September 1947 he reorganized the international communist movement into a Moscow-led organization, the Cominform, or Communist Information Bureau. Later that autumn he instructed east European communists to take control of their countries through extralegal means, a process that was completed by the following February when every east European state except Yugoslavia and Greece was governed by Moscow-directed communist regimes.

Despite these provocative actions, it is apparent that Stalin still believed he could reach some sort of accommodation over the German question. Indeed, the East German Communist Party had been deliberately left out of the first Cominform meeting, while even the French and Italian communists sent delegates. For Stalin the best outcome for Germany would have been a unified state that was politically nonaligned and disarmed. Indeed, there was much thought even among West German politicians (such as the leading Social Democrat, Kurt Schumacher) that was favorable to this approach. It was also possi-

THE BERLIN WALL

On 18 August 1961, five days after the East Germans began building the Berlin Wall, President John F. Kennedy wrote a letter to Willy Brandt, mayor of West Berlin. In the following excerpt, Kennedy expressed his feelings on the Soviet actions and outlined how the United States planned to respond.

The measures taken by the Soviet Government and its puppets in East Berlin have caused revulsion here in America. The demonstration of what the Soviet Government means by freedom for a city, and peace for a people, proves the hollowness of Soviet pretensions; and Americans understand that this action necessarily constitutes a special blow to the people of West Berlin, connected as they remain in a myriad of ways to their fellow Berliners in the eastern sector. So I understand entirely the deep concerns and sense of trouble which prompted your letter.

Grave as this matter is, however, there are, as you say, no steps available to us which can force a significant material change in this present situation. Since it represents a resounding confession of failure and of political weakness, this brutal border closing evidently represents a basic Soviet decision which only war could reverse. Neither you nor we, nor any of our allies, have ever supposed that we should go to war on this point.

Yet the Soviet action is too serious for inadequate responses. My own objection to most of the measures which have been proposed—even to most of the suggestions in your own letter—is that they are mere trifles compared to what has been done. . . .

On careful consideration I myself have decided that the best immediate response is a significant reinforcement of the Western garrisons. The importance of this reinforcement is symbolic—but not symbolic only. We know that the Soviet Union continues to emphasize its demand for the removal of Allied protection from West Berlin. We believe that even a modest reinforcement will underline our rejection of this concept. . . .

More broadly, let me urge it upon you that we must not be shaken by Soviet actions which in themselves are a confession of weakness. West Berlin today is more important than ever, and its mission to stand for freedom has never been so important as now. The link of West Berlin to the Free World is not a matter of rhetoric. Important as the ties to the East have been, painful as is their violation, the life of the city, as I understand it, runs primarily to the West—its economic life, its moral basis, and its military security. You may wish to consider and to suggest concrete ways in which these ties might be expanded in a fashion that would make the citizens of West Berlin more actively conscious of their role, not merely as an outpost of freedom, but as a vital part of the Free World and all its enterprises. In this double mission we are partners, and it is my own confidence that we can continue to rely upon each other as firmly in the future as we have in the past.

Source: *"Letter from President Kennedy to Governing Mayor Brandt,"* Foreign Relations of the United States, *14 (1961–1963): 352–353.*

ble that the dramatic economic and social reforms undertaken by the Soviet military administration in its zone, all of which were communist in complexion, could potentially lead to the full communization of the unified country.

Stalin had to find some way to stop the continued integration of the Western zones, a process started by Molotov's 1946 demand. The joint introduction of a reformed German currency in the Western sectors of Berlin was the immediate cause of Stalin's decision to declare a land and water blockade of the city in June 1948. He was creating a crisis over an anomalous feature of the occupation agreement in order to demonstrate his serious desire to promote a four-power solution to the German question (not a solution decided by three of the powers to his exclusion). In his strategic thinking the allies could either let West Berlin starve and fall under Russian control or come crawling to him for negotiations in which he would have the upper hand. Perhaps Stalin was also thinking about his own failure to prevent mass starvation during the siege of Leningrad. What he missed was that the West, especially the United States, had the capability and the will to risk aerial conflict and provide daily supplies of food, fuel, and consumer goods to a city of two million people for more than a year. The West carried out a tremendous feat. Its only alternative was to give in to Stalin either over Berlin or over Germany as a whole and look weak.

BERLIN CRISES

Stalin, however, was not fully estranged from a policy that would have resulted in German reunification. Even after the Western zones and the Soviet zone were made into two separate German states in 1949, East German officials were plagued by fears that Stalin would jettison their country if he could gain some strategic advantage by doing so. Indeed, the Soviet leader's "peace notes" on Germany, written in March 1952, proposed a scheme for German reunification according to which both German states would enter a confederate structure on equal footing, even though East Germany was about one third the size and had about one-third the population of the West. The Western allies did not accept the plan. In addition to its absurd equivalence of the two German states, the strategic disadvantage that losing West Germany's military and industrial potential was simply too great to countenance.

Stalin's death in March 1953 and other evolving features of the cold war changed the situation without reducing the tension that surrounded West Berlin. In the power struggle that followed, Stalin's designated successor, Georgy Malenkov, and his associates followed a "New Course" of developing a broad domestic economic base and trying to relax international tensions. Other Soviet leaders, led by Nikita Khrushchev, attacked this policy as weak and even as a betrayal of socialism. By 1955 Malenkov and his new strategic approach, which reached back to what appeared to be Stalin's, were no longer factors in the Soviet government. Significantly, one of Malenkov's associates, secret police chief Lavrenty Beria, was executed after a not-quite-so-fair trial in which he was accused of conspiring to sell out East Germany to the West.

Khrushchev's confrontational approach was important for the city of Berlin and for Germany as a whole. By the 1950s the dynamics of the Soviets' relationship with their East German allies became skewed. When Khrushchev began his de-Stalinization campaign in February 1956, the East German leadership, under the Stalinist Walter Ulbricht, once again feared for its survival. Seeking to compete with the West in order to demonstrate the superiority of socialism, Khrushchev simply could not afford to let East Germany be subsumed into a reunified German state, regardless of whatever strategic value that solution might have had for Stalin. Allowing a socialist state to revert to something other than socialism was not acceptable in an ideological struggle. The East German economy, moreover, was by far the best in eastern Europe. (Its geographic history as an integral part of industrial Germany predisposed it to be.) Khrushchev

believed East Germany would serve as a "display window" (*Schaufenster*) for socialism.

Keeping East Germany viable, however, was a terrible problem. While the borders of the occupation zones had been relatively free, millions of people simply left to assimilate into the socially and economically freer West Germany. When the borders were closed after East Germany became a separate state, the four-power presence in Berlin still allowed free transit to the West for any East German who took the Berlin subway into the Western sectors. As East German socialism continued to stifle initiative and personal liberty, hundreds of thousands of East Germans chose that way out.

The loss of what were predominantly young, educated people to the West; the ruthless exploitation of the East German economy by the Soviet occupation; and Ulbricht's continuing Stalinist communization of society and the economy raised serious questions about his regime's ability to survive without significant help from the USSR. Recent research has revealed that Ulbricht had considerable leverage in the alliance relationship between the two countries; for Khrushchev could either support him to his complete satisfaction or let his state collapse. Demanding that the West evacuate Ulbricht's capitol in November 1958, Khrushchev was attempting to shore up his ally's legitimacy. (Having half one's capital city occupied by mortal enemies does raise questions of legitimacy.) He was also trying to employ what many believed to be the Soviet advantage in strategic weapons to make a major play for Soviet foreign policy.

Khrushchev's ploy did not work. Recently released evidence shows that President Eisenhower almost certainly knew that Khrushchev's bluster about Soviet superiority in nuclear-missile technology was a bluff. Intelligence reports about the problems of the Soviet strategic-weapons program and the complete lack of aerial-espionage evidence to sustain the Soviet leader's claims of superiority enabled the West to ignore him without suffering undue consequences over Berlin.

By mid 1959 Khrushchev was aware that his bid for strategic-weapons superiority was at an end and that the success of the American strategic-weapons program might well leave the Soviet Union at a disadvantage. The Soviet leader began to approach the West with what seemed to be a desire to relax tensions. After a successful visit to the United States in the fall of 1959, relations warmed for a time. The downing of an American spy plane over Soviet territory in April 1960, however, threw a wrench into a planned summit between Khrushchev and Eisenhower in

Paris and caused the attempt at an early détente to founder.

Despite some efforts to renew the relationship with the Kennedy administration, which came into office in January 1961, the pressures of the East German alliance evolved into a major disruption. After a relatively unpromising meeting with Kennedy in Vienna in June 1961, it seemed apparent to Khrushchev that the best the Eastern bloc could hope for was a solution to the flight of East Germany's population. This problem became more pronounced in Soviet strategic thinking after Kennedy resisted attempts to lure him into firm American military commitments in Cuba and Laos. On 13 August 1961, with no real hope of dislodging the West from Berlin and the continuing exodus of East Germans for the West, the Soviet leader consented to the implementation of a plan code-named "Rose": building a wall around West Berlin. The stability crisis in East Germany was shored up, the battle lines of the cold war were solidified, and the Berlin crisis was over.

–PAUL DU QUENOY, GEORGE WASHINGTON UNIVERSITY

References

Michael R. Beschloss, *The Crisis Years: Kennedy and Khrushchev, 1960–1963* (New York: Edward Burlingame, 1991);

Campbell Craig, *Destroying the Village: Eisenhower and Thermonuclear War* (New York: Columbia University Press, 1998);

John Lewis Gaddis, *We Now Know: Rethinking Cold War History* (New York: Oxford University Press, 1997);

John P. S. Gearson, *Harold Macmillan and the Berlin Wall Crisis, 1958–62: The Limits of Interests and Force* (New York: St. Martin's Press, 1998);

Hope Harrison, "Ulbricht and the Concrete 'Rose': New Archival Evidence on the Dynamics of Soviet-East German Relations and the Berlin Crisis, 1958–1961," Working Paper of the Cold War International History Project, May 1993;

Nikita Khrushchev, *Khrushchev Remembers,* translated by Strobe Talbott (Boston: Little, Brown, 1974);

Vojtch Mastny, *The Cold War and Soviet Insecurity: The Stalin Years* (New York: Oxford University Press, 1996);

Norman Naimark, *The Russians in Germany: A History of the Soviet Zone of Occupation, 1945–1949* (Cambridge, Mass.: Harvard University Press, 1995);

Avi Shlaim, *The United States and the Berlin Blockade, 1948–1949: A Study in Crisis Decision-making* (Berkeley, Cal.: University of California Press, 1983);

Ann Tusa, *The Last Division: A History of Berlin, 1945–1989* (Reading, Mass.: Addison-Wesley, 1997);

Andreas Wenger, *Living With Peril: Eisenhower, Kennedy, and Nuclear Weapons* (Lanham, Md.: Rowman & Littlefield, 1997);

Vladislav Zubok and Constantine Pleshakov, *Inside the Kremlin's Cold War: From Stalin to Khrushchev* (Cambridge, Mass.: Harvard University Press, 1996).

CAMBODIA

Was the U.S. invasion of Cambodia in May 1970 justified?

Viewpoint: Yes, the American invasion of Cambodia was justified because the country was a center of Vietcong activity against South Vietnam.

Viewpoint: No, the U.S. invasion of Cambodia was not justified because it had only a marginal effect on North Vietnamese activities in South Vietnam.

The invasion of Cambodia by American troops in April 1970 marked the beginning of the end of U.S. involvement in the Vietnam War. President Richard M. Nixon, who had taken office the previous year, had campaigned on the promise that he would find a quick and honorable way to end the war. Indeed, during his first year in office some of the public clamor against the war had subsided somewhat, allowing the president and his national security adviser, Henry Kissinger, some breathing room. The administration could use this relative freedom from public scrutiny. Nixon and Kissinger wanted to extricate the United States from the war, but they did not want to appear to be capitulating to communist pressure. To achieve this end Kissinger used the improved relationship the United States was developing with the Soviet Union as part of the détente process to examine the possibility of Soviet pressure on the North Vietnamese to settle the war diplomatically. At the same time the administration was hoping to be able to shore up South Vietnam's military capabilities so that the South could assume an increasing share of the military burden.

From the vantage point of the president and his advisers, however, the situation on the ground was grim. Despite the massive losses the Vietcong had suffered during the 1968 Tet Offensive, the communists were winning the psychological war. After three years of escalating U.S. involvement and rosy "bringing the boys home by Christmas" predictions, the North Vietnamese could still mount well-coordinated attacks all over South Vietnam, with their soldiers reaching even the gates of the U.S. embassy compound in Saigon. The American public was forced to realize that the war was not going according to plan and that the gap between official U.S. pronouncements and reality was widening. Having come into office promising that he would "Vietnamize" the war, Nixon faced a problem: the South Vietnamese army was not up to the task of fighting the Vietcong and the North Vietnamese; yet, the gradual withdrawal of U.S. troops would depend on greater effectiveness of the South Vietnamese military effort. One way to allow the South Vietnamese more time to regroup and improve was to lessen the North Vietnamese pressure on the South. Much of the North Vietnamese military activity was launched from the sanctuaries the North Vietnamese had built over the years in eastern Cambodia. The border between Cambodia and South Vietnam was much longer than that between North and South Vietnam, and because of Cambodia's neutrality, the United States had abstained from attacking the North Vietnamese positions there. When Nixon took office, he launched a secret air campaign against the North Vietnamese bases in Cambodia, but without noticeable results.

Then, in April 1970, the decision was made to send U.S. troops into Cambodia. The news of the invasion (which the administration called an "incursion") galvanized the antiwar movement, and massive demonstrations followed. In one such demonstration, Ohio National Guardsmen opened fire on student demonstrators at Kent State University, killing four students. The antiwar protest never let up after that, increasing in intensity and volume. The invasion inflicted some setbacks on the North Vietnamese, but the damage to the Nixon administration's ability to continue controlling the pace of its gradual Vietnamization program was far greater, as was the damage to its credibility among many Americans. The administration also suffered from baseless accusations that the U.S. invasion of Cambodia helped the Khmer Rouge come to power there and, from 1975 until 1978, impose a brutal regime in which more than a million Cambodians perished.

Viewpoint:
Yes, the American invasion of Cambodia was justified because it was a center of Vietcong activity against South Vietnam.

In the spring of 1970 President Richard M. Nixon ordered American forces in South Vietnam to invade Cambodia. That decision had many ramifications for the Nixon presidency. Domestic critics alleged that Nixon's action widened the war unnecessarily and threatened to slow down the process of withdrawing American forces from Southeast Asia at a time when public opinion, and, indeed, the president himself, favored the reduction of the American presence there. In later years critics blamed Nixon's invasion for the genocidal horrors perpetrated by the Khmer Rouge regime. The secrecy of the decision compounded the criticism. Nixon looked as though he had something to hide, and many of his critics resented the exclusion of public opinion and a large part of the policymaking establishment from a major decision that was widely regarded as a mistake. In a broader strategic context, however, the invasion was entirely justified.

When Nixon entered office, he adopted an amazingly unusual approach to the Vietnam conflict. Unlike his predecessor, he pursued a strategy designed to win the war rather than merely repel the attacks of the North Vietnamese and their communist guerrilla cadres in South Vietnam. Under Secretary of Defense Robert S. McNamara's direction, the Johnson administration had consistently failed to take any decisive step toward eliminating the ability of the communist forces to continue fighting in South Vietnam. American forces never invaded the communist North, and Vietcong guerrilla bases in Cambodia and Laos were left untouched and inviolable.

Although a direct attack on North Vietnam risked provoking Chinese involvement, just as the invasion of North Korea had in 1950, respect for the neutrality of Cambodia and Laos was a moot point. The plain fact of the matter was that the main military effort of the communist forces in Vietnam was based exclusively in Cambodia and Laos for the first several years of the war, even though the neutrality of the two countries had been sanctified by the Geneva Accords of 1954. No direct North Vietnamese attack on the South came across the seventeenth parallel, which separated the two Vietnams, until the spring of 1970. Moving troops and supplies through Laos and Cambodia offered the communists a much broader front through which to attack the South. It also allowed them to maintain the pretense that the communist military activity in the South was an internal rebellion against the corrupt regime in Saigon, not an aggressive Northern attempt to conquer the South. From Hanoi's perspective these advantages were tremendous, but they inescapably involved the violation of Laotian and Cambodian neutrality. At the height of American involvement, the North Vietnamese had organized an extensive supply route through both countries along the "Ho Chi Minh Trail." The frontiers of the two neutral countries with South Vietnam were littered with Vietcong bases. The political pacification of the governments of Cambodia and Laos in the face of these obvious violations of their neutrality was complemented by economic exploitation. The North Vietnamese were able to extract as much as 40 percent of the Cambodian rice crop, for example. Arguing that the United States was obliged to respect the neutrality of Cambodia and Laos scrupulously is comparable to arguing that Britain and France should not have entered neutral Belgium when the Germans moved in without declarations of war in 1914 and 1940.

Despite the Johnson administration's reluctance to take the necessary steps, winning the Vietnam conflict was not an especially difficult proposition. First and foremost, North Vietnam manufactured little of its military hardware. During and after the war Hanoi relied on arms shipments from the Soviet Union to continue fighting. As relations between Beijing and Moscow deteriorated, Chinese support to the pro-Soviet North Vietnamese government dried up. The Soviet supply route over China was dependent on the use of Chinese railroads at a time when

CAMBODIA

NIXON ON THE CAMBODIAN INVASION

On 8 May 1970, President Richard M. Nixon held a televised news conference to respond to questions about his decision to send U.S. troops into Cambodia with the goal of "reducing American casualties and, also, of hastening the day that we can have a just peace." His complete remarks were entered into the Congressional Record on 11 May 1970. When he was asked: "On April 20th, you said Vietnamization was going so well that you could pull 150,000 American troops out of Vietnam. Then you turned around only 10 days later and said that Vietnamization was so badly threatened you were sending troops into Cambodia. Would you explain this apparent contradiction for us?" Nixon responded:

I explained it in my speech of April 20th, as you will recall, because then I said that Vietnamization was going so well that we could bring 150,000 out by the spring of next year, regardless of the progress in the Paris peace talks and the other criteria that I mentioned.

But I also warned at that time that increased enemy action in Laos, in Cambodia, as well as in Vietnam, was something that we had noted, and that if I had indicated, and if I found, that increased enemy action would jeopardize the remaining forces who would be in Vietnam after we had withdrawn 150,000, I would take strong action to deal with it. I found that the action that the enemy had taken in Cambodia would mean the 240,000 Americans who would be there a year from now without many combat troops to help defend them would leave them in an untenable position. That is why I had to act.

Source: *"The President's News Conference of May 8,1970,"* Congressional Record, *91st Congress, 2nd session, 116, 1970, part 11: 14826.*

---

mounting Sino-Soviet tension slowed down the delivery of matériel. The anti-Soviet proclivities of the Red Guards often led them simply to steal Soviet equipment intended for North Vietnam as it was in transit across their country. When strained diplomatic relations developed into significant frontier battles between the Soviets and the Chinese in the spring and summer of 1969, the movement of supplies to Hanoi by rail became a virtual impossibility.

The only way for the North Vietnamese to receive supplies at that time was by sea. The geography of the conflict is especially revealing in this respect, for there were only two possible ports to which supplies could be delivered. The North Vietnamese port complex at Haiphong gave the most direct access to North Vietnam, but the supplies would then have to be sent across the country and moved along the entire length of the Ho Chi Minh Trail to the main battleground. Since the Soviet military buildup along the Chinese border monopolized what little infrastructure existed in the Soviet Far East, ships sailing to North Vietnam had to leave from

the Black Sea ports, proceed through the Suez Canal or (after the canal was closed following the Arab-Israeli War of 1967) around the whole of Africa, cross the Indian Ocean, and skirt the South Vietnamese coast and American naval patrols. A simpler solution was to use the North Vietnamese political influence in Cambodia to gain access to the Cambodian port of Kompong Som, which was much closer to the battlefield than Haiphong. Reaching Kompong Som by sea, though almost as far as going to Haiphong, was much less risky because supply ships did not have to approach South Vietnam or the American patrols. The more direct access to South Vietnam was an advantage too great to be ignored.

For Nixon, the heavy North Vietnamese reliance on Soviet supplies was Hanoi's Achilles' heel. The importance of Kompong Som as the principal communist supply port in Southeast Asia made it the first target in his efforts to force the conflict to a favorable conclusion. Communist bases in Cambodia, the more immediate source of the Vietcong's ability to prosecute Hanoi's war in the South, were also vital targets for American military operations in Nixon's intervention. The initial success of the operation underscored its potential as a major strategic victory. Domestic reaction, however, ultimately destroyed whatever possibility Nixon's strategy had of ending the war. After knowledge of the invasion became public, the massive antiwar protests, compounded by the unfortunate deaths of four students at Kent State University, compelled Nixon to restrain American military activity in Cambodia. A congressional vote on 30 June 1970 forced the withdrawal of American troops from the country and forever prevented their return.

From a strategic standpoint, there is no question that Nixon's intervention in Cambodia was justified militarily. He was not simply a warmonger or an insecure individual who felt that he had to prove himself to the world through senseless aggression. One wonders what would have happened to the communist position in South Vietnam if their Cambodian bases had been permanently wiped out and their main supply port neutralized. Critics who argue that Nixon unnecessarily "widened" the war in his pursuit of that objective ignore the fact that the Johnson administration had achieved little during four years of massively increasing an American force that was used only to defend South Vietnam without ever attacking the root of the military problem. Critics also fail to take into account that the incursion into Cambodia and other acts of unnecessary "escalation" (for example, the bombing of Hanoi in December 1972)

CAMBODIA

Indochina during 1954–1975

were accompanied by the steady withdrawal of American troops from the region as a whole. It is not at all easy to explain logically how taking meaningful steps to end the war while reducing the American military presence represented a "widening" of the conflict.

The secrecy of the decision to invade was also upsetting to many of Nixon's critics. When the Judiciary Committee of the House of Representatives referred four impeachment charges against the president to the full House in 1974, the secret bombing of Cambodia was the basis for one of them. If the Washington foreign-policy establishment, Congressional leaders, and media resented their exclusion from the decision-making process, there were unmistakable and abundant reasons why it had to be confined to relatively few people. If Nixon had gone on television and announced what he was about to do, protests by the radical antiwar movement would almost certainly have anticipated the invasion rather than merely reacted to it. If the invasion had been publicized, its military success would have

CAMBODIA

been compromised. The communists would have known what was about to happen; no one would have understood the strategic importance of Nixon's decision better than they. Can one seriously imagine Franklin Delano Roosevelt announcing the Normandy invasion ahead of time and then elaborating its strategic importance in a fireside chat? The administration's foreign-policy organs, furthermore, were plagued by illegal leaks of secret material to the press. These breaches of security had the potential to release dangerously compromising information to the general public. Should something as crucial as the administration's strategy for ending the war emerge in that fashion, Nixon would probably have done just as well to announce it on television.

The critics' most serious moral objection to Nixon's decision to invade Cambodia is their charge that it caused the political destabilization of the country and opened the way for the barbarism of the native communist movement, Pol Pot's Khmer Rouge. This charge is patently ridiculous. That Cambodia did not even try to resist or seriously protest either the large-scale, blatant violation of its neutrality by the North Vietnamese or even refuse to cooperate in furnishing the logistical needs of communist forces for their war in South Vietnam does not present a picture of a stable country. Its domestic crisis was enhanced by the fact that before the American incursion took place, Prince Norodom Sihanouk was deposed by his own prime minister, Marshal Lon Nol, in a move sanctioned unanimously by the Cambodian legislature. In other words, Cambodia was in the throes of a constitutional, as well as military, crisis before the United States attacked the communist bases within its borders. In accordance with the criticism of Nixon and the congressional censure of his actions, the American presence in Cambodia was withdrawn by the end of June 1970; the Vietnamese communists returned to their base camps; and Cambodia's domestic political situation continued to deteriorate. It is indeed hard to imagine that the brief American incursion was a more significant factor in the destabilization of Cambodia than the years-long North Vietnamese presence there and their use of Cambodian territory as the main base for their war.

The rise of the Khmer Rouge had everything to do with the weaknesses of the existing political system and wider strategic interests. In an era of Sino-Soviet tension and Sino-American rapprochement, China had no interest in seeing Indochina united under the hegemony of the pro-Soviet Hanoi regime. As a result China supported Pol Pot's pro-Chinese forces to prevent

such a union from happening. Pol Pot and the other leaders of the Khmer Rouge, moreover, had developed their mad utopian vision and outlined their murderous and genocidal policies while they were young students in Paris in the 1920s and 1930s, not after the Americans intervened in their country in 1970. Nixon's critics themselves, who insisted on withdrawing even indirect American aid to Southeast Asia after 1973, did not exactly help the Khmer Rouge's millions of victims or do anything to right what they had called Nixon's wrong after they had succeeded in removing him from power.

For military and strategic reasons, any effective conclusion of the Vietnam War for the United States would have had to include direct involvement in Cambodia. For several years the North Vietnamese had violated its neutrality with impunity and made it the base of its military operations in South Vietnam. Those bases and the supply route through Kompong Som had to be neutralized. Nixon's invasion in the spring of 1970 was the only decisive step taken in that direction throughout the entire conflict. Had it succeeded, it would have been a tremendous blow to the communist war effort and made it possible to end the conflict in much more favorable circumstances. The fact that it was not allowed to succeed doomed the honorable peace Nixon sought so vigorously. In addition to its being a sound strategic approach, the allegations of critics that the invasion violated the Constitution, widened the war, and directly caused the rise of the Khmer Rouge have little basis in reality. The invasion was justified.

–PAUL DU QUENOY, GEORGE WASHINGTON UNIVERSITY

Viewpoint:
No, the U.S. invasion of Cambodia was not justified because it had only a marginal effect on North Vietnamese activities in South Vietnam.

The U.S. invasion of Cambodia in late April 1970 was an unmitigated disaster. Described by the Nixon administration as an "incursion," it revived and energized massive demonstrations on college campuses, largely dormant since the election of President Richard M. Nixon; it led to the shooting and killing of student demonstrators by the National Guard; and it prompted Congress to pass the Cooper-Church amendment mandating that all U.S. troops be pulled out of Cambodia by 1 July–

President Richard M.
Nixon announcing the
April 1970 invasion
of Cambodia

(Hulton Getty)

the first such military restriction voted by Congress against a president in time of war (declared or undeclared). Whatever goodwill the administration enjoyed since coming to power a year earlier, bolstered by candidate Nixon's promise to end the U.S. involvement in the war in Vietnam, disappeared completely, replaced by bitterness and rancor. The antiwar movement, and growing segments of the public, turned on the administration with a vengeance.

Historians agree. In the words of Seyom Brown, the invasion "marked the end of the administration's ability to convince wide segments of the policy community that the White House really did have a workable 'game plan' for ending the war. . . . Clearly, Nixon and [National Security Adviser Henry] Kissinger . . . had lost whatever intellectual and conceptual control over the situation they might have started out with in 1969, not to speak of the emotional control required to implement a strategy of deliberate, cool military disengagement." Nixon, who had published his autobiography in 1962 under the title *Six Crises,* described his Cambodia decision as his "seventh crisis."

What were the administration's aims in invading Cambodia? Were these aims achieved? Were they achievable? Cambodia had been a neutral country in name only: its weakness invited its neighbors to the east, North and South Vietnam, to violate its territory with impunity. North Vietnamese troops practically controlled the eastern border areas of Cambodia, using Cambodian territory for storing supplies and ammunition, as a roundabout way for its troops to get from North into South Vietnam, as staging areas for ground operations inside South Vietnam, and as sanctuaries for troops

retreating after hit-and-run operations in South Vietnam. Since March 1969, with the tacit approval of the Cambodian ruler, Prince Norodom Sihanouk, U.S. B-52 bombers regularly bombed these sanctuaries and staging areas, and these bombing campaigns were concealed from the American public. The bombing, however, did little to disrupt the flow of men and material from North to South. The administration considered this problem serious. Nixon began to implement his "Vietnamization" plan, which called for reducing the number of U.S. troops in Southeast Asia and shifting more and more of the burden of the fighting to the South Vietnamese military. American military planners were afraid that, as U.S. troops in South Vietnam were being drawn down, the country was becoming more and more vulnerable to attack by the North Vietnamese troops stationed in Cambodia. The South Vietnamese-Cambodian border was much longer than that between North and South Vietnam and much more difficult to defend. It was also closer to important South Vietnamese population centers. The administration thus wanted to do more to reduce the danger to the South from the North Vietnamese soldiers stationed in eastern Cambodia.

The opportunity presented itself in March 1970, when Prince Sihanouk was toppled in a military coup by Marshal Lon Nol. Lon Nol had a problem: the Cambodian communists, emboldened and strengthened with North Vietnamese training and matériel, were closing in on Phnom Penh, the Cambodian capital, in an effort to topple his regime and replace it with a communist government. Lon Nol wanted to move vigorously against the Cambodian communists, but

CAMBODIA

he realized that, in order to root them out, at the same time he would have to evict the North Vietnamese troops from Cambodian territory and destroy the North Vietnamese sanctuaries there. The North Vietnamese, however, were not willing to give up their commanding strategic positions inside Cambodia, which they had patiently built for many years, positions from which they were planning their final assault on the South Vietnamese regime to unite Vietnam under the leadership of Ho Chi Minh. The North Vietnamese also did not see any reason why they should make it easier for Lon Nol to move against local communist forces. In desperation, Lon Nol, tearing up the veneer of Cambodian neutrality, turned to the United States for help. Nixon, fearing that the North Vietnamese would use the gradual American withdrawal from the region to take over Cambodia and then South Vietnam, agreed. In announcing the decision to the nation, Nixon said: "If, when the chips are down, the world's most powerful nation, the United States of America, acts like a pitiful, helpless giant, the forces of totalitarianism and anarchy will threaten free nations and free institutions throughout the world. It is not our power but our will and character that is being tested tonight. If we fail to meet this challenge, all other nations will be on notice that despite its overwhelming power the United States, when a real crisis comes, will be found wanting."

On 30 June 1970, two months after the invasion began, American troops withdrew from Cambodia. U.S. troops achieved impressive military goals: 11,349 North Vietnamese troops were killed, and about 2,328 were captured; 22,892 individual weapons and 2,509 crew-served weapons were captured or destroyed, as were more than 15 million rounds of ammunition, 14 million pounds of rice, 143,000 rockets, more than 199,552 antiaircraft rounds, 5,482 mines, 62,022 grenades, 83,000 pounds of explosives, 435 vehicles, and 11,688 bunkers and military structures. These immediate military gains notwithstanding, the fact was that, as American troops were withdrawing after two months of intense military activity inside Cambodia, the Cambodian communists were in control of half of that nation—a much larger area than they had controlled at the beginning of April, when the invasion began. It was not long before the communist Khmer Rouge chased Lon Nol's forces out of Phnom Penh and took over the country. In the ensuing three years, the communist leader Pol Pot imposed a ghastly reign of terror on the small country. Inspired by a vision of turning Cambodia into a rural society untainted by urban, capitalist values, the Khmer Rouge was ruthless. All government employees and civil servants who served under previous governments—and the families of these employees—were executed. The large cities were emptied, and city dwellers—including the two mil-

lion inhabitants of Phnom Penh—were forced to march into the countryside, where they were told to fend for themselves. Hundreds of thousands of these people, unschooled in agriculture and exposed to the elements, died of starvation and disease. Entire segments of the population—including teachers, intellectuals, and artists—were systematically murdered in what came to be described as the "killing fields." Historians now estimate that Pol Pot orchestrated the killing of between one and two million Cambodians out of a population of six million.

The sheer scope of the Khmer Rouge's terror, and the fact that the organization's murderous campaign came on the heels of the U.S. incursion into Cambodia, led some to argue that the U.S. military activities in Cambodia caused the reign of terror. This contention does not stand up to scrutiny, and some who advanced this accusation later retreated from their earlier charges, chief among them William Shawcross, who covered the war for *The Sunday Times* (London) during 1970–1975. In 1994 he wrote that "those of us who opposed the American war in Indochina should be extremely humble in the face of the appalling aftermath: a form of genocide in Cambodia and horrific tyranny in both Vietnam and Laos." In reviewing his coverage, he concluded that he "concentrated too easily on the corruption and incompetence of the South Vietnamese and their American allies, was too ignorant of the inhuman Hanoi regime, and far too willing to believe that a victory by the Communists would provide a better future. But after the Communist victory came the refugees to Thailand and the floods of boat people desperately seeking to escape the Cambodian killing fields and the Vietnamese gulags. Their eloquent testimony should have put paid to all illusions."

Regardless of what the invasion did to Cambodia, it utterly failed to achieve its goals in Vietnam. Nixon wanted to shock North Vietnam into realizing that continuing the war would be extremely costly to it, but instead he found himself confronting the reality that the political costs of continuing the U.S. involvement in the war were becoming prohibitively high to his administration. Nixon and Kissinger were unprepared for the intense domestic reaction to the operation, but Hanoi was. North Vietnam intensified its military operations while becoming more intransigent at the negotiation table. The firestorm of protest reached Congress, which showed renewed interest in imposing legal limits on the ability of the administration to continue the military operations in Southeast Asia. Rather than increase Washington's freedom of action in the war and the diplomatic moves that accompanied it, the Cambodia operation limited U.S. freedom even more; rather than strengthen the U.S. hand in the intricate negotiations with the North, the operations weakened the U.S. position considerably. The United States subsequently made one concession after another, agreeing, among other things, to what was called a "cease-fire-in-place," a euphemism for allowing Hanoi to keep its forces in the South and accepting their control of territory they had already taken there. The U.S. insistence on the mutual withdrawal of forces from South Vietnam—both American and North Vietnamese—was abandoned in the wake of the Cambodian operation. The acceptance of the "cease-fire-in-place" spelled the death warrant for the South Vietnamese regime. It also legitimized the fundamental North Vietnamese contention that the only foreign troops that would have to leave South Vietnam as part of a peace agreement were the American forces. The United States thus tacitly accepted that what the North Vietnamese forces were doing in the South was a continuation of the Vietnamese war against outside colonial control.

The weakening of the American position did not translate into an immediate peace agreement. As the North Vietnamese kept insisting on conditions that Nixon felt he could not accept, there were periodic escalations in the fighting: the Easter bombing of 1972, the mining of Haiphong harbor in spring 1972, and the 1972 Christmas bombings. At the same time Kissinger tried to use the new relationship the United States was establishing with China and the Soviet Union to pressure Hanoi. After fits and starts, the peace agreement was finally signed on 27 January 1973. It was soon violated by both the North and the South Vietnamese. The administration, however, could no longer bring military pressure to bear in order to save the South. One reason was Nixon's increasing troubles as a result of the unfolding Watergate affair. The other reason was the increasing number of congressional limitations on the administration's control of the military effort in Asia. It started with Congress's angry reaction to the invasion of Cambodia and ended with a "nail-in-the-coffin" piece of legislation in June 1973, which barred any further U.S. military action in Indochina.

The Cambodia operation was a mistake. The only charitable thing that may be said about it is that it did not matter much one way or the other: U.S. policy in Vietnam was untenable, and by 1970 the handwriting was already on the wall. Perhaps, however, the operation did make a positive contribution, although not the one intended by its authors; by galvanizing public opinion and focusing its attention on the shortcomings of the administration's policies, it hastened the day of reckoning and quickened the end of a war that should have been ended long before.

—BENJAMIN FRANKEL, SECURITY STUDIES

References

Seyom Brown, *The Faces of Power: Constancy and Change in United States Foreign Policy from Truman to Reagan* (New York: Columbia University Press, 1983; second edition, revised, 1994);

David P. Chandler, *The Tragedy of Cambodian History: Politics, War and Revolution since 1945* (New Haven: Yale University Press, 1991);

Seymour M. Hersh, *The Price of Power: Kissinger in the Nixon White House* (New York: Summit, 1983);

Ben Kiernan, *How Pol Pot Came to Power: A History of Communism in Kampuchea, 1930–1975* (London: Verso, 1985);

Jeffrey Kimball, *Nixon's Vietnam War* (Lawrence: University of Kansas Press, 1999);

Henry Kissinger, *White House Years* (Boston: Little, Brown, 1979);

Guenter Lewy, *America in Vietnam* (New York: Oxford University Press, 1978);

Richard M. Nixon, *RN: The Memoirs of Richard Nixon* (New York: Grosset & Dunlap, 1978);

Stephen S. Rosenfeld, "The Shawcross Apology," *Washington Post*, 21 May 1999, p. A31;

William Shawcross, *The Quality of Mercy: Cambodia, Holocaust and Modern Conscience* (New York: Simon & Schuster, 1984);

Shawcross, *Sideshow: Kissinger, Nixon and the Destruction of Cambodia* (New York: Simon & Schuster, 1979);

Melvin Small, *Johnson, Nixon, and the Doves* (New Brunswick, N.J.: Rutgers University Press, 1988);

Richard C. Thornton, *The Nixon-Kissinger Years: Reshaping America's Foreign Policy* (New York: Paragon House, 1989).

CAMBODIA

CENTRAL AMERICA

Did the Reagan administration pursue the correct policies in regard to Central America?

Viewpoint: Yes, the Reagan administration's policies in Central America successfully blocked the expansion of communism in the region.

Viewpoint: No, the Reagan administration unnecessarily militarized U.S. policies in Central America at a time when communism was declining, and it substantially increased U.S. support to regimes that grossly violated human rights.

When President Ronald W. Reagan entered office in January 1981, his administration had to confront several challenges in Central America. Many countries in that region suffered from what seemed to be chronic political and economic instability. These conditions gave rise in some case to authoritarian governments that maintained order but had little in common with the democratic values of the United States and in other instances to largely Marxist revolutionary movements that advocated radical change.

Since regional instability had created the potential for the infiltration of Soviet influence, American policy throughout the cold war had been to support right-wing dictatorships that kept order and prevented communist expansion. The administration of President Jimmy Carter, however, had departed from that approach when it withdrew American support from the regime of Anastasio Somoza Debayle in Nicaragua and thus contributed to the rise to power of the revolutionary Sandinista movement. When it was discovered that the Marxist Sandinista regime had as little, if not less, respect for democracy and human rights as Somoza had, Carter withdrew support from it as well.

The Reagan administration predicated its approach to Central America on supporting pro-American dictatorships to prevent the expansion of communism and to turn back the gains that the USSR had already made there. Many authoritarian governments received American financial and military assistance. Support delivered to Marxist rebels in El Salvador—from throughout the communist world via Nicaragua—prompted a special American interest in sustaining the existing Salvadoran government. Within Nicaragua itself the Reagan administration supported and helped organize the "contras," anticommunist guerrillas who sought to overthrow the Sandinista regime. As the administration's broader strategy of turning back communism succeeded, it pursued a corollary to its Central American policy that aimed at replacing the authoritarian dictatorships with democratic regimes, a process that was largely completed throughout the region by the 1990s.

Viewpoint:
Yes, the Reagan administration's policies in Central America successfully blocked the expansion of communism in the region.

The Reagan administration's approach to foreign policy was controversial in its implications for Central America. To block the expansion of communist influence in the region, the administration often supported governments that hardly reflected American values. By affiliating itself with these governments and, consequently, with policies that grossly violated human rights, the administration compromised some of its domestic support and drew harsh criticism. Despite that outcome there can be no question that the policies of the Reagan administration were correct in the context of American strategic and security interests.

Since 1823, when President James Monroe elaborated the doctrine that carries his name, American foreign policy has been predicated on resisting the spread of great-power influence in the Americas. In the cold war, upholding that principle meant blocking the growth of communist influence supported by the Soviet Union and its allies. The election of the Marxist-supported government of Jacobo Arbenz Guzmán in Guatemala in 1954 presented the first such challenge. After Arbenz nationalized extensive American business interests and began to receive arms shipments from Czechoslovakia, the Eisenhower administration organized and supported an opposition movement through the Central Intelligence Agency (CIA) and precipitated Arbenz's fall from power. More important, earlier that year Secretary of State John Foster Dulles had received the overwhelming support of the Tenth Inter-American Conference for a resolution describing international communism as a threat to stability and democracy in the Americas and calling on the nations represented there to take steps to resist communism at home.

For the rest of the cold war, however, the emergence of a Marxist and pro-Soviet Cuba was the greatest threat to stability in Central America, and it is from that perspective that the Reagan administration's strategy must be understood. The Eisenhower administration made a series of mistakes in allowing the replacement of President Fulgencio Batista y Zaldívar of Cuba with a less corrupt and more effective pro-American leader. After rebel leader Fidel Castro took power in 1959, alienation from Washington and support from Moscow caused Cuba to move toward communism and a de facto alliance with the Soviet Union. Beset as they were with problems in developing an intercontinental ballistic

missile (ICBM) system, the Soviets perceived no uncertain opportunity in Cuba. The United States had missiles in Turkey and a functioning ICBM system of its own, both of which could strike Soviet targets. A base in the Caribbean offered the Soviets the ability to create a corresponding nuclear threat to American civilian targets.

Frustrated in their 1962 attempt to achieve that goal, the Soviets failed once again in 1970, when Washington confronted them over an attempt to establish a naval base capable of supporting nuclear armaments at Cienfuegos in western Cuba. Both the Cuban Missile Crisis and the Cienfuegos incident resulted in superpower "understandings" that eliminated Cuba as a base for Soviet missiles. In the late 1970s the Soviets were still interested in a strategic base near the continental United States, and, as part of a larger global strategy of communist expansion that reached from southern Africa to Southeast Asia, they saw opportunities for subversion in Central America. Conditions in several countries of that region were ripe for revolution, and there were no "understandings" to exclude Soviet strategic weapons. The policies of the strong, authoritarian regimes that ruled these countries had the effect of producing specifically Marxist revolutionary groups or broad left-wing reform movements with strong Marxist components.

The United States faced a strategic quandary. By backing authoritarian regimes to promote stability in its "backyard," it had to an extent opened the door for radicalized opposition movements that were favorably disposed to receiving Soviet aid and adopting policies influenced by Moscow. Washington had three choices. It could continue to support the pro-American dictators with full military aid, try to co-opt the opposition movements and support their bids to replace authoritarian regimes, or do nothing and allow the Central American nations to go communist.

All three options had proponents in Washington. The first opportunity to test the potential solutions came in Nicaragua, where the long-standing "Sandinista" movement (named for Nicaraguan revolutionary Augusto César Sandino, who had been executed in 1934) opposed the intergenerational dictatorship of the Somoza family. As the Sandinistas became stronger in the late 1970s, Anastasio Somoza Debayle's domestic position deteriorated, losing the support of even moderate elements of the population, and President Jimmy Carter allowed the rebels to force out Somoza and form a government, which Washington offered to support with large loans. In this case, however, Carter made the same mistake that the Eisenhower administration had made in Cuba. When the Sandinistas came to

Senator Daniel K. Inouye
and Representative
Lee H. Hamilton,
chairmen of the Senate
and House committees
formed in December 1986
to investigate the
Iran-Contra Affair

(Washington Post / Rich Lipski)

power in 1979, their regime was easily as brutal as the one they had replaced and American enthusiasm for supporting it collapsed.

President Ronald Reagan's election platform in 1980 included a promise to promote the creation of a free and democratically elected government in Nicaragua. Worsening relations between Washington and Managua placed the Marxist Sandinista regime in the Soviet orbit, while an impressive array of evidence confirmed that the armed revolutionaries of the Farabundo Martí National Liberation Front (FMLN) in neighboring El Salvador were receiving support from Nicaragua and several other pro-Soviet communist countries via Nicaragua. American M-16 assault rifles, for instance, were captured from the rebels, and an examination of their serial numbers indicated that they had been lost by American troops in Vietnam a decade earlier. It was clear that the Soviets and their allies were exploiting the instability in Central America to spread their ideological and strategic influence.

For an administration devoted to "rolling back" Soviet influence on a global scale, the situation was intolerable. How to rid Central America of that influence, however, was a difficult question. The psychological blow of U.S. failure in Vietnam was still relatively recent. The condition of the American military had declined, and only at the end of the Carter administration did

it begin to be restored, a process that took several more years to complete. A series of full-scale invasions was not a real possibility. Instead, the Reagan administration adopted a policy of supporting pro-American authoritarian dictatorships. Formulated by Jeanne J. Kirkpatrick, Reagan's ambassador to the United Nations, it gave defeating communist expansion precedence over immediate social reform and political democratization in Central America.

For the duration of the Reagan years, Washington preferred to conduct "low-intensity conflicts" and avoid large military commitments, which public opinion and the state of the military would not permit. In November 1981 Reagan applied that strategy toward Nicaragua and issued National Security Decision Directive 17 (NSDD-17), calling for the CIA to train and support "contra" freedom fighters in order to destabilize and overthrow the Sandinista regime. In response to the adoption of its own guerrilla tactics by the contras, the Sandinistas built up a large army with firm support from the communist world and even Western Europe. As the Nicaraguan communists escalated the conflict, CIA director William J. Casey used his mandate from NSDD-17 to bring the operations of the contras under closer agency control and expanded them to include assassinations of Sandinista officials, mining Nicaraguan harbors, and destroying industrial plants. Increasingly successful, the contras grew rapidly.

A major drawback to these tactics was that the military situation in various Central American countries was not always under American control. Their military training and American support notwithstanding, the contras, the national armies, and the military police of pro-American dictatorships lacked discipline. Together with the brutal and pervasive violence of the conflicts, discipline problems often led to atrocities that blacked American strategy in the eyes of world opinion and caused serious domestic criticism. Even before Reagan came to power, Carter briefly cut American aid to El Salvador in 1980, after the murder of four American nuns by Salvadoran soldiers had gone unpunished. Although Carter restored aid when the government's position became more precarious and support continued under Reagan, reprisals against civilians who sympathized with the rebels grew. Despite the Reagan administration's policy of trying to keep power out of the hands of extremists on the right or the left, the lack of direct U.S. involvement led to situations where the violence of the conflict harmed people who were working to end it through mediation. Such incidents as the suspicious assassination in 1981 of Oscar Cardinal Romero, the Roman Catholic archbishop of El Salvador, who had been an outspoken critic of social injustice and government brutality, and the murder in 1989 of six American Jesuit priests and two laywomen caused many to believe that the Reagan administration's policies were morally bankrupt regardless of the obvious strategic merits of resisting Soviet-supported communism in the region. Perhaps for the sake of expediency, critics also overlooked the atrocities of the FMLN and the Sandinista government. Nicaraguan leader Daniel Ortega Saavedra was feted like a celebrity by prominent critics of the Reagan administration when he visited the United States in 1990.

The failure of the administration to expand on the initial successes of the contras with more vigor did not result from the military situation, but rather from American domestic politics. When the extent of Casey's activities in Nicaragua became known to congressional investigators in late 1982, Congress was appalled. Also influenced by events in El Salvador, Congress adopted a series of measures to outlaw American support to the contras. Although military aid continued to be financed through private donations and arms sales to Iran, both of which were of questionable legality, the Reagan administration had to rely largely on economic sanctions to isolate and destabilize Nicaragua until Soviet support dried up and free elections removed the Sandinistas from power in 1990. El Salvador was

also stabilized after a decade of conflict and held free elections that firmly rejected communism.

Despite the bloodshed involved, firm American resolve in Central America not only blocked the spread of communism and Soviet acquisition of a new and viable strategic position in close proximity to the continental United States, but it actually ended with the full democratization of the entire hemisphere with the exception of one country, Cuba. Globally and regionally, Kirkpatrick's policy of tolerating authoritarian regimes until communism was no longer a threat and then easing them out when the threat ceased was fulfilled. As El Salvador democratized, the relatively stable and pro-American dictatorships of Jean-Claude "Baby Doc" Duvalier in Haiti in 1986 and Manuel Noriega in Panama were removed (in Noriega's case by American troops) by 1989. Further afield American pressure led to the collapse of Ferdinand Marcos's regime in the Philippines in 1986 and to the end of white minority rule in South Africa in 1994.

The fact that Reagan's policies ultimately succeeded in Central America, even though his domestic opponents tried hard to sideline them, should speak for itself. Had the contras been allowed to defeat the Sandinistas earlier and by military means, the bloody conflicts in Nicaragua and El Salvador might have ended sooner and with less destruction and loss of life. It is interesting that the only direct American military deployment in the area during the Reagan administration, the invasion of Grenada in October 1983, ended that country's Marxist regime, terminated its military agreements with the Soviet Union and Cuba, and restored democracy in a matter of days. Furthermore, the only place where Moscow achieved a firm and undisputed foothold in the Western Hemisphere is also the only nondemocratic country in the Americas today.

—PAUL DU QUENOY, GEORGE WASHINGTON UNIVERSITY

**Viewpoint:
No, the Reagan administration unnecessarily militarized U.S. policies in Central America at a time when communism was declining, and it substantially increased U.S. support to regimes that grossly violated human rights.**

Ronald W. Reagan took office as president in 1981 criticizing the policies of the Republican and Democratic administrations of the 1970s.

He faulted Richard M. Nixon and Gerald R. Ford, his Republican predecessors, for pursuing policies—such as détente with the Soviet Union and the opening of relations with China—that were too "pragmatic" and "amoral": If the United States treated the two communist powers just as it treated any other nations, and if the United States were solicitous of the communist powers' interests and preferences, would it not stand guilty of "moral relativism," even "moral equivalence"? The Soviet Union and China were not like other nations, Reagan charged. He described the Soviet Union—and, by implication, all communist regimes—as an "evil empire" with designs and policies that were not only inimical to U.S. interests but immoral as well. While Nixon supporters said that, in light of the increasing Soviet power, the United States might have to play the "China card" to balance the Russians, Reagan retorted that China was part of the problem, not part of the solution. "The inescapable truth," Reagan said, "is that we are at war, and we are losing that war simply because we don't or won't realize we are in it . . . [and] there can only be one end to the war we are in. . . . War ends in victory or defeat." In 1976 Reagan had challenged Ford, then the incumbent president, in the Republican primaries. One of his major lines of attack against Ford was criticism of the détente policies that Henry Kissinger had initiated under Nixon. Ford won, but went on to lose the election to Jimmy Carter in November 1976.

While Reagan criticized the Nixon and Ford administrations for being too pragmatic, he called the Carter administration too ideological, claiming that it had adopted the wrong ideology. President Carter emphasized two themes in his foreign policy: human rights and the North-South dimension of world politics—as distinct from the "old" East-West preoccupation of previous administrations. The Carter administration applied pressure on U.S. allies to improve their human-rights records and to introduce democratic practices. The administration also signed the Panama Canal Treaty, giving Panama control of the canal by the beginning of the twenty-first century. Reagan charged that the Carter administration's human-rights pressure was applied unevenly: regimes friendly to the United States—for example, South Korea, Argentina, Nicaragua, El Salvador, Brazil, Chile, Guatemala, the Philippines, Iran, and Pakistan—came under much harsher criticism than left-leaning regimes. The Carter administration also slowed down or suspended the flow of economic and military aid to friendly regimes because of their human-rights records and, in the cases of Nicaragua and Iran, actively lobbied for political reforms that ended in pro-American regimes being replaced by governments hostile to the United States and its interests.

Reagan also attacked the Carter administration emphasis on North-South issues. According to Reagan, this focus ignored the fact that the free world and socialist bloc were still engaged in a bitter and dangerous conflict, and the main goal of the United States should be to win that conflict first before turning its attention to Third World issues and human rights. Furthermore, Reagan accused the Carter administration of implicitly or explicitly conveying the impression that the developed world was to blame for the poor state of many countries in the Third World and that, out of guilt for past exploitation and mistreatment, the rich countries now "owed" the developing countries a debt. The Carter administration, Reagan said, pursued various measures aimed to compensate Third World countries for past exploitation by the colonial powers. The Panama Canal Treaty—as well as initiatives such as the Law of the Sea—transferred important assets and resources to the control of Third World countries. In short, according to Reagan, Carter's emphasis on human rights and North-South issues were both the results of misguided idealism, serving to weaken the United States and undermine its interests.

Reagan's views on Latin America were part and parcel of this worldview. His policies were a manifestation of his determination to make a stand against what he saw as communist encroachment in the hemisphere. His stress on the reassertion of American power was the result of his convictions that the East-West competition was at the core of world politics and that other concerns and issues should take a back seat relative to the need to prevent the USSR from expanding its power and influence. In his approach to Latin American issues, Reagan adopted the views of a conservative group known as the Committee of Santa Fe, which in 1980 issued a harsh indictment claiming that "America is everywhere in retreat" and charging the Caribbean "is becoming a Marxist-Leninist lake." Still worse, the committee added, "Never before has the Republic been in such jeopardy from its exposed southern flank. Never before has American foreign policy abused, abandoned, and betrayed its allies to the south in Latin America."

True to this alarmist view, the Reagan administration did not take long to make its positions known and to launch policies that were a sharp break from the policies of the preceding administration. On 23 February 1981, barely a month after Reagan took office, the State Department issued a White Paper charging the Soviet Union and Cuba with fomenting subversion and instability throughout the region. Some

NICARAGUA POLICY

In 1983 President Ronald W. Reagan established a special bipartisan commission, chaired by former secretary of state Henry Kissinger, to examine U.S. policy interests in Central America. The commission report included the following conclusions about Nicaragua.

The Sandinista military forces are potentially larger than those of all the rest of Central America combined. The government in Managua volunteered to this Commission an intelligence briefing which left no reasonable doubt that Nicaragua is tied into the Cuban, and thereby Soviet, intelligence network. The Commission encountered no leader in Central America, including democratic and unarmed Costa Rica, who did not express deep foreboding about the impact of a militarized, totalitarian Nicaragua on the peace and security of the region. Several expressed the view that should the Sandinista regime now be consolidated as a totalitarian state, their own freedom, and even their independence, would be jeopardized. In several countries, especially those with democratic traditions, we met leaders who expressed regret and outrage that the revolution against Somoza—which their own governments had supported—had been betrayed by the Sandinistas.

For all these reasons, the consolidation of a Marxist-Leninist regime in Managua would be seen by its neighbors as constituting a permanent security threat. Because of its secretive nature, the existence of a political order on the Cuban model in Nicaragua would pose major difficulties in negotiating, implementing, and verifying any Sandinista commitment to refrain from supporting insurgency and subversion in other countries. In this sense, the development of an open political system in Nicaragua, with a free press and an active opposition, would provide an important security guarantee for the other countries of the region and would be a key element in any negotiated settlement.

Theoretically, the United States and its friends could abandon any hope of such a settlement and simply try to contain a Nicaragua which continued to receive military supplies on the present scale. In practical terms, however, such a course would present major difficulties. In the absence of a political settlement, there would be little incentive for the Sandinistas to act responsibly, even over a period of time, and much inducement to escalate their efforts to subvert Nicaragua's neighbors. To contain the export of revolution would require a level of vigilance and sustained effort that would be difficult for Nicaragua's neighbors and even for the United States. A fully militarized and equipped Nicaragua, with excellent intelligence and command and control organizations, would weigh heavily on the neighboring countries of the region. This threat would be particularly acute for democratic, unarmed Costa Rica. It would have especially serious implications for vital U.S. interests in the Panama Canal. We would then face the prospect, over time, of the collapse of the other countries of Central America, bringing with it the spectre of Marxist domination of the entire region and thus the danger of a larger war.

Source: The Report of the President's National Bipartisan Commission on Central America *(New York: Macmillan, 1984), pp. 135–136.*

right-wing elements in Central America thought they understood the administration's message. On 3 March 1981 Colonel Roberto D'Aubuisson, leader of the Salvadoran right wing (and also, according to press reports, associated with the paramilitary "death squads" that killed thousands of Salvadoran civilians), announced his understanding that the Reagan administration would not mind if he wrestled the levers of power away from the elected leader of El Salvador, José Napoleon Duarte. The Reagan administration clarified its position, stating that it did not support a coup against Duarte, but Duarte's authority was undermined.

Not only did the Reagan administration encourage extragovernmental groups that looked at human rights with a jaundiced eye, but it also worked hard to reestablish good relations with human-rights-abusing regimes from which the Carter administration had distanced itself, restoring economic and military aid that the Carter administration had blocked. One example was Chile under the authoritarian rule of Augusto Pinochet Ugarte. The Reagan administration restored Chilean access to Import-Export Bank financing, and in August 1981 the U.S. ambassador to the United Nations, Jeanne J. Kirkpatrick, visited Chile. This move was symbolic: two years earlier Kirkpatrick had pub-

CENTRAL AMERICA

lished "Dictatorships and Double Standards," an article that had greatly influenced Reagan's thinking. Kirkpatrick's article suggested that the United States should distinguish between friendly authoritarian regimes and hostile totalitarian regimes, reserving most its criticism and punitive measures for the latter. The authoritarian regimes in Chile and Argentina were examples of regimes friendly to the United States, and, according to Kirkpatrick, human-rights violations were not as rampant or as severe in those countries as similar violations in leftist-totalitarian systems such as the Soviet Union, China, and Vietnam. In May 1981, General Vernon A. Walters, an aide to Reagan, visited Guatemala. The Reagan administration also invited General Roberto Eduardo Viola, president-elect of Argentina, to be the first visitor from Latin America to the White House. Viola was a member of the military junta that took over in 1977 and plunged his country into a "dirty war" in which tens of thousands of Argentinians suspected of leftist sympathies "disappeared" while many more were imprisoned and tortured.

The largest component of the Reagan administration's hemispheric policies was its emphasis on military activism, both overt and covert. The administration increased the sale of military hardware to countries in the region and increased the training of intelligence and counterinsurgency personnel, preparing them to fight effectively against communist insurgencies in their countries. The administration also stepped up direct involvement of the U.S. military and intelligence agencies in the region's affairs, as was the case with Grenada. On 13 October 1983 a faction of the Marxist regime on that island arrested the popular prime minister, Maurice Bishop. When Bishop and some of his supporters escaped from jail, they were captured and executed. In late October, the United States, with the token participation of six Caribbean nations, invaded Grenada and removed the coup leaders. The Reagan administration alleged that American university students who were studying in Grenada were in danger, but its real concern was the leftist character of the post-Bishop regime on the island.

The most conspicuous example of the Reagan administration's military activism against unfriendly regimes was the case of Nicaragua, where the Marxist Sandinista movement took over the country in 1979. During its first months in office the Reagan administration made the major decisions that shaped its policies toward Nicaragua, the administration's major preoccupation in Central America. The Carter administration had been initially accepting of, if not exactly enthusiastic about, the Sandinista regime, even offering it economic aid. After a few months, however, that aid was suspended in response to the Sandinistas' public criticism of the United States and the measures that regime took to bring Nicaragua closer to Cuba and Libya. The relationship deteriorated further when it was discovered that Nicaragua was aiding the leftist rebels in El Salvador. Beginning in March 1981 and accelerating in fall 1981, the Central Intelligence Agency (CIA) began to put together an anti-Sandinista force comprising various factions that opposed the new regime. Some were supporters of the former Nicaraguan ruler Anastasio Somoza Debayle while others were critics of both the Sandinistas and Somoza. On 14 February 1982 American papers reported that the Reagan administration had allocated $19 million to the anti-Sandinista effort, which included the arming and training of a group of fighters called the "contras," and support for middle-class politicians in Managua. When various mediation efforts failed to ease the tensions between the United States and Nicaragua, the administration increased its efforts on behalf of the anti-Sandinista forces. The United States covertly mined the Nicaraguan harbors to prevent aid from reaching the Sandinistas, and the CIA set up training and supply bases for the contras in neighboring Honduras, enabling them to increase their sabotage and disruption campaign against the Sandinista regime. After Congress passed the Boland Amendments in 1983 and 1984, prohibiting the administration from aiding the contras, members of Reagan's National Security Council (NSC) designed ways to work around it, first by secretly raising money for the contras from other countries. Then, in 1985—after Congress heard about these activities, and NSC members lied under oath about them—CIA director William J. Casey and NSC members John M. Poindexter, Robert C. McFarlane, and Oliver North came up with the idea that led to the Iran-Contra affair. Locked in a bitter and costly war with neighboring Iraq, Iran was under a tight embargo by Western countries because of its support for terrorism. Desperately in need of military supplies, it was willing to purchase military equipment at high prices. At the same time the Reagan administration was trying to win the release of a few American hostages held by pro-Iranian factions in Lebanon. Casey and the NSC came up with the idea of secretly selling Iran military hardware at highly inflated prices in exchange for the American hostages in Lebanon. The sales would strengthen the hands of moderate elements in the Iranian regime and

UNITED STATES

MEXICO
*Threatened by $80 billion
foreign debt 1980s*

Miami

Havana

BELIZE

Mexico
City

JAMAICA

GUATEMALA
*Arbenz
overthrown 1954
Castillo Armas
assassinated 1957*

HONDURAS

HAITI

CUBA
*Batista overthrown 1959
Attempted anti-Castro invasion 1961
Soviet military aid, U.S. quarantine 1962*

BAHAMAS
(Br.)

DOMINICAN REP.
*U.S. broke diplomatic ties 1960
Trujillo assassinated 1961
Diplomatic ties restored 1962
U.S. and O.A.S. intervention 1965*

PUERTO
RICO

*Pérez Jiménez overthrown 1958
Anti-Nixon riots 1958*

BARBADOS

GRENADA *Invaded by U.S. 1983*

TRINIDAD AND TOBAGO

EL SALVADOR

COSTA RICA
*Arias peace
plans, 1987–*

*Sandinistas
overthrow
Somoza 1979
U.S. supports
anti-Sandinista
"contras" 1981–*

U.S. naval and
air bases 1981–

NICARAGUA
Canal Zone

PANAMA
*Anti-U.S. riots 1959
U.S. returns
canal zone to
Panama by
treaty 1978
Noriega seizes
power 1983;
U.S. relations
strained, 1987*

*CARIBBEAN
SEA*

Caracas
VENEZUELA

Bogotá

COLOMBIA

GUYANA

SURINAM *(Neth.)*
FR. GUIANA

*U.S.-Colombian
military attacks
on drug cartels,
1988–1989*

Quito
ECUADOR

PERU

PACIFIC OCEAN

*Anti-Nixon riots 1958
Military coup 1962
Military coup 1968*

Lima

BRAZIL
*Military seizes power 1964
and rules 1964.
Threatened by $90 billion
foreign debt 1980s.*

BOLIVIA
La Paz

Brasília

PARAGUAY

*Salvador
Allende
elected 1970
Overthrown
by military
and died 1973*

Asunción

Rio de Janeiro

CHILE
Santiago

Buenos
Aires

URUGUAY
Montevideo

*Punta del Este Conferences
1961, 1962*

ARGENTINA
*Threatened by $50 billion foreign debt 1980s
Returns to civilian government 1983*

*ATLANTIC

OCEAN*

CENTRAL AMERICA

generate large profits that the administration could use to aid the contras, circumventing the limitations imposed by the Boland Amendments. Large amounts of hardware were sent to Iran through front corporations in Europe and Israel; large amounts of money were generated and deposited in Swiss banks; and some of that money reached the contras. In fall 1986 a Beirut newspaper reported the arrangement, resulting in the appointment of an independent counsel to investigate it.

The legacy of the Reagan administration's policies in Latin America is mixed. The thrust of those policies was preventing what the administration believed to be efforts by communist and pro-Soviet movements to gain power and influence. To achieve this goal the administration reemphasized covert and overt military means, including direct intervention by U.S. military and intelligence agencies in cases when local pro-American elements were not strong enough. At the same time the administration downgraded goals such as human rights, economic and social development, and political openness. The administration was not opposed to these goals; it just believed that winning the battle against communist encroachment was more important, and in any event many of the promoters of a reformist agenda had ulterior motives that should be examined carefully. Another characteristic of the Reagan administration was its unilateralism. It reduced U.S. support for and involvement with international and regional institutions to solve problems in the hemisphere, and it openly dismissed the relevance of international law and organizations when it came to fighting communist penetration in the region.

The Reagan administration pursued its narrow definition of U.S. security interests in the region in a single-minded fashion. There is little doubt that its military and intelligence activities made life more difficult for communist movements in Latin America. In Grenada, the United States forcibly removed a pro-Soviet regime. In Nicaragua the administration's support of the contras wreaked havoc on the economy and hindered the Sandinistas' attempts to strengthen their hold on the country. The training of counterinsurgency forces in Guatemala and El Salvador increased their efficiency. These successes, however, came at a price.

Domestically, the Reagan administration came close to creating a constitutional crisis over the issue of its aid to the contras. Whether or not this secret aid violated the letter of the Boland Amendments, it definitely violated its spirit. Moreover, Casey and North had more ambitious plans for the money generated by selling military hardware to Iran. Some of that money was supposed to go to the contras, but some of it was to be deposited in Swiss banks in order to create an "off-the-shelf" covert-action capability, that is, to fund covert activities without having to seek congressional funding and, hence, to be able to hide them from Congress and its oversight committees. Congress launched its own lengthy investigation of the Iran-Contra affair in 1987. The mining of the Nicaraguan harbors also was not duly reported to Congress, leading to harsh criticism of the administration. The zeal with which it pursued its anticommunist crusade in the hemisphere thus led the administration to play fast and loose with democratic principles and legislative controls at home. Moreover, in its effort to help the contras, the administration relied on unsavory characters, including drug traffickers. In the mid 1990s accusations surfaced that the CIA actually allowed these traffickers to ship cocaine to poor neighborhoods of American cities. These allegations were refuted by a CIA audit, but the agency admitted that it did not always look too carefully into the background of individuals with whom it was doing business and that it may have unknowingly worked with drug traffickers in its efforts to aid the contras.

The price paid by societies in the regions was also high. CIA-trained counterinsurgency forces became more effective at fighting insurgents, but they also became more brutal and deadly against tens of thousands of innocent civilians. On 11 March 1999 *The New York Times* reported many of these abuses, which had been uncovered by a human-rights investigative committee. The Reagan administration's diminished emphasis on economic, social, and political issues and its reluctance to distinguish between reformist and communist movements also slowed down the process of democratization in Latin America, although it already was too advanced to be stopped. A good example is the case of Argentina. In spring 1982, under the leadership of General Leopoldo Galtieri, the junta tried to shore up its sagging popularity and mask its mismanagement of the Argentinian economy by invading the Falkland Islands, a British colony off the coast of Argentina. (The Argentinians, who claim the islands, call them the Malvinas.) Alexander Haig, Reagan's secretary of state, supported a strong pro-British position. He won, but not without a behind-the-scenes disagreement with UN Ambassador Kirkpatrick, who favored a pro-Argentinian position. The ineptitude of the junta in running the military campaign, and their eventual defeat by the British, hastened their departure from the political scene and their replacement by the civilian government of Raúl Alfonsín. The Reagan administration took credit for helping to bring about democratic change in Argentina, but it is not clear why. The fact is, the Reagan administration came to its pro-British position hesitantly, after playing the neutral broker for a while. Prior to the war, when the administration wanted the Argentinians to help in its anticommunist campaign in Central America, it allowed the generals to understand that the United States would at least acquiesce, if not support outright, efforts by Argentina to seize the Falklands. That the Reagan administration improved relations with the Argentinian junta, that the generals understood Reagan to be encouraging of their reckless venture in the Falklands, that the United States then changed its mind, and that the generals were shamed into leaving office and allowed a civilian government to take over is not a compelling argument for the Reagan administration's having had a role in bringing about democracy in Argentina.

It may well be that the Carter administration exhibited a startling degree of naiveté when dealing with world affairs; the Reagan administration, however, exhibited a degree of simplemindedness, a lack of nuance, and a self-congratulatory toughness, along with its willingness to use the military instrument as a first rather than a last resort. These characteristics led it to define complex situations in black and white and to exaggerate the threats small countries such as Nicaragua and Grenada posed to a superpower such as the United States. This unidimensional vision did not admit differences between reformers and pro-Soviet communists, lumping them together as equally hostile to the United States. Its unwillingness to differentiate led the Reagan administration to support oppressive, murderous regimes that used the excuse of an anticommunist campaign to settle domestic scores at the expense of tens of thousands of lives. The Reagan administration also ran the risk of sparking a constitutional crisis at home. The administration assumed all these costs, ran all these risks, and actively supported repressive regimes, not during the height of the cold war but when that war was winding down and reformers were coming to power in the Soviet Union. The most negative verdict on Reagan's Central American policies, then, is that in all likelihood the extremes to which the administration went in pursuing the defeat of communism in Latin America was unnecessary. It was fighting a war that was already being won.

—BENJAMIN FRANKEL, SECURITY STUDIES

References

Richard E. Feinberg, "Overview, Testing U.S. Reassertionism: The Reagan Approach to the Third World," in *U.S. Foreign Policy and the Third World: Agenda, 1985–86,* edited by John W. Sewell, Feinberg, and Valeriana Kallab (New Brunswick, N.J.: Transaction Books, 1985), pp. 3–19;

Walter LaFeber, *America, Russia, and the Cold War, 1945–1996,* eighth edition (New York: McGraw-Hill, 1997);

Robert A. Pastor, "The Reagan Administration and Latin America: Eagle Insurgent," in *Eagle Resurgent? The Reagan Era in American Foreign Policy,* edited by Kenneth A. Oye, Robert J. Lieber, and Donald Rothchild (Boston: Little, Brown, 1987), pp. 359–392;

Peter Schweizer, *Victory: The Reagan Administration's Secret Strategy that Hastened the Collapse of the Soviet Union* (New York: Atlantic Monthly Press, 1994);

Caspar W. Weinberger, *Fighting For Peace: Seven Critical Years in the Pentagon* (New York: Warner Books, 1990);

Bob Woodward, *Veil: The Secret Wars of the CIA, 1981–1987* (New York: Simon & Schuster, 1987).

CHINA HANDS

Did the China Hands in the U.S. State Department play a positive or a negative role in shaping U.S. policy during the late 1940s?

Viewpoint: The China Hands accurately interpreted events in China and offered good advice on U.S. policy in China in the late 1940s.

Viewpoint: The role of the China Hands in shaping U.S. policy toward China during the late 1940s was largely negative because of their biased views about Mao Tse-tung.

The "China Hands" were individuals—scholars, writers, journalists, and diplomats—who, in the 1920s, 1930s, and 1940s, developed an interest in China, its history, culture, language, and politics. Many China Hands, especially those in the State Department, who were involved in fashioning U.S. policy toward the civil war between the Nationalists and Communists in post–Second World War China, came under sharp attack from conservative Republicans after the Communists defeated Chiang Kai-shek's Nationalists and took control over China in 1949. Many of these Republicans accused the administration of President Harry S Truman of policy mistakes that undermined the Nationalists and helped the Communists. Senator Joseph R. McCarthy (R-Wisconsin) charged that the Truman administration's policies were not mistakes or accidents: "There is a small coterie of men at the higher echelons of the State Department, concerting to deliver us to disaster," he claimed. "This is a conspiracy so immense, so as to dwarf any previous venture in the history of mankind."

The conservatives wanted the Truman administration to intervene on the side of the Nationalists in order to prevent a communist takeover of China. Truman, however, resisted these pressures. He based his decision on the unanimous recommendation of the China Hands at the State Department, who concluded that Chiang's regime was so corrupt and so unpopular that no amount of intervention from outside could save it from collapse. In response to mounting domestic pressure from the Republicans, Truman, on 5 August 1949—two months before the Communist takeover in China—ordered the release of a 1,054-page White Paper prepared by the China Hands for Secretary of State Dean Acheson. The White Paper detailed the corruption, ineffectiveness, and unpopularity of the Kuomintang (the Nationalists) and the futility of U.S. intervention to shore it up. Following the Communist takeover, McCarthy accused many China Hands of harboring communist sympathies, and several of them had to resign from the State Department as a result.

Viewpoint:
The China Hands accurately interpreted events in China and offered good advice on U.S. policy in China in the late 1940s.

The question "Who Lost China?" haunted the American political landscape for two decades. It gave rise to McCarthyism and made it difficult for American decisionmakers to address U.S.-Asian policies on their own merits. Democrats especially were exceedingly reluctant to "lose" another country in Asia to communism, lest such a "loss" would trigger another right-wing backlash. The charge of "losing" China to communism was a descendant of the accusation against the Yalta Agreements and President Franklin D. Roosevelt for "betraying" east European countries to communism. In both cases the president was accused of following policies that undermined the national interest because his advisers intentionally or naively gave him bad advice. In both cases, it was argued, a more steadfast and resolute American stand would have yielded better results for the United States and the West.

The charge that the Truman administration abandoned China to communism could certainly not be made on economic grounds. Between 1945 and 1949 the United States provided the Nationalist forces of Chiang Kai-shek with more than $1 billion in aid: Chiang received a total of $769 million in Lend-Lease aid; the U.S. Navy transferred to the Nationalist forces 131 naval vessels valued at $140 million and ordnance supplies worth $17.7 million; the Marines, as part of their retreat from north China, left 6,500 tons of ammunition for the Nationalists, while the Army left stocks worth $20 million in west China; and the United States also granted the Nationalists $50 million for "pipeline" goods. Thomas G. Paterson reports that the United States also provided China with $44 million in relief and rehabilitation aid and $69 million from the Export-Import Bank, while Congress authorized $338 million in economic assistance, of which $275 million was appropriated, and another $125 million for military use; finally, the Mutual Defense Assistance Act of 1949 provided China with another $75 million. In 1949 Secretary of State Dean Acheson correctly observed that China had received more aid from the United States than any other nation. By 1948–1949, however, it became clear to top decisionmakers within the Truman administration that the time had come for the United States to cut its losses and allow domestic Chinese forces to determine the course of events in China.

The civil war between Chiang's Kuomintang (Nationalist) forces and Mao Tse-tung's communist armies began in the 1930s. As was the case in other parts of the world, after the Second World War, the United States came to see the Chinese civil war as part of the larger cold-war struggle between East and West. The initial inclination of American analysts was to see Mao's Communists as willing puppets of Soviet premier Joseph Stalin. Soviet behavior during the last year of the war lent some support to this belief. The Soviets helped push the Japanese out of Manchuria but then impeded Nationalist forces from entering the territory. Rather than turn over the stocks of weapons, ammunition, and supplies they had captured from the retreating Japanese to Chiang's government, they handed these supplies to Mao's forces. According to J. P. D. Dunbabin and Steven Levine, these stocks included 300,000 rifles, 138,000 machine guns, and 2,700 artillery pieces. The Soviets also facilitated the recruitment into Mao's forces of 75,000 soldiers from the Japanese-puppet Manchukuo army. Dunbabin estimates that during the second half of 1946 the Soviets furnished Mao's forces with 1,200 to 1,800 artillery pieces and 370 to 700 tanks. (The Chinese provided the lower figures, the Soviets the higher figures.) Soviet gains in eastern Europe aroused suspicion in Washington that the USSR would rely on similar means to extend its power and influence in China. That is, the Soviets would use the presence of the Red Army to install a pro-Soviet regime, relying on local Communists and Mao's armies to extend their influence and eventually take over China.

Parallel to this typical cold-war reading of the situation in China, a new kind of thinking began to emerge, influenced in no small measure by the reports of the China Hands from the field, but it also found support in other quarters. This view held that the United States could not, and should not, continue to support Chiang in his war against Mao. Supporters of this view relied on five major arguments. First, it was not clear that Mao would be a Soviet puppet. Josip Tito of Yugoslavia had already demonstrated that a leader bent on domestic socialist reforms could be independent of Moscow in his foreign policies. Analysts of Chinese politics and Chinese-Russian relations said that traditional tensions between the two nations and China's suspicions of Russian imperialism in the Far East made it difficult to see how these two nations would end up as close collaborators. Stalin's assistance to Mao's forces was seen as an effort to balance the relative power of the nationalist and communist forces, thus prolonging the civil war and weakening China.

CHINA HANDS

CHINA HANDS

Another reason why the Truman administration decided it made more sense to cut U.S. losses rather than continue to invest them in blocking Mao from coming to power was that China was not perceived to be as vitally important to U.S. interests as Europe. Europe-first strategy characterized the U.S. military effort during the Second World War and was coming to dominate the U.S. cold-war strategy. The Joint Chiefs of Staff, for example, was asked to prepare a list of countries and rank them in order of importance to U.S. interests. China was ranked near the bottom, below Japan and Spain.

The Truman administration also realized that China's problems were too numerous and too large for the United States to do much about them. Reflecting on Truman's early 1947 speech on aid to Greece and Turkey—in which the president enunciated what would later be called the Truman Doctrine—a State Department official said that Greece was a "tea cup" while China was an "ocean." What made the task of dealing with China's problems even more onerous was that Chiang's government stood in the way. It did not take long for the Truman administration to conclude that Chiang's regime was hopelessly corrupt and singularly ineffective. It was like "corroded machinery that does not function," said Secretary of State George C. Marshall. American policymakers were also angry at Chiang for not fighting hard enough against the

Japanese occupiers. Chiang hoarded U.S. military supplies—and used his political influence in the United States to get even more—but did not use them to fight the Japanese. Rather, he was readying his forces for a postwar struggle against Mao's Communists. In the period before the nuclear bomb was tested, the prospect of an American invasion of the Japanese home islands was contemplated with great reluctance, and the fact that Chiang's forces did not do more to help weaken and defeat the Japanese Imperial Army rankled Washington.

In 1946 and the first half of 1947 it appeared that Chiang's forces might be able to hold their own against Mao, but by early 1948 the tide had turned. To win the war, Marshall said, "we would literally have to take over the country in order to insure that the [Chinese Nationalist] armies functioned with efficiency. . . ." The administration was unwilling to undertake such measures. Chiang, who always had strong political support on the right wing of the American political spectrum, appealed to Republicans for help. The Republican presidential nominee, Thomas E. Dewey, promised increased U.S. assistance, but Truman won the election.

In the late 1930s the Communists came to control the northern Chinese province of Yan'an. While engaged in an effort to form a coalition government between Chiang and Mao, American diplomats, including the China

Hands, visited the communist-run province in the early 1940s. The contrasts they saw between the decay, squalor, and corruption of the provinces under Chiang's control and the relative order in Yan'an, including basic health and education services for the poor and agrarian reforms, convinced some of them that a Maoist regime would be more preferable for China than a continuation of Chiang's rule. While they may have been naive about Mao's intentions and his capacity for systematic cruelty and repression, they were correct to assess the crippling weaknesses of Chiang and the inability of the United States to shore up his control over China. The China Hands' knowledge of Chinese history also helped them to make the case that an enduring Soviet-Chinese alliance was unlikely. Their motives and idiosyncrasies aside, on the major contours of policy and on the main issues in the debate swirling over China policy they were joined by clear-headed and hard-nosed cold warriors such as Acheson and Marshall. The China Hands were proven right. What is more, they had the courage of their convictions, which, in the climate prevailing in the late 1940s, was not easy to maintain, a fact to which their personal biographies bear witness.

—BENJAMIN FRANKEL, SECURITY STUDIES

Viewpoint:
The role of the China Hands in shaping U.S. policy toward China during the late 1940s was largely negative because of their biased views about Mao Tse-tung.

Most of the China Hands did not play an important role in U.S. policy toward China, which was more influenced by the cold-war desire to check the spread of international communism than by the China Hands' indictments of Chiang Kai-shek's corruption.

The China Hands were part of a long American tradition of missionary involvement with China, which goes back to the 1830s. The missionary community engaged in social-welfare and cultural activities as well as religious education, and their families became immersed in Chinese society and culture. Many of the China Hands were missionaries' children who spent their formative years and young adulthoods in China, where they developed strong anti-Nationalist views. Believing that the Nationalists' leader, Chiang Kai-shek, was an authoritarian, corrupt, and inept ruler, they wanted the United States to serve the Chinese

people as an engine for reform. The China Hands tended to see the leader of the Chinese Communists, Mao Tse-tung, as an agrarian reformer because, to ingratiate himself with the middle peasantry, he initially made proclamations that sounded more reformist than revolutionary.

The weaknesses the China Hands identified in Chiang's Nationalist regime became apparent during the Second World War. As General Joseph W. (Vinegar Joe) Stilwell was trying to push Chiang toward greater exertion against the Japanese, the China Hands, from their different posts throughout China, sent back reports that, rather than using U.S.-supplied arms to fight the Japanese—as the United States intended—Chiang was hoarding them for use against Mao's communist forces, which controlled a portion of northwestern China. The China Hands' knowledge of China led them to conclude that while Chiang's Nationalists and Mao's Communists were currently presenting a united front against the Japanese invaders, once the war was over the Communists would inevitably win a civil war against the Nationalists. The China Hands did not conceal their view that, short of major reforms in Chiang's style of ruling, China was likely to become a pro-Soviet communist country. Such reforms were unlikely, they predicted, and, even if made, the changes would probably come too late.

Among the China Hands who criticized Chiang was John Stewart Service, who in a 10 October 1944 memo to Stilwell described Chiang as "selfish and corrupt, incapable and obstructive" and added that the defeats of Nationalist troops fighting the Japanese demonstrated their "military ineffectiveness and will hasten the approaching economic disaster." He recommended that the United States support Mao's communist forces because they would be a more effective and disciplined opponent to the Japanese, thus reducing Allied casualties in the final phase of the campaign against Japan. The memo was leaked to the Chinese Nationalists who, in turn, activated the powerful pro-Chiang China Lobby in the United States. Roosevelt recalled Stilwell, who had lost all confidence in Chiang, and Service from China, and right-wing Republicans began to take note of the China Hands' skepticism concerning Chiang's chances of survival.

Service's problems continued in the United States. At the initiative of Mark Gayn, a freelance journalist who was doing some writing for *Amerasia* magazine, whose editor and publisher, Philip J. Jaffe, co-ordinated a spy network and used the magazine to dissemi-

DIVISIONS IN CHINA

After the Second World War, General George C. Marshall attempted to broker a peace in China between the Nationalist forces of Chiang Kai-shek (the Kuomintang) and the Communist forces of Mao Tse-tung, but both sides regularly broke agreements. Dean Acheson, at that time undersecretary of state, later wrote in a memoir about Marshall's frustration over his declining influence:

As the end of June [1946] approached, the general could report that hostilities had been pretty well brought under control and negotiations between the two sides resumed, although their positions seemed farther apart than ever. However, a new difficulty had developed, brought on by well-meant efforts in Washington to initiate measures for the aid of China. One was a proposal before Congress to establish a military advisory group to assist in the contemplated reorganization of the Chinese military forces. Another was an agreement, which had to be completed by the end of June, for carrying through lend-lease aid. These produced double trouble in China. Die-hard Kuomintang members, the General reported, used them to urge the Generalissimo to renew the war against the Communists, since American help would be forthcoming in any event. The Communists, reaching the same conclusion, used the proposed legislation as proof that concessions to the Nationalists in furtherance of unity were useless. Both sides attacked General Marshall, one from holding them back from victory, the other for selling them out by deceptive proposals designed to weaken them. "It would be helpful if government spokesmen in Washington seized a favorable occasion to explain the aims and development of American measures for aid to China," cabled the harassed General.

With the President's approval, I immediately issued a statement saying that press reports from China indicated the gravest misconceptions there of the preparations being made here to help carry out the agreements, some already reached in China, others under negotiation there to work out a plan and program for national unity. Illustrative descriptions of our efforts showed how they would fit into Chinese plans in several fields.

The General was grateful, but the negotiations begun in April, after sprouting hopefully, withered. The opening days of July found General Marshall in a rare period of discouragement. He was, he cabled me, "so closely engaged and so close to the trees" that he lacked perspective. He would appreciate a "frank and quite informal" appraisal of the situation as Vincent and I saw it. We sent a joint reply two days later, unhappily giving little comfort. The basic cause of trouble was plain enough—the total lack of any element of trust or confidence not only between the Kuomintang and the Communists but between both and the Chinese people. Only the extremists on both sides wanted war, but both sides feared the concessions that were necessary to compromise. Neither wished to incur responsibility for failure of the negotiations and the mission.

Source: *Dean Acheson,* Present at the Creation: My Years in the State Department *(New York: Norton, 1969), pp. 204–205.*

nate disinformation for the Chinese Communists, Service met with Jaffe and shared some of his China memos, several of which were classified top secret. Unbeknownst to Jaffe and Service, *Amerasia* was under Federal Bureau of Investigation (FBI) surveillance. In June 1945 six people affiliated with the journal were arrested by the FBI on charges of espionage for the Chinese communists. Jaffe and a colleague were convicted for possession of secret government documents, some of which had been given to them by Service and other China Hands. Service, who admitted his indiscretion, was cleared by a grand jury while others were indicted. To right-wing supporters of Chiang and the Nationalists, however, Service's admission was the proof they needed: a top State Department official, who had for years lobbied U.S. decisionmakers to shift their support from Chiang to Mao, was leaking top-secret documents to an anti-Chiang publication in order to change public opinion at home. The connection between the China Hands and *Amerasia* provoked the charge that the United States "lost China" because of what Senator Joseph R. McCarthy described as the "conspiracy so immense" of the China Hands and their allies. While some detractors charged that the China Hands were part of a vast communist conspiracy, others more charitably accused them of extreme naïveté with regard to communism and the Soviet Union. Both groups of critics agreed that the China Hands were elitist and detached from American realities, allowing their idiosyncrasies and esoteric preferences to come ahead of common sense and straight thinking.

Where did the China Hands go wrong? The major American objective in China during the Second World War was to defeat the Japanese, and it was not possible to win the war without Chiang, whether or not he and his generals were corrupt. It is also difficult to believe that the China Hands truly believed that Mao was a mild-mannered agrarian reformer. As early as 1931 China expert Edgar Parks Snow had written that Mao was a committed and unwavering Communist. The China Hands were so involved with China, so frustrated with the plight of the Chinese people, and so disgusted with the corruption and cruelty of the Chiang regime that they appear to have been unable to imagine that communism might impose worse conditions on the Chinese. They seem to have overlooked that Mao was a serious and dedicated revolutionary capable of killing and imprisoning tens of millions of Chinese in his effort to revolutionize Chinese society.

Chiang and his generals were the best option for China under the circumstances. The recalls of Stilwell and Service were but minor indications of Roosevelt's continued support for Chiang.

—AMOS PERLMUTTER, AMERICAN UNIVERSITY

References

J. P. D. Dunbabin, *International Relations since 1945: A History in Two Volumes,* volume 2: *The Post-Imperial Age: The Great Powers and the Wider World* (New York: Longman, 1994);

John Lewis Gaddis, *The Long Peace: Inquiries into the History of the Cold War* (New York: Oxford University Press, 1987);

E. J. Kahn Jr., *The China Hands: America's Foreign Service Officers and What Befell Them* (New York: Viking, 1975);

John Kifner, "John Service, a Purged 'China Hand,' Dies at 89," *New York Times,* 4 February 1999, p. B11;

Harvey Klehr and Ronald Radosh, *The Amerasia Spy Case: Prelude to McCarthyism* (Chapel Hill: University of North Carolina Press, 1996);

Steven I. Levine, *Anvil of Victory: The Communist Revolution in Manchuria, 1945–1948* (New York: Columbia University Press, 1987);

Thomas G. Paterson, *Meeting the Communist Threat: Truman to Reagan* (New York: Oxford University Press, 1988);

Lewis McCarroll Purifoy, *Harry Truman's China Policy: McCarthyism and the Diplomacy of Hysteria, 1947–1951* (New York: New Viewpoints, 1976).

CIA OPERATIONS

Did the CIA go too far in its covert operations during the 1950s and 1960s?

Viewpoint: Yes, CIA operations in the 1950s and 1960s discredited the United States.

Viewpoint: No, CIA operations during the 1950s and 1960s effectively limited full-scale military actions.

Since its creation in 1947, the Central Intelligence Agency (CIA) has been an instrument of American foreign-policy making. In the 1950s and 1960s its directors and the presidents who appointed them used its potential for covert operations as a strategic tool. Beginning in the late 1940s its capabilities were used to influence elections in Western Europe, and during the 1950s the administration of Dwight D. Eisenhower relied heavily on the CIA. Early in Eisenhower's presidency, his administration used covert CIA operations to topple regimes in Iraq and Guatemala that seemed to be leaning toward the Soviet Union. The administration also used the CIA to carry out espionage, both through conventional spy networks and intelligence gathering and with technologically advanced systems such as the U-2 spy plane. Although its use for such activities declined in importance during the administrations of John F. Kennedy and Lyndon B. Johnson, the CIA remained an important tool of American foreign policy.

CIA operations, however, were far from faultless. Its covert activities in Cuba during the late 1950s and early 1960s and its involvement in the overt invasion of that country in April 1961 alienated the revolutionary regime of Fidel Castro and was a factor in Castro's conversion to communism. Many critics have charged that the CIA's covert activities have been immoral and hypocritical. Its covert support for pro-American political parties in Western Europe during the 1940s and its role in toppling the ostensibly democratic, though Marxist, government of Guatemala in 1954 seemed to fly in the face of America's commitment to democracy. It can be argued, however, that there were crucial national interests at stake, which the activities of the CIA defended.

Viewpoint:
Yes, CIA operations in the 1950s and 1960s discredited the United States.

With the painful memory of the Japanese surprise attack at Pearl Harbor in 1941, the Truman administration created the Central Intelligence Agency (CIA) in 1947 to provide the president with timely and coordinated information on world threats. The mandate of the CIA, as spelled out in the National Security Act of 1947, was to gather, evaluate, and disseminate intelligence. The law placed at the head of the CIA a director with the responsibility to keep the president informed as his intelligence adviser on the newly established National Security Council (NSC).

A vaguely worded phrase in the statute permitted the president to turn to the CIA for the conduct of "other functions and duties" beyond its core mission of intelligence collection and analysis. Within the year the Truman administration drew on this catchall language to direct the CIA toward a leading role in the nascent war against international communism. President Harry S Truman vowed in 1947 to "help free peoples to maintain their free institutions and their national integrity against aggressive movements seeking to impose on them totalitarian regimes." This Truman Doctrine amounted to a declaration of cold war against America's onetime ally, the Soviet Union. In the cold war the United States resorted to overt political, economic, propaganda, and even military operations. It turned as well to a variety of covert operations, relying on the CIA for clandestine intelligence collection, counterespionage, and covert action.

Each of these intelligence activities can be highly intrusive against another nation. Collection of intelligence can entail violation of airspace, interception of telephone calls, and recruitment of indigenous peoples for espionage against their own countries. Counterespionage aspires to thwart hostile intelligence services through penetration operations, such as planting agents ("moles") inside enemy ser-

vices to inform the CIA of foreign recruitment efforts against Americans and to disrupt their success. More intrusive still, covert actions attempt secretly to disrupt and manipulate America's adversaries through the infiltration of secret propaganda into their media, schemes to shape their politics and economics, and even paramilitary operations to undermine their regimes (including assassination plots, until prohibited by executive order in 1976).

As the cold war intensified, CIA priorities shifted from the original statutory focus on collection and analysis toward stepped-up counterespionage and covert action in opposition to perceived Soviet intentions to spread communism around the globe. Even within the more-benign collection domain, operations grew more daring as U-2 reconnaissance airplanes began to enter Soviet airspace routinely in the late 1950s in the pursuit of reliable photographs of military bases.

Many of these operations proved valuable to American security. In some instances they were vital. Intelligence-collection activities provided warnings about Soviet missiles in Cuba in 1962. Counterespionage uncovered Soviet agents inside U.S. secret agencies. Radio Free Europe gave Soviet citizens a more realistic understanding of the world outside their walled empire, as well as helping labor

Former prime minister of Iran Mohammad Mosaddeq on trial for treason after his government was overthrown in a CIA-supported coup. He was found guilty and sentenced to three years in prison

(Wide World Photo)

CIA OPERATIONS

unions and political parties in Western Europe resist communist takeovers in the aftermath of the Second World War.

Yet, too often the CIA went beyond the pale of traditional American values (usually at the behest of presidential orders), carrying out covert operations that did more to harm the image of the United States than to advance its national security. During the 1950s and 1960s, the excesses were blatant within each of the covert-operation categories.

In the area of intelligence collection, twice during these decades the CIA dispatch of surveillance "platforms" into an adversary's home territory led to major international embarrassments for the United States. In 1960 the Eisenhower administration recklessly jeopardized an improvement in diplomatic relations with the Soviet Union by ordering the flight of a CIA U-2 spy plane deep into Soviet air space on the eve of an important superpower summit. A ground-to-air missile downed the plane over Russia and the pilot, Francis Gary Powers, was captured and put on public trial. The proposed summit conference collapsed, setting back a promising opportunity for détente with the Soviet Union. In 1968 the U.S. spy ship *Pueblo* cruised close to the North Korean shoreline and was captured by North Korean warships, causing another major international embarrassment.

The CIA also grew overzealous in its recruitment of American citizens to aid its collection mission. It funded the National Student Association until 1967, when a magazine disclosed the relationship, and it paid several U.S. journalists to engage in espionage abroad. These activities raised serious questions about the CIA's infiltration into the fabric of American society, and, stung by criticism, the CIA established tighter rules for its relations with groups inside the United States. Only in 1975 did congressional investigators discover that CIA intelligence gathering at home had gone even further. At the requests of Presidents Lyndon B. Johnson and Richard M. Nixon the CIA Operation CHAOS had spied on student dissenters against the Vietnam War, thereby violating its charter, which forbids espionage against American citizens.

CIA practitioners of counterespionage during the early stage of the cold war also engaged in overzealous operations. Investigative reporter Seymour M. Hersh maintained in a 1978 *New York Times Magazine* article that the CIA chief of counterespionage, James Jesus Angleton, acquired an early copy of Nikita Khrushchev's "secret speech" of 1954, in which the Soviet premier sharply criticized the excesses of the Stalinist era, and added to it even more inflammatory rhetoric against Joseph Stalin. Angleton then had his doctored version of the speech distributed throughout eastern Europe in an attempt to sully Stalin even more than Khrushchev had intended. Hersh argued that the CIA alterations of the text may have had the ironic effect of discrediting even the genuine criticism that Khrushchev leveled against Stalin.

In the area of covert action early, successful, and useful exercises of this secret power to block the communist capture of labor unions and political parties in Western Europe soon led to an overreliance on this so-called Third Option (between diplomacy and sending in the Marines). The CIA helped to depose Mohammad Mosaddeq of Iran in 1953, viewing him as unreliably pro-West and insufficiently protective of U.S. and British oil interests in Iran. The following year the CIA carried off another rapid coup, this time against President Jacobo Arbenz Guzmán in Guatemala—once more deposing a regime considered too Marxist in its political orientation for America's best interests. Arbenz was replaced by a CIA-backed oligarchy, while the Guatemalan people continued to live in abject poverty.

Had the CIA not intervened in these cases, the world would likely not have been much different for the United States. Iran would still have wanted to sell oil to the West, especially if diplomatic and economic agreements had been employed to draw Mosaddeq closer to the West. Poor and weak Guatemala was never a threat to the United States and, even more easily, could have been wooed with diplomatic and economic blandishments from the United States. Instead, the Eisenhower administration—like so many thereafter—chose the quicker remedy of covert action. The short-term results pleased the administration. In the long term, however, the world was left with the impression that the United States pursued its interests in a manner hardly distinguishable from the Soviets' use of the KGB.

After the successful covert operations in Iran and Guatemala, the Eisenhower, Kennedy, and Johnson administrations further increased funding and personnel for the CIA Operations Directorate, home of the Covert Action Staff and the Special Operations (that is, paramilitary) Group. Subsequent outcomes of U.S. covert actions during the 1950s and 1960s were far less "successful" than the results achieved in Iran and Guatemala. The best-known disaster occurred at the Bay of Pigs in Cuba (1961), when a CIA-spon-

CIA OPERATIONS

SECRET WARS

George W. Ball, former undersecretary of state in the Johnson and Kennedy administrations, argued against the use of covert action during a 1984 forum published in Harper's Magazine:

In principle I think we ought to discourage the idea of fighting secret wars or even initiating most covert operations. We throw away our considerable advantage over the Russians when we indulge in such things. At the moment, the Soviet Union has very limited assets to use in extending and maintaining it authority around the world. The Soviet assets consist almost entirely of military power. The United States, on the other hand, has assets that transcend that, the greatest of which is our reputation for upholding certain principles—noninterference in the affairs of other nations, respect for their sovereignty and self-determination, and so on. This is particularly true in the Third World, which is where most covert actions take place. When the United States violates those principles—when we mine harbors in Nicaragua—we fuzz the difference between ourselves and the Soviet Union. We act out of character, which no great power can do without diminishing itself.

I think it is a very foolish thing to do. Polls are taken in Europe today asking, What is the difference between the Soviet Union and the United States? And many people answer, Well, they are both great imperialists and they are both indulging in the same kinds of behavior. I think our covert war in Nicaragua has done us considerable harm in Europe and contributed to the problems we had there last fall with the deployment of NATO missiles. When we yield to what is, in my judgment, a childish temptation to fight the Russians on their own terms and in their own gutter, we make a major mistake and throw away one of our great assets. And we have been doing this more and more frequently in recent years. Vietnam contributed greatly to the process, but covert operations have contributed also.

Of course, part of the problem lies with our policy itself. We seem to have a Brezhnev doctrine of our own, which we apply to areas close to the United States. According to the Brezhnev doctrine, the Soviet Union will not accept the overthrow of any of the satellite regimes on its borders, even by popular revolution. I think we're applying a similar doctrine to Latin America, and I think that is the way it appears to the world. There's an old French proverb that says a man tends to acquire the visage of his adversary. What we are doing by indulging in operations of this kind is acquiring the visage of our adversary. . . .

In helping the insurgents in Nicaragua, I think we are being dishonest with ourselves, or else we are deceiving the contras. If the United States is really only trying to stop the movement of arms and supplies from the Sandinistas to the Salvadoran guerrillas, as we officially claim, then our purpose is very different from that of these poor devils fighting in the jungle. If the supplies are eventually stopped, does that mean the United States then say to the contras, "Sorry, chaps, we know we know you have been getting yourselves killed to establish a new government in Nicaragua, but now we are no longer going to help you"? This is what I mean when I say we get ourselves into positions that are contradictory and basically dishonest.

Source: "Should the U.S. Fight Secret Wars?: Overt Talk on Covert Action," Harper's, 269 (September 1984): 37, 39.

---

sored band of Cuban exiles invaded the island only to be defeated and captured by Fidel Castro's forces. The Kennedy administration then tried various means of assassinating the Cuban leader. All attempts failed—including one for which the CIA hired Mafia hit men. Castro proved well guarded, cautious, and elusive.

The CIA resorted to assassination plots against other foreign leaders as well, including Patrice Lumumba of the Congo, who was the target of a CIA poison plot but was slain by a rival African faction that got to him first. In its laboratories the CIA experimented with toxins from shellfish and exotic serpents that might be used for murder and developed instruments of death such as a poison-dart gun ("micro-bioinoculator"), ballpoint pens with tips that could be dipped in poison and then stuck into a victim, wet suits coated with the bacteria that cause botulism, and other "gifts" for undesirable foreign leaders—a laboratory full of inventions for "health alteration," "neutralization," and "executive action" (CIA euphemisms for murder).

During Johnson's presidency the spending and personnel allotted for covert action reached a level that has been surpassed only during the Reagan administration. The Johnson administration took aim at Salvador Allende Gossens, the Chilean socialist candidate in the 1964 presidential election, viewing him as another potential Castro. The administration infiltrated $2.6 million into opposition parties to besmirch the name of Allende and his party, a huge amount of money at the time for a Chilean presidential election and a subversion of the democratic process in that country. The CIA used television, radio, movies, pamphlets, posters, leaflets, direct mailings, paper streamers, and wall paintings to suggest that Soviet tanks and Cuban firing squads would soon become a way of life in Chile if Allende were elected. He lost that election, but ran again in 1970 and won. During the Nixon administration the CIA continued the crusade against Allende, even planning to assassinate him. Before the CIA plot was put into action, Allende was murdered, or committed suicide, in September 1973, during a successful military coup.

The Johnson administration also authorized the CIA to engage in major paramilitary operations in Southeast Asia during the long-term "secret war" in Laos (1963–1968) and the massive U.S. military operations in Vietnam (1965–1973). The analytic branch of the CIA forecasted the ultimate defeat of U.S. troops by forces of nationalism in the region, but its reports were ignored. The CIA recruited Meo tribesmen to fight under its guidance in Laos and South Vietnamese agents to aid in the Vietnam conflict, eventually abandoning them to imprisonment, torture, and death when the United States pulled its troops out of the region.

In Europe the CIA helped to incite Hungarians (1956) and Czechs (1967) into action against their communist suppressors, only to leave these brave rebels unaided when the Soviet tanks arrived to put down the uprisings. The CIA also abandoned the Khambas in Tibet, the Nationalist Chinese in Burma, the Bay of Pigs invaders, and the Kurds involved in CIA Middle Eastern operations. In Ferdinand Mount's view, these operations were "so many causes and peoples briefly taken up by the CIA and then tossed aside like broken toys."

Other wrong-minded covert actions proposed during this period included the undisclosed CIA sponsorship of books published in the United States and a CIA scheme to lace Moscow-bound Cuban sugar with a nasty-tasting chemical (vetoed by President John F. Kennedy). Among the sillier recommendations was a plan to incite rebellion in Cuba by shooting fireworks over the island and spreading leaflets proclaiming the Second Coming, which would supposedly lead the people of Cuba to rise up against Castro, the "Antichrist." (The CIA called this project "Elimination by Illumination" and it was also rejected by cooler heads outside the CIA Covert Action Staff.) Other fanciful schemes were carried out. During the 1960s the CIA covertly broadcast television programs into Cambodia (apparently without appreciating that only a few Cambodians owned television sets), and it lofted transistor radios into China by way of balloons and wind power, only to have many of them blow back to their point of origin in Taiwan.

It would be foolish to argue that all covert operations were inappropriate for the United States during the 1950s and 1960s. In the area of data collection, the ability of the United States to monitor the military capabilities and intentions of the Soviet Union, especially through sophisticated and reliable satellite and U-2 surveillance, probably contributed as much as nuclear deterrence to keeping a third world war at bay. With these surveillance capabilities in place on each side of the Iron Curtain by the late 1950s, each superpower could set aside its anxieties about a surprise military mobilization by the other side. Counterespionage is also an inescapable fact of life in a world of nation states. So long as nations have secrets to keep, they will have methods to protect this information. Even covert action cannot be dismissed out of hand. To thwart terrorist groups, CIA paramilitary capability could prove indispensable. Covert propaganda can also provide a beneficial result, as when secret radio transmissions from the outside world keep alive the hope for freedom among people ruled by totalitarian regimes, whether the Soviet Union during the cold war or modern-day Iraq.

The problem arises when a program in one of these areas of operation is carried to excess: collection missions that are unduly provocative or intrude into the rights of American society; counterespionage activities that discredit the United States more than the intended target, covert actions that rely on unrealistic paramilitary operations or seek to manipulate events in democracies. "In principle I think we ought to discourage the idea of fighting secret wars or even initiating most covert operations," concluded George W. Ball, who had been undersecretary of state during the Kennedy and Johnson administrations, in 1984. "When we yield to what is, in my judgment, a childish temptation to fight the Russians on their own terms and in their gutter, we make a major mistake and throw away one of our great assets." Even in the shadowy domain of intelligence operations, some limits must be maintained by the United States—even if its enemies play by different rules. Otherwise the United States will succeed only in becoming more like its enemies.

–LOCH K. JOHNSON, UNIVERSITY OF GEORGIA

Viewpoint:
No, CIA operations during the 1950s and 1960s effectively limited full-scale military actions.

Espionage and covert operations had an unusually prominent place in the conduct of the cold war. In the absence of direct conflict, the superpowers often had to rely on subtlety to advance their strategic aims. As the size and power of their nuclear arsenals grew, the adversarial relationship between the superpowers placed a premium on the defense of strategic interests and necessitated their advancement through means that would not provoke a general war with nuclear consequences. To achieve its goals American foreign policy in the 1950s and 1960s relied heavily on the use of covert operations directed by the Central Intelligence Agency (CIA) as opposed to direct military activity. There were legitimate reasons for that approach, and in the end CIA activity solved many problems that could have placed the United States and the Soviet Union in dangerous conflict situations or necessitated costly and expensive direct involvement. Examining the question from that perspective indicates that the CIA did not go too far.

In the first few years after its creation under the National Security Act of 1947, the CIA played a limited role in American foreign policy. Its early directors, Admiral Roscoe Hillenkoetter (1947–1950) and General Walter Bedell Smith (1950–1953), were old-school military officers who resented the fact that a civilian organization had been given authority over intelligence gathering and covert operations, which had traditionally been the province of the military. Their lack of enthusiasm caused them to lead the agency essentially as caretakers. Furthermore, President Harry S Truman's preference to use the military and the State Department (under

Dean Acheson) as the main conduits for foreign policy minimized the role of the CIA during his administration.

When Dwight D. Eisenhower entered office in 1953, his administration elaborated different ideas about strategy. Deeply concerned that excessive military spending would cause inflation and place a strain on the civilian economy, Eisenhower supported a budgetary policy that reduced military spending from $42 billion in Truman's last year in office to $34.5 billion, a decrease of nearly 20 percent. National Security Council memorandum 141 (NSC-141), a document prepared by Acheson and his top advisers shortly before Truman left office, had proposed an increase in the existing military budget by almost as much. Realizing what a heavily militarized cold war could mean for the American domestic economy and for the country's future ability to compete strategically with the Soviet Union, the new administration pursued military policies that could be sustained by a decreased budget.

Avoiding direct conflicts was a large part of that approach. The permanent armistice that ended the Korean War in July 1953 restored the rough status quo antebellum and closed a significant outlet for military spending. Avoiding expensive conflicts along the Sino-Soviet periphery was an important characteristic of the rest of Eisenhower's administration. Instead, he and his foreign-policy staff followed a policy based on deterrence. The structure of containment was globalized through strong regional collective-security agreements and Secretary of State John Foster Dulles's threat to respond to direct Soviet aggression with "massive retaliation." Relying on a strong diplomatic response to Soviet power and basing defense policy on flexibly deployed and comparatively inexpensive nuclear weapons permitted the necessary decreases in military spending. By 1955 Eisenhower had even begun to think seriously about balancing the federal budget.

There were, however, situations in which the United States could not avoid taking steps to protect its interests. The first threat to which Eisenhower had to react was the developing situation in Iran. The rise of the nationalist Mohammad Mosaddeq to power in 1951 created two problems for the United States. First, even though he undermined British influence in his country by nationalizing the Anglo-Iranian Oil Company, he failed to open Iran's lucrative oil fields to the United States. Part of American strategy was to distance Washington from European colonialism, but American oil companies had dreamed of gaining access to Iranian oil for decades, only to be shut out repeatedly by the British monopoly. Second, Mosaddeq began to undercut the power of the head of state, Mohammad Reza Shah Pahlavi, and there was evidence that he desired to rule in an authoritarian style of his own. One demonstration of Mosaddeq's independence was his gravitation toward the Soviet Union, either to become a permanent fixture in the nonaligned camp or to try to extract military and commercial benefits from the Soviets that the West was increasingly reluctant to give. Neither was a great prospect for American strategy. In any event Mosaddeq's continued rule of Iran was contrary to American interests.

Because fiscal considerations constrained his use of the military, Eisenhower relied on the CIA to implement the policy that removed the Iranian leader. Cooperation between the administration and the CIA was easy because Allen Dulles, the brother of Secretary of State John Foster Dulles, had been named head of the CIA when Eisenhower took office in 1953. In an efficient August 1953 coup, the forces of the shah—trained, supplied, and backed by the CIA—removed Mosaddeq from power. The restored government both opened a significant part of its oil fields to American business and remained one of America's staunchest allies until its collapse twenty-six years later. It is difficult to argue that CIA involvement in Iran exceeded the CIA's mandate, resulted in unnecessary brutality, cost more than a conventional American military intervention, or threatened to cause a direct military confrontation with the Soviet Union.

The same can also be said of Guatemala, where Eisenhower employed the CIA to achieve strategic ends the following year. In that country the democratically elected, Marxist-supported government of Jacobo Arbenz Guzmán presented a problem for American interests when it nationalized 178,000 acres of land belonging to United Fruit Company, a major American corporation that had been the source of much development and economic stability in Guatemala over the years. Despite some prior hints (as when the Guatemalan legislature stood for a minute of silence after hearing that Soviet premier Joseph Stalin had died), Eisenhower continued to follow his cautious policy toward using military power. After the nationalization, the United States discovered that Arbenz had received a major arms shipment from Czechoslovakia. How the weapons could have been shipped by water from landlocked Czechoslovakia to a Guatemalan port raised serious questions of Soviet involvement in the trafficking of arms.

Eisenhower declared a limited naval blockade and once again relied on the CIA to handle the problem. The details of Arbenz's

removal illustrate the desirability of using the CIA rather than direct military intervention. As few as 150 Guatemalan exiles under a disgruntled colonel, three planes piloted by CIA operatives, and diplomatic pressure from the United States toppled Arbenz in a matter of nine days in June 1954. Neither the Guatemalan army nor the left-wing and reputedly communist-controlled labor unions supported Arbenz. Once again a potentially serious threat to American interests was neutralized by covert operations and a dangerous and exacting military intervention was averted.

At the same time as these events unfolded in Guatemala, the French position in Indochina began to deteriorate. Even though the main body of the French army lay besieged at Dien Bien Phu, Eisenhower showed little interest or concern. No direct CIA involvement in Southeast Asia was authorized until after the French had pulled out, and it was largely oriented toward supporting army-sponsored efforts to train the armies of South Vietnam and Laos.

Elsewhere, the CIA engaged in a wide variety of espionage activities directed against the Soviet Union, but to say that these operations went too far is a vast overstatement. Even before a separate agency for foreign intelligence had been established, the international department of the KGB was actively infiltrating the Manhattan Project and other American programs developing atomic weapons and rocket technology. Since that activity began before the end of the Second World War, when the United States and Soviet Union were still allies, why should American espionage in the Soviet bloc not have been expected when the two countries were enemies? To say that recruiting spies, flying over Soviet missile-test sites with U-2 reconnaissance aircraft, tapping communications, or simply performing empirical analyses went too far in offending Soviet sensibilities is ridiculous.

One particular area in which the CIA has been said to have gone too far was in its involvement in the Bay of Pigs invasion of Cuba in April 1961. Although the issue is still mired in controversy, it appears that Eisenhower had approved the CIA plan to use Cuban exiles to overthrow Fidel Castro much in the same way that Guatemalan exiles had taken out Arbenz. When President John F. Kennedy entered office, the plan was still in development, and the new president had to decide what to do with the Cuban exiles who were expecting to be dropped off and supported in Cuba. Ultimately, Kennedy decided to allow the operation to take place. It was a disaster. Cuba was not Guatemala. Having

learned from Arbenz's fate, Castro had established firm control over the military and other
potentially independent institutions in his
country. In that sense the CIA miscalculated,
but the real failure of the landing in the Bay of
Pigs resulted from Kennedy's last-minute cancellation of promised air support. By and large
continuing the Eisenhower policy of not
allowing U.S. military power to be bogged
down in costly conventional conflicts,
Kennedy preferred not to commit a large
American force to Cuba. That decision was
made under especially acute pressure. Crises
were unfolding simultaneously over Berlin and
in Laos. Committing to one conflict could
well have meant losing the other two. None of
these valid considerations, however, changes
the fact that the annihilation of the Cuban
exile forces before they got off the beach happened because of Kennedy's cancellation of air
support.

The dynamics of foreign-policy making in
the Kennedy administration focused largely on
reducing the role of the CIA. During his election
campaign Kennedy had talked about atomizing
the CIA's functions, particularly because of its
failure to keep Cuba out of Castro's hands. Bear-
ing the blame for the Bay of Pigs disaster, Allen
Dulles was forced to resign in 1962. Strategic
policy throughout the rest of the Kennedy
administration focused on a conventional military buildup that accelerated under President
Lyndon B. Johnson. Gradually, direct CIA subversion in the Third World was replaced by an
emphasis on analysis, intelligence assessments,
and training missions for foreign counterintelligence services. While Kennedy was reluctant to
commit the restored American military to local
conflicts, his successor showed no such com-
punction, especially in regard to Vietnam. Yet,
other situations in which Eisenhower would
have relied on Allen Dulles's CIA were left to
the regular armed forces. In April 1965 the
Johnson administration deployed twenty-three
thousand U.S. Marines to the Dominican
Republic to prevent Juan Bosch Gavíño's revolu-
tionary-reform movement, believed by Johnson
and the Organization of American States to
include a strong communist element, from taking power in that country.

Although the covert activities of the CIA in
the 1950s were marked by some controversy,
they spared the United States the enormous cost
of supporting conventional military deployments in at least two countries, Iran and Guatemala. In both cases Washington also avoided
looking like an aggressor, as the Soviets did
when they marched into Afghanistan in 1979 to
solve an analogous problem with the domestic
politics of a strategically situated country. This
advantage was especially significant in Iran
because it allowed the United States to avoid
association with colonial powers. Furthermore,
the speed and efficiency with which the CIA
acted in Iran and Guatemala spared lives and prevented the subtleties of American strategic interests from developing into a direct confrontation
with the Soviet Union. Although Dulles and his
staff miscalculated in the Bay of Pigs invasion,
part of the blame for that bloody disaster must
also be placed on the Kennedy administration.
After this event, CIA covert operations by and
large declined as the agency was directed to
engage in more passive intelligence activity. The
Kennedy and Johnson administrations' preference to effect policy through the military proved
costly as it resulted in the kind of local war that
Eisenhower had gone to great pains to avoid. In
fact, he had specifically warned against a huge
commitment to Indochina. Covert activity in
defense of vital American interests during the
1950s and 1960s did not go too far.

–PAUL DU QUENOY, GEORGE WASHINGTON
UNIVERSITY

References

George W. Ball, "Should the CIA Fight Secret
Wars?" *Harper's,* 269 (September 1984):
33–47;

Frank Church, "Covert Action: Swampland of
American Foreign Policy," *Bulletin of the
Atomic Scientists,* 32 (February 1976): 7–11;

William Colby, *Lost Victory* (Chicago: Contemporary Books, 1989);

Peter Grose, *Gentleman Spy: The Life of Allen
Dulles* (Boston: Houghton Mifflin, 1994);

Seymour M. Hersh, "The Angleton Story," *New
York Times Magazine,* 25 June 1978, pp. 13–
15, 61–65, 68–69, 73;

Townsend Hoopes, *The Devil and John Foster
Dulles* (Boston: Little, Brown, 1973);

Loch K. Johnson, *America's Secret Power: The
CIA in a Democratic Society* (New York:
Oxford University Press, 1989);

Johnson, *Secret Agencies: U.S. Intelligence in a
Hostile World* (New Haven: Yale University
Press, 1996);

Walter LaFeber, *America, Russia, and the Cold
War, 1945–1996,* eighth edition (New York:
McGraw-Hill, 1997);

Tom Mangold, *Cold Warrior: James Jesus Angleton, The CIA's Master Spy Hunter* (New
York: Simon & Schuster, 1991);

Ferdinand Mount, "Spook's Disease," *National Review,* 32 (7 March 1980): 299–301;

Mark Perry, *Eclipse: Last Days of the CIA* (New York: Morrow, 1992);

Thomas Powers, *The Man Who Kept the Secrets: Richard Helms and the CIA* (New York: Knopf, 1979);

John Ranelagh, *The Agency: The Rise and Decline of the CIA,* revised edition (New York: Simon & Schuster; 1987) ;

Gregory F. Treverton, *Covert Action: The Limits of Intervention in the Postwar World* (New York: Basic Books, 1987);

United States Senate, Select Committee to Study Governmental Operations with Respect to Intelligence Activities, *Alleged Assassination Plots Involving Foreign Leaders: An Interim Report of the Select Committee to Study Governmental Operations with Respect to Intelligence Activities, United States Senate: Together with Additional, Supplemental, and Separate Views,* foreword by Clark R. Mollenhoff, introduction by Senator Frank Church (Washington, D.C.: Government Printing Office, 1975);

David Wise and Thomas B. Ross, *The Invisible Government* (New York: Random House, 1964);

Bob Woodward, *Veil: The Secret Wars of the CIA 1981–1987* (New York: Simon & Schuster, 1987).

CIVIL LIBERTIES

Did anticommunist measures at the onset of the cold war threaten civil liberties and domestic freedoms in the United States?

Viewpoint: Yes, civil liberties and domestic freedoms were threatened because of excessive fears about communist infiltration of the U.S. government.

Viewpoint: No, some measures were justified, and the Supreme Court stood guard over civil liberties and domestic freedoms by rejecting the more sweeping measures.

In the aftermath of the Second World War the portrayal of the competition between the United States and the Soviet Union as an apocalyptic struggle between democracy and communism intensified debates in the United States over the roles of the different branches of government and the rights of individuals when such rights might interfere with the ability of the state to defend the national interest.

Following the 1917 Bolshevik Revolution in Russia, many in the West, especially in intellectual and literary circles, viewed communism as the best solution to what they perceived as the inherent ills of the capitalist system. Support for communism increased during the 1930s, against the backdrop of economic depression and the rise of fascism. The heroic role the Soviet Union played in the war against Nazism garnered it even more sympathy in the West. Following the end of the Second World War, however, as U.S. policymakers came to the realization that the Soviet Union was no longer an ally against a common enemy but the enemy itself, questions were raised about the loyalty of individuals who, in the 1930s and 1940s, had looked to the Soviet Union as a model for a better society and to communism as a desirable alternative to Western ideology and institutions.

These questions were raised with increasing intensity toward the end of the 1940s and in the early 1950s, when a string of what appeared to be Soviet and Soviet-sponsored advances created the impression that communism and Soviet power were on the march: in violation of the Yalta Agreement, the Soviets refused to allow free elections in Poland; in 1948 they installed a pro-Soviet puppet regime in Czechoslovakia; they were actively supporting communist and separatist insurgencies in Iran, Turkey, and Greece; they helped Mao Tse-tung's communist forces reach power in China; and pro-Soviet politicians, trade-union officials, and journalists in Western Europe were agitating for pro-Soviet policies by their governments. The United States emerged from the Second World War as indisputably the most powerful nation in the world. These apparent setbacks, and the U.S. difficulty or even inability to intervene effectively to change the course of such events, led some in the United States, especially on the right-wing of the Republican Party, to charge that the U.S. government, especially the Department of State, was weakened in its resolve. They argued that U.S. global policies were based on bad advice and were ineffectively implemented because of the lingering pro-Soviet and procommunist sympathies of the individuals in charge of devising and implementing them.

This "red scare" forced the Truman administration to initiate procedures aimed at identifying and uprooting communists in government, and the Republicans in Congress used the red scare to justify legislation aimed at delegitimizing and curbing the influence of communist or left-leaning organizations. In April 1947, for example, Congressmen Karl E. Mundt (R-South Dakota) and Richard M. Nixon (R-California) sponsored the Mundt-Nixon Bill. This legislation called for the officers of the Communist Party and communist "front" organizations to register with the Justice Department; for the barring of communists from federal employment; and for the confiscation of the passports of members of the Communist Party. The bill passed the House but was stopped by the Senate Judiciary Committee. Many of its provisions, however, were included in the Internal Security Act of 1950, also known as the McCarran Act after its sponsor, Senator Patrick A. McCarran (R-Nevada). This bill passed both the House and the Senate on 17 September 1950. Truman vetoed it, claiming that the bill was too sweeping and that its provisions denied rights protected by the Constitution, but his veto was overridden.

The argument is also made that the emergence of the United States as a global power disrupted the balance among domestic institutions. The role of the executive branch increased dramatically. Many cold-war-specific agencies were created and added to the executive branch—including the various intelligence services such as the Central Intelligence Agency (CIA) and the National Security Agency (NSA)—while others, such as the Department of Defense, were reorganized and expanded. Technological developments—such as nuclear weapons and ballistic missiles—further enhanced the power of the presidency. The need to avoid the destruction of these weapons in a sudden, first-strike Soviet preemption, led to the adoption of a hair-trigger launch and predelegation of launch authority, giving the president unprecedented license to use force on a massive scale without Congressional approval or even consultation. Historian Arthur M. Schlesinger Jr. has called this period the age of the "Imperial Presidency."

Viewpoint:
Yes, civil liberties and domestic freedoms were threatened because of excessive fears about communist infiltration of the U.S. government.

In response to the onset of U.S.-Soviet rivalry after the Second World War, the U.S. government launched various oppressive domestic measures. The most abusive of these measures were the federal employee loyalty program of 1947, the Internal Security Act of 1950, the Immigration and Naturalization Act of 1952, and the Communist Control Act of 1954. They were the result of the complex interaction of three basic historical factors: the Truman administration's national-security ideology, underlying American fears magnified by this ideology, and the Republican and conservative bureaucratic opposition to Democrats and political progressives. These separate but related factors generated a series of events that threatened the freedom of Americans to express and pursue their political views.

The Truman administration's national-security rhetoric defined the cold war and manipulated domestic fear of communism to justify increased American involvement in foreign affairs. Republican politicians further exploited this fear by baiting their political opponents with reckless accusations of communist sympathy. President Harry S Truman's stance encouraged extremism, which drove the headlong cycle of propaganda, hysteria, and domestic political rivalry, generally known as the "red scare."

The catalyst to the red scare was what historian Michael J. Hogan has called "national security ideology." It developed from the shifting manner in which Americans understood the role of their country in foreign affairs following the Second World War. Despite the U.S. victory, the war left many Americans feeling relatively vulnerable. It had shown them that they could no longer depend on the great barriers of the oceans to ensure security in an age of aircraft carriers, long-range aircraft, and atomic weapons.

Furthermore, the peace that followed the war seemed brittle. In the imaginations of many Americans the Soviet Union was conflated with communism as a monolithic force bent on global domination. The immediate causes for this growing perception of a new threat to the United States were the Soviet blockade of Berlin, the expansion of Soviet influence into eastern and central Europe, the Maoist revolution in China, and a communist insurgency in Greece. To many Americans these events demanded new responsibilities and a new self-image for the United States.

GO TO HITLER UN-AMERICAN COMMITTEE

I AM A WRITER, Blacklisted By the Un-American Committee

As espoused by the Truman administration, national-security ideology envisioned the United States as a great military power and an international champion of democracy. It proposed that the United States engage in global efforts to contain communist aggression. Domestically, this thinking required that America redirect state resources toward military efforts, establish new, powerful government bureaucracies devoted to national-security issues, and cultivate new industries supporting military efforts. Internationally, it demanded foreign military aid, the stationing of U.S. troops and officials around the world, and huge foreign-aid programs such as the Marshall Plan, to bolster anticommunist governments and construct a pro-U.S. bloc of states.

The Truman administration justified such measures to Americans by rigidly defining U.S.-Soviet rivalry abroad in terms of the subversive dangers of communism at home. The administration manipulated postwar American anxieties over security, the USSR, and communism through key documents, such as the Truman Doctrine and George F. Kennan's widely circulated telegram of February 1946 from Moscow to the State Department. As Hogan has written, the common understanding of the cold war constructed by national-security rhetoric relied on a system of symbolic representations that defined the American national identity vis-à-vis an un-American "other." The other was generally characterized as the USSR or as a vague notion of a global communist entity led by

the Soviets. The Soviet-communist other was unreasonably aggressive, bent on hegemony, and antithetical to the freedom and righteousness represented by the United States. Furthermore, as Kennan's telegram proselytized, America had to assume the sacred "responsibilities of moral and political leadership" of the "free" democratic world by opposing the USSR and containing communism.

By linking dissent with communism the internal logic of this binary system made dissent difficult and the abuse of civil liberties relatively easy. In the Truman Doctrine, for example, the president declared that Americans "must choose between alternative ways of life"—the Soviet way versus the American way. By extension any criticism of American policy amounted to defiance of the United States and support for the communist enemy.

Truman's conception of U.S.-Soviet rivalry created an atmosphere of unreasonable fear of communism. It encouraged the development of political measures that abridged civil liberties. Republicans successfully exploited this atmosphere to serve their own agenda in the communist "witch hunt" that came to be called "McCarthyism," after its chief proponent, Senator Joseph R. McCarthy (R-Wisconsin). The projection of this fear onto the domestic political arena enabled Republicans to attack their opponents through "red baiting," the reckless accusation of communist sympathy.

In turn, Truman and other conservative Democrats adopted the same tactic for political

Picketers protesting the actions of the House Un-American Activities Committee. At center is John Howard Lawson, one of the writers and directors known as the Hollywood Ten, who were sent to jail for pleading First Amendment rights in refusing to testify before the committee

CIVIL LIBERTIES

self-preservation. This action a vicious cycle of progressively worse government abuses of domestic freedoms as each political faction attempted to prove its patriotism and righteousness by hunting and exposing communists and their alleged sympathizers. Conservatives in the government bureaucracy also facilitated this abuse.

The development of Truman's federal employee loyalty program exemplifies how the process curtailed fundamental domestic freedoms. Truman's national-security rhetoric provided Congressional Republicans with a readily available weapon with which to oppose Democrats—the danger of communist subversion in the United States. Republicans accused the Truman administration of harboring such communist sympathizers in the federal government and fought with Democrats over who would control a program to ferret them out.

The program enforced uniform procedures to screen the loyalty of prospective and current government employees. It could deny employment if any "reasonable" doubt of loyalty to the government existed. Reasons to deny employment included not only evidence of sabotage, espionage, or treason, but also evidence that an American advocated the violent overthrow of the U.S. government, or performed his or her duties in a manner that apparently served the interests of another state. Individual federal agencies implemented the program by establishing their own loyalty panels in accordance with the Loyalty Review Board. The Loyalty Review Board supervised agency panels and supposedly guaranteed an accused employee rights to counsel, to a hearing, to present evidence on his or her behalf, and to appeal decisions. Appeals were first made to agency panels, and finally to the Loyalty Review Board itself.

The program ultimately proved unconstitutional because it violated basic rights guaranteed to American citizens. In practice it attempted to suppress dissenting political viewpoints throughout the government rather than limiting itself to policing federal agencies directly involved in national security. The program tended to rely on hearsay, and it did not allow accused persons to confront their accusers. Furthermore, the program selectively targeted employees with past associations to organizations that Attorney General Tom C. Clark arbitrarily listed on an official Attorney General's List of subversive or communist groups, without reference to a reviewing authority.

By carrying out the loyalty program, conservative bureaucrats exacerbated the abuse of civil rights, particularly by specifically targeting the American Left. Both Clark and Federal Bureau of Investigation (FBI) director J. Edgar Hoover,

used the program to seize greater autonomy for themselves in attacking political opponents. Hoover leaked confidential information related to the loyalty program to congressional conservatives and tricked Truman into authorizing illegal wiretaps to support the program. Similarly, Clark used the Attorney General's List and the Justice Department to discriminate against leftist organizations that opposed U.S. policy and his own notions of patriotism. In Clark's own words, he had an inclination "to resolve all doubts in favor of security," leaving little room for consideration of personal rights.

Although he expressed belief in the necessity of some sort of loyalty program, Truman ultimately criticized the most serious abuses of the federal program, saying that it encroached "on the individual rights and freedoms which distinguish a democracy from a totalitarian country." He continued, however, to support the program, as well as other measures that circumscribed the rights of U.S. citizens. He did so in part to head off the extremism of Congressional Republican initiatives that might have enacted even greater abuses to civil rights. Truman, however, also realized that failure to satisfy the public appetite for internal security would leave him open to attack by Republicans. They could accuse him of being "soft on communism," perhaps even in collusion with it. Moreover, failure to support domestic anticommunist measures might weaken his public stand against communism, potentially jeopardizing his ambitious foreign-policy initiatives. In any case, whether measures proved abusive or not, Truman understood that they bolstered his administration by validating the communist threat with which he justified his foreign policy.

This general pattern of interaction between national-security ideology, the fear of communism it created, and conservative opposition to the American Left characterized the evolution of the other major domestic anticommunist measures developed in response to the cold war.

The Internal Security Act of 1950 focused on four issues: the mandatory self-registration of communist-related organizations with the government, the strengthening of anti-espionage laws, the amendment of immigration and naturalization laws, and the detention of potential subversives in times of national emergency. Its primary aim was to suppress the American Communist Party by forcing it to identify itself as an organization dedicated to the violent overthrow of the U.S. government. The U.S. Supreme Court ultimately concluded that this obligation conflicted with Fifth Amendment protection against self-incrimination.

CIVIL LIBERTIES

Fear of communism proved so entrenched that, despite the oppressive nature of the Internal Security Act, few politicians dared to oppose it. As Congressman Herbert H. Lehman (D-New York) later recalled, "A number of my liberal colleagues . . . said that if I voted against the measure it would mean my defeat for reelection that fall. They were wrong. But the fever of fear was on my colleagues."

The Immigration and Nationality Act of 1952 presumed a privileged status for native-born Americans by noting the high numbers of naturalized eastern Europeans represented in the American Communist Party and other leftist organizations. This act sought to deprive foreign-born radicals of their U.S. citizenship and legal immigrants with progressive political views of their residence permits. In some cases the government used the act to deport the accused to their countries of origin. The Supreme Court later recognized that this act violated the Constitution.

The Communist Control Act of 1954 circumvented the inherent inadequacies of the mandatory self-registration set up in the Internal Security Act. Rather than requiring communist organizations to do something they would almost certainly never do—register with the U.S. government as subversive—the Communist Control Act virtually made Communist Party membership illegal. The act established fourteen indications of Communist Party membership and arbitrarily stripped the party of "all rights, privileges, and immunities attendant upon legal bodies." Only one senator, Estes Kefauver (D-Tennessee), dared to vote against this act.

These measures and the cycle that produced them died, for the most part, in the backlash of the militant New Left, which emerged in the 1960s. Although fear of communism continued to exert an influence in U.S. policy making until the demise of the Soviet Union in 1990, the extremism generated by the Truman administration's national-security rhetoric disappeared as Americans recognized the spiraling abuses produced by the government's reaction to the perceived danger of the USSR. In retrospect, the vicious cycle that produced these measures marks a watershed in America's understanding of the relationship of civil rights and national security. It also serves as a sad commentary on the cavalier way in which politicians treated those rights in the face of political expediency. It is now generally recognized that most victims of the anti-communist measures had usually done nothing more "subversive" to American security than criticize U.S. policy or express pro-

gressive views—rights supposedly guaranteed to all American citizens by the Constitution.

—BARAK COHEN

Viewpoint:
No, some measures were justified, and the Supreme Court stood guard over civil liberties and domestic freedoms by rejecting the more sweeping measures.

During the early years of the cold war, Americans became increasingly preoccupied with internal security and the potential for communist subversion. Several measures adopted during this period encroached on civil liberties and constitutionally guaranteed rights. Legislation such as the Smith Act (The Alien Registration Act of 1940) and the Internal Security Act of 1950 (also known as the McCarran Act), and executive measures such as the federal employee loyalty program, Federal Bureau of Investigation (FBI) wiretapping, and the denial of passports to left-wing activists, all had an adverse effect on important constitutional freedoms and rights: the freedom of speech, the right to free assembly, and freedom from unwarranted search and seizure. Not until the Supreme Court issued a series of rulings in the late 1950s and early 1960s were most of these infringements of civil liberties overturned.

Efforts to prevent subversion inevitably require some sacrifice of civil liberties. A trade-off between freedom and security is necessary in every democratic society. The only real question is whether the right balance has been struck. The onset of the cold war and the discovery of a Soviet espionage network in the United States, consisting of dozens of members (as well as some nonmembers) of the U.S. Communist Party (CPUSA), gave ample grounds for concern about the prospect of domestic subversion in the period right after the Second World War. Measures to counter that threat were fully justified, but some of the actions that were taken, culminating in the excesses of the McCarthy period, went too far in the name of internal security. The Supreme Court was obliged to restore a proper balance.

Certain checks against domestic subversion had been in place well before the cold war started. The creation of the Martin Dies Committee on Un-American Activities (also known as the House Un-American Activities Committee, or HUAC) in the House of Representatives in 1938 and the passage of the Smith Act in 1940, were only the

TRUMAN'S LOYALTY PROGRAM

On 21 March 1947, President Harry S Truman issued Executive Order 9835, establishing procedures for the administration of an Employees Loyalty Program in the Executive Branch of the federal government. The order included the following provisions:

1. The standard for the refusal of employment or the removal from employment in an executive department or agency on the grounds relating to loyalty shall be that, on all the evidence, reasonable grounds exist for a belief that the person involved is disloyal to the Government of the United States.

2. Activities and associations . . . which may be considered in connection with the determination of disloyalty may include one or more of the following:

a. Sabotage, espionage, or attempts or preparations therefor, or knowingly associating with spies or saboteurs;

b. Treason or sedition or advocacy thereof;

c. Advocacy of revolution or force or violence to alter the constitutional form of government of the United States;

d. Intentional, unauthorized disclosure to any person, under circumstances which may indicate disloyalty to the United States, of documents or information of a confidential or non-public character obtained by the person making the disclosure as a result of his employment by the Government of the United States;

e. Performing or attempting to perform his duties, or otherwise acting, so as to serve the interests of another government in preference to the interests of the United States.

f. Membership in, affiliation with or sympathetic association with any foreign or domestic organization, association, movement, group or combination of persons, designated by the Attorney General as totalitarian, fascist, communist, or subversive, or as having adopted a policy of advocating or approving the commission of acts of force or violence to deny other persons their rights under the Constitution of the Untied States, or as seeking to alter the form of government of the United States by unconstitutional means.

Source: Eleanor Bontecou, The Federal Loyalty-Security Program *(Ithaca, N.Y.: Cornell University Press, 1953), pp. 275–281.*

most recent examples before the Second World War. Both HUAC and the Smith Act remained largely dormant until after the Second World War, when fears of communist subversion became far more pronounced.

The Smith Act made it illegal to advocate the violent overthrow of the U.S. government either in print or through membership in a group committed to that goal. The act gained little notice until 1949, when the top CPUSA leaders were convicted of conspiring to overthrow the government. Each of the defendants was also convicted of belonging to the party. The case, known as *Dennis* v. *United States* (1951), was affirmed by the Supreme Court.

The use of the Smith Act in the prosecution of Communist Party leaders infringed civil liberties on two main fronts. First, it inhibited freedom of association. For the first time since the Alien and Sedition Acts of the late eighteenth century, the U.S. government sought to limit the types of "legal" associations that citizens could join during peacetime. By ruling that the CPUSA, by virtue of its Marxist-Leninist orientation, was dedicated to the violent overthrow of the U.S. government (even though the party constitution explicitly denied such a goal) and that the party was, therefore, illegal, the government effectively sought to limit the scope of political competition in the marketplace of ideas. Furthermore, in *Dennis* v. *United States* the government argued (and the courts agreed) that it did not have to present evidence that the Communist Party was actually planning or preparing to overthrow the government. According to this interpretation, guilt under the Smith Act could be proven purely by arguing that the party subscribed to Marxist-Leninist ideology. The use of this standard of proof implied that members of the organization were being punished solely for their ideas about the desirability of overthrowing the government, rather than for any actions they may have taken (or been intending to take) toward this end.

Second, the prosecution of communist leaders inhibited freedom of speech and freedom of the press. By using published materials to show that the CPUSA sought to overthrow the U.S. government, the Truman administration engendered a chilling effect on the publication of antigovernment texts. The judge instructed the jury that they should consider whether the texts were being used to propagate the overthrow of the government. The conviction on the basis of this strategy was a signal that people who sought to spread subversive ideas to others by publishing them could face imprisonment. Under this ruling, unpublished statements advocating the overthrow of the government could likewise lead to imprisonment. In none of the trials of communist leaders was any evidence presented that party propaganda was effective in convincing anyone that the government should be overthrown. By the standards set forth in the Smith Act and approved by the Supreme Court in *Dennis* v. *United States,* such evidence was unnecessary. The simple publication or distribution of subversive materials was itself deemed illegal. In effect, the Supreme Court was rejecting the "clear and present danger" criterion set by Justice Oliver Wendell Holmes Jr., during his tenure on the court (1902–1932) to judge whether subversive speech was permissible.

At the same time that the executive branch was seeking to prosecute communist leaders under the Smith Act, Congress was taking on a prominent role in exposing alleged hidden communists in American public life. The key actors were HUAC, which gained significant public attention by holding hearings on communism in Hollywood and by breaking the Alger Hiss spy scandal, and Senator Joseph R. McCarthy (R-Wisconsin), who repeatedly claimed that the government had been extensively infiltrated by communists. The general notion that a substantial number of communist spies had penetrated the U.S. government was correct, but McCarthy had little interest in ferreting out genuine traitors. Instead, he resorted to false accusations and smear tactics to settle personal scores and promote his political career. The problem with HUAC was somewhat different. Almost all of those who were subpoenaed by the committee were, in fact, communists, as the committee members knew in advance. The purpose of the hearings was not to determine their guilt. The sessions were instead intended to coerce the disclosure of the names of other communists. Several witnesses refused to disclose the names of other communists on First Amendment grounds and were cited for contempt of Congress, eventually spending several years in prison. Witnesses were presented with the choice of aiding the investigation or going to prison. Furthermore, witnesses who claimed the Fifth Amendment right against self-incrimination were nonetheless denounced by HUAC members for being communists and were then blacklisted by the entertainment industry. Through these actions, Congress persecuted individuals who had done nothing wrong other than subscribing to a political ideology that the committee found odious. (It is noteworthy, for example, that comparable measures were not taken against American Nazis.)

The persecution of communists for their political views gained a legal foundation with the passage of the McCarran Act in 1950. It required all "Communist-front organizations" to register with the government and to disclose their membership lists. To determine which organizations were communist-front organizations, it set up the Subversive Activities Control Board (SACB). The McCarran Act also prohibited communists from entering the United States and authorized the government to detain potential subversives during a state of emergency or war.

This act had several damaging effects on civil liberties. The authority to treat organizations as communist fronts during a period when association with communism could lead to job loss, and even prison terms, was essentially an attack on the freedom of association. Being listed as a communist organization by the SACB was tantamount to a sentence of organizational death. Furthermore, as President Harry S Truman argued when opposing the act, it damaged freedom of expression by suppressing unpopular opinions and belief and through its chilling effect on the debate of controversial subjects. Finally, the creation of a mechanism for the detention of suspected subversives during an emergency was a clear violation of the right to due process, since no proof was required that genuine acts of espionage or sabotage had been committed.

The executive branch took actions of its own that resulted in limits on civil liberties, specifically by creating the loyalty-test program and by denying passports to American leftists. The Loyalty Order, issued by Truman in 1947, required all federal employees (including those without the need for access to classified information) to undergo loyalty checks or face dismissal. The order stated that employees could be dismissed for, among other things, belonging to or even sympathizing with an organization that was designated as "totalitarian, Fascist, communist, or subversive." Prior to this order, the federal government was specifically prohibited from selecting its civil-service employees on the basis of their political beliefs. By 1951 employees could be fired if there were "reasonable doubts" about their loyalty. The attorney general was instructed to create a list of subversive organizations, although no guidelines were provided for determining whether a particular organization was subversive; nor were hearings held on the classifications.

The loyalty program was detrimental to civil liberties both directly and indirectly. If the program had been limited to employees with the need for access to classified information, it would have been in accord with Holmes's criterion. The blanket application of the program to all federal employees, however, raised a host of problems. Because of the lack of standards and hearings, the process of determining whether government employees were disloyal, even when it worked as intended, was a violation of due process and an attempt by the government to judge the legitimacy of ideas. At the same time, the process was abused to attack people who advocated human rights, racial equality, and the redistribution of wealth—ideas that during the McCarthy era were sometimes considered suspect. Occasionally, a coworker with a grudge against a particular individual accused him or her of disloyalty. Such situations were not easily rectified because of the climate of suspicion that surrounded anyone who was accused and because suspects were not allowed to confront their accusers. The violation of due process in the administration of the loyalty program was compounded by its other adverse effects on civil liberties. The publication of the list of subversive organizations by the attorney general had the effect of significantly curtailing the freedom of association. Members of organizations on the list were fired from their jobs, prohibited from leaving the country, and denied eligibility for federal housing. The organizations themselves were denied meeting places. They lost contributions, members, and public support; and they generally found their ability to function severely impaired. In some cases, organizations were included on the list not because of subversive activities, but because they were opposed to government policy. In one case opposition to the Marshall Plan was cited as a loyalty violation. The compilation and publication of the Attorney General's List thus created a de facto loyalty program for the entire country, chilling political dissent and debate.

The Truman and Eisenhower administrations also infringed civil liberties by limiting the right to travel abroad. During the early cold-war period, many American intellectuals, scientists, and political figures were denied passports "on the grounds that their travel was not in the best interest of the United States." In 1952 the State Department issued a categorical restriction against foreign travel for members and sympathizers of the Communist Party and "anyone who gave reason for belief that he was going abroad to advance the [communist] movement." At the same time, the government sought to ban travel to several communist countries, including China, North Korea, and, later, Cuba. The Supreme Court later ruled that these restrictions on an individual's travel because of his or her political beliefs violated the First and Fifth Amendments of the Constitution.

The downfall of McCarthy in 1954, and the general easing of concern about communist subversion by the mid 1950s, put an end to the creation of new anticommunist laws and programs. At the same time, the Supreme Court, which until then had largely accepted anticommunist measures as constitutional, began to rule against the government. By the late 1960s it had reinstated almost all of the civil liberties lost during the early years of the cold war.

The Supreme Court's effort to restore a proper balance began with its decision in 1955 to circumscribe the power of congressional investigative committees. In *Quinn* v. *U.S.,* the Supreme Court ruled that Congress could not inquire into private affairs unrelated to a valid legislative purpose. In *Watkins* v. *U.S.* (1957), the court limited such committees still further, ruling that the purpose of their inquiries could not be to punish those being questioned. It allowed witnesses to refuse to answer questions outside the scope of the committee's activities and prohibited committee hearings from turning into name-gathering expeditions. After this ruling, Congress no longer had the power to expose communists (or others) purely for the sake of exposure. At the same time, in *Cole* v. *Young* the justices circumscribed the extent of the executive branch's loyalty test program, noting that the dismissal of federal workers without a hearing violated their rights. In 1956 the court outlawed the dismissal of public employees who invoked the Fifth Amendment when appearing before investigating committees. The justices held in *Slochower* v. *New York Board of Higher Education* (1956) that "the privilege against self-incrimination would be reduced to a hollow mockery if its exercise could be taken as equivalent either to a confession of guilt or a conclusive presumption of perjury."

The Supreme Court also took steps to restrict the scope of laws aimed at persecuting communists. In *Yates* v. *United States* (1957) the court ruled that Congress could not make it illegal to advocate the overthrow of the government in the abstract. After this ruling, communists were held to be in violation of the Smith Act only if they advocated specific illegal actions aimed at violently overthrowing the government. Furthermore, in *Scales* v. *United States* (1961), the court rejected guilt by association and ruled that simple membership in a subversive organization was not a violation of the Smith Act. An individual could be guilty only if he or she personally demonstrated active intent to overthrow the government and combined this intension with active membership in a subversive organization. In the companion case *Noto* v. *U.S.* (1961), the court ruled that teaching Marxism-Leninism or advocating violent revolution in the abstract was not a violation of the Smith Act. As a result of these two rulings, the Smith Act became practically unenforceable, and the government ceased to prosecute cases under its provisions. In 1965 the court struck down the registration requirements of the McCarran Act by allowing individuals to invoke the Fifth Amendment when refusing to register as members of communist organizations, on the grounds registration would expose the person to prosecution under the Smith Act.

The last of the infringements of civil liberties were lifted in the mid 1960s when the Supreme Court ruled that the right of U.S. citizens to travel abroad could not be restricted by the government. The court further limited the federal loyalty program by ruling that the government could not deny employment to individuals solely on the basis of Communist Party membership. Thus, as a result of the Supreme Court's actions, the steps that Congress and the Truman and Eisenhower administrations had taken to curtail civil liberties were in place for no longer than twenty years.

The fact that in the 1940s and early 1950s both of the elected branches of government were willing to enact measures that violated the Bill of Rights shows the extent to which the fear of communism affected American political opinion during this period. Concerns about communist subversion were well founded, and strong measures to deal with that threat were clearly justified. Several of the measures that were adopted, however, went well beyond what was needed and desirable, and the Supreme Court stepped in to right the balance, preserving constitutionally guaranteed rights and freedoms.

–MARK KRAMER, HARVARD UNIVERSITY

References

Michael R. Belknap, *Cold War Political Justice: The Smith Act, the Communist Party, and American Civil Liberties* (Westport, Conn.: Greenwood Press, 1977);

David Caute, *The Great Fear: The Anti-Communist Purge under Truman and Eisenhower* (New York: Simon & Schuster, 1978);

Richard M. Freeland, *The Truman Doctrine and the Origins of McCarthyism: Foreign Policy, Domestic Politics, and Internal Security, 1946–1948* (New York: Knopf, 1972);

Richard M. Fried, *Nightmare in Red: The McCarthy Era in Perspective* (New York: Oxford University Press, 1990);

John Earl Haynes, *Red Scare or Red Menace? American Communism and Anti-Communism in the Cold War Era* (Chicago: Ivan R. Dee, 1996);

Michael J. Hogan, *A Cross of Iron: Harry S. Truman and the Origins of the National Security State 1945–1954* (New York: Cambridge University Press, 1998);

Edward Pessen, *Losing Our Souls: The American Experience in the Cold War* (Chicago: Ivan R. Dee, 1993);

Richard Gid Powers, *Not Without Honor: The History of American Anti-Communism* (New York: Free Press, 1995);

Stanley N. Worton, ed., *Freedom of Assembly and Petition* (Rochelle Park, N.J.: Hayden Book Company, 1975).

CIVIL LIBERTIES

CONTAINMENT

Was universal containment preferable to strongpoint containment as a guide to U.S. foreign policy?

Viewpoint: Yes, universal containment, proposed by Paul H. Nitze, was preferable to strongpoint containment, advocated by George F. Kennan, because universal containment took a more realistic approach to communist expansion.

Viewpoint: No, universal containment was not preferable because it was expensive and indiscriminate.

Viewpoint: No, universal containment was not a viable policy option because it led to overextension of resources and to disaster in Vietnam.

The organizing principle of U.S. national-security policies during the cold war, containment was conceived and articulated by George F. Kennan in 1946, and given public expression in his famous "Mr. X" article in the July 1947 issue of *Foreign Affairs*. The head of the Policy Planning Staff at the U.S. State Department, Kennan argued that the Soviet Union wanted "to make sure that it has filled every nook and cranny available to it in the basin of world power." To meet the Soviet challenge the United States should adopt a policy of "a long-term, patient but firm and vigilant containment of Russian expansive tendencies" through "the adroit and vigilant application of counterforce at a series of constantly shifting geographical and political points, corresponding to the shifts and manoeuvers of Soviet policy."

In its different formulations and definitions, containment sought a middle course between all-out war with the Soviet Union and retreat in the face of rising Soviet strength. To many U.S. policymakers in the immediate aftermath of the Second World War, the choices did not seem so stark. The United States emerged from the conflict hoping there would be no return to the harsh power politics of the prewar decades. Many U.S. policymakers hoped that the alliance forged against the Nazi regime would hold during peacetime, serving to create a more stable and tranquil world.

Within a year or two following the end of the war, however, the Truman administration concluded that meaningful cooperation with the Soviet Union would not be possible and that the two countries were on a collision course. The administration interpreted a series of Soviet moves as indications of an expansionist, aggressive policy to which the United States had to respond. The Soviets were reluctant to allow free elections and democratic regimes in the areas of east and central Europe under their occupation. They assisted leftist elements in the civil war in Greece, fomented unrest in Turkey, supported separatist tendencies in northern Iran, and helped the communists, led by Mao Tse-tung, in the Chinese civil war.

Debates at upper levels of the Truman administration during the late 1940s revolved around what kind of containment the United States should adopt. Kennan proposed strongpoint containment, concentrating on preventing expansion of Soviet power and influence into areas of strategic importance to U.S. security and welfare. His successor as head of the Policy Planning Staff, Paul H. Nitze, advocated universal containment, which called for ringing the Soviet Union with a tight system of pro-Western alliances and preventing the extension of Soviet power anywhere, not only into areas of strategic or economic importance to the West. Supporters of universal containment won this debate, and Kennan became a trenchant critic of U.S. foreign policy.

**Viewpoint:
Yes, universal containment, proposed by Paul H. Nitze, was preferable to strongpoint containment, advocated by George F. Kennan, because universal containment took a more realistic approach to communist expansion.**

There are three principles of policy that policymakers ignore at their own peril. The first is that the best is the enemy of the good. The second is that in times of uncertainty a policymaker should err on the side of caution. The third is that policymakers, even (or, perhaps, especially) those devising foreign policies, should be aware of the domestic context of the policies they recommend. Especially with the benefit of hindsight, many criticisms may be leveled at National Security Council memorandum 68 (NSC-68), the document that established the strategy of universal containment, but a case can be made that, with the information available to its authors when it was written in 1950, NSC-68 adhered to these three principles.

In early 1950 President Harry S Truman created a committee of officials from the Departments of State and Defense to examine U.S. national strategy and write a coherent, comprehensive document that defined vital U.S. national interests, the major threats to these interests, and the best means to secure them. Truman's instructions came after a year in which the U.S. position in the world suffered a series of setbacks. In 1949 China was taken over by the communist forces of Mao Tse-tung; the Soviet Union exploded its first nuclear weapon; the Soviet grip over eastern and central Europe tightened; and Britain continued to decline as a world power. Truman wanted a clearly written document that could be distributed throughout the administration, focusing the attention of departments and agencies on what needed to be done to counter Soviet gains.

The interagency committee produced NSC-68, a document of sixty-six single-spaced pages that was meant to be more than a repudiation of the universalistic approach that had dominated U.S. policy in the immediate post–Second World War period. Although it differed from George F. Kennan's preferred version of containment, it was not meant to be a critique of Kennan. (In fact, Kennan was consulted on several points as the document was being written.) As

John Lewis Gaddis pointed out in 1982, however, the mandate the committee saw itself carrying out—to "systematize containment"—and the manner in which the document was written caused NSC-68 to be "more sweeping in content and implications than its originators had intended."

Kennan advocated containment based on "strongpoint" defense, that is, preventing the expansion of Soviet power and influence into a few selected regions. His recommendations were based on four assumptions. First, there was such a thing as an "irreducible" national interest—capable of being objectively and dispassionately calculated and determined; second, not every part of the world was of equal importance to the core national interests of the United States; third, the ideology governing the domestic politics, society, and economy of a state should be of little concern to the United States, unless such ideology was wedded to real material power; and fourth, the forces of nationalism and particularism were stronger than the unifying force of ideology, making it unlikely that a monolithic communist bloc would emerge to threaten the United States. These assumptions led Kennan to support a policy that would prevent the spread of Soviet power and influence to regions of potential industrial and military strength, such as western Europe and Japan, but would largely ignore other areas where levels of education and industrialization were insufficient to generate mighty industrial-military power. Since communism as an ideology was not in and of itself a concern to the United States unless it was wedded to power, Kennan argued, the United States should not waste its efforts trying to prevent the spread of communism to small or midsize countries in faraway places. The unifying theme of Kennan's "pick-and-choose" strategy was the notion of the limits of power: the United States was a rich and powerful country, but its power was not unlimited. Because its power was limited, the goals it pursued had to be limited as well. Kennan and his supporters later argued that his original formulation of containment should have been understood to mean that the threat from the Soviet Union was mostly political and psychological and that, therefore, the United States should emphasize political and economic means to contain that Soviet threat, rather than insist on primarily military measures.

The authors of NSC-68 argued, explicitly or implicitly, that Kennan's policy was wrong because it was based on a misunderstanding of the nature of power, a lack of appreciation of the means at the disposal of the United States, and a

CONTAINMENT

NSC-68

National Security Council memorandum 68 sought to justify the policy of universal containment by depicting communism as dedicated to the annihilation of individual freedoms.

The idea of freedom is the most contagious idea in history, more contagious than the idea of submission to authority. For the breadth of freedom cannot be tolerated in a society which has come under the domination of an individual or group of individuals with a will to absolute power. Where the despot holds absolute power—the absolute power of the absolutely powerful will—all other wills must be subjugated in an act of willing submission, a degradation willed by the individual upon himself under the compulsion of a perverted faith. It is the first article of this faith that he finds and can only find the meaning of his existence in serving the ends of the system. The system becomes God, and submission to the will of God becomes submission to the will of the system. . . . The same compulsion which demands total power over all men within the Soviet state without a single exception, demands total power over all Communist Parties and all states under Soviet domination. . . .

The antipathy of slavery to freedom explains the iron curtain, the isolation, the autarchy of the society whose end is absolute power. The existence and persistence of the idea of freedom is a permanent and continuous threat to the foundation of the slave society; and it therefore regards as intolerable the long continued existence of freedom in the world. What is new, what makes the continuing crisis, is the polarization of power which now inescapably confronts the slave society with the free.

The assault on free institutions is world-wide now, and in the context of the present polarization of power a defeat of free institutions anywhere is a defeat everywhere. . . .

Thus unwillingly our free society finds itself mortally challenged by the Soviet system. No other value system is so wholly irreconcilable with ours, so implacable in its purpose to destroy ours, so capable of turning to its own uses the most dangerous and divisive trends in our own society, no other so skillfully and powerfully evokes the elements of irrationality in human nature everywhere, and no other has the support of a great and growing center of military power.

Source: NSC-68: United States Objectives and Programs for National Security *(14 April 1950).*

therefore, the United States should invest its efforts in those areas judged more vital to its interests, power had more than material aspects. It was also a matter of psychology and perception. If country after country fell to communist rule and the leader of the free world were to watch this process without doing anything about it, it would increasingly become a problem for the United States—not because of the intrinsic value of each of the countries thus surrendered, but owing to the cumulative effect of the spectacle of these countries coming under communist rule in the face of Western indifference. Countries that were important to the West would inevitably conclude that Soviet power was on the rise, while the United States was in decline. Rather than support the United States in its struggle with the Soviet Union, such states would seek security either by aligning themselves with the Soviet Union or by adopting neutrality. The West would lose potential allies, markets, and access to resources, while the USSR would gain them. The United States thus had to adopt a perimeter—rather than strongpoint—defense, resisting Soviet expansion everywhere beyond the territories already under Soviet control. Not doing so would have deleterious material effects on Western security, as well as pernicious consequences for the self-confidence and resolve of Western societies. Perimeter defense was also easier to explain to the public than strongpoint defense. To ensure continuing public support for high defense budgets and high-profile foreign policy, the threat to America had to be portrayed in stark and consistent terms. If the struggle between the United States and the Soviet Union were portrayed as a zero-sum game and infused with a moral overtone, policymakers would have difficulty explaining why the United States chose to intervene against the spread of communism to one country but not to another. Kennan and other members of the sophisticated foreign-policy establishment could cope with the complexities and nuances of strongpoint containment, but it was not clear that American voters could. To make sure that they did not revert to prewar isolationism, containment had to be presented in more sweeping and compelling terms.

Moreover, the authors of NSC-68 argued, there was no need to distinguish between vital and peripheral issues—no need to opt for strongpoint over perimeter defense—because the means at the disposal of the United States were not as limited as Kennan had stipulated. The authors of NSC-68 were believers in Keynesian economics, in which government spending can play a positive role in fostering economic expansion. They pointed out that in time of crisis—the Second World War, for example—the American economy was able to meet the demands placed on it. "One of the most significant lessons of our World War

misreading of the American public's attitude toward foreign policy. Judging their discussion in terms of the knowledge and perspective available in 1950, one cannot say that the document they produced was implausible or unreasonable.

NSC-68 suggested that, while one could argue that not all parts of the world were of equal importance to the United States and that,

II experience," the report said, "was that the American economy, when it operates at a level approaching full efficiency, can provide enormous resources for purposes other than civilian consumption while simultaneously providing a higher standard of living." In comparison to Kennan, with his constricted view of U.S. economic capabilities and power potential, the authors of NSC-68 were exuberant indeed. Since there was no need to limit American goals because of limited resources, the United States could lead the West in challenging the Soviet Union everywhere.

Kennan also insisted on soberly defining vital national interests at the outset and only then turning to examine if these interests were threatened by the expansion of Soviet power and influence. The authors of NSC-68 appeared to offer a more undifferentiated version of American interests than Kennan: if any state were threatened by Soviet expansion, then preventing it was in the U.S. interest. Such an approach made sense for reasons of psychology and perceptions—which applied both at home and abroad. A pick-and-choose containment policy might have led to confusion, demoralization, and diminution of resolve.

These divergent assumptions led to three major policy differences between the versions of containment offered by the authors of NSC-68 and Kennan. First, whereas Kennan appeared to define the Soviet threat to the West as mostly political and psychological and appeared to offer mainly political and economic means to combat it, the authors of NSC-68 emphasized the military nature of the threat and the need for an American military response. The authors of NSC-68 argued that universal containment required a robust defensive system around the perimeter of the areas already controlled by the Soviets to prevent a Soviet break-out to regions not yet under their control. Moreover, the United States would have to become actively engaged in preventing communist movements from subverting pro-Western regimes anywhere around the world. Second, the authors of NSC-68 assumed that communism anywhere was threatening to the United States, and, therefore, their report did not emphasize the need to help dissenting and fragmenting forces within the communist camp, something in which Kennan put much store. Finally, Kennan and the authors of NSC-68 entertained different views about the nature of the world and how best to pursue U.S. interests in it. Kennan, a realist and a skeptic, believed that the relations among states were marked by competition and rivalry and that this constant jostling for position and advantage could not be changed. The best a country could do was to secure its own particularistic interests in an anarchic and unpredictable world, accepting that there would always be many regimes and situations that would violate its own sensibilities and preferences. The authors of NSC-68 believed that the best way for the United States to cope with these conditions was to change the international environment, making it more hospitable to U.S. interests and values. Animated by a typically American can-do, optimistic, expansive attitude, supporters of NSC-68 implied that the best way to serve American interests was to engage in a crusade to create a better world. NSC-68 emphasizes that the "overall policy" of the United States was "designed to foster a world environment in which the American system can survive and flourish," a policy "we would probably pursue even if there were no Soviet threat."

Some of the assumptions of NSC-68 were not convincing. Its arguments were not always presented in the most logical fashion, and its tone was certainly alarmist. In 1950, however, facing what appeared to be a rising communist tide and unsure whether the American public was willing to abandon its traditional isolationism and support high-level involvement in the world, the authors of NSC-68 were not unreasonable to argue as they did. Indeed, they may not have been so wrong about Soviet intentions. Recent scholars who have had access to Russian archives tend to view early Soviet designs as more aggressive than previous (mostly revisionist) scholarship on the cold war had asserted. Denied the knowledge now available, the authors of NSC-68 could only assume aggressive intentions on the part of the USSR, and they followed the safe policy path: when in doubt, err on the side of caution.

—BENJAMIN FRANKEL, SECURITY STUDIES

Viewpoint:
No, universal containment was not preferable because it was expensive and indiscriminate.

Compared to George F. Kennan's original conception of containment, National Security Council memorandum 68 (NSC-68) was unnecessarily costly and indiscriminate. Kennan advocated a strongpoint approach that distinguished between vital and secondary interests. He argued that the global balance of power would not be fundamentally altered unless the Soviet Union extended its influence to key centers of military and industrial power such as Japan, Germany, and Great Britain. Other strategic locations—such as Turkey, Iran, and the Philippines—were also considered of crucial value to U.S. security. In Kennan's view, however, the United States had neither the interest nor the ability to combat Soviet influence wherever it arose. NSC-68, issued on 7 April 1950 and written under the guidance of Paul H. Nitze, Kennan's successor as head of the Policy Planning Staff at the U.S. Department of State, reversed these priorities and declared that the United States had precisely such an interest. It became axiomatic that any Soviet or communist advance was an intolerable threat to American security. Such guidelines robbed the United States of criteria by which to measure the costs and benefits of each particular anticommunist effort. Clearly, the fall of Germany and the fall of Indochina to communism would not have been of equal significance for American interests—strategically, economically, or politically—and would not have called for equivalent responses. The "perimeter" approach to containment, as outlined in NSC-68, committed the United States to massive efforts at containing Soviet influence, even in regions where the concrete interests of the United States were minimal.

Part of the reason for the failure to distinguish vital from peripheral interests was an exaggerated concern over "credibility." According to NSC-68, diplomatic setbacks or retreats in regions of peripheral interest might be interpreted by allies and enemies alike as indicative of American weakness. It was, therefore, of paramount importance that the United States be seen as firm and vigilant in any given crisis, regardless of the particular issues at stake. This viewpoint, however, underestimated the ability of America's allies and the Soviet Union to make reasonably accurate, case-by-case judgments regarding American strength and interests. For example, Soviet premier Joseph Stalin did not take President Harry S Truman's refusal to intervene in the Chinese civil war as a sign that the United States might back down in Germany. Stalin understood that the interests at stake were obviously distinct and unequal.

Whereas Kennan had recommended that the United States strengthen local power centers in Europe and Asia through the use of economic aid and diplomatic support, NSC-68 went much further, encouraging the actual deployment of American ground forces abroad. These frontline commitments involved the replacement of indigenous forces with American troops, American bases, and American money. In some cases, such frontline deployments by American forces actually subtracted from the popular legitimacy of allied regimes by identifying them too closely with outside American influence. By emphasizing conventional military power, an area in which

the Soviet Union had considerable strengths on the ground, the authors of NSC-68 tended to downplay the utility of other policy tools, such as economic aid and atomic air power—areas in which the United States had clear advantages over the Soviet Union. The creative use of American economic power through the Marshall Plan had already helped to stabilize Western European economies, and America's nuclear arsenal was a powerful deterrent to Soviet aggression. There was no need to play to Moscow's strengths by attempting to match Soviet conventional military capabilities.

A further weakness of NSC-68 was its identification of international communism, rather than the Soviet Union, as the primary threat to American security. Kennan recognized that local communist movements, while they might be anathema to Americans, often reflected nationalist sentiments and would be difficult to turn into puppets of the Soviet Union. For this reason the United States had aided Josip Tito's Yugoslavia in its break from Moscow. There was considerable room for creative diplomacy to play on national rivalries within the communist world, thus encouraging disunity and relieving the West of some of the burden of containment. NSC-68, however, represented a shift in emphasis whereby any communist movement was assumed to be a tool of the Kremlin. Opportunities for creative diplomacy were, therefore, ruled out, notably with regard to China. The United States refused to recognize the new communist regime and instead stepped up political and military support to Chiang Kai-shek, Mao Tsetung's bitter rival, on the island of Taiwan. This assumption of communist unity also encouraged the fateful decision to treat the North Korean attack on South Korea in June of 1950 as if it had been directly ordered by Stalin. In Europe it might have been true that local communist regimes were Soviet puppet states. Asian communist regimes had domestic strength and legitimacy of their own and did not represent a simple extension of Soviet power. By the end of 1950 the European allies of the United States had grown increasingly alarmed at American policy in Korea, even though the United States had intervened in large part out of a desire to maintain credibility with its European allies.

NSC-68 was based on an overly pessimistic view of U.S. strength in relation to the Soviet Union and an overly alarmist view of Soviet aggressiveness. Nitze argued that the balance of power was shifting against the United States and that by 1954 the Soviet Union would be capable of launching a successful surprise attack against the United

States and its allies. The question of whether the Soviet Union had any intention of launching such an attack, or any interest in doing so, was no longer addressed. An objective assessment of the balance of forces would have revealed that the United States and its allies had massive strengths in terms of industrial production, technological superiority, ideological appeal, air power, naval power, and even land power. These advantages were not about to fade, and Stalin knew it. For all his brutality and paranoia at home, his foreign policy was notably cautious and realistic. Stalin probed for weaknesses, but whenever he was met by determined resistance from the United States—as in Turkey, Greece, or Iran—he withdrew. Certainly Stalin had no intention of launching a reckless and potentially disastrous military attack against the West. By failing to take American strengths, or Stalin's likely intentions, into account, the authors of NSC-68 encouraged an unnecessarily defeatist view of the strategic situation.

At its essence NSC-68 was not about restoring a balance of power in Europe and Asia. Rather, it was about asserting American preponderance internationally. Kennan had always maintained that a diverse, multipolar world was in America's interest and that such a world was the best defense against any Soviet plans for expansion. Such a relaxed view was unacceptable to the authors of NSC-68. In their view the only barrier to Soviet expansion was an assertive American presence.

All of these changes in emphasis—from a strongpoint approach to a perimeter defense, from an offshore strategy to a frontline military commitment, from flexible diplomacy to blanket anticommunism, and from atomic air power to conventional military forces—entailed a massive increase in U.S. defense spending. With the outbreak of the Korean War, NSC-68 became accepted government policy and military spending more than tripled. Only after that conflict turned into a lengthy, bloody stalemate did it become respectable to ask whether this particular form of containment was worth the cost.

It is sometimes argued that, whatever the flaws of NSC-68, the extremity of this document was necessary to win congressional and public support for the basic strategy of containment. In other words, while NSC-68 was a bit too militarized, global, and ideological in scope, such measures were required to prevent a relapse into isolationism. Such arguments do little credit to American democracy. In fact, the American public was strikingly rational and pragmatic in its approach to foreign policy during the late 1940s and was willing to defer to policy-making elites. Had these elites presented the case for a more restrained, practical, and modest form of containment, there is no reason to

assume that Congress or the public would have rejected it out of hand. The real problem by 1950 was that an elite consensus had developed under the lash of the anticommunist attacks of Senator Joseph R. McCarthy (R-Wisconsin). Allowing any communist advance overseas was perceived as not only unacceptable but downright treasonous. Such a consensus robbed policymakers of the ability to distinguish vital and secondary interests. Where elites led, public opinion followed.

The real reason for the adoption of NSC-68 as government policy was not that it represented the most balanced assessment of American security needs at the time but that it suited new budgetary priorities and the new psychological climate of official Washington. Influenced by economic adviser Leon H. Keyserling, Truman had decided early in 1950 to pursue a Keynesian policy of deficit spending, and a major military buildup was well suited to that purpose, regardless of its inherent merits. A series of events in 1949–1950 also led Americans to take an increasingly panicked view of the international situation. The Soviet atomic test of July 1949, the proclamation of the People's Republic of China in September, and the North Korean attack on South Korea in June 1950 seemed to suggest that containment had "failed" to stave off communist expansion. By 1950 the policy of containment had, in fact, achieved great success in balancing the strength of America and its allies against that of the Soviet Union, stabilizing the political and economic situation in Europe, and denying further gains to Soviet influence, all at relatively low cost to the United States. The underlying balance of power had not really altered significantly in 1949–1950; there was no need for a dramatic rethinking of Kennan's basic framework. Unfortunately, by 1950 steady nerves were in short supply, and American policymakers opted for an unnecessarily expensive, universal, and militarized version of containment. Its costs were so great that within three years it was rejected by the incoming Republican president in favor of a more restrained and economical approach.

—COLIN DUECK, PRINCETON UNIVERSITY

Viewpoint:
No, universal containment was not a viable policy option because it led to overextension of resources and to disaster in Vietnam.

A commitment to universal containment was one of the most significant—and ultimately flawed—decisions made by the United States at the onset of the cold war. The consequences of

President Harry S Truman outlining the Truman Doctrine before a joint session of the U.S. Congress, 12 March 1947

(CORBIS/Bettmann)

render the world "safe for democracy." With the world's financial center shifting to New York, Wilson also intended to make the globe safe for American capital.

Coinciding with the posture of "isolationism" that characterized U.S. foreign policy of the 1930s, the Great Depression inspired renewed determination to couple economic internationalism with great-power diplomacy at the end of the Second World War. It would have been out of character for the United States to have approached the cold war with a narrowly confined "realist" agenda. There was evil to confront and markets to reorient in the service of America's preponderant economic power. Consensus had to be mobilized in the customary fashion—through a national crusade. Americans were confident after their victorious campaign in Europe and Asia that theirs was a special destiny, which had given them alone the atomic weapon that had recently been deployed against Japan. Americans believed they had been summoned to achieve nothing less than an American Century.

The United States did not manufacture the cold war, but the nation was culturally predisposed to approach the East-West conflict in a universalist manner. Certainly Washington had legitimate reasons to be concerned about the potential economic, political, and cultural consequences of Soviet-style communism sweeping across Europe and Asia. Most historians agree that the European Recovery Program (also known as the Marshall Plan) was an effective approach to containment and economic recovery in western Europe. Having fought for the liberation of Europe, the United States could hardly have been indifferent to the economic and political turmoil in war-ravaged European states. While the Marshall Plan successfully addressed those concerns, there can be little doubt that U.S. action also helped cement the division of the continent because it did not give aid to the Soviet Union or the communist states of eastern Europe.

Europeans shared a community of interests with, and proved receptive to, U.S. intervention following the war, arguably even to the point of welcoming what Geir Lundestad has called an "empire by invitation." While sharply distinct from the United States in history and culture, Japan was extremely receptive to the models extended under U.S. occupation. U.S. national-security elites thus enjoyed remarkable success in their quest to ensure that postwar Europe and Japan evolved along liberal-capitalist lines.

Universal containment, however, represents a commitment extending far beyond what John Lewis Gaddis calls "strongpoint" regions such as Japan and western Europe. Given the powerful sense of mission, drive for economic supremacy,

crusading U.S. globalism resulted in "imperial overstretch" and undermined such cherished objectives as championing democracy and human rights. Instead, universalist pretensions encouraged militarization and intervention. The debacle in Vietnam was the logical culmination of cold-war universal-containment policy. American national interest would have been better served by a more restrained foreign policy in which the United States led by example and through mobilization of consensus.

Universal containment was less a product of geopolitics than of U.S. cultural imperatives. Central to the issue was the notion of America's "mission" in world affairs. Born of the Puritan quest to build a model "city upon a hill," this mission imperative gained legitimacy through the triumph of the American Revolution against imperial British despotism. Continental aggrandizement—defined as Manifest Destiny—encouraged what Richard Slotkin has called a sense of "chosenness," while confirming the utility of "regeneration through violence" against enemies who were viewed as racially inferior. Industrialization and impressive, though uneven, economic growth fueled the notion of American Protestant exceptionalism. No one better articulated this messianic impulse than President Woodrow Wilson, who, in 1917, justified intervention in the First World War as a crusade to

and penchant for mobilizing domestic consent through grand crusades, Washington could not remain committed to an agenda of such limited geographic and conceptual scope. The quest to undermine communism and promote "one world" dominated by liberal-capitalist values inevitably became global.

The Truman Doctrine, enunciated by President Harry S Truman on 12 March 1947, was not only an early milestone in the cold war, but a universalist manifesto as well. Truman declared in a speech to a joint session of Congress that it "must be the policy of the United States to support free peoples who are resisting attempted subjugation by armed minorities or by outside pressures." Congress readily approved the unelected president's request for $400 million in economic and military aid, an action that underscores the cultural receptivity of the new global mission. While Truman applied these funds to Greece and Turkey, the language he used was universal in scope. The logic of cold-war diplomacy was global intervention to ensure the American "way of life."

Strongpoint containment—according to which U.S. intervention to prevent the spread of Soviet influence should be limited to regions with significant industrial and military potential, such as Japan and western Europe—was not an option. Strongpoint containment not only contravened the universalist mission, but it also was seen as leaving U.S. interests dangerously vulnerable. The shocks of blitzkrieg, Pearl Harbor, total war, and continuing Soviet occupation of eastern Europe had left U.S. officials unwilling to settle for anything less than total security. Any and all regions of the world were seen as vital to U.S. national interests. Greece and Turkey, while hardly "core" urban-industrial states such as Germany or Japan, nonetheless occupied strategically significant positions in the Near East and on the Mediterranean Sea.

U.S. national-security elites also determined that Japan could not anchor containment across the "great crescent" of Asia unless the entire region evolved along liberal-capitalist lines. The universalist commitment to total security provoked a feverish domestic response to the "loss" of China to communism in 1949. By that time Washington had long since committed itself to ensuring an anticommunist—and often neocolonialist—orientation of regimes stretching from the Kurile Islands to Pakistan. Even states that were left outside of what Dean Acheson, secretary of state in 1949–1953, called the U.S. "defense perimeter," notably Korea, would be defended from communism.

The Korean War offers evidence of the supremacy of universal containment over more-limited foreign-policy objectives. Unwilling to accept the communization of Korea in the wake of Mao Tse-tung's triumph in China, the United States invested its blood, wealth, and prestige in the craggy hills of the onetime hermit kingdom. The war succeeded in "containing" communism but failed spectacularly when General Douglas MacArthur expanded the conflict in an effort to "liberate" the entire peninsula, leaving a divided Korea with the northern half under communist control. Ultimately, the war created two artificial states from a single nation, ensured a generation of Sino-American enmity, and wove the fabric of the cold war into the American national consciousness. The implementation of National Security Council memorandum 68 (NSC-68), authorizing a gargantuan "defense" buildup and sanctioning the global crusade against the evils of communism, was perhaps the most enduring legacy of the Korean War.

Throughout the 1950s Washington eschewed negotiations with communist regimes while amassing military force, building alliances, and wielding dominant economic power to anchor the American Century. Intervention, often covert, in the affairs of other nations was an inevitable corollary of empire building. After fomenting coups to establish friendly regimes in Iran (1953) and Guatemala (1954), Washington found its universalist ambitions mired in the swamps of the Bahìa de Cochinos (Bay of Pigs) in Cuba, where a covertly supported invasion by Cuban exiles failed to topple the regime of Fidel Castro. This defeat spurred no second thoughts about universal containment, but rather renewed the commitment of President John F. Kennedy to carry out his inaugural pledge in 1960 to "pay any price, bear any burden" to achieve victory in the cold war.

The subsequent and disastrous American war in Vietnam, waged by the administrations of Kennedy, Lyndon B. Johnson, and Richard M. Nixon, flowed directly from the logic of universal containment. An overextension concluding in a debacle was inevitable. Vietnam, determined to overcome a century of Western colonialism and hospitable to guerrilla resistance, was an especially unfortunate venue. Washington invested more than a decade of effort, billions of dollars, and the lives of 58,000 servicemen—only a fraction of the total casualties in the Indochina conflict—in an ultimately futile effort to prevent a communist regime from assuming power in a Third World nation of dubious strategic significance.

The Vietnam War was a textbook example of what Paul M. Kennedy calls "imperial overstretch"—the inevitable tendency, manifested throughout modern history, of a great power to overextend itself militarily and financially. The war destroyed the promise of Johnson's Great

Society (his strategy to address U.S. domestic issues), left economic "stagflation," and engendered a profound cultural malaise in its aftermath. The conflict, combined with the related Watergate scandal, confirmed the existence of an "imperial presidency" and spurred widespread public distrust of government. While the United States remained the preeminent power in world affairs, universal containment had exacted a high price and left deep scars on the body politic.

None of this argument is meant to suggest that the United States could or should have eschewed world leadership in the postwar era. Given the strength of its economy and the appeal of its democratic idealism, Washington emerged from the Second World War as the dominant power in world affairs. The tragedy is that the United States overinvested in military intervention and power politics. It adopted a missionary approach to world affairs and defined its security in global terms instead of pursuing more rational and geographically limited terms of engagement. By supporting an array of militaristic and dictatorial regimes around the globe, Washington sacrificed some of the appeal of its highly respected tradition of democratic idealism.

While such an assertion can never be proven, it is likely that U.S. economic strength, the allure of its consumer products, and the appeal of its democratic ideals would have gone a long way toward fostering the American Century even without global adventurism. It was precisely these sources of power, rather than intervention in the hallowed name of "national security," that ultimately led to the decline of the world communist movement. If, as seems likely, the national interest could have been served without embracing power politics as the trigger of global intervention, then the U.S. commitment to universal containment ranks as one of the great follies of the postwar era.

–WALTER L. HIXSON, UNIVERSITY OF AKRON

References

John Lewis Gaddis, "Mr. 'X' is Consistent and Right," in *Decline of the West? George Kennan and His Critics,* edited by Martin F. Hertz (Washington, D.C.: Ethics and Public Pol-

icy Center, Georgetown University, 1978), pp. 135–156;

Gaddis, *Strategies of Containment: A Critical Appraisal of Postwar American National Security Policy* (New York: Oxford University Press, 1982);

Gaddis, *We Now Know: Rethinking Cold War History* (New York: Oxford University Press, 1997);

George F. Kennan, "The Sources of Soviet Conduct," as X, *Foreign Affairs,* 25 (July 1947): 566–582;

Paul M. Kennedy, *The Rise and Fall of the Great Powers: Economic Change and Military Conflict from 1500 to 2000* (New York: Random House, 1987);

Melvyn P. Leffler, *A Preponderance of Power: National Security, the Truman Administration and the Cold War* (Stanford, Cal.: Stanford University Press, 1992);

Geir Lundestad, *The American "Empire" and other Studies of U.S. Foreign Policy in a Comparative Perspective* (New York: Oxford University Press, 1990);

Edward Mark, "Mr. 'X' is Inconsistent and Wrong," in *Decline of the West? George Kennan and His Critics,* pp. 157–172;

Ernest R. May, ed., *American Cold War Strategy: Interpreting NSC 68* (Boston: St. Martin's Press, 1993);

Yonosuke Nagai and Akira Iriye, eds., *The Origins of the Cold War in Asia* (New York: Columbia University Press, 1977);

Thomas G. Paterson, *Meeting the Communist Threat: Truman to Reagan* (New York: Oxford University Press, 1988);

Richard Slotkin, *Regeneration through Violence: The Mythology of the American Frontier, 1600–1860* (Middletown, Conn.: Wesleyan University Press, 1973);

Samuel F. Well Jr., "Sounding the Tocsin: NSC-68 and the Soviet Threat," *International Security,* 4 (Fall 1979): 116–158;

William C. Wohlforth, *The Elusive Balance: Power and Perceptions During the Cold War* (Ithaca, N.Y.: Cornell University Press, 1993).

CUBA POLICY

Has U.S. policy toward Fidel Castro in Cuba been prudent and effective?

Viewpoint: Yes, U.S. Cuba policy effectively limited communist expansion in Latin America.

Viewpoint: No, U.S. policy toward Cuba has failed to bring about the downfall of Fidel Castro.

From 1933 until the end of 1959 Cuba was ruled by strongman Fulgencio Batista y Zaldívar—at times directly, after he had arranged for himself to be elected president; at other times indirectly, through puppets and front organizations. In the years immediately after the Second World War, Cuba was ruled by the Auténtico Party, led by Ramón Grau San Martín and Carlos Prío Socarrás. Government corruption and incompetence were rampant, creating public unrest. On 10 March 1952 Batista seized power again. He improved relations with the United States, and direct investment by U.S. businesses in Cuba increased. Batista and his circle of cronies became rich and did little to alleviate poverty, illiteracy, and other ills. Soon, resistance to the government again found expression in strikes, demonstrations, and violence. A guerrilla war expanded in the mountains of eastern Cuba and in small cities in the west.

By the mid 1950s, the 26th of July Movement, led by Fidel Castro, had become the dominant antigovernment force in Cuba. Combining an appeal to nationalism with an emphasis on social justice, the movement attracted many followers. By 1958 the United States was losing its patience with Batista's reluctance to engage in necessary economic and social reforms. In March 1958 the United States imposed an arms embargo on Cuba and called the U.S. ambassador home for consultations. Castro and his followers saw these moves as signals that the United States was withdrawing its support from Batista. The armed struggle intensified, and on 31 December 1958 Batista fled to the Dominican Republic.

When Castro took over the government of Cuba in January 1959, it was not immediately clear that the United States and Cuba were on a collision course. In April 1959 Castro visited the United States, expressing his wishes for friendship, but relations between the two countries began to deteriorate rapidly. In May 1959 Castro nationalized the sugarcane industry, and by late 1959 he had dismissed the more moderate ministers from his cabinet and courted the support of the Cuban Communist Party. In the spring of 1960 Cuba had resumed diplomatic relations with the Soviet Union, and in February 1960 Cuba signed an economic treaty with the Soviets, which was followed by similar agreements with East European countries and China. In June 1960 the Cuban government seized all foreign-owned oil refineries and later that year expropriated all foreign-owned property. During the same period Castro began to accuse the United States of trying to undermine his regime. He claimed that the United States had bombed Havana in October 1959 and that it blew up a ship loaded with weapons in Havana harbor. There was no indication that the United States was involved in either of these incidents, but the leftward turn of the Castro government and its growing friendship with the Soviet Union led President Dwight D. Eisenhower to instruct the CIA on 17 March 1960 to begin training Cuban exiles in Florida for the task of overthrowing the Castro regime. With the approval of President John F. Kennedy, the exiles launched their attack at the Bay of Pigs in April 1961, but poor training and leadership, faulty intelligence, and an underestimation by the CIA of the degree of support Castro enjoyed among the Cuban people led to an easy defeat of the U.S.-sponsored forces by the Cuban military. During the first half of the 1960s the CIA also tried to assassinate Castro and on several occasions came close.

In addition to overt and covert military action the United States cut off all sugar imports from Cuba in July 1960 and later that year imposed a trade embargo on the island nation. In January 1961 diplomatic relations between the two countries were severed. The U.S. policy toward Cuba was set. For the next thirty years the goal was to isolate Cuba economically and politically in order to increase pressure on Castro through domestic shortages, denial of capital and technology, closing access to markets abroad, and disrupting Cuban relations with other countries. There were three purposes for this policy: first, to prevent the establishment of a socialist regime that other countries might want to emulate; second, to deny Castro the wherewithal to assist other revolutionary movements; and third, to increase the cost to the Soviet Union of supporting the Cuban regime.

Viewpoint:
Yes, U.S. Cuba policy effectively limited communist expansion in Latin America.

When Fidel Castro came to power in Cuba at the head of his guerrilla army in January 1959, the U.S. government took an initially positive attitude toward him. The past friendly relationship between the two countries, its geographic proximity to the United States (only ninety miles from Florida), and the lack of any overt Soviet involvement in Castro's successful revolution all pointed to a continued, if stylistically adjusted, alliance between the two countries.

What followed, however, was the swift and complete breakdown in relations, the alignment of Cuba with the Soviet Union, and a series of international crises that brought the world to the brink of nuclear war in the Cuban Missile Crisis, the opening of a new front in the cold war with guerrilla wars being waged across Latin America, and direct Cuban armed intervention in Africa.

Historians question whether this breakdown was inevitable and if U.S. policy toward Castro was prudent and wise. Might alternative U.S. policies have averted the deterioration in relations, and, after the breakdown, was American policy effective in containing Castro?

It may be argued that the breakdown in relations was unavoidable and that U.S. policies were reasonable in light of contemporary experiences and expectations. Furthermore, while no policy is perfect in retrospect, the

effect of the U.S. embargo and containment during the cold war did succeed in its essential goals of isolating and impoverishing Cuba, reducing Castro's utility to the Soviet Union, and marginalizing his role to that of a Soviet puppet and praetorian.

Before 1959 Cuba fell clearly within the U.S. orbit. The Monroe Doctrine of 1823, which warned European powers to stay out of the affairs of the New World, and the vast predominance of U.S. power in the region placed Latin America in general, and Cuba in particular, securely within the American sphere of influence. American investments in Cuba totaled $1.5 billion by 1959, and more than 70 percent of Cuban trade was with the United States. The resorts, casinos, hotels, and beaches of Cuba were the playgrounds of American vacationers. Cuba's substantial middle and upper classes were heavily influenced by American culture, often sending their children to school in the United States. The two societies were close and growing closer.

Throughout most of the 1950s Cuba was ruled by the corrupt military dictator Fulgencio Batista y Zaldívar, who had taken power in a 1952 coup, on the eve of national elections (coincidentally ending the electoral career of a young congressional candidate named Fidel Castro Ruz before it began). While initially supportive, American policy toward Batista underwent periods of profound ambivalence, especially as internal opposition mounted and civil war raged in Cuba throughout the late 1950s. While it applauded Batista's anticommunism, Washington disapproved of his lawlessness and corruption and the increasing instability he provoked in Cuba. Similarly, many in America, such as the editors of *The*

New York Times, saw Castro as an educated, upper-class nationalist, in the Cuban national tradition of José Martí, while others, such as Ambassador Earl E. T. Smith, saw him as a reckless and hostile revolutionary. This uncertainty about the situation in Cuba was reflected by the U.S. arms embargo imposed on Batista during the height of the insurrection.

In foreign relations, however, there was no ambivalence. Cuba and the United States were allies, united by the Rio Treaty (1947). The Americans possessed a major military base at Guantanamo Bay, and Cuba served as an important regional staging area for such American military ventures as the 1954 overthrow of Jacobo Arbenz Guzmán's regime in Guatemala. Cuba was tied militarily to the United States in the cold war.

With Batista's flight from Cuba and Castro's triumphant accession to power on 1 January 1959, the military state fell completely into Castro's hands. Although retaining all real power in his and his loyalists' hands, Castro, who had developed anti-American sentiments as early as the late 1940s, while he was a law student at the University of Havana, was nonetheless prudent enough to appoint to the government many noted moderates, such as Manuel Urrutia Lleó, who was named president. This outward moderation assuaged foreign and domestic fears of radicalism and initially earned Castro widespread praise for his broad-based, energetic, and youthful team.

Castro's closest advisers, his brother Raúl Castro Ruz and Ernesto "Che" Guevara de la Serna, were viscerally anti-American and ideologically committed communists. After his takeover Castro relied heavily on them and, more alarmingly to the Americans, on the cadres of the Cuban Communist Party to infiltrate and control the army and government. Castro quickly banned all political parties except the Communist Party.

Castro further alarmed the Americans with the wave of show trials and executions of his opponents in early 1959. Later that year, Castro's Agrarian Reform Law nationalized American-owned property valued at millions of dollars. Finally, feeling himself domestically secure, Castro purged his moderate allies, appointing former communist Osvaldo Dorticós Torrado as puppet president in July. Castro had embarked on a radical path, and, when his foreign policy began to mirror his domestic radicalism, conflict, and ultimately a showdown, with the United States became unavoidable. Castro's public denunciations of the United States became increasingly ferocious through 1959, and he began exploring

THE CUBAN DEMOCRACY ACT

On 23 October 1992, President George Bush signed into law the Cuban Democracy Act, which specified the following goals:

It should be the policy of the United States—

(1) to seek a peaceful transition to democracy and a resumption of economic growth in Cuba through the careful application of sanctions directed at the Castro government and support for the Cuban people;

(2) to seek the cooperation of other democratic countries in this policy;

(3) to make clear to other countries that, in determining its relations with them, the United States will take into account their willingness to cooperate in such a policy;

(4) to seek the speedy termination of any remaining military or technical assistance, subsidies, or other forms of assistance to the Government of Cuba from any of the independent states of the former Soviet Union;

(5) to continue vigorously to oppose the human rights violations of the Castro regime;

(6) to maintain sanctions on the Castro regime so long as it continues to refuse to move toward democratization and greater respect for human rights;

(7) to be prepared to reduce the sanctions in carefully calibrated ways in response to positive developments in Cuba;

(8) to encourage free and fair elections to determine Cuba's political future;

(9) to request the speedy termination of any military or technical assistance, subsidies, or other forms of assistance to the Government of Cuba from the government of any other country; and

(10) to initiate immediately the development of a comprehensive United States policy toward Cuba in a post-Castro era.

Source: "Title XVII—Cuban Democracy Act of 1992," United States Statutes at Large, volume 106 (Washington, D.C.: U.S. Government Printing Office, 1992), p. 2576.

and expanding contacts with the Soviet Union. The Soviets had dispatched KGB agent Aleksandr Alekseev to Cuba to open contacts, which were followed by a secret, June 1959 rendezvous in Cairo between Guevara and Soviet first deputy premier Anastas Mikoyan. Soviet military advisers and arms began arriving in the summer of 1959, and Castro engaged the Soviets in a series of mili-

CUBA POLICY

tary and trade negotiations to secure for Cuba a sugar market and weapons source other than the United States, with which Castro was already expecting trouble.

Castro also began to export revolution, training Nicaraguan, Dominican, and Haitian guerrillas in Cuba, and helping them to launch disastrous invasions of the Dominican Republic and Nicaragua during the summer of 1959. Although both assaults were swiftly crushed, Castro was becoming a regional security threat.

During this critical first year of Castro's government, the Eisenhower administration was often prickly and critical of Castro, with Ambassador Philip Bonsal filing formal protests about expropriation of the property of U.S. citizens in mid 1959; however, the fundamentals of American policy—a generous sugar quota, favorable trade relations, and nonconfrontation on security issues—remained the foundation of American policy.

In February 1960, however, Castro signed a massive trade deal with the Soviet Union during a visit by Mikoyan to Cuba, and already deteriorating relations between Cuba and the United States took a fatal turn. Miami was filling with Cuban exiles, fleeing the property confiscations and human-rights abuses of Castro's government. Some exiles chose to fight back with commando raids on Cuban ports and shipping. Alarmed by the flow of Soviet arms to Castro, the Central Intelligence Agency (CIA) began backing these commando raids, culminating most spectacularly in the March 1960 explosion in Havana harbor of the French ship *La Coubre,* loaded with imported arms.

With Castro increasing the pace of American property seizures and nationalizations, his constant public excoriation of the United States and its ambassador, and Soviet influence growing daily, the Eisenhower administration finally made the decision in March 1960 to arm and train secretly an exile army to topple Castro. The Soviet Union openly declared its intention to defend the Cuban revolution and signed a military treaty with Castro in July 1960. This agreement was reached against the background of the complete nationalization of the remaining American property, an increase in exile commando raids, and the American cancellation of Cuba's sugar quota. The United States broke off diplomatic relations with Cuba in January 1961.

Could any American policy have averted this breakdown? Given the context of the times, it is doubtful. Castro nurtured a deep anti-Americanism that sprang from resentment of American power and cultural domi-

nance in Cuba. With his youth, his diplomatic inexperience, and his heady intoxication with power, Castro's expectation of conflict with America became a self-fulfilling prophecy. Using the positive incentive of economic support and corrective public criticism, the United States might have influenced a reformist, but pro-American, regime in Cuba. With Castro, however, American economic supports enriched and emboldened him, while American criticism just enraged him.

The open collapse of U.S.-Cuban relations coincided with the inauguration of John F. Kennedy, whose administration approved the existing plans for an exile-army invasion of Cuba. The April 1961 Bay of Pigs invasion was a catastrophe. The principal long-term effect of the badly planned and hesitant invasion was to enable Castro to consolidate his grip on domestic power and to validate his membership in the Soviet bloc, giving the Soviets their first base of operations in the New World.

Castro enthusiastically supported the secret construction and placement of Soviet nuclear-missile facilities in Cuba. The resulting American naval blockade of Cuba in October 1962, and the superpower showdown of the Cuban Missile Crisis ironically completed the transformation of Cuba into a Soviet satellite. Tellingly, Soviet premier Nikita S. Khrushchev never consulted with Castro in the negotiations with the United States, in which the Soviets "blinked" and agreed to withdraw their missiles from Cuba and the United States agreed not to invade Cuba. Although safe from invasion, Castro had become marginalized as an appendage of the Soviet bloc.

American policy toward Cuba in the wake of Castro's alignment with the Soviet Union, and for the duration of the cold war, was to isolate Cuba diplomatically in the Western Hemisphere, to isolate Cuba economically and impoverish it through the use of trade embargo, and to provide military support to those threatened by Cuban-sponsored guerrillas or by direct Cuban armed intervention. Throughout the cold war the effect of these policies was startlingly successful. Castro backed guerrilla attacks on nations ranging from El Salvador and Guatemala to Argentina, but of the dozen guerrilla wars and direct interventions in which he engaged, the Sandinista takeover of Nicaragua was his only decisive success.

The Organization of American States (OAS) expelled Cuba in early 1962 and soon joined the American trade embargo, which dislocated much of the Cuban economy. Castro was forced to seek new markets in the Soviet bloc, and Marxist mismanagement ensured that problems in the Cuban economy were magnified by internal-planning fail-

ures. Castro increasingly depended on the Soviet purchase of his sugar and their supply of oil and machinery, ultimately amounting to a nearly five-billion-dollar annual subsidy. In trading a lucrative dependence on the United States for a poorer one with the Soviet Union, Castro impoverished Cuba, reducing his ability to afford military adventures and marginalizing Cuban economic independence.

Strategically, American policy sought to contain Castro militarily, first by assisting governments targeted by Castro and then by targeting pro-Castro governments. From the intelligence and training offered to the Bolivian government, which captured and executed Guevara in 1967, to the development of the Reagan Doctrine, which resulted in U.S. support for guerrilla wars against such Cuban-backed regimes as the Sandinistas in Nicaragua or the Dergue (or DERG) in Ethiopia, Cuban intervention was checked by countervailing American intervention.

For the Soviet Union, Castro's utility was his willingness to commit Cuban soldiers to distant battlefields, fighting proxy wars against American allies. At the peak of its foreign military involvement in the late 1970s, Cuba had more than fifty thousand troops fighting in Ethiopia and Angola, but nowhere did Cuban intervention decisively settle a conflict. While Cuban intervention did turn the tide of battle in favor of the MPLA in the Angolan civil war in 1975 and in the favor of the Dergue over its Somali and Eritrean rivals in 1977, these victories were notably fleeting.

In the wake of the Soviet invasion of Afghanistan in late 1979, and most dramatically with the adoption of the Reagan Doctrine, the United States and its allies stiffened their resolve and aggressively opposed Cuban intervention. In Central America, the United States supported aggressive efforts by El Salvador and Guatemala to defeat Cuban-supported guerrilla movements, and the United States armed and trained the Contra guerrillas to fight the Cuban-backed Sandinistas in Nicaragua.

In Africa, the Cuban army bogged down defending a series of corrupt and incompetent

Fidel Castro and Nikita Khrushchev embracing during a meeting of the United Nations General Assembly, 20 September 1960

(AP / Wide World Photos)

CUBA POLICY

governments against guerrilla movements sheltered by neighboring states. In Ethiopia, the Eritrean ELF and EPLF pounded the Cuban army, just as UNITA, backed actively by Zaire and South Africa, fought on in Angola. Ultimately, the Cuban presence in Africa became so significant that the 1988 Battle of Cuito-Cuanavale, at which the Cuban/MPLA army defeated the South African/UNITA army, was the largest tank battle ever fought in sub-Saharan Africa.

In the end, however, time caught up to Castro. Lacking the economic base to support his global projection of power independently as the Eastern Bloc began to break up in the late 1980s, Castro was forced to bring his troops home. After Cuban troops left Nicaragua, the Sandinistas risked a democratic election in 1990 and lost. In 1991 the Dergue was ousted in a bloody coup. In Angola the MPLA, propped-up by the oil revenues of Cabinda province, struggles still against UNITA.

The Cuban army returned home to a land made poor by thirty years of Marxist economic mismanagement and western economic embargo. Now a real danger only to those of his own people who dare to disagree with him, Castro's final war is with such enemies as poverty, malnutrition, political dissent, and the breakdown of the Cuban social order.

"There is no substitute for victory," noted General Douglas MacArthur, and by that objective measure, American policy toward Castro should be deemed a success. For more than thirty years, the thrusts of the Soviets' most aggressive praetorian were parried and checked. Although the conflict was objectively unnecessary, it was subjectively necessary for Castro, who picked a fight against the demon of his perceived imperial opponent. While the theater of this conflict allowed Castro to loom large on the world stage for a time, the prudent and wise strategy of the United States left Cuba prostrate and disarmed.

—GRANT M. LALLY, LALLY & LALLY, P.C.

Viewpoint:
No, U.S. policy toward Cuba has failed to bring about the downfall of Fidel Castro.

The U.S. policy toward Cuba is an outdated relic that has acquired sufficient inertia to become one of the most immovable and unalterable elements in American politics. The total embargo of Cuba by the United States began on 3 February 1962 as a reaction to Fidel Castro's moves to establish an increasingly authoritarian and communist regime. Over time the embargo has become a litmus test for a "strong" foreign policy and a source of significant domestic political support in certain key districts. In appealing to conservative anticommunists, liberal human-rights supporters, and politically charged Cuban expatriates, the embargo has become a self-sustaining force in the United States. For all its importance to American politicians, however, the embargo has been a dismal failure at improving the political situation in Cuba and at achieving its original aim of deposing Castro. The time has come for an innovative approach designed to achieve these goals, beginning with an end to this ineffective, counterproductive, and wasteful embargo.

During most of the embargo's existence, the Cuban economy was supported by massive subsidies of about $4.5 billion a year from the Soviet Union, and the embargo was more effective as a symbol than as an instrument of American foreign policy. After the end of the cold war and the collapse of the Soviet Union, American policymakers expected that, with the loss of Soviet aid, the Cuban economy would collapse within a few months. In December 1992 Representative Robert G. Toricelli (D-New Jersey), one of the most fervent embargo advocates, was quoted in the *Los Angeles Times* as saying that the Castro regime would fall "within weeks." Toricelli, who is now a U.S. Senator, was not the first, nor the last, person to prematurely predict Castro's imminent demise. In the years immediately following the end of the cold war, the embargo did have its greatest chance of succeeding. By all accounts Cuba was devastated by the loss of Soviet subsidies. From 1989 to 1993 the Cuban economy shrank by some 40 percent. Oil imports fell by half; spare parts and other materials were in scarce supply. This period was the pivotal moment embargo advocates had been awaiting for thirty years. In an effort to exert maximum pressure on the Cubans, the U.S. Congress passed the Cuban Democracy Act on 15 October 1992. This legislation, which went into effect that December, prohibits foreign-based subsidiaries of American companies from trading with Cuba and places restrictions on vessels carrying freight to the island. It also bars Cuban Americans from sending money to their relatives in Cuba, although exceptions for humanitarian reasons are included.

The impact of the Cuban Democracy Act was fairly significant. By the middle of 1993 the Cuban economy was in desperate need of reform. Embargo advocates had long claimed that Castro's obstinacy would make such reforms impossible. That summer, however, Castro began to implement several measures to try to salvage the Cuban economy. For the first time Cubans were allowed to hold U.S. dollars and shop in dollars-only stores. Self-employment was permitted in more than one hundred occupations. These steps were small, but important. In the short run, however, the Cuban economy continued to decline. Social unrest increased, as did the flow of refugees from Cuba. In 1994 rioting in some cities was reported. Castro reacted swiftly by stepping up internal security measures. He also threatened to lift all measures designed to prevent people from fleeing the island (a warning to the United States). In August 1994 Castro followed through on his threat, and in the one-month period that followed, the U.S. Coast Guard intercepted some thirty-two thousand Cuban refugees trying to reach the United States. The administration of President William J. Clinton reacted by sending the refugees to Guantanamo Bay, the U.S. naval base in Cuba, and negotiating a deal with Castro to halt the flood of refugees. For these and other reasons, foreign-policy analysts saw 1995 as a pivotal year. Either the situation would deteriorate enough to motivate Cubans to rid themselves of Castro, or the economy would turn around.

Supporters of the embargo were disappointed when the Cuban economy did in fact improve. By most estimates the post-cold-war collapse bottomed out in 1994, and some sources even show slight growth. Cuban officials claimed that the economy grew by 2 or 3 percent and forecasted that it would improve by 6 or 7 percent in 1996. This improvement dealt a lethal blow to the hopes of embargo advocates. In the one period when the embargo was most likely to succeed, it failed. With the Cuban economy recovering, the embargo had no chance of ever succeeding. Yet, it remains in place, strengthened by the passage on 12 March 1996 of the Helms-Burton bill, officially called the Cuban Liberty and Democratic Solidarity (Libertad) Act. President Clinton reversed his opposition to portions of the Libertad Act and signed it after Cuba shot down two civilian aircraft belonging to an American-based anti-Castro organization. The political benefits of such actions abound, but they come at the expense of a sound and effective policy toward Cuba. The embargo hurts the Cuban people and American citizens and companies. Even a strengthened embargo cannot succeed.

The U.S. government should lift the restrictions on trade with Cuba for the obvious reason that the embargo has not and will not work. Furthermore, Cuba is no longer able to pose a military threat to U.S. interests, and the embargo directly conflicts, not only with American interests regarding Cuba, but also with U.S. relations to its allies worldwide.

Cuba is receiving enough income from other countries to fuel its recovery. According to the U.S.-Cuba Trade and Economic Council, more than six hundred foreign businesses have offices in Cuba, and Cuba deals with about forty-five hundred businesses in more than one hundred countries. These companies have entered into some 350 joint ventures and economic associations with government-operated companies in Cuba, and by July 1998 foreign investments in Cuba totaled more than $5 billion. In 1998 Cuba also expected 1.4 million tourists to spend some $2 billion.

The two largest investors in Cuba are Canada and Mexico. European companies have also created lucrative businesses in Cuba, exploiting the gap created by the U.S. embargo. Advocates of the embargo reply that the United States should enact measures to penalize allies that trade with Cuba.

There is another, surprising source of income for Cuba—foreign subsidiaries of American companies. The U.S.-Cuba Trade and Economic Council estimated that from 1980 through 1992 legal trade between American-owned foreign subsidiaries and Cuban businesses amounted to $4.56 billion. While the Cuban Democracy Act of October 1992 banned dealings between U.S.-owned foreign subsidiaries and enterprises in the Republic of Cuba, it also provided opportunities for some industries. The number of U.S. businessmen traveling to Cuba grew from more than five hundred in 1994 to more than thirteen hundred in 1995, fifteen hundred in 1996, two thousand in 1997, and about twenty-five hundred in 1998. From 1994 to 1998, under the severest restrictions in the history of the embargo, American firms have conducted $600 million in trade with Cuba. Furthermore, despite limitations on Cuban exiles' gifts of money to relatives in Cuba, an estimated $400 to $500 million has been sent to Cuba each year.

How can embargo advocates think they can curtail foreign trade with Cuba when they cannot even stop all trade between Cuba and their own country? They cannot, and for this reason the embargo will never succeed in creating the economic disaster necessary to drive Castro from office.

As the only remaining great power in the world, the United States balances a wide range of interests. In the context of the cold war, Cuba was strategically important as well as an ideological adversary. An aggressive, communist regime ninety miles off the U.S. coast was a profound danger not only to the Western Hemisphere but also to the world. American policy toward Cuba had to be severe and consistent. In the games-manship of a bipolar world, small events were magnified and big events (most notably the 1962 Cuban Missile Crisis) brought the world to the brink of war.

The end of the cold war and the cessation of Soviet aid to Cuba have drastically altered the strategic importance of that island nation. It is far less a menace than when it was a Soviet client. Cuba's ability to threaten American interests has been reduced to rhetoric and a certain degree of embarrassment that Castro has not been deposed. Cuba no longer supports insurrections in Latin America or Africa, nor could it. According to a 31 March 1998 article in *The Washington Post*, a recent U.S. Defense Department assessment of the Cuban military threat "concluded that the Cuban armed forces have been significantly diminished, that its military is geared toward defending Cuba rather than making offensive moves and that severe shortages of fuel and spare parts have reduced its Soviet-built MIG jet fighter force." Release of the report was delayed because its assessment of the Cuban threat could not be reconciled with a continuation of the Cuban embargo policy. The Libertad Act was justified in part by the argument that Cuba "posed and continues to pose a national security threat to the United States." By the Pentagon's own conclusions, this argument is unfounded.

One might conclude that the failure of the embargo to effect change in Cuba and the disappearance of any Cuban military threat to the United States or its interests would be more than sufficient reasons to reassess the policy. Yet, the embargo lumbers on, pursuing aims that have become obsolete. If the embargo were merely ineffective, its continued existence might be acceptable, but in reality it works directly against American interests. As Wayne Smith, former chief of the U.S. Interests Section in Havana, has said, "Perhaps the most striking thing about U.S. policy toward Cuba is the near-total disjuncture between stated objectives and the means chosen to achieve them. Not only do the means not serve the ends, they seem designed to work against them."

In a global economy the effectiveness of a unilateral embargo will always be questionable. Without some form of international agreement, such embargoes are at best useless and at worst a source of friction between the nation imposing the embargo and its allies. When the Organization of American States (OAS) formally lifted its trade restrictions in 1975, the United States was left as the sole supporter of the Cuban embargo. Recent attempts to strengthen the embargo have led to increased friction between the United States and its important allies around the world. The Cuban Democracy Act of 1992 cut off virtu-ally all forms of financial exchange between the United States and Cuba. Though the Cuban Democracy Act of 1992 has had no noticeable effect on Cuba, it has had significant ramifica-tions around the world. In November 1995 the United Nations examined the legal and ethical nature of the U.S. embargo, and the General Assembly voted 117−3 against it. Only Uzbeki-stan and Israel voted with Washington—and they both trade with Cuba.

The Libertad Act includes two particularly contentious provisions, Titles III and IV. Title III allows American citizens to sue foreign inves-tors who conduct business on property that Cuba seized from Americans, and Title IV bars such foreign investors from obtaining entry visas to the United States. President Clinton has con-sistently suspended implementation of Title III, but officials of three companies have been barred from entering the United States under Title IV. Such actions have engendered much antipathy. The Congressional Research Service has reported that Canada, Japan, Mexico, European Union nations, and many other U.S. allies have been critical of the Libertad Act, contending "that the bill's provisions allowing foreign per-sons to be sued in U.S. courts constitute an extra-territorial application of U.S. law that is contrary to international principles." On 4 June 1996 the OAS approved a resolution opposing the act, ordering the Inter-American Juridical Commit-tee "to examine the legislation." By August the committee had "concluded that the law was not in conformity with international law."

At the same time Canada and the European Union lodged protests and threatened counter-measures in retaliation to any American actions under the law. The willingness of the U.S. gov-ernment to cause harm to its relationships with vital allies in pursuit of a doomed embargo raises serious questions about the soundness of U.S. foreign policy.

With regard to Cuba in particular, American goals generally fall into two areas. The United States does not want a dramatic increase in the number of Cuban refugees entering American territory. It also wants Cuba to undergo a peace-ful transition into a liberal and capitalist society. The embargo, paradoxically, works against both these aims. If the United States could actually coerce its allies into joining the embargo, thus making it achieve its stated purpose, the eco-nomic devastation in Cuba would likely unleash a flood of refugees to American shores. As for the second goal, Smith asserted in 1998 that Cas-tro will never "retire quietly and give up without a fight." In fact, writes Smith, "He would fight and a good percentage of the Cuban population and armed forces would fight with him. The result would be massive bloodshed, perhaps even

CUBA POLICY

civil war—with tens if not hundreds of thousand of refugees on our shores and intense pressures on the United States to intervene to stop the fighting. Intervention, however, could result in thousands of U.S. casualties." Instead, Smith asserts, "The objective should be a peaceful transitional process with or without Castro."

The embargo is, in effect, a lose-lose proposition for the United States. If successful, it would almost certainly lead to bloodshed, increased refugee displacement, and the involvement of American troops. If it never succeeds, it will continue to be an obstacle to the peaceful improvement of the Cuban economic, political, and human-rights situation.

Cuba has already achieved some significant reforms. While some embargo advocates cite these reforms as proof that the embargo is working, it actually serves as an obstacle to the success of these measures and the possibility of future reforms. In 1998 Cuba officially reinstated Christmas as a holiday after nearly thirty years. This change is the latest in a series of steps that has brought Cuba and the Catholic Church closer together. While limited in scope, these reforms stem from the constructive approach the Vatican has taken in engaging Castro and represent important concessions for the religious freedom of the Cuban people. It should come as little surprise that the Vatican is among the opponents of the U.S. trade embargo.

Beyond these social reforms, the Castro regime has undertaken economic measures that most Cuba experts believed it would never make, particularly those centered on integrating the Cuban economy into the global market. While it cuts off Cuba from its most logical trading partner, the embargo does not prevent other nations from benefiting from these reforms. In the 25 September 1997 issue of the *Christian Science Monitor,* Howard La Franchi reported that Cuba must make the transition to the global economy "without the giant market—the U.S.—that helped make it the second wealthiest country in Latin America before the 1959 revolution." He also noted Cuban complaints about this situation, quoting the assistant director of the Center for Research on the World Economy in Havana as saying, "We now have to go thousands of miles to sell products that without the embargo could be selling just 100 miles away. . . . That's a big extra cost." Embargo advocates would say the embargo is meant to have this kind of effect, but they are missing the larger point. The embargo does not prevent Cuba from trading, but it hinders Cuba's ability to integrate itself effectively into the world economy. In doing so, the embargo works directly against one of its stated aims—a more economically liberal Cuba.

The embargo cuts American firms out of a lucrative market they would otherwise be able to dominate and prevents American citizens from enjoying Cuban goods or tourism. In the words of Elizard Sanchez, a leading Cuban human-rights activist, "If you want to let some light into the island, then don't keep trying to keep all the windows shut." He argues that "the more American citizens on the streets of Cuban cities, the better for the cause of a more open system." The embargo forces the nation that once dominated 80 percent of the Cuban economy to watch from the sidelines as others reap the benefits that Americans once enjoyed. American tourists are deprived of experiencing the many pleasures of Cuba. A Johns Hopkins University study in the early 1990s estimated that resumed trade between the United States and Cuba would initially be worth around $2 billion and perhaps even more in subsequent years.

For thirty-seven years the United States has maintained its embargo on Cuba. The end of the cold war has served only to strengthen the embargo. Yet, despite the efforts of its supporters, the object of the embargo remains in power. During the cold war, Soviet subsidies sustained the Cuban economy and prevented the embargo from having any significant effect. With the end of the cold war trade with the rest of the world has replaced Soviet aid, and the embargo remains ineffective. For a brief moment following the end of Soviet subsidies, the embargo might have succeeded. But it did not, and now that moment has passed. Today the embargo serves only domestic political concerns while denying American businesses and the American people the ability to engage with Cuba and its people. Furthermore, the strengthening of the embargo through laws such as the Cuban Democracy Act have damaged relations with vital allies and diminished America's global influence. The embargo has been proven, by time and circumstance, to be utterly incapable of forcing the removal of Fidel Castro. In fact, it is argued that the best way to bring pressure to bear on the Castro regime is to open access to the island. Increased interaction with the United States and increased prosperity for the Cuban people would naturally lead to calls for greater freedoms and economic reforms. Castro has proven and continues to prove the impotence of the trade embargo. Rather than continue under such a legacy of failure, the United States should revisit its policy toward Cuba and act on the interests of American business, American consumers, and the Cuban people.

–JAMES REYNOLDS

CUBA POLICY

References

Jon Lee Anderson, *Che Guevara: A Revolutionary Life* (New York: Grove, 1997);

Andrew Bacevich, "Crazy Over Cuba," *National Interest,* 54 (Winter 1998/1999): 98–103;

Jules R. Benjamin, *The United States and the Origins of the Cuban Revolution: An Empire of Liberty in an Age of National Liberation* (Princeton, N.J.: Princeton University Press, 1990);

Leslie Bethell, ed., *Cuba: A Short History* (New York: Cambridge University Press, 1993);

Jorge G. Castañeda, *Compañero, The Life and Death of Che Guevara,* translated by Marina Castañeda (New York: Knopf, 1997);

Juan M. del Aguila, *Cuba, Dilemmas of a Revolution,* third edition (Boulder, Colo.: Westview, 1994);

Jorge Domínguez, *To Make the World Safe for Revolution: Cuba's Foreign Policy* (Cambridge, Mass.: Harvard University Press, 1989);

Georgie Anne Geyer, *Guerrilla Prince: The Untold Story of Fidel Castro* (Boston: Little, Brown, 1991);

Serge Kovaleski, "It's Christmas in Cuba," *Washington Post,* 2 December 1998;

Howard LaFranchi, "America's Embargo of Cuba: What Result After 35 Years?" *Christian Science Monitor,* 25 September 1997;

Carmelo Mesa-Lago, *Cuba after the Cold War* (Pittsburgh: University of Pittsburgh Press, 1993);

Andres Oppenheimer, *Castro's Final Hour: The Secret Story Behind the Coming Downfall of Communist Cuba* (New York: Simon & Schuster, 1992);

Thomas G. Paterson, *Contesting Castro: The United States and the Triumph of the Cuban Revolution* (New York: Oxford University Press, 1994);

Louis A. Pérez Jr., *Cuba and the United States: Ties of Singular Intimacy* (Athens: University of Georgia Press, 1990);

Dana Priest, "U.S. Report Delayed on Lack of Cuban Military Threat," *Washington Post,* 31 March 1998, p. A13;

Geoff Simons, *Cuba: From Conquistador to Castro* (New York: St. Martin's Press, 1996);

Earl E. T. Smith, *The Fourth Floor: An Account of the Castro Communist Revolution* (New York: Random House, 1962);

Wayne B. Smith, *Cuba After the Cold War,* International Policy Report, (Washington, D.C.: Center for International Policy, March 1993);

Smith, "Isn't It About Time for Washington to Accept That Castro Is in Power?" *Los Angeles Times,* 14 January 1996, p. 2;

Smith, *Wanted: A Logical Cuba Policy,* International Policy Report (Washington, D.C.: Center for International Policy, February 1998);

Jaime Suchlicki, *Cuba: From Columbus to Castro and Beyond,* fourth edition, revised and updated (Washington, D.C.: Brassey's, 1997);

Mark P. Sullivan, *Cuba: Issues for Congress* (Washington, D.C.: Congressional Research Service, Library of Congress, 2 December 1996);

John P. Sweeney, *Why the Cuban Trade Embargo Should Be Maintained,* Backgrounder, no. 1010 (Washington, D.C.: Heritage Foundation, 10 November 1994);

U.S. Information Agency, *Chronology of U.S.-Cuban Relations, 1958–1998* (Washington, D.C.: U.S. Government Printing Office, 1998);

U.S.-Cuba Trade and Economic Council, *Realities of Market Cuba* (August 1998).

DÉTENTE

Was détente a success?

Viewpoint: Yes, détente was a success because it reduced tensions and helped to end the cold war.

Viewpoint: No, détente was a failure because the United States and the Soviet Union never agreed on its fundamental meaning.

President Richard M. Nixon took office during the height of U.S. involvement in the Vietnam War. Public opposition to the war was growing, as was public discomfort with expensive and demanding foreign entanglements. Nixon chose Henry Kissinger as his national security adviser. As a Harvard professor in the 1950s and 1960s, Kissinger had criticized U.S. reliance on massive nuclear retaliation and pointed out the dangers attending to the pursuit of ideological "crusades" and total war in the nuclear age.

The term *détente* is used by historians to describe periods of relaxation of tensions between states. The détente Nixon and Kissinger launched was a response to the perceived decline in U.S. power, the rise in Soviet power, and the dangers of uncontrolled competition between the two nations. For the United States, détente had two purposes: first, to turn the Soviet Union from a revolutionary power bent on subverting the international order into a status-quo power with a stake in that order; and second, to find a way to regulate the nuclear-arms race.

With roots going back to President Franklin Delano Roosevelt's belief in a cooperative relationship with the Soviet Union and an always-present strain of thought in the American (and Western) political spectrum, détente was initially welcomed by the American public when it was launched in earnest in the early 1970s. The Soviet Union, however, appeared not to have moderated its foreign-policy conduct to the extent that many were led to believe it would. Also détente entailed trade-offs that many Americans found distasteful, such as the administration's reluctance to criticize human-rights violations by the Soviet authorities. The anti-détente forces gathered strength within the Republican party, coalescing around the stiff challenge of California governor Ronald W. Reagan to President Gerald R. Ford in the 1976 Republican primaries. Opposition to détente also had strong resonance in the Democratic Party, finding a champion in Washington senator Henry M. Jackson, who lost the 1976 presidential nomination race to Georgia governor Jimmy Carter. As president, Carter continued to pursue détente policies for a while, but with the Soviet invasion of Afghanistan in December 1979 the détente decade came to a close.

President Reagan continued to resist détente as a policy through much of his administration and even adopted policies designed to harm the Soviet Union economically and militarily, but by late 1986 changing Soviet attitudes under the leadership of Mikhail Gorbachev allowed détente to be renewed. In the last two years of the Reagan administration, and during the détente-oriented administration of George W. Bush, several agreements on arms control, human rights, and greater commercial and diplomatic ties gave the policy of cooperation a new chance.

Viewpoint:
Yes, détente was a success because it reduced tensions and helped to end the cold war.

In assessing whether détente in the cold war was a success, one must bear in mind that it is a multifaceted concept. Détente, a relaxation of tensions, has been a recurring historical fact, but it is also a perceived phenomenon, and public perception of it has not always corresponded to the objective reality. Détente is also a process as well as a state of international relations, and it affects internal as well as foreign relations. Finally, at times détente has been a policy objective. To be sure, a state may pursue détente; even adversaries may both pursue a relaxation of tensions, but they may not succeed. Objective foundations for détente may not exist, or subjective evaluations of the prospects for détente may be in error. Hence, in either case a policy of détente may not succeed. Furthermore, even when a relaxation of tensions can be or is achieved, détente as a policy objective may be overridden and discarded because of perceived security requirements with a higher priority. On the other hand, a détente in relations between adversaries may occur without having been pursued as a deliberate policy, although obviously it cannot occur if either adversary's policy is against détente.

During the cold war there were alternating intensifications and relaxations of East-West tensions. In one sense, neither détente nor confrontation "succeeded"—or failed—as each was reborn. Indeed, there were four periods of détente in the cold war. After the death of Joseph Stalin, the end of the Korean War in 1953, and the 1955 peace treaty that led to the withdrawal of foreign troops from Austria, the four-power East-West summit meeting in Geneva in 1955 gave rise to the Spirit of Geneva, the first cold-war détente. After Soviet leader Nikita Khrushchev, who had denounced Stalin, visited President Dwight D. Eisenhower in 1959, this first détente became known as the Spirit of Camp David (named for the presidential retreat in Maryland where they had conferred). This period of relative calm was ended by renewed tensions over Berlin, the shooting down of a U.S. U-2 reconnaissance aircraft over the Soviet Union in May 1960, and the Cuban Missile Crisis in October 1962. Soon after the missile crisis, however, a second détente gave rise to the Limited Nuclear Test Ban Treaty (LTBT), the U.S.-Soviet "hot line," and other steps in a relaxation of tensions.

After the intensification of the war in Vietnam, Warsaw Pact intervention in Czechoslovakia in 1968, and other sources of renewed tension in the late 1960s, a third détente followed in the early 1970s. When most analysts refer to cold-war détente, they are talking about this period. The earliest steps toward détente were taken by the West Europeans, first the French and then the Germans. The United States joined the effort in part to preserve a Western consensus. During the 1970s East-West bilateral meetings of leaders, five Soviet-American summits, and an all-European summit conference on security and cooperation accomplished many political agreements, including the first Strategic Arms Limitation Talks (SALT) agreement in 1972. There also was a growing normalization of trade, travel, and other relations between East and West, especially in Europe.

This "classic" cold-war détente declined in the late 1970s after renewed confrontations in the Third World and an intensification of the strategic-arms race. It finally collapsed after Soviet military intervention in Afghanistan at the end of 1979. The "decade of détente" had ended, and détente had failed (above all, in American eyes).

One important reason for the decline and fall of détente in the late 1970s, especially the U.S. policy of détente, was the discrepancy between the reality of continuing competition and the Nixon administration's overblown image of détente as "building a structure of peace." President Richard M. Nixon and his national security adviser, Henry Kissinger, were fully aware of the reality and "waged" détente vigorously to gain advantage in the global competition with the Soviet Union. They did not acknowledge this fact, however, and could not control adverse public reaction when the Soviet leaders sought to do the same, both by intervening in the Third World and by keeping up the arms race. Blame was attributed not only to the Soviet leaders but also to the policy of détente, especially in the Ford and Carter administrations.

Heightened tensions in the early 1980s led some to refer to a new or "second cold war," although it was really a continuation of the cold war that had waxed and waned since the late 1940s. The fourth and final period of détente came in the mid and late 1980s, with renewed summitry (five meetings of the U.S. and Soviet leaders during the last four years of the Reagan administration) and the achievement of new arms-reduction agreements. Although more progress toward reducing tensions was made during these years than during any of the preceding détentes, the United States studiously avoided calling this period a détente, owing to the bad name the word had acquired in influential circles. At that point the pattern of the cold war was broken, and the undeclared détente of 1985–1988 was succeeded in 1989–1990 not by renewed tension, but by a phenomenon that transcended détente: the end of the cold war.

Why did the détente of the 1980s succeed (apparently), while those of the 1950s, 1960s and 1970s had failed? Could an earlier détente have succeeded if it had been pursued more vigorously, as Deborah Larson contended in 1997? Or was the cold war brought to an end not as a development of the détente of the mid 1980s but as a result of President Reagan's hard-line policies in the early 1980s? Could the cold war have ended earlier not with greater efforts at détente, but with more vigorous competition and confrontation, as John Lewis Gaddis argued in 1997?

Although scholars differ, there is a growing consensus that the cold war rested on a foundation of ideological beliefs in ineluctable conflict, held by successive Soviet leaders from Stalin to Mikhail Gorbachev, and a reactive Western belief in an inescapable need to contain the Soviet expansive impulses fueled by those ideological beliefs. The cold war, to be sure, had dynamic geopolitical and geostrategic dimensions, and it was waged by both sides with a wide variety of means and specific objectives. It was marked by shifts in perceptions and policies within constraints of a common nuclear danger, leading to alternating periods of détente and confrontation, but always within an adversarial framework.

By the early 1980s Americans, in particular, generally viewed détente as a failure because it had not succeeded in bringing a lasting relaxation of tensions. Yet, détente was never an alternative to the cold war; détente was a less belligerent way to wage that conflict. In effect, détente was a palliative, reducing the dangers of confrontation and building on those elements of the adversaries' common interest

(above all, survival) that were never completely absent. Détente was also a continuing competition between rivals. There probably were missed opportunities for relaxation of some tensions, but those adherents and opponents of détente who saw it as a way to end the cold war were operating under a misconceived notion of the policy. Of course, détente failed to do what it never could have done and should never have been expected to do. Yet, it did ameliorate the dangers and costs, both societal and political, of the cold war while maintaining containment and deterrence.

A principal reason for the recurrent failures of détente during the cold-war decades was that the underlying suspicions and fears of the adversary could not be dispelled and were used by opponents of détente to discredit it for failing to do what it should never have been expected to do. Détente was vulnerable not because it caused real weakness, but because it could not (on either side) dispel the fears of the enemy.

In recognizing that the fundamental underpinning of the cold war was a reciprocated ideological belief in unavoidable conflict between two armed camps with different ideologies and political systems, historians can now see that the only way the mold could have been broken was by a Soviet leader's decisive recognition that the Marxist-Leninist-Stalinist ideological worldview was fundamentally flawed and must be discarded. Only then could Soviet and Western policymakers undertake through deeds, as well as declarations, to bring the cold war to an end.

Gorbachev brought such recognition to Soviet policy and deeds. After a cautious initial reception,

Presidents Leonid I. Brezhnev and Richiard M. Nixon toasting their agreement to the SALT I Treaty during their May 1972 summit meeting in Moscow

(CORBIS/Bettmann)

his overtures were reciprocated by Presidents Reagan and George Bush and other Western leaders in the late 1980s. It was that process—not the hard-line policies of the first Reagan administration or the undeclared transitional détente of the second—that led to the dismantling of the arms race, to the end of the division of Germany and Europe, and to the demise of the cold war by 1990 (even before the disintegration of the Soviet Union). As a relaxation of tensions within an adversarial framework of ideologically grounded worldviews, détente could not bring the cold war to an end, but that was not the true measure of its value.

Détente was a success in three important respects. First, it helped to keep the cold war from getting too "cold" or becoming a "hot" war. The second success of détente was its role in keeping alive the aspirations of people in eastern Europe and the Soviet Union who sought greater freedom. They valued the greater East- West contact fostered under détente. Although American political declarations of "bridge building" to the East in the 1960s and 1970s touched on this theme, the greatest achievements were contacts between eastern and western Europe and institutions in the framework of the Conference on Security and Cooperation in Europe (CSCE), which survives today as the Organization for Security and Cooperation in Europe (OSCE).

The most important success of détente, however, was its contribution to the gradual transformation of thinking in the Soviet Union that led to abandonment of the Marxist-Leninist ideological worldview, which posited an inevitable conflict between two contending worlds. This vitally important contribution of détente is still too-little recognized, but historians of the cold war are becoming increasingly aware of it by benefit of hindsight and greater information from declassified archives.

The lowered barriers to access to printed materials and the greater opportunity for travel and personal contacts under conditions of détente during the cold war, particularly in the 1970s, broadened the understanding of many Soviet officials, intellectuals, and other members of the Moscow establishment. Aleksandr N. Yakovlev, one of Gorbachev's key advisers, had been influenced by his experience as a graduate exchange student at Columbia University in the 1960s. So was Oleg Kalugin, a KGB intelligence officer and a notable early liberal "internal defector." Gorbachev himself was influenced by private travel in the early 1970s in France and Italy. Moscow institutes not only purveyed the official Soviet "line" to the West, but conveyed a much more nuanced and sophisticated picture of the West to Soviet leaders (and future Soviet leaders) in the 1970s and early 1980s. Official U.S. and other Western thinking on deterrence and strategic stability, as well as unofficial Western thinking on "nonoffensive" defense concepts and force structures,

for example, had a significant influence on the "new thinking" of the Gorbachev era. The access and exchanges afforded by détente significantly contributed to such developments.

Détente succeeded in playing a useful if limited role during the cold war, even though it failed to meet misconceived higher hopes. The most lasting success of détente, however, was its significant indirect role in helping to pave the way for the end of the cold war.

—RAYMOND L. GARTHOFF, BROOKINGS INSTITUTION

Viewpoint:
No, détente was a failure because the United States and the Soviet Union never agreed on its fundamental meaning.

Détente was a failure because the two superpowers never came to any agreement on the fundamental meaning of détente. On the American side, it was viewed as a means of reconciling the Soviet Union to the existing international order. President Richard M. Nixon and his national security adviser (later secretary of state) Henry Kissinger sought to "manage" Soviet behavior through the selective use of rewards and punishments, giving Moscow a stake in the existing international system and discouraging it from further expansion. Nixon and Kissinger hoped that habits of mutual restraint would evolve from this process of "linkage." Kissinger, in particular, also hoped that Moscow would eventually come to see itself as an established, or status quo, power with an interest in international stability.

Curiously, Kissinger had written his doctoral dissertation years earlier on the subject of diplomacy between revolutionary and status quo powers in nineteenth-century Europe. In that work he argued that Anglo-Austrian efforts to reconcile France were crucial to the success of the European Concert (an informal association of European monarchs)—but only after Napoleon's revolutionary regime had been defeated militarily. Kissinger may have come to believe that the Soviet Union of the 1970s was more akin to Restoration France than to Napoleonic France, but the Soviet Union remained a self-consciously revisionist power under the leadership of Leonid Brezhnev and would not be reconciled to Kissinger's design.

Like their American counterparts, Soviet policymakers had an interest in minimizing the risks of nuclear war. They also had a keen interest in countering Chinese influence, entrenching strategic parity with the United States, and gaining Western trade and technology. They had little interest, however, in joining the United States in defense of the international status quo. The Soviets were quite candid about their conception of détente: the arena of superpower cooperation would be expanded within an overarching framework of political and ideological struggle. Outside explicit oases of agreement, the conflict between capitalism and socialism would inevitably continue. In particular, it would continue in the developing world, through national liberation struggles aided by the Soviet Union and its allies.

Leonid I. Brezhnev and his advisers believed that the international balance of power—or the "correlation of forces," as they called it—was shifting in their favor. Moscow's nuclear deterrent made direct military aggression by the West unthinkable; socialist revolution could be promoted in the developing world without fear of nuclear war. Through détente Soviet policymakers sought recognition from the United States of their equal status in the international system. They also sought and expected further expansion of Soviet influence abroad. Their acceptance of détente did not indicate any recognition of an international status quo. If anything, it indicated a hope that the seeming decline of American power could be managed smoothly and peacefully.

Over the course of the 1970s, a series of crises revealed the lack of any agreement over the core meaning of détente. For the most part they were triggered by the extension of Soviet influence, arms, and aid to regions hitherto dominated by the United States and its allies. First in Angola and Mozambique, then in South Yemen, and finally in Afghanistan, the Soviet Union and Cuba acted to establish and support friendly communist regimes. Again, such active support of revolutionary activity in the developing world was entirely compatible with the Soviet conception of détente; Moscow had never made any secret of that. American policymakers, however, felt betrayed by these acts of Soviet expansion and responded with anger and resistance while questioning Soviet motives. In fact, the United States had no intention of letting the Soviets play an equal role in affairs outside eastern Europe. Kissinger, for example, did everything possible to shut the Soviets out of the Middle East, with considerable success. While the United States claimed the right to exclude Soviet influence from Latin America, it had no qualms about aiding armed rebels in Afghanistan, a nation bordering the Soviet Union.

Changes in the governments of Angola or Afghanistan might not alter dramatically the global balance of power, but such conflicts were symbolic of the larger struggle between the superpowers. By the 1970s the Soviet Union had built a blue-water navy capable of giving American naval authorities serious cause for concern. Moscow had began projecting its influence into traditional Western preserves. Soviet expansionism seemed to be on the

KISSINGER ON DÉTENTE

On 19 June 1972, Assistant to the President for National Security Affairs Henry Kissinger went before the U.S. Senate to explain the Nixon administration foreign policy in regard to the Soviet Union and progress in the arms-limitation talks. During this briefing Kissinger made the following remarks:

The President . . . decided that the United States should work to create a set of circumstances which would offer the Soviet leaders an opportunity to move away from confrontation through carefully prepared negotiations. From the first, we rejected the notion that what was lacking was a cordial climate for conducting negotiations.

Past experience has amply shown that much heralded changes in atmospherics, but not buttressed by concrete progress, will revert to previous patterns, at the first subsequent clash of interests.

We have, instead, sought to move forward across a broad range of issues so that progress in one area would add momentum to the progress of other areas.

We hoped that the Soviet Union would acquire a stake in a wide spectrum of negotiations and that it would become convinced that its interests would be best served if the entire process unfolded. We have sought, in short, to create a vested interest in mutual restraint.

At the same time, we were acutely conscious of the contradictory tendencies at work in Soviet policy. Some factors—such as the fear of nuclear war; the emerging consumer economy, and the increased pressures of a technological, administrative society—have encouraged the Soviet leaders to seek a more stable relationship with the United States. Other factors—such as ideology, bureaucratic inertia, and the catalytic effect of turmoil in peripheral areas—have prompted pressures for tactical gains.

The President has met each of these manifestations on its own terms, demonstrating receptivity to constructive Soviet initiatives and firmness in the face of provocations or adventurism. He has kept open a private channel through which the two sides could communicate candidly and settle matters rapidly. The President was convinced that agreements dealing with questions of armaments in isolation do not, in fact, produce lasting prohibitions on military competition because they contribute little to the kind of stability that makes crises less likely. In recent months, major progress was achieved in moving toward a broad-based accommodation of interests with the USSR, in which an arms limitation agreement could be a central element.

Source: "Congressional Briefing by Dr. Henry A. Kissinger," Congressional Record, 92nd Congress, 2nd Session, 118 (1972), part 17: 21307.

rise. Whatever their interest in détente, American policymakers had no intention of surrendering their hegemonic position in the international system to this self-described challenger. Nixon and Kissinger might admit Soviet nuclear parity, but in

DÉTENTE

practice they would not permit the Soviet Union to play a political role in regional affairs on par with that of the United States. Many leading Americans were unreconciled even to admitting nuclear parity. Impressive summitry could not conceal the fact that the two superpowers had agreed on no common code of conduct, or rules of the game, by which to regulate and moderate superpower rivalry in the developing world. At its heart the underlying political, military, and ideological rivalry between the two nations was simply too intractable to allow for any grand reconciliation through détente. Both sides would have preferred such reconciliation, but disagreed on its terms.

Managing détente successfully would have been an almost impossible challenge under any circumstances, but it should be added that the American political system in the 1970s was especially unlikely to sustain such a policy. The traditional American distaste for realpolitik is often mentioned as one cause of the failure of détente. Beyond that, the Vietnam War had shattered the cold-war foreign-policy consensus of the 1950s, and presidents from Nixon to Jimmy Carter had to deal with stinging attacks from both left and right. To liberals, détente seemed immoral, an excuse used to justify supporting right-wing dictators and a thin disguise for the old mentalities of the cold war; to conservatives, it seemed a sellout, offering too much to the Soviet Union without much benefit in return. Congressional critics complicated the process of "linkage" by censuring the Soviets on trade, emigration, arms control, and human rights, while simultaneously cutting domestic defense spending. By 1976 détente had become sufficiently unpopular that Ford refused to use the word in his campaign appearances. The policy suffered a lingering death over the next three or four years. Carter was ambivalent about its merits, preferring to emphasize human rights, a theme that could only alienate Soviet leaders. By the end of 1979, with the Soviet invasion of Afghanistan, Carter returned to a more traditional cold-war view of Soviet intentions and committed his administration to the reassertion of American military strength. Ronald W. Reagan's election in 1980 only confirmed and amplified this trend.

As frustrating as these domestic political complications were from Moscow's perspective, the critics of détente were on to something. Only a radical change in the nature of the Soviet regime would lead to a corresponding change in Soviet foreign policy. Only with the collapse of communism was there even a chance that Russia might become reconciled to the legitimacy of the existing international order. Beyond that, however, the critics of détente turned out to be right about something else: that America's relative decline in the international system was not inevitable. In fact, the United States was never as weak, and the Soviet Union never as strong, as policymakers of the 1970s

believed. The experience of Vietnam had encouraged a period of withdrawal and consolidation, but in the long run the United States was unlikely to accept the continued expansion of Soviet influence. In this sense, détente rested on a flawed perception of the relative strength of the two superpowers; a misperception that was sharply corrected over the course of the 1980s.

–COLIN DUECK, PRINCETON UNIVERSITY

References

S. R. Ashton, *In Search of Détente: The Politics of East-West Relations Since 1945* (New York: St. Martin's Press, 1989);

Mike Bowker and Phil Williams, *Superpower Détente: A Reappraisal* (London: Royal Institute of International Affairs / Newbury Park, Cal.: SAGE Publications, 1988);

Michael B. Froman, *The Development of the Idea of Détente: Coming to Terms* (New York: St. Martin's Press, 1991);

John Lewis Gaddis, *We Now Know: Rethinking Cold War History* (New York: Oxford University Press, 1997);

Raymond L. Garthoff, *Détente and Confrontation: American-Soviet Relations from Nixon to Reagan,* revised edition (Washington, D.C.: Brookings Institution, 1994);

Garthoff, *The Great Transition: American-Soviet Relations and the End of the Cold War* (Washington, D.C.: Brookings Institution, 1994);

Kjell Goldmann, *Change and Stability in ForeignPolicy: The Problems and Possibilities of Détente* (Princeton, N.J.: Princeton University Press, 1988);

Fred Halliday, *The Making of the Second Cold War* (London: Verso, 1983);

Henry Kissinger, *White House Years* (Boston: Little, Brown, 1979);

Kissinger, *Years of Upheaval* (Boston: Little, Brown, 1982);

Deborah Welch Larson, *Anatomy of Mistrust: U.S.-Soviet Relations during the Cold War* (Ithaca, N.Y.: Cornell University Press, 1997);

Robert S. Litwak, *Détente and the Nixon Doctrine: American Foreign Policy and the Pursuit of Stability, 1969-1976* (New York: Cambridge University Press, 1984);

Keith L. Nelson, *The Making of Détente: Soviet-American Relations in the Shadow of Vietnam* (Baltimore: Johns Hopkins University Press, 1995);

William Curti Wohlforth, *The Elusive Balance: Power and Perceptions During the Cold War* (Ithaca, N.Y.: Cornell University Press, 1993).

FINLANDIZATION

Could a "Finland" status have been attained for some eastern and central European states?

Viewpoint: Yes, some eastern and central European states could have remained neutral like Finland.

Viewpoint: No, Soviet insecurities and historical conditions made it unlikely that the Soviet Union would have agreed to a Finland status for eastern and central European countries.

Finland became independent from Russia in 1917, but relations with Russia (and its successor, the Soviet Union) remained uneasy. In 1939, following the signing of the Nazi-Soviet Nonaggression Pact (also known as the Molotov-Ribbentrop Pact), in which the Baltic states of Lithuania, Latvia, and Estonia were given to the Soviet Union, the Soviets invaded eastern Finland. In the Winter War that ensued, the outnumbered Finns fought courageously, but in March 1940 they were forced to cede a large area of southeastern Finland to the Soviets in the Treaty of Moscow. When Germany invaded the Soviet Union in June 1941, the Finns resumed hostilities, hoping to reclaim the territory they had lost earlier. Finland also adopted a pro-German foreign policy, and Finnish president Risto Ryti refused to change his position even as the tide of the Second World War turned against Germany.

Finland emerged from the war with its freedom of action in foreign policy and defense matters curtailed. Although independent, Finland was within the Soviet sphere of influence, leading it to sign a treaty with the Soviet Union in which it promised to remain neutral in the struggle between East and West. Finland did not join the European Recovery Plan (the Marshall Plan), the North Atlantic Treaty Organization (NATO), or other initiatives or organizations that the Soviets deemed hostile.

Soviet influence on Finnish foreign and defense policy led to the coining of the term *Finlandization,* to distinguish such indirect domination from the Red Army's occupation of countries such as Poland, Czechoslovakia, and Hungary. During the cold war U.S. policymakers often suggested that, if the United States were to waver in its support of countries threatened by the Soviet Union, these countries might decide to "Finlandize," that is, settle for a compromise with the Soviets that would have allowed them to retain their domestic freedoms in exchange for neutrality in foreign policy and defense issues.

Viewpoint:
Yes, some eastern and central European states could have remained neutral like Finland.

From the end of the Second World War until the late 1980s six eastern European countries—Poland, Czechoslovakia, Hungary, Romania, Bulgaria, and East Germany—were completely dominated by the Soviet Union (as were Yugoslavia until 1948 and Albania until 1968), emulating the Soviet model in their domestic, political, and economic practices. This result was not a foregone conclusion in 1945. At least some of the six Soviet-bloc nations might, under certain circumstances, have struck out in a different direction, one more similar to the path followed by Finland or Austria.

Both Finland and Austria managed to maintain domestic freedom while adhering to a neutral line in foreign policy and did so as a result of Soviet security and political concerns. Annexed (without any meaningful resistance) by Nazi Germany in 1938, Austria was occupied by the Allies in 1945 and divided into four occupational zones. Austria joined the Marshall Plan, but early hopes for an end to the occupation were dashed by the onset of the cold war. After Joseph Stalin's death in March 1953, the Soviet line on Austria became more flexible. The Soviets watched with increasing alarm the West's plans to admit West Germany into the North Atlantic Treaty Organization (NATO) and permit West German rearmament. Probably hoping to forestall both, the Soviets allowed Austria to become a model of a central European nation that was accorded its freedom in a manner Moscow did not view as threatening. Thus, in May 1955 Austria and the Allies signed the Austrian State Treaty, in which Austria pledged its neutrality in world affairs. The treaty ended the occupation of the country, and foreign forces withdrew. While politically neutral, Austria joined Western economic institutions such as the European Free Trade Association (EFTA) and later reached a special arrangement with the European Community (EC).

Finland followed a similar course to Austria, with slightly less freedom in its foreign economic policies. The Finnish-Soviet Winter War of 1939–1940 and the active collaboration of the Finns with the Nazis made the Soviets assert their wishes vis-à-vis Finland firmly and early. In 1947 Finland and the USSR signed a treaty establishing Finland's neutrality in foreign and defense matters. In return, the Soviets abstained from intervening in Finnish domestic affairs. Because of objections from Moscow, Finland did not join the Marshall Plan but was allowed to receive large loans from the U.S. Export-Import Bank. This pattern of neutrality on foreign-policy and defense issues, care not to offend Soviet sensibilities, abstention from membership in Western organizations such as NATO or the EC, domestic political freedom, and access to Western markets and technology gave rise to the term *Finlandization* (which acquired a derogatory connotation in Western political discourse, implying that a state was a "free

rider" or a "fence sitter"). Was it reasonable to expect the states of central and eastern Europe to be able to enjoy the status gained by Austria or Finland rather than be subjected to the oppressive Soviet domination?

It is true that there were many conditions that facilitated Soviet penetration and domination of the central and eastern European countries. First, while driving the Nazi forces west, the Red Army came to occupy many of these countries. In 1945 the Soviet Union was in physical control of much of central and eastern Europe. Second, in successive meetings of the leaders of the anti-Nazi alliance—at Moscow and Tehran in 1943 and Yalta in 1945—it became clear that the United States and Britain would demand greater freedom for the central and eastern European states but would not be willing to do much about securing it. As Marc Trachtenberg has noted, the two Western allies were not merely making speeches about freedom in eastern Europe in order to pacify domestic constituencies. They truly hoped for a better deal for eastern Europe, but there was just so much they were willing to do about it. Third, the regimes of some of these countries had lost their legitimacy during the war. They were corrupt and ineffective, and the collaboration of some of them with the Nazi occupiers damaged their nationalist claims or Western support. Fourth, and in contrast, members of the communist movement were central in the underground resistance to the German occupiers. These movements were thus able to portray themselves as truer to national aspirations and honor than the regimes in power. The role of these anti-Nazi partisans in defeating the Nazi armies had been exaggerated (for example, by Josip Tito in Yugoslavia), but the communists did play a part in the anti-Nazi campaign. Fifth, at least initially, the communists in these countries offered policies that enjoyed broad support, especially in light of the corruption and favoritism of the old regimes, which were swept aside after the war. Agrarian reform, changes in the educational and health provision systems, and industrialization were all popular with the masses. In short, as Charles Gati has pointed out, the Soviet Union was able to expand into the territory of eastern Europe because there were no countervailing pressures to make such an expansion too costly or onerous.

There were obstacles—real or perceived—to Soviet domination of eastern Europe. First, Gati notes, as the cold war intensified, it was not clear if the West would accept complete Soviet domination of the region. The West did protest Soviet denial of free elections and

Workers demonstrating in Prague, February 1948

(Popperfoto)

democratic procedures in the countries that came under Red Army rule. In February 1947 President Harry S Truman, enunciating what came to be called the Truman Doctrine, committed the United States to supporting "free peoples who are resisting subjugation by armed minorities or by outside pressures." Poland and East Germany were the most strategically important countries for the Soviet Union, and it was difficult to see how Stalin would allow for regimes there that would be less than completely obedient to Moscow. Other countries, however, were not as important to the USSR, and there might have been an opportunity for the West to gain greater freedom from Moscow for these countries in exchange for accepting most of the Soviet demands concerning Poland and Germany. Indeed, Gati quotes Zoltán Vas, a former member of the politburo of the Hungarian Communist Party, as stating that, as late as 1946, the leadership of the party was not sure whether or not Stalin "might not let Hungary [and presumably Czechoslovakia] come under the political influence of the [Western] allies in exchange for Soviet demands on Poland and Germany."

With the exception of the Czechoslovakian party, the communist parties in the eastern European states did not enjoy a large following. The Soviet Union thus could not rely on indigenous mass popular movements effectively to govern the countries it wanted to

rule. To increase the popularity of the local communist parties Stalin advised them to begin attending to local issues first and to worry about matters pertaining to the international communist movement later. This attention to local issues—and the fact that, for example, Czech communists ruled as Czech first and communist second in this period of "national" communism—created a situation in which the diversity of the region and the differences among its countries increased rather than decreased. To the Soviets' chagrin, in summer 1947 three of those countries—Poland, Czechoslovakia, and Hungary—expressed interest in accepting the U.S. invitation to take part in the Marshall Plan. Stalin had to remind the leaders of these countries that he would allow freedom from Moscow—and the focus on domestic needs—to go just so far.

There was a vivid example in eastern Europe of a communist state that defied Moscow and survived. Tito, the leader of the anti-Nazi Yugoslav partisans and ruler of Yugoslavia after its liberation, was not a man accustomed to taking orders. Although he admired Stalin, he rejected Stalin's advice about how to run Yugoslavian internal affairs. The Soviet Union launched an intense campaign to vilify Tito and undermine his regime, using propaganda, subversion, and even hints of military action against the defiant regime. Stalin misjudged Tito, however; the greater

FINLANDIZATION

the Soviet pressure and the more intense the anti-Yugoslav campaign, the more determined Tito became. In 1948 he officially broke with the Soviet camp. While loyal to communist doctrines on economics and politics, he charted an independent course in foreign policy between the Western and Eastern blocs. In the mid 1950s he joined with President Gamal Abdel Nasser of Egypt, Kwame Nkrumah of Ghana, and Sukarno of Indonesia to form the nonaligned movement.

The example of Yugoslavia was important for the West and dangerous for Moscow. It proved a point made by George F. Kennan, the author of containment policy, that communism was not a monolithic ideology and that communist rulers would still pursue the national interests of their countries. The United States, Kennan argued, should be willing to overlook the particular nature of a regime and consider its foreign-policy positions. For the Soviets the case of Yugoslavia was threatening because it showed that a country could stand up to Moscow and the pressure it applied and not only survive but gain standing and esteem in world councils. According to Gati, Yugoslavia's ability to withstand Stalin's brutal pressure "revealed for all to see the limits of Stalin's power even in his own backyard. . . . Perhaps most important, Yugoslavia's independence offered an alternative to others in Soviet-controlled Eastern Europe." It is fair to say that the example of Yugoslavia inspired attempts by Imre Nagy in Hungary in 1956, Wladyslaw Gomulka in Poland in the late 1950s, and Alexander Dubček in Czechoslovakia in 1968 to reform domestic politics and introduce greater freedoms. Similarly, the success of Nicolae Ceausescu in Romania to establish greater freedom for his country in defense and foreign-policy matters (without, however, a corresponding increase in domestic freedoms) probably also owes much to Tito's example.

The potential for different paths for the central and eastern European countries was there, but it was never fully explored. The sorry state of the Western European economies, and the potential for political turmoil there; the civil war in Greece and the difficulties in Turkey and Iran; the civil war in China; and wrangling over the future of Germany all consumed the attention of the Truman administration. Moreover, the developments in central and eastern Europe were taking place while the United States was rapidly demobilizing. (In 1945 the United States had ninety-seven divisions, combat ready and tested; in 1947 it had only twelve, most understrength and tied down in occupation duties.)

It is thus not clear that the United States was in a position to demand of Stalin the kind of deal that would have allowed for greater freedom for some of those countries. It was also not clear that the domestic political situation would have allowed the administration much freedom of maneuver: the largest domestic constituency attentive to the affairs of east and central Europe was the Polish American community, but it was probably over Poland that Stalin would have been most intransigent. It would have been difficult to explain a fight for greater freedom for Bulgaria and Hungary while conceding greater Soviet control over Poland. The Truman and Eisenhower administrations thus chose to issue general proclamations about the desirability of greater freedom and independence for the countries that they came to call "captive nations" but not to do much by way of concrete policies. The fight, if there was to be a fight, would have to come another day.

—BENJAMIN FRANKEL, SECURITY STUDIES

Viewpoint:
No, Soviet insecurities and historical conditions made it unlikely that the Soviet Union would have agreed to a Finland status for eastern and central European countries.

At the allied conferences during the Second World War, the Western allies promised Joseph Stalin that the postwar settlement would respect Soviet security interests around the entire periphery of the USSR. Indeed, the conferences at Tehran in 1943 and Yalta in 1945 specifically conceded influence over vast stretches of territory bordering on the Soviet Union to Stalin, either directly or indirectly.

In eastern Europe both kinds of concessions were made. First, it was established that the Soviet Union would retain the territories it had acquired as a secret provision of the Molotov-Ribbentrop Pact (or Nazi-Soviet Nonaggression Pact) of 1939 (that is, eastern Poland and the Baltic states) or as a result of its independent military moves against Finland and Romania (parts of Karelia and all of Bessarabia) in 1939–1940. Second, it was acknowledged that states bordering on the Soviet Union should be controlled by what the allies described as "friendly" governments.

The Soviet Union's relationship with Finland was a potential model for what this agreement would mean in practice. Throughout the

NATO, Warsaw Pact, and
neutral countries in
Europe during the cold
war

Neutral Country

Warsaw Pact Organization

Communist Country. *Not Members of Warsaw Pact*

North Atlantic Treaty Organization *Plus Canada and The United States*
Greece and Turkey joined in 1952   Germany joined in 1955   Spain joined in 1982
France withdrew from Integrated Military Command in 1966

cold war, Finland retained full independence; yet, its foreign policy of firm nonalignment was one shared by few countries in Europe. It was made even more unusual in noncommunist Europe by its perceivable tilt toward Moscow in nonmilitary relations. Apart from the cold-war superimposition of superpower conflict over much of world diplomacy, there were other reasons why this relationship did not and could not have become the model of Soviet relations with the rest of eastern Europe.

Probably the most important reason is that Finland did not by itself present any significant challenge to Soviet security. Although the Germans had used Finland as a staging ground for an element of their invasion of the Soviet Union in 1941, the difficult logistics of supplying their troops there seriously limited their effectiveness. Neither Leningrad nor the strategic port of Murmansk, where much Allied military support to the Soviet Union arrived by sea, were ever captured by the German and Finnish forces despite the spectacular successes of the German army everywhere else on the eastern front in the early phases of the campaign. For the same reason an attack through Finland would not have been much more of a threat after 1945, even if Finland had joined NATO or otherwise allied itself with the United States. The territorial modifications that were restored and expanded in Soviet favor after Finland surrendered in September 1944 reduced that negligible threat further by giving the Soviets control of strategic territory along the border and of the Finnish naval bases on the Arctic Sea. Eastern Europe, on the other hand, was the historic route for invasions of Russia. Germany had used it twice in twenty-seven years.

Second, for economic reasons it was clearly in the Finns' interest to maintain favorable relations with the Soviet Union. Geographic factors alone predisposed Finland to conduct most of its foreign trade with Moscow. Finland had been an integral part of the Russian Empire for more than a century before it declared its independence in 1917, a fact that had not been without its effect on the country's commercial orientation. These circumstances were patently absent from Soviet relations with the rest of the European countries with which it shared a border. Situated in the center of the continent and enjoying a much more developed infrastructure than could be found on the Soviet-Finnish border or between Finland and the West, these nations were well placed to conduct a high volume of trade with Western Europe. Historically, with the exception of Poland, they had been either entirely or in large part outside the grasp of the Russian Empire. Well before the First World War there was an economic gravitation of these states and of the Hapsburg Empire (from which several states in the region later emerged) toward Germany. The relative instability of the new eastern European states in the interwar period and their general hostility toward the USSR exacerbated that dependence.

Furthermore, immediate security was Joseph Stalin's principal motivation in foreign policy, regardless of whether challenges to it were real or perceived. Mirroring his approach to domestic politics, in which even perfectly loyal and innocent Soviet leaders were subject to ruthless purges simply because of their potential for success should they present a challenge to his leadership, Stalin's approach to international politics attempted to neutralize external situations that had the potential to compromise Soviet security. Stalin had no real reason to fear that Finland's political independence would be a future threat, especially considering the historically close nature of its economic relationship with its eastern neighbor.

For a variety of strategic and historical reasons, Stalin's ideas about eastern Europe were different. Their independence plainly presented the possibility that given the right turn of events, the "friendly" democracies in eastern Europe could turn on the USSR in the future, even if they were economically oriented toward Moscow and officially neutral. The lure of their historically beneficial trade relationships with the West and the prospect of postwar American financial assistance to rebuild their countries were factors

Stalin could not ignore. American financing was especially dangerous from his perspective because he quite correctly perceived that it was designed to marginalize political extremes and encourage domestic, political, and economic stability. In any democracy with pretensions to freedom such stability would and did diminish the political influence of communism and consequently blight the disposition of those countries toward the Soviet Union. The popularity of communism in France and Italy, for example, declined after their economies began to boom with the massive infusion of American foreign aid from the Marshall Plan.

From the beginning it was clear that Stalin had no intention of allowing eastern Europe to owe its future stability and prosperity to the United States. Rather, he pursued policies that broadened Soviet influence as extensively as possible. The geographical changes are an important consideration on this point because the retention of eastern Poland and the annexation of Subcarpathian Ruthenia gave the Soviet Union direct frontiers on Czechoslovakia and Hungary, two countries that had no prewar border with the Soviet Union. If Moscow were entitled to "friendly" governments in neighboring countries, those two could now be added to the list.

Although the West had extracted promises from Stalin that these "friendly" governments would provisionally include noncommunist elements and then hold free and democratic elections, the reality was quite different. The presence of the Red Army throughout the region gave Stalin enormous power to influence the provisional political complexion of those countries. In every case parties of the moderate right, and sometimes even the political center, were dissolved or outlawed on the grounds that their philosophical opposition to communism, their legality during the war, or the interests they were said to represent made them "fascist" or "reactionary." Legal noncommunist parties were customarily given a disproportionately small amount of the political resources administered by the Red Army in liberated countries.

The Soviets also distorted the composition of the provisional governments so that communists were disproportionately given control of key ministries such as information (which controlled the media) and interior (which controlled the police). The communists of the region were themselves beholden to Stalin as many of them had spent years before and during the war in Moscow. The especially ruthless and capricious victimization of foreign communists in the Soviet purges left those who survived under no uncertain impression of Stalin when they returned to eastern Europe in the train of the Red Army.

The "democratic" elections that were held in these countries made it illegal for a large part of the electorate to express itself politically and biased the outcome of what competition remained by placing a disproportionate amount of power in the hands of the communists. Within a short period of time, all of the countries in eastern Europe that had been occupied by the Red Army at the end of the war became monolithically communist states. The remaining noncommunist parties were outlawed, forcibly assimilated by the communist parties, or reduced to purely nominal independence. Independent economic and social institutions were quickly brought under control.

It is possible that Stalin wished for the transition to communism to come without direct coercion. The advantages enjoyed by the communist parties did allow them to receive large percentages of the vote in what seemed to be freely contested elections. Even though it would have been a legal fiction, communist parliamentary majorities were not beyond the realm of possibility and even had a serious chance of independent success. Ultimately, however, drastic measures were taken to accelerate the effects of that predisposition.

Scholars who tend to blame the United States for the origins of the cold war argue that Western misperceptions of Soviet activity reinforced Stalin's misinterpretation of Western intentions and pushed him into communizing eastern Europe. This argument is fundamentally flawed because it fails to address what Stalin was doing elsewhere. Much of the scholarship on postwar eastern Europe does not consider that well before the announcement of the Marshall Plan and the economic consolidation of the Western allies' occupation zones of Germany, the Soviet dictator had been testing how far he could push the limitations of the wartime agreements. In 1946 Stalin attempted to extract territorial concessions from Iran and military-base rights from Turkey, two countries that had remained benevolently neutral during the Second World War and whose futures had not been the subject of negotiations during the wartime conferences. President Harry S Truman's response in both cases was firm, and the Soviets were forced to withdraw their demands. That same year Soviet foreign minister Vyacheslav Molotov presented a Soviet demand for four-power occupation of Germany's industrial Ruhr region in order to give the Soviets partial control over West German productive capacity. In addition to prompting a curt refusal, Molotov's approach actually contributed to their decision to combine their occupation zones into a single economic unit that excluded Soviet influence over occupation policy for West Germany. In that sense Stalin reacted to Western resolve in his policy toward eastern Europe, but it is important to realize that the collapse of the cooperative relationship that had existed during the war was owing in large part to his skirting the spirit of the wartime agreements about the future of the region and the expansionist pressure he applied elsewhere in the world.

The dispatch with which that resolve was presented made the Soviet leader realize that his security interests were better served by consolidating control over what was already in his possession. A gradual communist takeover that was legal at least in form could not be reconciled with that goal. The firm communist consolidation in eastern Europe in late 1947 and early 1948 dovetailed with Stalin's changing approach to international politics. After following his instructions not to participate in the Marshall Plan, which even countries not yet dominated by communism were diplomatically compelled to obey, the national communist parties of the region were organized under the Communist Information Bureau (Cominform). Its purpose closely resembled that of the Communist International (Comintern), which had coordinated the policies of foreign communist parties under Moscow's direction before Stalin ordered its dissolution, ironically as a goodwill gesture to the West, in 1943. "Nationalist" deviations from a pro-Moscow orientation, like that of the Yugoslavian communists under Josip Tito, were regarded as treason. While Belgrade and Moscow entered a period of estrangement, the eastern European countries under closer Soviet control purged Communist Party members who were not unswervingly loyal to the Soviet Union and its aims.

Even though growing superpower tension clouded the development of the issue, there is no doubt that Stalin associated the vital security interests of his country with his ability to control eastern Europe. The obvious strategic factors that made hegemonic domination of that region essential for the Soviet leader's concept of security rendered the Finland model an impossible option. The great pains to which Stalin went to justify the expansion of his influence in the region before superpower cooperation became a lost cause laid the groundwork for its full communization. Despite his bestowal of tremendous domestic-political advantages on national communist parties, the "natural" development (given the immediate postwar political conditions) of communist governments elected in biased, yet ostensibly democratic, political systems was disturbed by the rapidity of the strategic partnership's decline. Although the consolidation of eastern Europe under communist leadership had to be accelerated and effected forcefully, these factors did not change the illusory nature of the alternative of a "Finlandized" eastern Europe.

—PAUL DU QUENOY, GEORGE WASHINGTON UNIVERSITY

References

Lynn Davis, *The Cold War Begins: Soviet-American Conflict over Eastern Europe* (Princeton, N.J.: Princeton University Press, 1974);

John Lewis Gaddis, *We Now Know: Rethinking Cold War History* (Oxford: Clarendon Press / New York: Oxford University Press, 1997);

Charles Gati, *The Bloc that Failed: Soviet-East European Relations in Transition* (Bloomington: Indiana University Press, 1990);

Beatrice Heuser, *Western "Containment" Policies in the Cold War: The Yugoslav Case, 1948–53* (London & New York: Routledge, 1989);

Walter LaFeber, *America, Russia, and the Cold War, 1945–1996,* eighth edition (New York: McGraw-Hill, 1997);

Vojtech Mastny, *The Cold War and Soviet Insecurity: The Stalin Years* (New York: Oxford University Press, 1996);

Robert Reinhart, ed., *Finland and the United States: Diplomatic Relations through Seventy Years* (Washington, D.C.: Institute for the Study of Diplomacy, Georgetown University, 1993);

Bruce Olav Solheim, *The Nordic Nexus: A Lesson in Peaceful Security* (Westport, Conn.: Praeger, 1994);

Marc Trachtenberg, *A Constructed Peace: The Making of the European Settlement, 1945–1963* (Princeton, N.J.: Princeton University Press, 1999).

FLEXIBLE RESPONSE

Was Kennedy's policy of flexible response preferable to Eisenhower's doctrine of massive retaliation?

Viewpoint: Yes, Kennedy's flexible-response doctrine was preferable to Eisenhower's doctrine of massive retaliation because Kennedy's position avoided civilian targets and tailored responses to fit the provocation.

Viewpoint: No, Kennedy's flexible-response doctrine was not preferable to Eisenhower's massive retaliation, because flexible-response led to the Berlin Crisis and the Cuban Missile Crisis.

The United States was the first country to develop and acquire nuclear weapons. In the late 1940s it enjoyed a nuclear monopoly, and during the 1950s and early 1960s it maintained a clear nuclear dominance vis-à-vis its adversaries.

The Eisenhower administration, coming to power eight years after the costly U.S. participation in the Second World War, and in the midst of a long and inconclusive military intervention in Korea, adopted a strategic posture that stressed technological advantages in air power and nuclear weapons. Central to Eisenhower's New Look doctrine, as it was called, was the concept of "massive retaliation." It said that the United States would use its nuclear weapons, in a massive fashion and early in any conflict, to destroy the society of an adversary who challenged U.S. security or interests. At least in part the New Look doctrine was motivated by economic considerations: the Republican Eisenhower administration was dedicated to fiscal responsibility and balanced budgets, and nuclear weapons were cheaper than large conventional armies during the post–Second World War period. As a senior Eisenhower administration official said at the time, nuclear weapons gave the United States "more bang for the buck."

The Kennedy administration came to power in 1961, determined to replace Eisenhower's massive-retaliation policy with the doctrine of "flexible response." The new doctrine emphasized the need for multiple military options, a greater number and variety of military instruments, and flexibility in their employment. Accordingly, the Kennedy administration, in addition to developing more limited and refined nuclear options, also enhanced U.S. conventional military capabilities and covert-action operations.

Viewpoint:
Yes, Kennedy's flexible-response doctrine was preferable to Eisenhower's doctrine of massive retaliation because Kennedy's position avoided civilian targets and tailored responses to fit the provocation.

The debate over flexible response was part of a larger debate over the advantages and disadvantages of two possible approaches to contending with a military challenge from an adversary: symmetrical and asymmetrical. President Dwight D. Eisenhower's administration adopted the policy of massive retaliation—an example of an asymmetrical response. Flexible response, the symmetrical option, was espoused by officials in

DULLES ON MASSIVE RETALIATION

In a 12 January 1954 speech to the Council of Foreign Relations in New York City, Secretary of State John Foster Dulles defined the Eisenhower administration's policy of massive retaliation.

We live in a world where emergencies are always possible, and our survival may depend upon our capacity to meet emergencies. Let us pray that we shall always have that capacity. But, having said that, it is necessary also to say that emergency measures—however good for the emergency—do not necessarily make good permanent policies. Emergency measures are costly, superficial, and imply that the enemy has the initiative. They cannot be depended on to serve our long-term interests.

This "long-term" factor is of critical importance. The Soviet Communists are planning for what they call "an entire historical era," and we should do the same. They seek, through many types of manoeuvres, gradually to divide and weaken the free nations by over-extending them in efforts which, as Lenin put it, are "beyond their strength, so that they come to practical bankruptcy." Then, said Lenin, "our victory is assured." Then, said Stalin, "will be the moment for the decisive blow."

In the face of this strategy, measures cannot be judged adequate merely because they ward off an immediate danger. It is essential to do this, but it is also essential to do so without exhausting ourselves.

When the Eisenhower Administration applied this test, we felt that some transformations were needed. It is not sound military strategy permanently to commit U.S. land forces to Asia to a degree that leaves us no strategic reserves. It is not sound economics, or good foreign policy, to support other countries permanently, for in the long run that creates as much ill-will as good-will. Also, it is not sound to become permanently committed to military expenditures so vast that they lead to "practical bankruptcy." . . .

We need allies and collective security. Our purpose is to make these relations more effective and less costly. This can be done by placing more reliance on deterrent power and less dependence on local defensive power. This is accepted practice so far as local communities are concerned. We keep locks on our doors, but we do not have an armed guard in every home. We rely principally on a community security system so well-equipped to punish any who break in and steal that, in fact, would-be aggressors are generally deterred. That is the modern way of getting protection at a bearable cost.

What the Eisenhower Administration seeks is a similar international security system. We want, for ourselves and the other free nations, a maximum deterrent at a bearable cost. Local defense will always be important. But there is no local defense which alone will contain the mighty land power of the Communist world. Local defenses must be reinforced by the further deterrent of massive retaliatory power. A potential aggressor must know that he cannot always prescribe battle conditions that suit him. Otherwise, for example, a potential aggressor who is glutted with manpower might be tempted to attack in confidence that resistance would be confined to manpower. He might be tempted to attack in places where his superiority was decisive. The way to deter aggression is for the free community to be willing and able to respond vigorously at places and with the means of its own choosing.

Source: *Keesing's Contemporary Archives, 9 (16–23 January 1954): 13361.*

the administration of President John F. Kennedy. Massive retaliation and flexible response were both conceived as military doctrines, but they represented a broader understanding of conflict and how to fashion policies to cope with its exigencies.

Supporters of the asymmetrical response emphasized three things. First, a country should lead with its strength. In fashioning its policies it should rely on its advantages vis-à-vis the adversary. Second, a country should be mindful of what it can afford and what it cannot. In a democracy the leadership should be aware of what policies public opinion would, and would not, accept. Finding a perfectly calibrated response to any initiative by an adversary is likely to be expensive. Because they tend to be more complex and nuanced than asymmetrical responses, symmetrical responses are more difficult to explain to citizens, and public support for such decisions is harder to rally. Third, the symmetrical approach, by its nature, is a defensive,

FLEXIBLE RESPONSE

reactive policy that allows the adversary to dictate the pace and scope of conflict, and of responses to it.

Massive retaliation, which was incorporated into Eisenhower's New Look doctrine, was enunciated by Secretary of State John Foster Dulles in a series of speeches and articles in the early 1950s. This policy stated that the United States would rely on its technological advantages—specifically, air power and nuclear weapons—to contain the spread of Soviet influence and power. Rather than trying to match the Soviet Union soldier for soldier or tank for tank, and rather than allowing the Soviets to decide on their own what means to use in each point of conflict with the expectation that the United States would choose similar means, the Eisenhower administration asserted that the Soviets could not expect such a luxury. The United States was not going to play tit for tat with the Soviet Union. The Soviet Union would not be allowed to decide how the United States should respond to Soviet provocation. Pointing to U.S. advantages in air power and nuclear weapons, the Eisenhower administration announced that it would likely use nuclear weapons in a massive attack on the Soviet homeland in response to any Soviet breach, large or small.

Opponents of asymmetrical response and, hence, of massive retaliation contended that there were three problems with both. First, massive retaliation was simply not credible as a military doctrine. Wars are costly, and even winners pay a heavy toll. The goal of a country's military posture should be to deter an adversary from attacking by convincing him that he cannot win. Asymmetry fails this test. Soviet leaders did not believe that the United States would incinerate tens of millions of Soviet citizens in response to anything short of a massive Soviet attack on the American homeland or, perhaps, on a vital U.S. interest.

The second problem with massive retaliation is related to the first. Because of the heavy reliance on nuclear weapons, the bar for U.S. retaliation to Soviet provocations was raised so high that the Soviet Union could systematically "nibble" on the margins of U.S. power and interests, steadily expanding its power and influence. Aware of the threat of massive retaliations, Soviet leaders calibrated each provocation to bring them a meaningful gain while remaining below the high bar of massive nuclear reprisal from the United States.

The third problem with adopting the policy of massive retaliation had to do with the nature of American society. Advocates of symmetrical response argued that owing to the liberal, democratic principles undergirding the American polity, no president would order a military attack that would result in the deaths of tens of millions of innocent civilians, unless the attack was in response to a catastrophic assault of historical proportions inflicting massive casualties on the American population. Consequently, heavy reliance on nuclear weapons resulted in "self-deterrence": because of their own moral principles, American decisionmakers were deterred from using the very military means they had built for the national defense.

Critics of massive retaliation argued that the rigidity of that doctrine brought on a paralysis in the exercise of American power. They charged that reliance on the threat of massive use of nuclear weapons caused the Eisenhower administration not to stand tough in the face of Soviet advances but only to talk tough, as was the case with Dulles's talk about the "captive nations" of eastern Europe and his call for a "roll back" of communist sway over the continent. The fact was that the Eisenhower administration judged each Soviet advance to be too small, in and of itself, to trigger a massive nuclear retaliation. Consequently, the Soviets adopted "salami tactics," incremental measures designed to erode Western power and influence in the face of self-induced inaction on the part of the United States.

Officially announced by Secretary of Defense Robert S. McNamara in a commencement address at the University of Michigan in May 1962, the Kennedy administration's policy of flexible response offered a solution to the problems that hobbled massive retaliation. Flexible response included three major departures in U.S. military policy. The first was a large-scale rebuilding of U.S. conventional, nonnuclear forces. The second was the calibration and refinement of U.S. nuclear options, and the third was the augmentation of U.S. covert-action capabilities. The purpose of these dramatic departures was to increase the number and variety of military instruments that American decisionmakers had at their disposal, allowing them to use U.S. power in a wider range of contingencies.

The building up of U.S. conventional forces was meant to bring the nonnuclear elements of the U.S. military to a level closer to that of the Red Army. The Soviet Union had fielded a large nonnuclear military force, and the Kennedy administration wanted to contain that force, at least in the initial phases of a conflict, without resorting to nuclear weapons, as was the plan of the Eisenhower administration. Moreover, the European theater was no longer the only place where the Soviet Union might try to expand its power. In the late 1950s and early 1960s, as the British and French empires began to crumble, the process of decolonization gathered momentum. More and more countries in Africa and Asia were gaining independence, and the Soviet

Union was eager to extend its influence over them. Enhanced conventional capabilities would allow the United States more ways to intervene in Third World areas of contention.

The refining of U.S. nuclear capabilities by creating "limited nuclear options" would allow the president greater flexibility in the use of nuclear weapons. The Eisenhower administration had threatened cataclysmic destruction of the Soviet Union if it endangered American interests; the Kennedy administration wanted to tailor U.S. nuclear responses to fit provocations—to make a response more symmetrical with the violation that prompted it. There were three purposes for adopting limited nuclear options. The first was to increase the credibility of U.S. deterrence. If it is similar to a provocation in scope and size, a deterrence threat is more believable. Second, the new administration saw a need not only to lower the bar for U.S. nuclear employment, which the Eisenhower administration placed so high that it had lost its effectiveness, but to introduce new rungs on the "escalation ladder." In other words, the Kennedy administration believed that there was a need to create a variety of nuclear responses, each different in scope and scale, to meet any possible Soviet attack. These different nuclear responses would convince Soviet military planners that they could not find a "window of vulnerability" in the U.S. military posture or enjoy "escalation dominance." The side with a greater variety of nuclear options enjoys escalation dominance, which allows the fine-tuning of nuclear options. The side with fewer nuclear options is at a disadvantage, because at key junctures of a war it must decide between absorbing the punishment its adversary has inflicted or escalating the war to

even higher levels of destruction. Supporters of flexible response argued that, if the distance between the rungs on the escalation ladder were too great, U.S. leaders might be deterred from moving up to the next rung.

Third, military planners in the Kennedy administration wanted to be able to use nuclear weapons without killing tens of millions of Soviet citizens. (When McNamara introduced this doctrine in 1962, it was called the "city-avoidance doctrine.")

According to this doctrine, nuclear weapons, at least in the initial phases of a war, should be used against military targets, not civilian populations. This approach fits Judeo-Christian notions of proportionality in war, and it was also seen as beneficial to the United States. The Soviet Union was by then building its own nuclear arsenal and delivery systems, thus acquiring the ability to retaliate in kind to any U.S. nuclear attack on the Soviet Union, if not yet on quite the same scale. McNamara believed that if the United States abstained from targeting Soviet population centers the Soviet Union would abstain from retaliating against American cities, not because of humane considerations but because they would not want their own cities destroyed. (This approach was thus described as "intra-war deterrence" and as holding the adversary's population "hostage.")

The building up of U.S. conventional capabilities and the augmentation and refinement of its nuclear capabilities were intended to create a "seamless web" of escalation—from the smallest conventional encounter to an all-out nuclear war. The seamless quality of U.S. military capabilities would make it easier for an American president to move to the next rung on the ladder of military escalation. This seamlessness of military posture would be beneficial in two ways. First, its deterrence value would be enhanced because it would be more credible as a military doctrine. An adversary would recognize the ease with which an American president could escalate and be less likely to initiate a war. Second, if a war did break out, the new doctrine would allow an American president to inflict only the level of punishment necessary to make the enemy stop its aggression.

To add to U.S. policy instruments the Kennedy administration also ordered the strengthening of covert-operations capabilities, including special forces (the Green Berets were created), commando and reconnaissance units, and augmented CIA capabilities. Kennedy was particularly interested in this aspect of his administration's military buildup.

The manner in which the Kennedy administration handled the crises in Berlin (1961) and Cuba (1962) reflected its approach to the use of military means on behalf of U.S. national-security policies. In both cases the president rejected the extreme measures offered to him—a nuclear confrontation with the Soviets over the erection of the Berlin Wall or an aerial bombardment or invasion of Cuba. Especially in regard to Cuba, the administration devised a military plan that demonstrated U.S. resolve, yet allowed time and room for negotiations. Also, the administration coupled its demand for a Soviet withdrawal of the missiles installed in Cuba with a face-saving offer to have American Jupiter missiles in Turkey removed as part of a tacit bargain. Flexible response, as a military doctrine, was not directly tested in either situation, but the spirit that had animated it had prevailed and produced good results.

–JOMO KASSAYE, HENRY L. STIMSON CENTER

Viewpoint:
No, Kennedy's flexible-response doctrine was not preferable to Eisenhower's massive retaliation, because flexible-response led to the Berlin Crisis and the Cuban Missile Crisis.

During the latter part of the 1950s President Dwight D. Eisenhower enacted a military policy of all-or-nothing massive retaliation, whereby the United States would quickly escalate to total thermonuclear attack in a war with the Soviet Union. Eisenhower believed that a limited war was impossible, so he sought to remove all limited military options from official U.S. national-security policy. By 1958 and 1959 Eisenhower had succeeded in this objective.

A large group of influential Americans emerged to oppose Eisenhower's all-or-nothing policy. The prominent Harvard political scientist Henry Kissinger, who later became national-security adviser and secretary of state during the administrations of Richard M. Nixon and Gerald R. Ford, argued in his major 1957 study, *Nuclear Weapons and Foreign Policy,* that the Eisenhower administration was too preoccupied with saving money and too fixated upon total war. Americans, Kissinger contended, had to get used to the idea of fighting expensive, limited wars. The alternative was either defeat at the hands of the Soviet regime or a suicidal thermonuclear holocaust. At the RAND Corporation, a California think tank affiliated with the U.S. Air Force, analysts such as Henry Rowen and Herman Kahn argued that a nuclear war with the Soviet Union did not have to descend inevitably into all-out war. Rowen, Kahn, and others completed intricate and technical studies in which they attempted to demonstrate that a nuclear war could be fought in a limited way and could be won. Retired military officials, such as John Galvin and Maxwell D. Taylor, opposed Eisenhower's severe diminishment of the U.S. Army role in a future war with the Soviet Union. They believed that a war fought only with thermonuclear weapons was both immoral and suicidal. In his best-selling book *The Uncertain Trumpet* (1960) Taylor called for a rejuvenation of American conventional forces and new strategies of limited war, coining the phrase "flexible response."

These arguments attracted the attention of leading Democrats in Washington. Senators W. Stuart Symington (Missouri), Lyndon B. Johnson (Texas), Henry M. Jackson (Washington), and John F. Kennedy (Massachusetts) each attacked Eisenhower's military policies, often borrowing the arguments of Kissinger, Kahn, and Taylor. These congressional leaders, many of whom had close ties with American aviation industries, accused Eisenhower of allowing American defenses to slip dangerously. Not only had the United States neglected its capabilities for fighting smaller, limited wars, they charged, it had also allowed the Soviet Union to gain a decisive advantage over the United States in their production of ballistic nuclear missiles. It was this military weakness, these leaders suggested, which had prevented the Americans from effectively confronting the Soviet Union in cold-war conflicts such as Suez, Hungary, the Taiwan Straits, and Berlin.

This accusation became a central feature of Kennedy's 1960 presidential campaign against

TAYLOR ON FLEXIBLE RESPONSE

General Maxwell D. Taylor, former U.S. Army chief of staff, defined the concept of Flexible Response in The Uncertain Trumpet (1960).

Having recognized the limitations of our atomic deterrent forces, we should, in consistence, redefine general war as being synonymous with a nuclear exchange between the United States and the USSR. Limited war would then be left to cover all other forms of military operations. The question of using atomic weapons in limited wars would be met by accepting the fact that primary dependence must be placed on conventional weapons while retaining readiness to use tactical atomic weapons in the comparatively rare cases where their use would be to our national interest.

The National Military Program of Flexible Response should contain at the outset an unqualified renunciation of reliance on the strategy of Massive Retaliation. It should be made clear that the United States will prepare itself to respond anywhere, any time, with weapons and forces appropriate to the situation. Thus, we would restore to warfare its historical justification as a means to create a better world upon the successful conclusion of hostilities.

Source: Maxwell D. Taylor, The Uncertain Trumpet (New York: Harper, 1960), pp. 145–146.

Republican candidate Richard M. Nixon, who was Eisenhower's vice-president. After Kennedy won the election, he appointed officials such as McGeorge Bundy, Walt W. Rostow, and Robert S. McNamara to develop a new American military policy of flexible response. The job of Bundy, Rostow, McNamara, and other top administration officials was to increase defense spending considerably, particularly in the areas of conventional forces, limited nuclear weapons, and missile development. Kennedy believed that with a new policy of flexible response the Americans could stand up to the Soviets and compel them to back down during potential cold-war crises.

Despite this new policy, Kennedy chose conciliation over confrontation during the two major crises of his administration—the Berlin Wall Crisis of 1961 and the Cuban Missile Crisis of 1962. Traditional interpretations of the Kennedy administration's management of these events emphasized American toughness and resilience, suggesting that the Soviet Union was forced to back off, but new evidence and documentation show that these interpretations are wrong.

After the Second World War the victorious allied powers occupied and administered Berlin,

the capital of the defeated Nazi regime. Berlin, however, lay in the middle of the Soviet-controlled sector of Germany. As the cold war progressed, the Western nations—the United States, France, and Great Britain—refused to leave Berlin. As a result, the western sections of the city became a kind of Western enclave in the larger Soviet sector. This situation was unacceptable to East German leader Walter Ulbricht and Soviet premier Nikita S. Khrushchev. In 1958 the Soviets gave an ultimatum demanding that the Western powers leave Berlin, but Khrushchev settled instead for a summit meeting with Eisenhower.

In June 1961 Khrushchev decided to test Kennedy's resolve. Meeting with Kennedy in Vienna, Khrushchev told the new American president that the Western powers must leave Berlin in six months. The United States rejected this ultimatum. During the summer of 1961 the United States and its North Atlantic Treaty Organization (NATO) allies declared that the West would fight rather than quit Berlin. In response Khrushchev and Ulbricht decided in August to erect a large wall around the entire western sector of Berlin. This wall not only kept East Germans and other eastern Europeans from defecting to West Berlin, it also imprisoned West Berliners, forcing them to live their lives inside a walled city.

Many Americans and Europeans saw the Berlin Wall as a clear signal of Soviet aggression, and they urged the Kennedy administration to destroy it—even at the risk of initiating a war with the Soviet Union. Supporters of American action pointed to Kennedy's policy of flexible response: what was the new policy for, if not to deal decisively with provocations such as the Berlin Wall? Surely, the new American president, who had condemned so clearly Eisenhower's cold-war inaction, would use his new military policy to act immediately in this crisis.

Instead, the Kennedy administration welcomed the construction of the Berlin Wall. Kennedy and his military advisers had not yet had time to develop and implement flexible military forces in Europe. Eisenhower's policy of all-or-nothing thermonuclear war continued to constrain the options of the Kennedy White House: despite the rhetoric of flexible response, in the event of war over Berlin the United States, in fact, had few options other than an all-out thermonuclear attack. The commander of NATO forces, General Lauris D. Norstad, made this fact abundantly clear to Kennedy and his advisers during the fall of 1961. Therefore, the Kennedy administration, as well as Soviet leadership, saw the Berlin Wall as an expedient solution to a difficult problem. The West did not want to leave Berlin under duress. The Soviet Union and its East German ally could no longer tolerate the flight of East German citizens into West Berlin. Neither side wanted to push matters too close to thermonuclear war. The Berlin Wall accommodated all these concerns.

The American decision to tolerate the Berlin Wall might be viewed as a tacit compromise with the Soviet Union and interpreted as a successful example of cold-war negotiation. Kennedy and his advisers, especially Secretary of Defense McNamara, however, saw the situation as proof that the administration had to complete its policy efforts and make flexible response operational. Following the ideas of the political scientist Thomas C. Schelling, McNamara hoped to develop a military posture in Europe and around the world that would allow the United States to confront the Soviet Union confidently and creatively in future crises. Accordingly, in late 1961 and early 1962, McNamara successfully introduced a new American and NATO nuclear policy, which he called the "city-avoidance doctrine."

McNamara's new doctrine broke from the long-standing American policy of destroying the Soviet Union utterly and immediately in the event of general war. Rather, the United States and its NATO allies would seek, once hostilities with the communist bloc commenced, to destroy Soviet nuclear and conventional forces. Such a strategy would spare Soviet and East European population centers and, if executed well, put the West in a position to dictate terms to the Soviet regime. By attacking Soviet missile sites and other military targets at the outset of a war—even, perhaps, before the communists had begun to fight—the United States could prevail in a war with the Soviet Union and do so without blowing up much of the world. McNamara, Kennedy, and other administration officials found this policy an attractive option in the wake of the Berlin Wall compromise, and by the summer and fall of 1962 the Pentagon had begun to refashion its military forces to fulfill the mission of taking out Soviet forces at the beginning of a crisis rather than retaliating for a Soviet move with all-out thermonuclear war.

In 1959 and 1960 Cuban rebels led by Fidel Castro overthrew the government of Fulgencio Batista. By 1961 Castro had begun to turn toward the Soviet Union for military and economic assistance, and, after the failed American attempt to overthrow his regime in April of that year, Castro established a full alliance with the Soviet Union.

In the summer of 1962 the Kennedy administration began to receive intelligence reports of heavy Soviet naval activity around Cuba. On 13 September Kennedy told Khrushchev that the United States would not allow the Soviets to make Cuba into a military base. Khrushchev ignored this warning, and in early October Soviet officials began to construct missile installations on the island.

Kennedy and his advisers immediately decided that either they had to force the Soviet Union to remove the missiles from Cuba, or they must attack the installations. The president convened "Ex Comm," an executive committee of the National Security Council, to manage the Cuban crisis. During the week of 16–22 October, Ex Comm decided to establish a selective naval blockade around Cuba, preventing Soviet ships from entering Cuban waters. Ex Comm rejected more-belligerent options, such as an air strike against the missile installations, an invasion of the island, a full blockade of Cuba, or military action against Soviet allies in Europe or elsewhere.

On 22 October Kennedy announced on television that the United States had discovered the missile installations and had demanded they be removed. Yet, while Soviet and American ships confronted one another in the Caribbean, Kennedy and his advisers decided to adopt a more conciliatory stance, hoping that both sides could avoid direct confrontation and the possibility of war. Attorney General Robert F. Kennedy, the president's brother, arranged a deal with a Soviet agent in Washington whereby the Americans would quietly agree to dismantle and remove shorter-range nuclear missiles it had deployed in Turkey. At the same time the Americans would promise publicly never to invade Cuba. In exchange Khrushchev would terminate the installation program in Cuba. On 27 October, Khrushchev, who was not yet aware of the American decision to accept all these terms, sent a telegram angrily demanding that the United States publicly dismantle its Turkish missiles. The Kennedy administration simply ignored this telegram and accepted the original deal. On 28 October the United States announced that in exchange for an American promise not to invade Cuba, the Soviets were dismantling their missile installations there. Not publicly revealed was the additional American promise to remove the Turkish missiles.

Absent from the American decision-making process during the Cuban Missile Crisis was any serious consideration of initiating major war against the Soviet Union. McNamara and Kennedy had developed the city-avoidance doctrine in order for the Americans and their allies to have creative options during a crisis such as the one in Cuba. The main architects of this new policy, however, declined during the actual crisis to advocate more-offensive courses of actions. Ex Comm transcripts reveal quite clearly that administration officials were far more eager to find some kind of compromise that saved face for both sides than to put the new American strategies to use.

After the Cuban crisis, Kennedy and McNamara no longer spoke of flexible response and the city-avoidance doctrine. Instead, they developed a new American nuclear policy that would retaliate against Soviet cities in the event of major communist attack. At the same time officials would seek to avoid direct confrontation with the Soviet Union. These policies resembled those of President Eisenhower in the late 1950s.

—CAMPBELL CRAIG, UNIVERSITY OF CANTERBURY, NEW ZEALAND

References:

Desmond Ball, *Politics and Force Levels: The Strategic Missile Program of the Kennedy Administration* (Berkeley: University of California Press, 1980);

Campbell Craig, *Destroying the Village: Eisenhower and Thermonuclear War* (New York: Columbia University Press, 1998);

Lawrence Freedman, *The Evolution of Nuclear Strategy* (New York: St. Martin's Press, 1981);

Aleksandr A. Fursenko and Timothy Naftali, *One Hell of a Gamble* (New York: Norton, 1997);

John Lewis Gaddis, *Strategies of Containment: A Critical Appraisal of Postwar American National Security Policy* (New York: Oxford University Press, 1982);

Robert Jervis, *The Meaning of the Nuclear Revolution: Statecraft and the Prospect of Armageddon* (Ithaca, N.Y.: Cornell University Press, 1989);

Philip Nash, *The Other Missiles of October: Eisenhower, Kennedy, and the Jupiters, 1957–1963* (Chapel Hill: University of North Carolina Press, 1997);

Scott Douglas Sagan, *Moving Targets: Nuclear Strategy and National Security* (Princeton, N.J.: Princeton University Press, 1989).

FLEXIBLE RESPONSE

GUATEMALA AND CHILE

Did the United States pursue the correct policies toward the governments of Jacobo Arbenz in Guatemala and Salvador Allende in Chile?

Viewpoint: Yes, U.S. policies toward Guatemala in 1954 and Chile during the early 1970s blocked the spread of communism in Latin America.

Viewpoint: No, U.S. intervention in the internal affairs of Guatemala and Chile was wrong because it only postponed future instability.

In 1944 the government of Guatemalan dictator Jorge Ubico Castañeda was toppled and succeeded by the elected, reformist government of Juan José Arévalo. The elections of 1950 brought to power another pro-reform candidate, Jacobo Arbenz Guzmán. Arbenz initiated a series of economic and land reforms, many of which came at the expense of the United Fruit Company, an American-owned business that was the largest landowner and employer in Guatemala. On 17 June 1952 the Agrarian Reform Law allowed the government to take over land that was not under cultivation, compensating the owner with government bonds. For the purpose of compensation, the value of property was determined by tax assessments. Because of the economic might and political muscle of the United Fruit Company, the valuation of its landholdings had been set artificially low by friendly tax assessors. Thus, while the Arbenz government paid United Fruit $630,000, the U.S. government, acting on behalf of United Fruit, claimed that the land taken from the company was actually worth $15.9 million.

Tensions mounted. Because Arbenz had asked communists for help in passing the Agrarian Reform Law, the United States began to suspect that he was a communist sympathizer. The administration of President Dwight D. Eisenhower ordered the Central Intelligence Agency (CIA) to arrange for his replacement with a more pro-American ruler. The CIA recruited and trained about two hundred Guatemalan troops in Honduras to lead a coup.

On 17 May 1954 it was announced that the Guatemalans were importing arms from Czechoslovakia, leading President Eisenhower to declare a blockade of Guatemala and to ship arms to Nicaragua and Honduras. The American-trained invasion force entered Guatemala on 18 June 1954 under the leadership of Colonel Carlos Castillo Armas. The expected popular uprising did not occur, and two of the three planes providing support to the invaders were shot down. After intense discussions the Americans publicly committed their support to Castillo Armas, causing the Guatemalan army to turn on Arbenz. He resigned on 27 June, escaped to Mexico, and then went on to Czechoslovakia. Castillo Armas finally came to power after a series of coups, reversing the agrarian reforms and returning the nationalized property to United Fruit.

In the 1970 presidential elections in Chile, Salvador Allende Gossens—leader of the Popular Unity Coalition, a group of left-wing parties that he had cobbled together a few months earlier—won the election with 36.3 percent of the popular vote. Allende had lost three previous attempts to win the presidency (in 1952, 1958, and 1964). Alarmed by Allende's leftist rhetoric and his alliance with the Communist Party, the U.S. government and business interests had funneled money to his opposition, the conservative Christian Democratic Party (CDP). In 1964 the Central Intelligence Agency (CIA) spent $2.6 million to support Allende's rival, the Christian Democrat Eduardo Frei Montalva. The situation in 1970 was more complicated. There was a debate within the administration of Richard M. Nixon about whether to support the conservative candidate Jorge Alessandri Rodríguez, who as president from 1958 to 1964 had proposed mild agrarian reforms, or Radomiro Tomic, who represented the left wing of the Christian Democratic Party. The CIA was authorized to spend $300,000 in a campaign of disruption and propaganda against Allende, without direct support to any of his rivals. The International Telephone and Telegraph Corporation (ITT) and other American businesses, however, funneled $600,000 to Alessandri. Since Allende failed to get an absolute majority, his election had to be confirmed by the Chilean congress. Despite vigorous American pressure, the congress approved his election to office.

On entering office Allende proceeded to nationalize the shares of American companies, especially ITT and Kennecott Copper Corporation, in Chilean copper mines and deducted "excess profit" from U.S. companies' revenues. The Chilean government also took over most of the other American companies operating in Chile. Allende's foreign policies further irked Washington. After barely two weeks in office, Allende tightened relations with Fidel Castro's Cuba. He also began talks with North Korea and North Vietnam. In retaliation the United States exerted pressure on the World Bank and the Inter-American Development Bank to deny Chile's requests for loans. The United States was also active in discouraging private loans to Chile.

The Chilean economy deteriorated rapidly, leading to labor unrest and a series of crippling strikes in 1972 and 1973. On 10 January 1973 Allende announced a new system of rationing basic foodstuffs. The March midterm elections resulted in a tie, with Allende's coalition winning just under 44 percent of the vote. In June there was an attempted military coup. The summer was marked by ever more severe strikes and riots, ending in a military takeover of the government on 11 September 1973. Allende was killed—or committed suicide—in the presidential palace while it was under attack. General Augusto Pinochet Ugarte, the leader of the coup, imposed a harsh authoritarian rule over Chile, leading the U.S. Senate, in June 1976, to pass the Kennedy Amendment prohibiting military aid to Chile unless there were improvements in human-rights conditions there.

It is not clear whether the CIA had any direct involvement in the September 1973 coup, but declassified documents do show that between 1970 and 1973 the CIA spent $8 million on a campaign to destabilize the Chilean economy and support Allende's political opponents. In 1974 the CIA activities in Chile were investigated by the Senate Select Committee on Intelligence Activities, leading to new restrictions on the agency's covert operations.

Viewpoint:
Yes, U.S. policies toward Guatemala in 1954 and Chile during the early 1970s blocked the spread of communism in Latin America.

Among the more troubling episodes of the cold war were the American interventions in Guatemala in 1954, where an American-sponsored rebel general ousted the elected government of President Jacobo Arbenz Guzmán, and in Chile in 1973, where American support encouraged the Chilean military to execute a coup against the elected president, Salvador Allende Gossens. In both cases the American government found itself undermining the results of democratic elections, overthrowing democratically elected leaders and creating military dictatorships in their places.

This paradox is particularly startling in the ideological context of the cold war, with the United States heading the North Atlantic Treaty Organization (NATO) of liberal and democratic nations against countries that these Western allies portrayed as the totalitarian, one-party dictatorships of the Soviet bloc. In both Guatemala and Chile, the postcoup regimes proved to be brutal and antidemocratic. In Chile the military junta killed nearly three thousand opponents, while in Guatemala a series of unstable governments led to two decades of instability followed by civil war and the slaughter of some two hundred thousand Guatemalans.

Given the context of the cold war, however, American intervention against these radical and deeply flawed regimes was well justified. Furthermore, while the excesses of the successor regimes were deplorable, they were never American policy. They are more attributable to regional polarization in Guatemala and domestic polarization in Chile than to any inherent effect of the American policy.

The American interventions against Arbenz and Allende occurred twenty years apart, but both are joined by a common theme. Under the Monroe Doctrine—which the United States had declared in 1823 to warn European powers away from interference in the countries of the New World—the United States came to dominate the Western Hemisphere. During both the Arbenz and Allende episodes, U.S. world dominance was challenged by the Soviet Union. In each case a self-proclaimed radical had taken power, creating social chaos and attracting supporters who were openly pro-Soviet.

There were also vast differences between the interventions. Guatemala is located in Central America, a region of small, poor, weak, oligarchical, and deeply divided societies, where the United States has played a traditionally paternalistic and powerful role. American business interests, such as the United Fruit Company, dominated the economies and to a significant degree the politics of Central America. The use of direct American military intervention in the Caribbean Basin (Cuba in 1898, Panama in 1903, Haiti in 1915, Nicaragua in 1912 and 1926, and the Dominican Republic in 1916 and 1965) was an established tradition. Although President Franklin D. Roosevelt's Good Neighbor Policy sought a means short of direct military intervention to maintain American influence in the region, American dominance was in no way lessened.

American hegemony has also had the decidedly positive effect of imposing a Pax Americana on Central America, preventing the outbreak of regional wars. In 1949 and 1955 American pressure halted Nicaraguan efforts to invade Costa Rica, and in 1969 American influence was important in ending the bloody two-week Soccer War between El Salvador and Honduras.

In South America, by contrast, the United States has had little history of direct intervention. Composed of countries larger, wealthier, older, more settled, and geographically more distant from the United States than the Central American states, South America has enjoyed many of the benefits of the Monroe Doctrine (such as U.S. support for Venezuela in its 1895 border dispute with Britain over British Guiana (Guyana) with little of the outright military dominance evident further north. The concomitant of regional independence and relative isolation, however, was a series of internecine territorial wars, such as the devastating War of the Triple Alliance (1864–1870), in which 90 percent of Paraguay's male population was killed in its war against Argentina, Uruguay, and Brazil; and the Chaco War (1932–1935) between Bolivia and Paraguay in which more than one hundred thousand combatants died fighting over the desert scrub lands of the Chaco region.

Latin America represents the "backyard" of the United States—its strategic rear. American security, and to a degree its prosperity, have been ensured by the lack of hemispheric rivals since the departure of the French army from Mexico in 1867. The strategic importance of a secure rear should not be underestimated. It has allowed the United States to develop and thrive without a large standing army, permitted American intervention in both world wars without fear of serious territorial attack, and allowed for American leadership in the cold war on the cheap. During most of the cold war, America dedicated less than half the percentage of its gross national product (GNP) to military expenditures than did the Soviet Union.

The intrusion of the cold war into Latin America and the two successful pro-Soviet takeovers in Cuba and Nicaragua reinforce the strategic importance of the region. Fidel Castro, who came to power in Cuba in 1959, brought the world to the brink of nuclear war in the 1962 Cuban Missile Crisis and sponsored invasions and guerrilla attacks on pro-American regimes throughout the New World. Similarly, following the Sandinista takeover of Nicaragua in 1979, civil war engulfed Central America, with the loss of hundreds of thousands of lives and the expense of billions of dollars in damage and armaments.

The realignment of either Guatemala or Chile to the Soviet camp would have been damaging to the West. In Guatemala the establishment of a Soviet client in the New World would have increased the likelihood of regional and civil wars in Central America. In Chile, with the nearby states of Argentina, Brazil, and Uruguay each experiencing the collapse of its democratic institutions and facing serious Marxist urban-guerrilla movements, the emergence of a Marxist Chile would have injected massive instability into the southern cone. In either case the regional and global impact could have been drastic, opening the New World to cold-war strife.

Nonetheless, the American interventions in Chile and Guatemala have attracted a great deal of criticism. The common reproach has been that the United States was hostile to reformist governments in Latin America and more interested in protecting American business investments than in promoting human rights or democracy. An analysis of the Arbenz and Allende cases in the context of other reformist regimes reveals a different story, however. The United States faced the dilemma of radically reformist governments elsewhere in Latin America—for example, in Bolivia in 1952—but did not intervene.

In Bolivia in 1952 an armed uprising led by the tin miners and other workers brought Víctor Paz Estenssoro back from exile and to power at the head of his Movimiento Nacionalista Revolucionario (National Revolutionary Movement, or MNR). Launching a fundamental social revolution, Paz Estenssoro and Hernando Siles

Zuazo, who succeeded Paz Estenssoro in 1956, nationalized the tin and silver mines, broke up the large estates, and redistributed land to the peasants. American business interests were nationalized, albeit with some compensation, and the domestic power of the "tin barons" and other domestic elites, was supplanted by radical groups such as the tin-miners' unions.

Yet, the Bolivian revolution was explicitly noncommunist, a fact that was widely appreciated in Washington. Representing one of the largest aid programs in history, American support through the Alliance for Progress helped to stabilize the Bolivian economy. In fact, the success of the Bolivian social revolution and generous American support for the reformist governments of the MNR have been credited with inoculating Bolivia against the later appeals of Castro and Ernesto "Che" Guevara for a Marxist revolution in Bolivia. Guevara's ill-fated attempt to create a guerrilla uprising in Bolivia in 1967 received virtually no support from the local peasantry, and his miserable death there in October 1967 was as much a testament to the prudence of American policy as to his own poor planning and self-delusions.

In the context of contemporary expectations and experience, the American interventions in Guatemala and Chile were reasonable and measured. While the critics of American policy may claim that the United States acted unreasonably, the fact that it had dealt favorably with some social revolutions while opposing the radical variety evinces a nuance to American policy that should not be ignored.

When Arbenz took office as president of Guatemala in 1951, he succeeded the reformist Juan José Arévalo, who had governed since 1945. Arévalo, a teacher and writer, had implemented his "spiritual socialism," bringing a social-security system and new labor laws to Guatemala. He also faced an average of one military-coup attempt every six months, and he presided over a deeply fractured, predominantly Indian, and in many ways still feudal, society.

Arbenz, who had strong leftist sympathies, had been a colonel in the Guatemalan military. On becoming president he sought to carry out his own reforms, quickly legalizing the Communist Party and, with strong Communist backing, securing the passage of the Agrarian Reform Law in 1952. This law allowed the nationalization of large estates as well as more than four hundred thousand acres of property owned by the United Fruit Company, with compensation at only a fraction of market value.

The expropriations created instant internal opposition and deeply polarized Guatemalan society. They also gave United Fruit and other business interests many domestic and military allies against Arbenz, whose relations with the Communists similarly alienated the Catholic Church. In 1953 a bloody uprising against Arbenz was put down in the city of Salamá.

Across Latin America the Arbenz regime was gaining notoriety as the Latin "socialist" experiment. Arbenz welcomed hundreds of Latin American leftist political exiles to the capital, Guatemala City. Among these Marxists and revolutionaries was the young Argentine Che Guevara, who was introduced in Guatemala to the exiled followers of a young Cuban rebel named Fidel Castro. Guatemala was rapidly becoming the focal point of Latin American revolution.

Arbenz was also attracting the hostility of neighboring states and leaders, such as Anastasio Somoza of Nicaragua, who feared the example of land expropriations and the sanctuary given to anti-Somoza exiles. By early 1954 the presidents of Honduras, El Salvador, and Nicaragua were united in their determination to oust Arbenz.

As Arbenz struggled in Guatemala, the Eisenhower administration took office in Washington. Two brothers, John Foster Dulles and Allen Welsh Dulles, became, respectively, secretary of state and director of the CIA. Both had ties to United Fruit and were receptive to the opponents of Arbenz. As a war of words escalated between Arbenz and Washington, Dwight D. Eisenhower decided to oust Arbenz in a mission dubbed Operation Success.

With regional tensions rising, Arbenz approached the Soviet bloc for arms, receiving several tons of Czech weapons on the Polish freighter *Alfhem* in 1954. The arrival of these weapons thoroughly alarmed Guatemala's neighbors and triggered Arbenz's ouster. A rebel colonel, Carlos Castillo Armas, had organized a paramilitary force in Nicaragua, and with heavy regional and CIA support, he invaded Guatemala via Honduras on 18 June, proclaiming himself provisional president. After several days of confusion, the Guatemalan military pressured Arbenz to resign, and on 27 June, Arbenz stepped down.

Guatemala did not settle into a stable democracy, but then it had no established democratic tradition. The pattern of military coups and oligarchic politics continued until the late 1970s, when the ascent of the Marxist Sandinistas to power in Nicaragua brought a new level of violence to Central America. With social polarization ripping apart the region and Guatemalan rejection of American arms and supervision, mass killings began in Guatemala.

Given the history of Central America as a virtual American protectorate, the American decision to oust the Arbenz government was not difficult or unreasonable. Arbenz had made overtures to the Soviet bloc, had purchased Czech weapons, and had made Guatemala a refuge for communists and revolutionaries. By menacing his neighbors in Central America and by nationalizing the property of Americans and the Guatemalan elite without real compensation, he had alienated powerful regional interests. Arbenz had become hostile to America and destabilizing to the region, while leaving himself domestically vulnerable. His ouster was not only reasonable, but predictable.

The overthrow of Dr. Salvador Allende in Chile in 1973 occurred in an atmosphere even more poisoned by years of violence, social polarization, civil unrest, politically inspired economic collapse, and the beginnings of civil war. The established tradition of democratic government in Chile made this political collapse all the more startling. Yet, without Allende's destruction of Chile's social consensus and his creation of a virtual civil war, the American efforts against Allende would have been unnecessary and ineffective.

Chilean democracy evolved from a caudillo system that by the 1870s had developed a tradition of political tolerance. Power was balanced between a president and a congress. By the mid 1900s Chile had become a relatively prosperous country with a substantial middle class and a militant, radical working class.

Even before Allende's election, however, Chile had become a deeply polarized society. Socialists, leftist radicals, and communists represented a solid third of the electorate and were dedicated to profound social revolution. Another third traditionally supported parties of the Right. Since their emergence in the late 1950s, Christian Democrats uneasily occupied the reformist center.

After the presidencies of the rightist Jorge Alessandri Rodríguez (1958–1964) and the Christian Democrat Eduardo Frei Montalva (1964–1970), the Chilean election of 1970 loomed as a three-cornered struggle. The Marxist Left had united under the Popular Unity (UP) banner, openly calling for "transition to socialism," with Allende, an avowed Marxist, as their candidate. Winning a plurality of 36.3 percent of the vote, Allende was confirmed by the congress after an agonizing round of negotiations between the UP and the divided Christian Democrats, who sought to somehow restrain Allende's radicalism.

On taking power Allende immediately launched into a radical program of land and business expropriations. He authorized hundreds of state takeovers of private businesses. His proposed takeover of the trucking sector affected forty thousand independent truckers. In the rural sector squatters routinely seized lands,

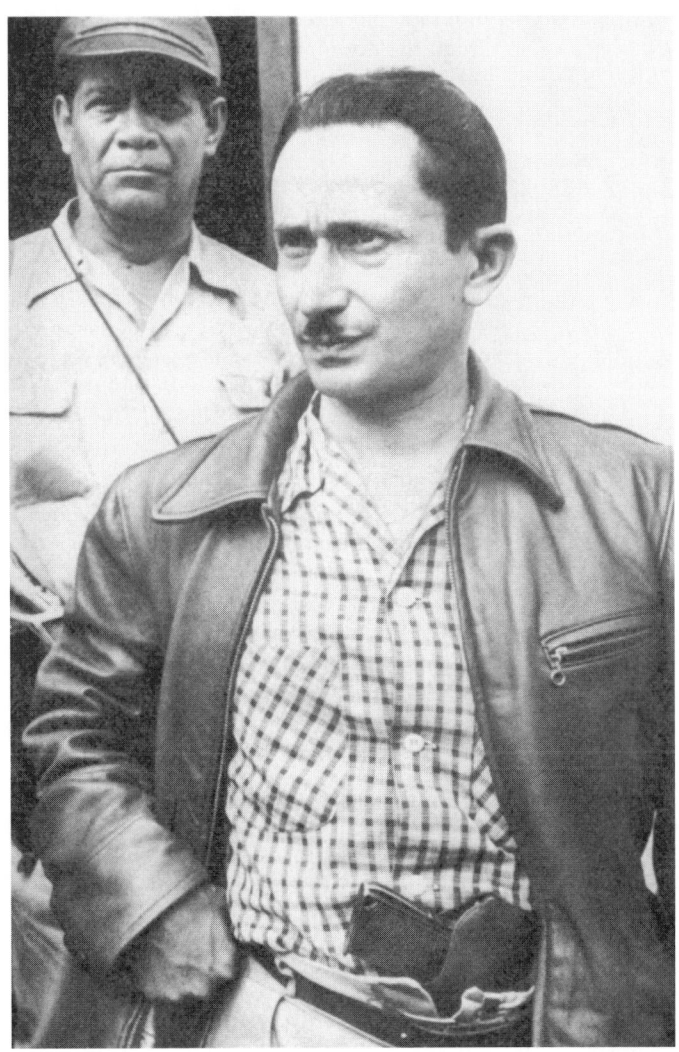

Carlos Castillo Armas after his successful U.S.-backed coup against the government of President Jacobo Arbenz Guzmán

often supported by the radical and armed Movimiento de Izquierda Revolucionaria (Revolutionary Left Movement, or MIR).

These massive expropriations shattered Chilean society, generating intense, disruptive, and sometimes violent reactions. Landowners resisted land seizures by setting up local commando groups, known nationally as the Gremial movement. A series of industrial and general strikes, most notably the truckers' strike and massive general strike of October 1972, crippled the economy. Agricultural production plummeted, and inflation soared to more than 300 percent. The MIR, the Mapucistas (members of the militant Movement of Popular Action, or MAPU), and other leftist groups launched bank robberies and a terror campaign that killed scores of people. Chile was on the brink of collapse.

Countering the resistance and the massive social disruptions, Allende took the fateful step of bringing senior military officers into his cabinet, involving them directly in the poisoned politics of the time. He also instituted a national system of price controls, to be monitored by his own local block committees, and turned a blind eye to the development of the "cordones populares"—armed leftist workers militias. Further alienating the United States, Allende established close relations with Cuba, bringing Cuban advisers to Chile.

Amid the mounting violence and chaos, a congressional election was held in 1973, with the opposition coalition of rightists and Christian Democrats winning a narrow margin. Faced with what they believed to be an outlaw president and national collapse, the congress voted in August 1973 for the military to defend the "constitution and law" against Allende. Three weeks later, General Augusto Pinochet Ugarte led the bloody coup that ousted Allende.

American support for Allende's opponents was important, but hardly the only factor precipitating his overthrow. In 1970 American pressure on the Chilean Congress to prevent Allende's election was ineffective, and American support that did matter—aiding the striking truckers for example—merely built on existing social forces. Given the strategic importance of Chile and the radicalism of Allende, this American support was entirely responsible and reasonable.

The Chilean military took power by force, and far from reestablishing the Right in power, they completely supplanted it. Determined to stamp out the Marxist forces that had seized property, committed terrorist acts, and even infiltrated parts of the military, the military junta under Pinochet was brutal and ruthless, killing some three thousand people. This violence reflected the deep scars within Chilean society after Allende, however, and was not an underlying American objective.

Chile returned to democracy in the 1990s, after Pinochet stepped-down in 1989, and the Christian Democrats Patrico Alwyn Azócar, and then Edwardo Frei Ruiz-Tagle, were elected president. After the bloody disruptions of the Allende and Pinochet years, Chilean democracy had returned to a more stable, and traditional, equilibrium.

—GRANT M. LALLY, LALLY & LALLY, P.C.

Viewpoint:
No, U.S. intervention in the internal affairs of Guatemala and Chile was wrong because it only postponed future instability.

In 1954 and 1973 the United States used its power to overthrow democratic governments in Latin America. Though they were separated by two eventful decades, the military coups d'état in Guatemala in 1954 and Chile in 1973 had many things in common. Both coups were bloody affairs that ushered in long-term, brutal military dictatorships and deepened social and political polarization. Members of opposition organizations, suspected sympathizers, or others deemed enemies of the state were rounded up, tortured, murdered, or made to "disappear." In Guatemala 1954 marked the point of departure at which an entire society plunged headlong into a devastating process of self-mutilation and national prostration (fanned by outside meddling), consuming the lives of hundreds of thousands of citizens. Their feeble transition to democracy since 1986 indicates that Guatemalans have yet to recover from the aftereffects. For Chile military rule had an equally deep impact despite economic prosperity before and after the return to democracy in 1989. Military rule left Chile divided, and Chilean democracy was deformed by constitutional engineering before the military government left power. The United States had pledged itself to the promotion and collective defense of democracy, but it was so threatened by the democratic governments of Guatemala and Chile that it subverted the ideals it had promised to protect.

Both military coups resulted from active American collusion. Although these events have been labeled cold-war episodes, they are consistent with the long historical pattern of U.S. interventionism in Latin America. The essential difference is that during the cold war the United States turned away from sending in the Marines to using covert operations and training Latin American troops. The underlying goals, motives, and pathologies never changed, even if U.S. intervention, was dressed in anticommunist garb after 1945. While the scale of participation differed and while each coup was the culmination of deeper, persistent political crises with local origins, U.S. actions in Guatemala and Chile were driven by the same historical obsession with immunizing the hemisphere against "foreign" intervention, by underlying pathologies engendered at times by well-intentioned crusading universalism, and by mostly negative, ethnocentric images of Latin Americans and their societies as unruly, unstable, and in need of supervision, as people easily duped by foreigners and their subversive ideologies. The circumstances surrounding the overthrow of democratically elected, constitutional governments in Guatemala and Chile should cause citizens of the United States to examine the purposes and uses of U.S. national power. Rather than discussing the moral costs, however, this essay focuses on how such interventions were ineffective in protecting short-term concrete interests and how they undermined long-term U.S. political and national-security objectives in the region.

The interventions in Chile and Guatemala involved concerted planning and conspiracy at the highest levels of the U.S. government. The active participation, complicity, and encouragement of the United States in both coups are confirmed by declassified documents. The decisions to overthrow Arbenz and Allende were made years before actual events transpired. The administration of President Richard M. Nixon, for instance, decided to topple the Allende government only days after the 1970 Chilean presidential elections, before Allende was confirmed and sworn in by the Chilean congress, but he was not ousted until September 1973. U.S. unease with Guatemalan reform and Arbenz's supposed communist tendencies started during the administration of Harry S Truman. Prior to assuming office in 1953, President Dwight D. Eisenhower had already decided to overthrow Arbenz.

U.S. intervention also included direct coordination with local conspirators, as well as sustained covert operations aimed at "destabilizing" each country's political and economic situation and demonizing the new governments. The United States not only contacted extremists in the Chilean military, such as the volatile General Roberto Viaux Marambio, but spent millions of dollars to promote strikes and business stoppages, as well as financing the political opposition. In its efforts to isolate and discredit Arbenz the United States manipulated the local media (through its covert broadcast of Radio Liberty) and the U.S. press. Americans organized, armed, and trained paramilitary rebel forces in Guatemala, coordinating aerial support for their invasion and producing a potent psychological warfare campaign before and during the attack. Though it exceeded later U.S. involvement in Chile, this explicit role in equipping and coaching the "liberators" or "freedom fighters" was not unusual for American governments, as evidenced by U.S. activities in the Panamanian isthmus (1903), Cuba (1961), and Nicaragua (1980s). The U.S. interventions in Guatemala and Chile are the clearest examples of corporate influence in the making of U.S. foreign policy.

Despite the similarities of the interventions in Guatemala and Chile, the extent of U.S. participation in each nation was not equal. The U.S. role was far more direct and determining in Guatemala than in Chile, which was heading toward political rupture with or without U.S. involvement. The underlying political crises leading up to these interventions were not the making of the United States. Since the early 1940s the political situation in Guatemala had been deteriorating. Political struggles centered largely on redistributive politics and mounting pressures to redress longstanding social and economic inequities. In other words, the roots of political insta-

COUP IN CHILE, 1973

U.S. attaché Patrick Ryan was in Valparaiso, Chile, during the successful military takeover led by General Augusto Pinochet on 11 September 1973. Ryan's report includes an account of his attempt to warn U.S. citizens to stay under cover and an assessment of the rebels' effectiveness.

Moving about the city even in military uniform, driving a diplomatic auto and flashing a Chilean Navy I.D. card wasn't easy. Roadblocks had been established at all key intersections. Most were manned by nervous young soldiers/sailors with semi-automatic weapons, round in chamber and weapon OFF safe. They had been briefed to expect a violent combat reaction from Marxist forces and itchy trigger fingers were the rule rather than the exception. In my appointed rounds I used back alleys and side streets where possible—where not, maximum discretion coupled with an extremely friendly "Buenos Dias" in my best Irish brogue, managed to reach all but one American family before Russian Roulette game with roadblocks ran out of luck. Apparently final roadblock didn't "sabe" my Irish-Spanish. However, I clearly understood their pointed signals with Grease Guns, which in any language translated into: "Get Going, Gringo." . . .

Chile's coup d' état was close to perfect. Unfortunately, "close" only counts in horseshoes and hand grenades; consequently there were problems. H-hour was set in cement countrywide for 0600, but as often happens in such people-controlled operations, someone doesn't follow the script. For reasons too labyrinth to explain here, H-hour in Santiago was slipped to 0830.

Original plan called for President Allende to be held incommunicado in his home until the coup was a fait accompli. H-hour delay in Santiago permitted Allende to be alerted at 0730. Allende immediately dashed to the RONEDA (palace) under escort of a heavily armed personal security force, Grupa de Amigos Perzonales (GAP). At the Raneda he had access to radio communications facilities which permitted him to personally implore "workers and students to come to the Raneda and defend your Government against the Armed Forces." The hour was 0830.

Source: *Situation Report #2, U.S. Department of Defense, U.S. Milgroup, 1 October 1973, National Security Archive Electronic Briefing Book 8.*

bility lay in historic, vast socioeconomic inequalities. Arbenz's policies were perceived as threatening not just by United Fruit and its subsidiaries but also by the landed oligarchy and ruling class of Guatemala.

Allende came to power in a much more polarized, unstable political context, a deeply divided society and political system. Moreover, he won the presidency with the thinnest of electoral victories (36.3 percent of the popular vote), in a country that had been practically divided

GUATEMALA AND CHILE

into three even political sectors—left, right, and center—since the 1940s. By the 1970 presidential elections the splits among and within the parties had deepened, and Chileans continued to move toward the extreme right or left, leaving a void in the center. The principal center party, the Christian Democratic Party, simply imploded, leaving no viable moderate political alternative. By this time political violence and terrorism had escalated, carried out mostly by leftist groups such as the Movimiento de Izquierda Revolucionaria (Revolutionary Left Movement, or MIR). Allende contributed to his own downfall with some of his policy choices and responses to the maneuvers of his opponents. In the context of polarized politics, class warfare, and his thin electoral base of support, greater moderation and compromise might have been what Chile needed most. (It is not certain, however, that such measures would have dampened the plans of the pro-coup forces and the Nixon administration.)

Though in Guatemala and Chile the United States was motivated by what it perceived as instances of "communist subversion," private American economic interests and the influence exerted by U.S. multinational corporations were central in both cases. Corporate officers not only had privileged access to high-level policymakers, but government officials were even investors in businesses that were directly affected by political changes in the region. For example, John Foster Dulles, secretary of state during the Eisenhower administration, and his brother Allen Dulles, director of the CIA in 1953–1961), had conflicting interests because they had legal or financial stakes in companies that actively campaigned for U.S. intervention. Executives of companies such as the United Fruit Company, ITT, the Anaconda Corporation, and Kennecott Copper Corporation exerted significant influence in fashioning interventionist policies through direct access to policymakers. Furthermore, a "revolving door" between these businesses and high-level government offices created conflicts of interest. For example, John A. McCone, who was director of the CIA under Presidents John F. Kennedy and Lyndon B. Johnson, was later a CIA consultant while employed as a senior executive of ITT. Though it remains unclear if any funds were actually passed on, it has been established that ITT offered to contribute $1 million to any CIA plan to overthrow Allende.

To claim that private business highjacked U.S. hemispheric policy may be an exaggeration; policymakers were also driven by other concerns and obsessions. The actual losses of profit suffered by multinational corporations in Guatemala and Chile were far less than those incurred by U.S.-owned operations nationalized by Mexico in the 1930s or by Cuba in the 1960s. The

reformist governments in Chile and Guatemala were committed to modest redistributive policies—ranging from giving workers the right to strike and collective bargaining to implementing more assertive nationalization policies. At no point did either government attempt to expropriate U.S.-owned property without prompt, reasonable compensation (as determined by U.S. law), nor did the reformism of either threaten to eliminate the private market and introduce socialism, as critics of Allende charged. While Allende's reformism and nationalization programs were more sweeping, the reforms carried out by Arbenz were no more "radical" than those the United States later encouraged under the Alliance for Progress.

The peculiarly cold-war element is apparent in an almost fanatical ideological obsession and proclivity not only to cast the new governments in Guatemala and Chile as "communistic" but to treat events in these nations as consequential for the global balance of power. Richard Immerman has called this manner of thinking the "Cold War ethos." The cold-war atmosphere led U.S. policymakers to exaggerate developments on the periphery and to define "threat" in exceedingly ideological terms. Fears of communist subversions and the belief that governments would fall to communism like dominoes led the United States to costly miscalculations not just in Latin America but in Southeast Asia. Just as Arbenz was being overthrown in Guatemala, U.S. advisers were making their first appearance in Vietnam. Cold-war blinders increased U.S. inability to understand local developments, to have a measured appreciation for postwar nationalism and radicalism in Latin America. Throughout the cold war, the United States exhibited an excessive ideological preoccupation and a ready-made proclivity to misinterpret regional developments in the most malign fashion and exaggerate the implications of events in the remotest of villages or smallest of Caribbean islands. The U.S. overreaction in Guatemala and Chile demonstrated a misreading of Soviet aims, influence, and capacity to control communist and nationalist groups in Latin America and elsewhere. As George F. Kennan feared, this perception dragged the United States into a series of civil wars from which it had difficulty extricating itself.

At worst the governments of Arbenz and Allende, both elected by recognized free and fair elections, were nationalist and reformist, including only small numbers of communists. In Guatemala a few communists in the lower rungs of the state administration were active in the politically charged agrarian-reform agencies.

In fact, the policies of Arbenz and Allende were consistent with those of their reformist predecessors (if a bit faster paced and wider in scope). Nor were they significantly different from the nationalist, assertive policies of governments (including staunch U.S. allies) all over the region. Neither Arbenz or Allende represented an actual threat to the United States. In principle the presence of antagonistic regimes in the hemisphere, especially if they are allied with an extra-hemispheric power, has the potential to present serious strategic concerns. Few can quarrel with the strategic significance of the Soviet placement of nuclear missiles in Cuba in 1962 or the presence of French imperial troops in Mexico a hundred years earlier. Yet, it stretches credulity and imagination to make similar arguments about the leftist governments and politics of Arbenz and Allende. Neither Arbenz nor Allende established significant economic or military ties to the Soviet Union. Neither government could be described as communist. Nor did either country represent an actual or potential threat to its neighbors or to regional stability. Both governments came to power at times of high levels of domestic instability and social strife (long in the making in both countries). It is important to recognize that the United States contributed as much to the instability as the often misguided policies of Arbenz and Allende.

In a narrow sense U.S. covert interventions in Guatemala and Chile were "successful." Colluding with local conspirators, the United States toppled Arbenz and Allende. As far as some U.S. officials were concerned, communism had been rolled back, and U.S.-owned corporations were able to regain their high profits and unhampered operations. What did the United States really achieve, however? Was there a credible threat to U.S. strategic and economic interests? Were there other means, short of intervention, to protect those interests? Were the means employed commensurate with the ends, and were these ends achieved in the long run? Though the interests of individual U.S. citizens and business were substantial, U.S. national interests in Guatemala and Chile were minimal, and the long-term results were not worth the costs.

In fact, U.S. interventions in Guatemala, Chile, and elsewhere in Latin American have actually damaged U.S. interests and have ultimately been unsuccessful. Direct military and covert interventions were counterproductive, even if private economic interests gained temporary advantages.

After such interventions U.S. relations with Latin American governments have deteriorated, obstructing or increasing the cost of other U.S. policy goals in the region. Anti-U.S. sentiment also increased, especially among the politicized youth. In fact, one might argue that American interference indirectly promoted, not discouraged, revolutionary and socialist activities. The extent of the anti-U.S. sentiment sparked by the intervention in Guatemala was made plain by angry demonstrations during Vice-president Richard M. Nixon's visit to the region four years later. To its credit the United States responded by reorienting its regional policy during the last years of the Eisenhower administration, laying the groundwork for the Alliance for Progress.

There were other damaging side effects of U.S. interventionism. Policymakers and academics alike often overlook the fact that U.S. interventions tend to lead to vicious circles of interventionism. The installation or propping up of "friendly" dictators and governments merely deepened underlying sources of political and social tensions, postponing events that required new interventions. U.S. military incursions in Latin America during the 1920s sowed the seeds of political crises of the 1980s, engendering greater instability in the long term. Such a dynamic is inherent in spheres of influence, its logic reinforced by the fact that the United States became a prized political resource for local contending forces. U.S. interventions in Latin America have always had local co-conspirators, often allied, elite classes and political factions that ably manipulated U.S. policy, playing on U.S. fears and courting intervention as a means to protect or advance their own particular interests. In Guatemala, as elsewhere in Latin America, U.S. interventionism made local contending elites look to the United States to shore up their weaknesses and protect their concerns. The oligarchic class and political elite, accustomed to relying on U.S. backing, straddled societies marked by vast inequalities and poverty and where social and political orders were brittle. The United States often installed weak, unpopular, corrupt military dictatorships whose only source of support, legitimacy, and survival was the United States and its taxpayers. The hand-picked strongman in Guatemala, U.S.-trained Carlos Castillo Armas, was assassinated only a few years after he was installed as president. By the mid 1960s civil wars and right-wing death squads had become the norm in the country, costing the United States ever greater amounts of money (and prestige) to prop up corrupt, repressive military dictatorships in the name of anticommunism. The instability in Guatemala only increased, and by the 1980s its social and political crises caused waves of refugees to seek and receive asylum in the United States. The U.S. not only misread the local situation (and failed to distinguish actual threats to its interests), but it repeatedly turned to militarized and covert "quick fixes" during the cold war—for problems that required long-term solutions.

Just as these interventions have tended to undermine U.S. interests in the region, their negative consequences also reverberated domestically. As illustrated by the Iran-Contra scandal and the incursions of the 1980s, U.S. interventionism has tarnished the U.S. constitutional order, violated the law, fragmented the political process, and divided the public. As Kennan had feared, U.S. intervention in the domestic affairs of other nations, and U.S. obsession with halting the spread of communism worldwide, could not but diminish the constitutional role and political values of the U.S. government at home. The interventions in Guatemala and Chile also demonstrate the degree to which private, particularistic interests exert inordinate influence on U.S. foreign policy. In principle U.S. power and policy ought to serve and promote the interests of its citizens abroad, but in practice private and national interests often collide, and myopic, short-term calculations can undermine both. In the cases of Guatemala and Chile, U.S. businesses influenced U.S. policies for their own particular gains and to the detriment of long-term U.S. interests.

From the beginning of its interaction with the independent nations of South and Central America, the United States declared that it had a unilateral "right" to concern itself with the affairs of Latin America, especially those it deemed essential to its "safety and security." The language of the Monroe Doctrine (1823) and its later amendments asserts that the United States has the unilateral right to intervene in the region to prevent "foreign" incursions and ideologies. As in all spheres of influence, the United States was preoccupied with the external behavior, stability, and ideological makeup of subordinate Latin American countries. In the course of protecting its interests the United States became deeply involved in the domestic affairs of these countries. The logic of interventionism was unavoidable. Intervention and interference became a certainty with the penetration of the region by private U.S. economic and commercial interests, which often enjoyed monopoly profits and constituted the bulk of economic activity in many countries. Therefore, even the mildest reforms negatively affected their operations and set the stage for U.S. intervention. Yet, as the Good Neighbor Policy and the Alliance for Progress suggest, the United States was aware that there were other options for maintaining regional stability and promoting its interests in Latin America.

A principle feature of U.S. policy toward its southern neighbors has been the image of Latin America as a region responsible for "chronic wrongdoing," as President Theodore Roosevelt put it, requiring not only supervision but intervention. This interpretation reflects something deeper about the U.S. self-image as a world power, its political mythologies, and its "arro-

gance of power." The underlying pathologies in U.S. policy toward Latin America have not changed from the time of the Monroe Doctrine. The United States has seen itself as the natural protector, or policeman, of the hemisphere, presuming to know what is best for the region. The cold war heightened sensibilities and intensified trends that were already deeply embedded in U.S. attitudes toward Latin America. The interventions in Guatemala and Chile were not unique, isolated episodes, but links in a long chain of U.S. activities in the hemisphere.

To characterize the U.S. interventions in Guatemala, Chile, and elsewhere as right or wrong, successes or failure, misses the much larger point. Interventions in Guatemala, Chile, Turkey, Greece, and Iran were "successful." In Guatemala and Iran, U.S. intervention merely postponed and magnified future catastrophe. For the most part the deeply rooted impulse of the United States to interfere in the affairs of others, to mold the world in its own image—together with new pathologies engendered by the cold war—led the United States into costly expenditures of national treasure and lives in distant places of no strategic value. U.S. intervention in Guatemala involved minimal costs in terms of national effort and resources, but neither did it contribute to stability in Latin America. Neither Guatemala nor Chile proved anymore compliant to U.S. wishes after the coups, even if U.S. investors profited. Conditions abroad often necessitate intervention as a tool of national policy. They did not in Guatemala and Chile. Given its historical impulses, its image of itself, and its role in the world, the United States may long continue to make intervention the dominant deature of its foreign policy. Ultimately U.S. citizens may have to decide if the proper ends to which U.S. national power is employed should include participating in or supporting the murders of citizens of other countries or if such uses of power subvert U.S. political values.

–JOÃO RESENDE-SANTOS, UNIVERSITY OF PENNSYLVANIA

References

Jon Lee Anderson, *Che Guevara: A Revolutionary Life* (New York: Grove, 1997);

Simon Collier, Harold Blakemore, and Thomas E. Skidmore, eds., *The Cambridge Encyclopedia of Latin America*, second edition (Cambridge & New York: Cambridge University Press, 1993);

Nathaniel Davis, *The Last Two Years of Salvador Allende* (Ithaca, N.Y.: Cornell University Press, 1985);

Jonathan L. Fried, ed., *Guatemala in Rebellion: Unfinished History* (New York: Grove, 1983);

Seymour M. Hersch, "The Price of Power: Kissinger, Nixon, and Chile," *Atlantic Monthly*, 250 (December 1982): 31–58;

Michael H. Hunt, *Ideology and US Foreign Policy* (New Haven: Yale University Press, 1987);

Richard H. Immerman, *The CIA in Guatemala: The Foreign Policy of Intervention* (Austin: University of Texas Press, 1982);

Brian Loveman, *Chile: The Legacy of Hispanic Capitalism*, second edition (New York: Oxford University Press, 1988);

Ivan Musicant, *The Banana Wars: A History of United States Military Intervention in Latin America from the Spanish-American War to the Invasion of Panama* (New York: Macmillan, 1990);

Stephen G. Rabe, *Eisenhower and Latin America: The Foreign Policy of Anticommunism* (Chapel Hill: University of North Carolina Press, 1988);

Stephen Schlesinger and Stephen Kinzer, *Bitter Fruit: The Untold Story of the American Coup in Guatemala,* second edition (Garden City, N.Y.: Doubleday, 1983);

Paul E. Sigmund, *The Overthrow of Allende and the Politics of Chile, 1964–1976* (Pittsburgh: University of Pittsburgh Press, 1977);

Gregory F. Treverton, *Covert Action: The Limits of Intervention in the Postwar World* (New York: Basic Books, 1987);

United States Senate, Select Committee to Study Governmental Operations with Respect to Intelligence Activities, *Covert Action in Chile, 1963–1973: Staff Report of the Select Committee to Study Governmental Operations with Respect to Intelligence Activities, United States Senate* (Washington, D.C.: U.S. Government Printing Office, 1975).

HITLER AND STALIN

Is the comparison between Hitler and Stalin valid and justified?

Viewpoint: Yes, Hitler and Stalin both established brutal totalitarian regimes.

Viewpoint: No, Hitler and Stalin were more dissimilar than alike.

Adolf Hitler and Joseph Stalin have the distinction of being history's most infamous dictators. Each enjoyed absolute power over his country, power that ended only with his death. Both were also driven by a strong desire to preserve their power and expand their influence in the world.

It is clear that both Hitler and Stalin were dominated by the desire to rise to power and maintain it. Both men were known for incisive political calculations and seemingly arbitrary acts of ruthlessness and cruelty in the service of this end. Much scholarship suggests that such behavior by one may even have inspired it in the other. Scholars have drawn a correlation, for example, between Hitler's purge of the Nazi Brownshirts in 1934 and Stalin's purges of the Soviet leadership over the successive years. Their foreign policies share the traits of shrewd diplomacy and naked aggression.

Yet, it is also easy to recognize crucial differences between the two men. Hitler's rise to power was based on mass political appeal, while Stalin's was based largely on his ability to manipulate the administration of the Communist Party. The personal ruling styles of both rulers were different in many ways as well. Stalin is often remembered for his cold rationality. Hitler, by contrast, was known for his highly emotional approach to statecraft. Translated into practical politics, this distinction is important. Stalin's rationality allowed him to avoid the consequences of his mistakes and to die of old age, while Hitler's irrationality caused him to become trapped by his mistakes and to take his own life.

Viewpoint:
Yes, Hitler and Stalin both established brutal totalitarian regimes.

Violence and bloodshed in the twentieth century have been so common that it is hard to single out one or two individuals who best personify that destruction. Mao Tse-tung, Pol Pot, Tojo Hideki, and other dictators all contributed their share to the record of human atrocities. The most infamous perpetrators of orga-

nized cruelty in the twentieth century, however, are two men whose fates were intertwined during the 1930s and 1940s: Adolf Hitler and Joseph Stalin.

The parallels between Hitler and Stalin, and between the dictatorships they created, were evident as early as the 1930s, but the two were not compared systematically until after the Second World War. The new notion of totalitarianism was reintroduced in the early 1950s. The term *totalitarian* was coined in Italy in the 1930s to describe what Benito Mussolini regarded as an ideal regime—one that unified the

RENDEZVOUS

population within its territory and eliminated all opposition, debate, and factionalism. After Hitler's rise to power in 1933, many observers of Germany informally used the term to describe the new Nazi state and its desire to place society under the strict control of the National Socialist (Nazi) Party. The formal concept of *totalitarianism*, and the likening of the Soviet Union under Stalin to Nazi Germany, emerged in 1951 with the publication of Hannah Arendt's book *The Origins of Totalitarianism*. Arendt argued that neither Stalin nor Hitler sought power for its own sake; instead, they used it to reconstruct the world and the individuals therein.

Building on Arendt's thesis, Carl Friedrich and Zbigniew Brzezinski sought to provide a more elaborate definition that would encompass all the relevant similarities of totalitarian regimes and would distinguish such regimes from ordinary dictatorships. They isolated several core features of totalitarianism: the presence of an official ideology that sought to control "all vital aspects of man's existence," the creation of a "mass party" based on the ruling ideology and led by a dictator, the use of widespread terror, and the technological control and manipulation

of mass communications, the armed forces, the economy, and other facets of human life.

This definition of totalitarianism not only provided the basis for comparing the Soviet Union and Nazi Germany but also offered insights into the similarities between Hitler and Stalin. The labeling of such men as mere "dictators" seemed inadequate; their regimes were a particular form of dictatorship that went beyond authoritarianism and evoked images of violent tyranny unseen since Genghis Khan or Ivan the Terrible. Totalitarianism helped specify the many parallels in the slogans, speeches, and cultlike adoration surrounding Stalin and Hitler, as well as the brutal policies that the two men pursued.

The regimes that Hitler and Stalin established were both equipped with all-encompassing ideologies. Stalin embraced, without much modification, a Marxist ideology shaped and interpreted by Vladimir Lenin, and even at the height of his power Stalin paid homage to Lenin as the ideological wellspring of the Soviet Communist Party. Hitler had to cobble together his own rather incoherent ideology, based on violent racism and a messianic German nationalism whose only consistent element seemed to be

Adolf Hitler and Joseph Stalin meeting over the "corpse" of Poland, September 1939; editorial cartoon by David Low for the *Evening Standard* (London)

extreme anti-Semitism. Each man professed an absolute devotion to the ideas he espoused and claimed that the implementation of his particular ideology would mean the ultimate salvation of humanity, a task worthy of the "god of history."

For each man, his ideology was the only acceptable way of viewing the world. Each regarded opposition and dissent not as a legitimate difference of opinion, but as treachery and turpitude. Conflict, whether "class" conflict in the Soviet Union or "racial" conflict in Nazi Germany, was seen as a total war in which the opposing side was to be destroyed, not just defeated. In each state, entire groups of people were regarded as enemies of the reigning ideology because of their identities. The so-called kulaks (prosperous peasants) in the Soviet Union and the Jews in Nazi Germany were deemed so inimical to the new society that they had to be removed: through exile, forced starvation, or shooting in the Soviet case, and through the industrialized slaughter of the gas chambers in the German case.

In carrying out these policies Stalin and Hitler exercised ruthless control over their governments through their leadership of the ruling party, which was the protector of state ideology. The Nazis and the Soviet Communist Party each claimed to be the ultimate representative of the popular will, and each dictator asserted that his party was the only defense against "enemies of the people." The entrenchment of highly centralized, one-party rule ensured that power would not be diluted by the large bureaucracy that each regime had built to implement its goals.

Both Stalin and Hitler sought to foster a mythlike cult around themselves to justify, to themselves and to others, their seemingly fantastic schemes for destroying and remaking society. They personally supervised the writing of their biographies so that they were portrayed as revolutionary heroes and supremely wise and courageous leaders. Both developed murderous hatreds for anyone who challenged their leadership or even portrayed them in a less-than-flattering way. They relied on the mass media to convey images of themselves as the saviors of their nations, and both went to great lengths to stage scenes of mass adulation for themselves.

By the same token, Stalin and Hitler were obsessed by purported "enemies" and by alleged "conspiracies" against their regimes, and they justified violence and slaughter as the only way to overcome those suspected threats. For both men, enemies served a dual function. On the one hand, they could be depicted as "wreckers" and "back-stabbers" who were responsible for the failure of certain policies. On the other hand, the alleged presence of enemies and conspiracies could bolster the regime's claim to exercise an "iron hand." Stalin's and Hitler's murderous antipathy toward enemies was similar; only their

identities differed. For Hitler, the prime enemy of Germany was the "Jewish race," which he believed posed a mortal threat to the "Aryan" German "race." Although other marginal groups, such as Gypsies, homosexuals, and disabled people, also were the target of Hitler's murderous wrath, his chief goal was to exterminate the Jews. Stalin, by contrast, had a less discriminating view of his enemies and believed they might be lurking anywhere, even among his most loyal supporters. Not only did Stalin want to "eradicate kulaks as a class" and "annihilate the bourgeoisie," he believed that a host of "secret" enemies were pervading the Soviet Union. These were the "wreckers" responsible for the failure of industrial or agricultural enterprises, "Trotskyites" who voiced opposition to Stalin's policies, and the "traitors" within the security apparatus and armed forces.

It was a peculiarity of both the Soviet Union and Nazi Germany that scientific terminology and the latest technological methods were adopted to implement the official ideology. Both Stalin and Hitler insisted that all aspects of society be conducted in a regimented and "scientific" manner. The Soviet Union implemented "five-year plans," collectivized of agriculture, and created an elaborate organization of prison and forced-labor camps. In Nazi Germany the "scientific" approach was expressed in a "four-year plan" (borrowed explicitly from the Soviet model), the swift rebuilding and modernization of the army, and the clinical and methodical nature of the death camps. All these measures reflected the desire of Hitler and Stalin to justify their programs in the name of scientific and technological progress.

Although Stalin and Hitler each often depicted the other as the exemplar of evil, they also had a grudging admiration for one another. Despite Hitler's aversion to "Bolshevism" (which he associated with Jews) and Stalin's denunciations of "fascism," the two men sought a rapprochement on the eve of the Second World War. After the Nazi-Soviet Pact was signed in August 1939, the two leaders praised one another. Hitler indicated that he approved of Stalin's purges of the Soviet Communist Party in the 1930s, which in Hitler's view had been directed against the "Jews" in the party. Both Stalin and Hitler freely borrowed tactics from one another: Hitler used communist mobilization techniques in election campaigns, and from Hitler's exploitation of the Reichstag fire of February 1933 Stalin learned how to use the murder of Sergey Kirov in December 1934 as a pretext for the Great Purges.

It is true, of course, that the Nazi and Soviet states were not identical, either in their structures or in the way they were formed. The pre-existing economic and social structures of the tsarist empire and Weimar Germany helped shape the methods by which Stalin and Hitler created their regimes. Thus, their tactics were quite dissimilar. Nevertheless, the variations between the two should not obscure the basic fact that Hitler and Stalin both worked relentlessly toward the murderous reshaping of society, resulting in death, destruction, and suffering for millions. The two men sought to destroy whole classes and races of people on a scale unknown before them. This point has been emphasized by Peter Kenez: "Terror was not an epiphenomenon. It is not a topic like the history of Soviet sports or Soviet opera. Because of the terror, parents talked differently to their children, writers wrote differently, workers and managers talked to one another differently. Because of the terror, social mobility increased. Because of the terror, millions perished."

No comparison is ever ironclad, but, as Charles Maier has pointed out, scholars are "condemned to compare" historical phenomena and events. Although it is important to make distinctions, it is impossible to understand historical figures without comparing them to others. In this particular case, a comparison of Hitler and Stalin underscores the common features of their regimes: millenarian ideologies that justified any means in pursuit of the ultimate goal; charismatic leaders who claimed the ability to reshape individuals and societies and stopped at nothing to achieve that end; and the profoundly destructive effects of their policies on other societies.

—MARK KRAMER, HARVARD UNIVERSITY

Viewpoint:
No, Hitler and Stalin were more dissimilar than alike.

In some ways the comparison between Adolf Hitler and Joseph Stalin is inevitable. The two dictators have become personifications of modern evil. Both men wielded nearly absolute power. The depth and reach of their brutality remains unprecedented, even in a century defined by violence. Each was driven by radical ideological beliefs about the structure of society and the guiding forces of history. Despite these apparent similarities, however, Hitler and Stalin and the regimes they created were more dissimilar than alike. Comparisons between the two men and their regimes are often overdrawn. Indeed, so powerful were their differences that each man came to view the other as his own antithesis and mortal enemy. Their ultimate confrontation led to the bloodiest war in human history, the reverberations of which are still being felt today.

The comparison of Hitler and Stalin has focused first and foremost on their use of ter-
ror and violence. Both were prodigal killers. Exactly how many innocent people died as a result of their polices will never be known. Estimates of the civilian death toll under Stalin range from a few million (almost certainly an underestimation) to more than 60 million (almost certainly an exaggeration). Hitler was probably responsible for between 8 million and 16 million civilian deaths, including more than 5 million Jews. Even the lowest of these estimates establishes that both dictators relied on the extensive use of violence to achieve their political and military goals both at home and abroad. This unimaginable slaughter has formed the basis of many comparisons between the Nazi concentration-camp system and the Soviet gulag. In fact, some scholars have pushed this comparison to a disturbing extreme, suggesting that Hitler's brutality was in part a defensive response to the fear inspired by Soviet atrocities. A closer look at the use of violence and terror under Hitler and Stalin, however, reveals strikingly different patterns in both its means and its ends.

Stalin unleashed his terror on the Soviet Union in three massive waves of violence, first during the collectivization of agriculture in 1929–1933, then in the Great Terror of 1936–1938, and finally during the deportation of suspect nationalities beginning in the late 1930s and continuing until Stalin's death in 1953. Stalin's use of violence in each of these episodes is perhaps best described as instrumental. Although characterized by its excessive and exceptionally brutal application, Stalin's violence aimed to achieve ends beyond the destruction of the individuals and groups it targeted. His brutality was primarily directed at achieving domestic goals, and its victims were primarily Soviet citizens. He used violence to crush opposition—sometimes real and often imagined—to his authority or his policies. He used it to spread terror among potential enemies and ensure complete obedience. Even Stalin's demand for the total elimination of the so-called kulak class was calculated to achieve the rapid collectivization of agriculture and consolidate his political control over the countryside.

Hitler also used violence instrumentally, particularly in the effort to crush political opposition soon after his rise to power. Yet, this kind of violence played a much smaller role for Hitler than it did for Stalin. While Stalin used terror primarily to secure his power and implement his polices within the Soviet Union, the majority of Hitler's victims were foreigners, and their destruction often seems closer to an end in itself. Hitler viewed violence as a positive force, part of a struggle for self-preservation between races that would ultimately result in the betterment of mankind.

STALIN

George F. Kennan, who worked at the U.S. embassy in Moscow in 1933–1937 and 1944–1946, recorded his impressions of Premier Joseph Stalin in Memoirs, 1925–1950.

His was a low-slung, smallish figure, neither markedly stout nor thin, inclining, if anything, to the latter. The square-cut tunic seemed always a bit too large for him; one sensed an effort to compensate for the slightness of stature. Yet there was also a composed, collected strength, a certain rough handsomeness, in his features. The teeth were discolored, the mustache scrawny, coarse, and streaked. This, together with the pocked face and yellow eyes, gave him the aspect of an old battle-scarred tiger. In manner—with us, at least—he was simple, quiet, unassuming. There was no striving for effect. His words were few. They generally sounded reasonable and sensible; indeed, they often were. An unforewarned visitor would never have guessed what depths of calculation, ambition, love of power, jealousy, cruelty, and sly vindictiveness lurked behind this unpretentious facade.

Stalin's greatness as a dissimulator was an integral part of his greatness as a statesman. So was his gift for simple, plausible, ostensibly innocuous utterance. Wholly unoriginal in every creative sense, he had always been the aptest of pupils. He possessed unbelievably acute powers of observation and, when it suited his purposes, imitation. (If he later destroyed his teachers, as he usually did, this was really the mark of his high respect for them.) By the same token he was, of course, a great, if terrible (in part: great *because* terrible), teacher of politics. Most impressive of all was his immense, diabolical skill as a tactician. The modern age has known no greater master of the tactical art. The unassuming, quiet facade, as innocently disarming as the first move of the great master at chess, was only a part of this brilliant, terrifying tactical master.

Source: George F. Kennan, Memoirs: 1925–1950 *(Boston: Little, Brown, 1967), p. 279.*

The complete extermination of the Jews was the most essential and urgent aspect of this struggle. Hitler sought the elimination of every Jewish man, woman and child, not their acceptance of his authority or compliance with his policies. For him their existence represented a threat to Germany's survival. Similar motives inspired the murder of the Gypsies, the mentally and chronically ill, homosexuals, and the Poles, although none of these groups was pursued as mercilessly as the Jews. These genocides have no true analogue on the long list of Stalin's crimes.

The differences between the ultimate ends of Stalin's and Hitler's brutality are high-lighted by the institutional means they created to carry it out. The camps of Stalin's vast gulag were places where labor was produced and death was expected. In Hitler's killing centers, death itself was the product. A surprisingly small percentage of Stalin's victims were actually executed outright. The great majority died of starvation, exposure, and overwork, both inside and outside of the camps. The gulag had no equivalent to the industrialized killing centers of the Nazi death camps. Although this fact hardly diminishes Stalin's responsibility for his victims, it does suggest that the gulag and the Nazi death camps were built to serve different purposes. Not all Nazi concentration camps were death camps, of course, and forced labor was performed even in Auschwitz and Treblinka. Millions of Jews also died of starvation, exposure and disease, both in the camps and in overcrowded ghettos. Yet, in Hitler's death camps, labor was a byproduct, and nearly every person sent there was destined to die.

Scholars have often compared Nazi Germany and the Soviet Union as archetypes of modern totalitarian states and Hitler and Stalin as archetypal totalitarian leaders. This broad generalization, however, often applied during the cold war in the effort to link the Soviet system to the evils of Nazism, obscures profound differences in the nature of the two regimes and the ways their leaders ruled.

Stalin's Soviet Union was much closer to the ideal totalitarian state than Nazi Germany, although the term *totalitarianism* remains inadequate even to describe the Soviet regime. In Stalin's Russia, terror of one form or another touched nearly every segment of society. Its victims were selected with striking unpredictability. Even the regime's most decorated heroes and enthusiastic communists could become "traitors," "saboteurs," or "enemies of the people." More than half of the delegates to the twenty-seventh Communist Party Congress of 1934, for example, were arrested for counterrevolutionary crimes during the Great Terror, and 98 out 139 Central Committee members (full and candidate) were shot. More than 43,000 military officers were purged, and the majority of senior officers arrested and killed.

These brutal methods supported an economic, political, and social program that sought an astonishing degree of control over the daily life of ordinary Soviet citizens. The state exercised a virtual monopoly of the media, art, science, and education. Organized religion was effectively abolished. It was in the economic sphere, however, that Stalin sought the most extensive powers over daily life. The most massive program designed to bring Soviet economic production under Stalin's command was the collectivization of agriculture. Collectivization ravaged more than half the Soviet population and shattered a way of life that had existed for hundreds of years. Decisions about what, when, where, and how to plant—once made individually by millions of peasant households—were centralized under the Soviet command system. Collectivization was perhaps the largest attempt at social engineering in human history.

Hitler believed that Stalin's purges must have been motivated by madness. Apart from his purge of the SA (storm trooper) leadership on the "Night of the Long Knives" in 1934, Hitler never launched a systematic attack on members of his own regime. Hitler's domestic enemies fell into clearly identified social and political groups. Germans outside these groups could remain reasonably secure as long as they refrained from open opposition to the regime. Nor did Hitler's social projects intrude so deeply into the life of the average German citizen. Hitler never secured complete control over education, science, or the Church. His intervention in the German economy, which focused primarily on military production, was modest by Soviet standards. There was no equivalent to Stalin's collectivization campaign in Hitler's Germany. Even Hitler's program of racial purification directly affected a relatively small portion of German society. Jews (including the so-called Mischlinge, or mixed-breed Jews) and Gypsies, for example, amounted to only about 1 percent of the total German population in 1933.

The differences between the Nazi and Soviet regimes were reflected in the leadership styles of Hitler and Stalin. Stalin was the ultimate interventionist, seeking maximum control over nearly all aspects of political power. He reviewed hundreds of official documents every day. Even the most minute and seemingly inconsequential details of policy were not beyond his purview. In comparison, Hitler remained surprisingly aloof from the formal bureaucracy he headed. He detested paperwork. Many issues and aspects of the policy-making process did not interest him. With the partial exceptions of foreign policy and military affairs, Hitler preferred to issue broad policy directives, leaving it to others to interpret the details of implementation.

Cults of personality, often identified as an integral element of totalitarian leadership, emerged around both Hitler and Stalin. Yet, the cults that surrounded the two dictators were fundamentally different. Hitler's personal leadership was always more central to Nazism in Germany than Stalin was to communism in the Soviet Union. Stalin rose to power from within the Soviet system, and, as a result, he shared public adulation with previous icons such as Vladimir Lenin and Karl Marx. Stalin and the communist ideology he espoused could be separated. Soviet communism survived Stalin's death and cults of personality never developed around his successors. It is nearly impossible, on the other hand, to imagine Nazism without Hitler or the cult that surrounded him. The Führer principle, personified in Hitler, practically defined the Nazi system of governance. The almost religious exaltation of Hitler was perhaps the Nazis' most powerful political tool, generating consensus behind radical and costly policies without the reliance on massive domestic coercion that characterized Stalin's rule.

–BENJAMIN A. VALENTINO, MASSACHUSETTS INSTITUTE OF TECHNOLOGY

References

Hannah Arendt, *The Origins of Totalitarianism* (New York: Harcourt, Brace, 1951);

Stéphane Courtois and others, *Le livre noir du communisme: crimes, terreurs, and et répression* (Paris: Robert Laffont, 1997); translated by Jonathan Murphy as *The Black Book of Communism* (Cambridge, Mass.: Harvard University Press, 1999);

Carl J. Friedrich and Zbigniew K. Brzezinski, *Totalitarian Dictatorship and Autocracy* (Cambridge, Mass.: Harvard University Press, 1956; revised, 1965);

Abbott Gleason, *Totalitarianism: The Inner History of the Cold War* (New York: Oxford University Press, 1995);

Alexander J. Groth, "The 'ISMS' in Totalitarianism," *American Political Science Review,* 58 (December 1964): 888–901;

Peter Kenez; "Stalinism as Humdrum Politics," *Russian Review,* 45 (October 1986): 395–400;

Ian Kershaw, "'Working Towards the Führer': Reflections on the Nature of the Hitler Dictatorship," in *Stalinism and Nazism: Dictatorships in Comparison,* edited by Kershaw and Moshe Lewin (New York: Cambridge University Press, 1997), pp. 88–106;

Charles S. Maier, *The Unmasterable Past: History, Holocaust, and German National Identity* (Cambridge, Mass.: Harvard University Press, 1988);

Steven Wheatcroft, "The Scale and Nature of German and Soviet Repression and Mass Killings, 1930–1945," *Europe-Asia Studies,* 48 (1996): 1319–1353.

HUMAN RIGHTS

Was Jimmy Carter's emphasis on human rights a sound basis for foreign policy?

Viewpoint: Yes, Jimmy Carter's emphasis on human rights was an effective response to changing geopolitical realities.

Viewpoint: No, Jimmy Carter's emphasis on human rights undermined vital alliances and increased international tensions.

From its inception the United States understood itself as a nation dedicated not only to securing its interests and enhancing its welfare but also to securing human rights and enhancing political freedom, civil liberties, and individual rights in the world. There were two competing theories, however, regarding how best to advance these goals. One theory emphasized the power of example, asserting that the United States would best serve the cause of expanding human rights by building "a more perfect union" at home, "a city upon a hill" that other peoples would want to emulate. The other theory emphasized U.S. missionary responsibilities. It was not enough to build a perfect society in America; it would be a betrayal of American ideals not to spread these ideals actively worldwide, taking action where they were violated.

Until the mid 1970s, American policymakers viewed the advancement of human rights as secondary to, but derivative of, the pursuit of general U.S. foreign-policy interests. The perception was that, as the leader of the Free World in its struggle against communism, everything that served U.S. interests also served the cause of human rights, even if not immediately. This rationale was used to justify U.S. support for authoritarian and dictatorial regimes that were anticommunist. This line of thinking was also behind U.S. intervention against popularly elected governments when they adopted policies deemed inimical to the interests of the United States or U.S. business (for example, in Iran in 1953 and Guatemala in 1954). Thus, in 1970, shortly before the election of the left-leaning Salvador Allende as president of Chile, Henry Kissinger, national security adviser to President Richard M. Nixon, reportedly told a secret White House gathering, "I don't see why we need to stand by and watch a country go Communist due to the irresponsibility of its own people." The United States was active in trying to prevent Allende from coming to power, and then in efforts to destabilize his regime.

Human rights became a more prominent issue in the early 1970s as a result of congressional action. There were several reasons for this change, among them the prominence of the civil-rights struggle at home and the experience of the Vietnam War, which caused many Americans to question the priorities of U.S. foreign policy. Another contribution was the effort by the Nixon administration, under the influence of Kissinger, to advance a more realpolitik kind of foreign policy. Trying to normalize relations with the Soviet Union under détente, the administration tacitly accepted that the issue of Soviet citizens' political, religious, and other rights were an internal matter of the Soviet Union. Leading senators and congressmen disagreed, focusing their attention especially on the issue of Jewish emigration from the Soviet Union. In 1974 Congress passed the Jackson-Vanik Amendment, tying trade liberalization for the Soviet Union to its treatment of Soviet Jews who wanted to leave that country. In 1975 Congress mandated that U.S. economic aid be conditioned on the recipient's human-rights record. Congress also required the Department of State to prepare an annual report on the state of human rights in countries receiving U.S. aid.

The executive branch joined the legislative branch in its stand on human rights when President Jimmy Carter took office in January 1977 and made the issue a central feature of his administration's foreign policy. A month after assuming office Carter ordered the reduction by two-thirds of military aid to Uruguay and Argentina, both then military dictatorships. U.S. military aid to Guatemala was banned in 1978. The Carter administration also launched a series of diplomatic initiatives against the regime of Augusto Pinochet in Chile and also reduced its involvement with Nicaraguan leader Anastasio Somoza. In July 1979, when the leftist Sandinista movement took over Nicaragua after popular unrest forced Somoza to flee the country, the United States gave the new regime more than $100 million in aid during its first eighteen months in power, even though the Sandinistas espoused radical-socialist economic and social policies. In October 1979 the Carter administration supported a coup by reformist military officers in El Salvador.

Beginning in 1978 the administration also exerted increasing pressure on the shah of Iran to allow greater freedom of expression to the Muslim opposition to his regime. As the anti-shah forces—including not only Muslim clerics but Western-educated professionals—gathered strength, the Iranian military turned to the United States for help. The military feared that the mullahs were the driving force behind the anti-shah movement and that, once in power, these Muslim clerics would dominate the new regime and turn Iran into a theocracy. Leading Iranian military officers, many of them U.S.-trained, said they would seize power only with the support of the United States. Carter, though, warned the Iranian military not to intervene and let the political struggle unfold on its own. For a short while it appeared as if Carter's gamble had worked, as Mohammad Reza Shah Pahlavi was succeeded by liberal politicians such as Shapour Bakhtiar and Mehedy Bazarghan. Soon, however, the mullahs took over and installed the Ayatollah Khomeini as leader of Iran, turning it into a theocracy.

Carter's emphasis on human rights as "the heart and soul" of U.S. foreign policy now alarmed many in Congress, who felt he went too far. In June 1979 more than one hundred members of Congress signed a full-page advertisement in *The New York Times,* warning that Carter's policy toward Nicaragua was leading to the creation of another Cuba in the hemisphere. In the presidential election of 1980 one of the major themes of the successful Republican candidate, Ronald Reagan, was that Carter's human rights policies were undermining U.S. interests.

Viewpoint:
Yes, Jimmy Carter's emphasis on human rights was an effective response to changing geopolitical realities.

Jimmy Carter entered office in January 1977 promising to make human rights an "absolute" in his administration's foreign policy. Although many perceived the new president's resolve as either idealism or naïveté, his ideas about shifting the basis of American foreign relations to human rights in many ways reflected a continuation of themes developed during the administrations of his two immediate predecessors, Presidents Richard M. Nixon and Gerald R. Ford. Over the course of Carter's administration, human-rights considerations played crucial roles in several critical foreign-policy decisions and provided a sound basis for the president's strategic approach in general, even if the application of these decisions is not known to have led to efficient results.

Fundamental changes in the geopolitical structure had begun to manifest themselves by the end of the 1960s. Certainly the most momentous transition for American strategic planners was the opening of a serious rift between the Soviet Union and mainland China. While the relationship between the two largest communist powers had never been without tension, Mao Tse-tung's growing assertions of his country's political independence from Moscow and his pretensions to a leadership role in the communist world exacerbated the situation. In the spring of 1969 the diplomatic estrangement between the two countries broke out in armed border clashes.

Many American strategists recognized a substantial opportunity in the Sino-Soviet split. If China could be drawn away from the Soviet orbit, the strategic situation of the United States could be dramatically improved. A series of positive diplomatic signals from the Nixon administration, followed by well-received visits to Beijing by national-security adviser Henry Kissinger in July 1971 and the president himself the follow-

CARTER'S HUMAN-RIGHTS MESSAGE

At his inauguration on 20 January 1977 President Jimmy Carter called for a new emphasis in U.S. foreign policy:

To be true to ourselves, we must be true to others. We will not behave in foreign places so as to violate our rules and standards here at home, for we know that the trust which our Nation earns is essential to our strength.

The world itself is now dominated by a new spirit. Peoples more numerous and more politically aware are craving and now demanding their place in the sun—not just for the benefit of their own physical condition, but for basic human rights.

The passion for freedom is on the rise. Tapping this new spirit, there can be no nobler nor more ambitious task for America to undertake on this day of a new beginning than to help shape a just and peaceful world that is truly humane.

We are a strong nation, and we will maintain strength so sufficient that it need not be proven in combat—a quiet strength based not merely on the size of an arsenal, but on the nobility of ideas. We will be ever vigilant and never vulnerable, and we will fight our wars against poverty, ignorance, and injustice—for those are the enemies against which our forces can be honorably marshaled.

We are a purely idealistic Nation, but let no one confuse our idealism with weakness.

Because we are free we can never be indifferent to the fate of freedom elsewhere. Our moral sense dictates a clear cut preference for these societies which share with us an abiding respect for individual human rights. We do not seek to intimidate, but it is clear that a world which others can dominate with impunity would be inhospitable to decency and a threat to the well-being of all people..

Source: "In Changing Times, Eternal Principles: President Carter's Inaugural Address," New York Times, *21 January 1977, p. B1.*

---

ing February, were highly successful in engineering Sino-American rapprochement.

Nixon's crucial problem was that his domestic political credentials had been built on aggressive anticommunism, and Mao's China remained a brutal communist dictatorship. To facilitate the strategic victory that his administration was trying hard to engineer, Nixon was obliged to soft-pedal his anticommunist rhetoric. If Beijing were to become an important American ally against Moscow, a new vehicle for ideological opposition to the Soviet Union had to be found.

The advent of détente—a relaxation in the tension between the United States and the Soviet Union based on close diplomatic and commercial ties—coincided with the need to resolve the emerging contradiction in American foreign policy. This diplomatic engagement, which Kissinger and other prominent American leaders advocated, was expected to result in Soviet geopolitical restraint and eventually in the domestic reform of the Soviet system. As with China, no constructive engagement of the Soviet Union could be expected to bear fruit if the galvanizing force behind American foreign policy remained a fundamental and highly ideological rejection of the values of the Soviet system of government.

Human rights was a convenient vehicle to further American diplomatic goals. Many who either opposed détente or wished to hold it in check should it not produce effective results began to criticize the Soviets' human-rights record for the first time in the cold war. Such measures as the Jackson-Vanik amendment, passed in 1974, linked the growth of commercial ties and the extension of most-favored-nation status to human-rights issues such as Jewish emigration. The Helsinki Conference of 1975 created international human-rights standards to which all signatory countries, including the Soviet Union, were obliged to adhere.

When Carter entered office, human rights became crucial to American policy making. By 1977 serious problems had developed in the détente relationship with the Soviet Union. Although recent scholarship debates to what extent Moscow was responsible, it is plain that countries closely associated with and supported by the Soviet Union embarked on several provocative steps internationally. In 1975 the pro-Soviet government of North Vietnam conquered South Vietnam, blatantly violating the Paris Peace Accords that had ended the Vietnam conflict. Later that year Fidel Castro began to dispatch the first of thousands of Cuban troops to Third World countries with substantial Marxist revolutionary movements. Moscow's assistance was a major factor in many of these deployments. Within the first few weeks of the Carter administration, there was also intelligence that the Soviets were accelerating the development of their nuclear-missile programs to achieve either strategic parity with or an outright advantage over the United States.

Since détente was not producing the kind of restraint its proponents had believed it would, many members of the American foreign-policy-making establishment advocated military and diplomatic policies that more closely reflected containment thinking. Although some of these policies involved the increased deployment of

HUMAN RIGHTS

raw military power in forward strategic positions, human rights added an interesting new dynamic to their approach.

The concept was extremely useful because unlike communism, human-rights violations could be argued by degrees, giving the Carter administration a great deal of flexibility in its approach to foreign affairs. Theoretically, he could use attacks on the human-rights records of certain countries as leverage to elicit cooperation with Washington and at the same time turn a blind eye to the human-rights records of countries with which the United States desired good relations for strategic reasons. In a world where the American strategic interest was being redefined, human rights had the potential to make transitions much easier and more flexible.

Superpower diplomacy offers perhaps the most important application of that principle. The second round of the Strategic Arms Limitation Talks (SALT), arms-control negotiations that had been under way for several years before Carter took office, became inextricably linked with the Soviet human-rights record. Although some have argued that the president's denunciations of the persecution of individual Soviet dissidents angered Moscow with what it viewed as undue meddling in its internal affairs and actually led to harsher measures against the dissidents, the balance of evidence indicates that Carter and many in his administration believed the terms offered by the Soviets to be a bad deal. Attacking the Soviet Union on apparently unrelated human-rights grounds is best understood as an attempt either to extract concessions in the negotiations or to avoid signing an agreement to the disadvantage of the United States. As it was, SALT II negotiations dragged on in great difficulty until the treaty was finally signed in 1979. It still has not been ratified by the Senate.

With China the situation was fundamentally different. The Chinese were certainly not known for a stellar human-rights record. Beijing's treatment of its political dissidents, its minority Christian and Muslim populations, and the Tibetans, among others, were easily as objectionable as Soviet human-rights abuses. Despite these facts, however, the Carter administration pursued the fulfillment of Nixon's policy toward China. Although Secretary of State Cyrus R. Vance and national-security adviser Zbigniew Brzezinski disagreed about the precise timetable for the formal normalization of diplomatic relations with China, the process was ultimately brought to completion and announced on 1 January 1979. Human-rights concerns played no serious role in the process or in Sino-American relations for years after.

The transition to a foreign policy based on human rights was also relevant to more peripheral strategic areas. Unlike doctrinaire anticommunism,

Carter's human-rights policy provided him with a means of stabilizing or altering the governments of noncommunist and pro-American countries to try to prevent more radical changes that might endanger their relationships with the United States. Ideally, this approach was a sound means of securing the domestic situations of those countries and eliminating the stigma implicit in American alliances with brutal regimes. With such countries as Brazil, Chile, and Argentina, favorable relations predicated on improvements in human rights met with success over time.

While it is true that the approach resulted in some notable and embarrassing failures, it is simplistic to dismiss the construct of foreign policy based on human rights as flawed. The unfortunate developments in Iran and Nicaragua, for instance, had much to do with American docility in supporting and encouraging regime-sponsored reform. There was also a serious lack of intelligence on and political understanding of the opposition movements. Had these flaws been avoided, there was a good chance that these countries could have become stable and effective allies through reform.

Although the Carter administration's foreign policy was, for a variety of reasons, not generally successful, its reliance on human rights as a mobilizing ideology was not misguided. It was an effective response to changing geopolitical realities and a continuation of a theme established in the foreign policies of two previous administrations. In superpower relations human rights provided a sound strategic basis, as it gave the administration the flexibility to place a brake on the negative aspects of détente with the Soviet Union and simultaneously explore its coincidences of strategic interest with China. In the Third World success was somewhat more limited, but several pro-American governments became more stable and less heinous because their relations with the United States had to accommodate human-rights considerations. The administration's abundant foreign-policy blunders had much more important causes than the importance it attached to human rights.

–PAUL DU QUENOY, GEORGE WASHINGTON UNIVERSITY

Viewpoint:
No, Jimmy Carter's emphasis on human rights undermined vital alliances and increased international tensions.

No American president is more closely identified with human rights than Jimmy

Presidents Jimmy Carter (left) and Leonid Brezhnev (right) at the Vienna Summit of June 1979, where the two leaders signed the SALT II Treaty

Carter. During his campaign for the presidency, Carter repeatedly invoked the language of human rights as part of his appeal for a foreign policy that was moral in its conception and its execution, or, as he put it in a major address at the University of Notre Dame within a few months of his inauguration, a foreign policy that would make us "proud to be Americans." This emphasis on human rights specifically, and public virtue more generally, emanated from Carter's personal convictions and from the political necessity of restoring public faith in institutions that had been seriously weakened by Watergate and the Vietnam War. The return to Wilsonian idealism was, in other words, a reaction against the realpolitik of the Nixon-Kissinger era.

Carter came into office believing that the United States was obsessed with the concept of containment and that Kissinger's "grand design," with its almost exclusive focus on the Sino-Soviet-American triangular relationship, was myopic. He believed that East-West issues, although important, could not be allowed to dominate completely the U.S. foreign-policy agenda. In Carter's view—and, by the mid 1970s, he had considerable scholarly support for this belief—North-South issues were becoming increasingly important. There was, he said, a need to come to grips with changes in the Third World. The failure to deal with these matters was, according to Carter's analysis, responsible for many of the weaknesses of the détente policy.

In his memoir *Keeping Faith* (1982) Carter set out several reasons for attempting to promote human rights abroad. He argued that support for human rights within totalitarian regimes would enhance freedom and democracy while "helping to remove the reasons for revolutions that often erupt among those who suffer from persecution." A strong human-rights policy "would also help strengthen our influence among some of the developing nations that were still in this process of forming their own governments and choosing their future friends and trading partners." Carter added, "And it was the right thing to do."

During his single term in office, President Carter attempted to transform words into deeds by creating an institutional framework for human-rights policy within the executive branch, by engaging in quiet diplomacy to encourage American allies and client states to improve their human-rights records, by rewarding governments that showed progress in human-rights observance, and by making human-rights progress a condition of U.S. military and economic assistance in selected cases. His administration also attempted to make human rights a significant factor in the work of multilateral institutions by directing American representatives to organizations such as the World Bank to vote against loans to countries with patterns of human-rights violations, by working to strengthen the Inter-American Commission on Human Rights and other regional human-rights organizations, and by increasing the human-rights emphasis of the United Nations.

To a considerable extent criticisms of Carter's human-rights policy parallel those leveled against its historical model, namely, Woodrow Wilson's efforts to inject moral considerations into American foreign policy. Carter, like Wilson, designed and implemented a policy that was seriously flawed because it was moralistic, inconsistent, and, ultimately, counterproductive.

Like Wilson, Carter believed in American exceptionalism and articulated this belief on many occasions. Early in his administration, Carter stated that "no other country is as well qualified as we to set an example" of human freedom and human rights. Secretary of State Cyrus R. Vance often pursued the same theme. In his memoir *Hard Choices* (1983) he linked faith in American virtue with support for human rights internationally: "Historically, our country had been a force for progress in human affairs. A nation that saw itself as a 'beacon on the hill' for the rest of mankind could not content itself with power politics alone. It could not properly ignore the growing demands of individuals around the world for the fulfillment of their rights." Naturally, such a self-conception, no matter how often it was qualified by references to the need for improvement in the United States, was offensive to other countries. In addition to being advanced with rhetoric that often sounded self-righteous and arrogant, the Carter administration's human-rights policy appeared selective. The administration advocated observance of civil and political rights far more ardently and consistently than it advocated observance of economic and social rights. Inevitably, the policy and its public justification created an impression that Carter was demanding that other countries meet an American standard that had long been surpassed in the United States rather than a universal standard that the United States, too, often failed to meet.

The requirement imposed by Congress that the State Department submit annual reports on the status of human rights in all countries receiving U.S. assistance—and the brutally frank manner in which the State Department complied during the Carter years—was indicative of the moralism that characterized the Carter administration's human-rights policy. On balance the reporting requirement had a deleterious effect on American foreign policy. There was, after all, nothing quiet about this aspect of American diplomacy. Making foreign governments the objects of a subjective and public grading of compliance with human-rights standards created much resentment and set up the United States government for the charge that it had appointed itself the world's judge. The resentment aroused by the "grading policy" increased when the State Department raised the standards, and Carter made it clear that the grades mattered.

Perhaps the most insistent criticism of Carter's human-rights policy was that it was inconsistently applied. The Soviet Union came under heavy criticism for its suppression of political dissent, but the People's Republic of China (PRC), with which the United States was in the process of normalizing diplomatic relations, did not. Also because of the rapprochement with the PRC, the Carter administration failed to punish or even isolate the Pol Pot regime in Cambodia, perpetrator of one of the worst genocides in history. In the Philippines, the desire to preserve rights to important military bases at Clark Field and Subic Bay caused Carter to tone down criticism of the abysmal human-rights record of Ferdinand Marcos's regime. Iran's strategic significance as a listening post and a military ally on the Soviet Union's southern flank protected it from the moral condemnation that Mohammad Reza Shah Pahlavi's repression deserved. As national-security adviser Zbigniew Brzezinski noted in his memoir *Power and Principle* (1983), "In practical terms, our influence was greater with weak and isolated countries than with those with whom we shared vital security interests." Of course, it was not the difference in influence that was objectionable to critics of the policy as much as it was the difference in effort. The Soviet Union and other states regularly pilloried the United States for the inconsistency of its human-rights policy.

In the United States (and even within the administration), the Carter human-rights policy was subject to criticism from opposite sides. On the one hand, the policy was attacked for its failure to go far enough in its attempt to improve the behavior of repressive regimes. This criticism was especially prevalent in cases such as those involving Iran and communist China in which American pressures were lessened in order to avoid undermining other important foreign policy goals. On the other hand, the policy was faulted for going too far in its efforts to inject such controversial political goals into international relations. According to this critique, such interferences in the internal affairs of sovereign states could only cause resentment in those states censured for human-rights violations and serve to impede more essential foreign-policy objectives.

Carter's human-rights policy could be either morally consistent but utterly indifferent to the national interest or morally inconsistent but at least partially cognizant of the difference between allies and enemies and thus somewhat considerate of the national interest. It could not be both.

All too often, Carter's emphasis on human rights was not only moralistic and inconsistent, it was counterproductive as well. American criticism of the human-rights records of other governments invariably tended to put those governments on the defensive, and, in so doing, it injected into bilateral relationships tensions that might not otherwise have been present. This additional tension sometimes impeded progress on other important foreign-policy goals. With the Soviet Union the Carter administration was forced to try and steer a course between support for human rights and the desire for a comprehensive arms-control treaty. Because the United States had few means of influencing the Soviet Union directly, public criticism of human-rights abuses and symbolic shows of

support for dissidents were the primary tactics used. Early in his administration Carter criticized the Soviet Union and Czechoslovakia for intimidating citizens who were attempting to protest. In February 1977 Carter responded publicly to a letter from Andrey Sakharov, a noted Soviet physicist and dissident. Carter also met with Vladimir Bukovsky in the Oval Office in March, an act that contributed to Soviet intransigence later that same month, when Vance went to Moscow to present an ambitious arms-control proposal. In spite of Carter's efforts to "de-link" arms control and human rights, the Soviets refused to compartmentalize issues in the bilateral relationship, and, as a consequence, completion of the SALT II Treaty, which had seemed so close in 1977, was delayed until 1979. By then the domestic and international political environments had changed to such an extent that the U.S. Senate was no longer prepared to ratify such an agreement.

Although direct links are difficult to establish, American support for human rights no doubt encouraged revolutionary movements in some parts of the world. While this result may have been helpful (both from the standpoint of American national interests and of human rights) in Latin America, in Iran it proved to be an unmitigated disaster. The overthrow of Mohammad Reza Shah Pahlavi resulted in the loss of a strategically situated ally, the national embarrassment of the hostage crisis, and human-rights violations in Iran that were different in character but not necessarily in severity from those committed by the shah's regime.

Carter's well-intentioned effort to make the promotion of human rights a priority in American foreign policy, like Wilson's appeal to moral principles sixty years earlier, ultimately created more problems than it solved. Essential foreign-policy objectives—such as nuclear-arms control, containment of communism, and the promotion of stability in the world—were frequently undermined by the effort to punish human-rights violators. Because of its moralistic and interventionist nature, Carter's emphasis on human rights frequently increased tensions in international relations while failing to achieve many tangible results. In sum, American foreign policy and the cause of human rights would have been better served by leaving human-rights issues to international governmental organizations such as the United Nations and the Organization of American States and to international nongovernmental organizations such as Amnesty International.

–ROBERT E. WILLIAMS, PEPPERDINE UNIVERSITY

HUMAN RIGHTS

References

Peter R. Baehr, *The Role of Human Rights in Foreign Policy* (New York: St. Martin's Press, 1994);

Zbigniew Brzezinski, *Power and Principle: Memoirs of the National Security Adviser, 1977–1981* (New York: Farrar, Straus & Giroux, 1983);

Jimmy Carter, *Keeping Faith: Memoirs of a President* (New York: Bantam, 1982);

Anatoly Dobrynin, *In Confidence: Moscow's Ambassador to America's Six Cold War Presidents (1962–1986)* (New York: Times Books / Random House, 1995);

Jack Donnelly, *International Human Rights,* second edition (Boulder, Colo.: Westview Press, 1993);

Walter LaFeber, *Russia, America, and the Cold War, 1945–1996,* eighth edition (New York: McGraw-Hill, 1997);

Linda B. Miller, "Morality in Foreign Policy: A Failed Consensus?" *Daedalus,* 109 (Summer 1980): 143–158;

A. Glenn Mower Jr., *Human Rights and American Foreign Policy: The Carter and Reagan Experiences* (New York: Greenwood Press, 1987);

Gaddis Smith, *Morality, Reason, and Power: American Diplomacy in the Carter Years* (New York: Hill & Wang, 1986);

Tony Smith, *America's Mission: The United States and the Worldwide Struggle for Democracy in the Twentieth Century* (Princeton, N.J.: Princeton University Press, 1994);

Richard C. Thornton, *The Carter Years: Toward a New Global Order* (New York: Paragon House, 1991);

Cyrus R. Vance, *Hard Choices: Critical Years in America's Foreign Policy* (New York: Simon & Schuster, 1983).

HUMAN RIGHTS

IDEOLOGY

Did ideology play an important role in the U.S.-Soviet conflict?

Viewpoint: Yes, ideology played an important role in the cold war because the United States and the Soviet Union both framed their foreign policies in terms of their ideological perceptions.

Viewpoint: No, ideology was less important than strategic interests in the cold-war conflict between the United States and Soviet Union.

One of the major debates among Western policymakers and scholars during the cold war was over the role of ideology in Soviet foreign policy: was the USSR motivated primarily by traditional Russian impulses, which had been pursued by previous rulers of this large land, or was it driven by a messianic Marxist ideology? This question derived from a broader question about communism and its relationship to the histories, cultures, and traditions of the countries in which it had taken root.

The answer to both questions had profound implications for U.S. foreign and defense policies. If the Soviet Union were a traditional power motivated by traditional considerations of power politics, then it would be possible to deal with the Russians by relying on a combination of traditional policy means. Such means would have to take into account the sheer size and strength of the Soviet state, but they would still fall within the normal range of policies one great power pursues vis-à-vis another. Moreover, if the Soviet Union were a traditional power, then the struggle between it and the West would be a traditional competition over resources and influences, not a do-or-die struggle between two alternative ways of life. If the communist movements that seized power in eastern European and Asian countries were motivated mostly by national and parochial interests, then the United States did not have to fear the creation of a vast, monolithic communist camp directed from Moscow.

The U.S. response to these questions unfolded in three stages. In the immediate aftermath of the Second World War the prevailing view was that the Soviet regime was not essentially different from other regimes, and that it would be possible to do business with the communist state, just as it had been possible to craft a military alliance with the Soviet Union against Nazi Germany. This view was held by some leading American policymakers and politicians even after it was abandoned by the administration of Harry S Truman. Among the chief proponents of this viewpoint was Henry A. Wallace, who served as vice-president from 1941 to 1945 and who ran a left-leaning presidential campaign in 1948 to challenge Truman's change of direction. The Russia-as-a-normal-state view was challenged early on by George F. Kennan, who, from his post at the U.S. embassy in Moscow, sent long and detailed analyses of Soviet foreign policy. His views were made public in "The Sources of Soviet Conduct," an article he published under the name "Mr. X" in the July 1947 issue of *Foreign Affairs.* He warned that viewing the Soviet Union as just another state was naive: the Soviets were motivated by a dangerous combination of traditional Russian impulses and the messianic fervor of Marxism. Kennan emphasized that communism would eventually give way

148

to national and parochial interests, if it did not collapse earlier under the weight of its own economic inefficiencies. Communism as an ideology was not, in and of itself, a threat to the United States; it was unlikely that communist regimes in different countries would form a cohesive block of states hostile to U.S. interests because communism was not strong enough to paper over the real differences in interest and outlook that divided states. Kennan, therefore, recommended a policy of patient, vigilant containment of the Soviet Union, which would prevent the spread of Soviet influence to key industrial regions and the establishment of working relationships with communist regimes.

Kennan's cautious, realpolitik views were soon overtaken by a third reading of the role of ideology in Soviet foreign policy, an interpretation that came to dominate U.S. policy for the next two decades. That view, articulated by analysts such as Paul H. Nitze in National Security Council memorandum 68 (NSC-68), portrayed communism in the most alarming colors as a pervasive, predatory menace for the United States, the West, and the Judeo-Christian way of life. Communist countries were viewed as part of a tightly monolithic block of states, controlled and masterminded from Moscow. Because a country that came under communist control also became a pawn in the Soviet scheme to take over the world, communism had to be vigorously resisted everywhere.

This Manichaean view of U.S.-Soviet competition gave way, in the late 1960s, to a more realistic, realpolitik vision under President Richard M. Nixon and Secretary of State Henry Kissinger. It was revived, however, in the 1980s under President Ronald W. Reagan, who, echoing John Foster Dulles's 1950s reference to "Godless communism," described the Soviet Union as "an evil empire."

Viewpoint:
Yes, ideology played an important role in the cold war because the United States and the Soviet Union both framed their foreign policies in terms of their ideological perceptions.

The U.S.-Soviet conflict cannot be understood without reference to ideology. The cold war began in large part because the United States interpreted Soviet premier Joseph Stalin's refusal to allow free elections in eastern Europe as a hostile act. The conflict intensified and spread as each side tried to export its ideological system to the Third World. The cold war ended because domestic political changes within the Soviet Union obviated the reason for continuing the conflict.

Ideology served as the lens through which both sides viewed the world, defined their identities and interests, and justified their actions. U.S. leaders perceived the Soviet Union as threatening not simply because the USSR was powerful but because the entire Soviet enterprise was predicated on implacable hostility to capitalism and dedicated to its ultimate destruction. From the earliest days of the Russian Revolution until the end of the cold war, Moscow viewed the United States as unalterably hostile. Even when both nations were fighting a common enemy, Nazi Germany, the Soviets were certain that the Americans were determined to destroy the Soviet Union. To believe otherwise undermined the whole rationale for the one-party communist state. A brief examination of the role communism and liberalism played in Soviet and

American foreign policies will demonstrate these points.

Despite the breadth and depth of the writings of Karl Marx and Vladimir Lenin, the crux of communist ideology can be reduced to four essential tenets.

First, communism claims to be universal: the main factor said to be underlying all human behavior everywhere is the individual's relationship to the means of economic production. Class interests, therefore, supersede national, ethnic, religious, and all other interests. The universal concern of all workers regardless of nationality is known as proletarian internationalism.

Second, the capitalist system is pernicious and leads to the exploitation of the working class.

Third, because of its inherent defects, capitalism, like feudalism before it, will inevitably give way through violent revolution to the power of the working class. Marx and Lenin believed that history verified this claim.

The inability of proletarian internationalism to prevent the First World War, an apparent failure of the theory, led to the fourth tenet: imperialism, the final phase of capitalism, leads inevitably to war and revolution. The failure of the universal proletarian revolution to materialize at the same time as the Russian Revolution near the conclusion of the First World War led to a corollary: international relations are a reflection of the class struggle in which socialist countries represent the working class and capitalist countries represent the exploiting class. Socialist internationalism referred to the common class interests of all socialist states; these concerns trumped other interests, at least in the minds of Soviet leaders.

IDEOLOGY

Liberalism is by definition much less constraining and proscriptive than communism. Nevertheless, the United States identified as threatening those states that combined a hostility to liberal principles with the power to act on that hostility. In practical terms, while this criterion generated considerable domestic debate, it also produced clear antipathies to autocratic states, including most notably Nazi Germany and the Soviet Union.

Even before the cold war the United States felt threatened by the rapid growth in military capacity of the three avowedly antidemocratic states of Japan, Germany, and the Soviet Union. The United States allied itself with the Soviet Union against Adolf Hitler because the power and proximity of Germany to Western democra-

cies with which the United States traded and shared political, ideological, cultural, and historical affinities outweighed President Franklin Delano Roosevelt's fears of the Soviet Union. Roosevelt, however, greatly underestimated the degree to which communist antipathy to capitalism directed Soviet behavior, a point George F. Kennan, who became director of policy planning at the U.S. State Department in 1947, made strikingly clear in his well-known long telegram of 1946 and in his 1947 *Foreign Affairs* article "The Sources of Soviet Conduct." Kennan argued that Soviet hostility to American interests was deeply rooted in the Soviet leader's ideology, which justified a dictatorship of the proletariat in large part because of a "capitalist menace" abroad. Soviet antagonism to the

United States would be mitigated, Kennan argued, when Soviet ideology changed. That is, in fact, what happened.

The first great issue dividing the Second World War allies was Stalin's refusal to allow free elections in eastern Europe. Though Soviet dominance of eastern Europe was undoubtedly viewed as a military necessity after the Russians' experience of two catastrophic wars within a quarter century, the desire to prevent a repeat of history did not require the imposition of communism on the region. The Soviet relationship with Finland demonstrated that strict security considerations did not require the Soviet Union to force its ideological model on its neighbors. The Soviets imposed their model on eastern Europe because the spread of communism validated and legitimized communist rule at home.

Moreover, the United States attached an importance to the Soviets' antidemocratic activities in the region that colored all subsequent interpretations of Soviet behavior. Power and capabilities may contribute to perceptions of the intentions of other actors in the international system, but, as Robert Jervis noted in 1985, "the actual gains the other makes—or the losses it inflicts on the state—are often less troublesome than the methods by which they are pursued. A state is likely to be seen as a threat if it displays a willingness to ignore accepted procedure, a disregard of what are usually considered the legitimate rights of others, and an exceptionally high propensity to accept risks in order to improve its position."

American and Soviet policymakers defined and understood the bounds of what was legitimate and acceptable in different, ideologically conditioned ways. Thus, American perceptions of Soviet hostile intentions in the aftermath of the Second World War derived not from Soviet power, but from what the Soviets did with that power; Moscow's repression of democratic movements in eastern Europe conflicted with the promises to permit elections that Stalin made at Yalta and Potsdam. Western estimates of Soviet strength followed, rather than preceded, their perceptions of Soviet behavior.

The policy developed for containing Soviet power, the Truman Doctrine, was articulated in ideological terms: "It must be the policy of the United States to support free peoples who are resisting attempted subjugation by armed minorities or outside pressures." As the U.S.-Soviet conflict progressed through the decades, the actions and ideological rhetoric of each side seemed to confirm the correctness of its view and the necessity to continue, if not intensify, the struggle. The Marshall Plan, implemented in 1948–1951 to rebuild the economies of seventeen nations in western and southern Europe,

and the establishment of the North Atlantic Treaty Organization (NATO) in 1949 fulfilled Lenin's predictions about imperialism: the capitalist West was engaged in a plan to encircle and crush the embodiment of socialism. Like his predecessor, President Dwight D. Eisenhower framed the struggle in ideological terms, as when he explained the global nature of the struggle: "Conceiving the defense of freedom, like freedom itself, to be one and indivisible, we hold all continents and peoples in equal regard and honor."

The focus by both sides on the consequences of spreading their ideological systems contributed to the globalization of the cold war. Stalin and his successors were convinced that the legitimacy of their rule depended on validating Marxist-Leninist predictions of world revolution. The beginning of the nuclear standoff in Europe made it apparent that fomenting revolution in the industrialized, democratic states of the West was either impossible or too dangerous. As a result the Soviets turned their efforts to exporting revolution to less developed countries. They tended to view all anti-Western movements throughout Latin America, Asia, Africa, and the Middle East through the single lens of Lenin's theory of imperialism. Thus, despite the diverse motives behind revolutions, coups, and civil wars in China, Laos, Cuba, Vietnam, Congo, Ethiopia, Somalia, Afghanistan, Libya, and elsewhere, Stalin, Nikita S. Khrushchev, and Leonid I. Brezhnev characterized them all in anti-imperialist terms.

Soviet exploitation of decolonization created a painful dilemma for the United States. On the one hand, the United States felt tremendous sympathy for Third World nations seeking self-determination and independence. This sentiment had a pedigree dating from the presidency of Woodrow Wilson. Moreover, the United States had always regarded itself as a freed colony. (This self-concept is ironic because the United States, as a settler nation, belongs in a different category from India, China, Vietnam, and Algeria.) On the other hand, many Third World leaders of coups and revolutions were rebelling against domination from Western or Western-supported allies of the United States—mainly the United Kingdom and France—and were often attracted to the Soviet model of apparently accelerated industrial development. Thus, the United States found itself in the uncomfortable position of opposing nationalist revolutions because of the perceived benefit they would provide to the Soviet Union.

The Soviet-American contest in the Third World was an example of both balance-of-power considerations and ideological zeal. The Soviets supported coups and revolutions that were communist in name only, as in Libya and Angola, because they were perceived to weaken the United States. The United States opposed popular, nationalist movements, for example, in Vietnam and Chile, because of the fear that they would ultimately benefit the Soviet Union. The point, however, is the constraining role ideology played. Had the conflict been purely one of national power, it would have been difficult to explain why the alliances always formed along ideological lines.

Like its beginning and middle, the end of the cold war was driven primarily by ideological change within the Soviet Union. Beginning cautiously in 1986 and 1987, and then advancing more boldly over the next four years, General Secretary Mikhail S. Gorbachev introduced economic and political reforms that were designed to make the Soviet Union stronger, though they actually produced a quite different effect.

The first foreign policy consequences of glasnost (openness), perestroika (restructuring), and demokratizatiia (democratization) at home were an increasing Soviet tolerance for ideological experimentation in Hungary and Poland and the Soviets' desire to reduce tensions with the West. Gorbachev's plans for economic change proved impossible without political reform, specifically making the bureaucracy more open and subject to popular pressure from below. This experiment with limited democracy, however, developed a momentum of its own and became too strong for Gorbachev, or his more hardline opponents within the Communist Party, to control. Fealty to Marxist-Leninist principles had been discredited; legitimacy required popular support. "Deideologization" and "universal human values" replaced "socialist internationalism" as guiding foreign-policy principles. Without the need to validate old Marxist-Leninist prescriptions, the rationale for the cold war collapsed. Aleksandr Yakovlev, one of Gorbachev's closest advisers, responded to critics of the newly accommodating Soviet foreign policy by asking "if we proclaim principles of freedom and democracy for ourselves can we deny others the same thing?" (*Pravda*, 8 February 1990).

Ideology was not the only factor that drove the cold war, but it is difficult to overstate its importance. For those who see nothing but power at the root of the conflict, it is striking that, despite the fact that the capacity of Russia to destroy the United States remained in place, the U.S. relationship with Russia changed from hostile to cautiously friendly after the Soviet Union disintegrated and the communists lost power. Put more simply, while deliverable destructive power did not effectively diminish, changes in ideology ended the conflict.

–GLENN CHAFETZ, U.S. DEPARTMENT OF STATE

Viewpoint:
No, ideology was less important than strategic interests in the cold-war conflict between the United States and Soviet Union.

The emergence of the cold-war conflict between the United States and Soviet Union was fundamentally a contest of interests. The competition between these two countries took center stage for the second half of the twentieth century. Their clash of interests, however, had been foreseen for more than a century. The observations of the Frenchman Alexis de Tocqueville about the two states in the 1830s might just as well have been written in the aftermath of the Second World War. In his *Democracy in America* (1835) de Tocqueville wrote of the United States and Russia relative to the other great powers: "All the others have halted or advanced only through great exertions; they alone march easily and quickly forward along a path whose end none can yet see." De Tocqueville and other astute nineteenth-century observers, including William Henry Seward, U.S. secretary of state from 1861 to 1869, predicted a competition between the two not based on ideology, but rather on the clash of interests that would emerge based on their power-projection capabilities. To understand both the alliance between the United States and the Soviet Union during the Second World War and the conflict that arose between them after the war, an explanation focusing on interests is the most compelling.

The United States and Soviet Union clashed ideologically throughout the twentieth century. Yet, the two nations forged a critical wartime alliance to fight Nazi Germany. The most credible explanation for this phenomenon is that the United States and the Soviet Union joined forces to achieve the compelling objective of combating an adversary perceived by both states as a threat to their vital national interests.

Despite the success of the U.S.-Soviet alliance, antagonisms between the two states began emerging during the Second World War. Those tensions reflected competing ideological claims regarding the contours of the postwar system. More important, however, they revealed a deep-seated divergence of interests concerning power claims and power projection, especially in Europe. Once the German threat was destroyed, and the multipolar European system along with it, a bipolar configuration of power in the international system began to emerge. The two main powers of that bipolar structure were the United States and the Soviet Union. Therefore, each would increasingly seek to balance the power of the other, a process that emerged immediately after the war through the articulation of their competing interests and prerogatives on the European continent.

Several theoretical assumptions about the behavior of states in the international system—drawn from two related approaches to international relations, realism and structural realism—are relevant in explaining the cold war between the United States and Soviet Union.

First, all states exist in a condition of anarchy. That is, there exists no authority above that of the sovereign state. Because of that permanent condition, each state is left to defend its own interests in an environment of competing interests among states. The international system is thus one of self-help. Further, because every state must fend for itself, there exists among states a security dilemma in which one state's gain in security or power is necessarily the next state's loss.

Second, all states, therefore, perform analogous functions in the international system. The highest priority of every state is to maintain or enhance its security position vis-à-vis other states. While ideological considerations and domestic factors may influence a state's particular approach to foreign-policy matters, the concerns of high politics, or national security, will define its vital interests.

Third, when faced with an external threat from another state or group of states, a state will seek to preserve its security by balancing against the threat, by either internal mobilization or allying with other states, or both. When vital interests are threatened, states will ally with others on the calculation that the alliance will be sufficient to counter or defeat the challenging state.

Fourth, all states will be constrained according to their relative power position in the international system. Briefly, hegemons and great powers will be less constrained in their behavior than medium-sized or small states. To determine the ranking of states in the system, their power capabilities are measured through examination of factors such as military, economic, and technological capabilities, as well as geographic size, location, and population. The distribution of power among states also determines the structure of the system, be it multipolar, bipolar, or more rarely, unipolar in configuration. Balancing behavior in the system will conform to the pattern of power distribution among the states. Alliance formations will be largely determined by the structure. Thus, alliances in a bipolar configuration will reflect the overwhelming power of the two major players, and the pattern of alliance formation will be forged around those two powers. Furthermore, the two major players will find themselves in constant competition with one another, since the vital interests and security of each can be directly challenged or damaged only by the other. It is also the case, however, that bipolar structures tend to be more stable

THE BREZHNEV DOCTRINE

In 1968 Leonid Brezhnev proclaimed in a speech to Polish laborers that the Soviet Union was responsible for maintaining existing socialist states. This declaration, which was published in Pravda *on 25 September 1968, became known as the Brezhnev Doctrine and included the following remarks:*

The peoples of the socialist countries and Communist parties certainly do have and should have freedom for determining the ways of advance of their respective countries.

However, none of their decisions should damage either socialism in their country or the fundamental interests of other socialist countries, and the whole working class movement, which is working for socialism.

This means that each Communist party is responsible not only to its own people, but also to all the socialist countries, to the entire Communist movement. Whoever forgets this, in stressing only the independence of the Communist party, becomes one-sided. He deviates from his international duty.

Marxist dialectics are opposed to one-sidedness. They demand that each phenomenon be examined concretely, in general connection with other phenomena, with other processes.

Just as, in Lenin's words, a man living in a society cannot be free from the society, one or another socialist state, staying in a system of other states composing the socialist community, cannot be free from the common interests of that community.

The sovereignty of each socialist country cannot be opposed to the interests of the world of socialism, of the world revolutionary movement. Lenin demanded that all Communists fight against small-nation narrow-mindedness, seclusion and isolation, consider the whole and the general, subordinate the particular to the general interest.

Source: *Leften Stavros Stavrianos,* The Epic of Man *(Englewood Cliffs, N.J.: Prentice-Hall, 1976), p. 465.*

than multipolar structures. Because there are only two major players under conditions of bipolarity, their efforts to balance one another become more manageable and predictable over time. Under conditions of multipolarity the actions of states are more unpredictable because the system is more complex and thus more difficult to manage.

At the close of the Second World War in 1945, the multipolar European system that had dominated world politics for more than a century lay in ashes. In its place emerged a bipolar structure that lasted until 1990. Following the assumptions of realism and structural realism, and as predicted by observers a century earlier, the United States and the Soviet Union met for the first time in the 1945–1950 period as the two superpowers in the international system. Their relative positions in that system predisposed each to perceive the other as the dominant threat to its own national security. The conflictual nature of that competition derived predominantly from constraints placed on both states in their newly assumed roles as the two major players of the bipolar structure. Their contest was largely played out according to competing and irreconcilable interests, and both began to pursue policies that turned their relations into a cold war.

In an action-reaction pattern, and in an evolutionary manner, the two superpowers began mobilizing against one another. Caught in the security dilemma, each side pursued policies aimed at balancing the power of the other, creating an arms race that lasted throughout the cold war. Each state also promoted domestic political policies aimed at mobilizing its citizens to remain vigilant and distrustful of the other. For example, one of the first clarion calls of the cold war, meant to mobilize American and Western sentiments against the Soviet threat, occurred in 1946, when Winston Churchill gave one of his best-known speeches in Fulton, Missouri. He warned the West, and especially the United States, of the expansionist desires of the Soviet Union, declaring that an "iron curtain has descended" across Europe. Earlier that year Soviet premier Joseph Stalin had given a speech that issued a call to mobilize the Soviet Union against its capitalist enemies, demarcating the division of the world according to the U.S.-Soviet competition.

Following the logic of bipolarity, each state began mobilizing other states, trying to form alliances and balance against the other. Most important was the cold-war contest in Europe, where the alliance pattern conformed to bipolarity. The clear demarcation of interests there created well-defined spheres of influence, and the centrality of Europe in the cold war is supported by critical documents of the period. While stationed at the U.S. embassy in Moscow in the Soviet Union, for example, George F. Kennan sent his historic 1946 telegram warning the Truman administration of the expansionist tendency of the Soviet Union in Europe. Kennan advised Washington to abstain from talk of universalistic aspirations in the world and to draw a line in Europe, articulating clearly American interests on the continent. Kennan's telegram had an immediate and long-lasting impact on American foreign policy, giving birth to the policy of containment. As John Lewis Gaddis observed in 1982, "It followed, therefore, that

the objective of containment should be to limit Soviet expansionism, and that communism posed a threat only to the extent that it was the instrument of that expansion." Following the logic of containment, the North Atlantic Treaty Organization (NATO) was created in 1949. After the newly formed West Germany was admitted to NATO in 1955 the opposing Warsaw Pact, or Warsaw Treaty Organization (WTO), was founded in response. Europe thereby divided into two opposing cold-war camps. The United States and the Soviet Union were the unquestioned leaders of their respective alliance systems, and that system stood, albeit loosely, until the collapse of bipolarity. Outside Europe, the epicenter of the cold war, the United States and Soviet Union forged a series of global alliances throughout the cold-war period, registering the greatest flurry of activity in the 1950s. Both states, in their roles as sole superpowers, projected power interests on a global scale and met each other wherever they went. Caught in the security dilemma, the United States and Soviet Union each sought to check the power of the other wherever necessary.

Over time the bipolar structure dominated by the United States and the Soviet Union became stable, as each came to stop at the edge of the other's sphere of influence. Through their iterated interactions with one another, the bipolar competition actually created shared interests between the two states and led to their joint management of the international system. Such an outcome could not be predicted by analyses that emphasize intense ideological rivalry as the dominant explanation for the cold war. Arguments that seek to explain the cold-war competition in terms of ideology, for example, should anticipate that the United States would have supported democratic reform movements and uprisings throughout eastern Europe in this period, such as those that occurred in East Germany in 1953 and in Poland and Hungary in 1956. In fact, the Soviet Union resolved these crises without intervention from the United States or its Western allies. Furthermore, the nuclear-arms race also had a stabilizing effect on the bipolar competition by creating the conditions of nuclear deterrence. The reality of the nuclear world led over time to more prudence in the power competition between the superpowers. The peaceful resolution to the Cuban Missile Crisis of 1962 is one example. The two states went to the precipice of war and backed away. The nuclear-arms race between the United States and Soviet Union resulted in rough parity by the end of the 1960s. As a result, the policy of Mutual Assured Destruction (MAD) emerged, impelling both

IDEOLOGY

states to seek even more predictability and caution in their relations and to manage their relationship more carefully. The reality of nuclear deterrence, therefore, created a situation in which both superpowers came to share an interest in avoiding a direct confrontation that could lead to a nuclear exchange. Again, bipolarity produced shared as well as competing interests between the ideologically opposed superpowers.

The ideological differences between the United States and the Soviet Union certainly colored their competition throughout the cold war. Ideological differences, however, did not cause the cold war, nor did they drive the competition in a compelling manner. Had ideology been the sustaining force of the cold war, the stability and predictability of the relationship between the two states would not have emerged. Their mutual respect for spheres of influence, the prudent management of their nuclear relationship, and their consistent policy of checking global expansion without resort to direct confrontation are best explained by an analysis based on interest-motivated behavior. In short, what drove the cold war was the logic of bipolarity. Both superpowers defined their interests according to the constraints derived from their position in the anarchic international system. From 1946 to 1990 the relationship between the United States and Soviet Union included both diverging and shared interests, and it was a combination of these interests that governed their conduct during the cold war.

–MARY HAMPTON, UNIVERSITY OF UTAH

References

Michael E. Brown, Sean M. Lynn-Jones, and Steven E. Miller, eds., *The Perils of Anarchy: Contemporary Realism and International Security* (Cambridge, Mass.: MIT Press, 1995);

John Lewis Gaddis, *The Long Peace: Inquiries into the History of the Cold War* (New York: Oxford University Press, 1987);

Gaddis, *Strategies of Containment: A Critical Appraisal of Postwar American National Security Policy* (New York: Oxford University Press, 1982);

Robert Jervis, Richard Ned Lebow, and Janice Gross Stein, *Psychology and Deterrence* (Baltimore: Johns Hopkins University Press, 1985);

Deborah Welch Larson, *Origins of Containment: A Psychological Explanation* (Princeton, N.J.: Princeton University Press, 1985);

Vojtech Mastny, *Russia's Road to the Cold War* (New York: Columbia University Press, 1979);

Miroslav Nincic, *Democracy and Foreign Policy: The Fallacy of Political Realism* (New York: Columbia University Press, 1992);

William Taubman, *Stalin's American Policy: From Entente to Detente to Cold War* (New York: Norton, 1982);

Kenneth N. Waltz, *Theory of International Politics* (New York: McGraw-Hill, 1979).

IDEOLOGY

ISRAEL

Has the close alliance between the United States and Israel been helpful to U.S. policies in the Middle East?

Viewpoint: Yes, the close alliance with Israel has helped the United States to contain the spread of communism in the Middle East.

Viewpoint: No, the close alliance between the United States and Israel has hurt U.S. relations with Arab nations.

Beginning in the mid 1960s and accelerating after the 1967 Six Day War, U.S. support for Israel has become ever stauncher. Massive amounts of economic aid and military assistance have been coupled with unyielding U.S. political support for Israel in international institutions. Both sides describe the bonds between the United States and Israel as a "special relationship."

This special relationship has posed problems for U.S. diplomacy in the Middle East and in the Third World at large. Arab countries have resented U.S. defense of Israel, and the resentment has been shared by many Muslims around the world. Israel is a small country with a population of slightly more than 5 million people. It has no natural resources. The Arab world comprises some twenty countries with more than 150 million inhabitants. These countries control vast resources. Beyond the Middle East, there are more than one billion Muslims in the world. The Third World has seen U.S. support of Israel as but another example of a Western power supporting a European outpost against the interests of the native populations. These feelings were intensified after the 1967 war, as Israel came to control millions of Palestinians in the territories it had captured from Jordan (the West Bank) and Egypt (the Gaza Strip). Since the late 1970s the anti-American feelings created by U.S. policies in the Middle East have engendered increasingly violent acts of terrorism against Americans and American interests. Yet, the United States has continued its staunch support of Israel.

Viewpoint:
Yes, the close alliance with Israel has helped the United States to contain the spread of communism in the Middle East.

The reasons why the United States provided economic and military aid, as well as political support, to Israel may be illustrated by a brief overview of the Middle Eastern crisis of September 1970. The Palestine Liberation Organization (PLO) was created in 1964, aiming to replace Israel with a Palestinian state. In June 1967 Israel occupied the two main bases of PLO operations—the West Bank of the Jordan River and the Gaza Strip—in the Six Day War. During the following three years the PLO increasingly turned Jordan into its main base of operations against Israel. Relying on the support of Palestinians in the refugee camps on the eastern side of the Jordan River, the PLO turned a slice of Jordan into a state-within-a-state with its own military and police force outside Jordanian control. King Hussein of Jordan

finally decided that this situation must not be allowed to continue when in September 1970 PLO guerrillas hijacked several passenger planes belonging to Western carriers and landed them at the airport in Zarqa, Jordan. The PLO soldiers removed the passengers and then blew up the planes as the world watched on television. The king did not wait long before launching a military campaign against the PLO, destroying its bases and forcing it out of Jordan. Syria, a neighbor of Jordan and a supporter of the PLO, decided to intervene, moving armored columns south toward the Jordanian border. Several of its tank formations crossed into Jordan. The United States was heavily involved in Vietnam at the time and sending an expeditionary force to the Middle East to defend the territory of an ally was politically, and probably militarily, not a viable option. Instead, Israel mobilized its own military, moved it closer to the Israeli border with Jordan and Syria, and issued an ultimatum to Syria to withdraw its forces from Jordan. Syria had lost the Golan Heights to Israel only three years earlier in the Six Day War and was in no mood to confront the Israeli military again, this time alone. It withdrew its army from Jordan, moved its remaining forces back from the border, and allowed Hussein to complete unhindered the expulsion of the PLO from Jordan.

This example shows why states cooperate and enter alliances with each other: because it serves their interests. The tacit thirty-year alliance between the United States and Israel has served U.S. interests well. Specifically, the U.S.-Israeli alliance helped the United States to limit the influence of radical Arab regimes, made it more difficult for the Soviet Union to expand its power and influence in the Middle East, and offered protection, both direct and indirect, to Arab regimes friendly to the United States. Because of its tacit arrangement with Israel, the United States was able to achieve these goals relatively cheaply, without involving American troops. Between 1958, when the U.S. Marine Corps landed in Lebanon to shore up the pro-Western regime there, and 1990, when the United States sent troops to Saudi Arabia during Operation Desert Storm, American troop deployment in the region was minimal, confined mostly to the offshore presence of the U.S. Navy.

There are many factors that predisposed the United States to be friendly to Israel. First, both countries adhere to democratic principles. In the case of Israel such adherence is marred by the fact that its Arab citizens, although legally equal to the Jewish citizens, are less than equal, a status that can be partly explained by the existence of a state of war between Israel and its Arab neighbors. Another factor that has contributed to the

President Anwar Sadat, President Jimmy Carter, and Premier Menachem Begin signing the Camp David agreement, 17 September 1978

ISRAEL

close relationship between the two countries is the presence in the United States of a vocal and politically astute Jewish community that, using all available levers of democracy, forcefully conveys to American politicians its interest in a safe and secure Israel. It is difficult to imagine, however, that these strong motivators would be powerful enough on their own to push the United States into a close alliance with Israel in the absence of an equally compelling strategic rationale for such a relationship. In fact, strategic reasons provide the bedrock on which the United States has built its special relationship with Israel, and those considerations are, in turn, the reasons that pro-Israel domestic factors are allowed to wield so much influence.

The fact is the United States does not have a reasonable alternative to its close relationship to Israel. When the United States made a strategic decision to contain the spread of Soviet power and influence, it had to build an infrastructure on which such containment could be based. In the Middle East no Arab country with which the United States could possibly have collaborated could offer the United States a better-trained military establishment, a more-educated population, and a more-compatible culture and political climate than Israel. The Arab countries that sided with the United States (such as Saudi Arabia, Jordan, and the Gulf sheikdoms) were either too small or traditional to provide for large, modern militaries. Moreover, too close and open an involvement with the United States might have delegitimized and destabilized pro-Western regimes. Other pro-Western countries, such as Tunisia and Morocco, were too far from the heart of the region, while Lebanon was too small and lacking in power resources. During the 1950s and 1960s other countries in the region—for example, Egypt, Syria, Iraq, Yemen, and Libya—were taken over by revolutionary regimes interested in developing an Arab version of socialism. They were hostile to Western interests (which they equated with colonialism) and sympathetic to Soviet attempts to weaken Western influence in the Middle East. The only countries that were friendly to American interests, in possession of large modern militaries, and willing to side openly with the United States were Israel and Iran (until Ayatollah Khomeini's takeover in 1979). If the United States, rather than rely on the Israeli or Iranian military to help protect Western interests in that region, had wanted to station tens or even hundreds of thousands of American troops in the Middle East—as it did in Europe after the Second World War and on the Korean peninsula after the Korean War—it would have been impossible to find an Arab country willing to allow American troops in its territory for any length of time.

Israel's role in helping the United States carry out its ambitious containment policy came at a relatively modest price. Although many critics of the close relationship between the United States and Israel assume that the United States has given Israel an inordinate amount of aid over the years, A. F. K. Organski calculates that West Germany has received seventeen times the amount of assistance given Israel and that South Vietnam received ten times that amount. Israel does not even stand out as a large aid recipient when compared to other countries in the region. Counting the aid received from the United States and other sources, Arab countries received nine dollars' worth of arms for each dollar's worth Israel received.

The special relationship of the United States and Israel has convinced many Arab states that their dream of "throwing Israel into the sea" is not going to be realized and that they should accept the existence of Israel and make peace with it. In this regard it is important to note the attitude of the United States toward Israel's nuclear-weapons program. In 1961 and 1963 the Kennedy administration pressured Israel to abandon the program, but the Johnson administration largely looked the other way when it came to Israel's effort to acquire nuclear weapons (which were successful by spring 1967). The Nixon administration tacitly accepted Israel's status as a nuclear-weapons state. Many in the arms-control community in the United States have expressed their displeasure at this state of affairs, pointing out a "double standard" in U.S. nuclear-nonproliferation policies that weakens efforts to check the spread of nuclear weapons and makes it more difficult to persuade other nations not to develop them. The United States has applied political pressure, imposed economic sanctions, and even taken military action against countries developing, or suspected of developing, nuclear weapons. For example, the United States applied political pressure to Taiwan and South Korea in the mid 1970s. It used political pressure and economic sanctions against Pakistan in the late 1970s, the early 1990s, and the late 1990s and against India in the late 1990s as well. In the 1990s the United States also took military action against Iraq and threatened to use force against North Korea. Supporters of universal nuclear disarmament thus perceived the U.S. acceptance of Israel's nuclear status as hypocritical. While this charge may be true, there is no denying that the Israeli nuclear program—and tacit U.S. approval of it—had the intended effect on Israel's neighbors and advanced the cause of peace in the region.

Over time the unwavering U.S. support of Israel strengthened the position of the United States in the region and weakened that of its

ISRAEL

main rival, the Soviet Union. Many Arab countries shifted their allegiance from the Soviet Union to the United States because only the United States could persuade Israel to make the political and territorial concessions those Arab states desired. The only way in which the Soviet Union could have helped the Arabs would have been by supplying them with ever larger quantities of ever more sophisticated weapons. Yet, U.S. military supplies to Israel, indigenous Israeli military industries, and Israel's nuclear arsenal made the military option unrealistic. Beginning in the early 1970s, therefore, Arab states led by Anwar Sadat of Egypt came to the realization that the solution to their conflict with Israel lay with the United States. Sadat ordered tens of thousands of Soviet military personnel out of Egypt in 1972 and 1973. After military efforts by Egypt and Syria in October 1973 failed to win back the territory they had lost to Israel in the Six Day War, Sadat encouraged Secretary of State Henry Kissinger to engage in the arduous "shuttle diplomacy" that brokered the cease-fire and troop-separation agreements between Israel and Egypt and Israel and Syria. By the late 1970s, another U.S. president, Jimmy Carter, served as the mediator for the 1978 Camp David agreement between Israel and Egypt that led to a formal peace treaty between the two nations in March 1979—the first such agreement between Israel and any of its Arab neighbors. In the early 1990s President William Clinton was instrumental in helping Israel and Jordan and Israel and the Palestinians—represented by PLO leader Yasser Arafat—conclude another set of peace agreements. Even Syria, one of the most implacable foes of Israel and the United States, has softened its stance, becoming more engaged in American diplomatic initiatives and more amenable to American inducements. U.S. support for Israel has thus paid handsomely in strengthening the U.S. position in the Middle East.

The United States did not arrive quickly at the idea that support for Israel was good for U.S. interests. In 1948 leading American decisionmakers—among them Secretary of State George C. Marshall and Secretary of Defense James V. Forrestal—opposed the creation of the State of Israel and tried to persuade President Harry S Truman not to recognize the young nation. In 1956 the United States joined with the Soviet Union to pressure Israel to withdraw from the Sinai peninsula. The policy of keeping a distance from Israel did not work, as one pro-Western regime after another in the Arab world was toppled by forces hostile to the United States and its

interests. In the mid 1960s, under President Johnson, that policy began to change, and the transition was completed under Nixon in the late 1960s. The vocal domestic support for Israel followed, rather than initiated, the strategic reorientation of U.S. policy toward the region.

A policy should be judged by its results. For the first fifteen to twenty years following the creation of the State of Israel, the United States pursued a policy in the Middle East that was cool toward Israel and eager to satisfy Arab demands. Whether as a direct result of that policy or not, during the same period a series of pro-Western regimes in the region were overthrown; an active subversion campaign against the remaining few was set in motion; and the Soviet Union became increasingly involved in Middle Eastern affairs. During the two and a half decades after the United States became more openly supportive of Israel and increased military and economic aid to it, important Arab states such as Egypt came back to the Western fold. Once-radical states and organizations such as Syria and the PLO moderated their views and became more constructive actors in the region, and before collapsing altogether, the Soviet Union was pushed out of the Middle East. Recalcitrant leaders such as Saddam Hussein of Iraq and Mu'ammar Gadhafi of Libya became largely isolated, making it easier for the United States to contain them. The verdict is in: U.S. support for Israel served U.S. strategic interests, enhanced its position in the Middle East, and bolstered the standing of pro-Western regimes in the region.

—BENJAMIN FRANKEL, SECURITY STUDIES

Viewpoint:
No, the close alliance between the United States and Israel has hurt U.S. relations with Arab nations.

During 1947–1948 the U.S. government was sharply divided over whether to support the creation of the State of Israel. Most of President Harry S Truman's political advisers strongly supported U.S. recognition of and support for the fledgling state, but almost the entire foreign-policy establishment was bitterly opposed—including Secretary of Defense James V. Forrestal, Secretary of State George C. Marshall, Undersecretary of Defense Robert A. Lovett, State Department Chief of Policy Planning George F. Kennan, Undersecretary of State Dean G. Acheson, Office of Special Political Affairs director Dean Rusk, and Charles E. Bohlen, who was Marshall's personal assistant and future ambassador to the Soviet Union. Indeed, Marshall came close to resigning in protest over Truman's decision in favor of recognition.

In early 1948 Kennan summed up the case against recognizing Israel in an internal State Department analysis: "Supporting the extreme objectives of political Zionism," he said, would be "to the detriment of overall U.S. security objectives" in the Middle East. Such an American policy, he warned, would increase the opportunities for the expansion of Soviet influence, endanger profitable oil concessions, and threaten U.S. military-basing rights in the region.

Kennan's arguments were not seriously engaged by supporters of Israel, and in the end Truman did not refute them but simply overrode them. As all Truman's biographers agree, Truman acted (to his everlasting credit) mainly for moral reasons. He was deeply moved by the plight of the Jews, was horrified by the Holocaust, and was a profound believer in the biblical basis of the Zionist claim on Palestine. Of course, it did not hurt that Truman's moral beliefs coincided with his domestic political interests: his need for Jewish electoral and financial support in the 1948 presidential elections.

The basis of the American alliance with Israel has not changed since 1948. Nearly all American presidents and continuing large majorities in Congress and public opinion believe that the United States has a deep moral obligation to support the existence and basic security of Israel. In turn, the widespread public support of Israel ensures that it is in the domestic political interest of every American politician, regardless of party, to support Israel strongly. Nonetheless, the national-interest arguments for American support of Israel have always been less than compelling.

Clark M. Clifford, Truman's leading political adviser in 1948 and a strong advocate of U.S. support of Israel, later wrote that Marshall, Acheson, and the other leaders of the foreign-policy establishment remained convinced for the rest of their lives that Truman had made the wrong decision. Clifford seemed bemused by this attitude, but he should not have been. The highest responsibility of foreign-policy professionals is to serve U.S. national interest as they understand it. For that reason, it is hardly surprising that they did not change their minds, for Kennan's arguments—based strictly on the U.S. national interest rather than on moral or domestic political considerations—were not only essentially irrefutable, they were largely if not entirely prescient.

What were America's national interests in the Middle East? During the cold war they were the containment of possible Soviet expansion in the area, the maintenance of Western access to oil at favorable prices, the avoidance of major war, and the continuance of general stability in the region. The only change in the post-cold-war era is that the containment policy has been directed against Iraqi or fundamentalist Islamic expansionism rather than against the departed Soviet Union. Then and now, the American alliance with Israel actually or potentially endangers those interests rather than serving them.

Despite their initial belief that support of Israel would be inconsistent with the national interest in containing Soviet expansionism, most U.S. officials had changed their minds by the 1960s and had come to regard Israel as a "strategic asset" for the United States in the cold war. Although this point of view remains the overwhelming consensus, it is unpersuasive. The historical evidence does not support the view that the Soviet Union had expansionist objectives in the Middle East. If it did have such goals, then the American alliance with Israel did far more to facilitate Soviet expansionism than it did to contain it—just as Kennan had predicted.

The dominant view of Soviet policy was that it aimed at dominating the Middle East, motivated by a combination of revolutionary Marxist ideology and traditional Russian imperialism and expansionism. In this view the Soviets sought to take advantage of the post–Second World War "vacuum" left by the decline of Western power and the resulting political instability in the Middle East by tactically aligning themselves with emerging radical, nationalist, anticolonialist forces in the area and using the Arab-Israeli conflict as a means of penetration. The Soviet goals, the consensus ran, were to eliminate Western influence, establish Moscow as the dominant power in the area, threaten vital Western communications and sea routes, outflank the North Atlantic Treaty Organization (NATO), and gain control over the region's oil, thereby putting severe economic pressure on Western Europe, Japan, and the United States.

The problem with this view is that there is next to no evidence to support it. Rather, all actual Soviet behavior in the Middle East during the cold war is best explained in terms of a combination of traditional Russian defensive concerns, the dynamics of the geostrategic rivalry between the United States and the Soviet Union, and Soviet aspirations to be recognized and accepted as a superpower equal in influence and prestige to the United States.

Soviet defensive objectives included Russia's traditional concern with the safety of its southern flank along the 1,800-mile-long border it shares with countries of the Middle East, its cold-war worries about "capitalist encirclement," its desire for secure access to the Mediterranean, its need to protect sea lanes and lines of communications with the Soviet far east, and probably, above all, its fear of the direct nuclear threat to the Soviet homeland that was posed by American aircraft carriers and submarines in the Mediterranean. This final concern alone can account for the Soviets' drive to secure land, sea, and air bases in the Middle East so that they could monitor U.S. naval forces and counterbalance the U.S. strategic threat.

In addition, the Soviets clearly were motivated by the desire to be accepted as a superpower of equal standing and influence to the United States. Indeed, much of their behavior was simply an emulation of their cold-war rival. The Soviet military presence in the Middle East played the same function in Soviet policy as military projection played in American policy: to show the flag, to deter intervention against allied states by the superpower rival, and to maintain the capability to intervene if necessary to protect client states threatened by allies or proxies of the adversary. On the other hand, there is no evidence that the Soviets ever sought to seize the oil resources of the Middle East or otherwise deny the West access to them. Rather, to the extent that oil played any role at all in Moscow's policies, the Soviets' concern was to maintain future access for themselves against the time when their domestic oil production would no longer meet its needs.

In the standard cold-war interpretation the Soviet Union deliberately sided with the Arab states in the Arab-Israeli conflict, seeking to exploit the situation in order to drive the United States from the Middle East and secure Soviet domination over the entire region. While the Soviets did not want Arab-Israeli wars to get out of control and precipitate a superpower confrontation (the argument goes), they did seek "to keep the pot boiling" and therefore opposed any political settlement of the conflict.

No part of this interpretation stands up to historical examination. To begin with, in the 1947–1949 period the Soviets supported Israel rather than the Arabs. The Soviet Union was the first state to recognize Israel. The Soviets allowed substantial Jewish emigration from the Soviet Union and eastern Europe to Israel, and, through Czechoslovakia, they were the most important supplier of heavy weapons to Israel during the 1948 war.

By the early 1950s Soviet support for Israel had ended—surely a consequence of Israel's fateful decision in 1950 to shift its initial foreign policy of neutrality in the cold war to one of alliance with the West. This new Israeli policy then led to an Israeli effort to buy Western arms. Even so, despite the end of

Soviet political and military support for Israel, initially the Soviets simply withdrew from the Middle East and the Arab-Israeli conflict. They did not immediately shift their support to the Arabs or actively seek the expansion of Soviet influence in the region.

Soviet noninvolvement ended in the mid 1950s as a direct consequence of the Eisenhower administration's decision actively to extend its containment policy to the Middle East by linking NATO with the Baghdad Pact states of Britain, Turkey, Iraq, Iran, and Pakistan. Had the plan succeeded, it would have completed a ring of pro-Western, American-armed states around the entire European, Middle Eastern, and southern periphery of the Soviet Union. (It fell apart when conservative monarchies in Iraq, Iran, and Pakistan were overthrown.) It is hardly surprising that the Soviets saw this alliance as a direct threat to their national security; thus, their response was not evidence of "expansionism."

The initial Soviet counter to the Eisenhower policies was to propose the demilitarization and neutralization of the Middle East by means of a superpower agreement to refrain from arming client governments. When the United States ignored these proposals and began arming the conservative states in the region, the Soviets responded by developing their own alliances with radical nationalist regimes, principally in Egypt and Syria.

ISRAEL

While Moscow's clear motivation was to counter Western moves in the Middle East, the consequence was to align the Soviet Union with the leading opponents of Israel. Soviet policies in turn precipitated closer U.S. ties with Israel, and the deepening action/reaction cycle nearly ended in a superpower confrontation in 1967 during the Six Day War.

Because of their fear of such a confrontation, after 1967 the Soviets sought a political settlement of this Arab-Israeli conflict, so long as the consequence of such a settlement would not be the elimination of Soviet influence in the Middle East and the unilateral domination of the region by the United States. Thus, Moscow repeatedly proposed that the two superpowers work together jointly to negotiate and guarantee peace in the Middle East. The primary goal of President Richard M. Nixon and Secretary of State Henry Kissinger, however, was not to settle the Arab-Israeli conflict but to drive out the Soviets. The Nixon administration refused to pursue peace on the basis of an institutionalized, co-equal role for Moscow. As a result, a golden opportunity for ending the Arab-Israeli conflict was lost.

Even if Soviet goals had been truly expansionist, it is hard to understand why American policymakers came to believe that Israel was a strategic asset, rather than a liability, to containment. If policymakers feared outright Soviet military expansionism—a Soviet invasion of the region—then there might at least have been a plausible case for regarding Israeli military power as an important component of the Western defense effort. By the time Israeli armed forces became significant, however—in the late 1960s—the U.S. concern was not so much about Soviet invasion but the extension of Soviet military, economic, and political influence. For that reason, it is hard to see why American policymakers failed to realize that Israel was a liability rather than an asset in the effort to contain the expansion of Soviet influence.

The American alliance with Israel gave the Soviets the opportunity to forge alliances in the Arab world. Indeed, President Gamal Abdel Nasser of Egypt, not the Soviet leadership, initiated the 1955 Soviet-Egyptian pact that led to Soviet influence in the Middle East. If not for U.S. support of Israel (which then took the form of encouraging France to provide Israel with modern arms), Nasser probably would not have turned to the Soviet Union as a counterbalance. Even if he had, there would have been no reason for the Soviets to have agreed to arm Egypt in exchange for base rights. At that time their overall goal was not to escalate the cold-war competition in the region but to seek joint superpower disengagement.

Moreover, American support of Israel in the Arab-Israeli conflict exacerbated the growing radical nationalism and anticolonialism in the Middle East and contributed to the destabilization of conservative, pro-Western states in the region. Together with Eisenhower's decision to throw down the gauntlet to the Soviets in the Middle East, U.S. support of Israel ultimately undermined rather than supported the traditional Western domination of the region, providing a basis and an opportunity for the expansion of Soviet influence.

The most concrete, tangible, and unambiguously clear American national interest in the Middle East is to maintain access to Arab oil at reasonable prices, both for the United States and its major allies, particularly Japan and Western Europe, who for decades have imported most of their oil from the Persian Gulf area. Nothing could be more obvious than the fact that American support for Israel in its conflict with the Arab world potentially puts this national interest in jeopardy.

Even in the 1940s, at a time when the United States imported less than 3 percent of its oil from the Middle East, foreign-policy professionals worried about future access to Arab oil for America and its major allies. In the ensuing decades, as the U.S. economy expanded and domestic oil production dropped, access to the oil in the Middle East became increasingly important. At the same time, growing American support of Israel deepened Arab anger. In the early 1970s, the predicted risks of this policy materialized. To be sure, the Arab oil embargo of the United States and Western Europe in 1973—precipitated by Western support of Israel in the Yom Kippur War—was short-lived and, in retrospect, less damaging than the near-panicked reaction at the time warranted. Various alternatives to Middle Eastern oil quickly materialized; the "embargo" turned out to be ineffective; and the accompanying 400-percent price rise was largely rolled back within a decade.

The 1973 scenario has not been repeated, both for economic reasons and because Saudi Arabia and the other oil-producing sheikdoms of the Persian Gulf came to realize their dependence on U.S. military might to ensure their continued independence. Thus the continuing conflict between U.S. support for Israel and access to Arab oil has remained potential rather than actual. Even so, it is far from implausible that the risks could substantially increase in the future. For example, rising demand for petroleum together with decreasing world oil supplies, resulting in an increased U.S. or Western dependence on Middle Eastern oil, would give the Arab states considerably more economic leverage than they have. This leverage could be employed in ways that would damage Western economies, especially if the oil-producing states are motivated not only by economic reasons but also by anger at continued U.S. support of Israel in an unresolved Arab-Israeli conflict.

The danger to U.S. access to Persian Gulf oil would be even greater should a continued Arab-Israeli conflict be accompanied by a rising tide of Islamic fundamentalism in the Middle East. In the worst case, for example, the Saudi monarchy might be overthrown by a radical Islamic revolutionary movement, and the new rulers might decide for ideological reasons to throw Western oil companies out of the country and cut off oil shipments to America and its allies. Of course, Islamic fundamentalist rage at the United States is by no means just a reaction to the American support for Israel. For that reason a settlement of the Arab-Israeli conflict or even the withdrawal of American support from Israel would not necessarily end the risks—but it would certainly diminish them substantially.

With the brief exception of 1973, the potential conflict between U.S. support for Israel and U.S. access to Arabian oil has not materialized. Be that as it may, except for American support of Israel, there would be little or no risk at all. Nor does U.S. support of Israel provide offsetting advantages to U.S. national interests. Despite all the rhetoric about the "strategic" importance of Israel to the Americans, it is hard to imagine circumstances in which Israeli military power might be employed to "solve" the potential oil problem. In light of the Israeli experience in tiny, neighboring Lebanon, for example, it is wildly implausible that Israel would intervene in Saudi Arabia to reverse a radical Islamic overthrow of the monarchy.

By far the most important American national interests in the Middle East are the maintenance of regional stability, containment of Islamic fundamentalism, and—above all else—the avoidance of international terrorism, as well as an interstate war in an environment where weapons of mass destruction and the means to deliver them are rapidly spreading. American support of, or de facto collaboration with, current Israeli policies in the Arab-Israeli conflict, especially in regard to the Palestinians, undercuts all these interrelated interests.

Fundamentalist movements are increasingly strong in Jordan, Egypt, and perhaps Saudi Arabia. Specialists also worry about Syria when the rule of President Hafiz al-Assad ends and even Iraq after the reign of Saddam Hussein. So far, however, the rise of Islamic danger to the Middle East has reinforced rather than undercut the standard American view that Israel is an important strategic asset of the United States in the effort at "containing" fundamentalism—the fundamentalist danger has simply substituted for the Soviet or communist threat of the cold war as the basis for the U.S.-Israeli de facto military alliance.

A strong case can be made that Middle Eastern fundamentalism is a true danger not only to U.S. national interests but to basic U.S. national security. Indeed, Islamic fanaticism is a considerably greater danger than either communist revolution or Soviet expansionism ever was. The U.S.-Israeli alliance, however, is part of the problem, not the solution.

Clearly the causes of fanaticism—a general global revival of religious fundamentalism, ongoing poverty in the Middle East, corrupt and authoritarian misrule—are far deeper than the Arab-Israeli conflict and will continue even if the conflict is settled. It is equally clear, however, that populist rage at Israel, America, and the pro-Western governments of President Hosni Mubarak in Egypt, King Abdallah in Jordan, and perhaps even the Saudi monarchy, substantially increases the mass appeal of the fundamentalists.

Nor does Israeli military power provide offsetting advantages to the United States in dealing with these problems. Unless one believes that Israel and the United States might join forces, for example, to reverse fundamentalist revolutions in Jordan, Egypt, or Saudi Arabia, that power is either irrelevant or not available to "contain" the threat militarily. It is instructive that, for obvious political reasons, Israeli military power was of no relevance—indeed, was strongly unwanted—during the Gulf War and subsequent military confrontations between Iraq and the United States.

The greatest dangers to the national security of the United States today are posed by weapons of mass destruction, which could strike America in the future, either by international terrorism or by spreading interstate war. The American alliance with Israel increases these dangers. The greatest danger stems from Islamic fundamentalists—such as the bombers of the World Trade Center in New York or the followers of Osama bin Laden—whose hatred of the United States is a direct consequence of continuing American support of Israel. It is a virtual certainty that terrorists will strike American cities again, and sooner or later it may be with weapons of mass destruction.

Finally, there continues to be a significant danger of an Arab-Israeli war, perhaps with nuclear weapons, an engagement that, by one route or another, could involve the United States. If such war comes, its most likely cause will be the ongoing Israeli intransigence with the Palestinians and with the Syrians over the Golan Heights, which have been main obstacles to a comprehensive settlement of the Arab-Israeli dispute for at least the last decade.

As in the internal U.S. government debate over support for the creation of Israel in 1948, the case for American support of Israel on moral grounds has always been stronger than the national-interest argument. In the early years of the U.S.-Israeli alliance, the American government supported Israel despite its perceived national interests, not because of them. Since the 1960s most policymakers have come to believe that American national interests and moral values are congruent, both requiring support of Israel. However genuine this belief, it was and remains unpersuasive. Strictly defined and coldly calculated, the American national interest has never included supporting Israel rather than its opponents in the Arab-Israeli conflict.

In addition, the United States has oversimplified the moral issues in the Arab-Israeli struggle. The core issue, the conflict between Palestinian Arabs and Israeli Jews over the ancient land of Palestine, is far more morally complex than either the Israelis or their American supporters have been willing to acknowledge. Moreover, there is no doubt that mainstream Palestinian leaders and a majority of the Palestinian people are prepared to resolve their conflict on the basis of a genuine and morally compelling compromise: the division of the land of Palestine into two independent states, one Jewish, the other Arab. It is Israel that blocks this settlement, thereby ensuring the continuation of the overall Arab-Israeli conflict.

Today, as in the past, the United States has powerful, moral reasons to support the basic national security and survival of Israel. Yet, the main threat to Israeli survival is not Arab policies but Israel's own shortsighted intransigence, especially, but not exclusively, in its conflict with the Palestinians. Traditionally the United States has provided near-unconditional support of the Israeli government, whatever its policies. Continuing that stance endangers Israel, American national security, and international peace and stability.

–JEROME SLATER, STATE UNIVERSITY OF NEW YORK COLLEGE AT BUFFALO

References

Abraham Ben-Zvi, *Decade of Transition: Eisenhower, Kennedy, and the Origins of the American-Israeli Alliance* (New York: Columbia University Press, 1998);

Robert Jervis, Richard Ned Lebow, and Janice Gross Stein, with contributions by Patrick Morgan and Jack L. Snyder, *Psychology and Deterrence* (Baltimore: Johns Hopkins University Press, 1985);

A. F. K. Organski, *The $36 Billion Bargain: Strategy and Politics in U.S. Assistance to Israel* (New York: Columbia University Press, 1990);

William B. Quandt, *Peace Process: American Diplomacy and the Arab-Israeli Conflict Since 1967* (Washington, D.C.: Brookings Institution / Berkeley: University of California Press, 1993);

Cheryl A. Rubenberg, *Israel and the American National Interest: A Critical Examination* (Urbana-Champaign: University of Illinois Press, 1986).

Nadav Safran, *Israel, The Embattled Ally* (Cambridge, Mass.: Belknap Press, 1978);

David Schoenbaum, *The United States and the State of Israel* (New York: Oxford University Press, 1993);

Alan R. Taylor, *The Superpowers and the Middle East* (Syracuse, N.Y.: Syracuse University Press, 1991);

Seth P. Tillman, *The United States in the Middle East, Interests and Obstacles* (Bloomington: Indiana University Press, 1982).

ISRAEL

LIMITED NUCLEAR WAR

Do limited-nuclear-war doctrines make nuclear wars more likely?

Viewpoint: Yes, the adoption of limited-nuclear-war doctrines makes nuclear war more likely because such wars may be easier to initiate but are difficult to contain.

Viewpoint: No, limited-nuclear-war doctrines do not weaken nuclear deterrence.

Early in the nuclear age, Bernard Brodie, one of the preeminent theoreticians studying nuclear weapons, said that they had changed the role of weapons in warfare: the task of weapons had always been to win wars; with the nuclear revolution, the task of weapons would be to deter war. There were some early grumblings about this formulation, especially while the United States enjoyed a nuclear monopoly. As the Soviet Union began to build up its nuclear arsenal, however, and as it acquired the capability, sometime in the early to mid 1960s, to inflict truly heavy damage on—in fact to destroy—the United States, the debate over using weapons to win wars and using weapons to deter them gave way to a debate over what kind of strategy to employ these new weapons would best deter war.

Two schools emerged. The first emphasized the punishing quality of nuclear weapons: these weapons were so destructive that, in order to use them for deterrence purposes, it was best to promise an adversary an unacceptable retaliation if he attacked the United States. Nuclear weapons would make sure that the damage inflicted in such retaliation would outweigh any possible gains the adversary was hoping to achieve by initiating war against the United States or its vital interests. This school was called "deterrence by punishment," "minimal deterrence," and similar names.

The second school argued that, beyond a certain point, the promise of ever-greater violence became incredible, especially as the other side was acquiring the ability to respond in kind: for example, the United States offered a nuclear "umbrella" to its European and Asian allies. If the Soviet were to overrun Paris, would the United States attack Leningrad with nuclear weapons, if in response the Soviets were sure to attack New York and Chicago? In other words, would U.S. threats to take action on behalf of Paris be credible if that action meant the sacrifice of New York and Chicago? Would the other side abstain from attacking Paris? This second school answered with a resounding "no." Moreover, its proponents argued, was it unlikely that an American president would order a nuclear attack on hundreds of millions of innocent civilians for anything short of retaliation for the total devastation of the United States? Relying on deterrence by punishment thus amounted not to deterrence—but to self-deterrence: the United States would be deterred from using its own nuclear weapons because of the horrendous cost they would inflict and because of the retaliation that using them was sure to bring.

The solution was a move to a deterrence-by-denial posture, also known as war-fighting doctrine. Rather than build big bombs and target them against the urban centers of the adversary, the United States ought to build smaller, more precise weapons aimed to destroy the military capabilities of the adversary, while minimizing "collateral" damage to his population. Such a posture would have three advantages over deterrence by punishment. First, it would limit the damage done to the adversary because the United States would target his military installations, not his population, and, thus, to the United States (because the adversary was not likely to retaliate against the U.S. civilian population, knowing that the United States could destroy his own civilians. Second, because the level of damage would be relatively low, it was more likely that a president would resort to nuclear weapons when necessary; and, because the adversary knew that fact, this strategic posture would as a result be more credible as a deterrence. Third, this posture was moral because it promised the destruction of fewer people, and more effective because, if nuclear weapons were ever used, they would aim to win the war by destroying the military assets of the other side.

Critics of this war-fighting doctrine said that there were two major flaws in the thinking behind it. First, precisely because the damage associated with the use of nuclear weapons under this doctrine, at least initially, was relatively low, it was more likely that leaders of states would have fewer compunctions about using weapons in a way that did not promise the end of the world. Second, despite the promise of "limits" and "control," there was no way to keep a nuclear exchange limited and controlled. Even the most "limited" nuclear exchange would be hugely destructive, unleashing unimaginable emotions and fears. Second, nuclear exchanges, especially against command-and-control and communication systems would so disrupt the ability of the central command authorities to control their nuclear forces, that the United States might face a situation in which isolated nuclear launch crews, to whom launch authority had already been delegated, would engage in "private" nuclear wars against their preassigned targets. Limited-nuclear-war doctrines, by falsely promising "limits," "control," and "proportionality," would thus make it more, not less, likely that an all-out nuclear war would break out.

Beginning in the early 1960s, the United States opted for ever-more limited and refined nuclear-employment doctrines, relying on improvements in technology. High officials periodically gave expression to this trend—from Robert S. McNamara in his 1962 "city avoidance" doctrine, to James R. Schlesinger in his 1974 "Limited Nuclear Options," and Harold Brown in his 1979 "countervailing strategy." Fortunately, the United States and the Soviet Union ended the cold war without shooting nuclear missiles at one another in anger. Whether or not this positive outcome was because of U.S. and Soviet adoption of more limited nuclear employment approaches is a matter of speculation.

Viewpoint:
Yes, the adoption of limited-nuclear-war doctrines makes nuclear war more likely because such wars may be easier to initiate but are difficult to contain.

The apocalyptic specter of all-out thermonuclear exchange has led many scholars, strategists, and policymakers to advocate policies of limiting nuclear war so as to keep a war between nuclear powers from escalating to a world-ending holocaust and to make the threat of nuclear war credible during an international crisis. For the fortunate reason that there has never been a nuclear war, the questions of whether it is possible to limit a war between nuclear powers, and whether limited-war policies make nuclear war more likely, remain hypothetical. This essay will, nevertheless, offer two propositions: first, that a war between nuclear powers is highly unlikely to remain limited; second, that limited-nuclear-war policies, by making the notion of nuclear war "thinkable," do indeed make the actual outbreak of war between nuclear powers more, not less, likely. If these propositions are both true, lim-

ited-nuclear-war policies are inherently and unacceptably dangerous, for they run the risk of lulling statesmen into starting a war that is bound to escalate into absolute destruction. The first proposition is conceptual, based largely on the ideas of the Prussian strategist Carl von Clausewitz and other students of modern war; the second rests on a brief historical case study.

One apparent advantage of limited-nuclear war, and the typical reason why some strategists and policymakers have supported it, is its promise of keeping a nuclear war somewhere below the level of global nuclear holocaust. If powerful nations in an anarchical world are likely to end up sooner or later going to war, then it is imperative to develop, and then implement, strategies of limited-nuclear war so as to control the amount of destruction and death. A fatal defect of this argument, however, is its assumption that political and military leaders will be able to limit their attacks once an actual nuclear war breaks out.

The greatest theoretician of modern war, Clausewitz describes in his *On War* (1833) the problems facing military officers who were trying to understand what was going on in the Napoleonic Wars (1793–1815). The immense armies, the vast battlefields, the widespread use

of gunpowder, and the logistical problems of feeding and equipping a large citizen army all raised the destructiveness and chaos of war to the point where it became virtually impossible for officers to assess whether their strategies were failing or succeeding. While it was possible in premodern warfare for capable officers in the field to grasp the dynamic of a battle and act with strategic rationality, in the era of mass-produced cannon, million-man armies, and military theaters the size of small nations, field officers were overwhelmed by the noise, smoke, movement, scope, violence, and sheer tumult of any significant battle. Clausewitz termed this new phenomenon the "fog" of modern war.

Compounding this fog, Clausewitz continued, were the increasing stakes of victory or defeat. Napoleon Bonaparte had demonstrated that a powerful citizen army can devour nations whole, making the consequences of defeat in a decisive battle against an adversary such as Napoleonic France not simply the dishonor of a given prince, a change in national religion, or even the gradual alteration of international relations, but rather the rapid military subjugation of an entire people. With such momentous consequences looming, military leaders act with urgency, demanding of their subordinates in the field success at any cost.

When military officers in the field are unable to discern what is actually happening—and at the same time are being deluged with demands to win at all costs—their natural reaction will be to deliver as much firepower and deploy as many soldiers as are available in the general direction of the enemy. The result of this mass strategy, apart from causing vast destruction, will be to disorient and terrify the other side that much more, leading them to respond in kind. Having observed this kind of disorientation and panic at first hand, Clausewitz concluded that modern war tends toward the absolute because in the fog of modern war, leaders are bound to err on the side of overkill, forcing the other side to do the same.

What sort of "fog" would descend in a nuclear war? The answer to this question, once again, must be speculative, but Clausewitz's view would be unambiguous. The attempt to limit a nuclear war to a "battlefield," such as central Europe, would hopelessly fail, as military commanders on the scene either would be instant casualties or be so far removed from the action as to be unable to discern what is happening. The temptation to escalate the war, by using whatever nuclear weapons remain available, would be irresistible to commanders who are hearing only screams and static from the front. Allies whose

East German soldiers standing guard at the Friedrichstrasse border crossing, 4 December 1961, as workers build tank traps and reinforce the Berlin Wall, erected a few months earlier in response to the refusal of the Western Allies to withdraw their troops from West Berlin

(Corbis/Bettmann)

LIMITED NUCLEAR WAR

countries have been physically obliterated would demand retaliation. A determination to match the other side's escalation would lead commanders to overestimate incoming assaults, a reaction hard to avoid given the novel experience of being attacked with thermonuclear weapons. In general, the visceral desire not to be the only side that respects limits to the war (and risk annihilation by the side that does not) would overwhelm any calls for moderation once the war has begun. A limited war in a supposedly contained theater would spill over quickly into other parts of the world. Since neither side would be likely to want to surrender at this point, as both would still possess their strategic arsenals, a limited-nuclear war would in all likelihood escalate rapidly into general war.

If a limited-nuclear war were to escalate into a general war between the major nuclear belligerents, the impulses toward immoderation evident in the original conflict would only intensify. Political and military leaders who have relocated deep underground would become like Clausewitz's field officers, entirely unable to discern with any degree of confidence whether a given incoming attack is "limited," merely the first wave of an all-out assault, or an all-out attack that has been insufficiently monitored. News that the fifty to one hundred largest cities of one's nation have been destroyed, leaving tens or hundreds of millions dead, would make it unimaginably difficult for anyone in a command bunker to argue that the other side's attack has been "limited" and hence worthy of only a "limited" reprisal.

The disinclination of a political leader of a great power in the nuclear age (and, indeed, in the twentieth century) to err on the side of national defeat makes the notion of limited-nuclear war dubious from the outset. Once the first nuclear weapon explodes, even in a supposedly "local" conflict, statesmen are going to think seriously about the colossal risks of unilaterally moderating their next move. Acutely aware that the simplest, and perhaps only, way to be the only loser in a great war between two nuclear powers would be to limit one's own strikes while the other side launches everything it has, the statesman who at the outset refuses to authorize a general strike would have to have a religious kind of faith in the limitability of nuclear war. He would have to fend off political and military aides who do not share this faith, and who see his moderation as a certain recipe for national suicide. Every emotion in the underground bunker during the seconds or minutes of decision-making time would be visceral, apocalyptic, and fear crazed. It is highly unlikely in our current political culture that any reasonable leader of a great power would, in such circumstances, do anything other than immediately launch the general arsenal.

While an advocate of limited-nuclear war might concede that nuclear war between large nuclear powers is, in all likelihood, not limitable, they might still contend that a nation that develops limited-nuclear-war strategies is less likely to get into a war with another nuclear power. The typical argument is that all-or-nothing nuclear strategies are inherently incredible. Because no nation would really initiate a global thermonuclear holocaust over a minor conflict, adversaries will be encouraged to commit aggression, aware that the other side can only retreat or put an end to the world. This strategy is a formula for greater instability, perennial conflict, and eventual all-out war.

During the period 1958–1962, the Soviet Union and its ally communist China, bolstered by the Soviet acquisition of a thermonuclear arsenal capable of destroying much of the United States, instigated cold-war crises in the Taiwan Straits (1958), Berlin (1958–1959 and 1961), and Cuba (1962). Because of President Dwight D. Eisenhower's decision to eliminate limited-nuclear-war strategies, in the first three crises the United States had no effective options other than seeking some sort of compromise with the Soviet Union or instigating an all-out nuclear war. If the limited-war theorists are correct, Eisenhower's all-or-nothing approach should have made war more likely during this period. Instead, it made war much less likely.

Soviet premier Nikita S. Khrushchev's ultimatum in November 1958 gave the Western powers six months to get out of Berlin. The United States and its European allies refused to accede to this ultimatum, and in May 1959 they made formal preparations for meeting the Soviet challenge with force. Because at this moment the United States and NATO had no strategy of limited-nuclear warfare, nor the necessary weaponry, they had to accept that if a confrontation over Berlin expanded beyond minor skirmishes, the West would have no alternative but to ask for terms or unleash all-out thermonuclear war. The world would face thermonuclear holocaust over rights of occupation.

Eisenhower was privately opposed to the idea of waging thermonuclear war over occupation rights in Berlin, but he had decided that a public declaration of this conclusion would destabilize the Western position in Europe. A student of Clausewitz, Eisenhower was convinced as well that any significant war with the Soviet Union over Berlin would inevitably escalate into all-out destruction. Therefore, he would have to seek a compromise with the Soviets without openly appearing to do so.

As Eisenhower had intended with his earlier decision to eliminate limited-nuclear-war strategies, having only the alternative of compromise or all-out holocaust turned out to be an advantage in his attempts to cut a quiet deal over Berlin. It allowed Eisenhower to put off contingency plans for the defense of Berlin and to deflect those military and political aides who urged him to prepare for war. By presenting to his subordinates the simple choice of compromise and negotiation or nuclear apocalypse he was able to evade a formal commitment to war while quietly seeking a deal. He achieved this goal in the summer of 1959 by beginning negotiations with the Soviet Union (despite the public policy of refusing to negotiate under ultimatum).

Had the United States had limited-war strategies available during this period, Eisenhower's efforts to evade war and quietly seek compromise would have been more, not less, difficult. The key to his procrastination was the stark scenario he presented to his advisers: in the event of war over Berlin the United States would launch its entire arsenal and face the inevitable, all-out Soviet retaliation. This dire prospect allowed him to ridicule confrontational plans as suicidal and proposals for limited war as naive. Eisenhower's all-or-nothing strategy created a "box" of decision making, in which he could easily brush aside proposals for military confrontation that would have seemed much less controversial had limited-nuclear-war strategies and weaponry been available.

The Berlin crisis of 1958–1959 shows—as do the 1958 Taiwan Straits and 1961 Berlin crises—how Clausewitz's skepticism about limiting modern war applies to the nuclear era. Eisenhower (the only great-power political leader during the cold war with actual wartime command experience) shared Clausewitz's belief that war between great powers could not be limited. Eisenhower added to Clausewitz's main argument two new points about war between great powers in the nuclear age: one, that limitation of war was not simply unlikely but impossible and that escalation would occur almost instantly; two, that the consequences of unlimited thermonuclear war—the absolute destruction of nations waging it, and perhaps the human race as well—made it imperative to avoid war at all costs. To escape such consequences Eisenhower had to eliminate and discredit the idea of limited-nuclear-war.

–CAMPBELL CRAIG, UNIVERSITY OF CANTERBURY, NEW ZEALAND

Viewpoint:
No, limited-nuclear-war doctrines do not weaken nuclear deterrence.

In 1970 President Richard M. Nixon posed the following question in his foreign-policy report to Congress: "Should a president, in the event of a nuclear attack, be left with the single option of ordering the mass destruction of enemy civilians, in the face of certainty that it would be followed by the mass slaughter of Americans?" The nuclear doctrine to which Nixon was referring is called "mutual assured destruction" (MAD). Those who are unfamiliar with MAD may be shocked to learn that an American president might find himself complaining that his only retaliatory option once the nuclear threshold had been crossed would ensure the annihilation of the Soviet and American people. This dilemma has been captured in the phrases "suicide or surrender" and "humiliation or holocaust." Yet, notwithstanding its narrowing of choices to those grim alternatives, MAD was endorsed by many influential experts on nuclear policy. They based their support of the doctrine on the claim that any deviation from MAD would intensify the nuclear-arms race, and even worse, would increase the risk of nuclear war.

Despite their arguments, those actually responsible for coping with a Soviet attack were understandably uncomfortable with the single option offered by MAD. Presidents from John F. Kennedy onward sought alternatives, all of which can be placed under the general designation of "limited-nuclear war." Contrary to the claims of MAD advocates, such limited-nuclear options in no way weakened deterrence, nor can they be held accountable for driving the nuclear-arms race. Instead, efforts to limit the destructive consequences of war represented a more prudent and moral approach to nuclear strategy than that offered by MAD purists.

The heart of the case for what might be called a policy of "mutual assured destruction only" was that deviations from MAD would weaken nuclear deterrence. MAD advocates feared that having limited-nuclear options might tempt some misguided leader into launching a small-scale nuclear attack during a cold-war crisis, based on the belief that escalation could be contained well short of the devastation of his country. Such a limited war, however, was bound to get out of control, quickly reaching the level of all-out thermonuclear war. So long as the superpowers employed a MAD-only policy, they argued, the consequences of any breakdown of deterrence would loom as self-evidently unacceptable, ensuring that even the most minimally rational leader would refrain from starting a superpower war. Put another way, presidents need not have worried about the "humiliation or holocaust" dilemma because their public commitment to destroy the attacker's society in retaliation ensured that no attack would ever occur.

But was MAD really 100 percent reliable? If not, was it feasible to pursue options short of the wholesale murder of the enemy's population? Would such efforts to limit the consequences of a superpower war inevitably make the outbreak of nuclear war more likely?

If the answer to the first and third questions is "no," it follows that the case for an assured-destruction-only posture is both morally and practically unsupportable. In moral terms it is sufficient to note that MAD calls for the deliberate targeting of tens of millions of innocent civilians. Not only is it obviously unethical to plan for the mass murder of noncombatants, but the U.S. government has supported the international legal prohibition of such a policy. Thus, a 1977 protocol to the 1949 Geneva Convention, signed by the United States, prohibits "making the civilian population . . . the object of attack," a ban that includes any plan that "may be expected to cause . . . injury to civilians . . . which would be excessive in relation to the concrete and direct military advantage anticipated." Under MAD, of course, there would be no military advantage in killing off the enemy's population. Indeed, actually executing the plan would in effect amount to a case of "murder-suicide" on a gigantic scale.

In practical terms the tragically absurd nature of a decision to retaliate under conditions of MAD is precisely what called into question the claim that MAD was essential or even useful for deterrence. During the cold war three successive provocations were invoked by U.S. policymakers as triggers for the "assured destruction" of the Soviet Union: aggression against small countries, an attack on Europe, or a limited strike at the United States itself. In each case, decisionmakers found themselves unsure of the credibility of such an ultimate threat, and they were certain they wanted more-flexible options if deterrence failed and they found themselves at war.

The first case of explicit U.S. reliance on mass-destruction threats was the 1954 doctrine called "massive retaliation." Its purpose was to prevent a repetition of conflicts such as the 1950 invasion of South Korea by the communist North Korea, which had led to a costly conventional war that had ended in stalemate. Under this doctrine, the United States threatened to respond "massively" to unspecified acts of aggression by the Soviet Union or its communist allies. U.S. nuclear-war plans of that year in fact included only one option: an all-out simultaneous attack against the Soviet Union by more than seven hundred bombers, designed to destroy both military targets and population centers. What provocation, however, would have actually convinced a U. S. president to launch a massive nuclear strike at the Soviet Union: a communist-led revolution in

Cuba? A guerrilla war in Vietnam? Critics of massive retaliation quickly pointed out that the communists could pursue aggression by using "salami" tactics, cutting off one thin slice at a time to avoid provoking massive retaliation. As President Kennedy later complained, the Soviets would "nibble us to death."

This critique was sufficiently compelling to prompt a search for flexible military options, including limited conventional and nuclear alternatives. While it is true that some analysts (most memorably Henry Kissinger) briefly flirted with developing limited-nuclear-war options in response to salami tactics, they soon realized that credible deterrence and effective war-fighting in such cases required reliance on robust conventional power. In any event the case for massive retaliation collapsed even before the Soviets had achieved their own capability to respond by destroying the United States.

If it had quickly become apparent that such all-or-nothing threats would be insufficient to deter communist probes at the periphery of American power and interests, what about the utility of massive retaliation for deterring an attack on Western Europe? After all, the security of Europe was unquestionably a vital American interest, as recognized by the formation and durability of the North Atlantic Treaty Organization (NATO). Yet, as the Soviets pursued their own nuclear buildup throughout the 1950s and early 1960s, threats to annihilate the Soviet Union in response to an invasion of Western Europe sounded increasingly hollow.

Starting in the 1950s, low-yield nuclear weapons had been developed and deployed in Europe for potential use in stopping the advance of the Red Army. The other key technological change was the increasing accuracy of nuclear missiles, a development that steadily improved prospects for destroying military targets while limiting civilian deaths. In 1967 NATO formally dropped its reliance on massive retaliation, substituting a flexible-response doctrine, which offered both conventional-defense and limited-nuclear-war options.

The third, and most convincing, trigger for unleashing an assured-destruction attack against the Soviet Union would be a direct nuclear attack against the United States. Yet, even here, as President Nixon's complaint revealed, the "humiliation or holocaust" dilemma was unbearable for American leaders. What if the Soviet attack was directed solely against a few military targets, such as an intercontinental-ballistic-missile (ICBM) base in a sparsely populated state such as North Dakota? Blast and fallout effects would no doubt produce horrific damage, including perhaps hundreds of thousands of deaths. Would the proper response, however, be the complete destruction of Moscow, Leningrad, and dozens of other Soviet cities—that is, the response envisioned by the doctrine of MAD?

As early as 1961 Secretary of Defense Robert S. McNamara had proposed what became known as the "no-cities doctrine," offering the hope that even if nuclear deterrence failed, the availability of limited-nuclear-war plans might enable a president to avert the end of human civilization. McNamara himself became disillusioned with all types of efforts to limit the extent of damage in a nuclear war, and in the mid 1960s became the leading advocate of MAD. Yet, the emergence of MAD as the declaratory nuclear doctrine of the United States in the late 1960s and early 1970s obscured the continued support for limited-nuclear-war options by the U.S. leadership. According to McGeorge Bundy, national security adviser under Presidents Kennedy and Lyndon B. Johnson and the leading ally of McNamara in lobbying for MAD, "We may have spread confusion by using the measuring stick of 'assured destruction' . . . . This measurement lent itself to the erroneous conclusion that the population itself would be the preferred target of any actual attack." Even decisionmakers who publicly condemned limited-nuclear-war doctrines understood that presidents needed options.

During the Carter administration, planning for limited-nuclear war became highly publicized by the 1980 release of Presidential Directive (PD) 59, which included the underlying argument that limited-war options would strengthen deterrence, particularly by threatening to destroy targets that an aggressive Soviet leadership might value more than the lives of its own people. PD 59 consequently called for targeting Soviet military forces, even the bunkers in which the Soviet leadership would be hiding, during a nuclear exchange. In short, at least since 1961, limited-nuclear-war options have formed a continual component of U.S. deterrent and war-fighting strategy.

The manifest desire of every U.S. president since Kennedy for nuclear-war options beyond "humiliation or holocaust" does not, of course, prove that MAD purists were wrong in condemning limited-nuclear-war options. It does demonstrate, however, that limited-nuclear-war planning did not fatally weaken deterrence. Nuclear war has been avoided despite periods (such as the years of the Carter administration) of highly publicized limited-nuclear-war doctrines. Yet, the discrepancy between reality and the fears of opponents of limited-war doctrines does point to one faulty premise underlying MAD.

A good representation of that error is this 1962 statement by the noted psychologist Erich Fromm, who was writing in opposition to a U.S. civil-defense program: "thermonuclear war has been avoided until now because neither side believed it was possible to survive such a war. . . . It is precisely for this reason that we consider it so dangerous to underemphasize the fantastic damage that a thermonuclear war would surely

NUCLEAR STRATEGY

During the Berlin Crisis of 1961 strategic-arms theorist Thomas C. Schelling prepared a paper for the Kennedy administration on how its policy of limited nuclear war could be applied in that crisis. Schelling's paper includes the following observations:

The important thing in limited nuclear war is to impress the Soviet leadership with the risk of general war—a war that may occur whether we or they intend it or not. If nuclear weapons are introduced the main consequence will not be on the battlefield; the main consequence will be the increased likelihood and expectation of general war. The state of the local battlefield will receive less attention than the state of our strategic forces and the enemy's. Nuclears should therefore be used—if they are used at all in Europe—not mainly to destroy tactical targets but to influence the Soviet command.

Nuclears should be used to impress the Soviets with the fact that they cannot win a regional war—that it is unlikely to remain regional if it is fought with nuclears on the scale that tactical military considerations would dictate. The purpose of nuclears is to convince the Soviets that the risk of general war is great enough to outweigh their original tactical objectives, but not so great as to make it prudent to initiate it pre-emptively. . . .

We should plan for a war of nerve, of demonstration, and of bargaining, not of tactical target destruction. Destroying the target is incidental to the message the detonation conveys to the Soviet leadership. Targets should be picked with a view to what the Soviet leadership perceives about the character of the war and about our intent, not for tactical importance. A target inside the USSR is important because it is inside the USSR, not because of its tactical contribution to the European battlefield. A target in a city is important because a city is destroyed, not because it is a local supply or communication center. The difference between one weapon, a dozen, a hundred, or a thousand, is not in the number of targets destroyed but in the Soviet (and American) perception of risks, intent, precedent, and implied "proposal" for the conduct or termination of war.

Extra targets destroyed by additional weapons are not a local military "bonus"; they are noise that may drown the message. They are a "proposal" that must be responded to. And they are an added catalyst to general war. This is an argument for a selective and threatening use of nuclears rather than large-scale tactical use. (It is an argument for large-scale tactical use only if such creates the level of risk we wish to create.) Success in the use of nuclears will be measured not by the targets destroyed but by how well we manage the level of risk. The Soviets must be persuaded that the war is getting out of hand but is not yet beyond the point of no return.

Source: Thomas C. Schelling, "Nuclear Strategy in the Berlin Crisis," Foreign Relations of the United States, 14 (1961–1963): 170–171.

LIMITED NUCLEAR WAR

bring about." In other words, Fromm believed that efforts to defend the American population by providing bomb shelters were like efforts to provide options short of all-out nuclear war: both would delude leaders into thinking they could safely engage in a nuclear war.

There is no empirical support for this MAD view of the requirements of nuclear deterrence. First, the United States did not launch a nuclear war during the 1950s, even when it was highly confident that it could "survive"; war was avoided across the whole range of growing U.S., and later Soviet, offensive capabilities. That error became the basis for the fundamental misconception underlying MAD. To be deterred, a rationally acting state obviously does not need to know that it will be utterly destroyed; what is required is a conviction that any possible gains from aggression are outweighed by the prospective costs and risks. Indeed, it is plausible that anyone whose restraint from launching nuclear war depends on nothing less than the certainty of national "death" might not even be deterred by that prospect.

Limited-war plans, like efforts at homeland defense, are highly unlikely to weaken deterrence of rational leaders. Even the most limited damage by nuclear weapons is going to be seen as unacceptable, because no rational decisionmaker would ever assume that his country could escape escalation toward an irreparable level of destruction. The need for such efforts to limit damage would arise only if war came about because of factors such as technological failure during the stress of a crisis or other circumstances in which both sides found themselves desperately searching for ways to avoid destroying one another's cities.

Because nuclear war has not occurred, we do not know if the existence of limited-nuclear-war doctrines could have helped to channel a failure of deterrence away from inexorable escalation to the mutual destruction of the American and Soviet societies. We can, however, be reasonably sure that limited-war doctrines have not encouraged any American or Soviet leader to believe that nuclear war was a viable option. If nuclear weapons are one day used, we should all join in hoping that world leaders will have pursued every option—reducing offensive forces, cooperatively enhancing defenses, and employing limited-war options that spare population centers that might minimize the scale of the catastrophe.

—DAVID GOLDFISCHER, UNIVERSITY OF DENVER

References

Raymond Aron, *Clausewitz: Philosopher of War*, translated by Christine Booker and Norman Stone (London: Routledge & Kegan Paul, 1983);

Desmond Ball, *Politics and Force Levels: The Strategic Missile Program of the Kennedy Administration* (Berkeley: University of California Press, 1980);

Ball and Jeffrey Richelson, eds., *Strategic Nuclear Targeting* (Ithaca, N.Y.: Cornell University Press, 1986);

Christoph Bertram, ed., *The Future of Strategic Deterrence* (Hamden, Conn.: Archon, 1981);

Bernard Brodie, *The Absolute Weapon* (New York: Harcourt, Brace, 1946);

Campbell Craig, *Destroying the Village: Eisenhower and Thermonuclear War* (New York: Columbia University Press, 1998);

Lawrence Freedman, *The Evolution of Nuclear Strategy* (New York: St. Martin's Press, 1981);

David Goldfischer, *The Best Defense: Policy Alternatives for U.S. Nuclear Security from the 1950s to the 1990s* (Ithaca, N.Y.: Cornell University Press, 1993);

Morton H. Halperin, *Limited War in the Nuclear Age* (New York: Wiley, 1963);

Robert Jervis, *The Illogic of American Nuclear Strategy* (Ithaca, N.Y.: Cornell University Press, 1984);

Herman Kahn, *On Thermonuclear War* (Princeton, N.J.: Princeton University Press, 1960);

John Keegan, *The Mask of Command* (New York: Viking, 1987);

Henry Kissinger, *Nuclear Weapons and Foreign Policy* (New York: Published for the Council on Foreign Relations by Harper, 1957);

Sir Basil Henry Liddell-Hart, *The Way to Win Wars: The Strategy of Indirect Approach* (London: Faber & Faber, 1942);

Thomas C. Schelling, *The Strategy of Conflict*, revised edition (Cambridge, Mass.: Harvard University Press, 1980);

Herbert Scoville Jr., "Flexible Madness?" *Foreign Policy*, no. 14 (Spring 1974): 164–177.

MARSHALL PLAN

What were the true motivations behind the Marshall Plan?

Viewpoint: The motivation behind the Marshall Plan was to divide Europe between East and West and strengthen European markets for U.S. goods.

Viewpoint: The chief motivation behind the Marshall Plan was a desire to reunify Western Europe.

The Second World War devastated the countries of Europe. Victors such as Great Britain and France were as exhausted by the war as the defeated nations of Germany and Italy, or the countries caught in the middle, such as Poland and Czechoslovakia. The collapsed infrastructure, economic and social dislocation, diminished productive capabilities, and massive waves of refugees were exacerbated by the especially harsh winter of 1946–1947.

U.S. policymakers viewed these economic and social problems with special urgency. In eastern and central Europe the Soviet Union was tightening its grip on the countries that had come under the occupation of the Red Army during the war. In Western European countries, local Communist parties were actively exploiting the miserable conditions to advance their political agenda and their standing in public opinion.

For decisionmakers in the Truman administration these conditions bode ill for the ability of the United States to keep some of the countries of Western Europe in the Western column. Moreover, for these countries to make meaningful contributions to a U.S.-led effort to contain the Soviet Union, they had to be revived economically and stabilized politically. In addition, the economic welfare of the United States—and the fate of the global free market that the United States was trying to promote—were also at stake in the economic and political well-being of Europe. In June 1947, with these considerations in the background, the Truman administration launched the European Recovery Program (ERP), better known as the Marshall Plan after Secretary of State George C. Marshall.

The transfers of monies from the United States to Europe began in April 1948 and ended on 31 December 1951. During that period, the United States transferred about $12.5 billion to Europe, or about 1.2 percent of the U.S. Gross National Product (GNP) for 1948–1951. Most of the money was given out as grants to the recipient states.

Viewpoint:
The motivation behind the Marshall Plan was to divide Europe between East and West and strengthen European markets for U.S. goods.

When Secretary of State George C. Marshall spoke at Harvard University commencement ceremonies on a balmy day in June 1947, he described at great length the harsh economic and social conditions on the European continent. He used the occasion to announce that the United States would help Europe recover from the

THE MARSHALL PLAN

The following list gives aid allotments by country in millions of dollars for the period 3 April 1948 – 31 December 1951. Yugoslavia was not a member of the Organization for European Economic Cooperation and Development but nonetheless received aid under the Marshall Plan.

Austria	634.8
Belgium-Luxembourg	546.6
Denmark	266.4
France	2,576.8
Germany (Federal Republic)	1,317.3
Greece	614.1
Iceland	26.8
Ireland	146.2
Italy	1,315.4
The Netherlands	1,000.7
Norway	241.9
Portugal	50.5
Sweden	118.5
Trieste	33.0
Turkey	176.5
United Kingdom	2,865.8
Yugoslavia	61.5
Prepaid freight account	42.5
European Payments Union –capital fund	350.0
Total	12,385.2

Source: First Report to Congress on the Mutual Security Program. U. S. President *(Washington, D.C.: U.S. Government Printing Office, 1952).*

devastation of war and "return to normal economic health" by initiating a program designed to provide "a cure rather than a mere palliative."

The situation in Europe was indeed dire. On 27 May 1946, a week before Marshall's speech, Undersecretary of State for Economic Affairs William L. Clayton wrote a memo to Undersecretary of State Dean Acheson saying that "Europe is steadily deteriorating.... Millions of people in the cities are slowly starving.... Without further and substantial aid from the United States, economic, social, and political disintegration will overwhelm Europe.... Aside from the awful implications which this would have for the future of peace and security of the world, the immediate effects on our domestic economy would be disastrous." American officials were justifiably worried about the situation in Europe. From without, the Soviet Union was exploiting the presence of the Red Army in the countries of east and central Europe to help local communist organizations take over and impose a Soviet-like system there, making them into obedi-

ent satellites of the USSR. From within, the Communist parties in Western European countries—especially Italy, France, Belgium, and Greece—were large and popular. The standing of communist organizations was augmented further by the fact that in many countries under Nazi occupation during the war the communists had been the backbone of the resistance movements, fusing the fight for national independence with a quest for social justice. The Truman administration was afraid not only of the likelihood that deteriorating economic and social conditions would make the radical messages of the communists more appealing, but also that, if these parties were to join coalition governments in Western European countries, they would demand increases in social benefits and redistributive policies that ravaged European economies could ill afford, while blocking the austerity measures necessary for long-term recovery. American policymakers believed that the way to recovery entailed short-term sacrifices such as keeping wages low, controlling inflation, limiting domestic consumption, balancing budgets, lowering welfare outlays, and stabilizing currencies. Such policies were anathema to the communists. The administration was also worried that the continuing one-sided flow of goods from the United States to Europe was creating dangerous inflationary pressures in the United States, where demand was beginning to outpace the supply of goods and services.

To help European governments embark on the road to recovery the United States had to do something. The result was the European Recovery Program (ERP), which became better known as the Marshall Plan. Congress passed the ERP in April 1948, calling for the European nations to revive their economies so that by 1952 they would no longer require massive assistance from non-European nations. Some historians, including Alan S. Milward, argue that the ERP was not truly necessary because Western European economies, except that of West Germany, were already growing by the time the ERP was launched. While this statement is true, this growth was largely the result of generous supplies of fuel and food from the United States. In 1947, even before the Marshall Plan began, Europe was already dependent on the United States. European nations imported $3 billion more from the United States in 1947 than they did the year before the Second World War, while importing $3.7 billion less from the rest of the world. In 1946 Europe imported goods worth $4.4 billion from the United States, while exporting only $900 million, creating a merchandise deficit of $3.5 billion and a payment deficit of $4.2 billion. According to Melvyn P. Leffler, in 1947 40 percent of west European countries' consumption of bread grains, aluminum, and cotton—as well as 30 percent of lead, petroleum, and zinc; 15 percent of fats and oils; and 10 percent of meat and solid fuels—came from the Western

Hemisphere. In addition to its concerns about inflationary pressures at home, the Truman administration was worried about growing trade imbalances. If Western European governments were unable to produce and sell enough to finance their essential purchases abroad, they might have tried to resort to greater government regulation of their economies, curbing free markets and the free flow of goods.

There were thus multiple reasons for the launching of the Marshall Plan. The economic recovery of Western Europe was only one, and it was as much a means toward achieving other goals as it was an end in itself. The many reasons for the ERP were the result of the gravity of the crisis the Truman administration was facing. George F. Kennan wrote that this crisis was threatening traditional concepts of U.S. security, which postulated "a reasonable number of free [European] states subservient to no great power." The Joint Chiefs of Staff said that without "the support of some of the countries of the Old World . . . our military strength [would] be overshadowed by that of our enemies." The ERP was launched to arrest the changes in the global balance of power that would have resulted from the continuing economic decline of Western Europe. The plan aimed to alleviate Europe's economic distress, but to do so in a way that would advance specific U.S. objectives.

One such objective was to try and lure eastern European countries away from Soviet clutches. Soviet specialists in the State Department, such as Kennan and Charles Bohlen, knew that the Soviet Union would probably not accept an invitation to join the Marshall Plan and would likely try to sabotage it. On 27 June 1947 Ernest Bevin and Georges Bidault, the foreign secretaries of Great Britain and France, met in Paris with Vyacheslav Molotov, the Soviet foreign minister. The USSR, predictably, objected to the Marshall Plan as intervention in Soviet domestic affairs. They also prohibited the countries under their control from joining. With the possibility of Soviet participation out of the way, the Marshall Plan proceeded to accomplish what it had been designed to do: it shored up the economy of Western Europe, making the political systems of those nations more stable and their voters less susceptible to communist appeals. The plan also achieved other goals. It made the Western European countries more amenable to the idea of joining an alliance led by the United States, and it planted the seeds for greater Western European economic and political integration. The intensification of the cold war, as well as the war in Korea, led to a greater emphasis on the security aspects in the relationship between the United States and Western Europe. The March 1947 enunciation of the Truman Doctrine, the April 1949 signing of the agreement creating the North Atlantic Treaty Organization (NATO), and the October 1951 Mutual Security Act were but manifestations of the growing preoccupation of the West with competition with the USSR. While the United States did not present the Marshall Plan as an anti-Soviet instrument (indeed the Soviet Union was invited to join), the anti-Soviet emphasis of subsequent U.S. initiatives was unmistaken. Indeed, by 1951 the Marshall Plan was terminated and replaced with the Mutual Security Program (MSP), which shifted the emphasis in U.S. aid policies to defense-related programs.

The Marshall Plan achieved impressive political and strategic objectives. As Imanuel Wexler pointed out in 1997, its record of economic achievement is less clear, both with regard to the economic performance of the countries that received the aid and with regard to the more fundamental question of whether or not the ERP was necessary for the attainment of these goals. The plan set for itself the goal of helping Europe become economically viable, without substantial U.S. aid, by 1952. Industrial production and foreign trade both made gains beyond expectations by the time the ERP was terminated. Agricultural production, however, faltered, and personal consumption lagged behind expectations. Trade among European states and between Europe and the rest of the world expanded, but Europe was still facing a severe balance-of-payment deficit at the end of 1951. Initial gains in the fight against inflation were lost as European governments increased their defense budgets and the importation of raw materials. Wexler rightly points out that the expectations of attaining Western European economic viability in four years were not realistic, because the two essential conditions—favorable balance-of-payments equilibrium and adequate per capita income reached through high levels of domestic production—could not have been secured in such a short period of time without unacceptable political measures.

The Marshall Plan succeeded in helping to stabilize the political situation in Western Europe and in laying the foundation for a concerted Western effort to contain communist influence and Soviet expansion. The United States never seriously pursued the goal of reviving the economy of the entire European continent, and the more limited objective of rehabilitating the economies of the countries of Western Europe was partially achieved. That the record of the Marshall Plan is thus uneven at best, however, does not mean that it should not have been launched, but it does mean that it was not as indispensable or without alternatives as has at times been argued.

—BENJAMIN FRANKEL, SECURITY STUDIES

Viewpoint:
The chief motivation behind the Marshall Plan was a desire to reunify Western Europe.

There were two main motivations behind the American decision to offer Marshall Plan assistance to Europe in 1947. First and foremost, the Truman administration had become convinced that continuing economic disarray in Western Europe might lead to communist electoral gains and even democratically elected communist governments in major Western European nations. In order to prevent damage to American interests—and the cause of freedom and democracy—that would follow from communist control of major Western European countries, some U.S. effort was essential to facilitate not only economic recovery but the revival of hope among the general population. The Truman administration also hoped that participation in the American-led program might open up the economies of eastern Europe and conceivably even the Soviet Union. A program of assistance offered to all Europe might facilitate the integration of the Europeans into an American-led capitalist economic group. If this integration did not happen, such a program might drive a wedge between the Soviets and some of their eastern European neighbors, or at least it might permit the United States to generate political capital by advertising Soviet responsibility for the division of Europe and making clear that the United States sought to assist European recovery while the Soviets impeded it.

Apparent Soviet disregard for the deteriorating economic conditions in Europe during the April 1947 meeting of the Council of Foreign Ministers greatly disturbed U.S. secretary of state George C. Marshall. Scott Parrish argues that Joseph Stalin was not convinced of the desperate state of the Western economies and was concerned about obtaining reparations from Germany and preventing a German resurgence. Marshall, however, concluded that Stalin expected the continuing economic problems to heighten the popular appeal of communists in countries such as France and Italy and that the Soviet leader was delaying any response to the deteriorating conditions to help the communists in those and other countries. Accordingly, Marshall decided that some U.S. action was necessary to show Europeans that the Americans were not planning to adopt a policy of official aloofness toward Europe, as they had done after the First World War. This clear signal that they need not fear abandonment by the United States was calculated to boost the sagging morale of the Europeans, to give them confidence in America's

commitment to them, and to convince them of the possibilities for economic recovery and prosperity under democratic regimes.

As the U.S. State Department was contemplating ways to assist European recovery, many Americans thought that Europe had to function as an economic unit if it were to thrive. Without the food and raw materials of eastern Europe, it seemed unlikely that the industrial capacity of Western Europe could be utilized fully. Although there were obvious potential problems in any recovery program involving eastern European participation, the Americans did not assume that Europe would be divided. As George F. Kennan, director of the State Department Policy Planning Staff, later recalled, it was decided that the program should work "in such a way that the Eastern European countries would 'either exclude themselves by unwillingness to accept the proposed conditions or agree to abandon the exclusive orientation of their economies'." The American planners realized that recovery aid might appeal to eastern European states and provide a means by which their economies could be turned away from their pro-Soviet orientation.

Given the hostility toward Soviet-style communism that President Harry S Truman had expressed in his Truman Doctrine speech of March 1947, the possibility of Soviet participation in the Marshall Plan was problematic. Some contemporary domestic critics attacked the Marshall Plan for proffering assistance to the USSR while at the same time the United States was providing aid to Greece and Turkey to help them resist Soviet influence. The State Department Policy Planning Staff realized that the Soviets might possibly attempt to participate in the program solely to disrupt it or dominate it for their own ends. The staff concluded, however, and Marshall agreed, that the Soviets should be offered the opportunity to participate if they were willing to do so constructively. As Kennan later recalled, they decided to "play it straight": "If they responded favorably, we would test their good faith by insisting that they contribute constructively to the program as well as profiting from it. If they were unwilling to do this, we would simply let them exclude themselves. But we would not ourselves draw a line of division through Europe." According to Kennan, the staff suggested "that American effort in aid to Europe should be directed not to the combating of communism as such but to the restoration of the economic health and vigor of European society. It should aim, in other words, not to combat communism but the economic maladjustment which makes European society vulnerable to exploitation by any and all totalitarian movements

and which Russian communism is now exploiting." The Harvard commencement speech in which Marshall proposed the European reconstruction program demonstrates that he agreed with the staff's suggestion. Echoing Kennan's language, Marshall explained, "Our policy is directed against hunger, poverty, desperation and chaos. Its purpose should be the revival of a working economy in the world so as to permit the emergence of political and social conditions in which free institutions can exist." Marshall further mentioned that "Any government that is willing to assist in the task of recovery will find full cooperation, I am sure, on the part of the United States Government. Furthermore, governments, political parties, or groups which seek to perpetuate human misery in order to profit therefrom politically or otherwise will encounter the opposition of the United States."

The Soviet Union obviously stood to gain from continuing economic dislocation in the West and arguably was the target of this policy. Communist parties in countries such as France, however, could not afford politically to be seen impeding economic recovery.

Despite the apparent harshness of the anticommunist rhetoric in the Truman Doctrine, Parrish argues that the Soviets did not see the promulgation of that doctrine as an irreversible decision by the United States for a confrontational policy toward the Soviets. The USSR was given the opportunity to participate in the program in good faith, and the Kremlin leadership apparently considered participation seriously. When the British, French, and Soviet delegations met in Paris in June 1947 to consider how to respond to the American invitation to develop a program of assistance, Soviet foreign minister Vyacheslav Molotov brought a much larger delegation than he would have needed if his intention were to disrupt the proceedings. The Soviets appear to have considered seriously whether participation in the program might provide them with credits on favorable terms. Parrish has identified two conflicting views of the Marshall Plan among Soviet officials. Some of them argued that the capitalists faced an inevitable postwar depression and were forced to provide credits so that they could unload their surplus production. Consequently, these

President Harry S Truman discussing the Marshall Plan with Secretary of State George C. Marshall, plan administrator Paul Hoffman, and W. Averell Harriman, who supervised the plan in Europe, 1948 (U.S. Information Agency, National Archives)

MARSHALL PLAN

officials argued, the United States was employing the Marshall Plan in hopes of exacting some benefit from the necessary provision of credits. This line of thought led to the conclusion that American desperation might permit the Soviets to obtain credits cheaply. Other Soviet officials, including ambassador to the United States Nikolay Novikov, saw Marshall's injunction against "groups which seek to perpetuate human misery" as an attack on the Soviet Union. He interpreted the Marshall Plan as part of an attempt to construct an anti-Soviet alliance.

Despite serious Soviet consideration of the American offer, and American openness to good-faith Soviet participation, the Kremlin ultimately concluded that it would gain too little from the program. Of particular concern in Moscow was the American interest in the economic integration of Europe. The U.S. leadership saw integration as essential to European recovery and prosperity; the Soviets saw it as an infringement on sovereignty and an attempt to trap nations into a U.S.-dominated capitalist group. Rather than participate constructively in a U.S.-led program to foster prosperity and democracy, the Soviets decided that their interests required them to reject the program and to attempt to prevent it from working properly.

Even after the Soviets decided against participation in the Marshall Plan, for a brief spell in early July 1947 they considered encouraging some eastern European nations to take part in the organizational conference that began later that month, with the aim of preventing the development of a European consensus and disrupting the conference. The Soviets, however, quickly changed their minds about this gambit. The Kremlin feared that the appearance of eastern European governments at the conference would suggest the diplomatic isolation of the Soviet Union in Europe. Perhaps more important, the Soviets realized that the prospect of western credits could become too tempting to the eastern Europeans. The governments in Poland and Czechoslovakia apparently found participation appealing in precisely the ways Americans hoped the eastern Europeans might, as a way to obtain access to increased capital and higher quality goods on more favorable terms than the USSR could supply. This possibility threatened to reorient eastern Europe toward the West economically, with the likelihood that political connections would follow. Such a development would deprive the Soviets of the cordon of sycophantic states on their borders that had been Stalin's prime diplomatic goal. Accordingly, the Soviets not only pressured the Poles, the Czechoslovaks, and others into rejecting participation in the Marshall Plan but initiated the crackdown that ended coalition governments and solidified the control of pro-Soviet communists throughout eastern Europe. The Soviets also countered with their own "Molotov Plan" and the establishment of the Cominform, which were designed to keep the eastern Europeans focused eastward and under Soviet domination. Additionally, the Soviets ordered the Communist parties in the Western democracies to reject participation in coalition governments and to resist the Marshall Plan; in effect, they were ordering those parties to object suicidally to economic recovery.

As Kennan claimed, the Americans had "play[ed] it straight" and given the Soviet Union the opportunity to participate in the Marshall Plan as long as it was willing to contribute constructively to European economic recovery. The Kremlin leadership, however, had decided it could not afford to do so. The Soviets' unwillingness to support the program on these terms makes clear that it was their concerns and insecurity, not American policy, that prevented Soviet and eastern European participation in the Marshall Plan and sharpened the division of Europe into ideologically hostile camps.

–JOHN A. SOARES JR., GEORGE WASHINGTON UNIVERSITY

References

David W. Ellwood, *Rebuilding Europe: Western Europe, America, and Postwar Reconstruction* (London & New York: Longman, 1992);

Susan M. Hartmann, *The Marshall Plan* (Columbus, Ohio: Merrill, 1968)

Michael Hogan, *The Marshall Plan: America, Britain and the Reconstruction of Western Europe, 1947–1952* (Cambridge: Cambridge University Press, 1987);

George F. Kennan, *Memoirs, 1925–1950* (Boston: Little, Brown, 1967);

Melvyn P. Leffler, *Preponderance of Power: National Security, the Truman Administration, and the Cold War* (Stanford: Stanford University Press, 1992);

George C. Marshall, "European Initiative Essential to Economic Recovery: Remarks by the Secretary of State," *Department of State Bulletin*, 16 (15 June 1947): 1159–1160;

MARSHALL PLAN

Alan Milward, *The Reconstruction of Western Europe 1945–1951* (London: Methuen, 1984);

Scott D. Parrish, "The Turn Toward Confrontation: The Soviet Reaction to the Marshall Plan, 1947" and Mikhail M. Narinsky, "The Soviet Union and the Marshall Plan," in *New Evidence on the Soviet Rejection of the Marshall Plan: Two Reports,* Cold War International History Project, Working Paper no. 9 (Washington, D.C.: Woodrow Wilson International Center for Scholars, March 1994);

Harry Bayard Price, *The Marshall Plan and Its Meaning* (Ithaca, N.Y.: Cornell University Press, 1955);

Imanuel Wexler, "Marshall Plan, 1948–1951," in *Encyclopedia of U.S. Foreign Relations,* edited by Bruce W. Jentleson and Thomas G. Paterson (New York: Oxford University Press, 1997), pp. 113–117;

Wexler, *The Marshall Plan Revisited: The European Recovery Program in Economic Perspective* (Westport, Conn.: Greenwood Press, 1983).

MARSHALL PLAN

MILITARIZING CONTAINMENT

Did the United States unnecessarily militarize the conflict with the Soviet Union?

Viewpoint: Yes, the United States government vastly overestimated Soviet military strength.

Viewpoint: No, the United States militarized the conflict in response to Soviet expansionism.

The cold war generated an arms race between the superpowers. The United States and the Soviet Union spent large sums on military capabilities that went largely unused. At different times both countries suffered economic difficulties because of military spending. Many scholars attribute the collapse of the Soviet Union at least in part to its devotion of an abnormally large percentage of its national wealth to the development and maintenance of its military. While not spending nearly as much in per capita terms, the United States still struggled with budget deficits and recessions that were at least partially caused by its military spending.

Regardless of whether or not the United States was responsible for this militarization, it clearly attached enormous importance to achieving and maintaining military superiority over its adversary. So did the Soviet Union. In a strategic sense the militarization of the cold war created a state of permanent tension in international politics. Since it never erupted into a full-scale war between the two countries, some have argued, the tension was the factor that kept the peace. Others charge, however, that luck was the only reason for the absence of direct conflict and the avoidance of what would have been by far the most destructive war in world history.

Viewpoint:
Yes, the United States government vastly overestimated Soviet military strength.

The cold war spawned many excesses in American life, none more consequential than the militarization of U.S. foreign policy. Washington spent billions of dollars, spurned negotiations with communist governments, intervened in peripheral wars, and fueled a nuclear-arms race—all in deference to a foreign policy dominated by military considerations. In the final analysis militari-

zation was based on flawed perceptions. The "communist threat" was not primarily military, but ideological. No amount of weaponry could attain victory in a struggle for hearts and minds.

The genesis of cold war militarization was the Second World War. "Military Keynesianism"—priming the economic pump through government spending on defense—fueled the massive global war effort and brought an end to the most severe depression in U.S. history. Defense spending not only ended the Great Depression but also forged an enduring link between prosperity and militarization.

Vast federal bureaucracies, including the Pentagon itself, emerged during the war and became fixtures in American life. The four service branches assumed unprecedented power and prestige on the basis of their courageous war effort, and they were determined to maintain their elevated position in national affairs. The lesson that both civilian and military officials took from the Second World War was that weakness had fostered the appeasement of the Axis powers, thereby inviting their aggression. A powerful military establishment, U.S. officials averred, was vital to deterring future aggressors.

Powerful lobbies, both public and private, emerged from the war determined to maintain the high levels of American defense spending on which they had become dependent. In addition to the federal government and the military establishment, hundreds of private corporations had prospered during the war on the basis of defense contracts. States and, indeed, entire regions of the country had achieved affluence. The California economy, for example, skyrocketed on the basis of aircraft, armament, and defense-technology industries. University and defense "think tanks" emerged from the war with a vested interest in maintaining a powerful defense establishment. As far as all these entities were concerned, there was no going back to the peacetime economy and its legacy of economic depression.

With the defeat of Nazi Germany and Imperial Japan, the Soviet Union and world communism became the logical focus of attention for the defense establishment. The United States and its chief allies had good reasons to reject the legitimacy of the continuing Soviet occupation of eastern Europe. Another concern was the militarization of the Soviet economy as a result of the ultimately successful effort to fend off near defeat at the hands of Hitler's armies. The Soviet Red Army emerged from the war as the largest such force in history. Juxtaposed with the pledge to support communist revolution across the globe, the heavily armed Soviets represented a formidable force that had to be "contained."

Such perceptions notwithstanding, the "Soviet threat" was not primarily military, and the U.S. preoccupation with militarization thus represented a diversion of effort and resources from areas of greater priority. Western militarization frightened the Soviets, who had, after all, been attacked from the West twice in a single generation and who were keenly conscious of the hostility to Bolshevism that had emanated from the United States and its European allies since 1917. It should have been obvious from the outset that militarization would set into motion an action-reaction cycle and provide an enduring obstacle to a more peaceful world. Militarization also offered a wasteful and dangerous model for a variety of Third World nations that could ill afford the effort but, nevertheless, all too often gave in to its temptations.

As the creators of the Marshall Plan to rebuild postwar European economies (1947) understood, the primary "Soviet threat" had little to do with the prospect of military aggression. For a nation that had suffered at least twenty million wartime deaths and massive physical destruction during the prolonged war of occupation and liberation, military aggression against the West was unthinkable. Continued Red Army occupation of eastern Europe was one thing—especially since there was no place to put the troops back home—but invasion of Western Europe or any other area beyond Soviet control was not a realistic possibility in the immediate postwar years. Yet, planners in Washington became preoccupied with just such a chimerical possibility.

The real communist threat was that of subversion and political action to exploit the economic weakness and psychological malaise in the aftermath of a devastating military conflict. Loans, foreign aid, inspiration, and reforms had fended off this threat and brought recovery in Western Europe and Japan. Early U.S. cold-war planning thus offered a reasoned and effective response to a legitimate challenge to American national interests. Panic soon set in, however, as the legacy of the Second World War joined with powerful public and private defense lobbies to spur an unnecessary militarization of U.S. foreign policy.

A crucial event in this chain of developments was the Soviet clampdown on Czechoslovakia in response to the Marshall Plan. Determined to prevent their own falling dominoes, the Soviets not only forbade Czech participation in the American-sponsored recovery program, but launched a coup in Prague in February 1948 to ensure the continued membership of Czechoslovakia on the communist side of divided Europe. Efforts to reunite Germany had long since broken down, and the cold war emerged in full force. Perceptions on both sides of the "iron curtain" were uniformly hostile and the threat of war, as opposing armies faced off in divided Berlin a few months later, was palpable.

The Western response to Soviet efforts to secure control of their own postwar sphere was the North Atlantic Treaty Organization (NATO), created in 1949, the embodiment of militarization. NATO was a mistake that ensured generations of militarization and waste. This military alliance fostered unrealistic fears of direct Soviet military aggression while, at the same time, encouraging the Soviets' worst fears about Western intentions. Soviet dictator Joseph Stalin had little choice but to sacrifice everything else to rebuilding his defenses and planning for the possibility of another war with the West. Both sides ceased to practice diplomacy.

While the Czech coup and the creation of NATO set the process in motion, subsequent events cemented the trend toward militarization.

The twin shocks of 1949—the "loss" of China to communism and the successful Soviet test of an atomic weapon—encouraged panic and the adoption of worst-case scenarios in the West. Heading off the nuclear-arms race was well beyond the capabilities of either superpower. Both worked feverishly on research and development of the incomparably destructive new weapons, and it is difficult to conceive that any amount of persuasion would have succeeded in compromising such efforts. The historic and apocalyptic U.S. National Security Council memorandum 68 (NSC-68) authorized the development in 1950 of the hydrogen "super" bomb, a project to which the Soviets were likewise committed.

The outbreak of war in Korea assured President Harry S Truman's approval of NSC-68 and spurred the most intense militarization in American history. Washington immediately assumed that the northern Korean "invasion" of southern Korea had been ordered from Moscow. Actually, the Korean communist leader, Kim Il-Sung, acted at his own behest, but not without eventual approval of the Soviets, on whom he modeled his regime. NSC-68 was a blueprint for massive militarization. The document depicted the United States as locked in a death struggle with the communist world. National-security elites put in motion plans for a mind-boggling threefold increase on national defense, levels that were indeed attained during the Korean War.

These events and perceptions established the framework for cold-war militarization—a militarization so powerfully entrenched that it has survived even the passage of the cold war itself. There was no turning back after 1950. Washington had committed itself. Uncompromisingly hostile perceptions of the USSR and powerful lobbies perpetuated the phenomenon. The Soviets, at least under Stalin, did little to change Western perceptions for the better and much to encourage them. Both Stalin's successor, Nikita S. Khrushchev, and U.S. president Dwight D. Eisenhower came to perceive the excesses, if not the fundamental folly of militarization, but neither had the ability to stop the machine. Eisenhower's farewell address of 17 January 1961 warned Americans about the "unwarranted influence . . . by the military-industrial complex" and was a confession of his powerlessness.

By the time of Eisenhower's address, Washington was already engaged in another paroxysm of military spending, this one fueled by the 1957 Soviet launch of Sputnik, the first man-made satellite to orbit the Earth, and partisan politics. Democrats attacked Republican foreign policy over a "missile gap" that later proved to be mythical. The subsequent buildup, the war of words with the Soviets and Chinese communists, and the ongoing nuclear-arms race nearly produced catastrophe during the October 1962 Cuban Missile Crisis. Then, anxious to win victories in the cold war, President John F. Kennedy committed thousands of advisers and employed counterinsurgency tactics to contain the nationalist movement in Vietnam, led by the communist Ho Chi Minh. When such efforts proved insufficient, the Pentagon, private corporations, and the militarized culture at large supported the introduction of bombing, ground troops, and other tactics such as forest defoliation. None of these methods worked, but the sheer destructiveness of American power was breathtaking.

The Vietnam War was the ultimate commentary on the folly of U.S. militarism. Washington deployed the full panoply of its military power, save nuclear weapons, and dispatched more than a half million troops at one point. It pummeled three tiny Third World countries (Vietnam, Laos, and Cambodia) with more bombing tonnage than was used by all the belligerents in all combined theaters of the Second World War. None of these tactics produced the desired results because they did not address the fundamental issues—the legacy of Western colonialism and the corruption of the client regime in Saigon. Washington's preoccupation with cold-war militarization was so complete that it lacked the ability to understand the crucial issues involved in the conflict, in which it had nonetheless invested enormous resources and prestige while undermining U.S. national unity.

The rethinking of American priorities after Vietnam was ephemeral at best. Defeat in Southeast Asia, combined with the Iran hostage crisis and the Soviet invasion of Afghanistan in 1979, led to another wave of hysterical defense spending reminiscent of the NSC-68 and "missile gap" buildups. Washington was addicted to militarization and was nowhere near recovery. President Ronald W. Reagan then catapulted the nuclear-arms race to unparalleled heights of absurdity, until the reform-minded Soviet leader Mikhail Gorbachev offered a spate of unilateral concessions that proved impossible either to ignore or dismiss as communist propaganda. Even then arms-control measures were extraordinarily modest.

Can militarization be credited with helping to bring an end to the cold war? Perhaps the answer is "yes," to the extent that the burden of perpetual spending for weapon systems contributed to fundamental Soviet economic weakness, forcing Gorbachev to call off the cold war and ultimately to preside over the liquidation of the Soviet empire. Yet, the "peace through strength" argument, used by some to vindicate militarization, is shallow in the extreme. It overlooks the fundamental reality that cold-war militarization was a misguided response to a misperceived

threat. It fails to comprehend that the cold war might have been far less costly, conflictual, and risky—as well as shorter—had military considerations not dominated Washington's foreign policy. Perhaps, most of all, this perspective obscures the colossal waste of resources and the opportunities for domestic and international progress that were sacrificed to an obsession with militarist solutions to what were, in essence, nonmilitary problems.

—WALTER L. HIXSON, UNIVERSITY OF AKRON

Viewpoint:
No, the United States militarized the conflict in response to Soviet expansionism.

The cold war earned its name because its two major protagonists, the United States and the Soviet Union, never engaged in direct military conflict. Although there were many "proxy" conflicts fought by partisans of both powers, the predominant source of tension in postwar international politics never found military expression on any large scale. It is nevertheless true that both superpowers maintained large military establishments, including large nuclear arsenals, partially to be prepared for the possibility of a war and partially to deter that possibility.

Some of the historiography suggests that the military tension of the cold war was largely the fault of the United States. Even George F. Kennan, the American diplomat whose observations of Soviet behavior and attitudes strongly influenced the decision of the Truman administration to adopt a containment strategy toward the Soviets, later lamented that the military aspects of containment were a distortion of his original recommendations. Some contemporary scholars have seized on Kennan's remarks and argued that the United States was responsible not only for the militarization of the conflict, but for its origins. The plain fact is that military power was an important factor in the cold war, and its use by the United States was both necessary and justified.

Perhaps the most defining feature of the cold war was the specter of nuclear weapons. The United States was not responsible for introducing this element into the cold war because its invention and use of the atomic bomb was designed to end the conflict with Japan as quickly as possible and with minimal loss of life. The successful use of these weapons against Japan, however, prompted Soviet premier Joseph Stalin to embark in earnest on his own nuclear-weapons program. While the United States actually put its atomic-weapons-construction program on hiatus for several years after the Second World War, Stalin lost no time in catching up with the West. With the assistance of his chief of secret police, Lavrenty Beria, Stalin rapidly achieved his goal of making the USSR an atomic power, mainly by employing a large nuclear-espionage network in the West, forcing kidnapped German civilian scientists to develop Soviet nuclear technology, and using the enormous Soviet slave-labor pool to construct the necessary facilities.

America's eventual military build-up was largely reactive. The United States rapidly demobilized its conventional armed forces even as the cold war became a divisive reality. The emphasis of American strategy was to broaden the domestic industrial base to compensate for the decline of war production as a sector of the American economy. The Soviet Union, on the other hand, demobilized relatively far fewer troops and maintained an economic base heavily weighted toward war production and heavy industry. This "militarization" of the Soviet economy remained a consistent feature of Soviet policy until the demise of the USSR in 1991.

The success of the communist revolution in China in October 1949, Mao Tse-tung's alliance with the Soviet Union in February 1950, and the Soviet-sanctioned invasion of South Korea in June 1950 caused Congress to vote funding for military expansion. The prudent nature of Washington's approach to postwar rearmament was not reflected in Moscow, however. During the post-Stalin succession struggle, the leading candidate, Georgy Malenkov, was forced to resign as premier after he stated with trepidation that nuclear war would result in the extinction of the human race. His critics, led by Nikita Khrushchev, excoriated him for not having said instead that nuclear war would result in the destruction of capitalism. Malenkov's rhetoric reflected a "New Course" that would have involved a relaxation of diplomatic tension with the West and a concentration on light-consumer industry at home.

The dynamics of the post-Stalin succession, however, favored Khrushchev's rise to power and the general continuation of policies that involved high spending on the military and heavy industry. Khrushchev's outspoken desire to overtake the U.S. militarily actually caused American fears that there would be a "missile gap" in the Soviet Union's favor. With the Soviets promising to produce missiles "like sausages," it seemed that Khrushchev's policies would create an undisputed military advantage for the Soviet Union. Khrushchev also pursued aims in the Third World that were intended to enhance

the Soviet position worldwide. In 1962 these efforts culminated in his failed attempt to place Soviet missiles in Cuba in order to gain strategic nuclear leverage over the United States. Despite Khrushchev's gambits in Cuba and elsewhere in the world, containment remained a reactive strategy designed to prevent further Soviet expansion. Its military component grew larger during the Eisenhower and Kennedy administrations.

Another important consideration in refuting the supposition that the militarization of containment was unnecessary is that for the United States competitive military spending had no consequences for the development of its domestic economy. Indeed, the overall picture of the American economy during the cold war was one of steady growth, complemented by a standard of living that rose faster and higher than in any other country in the world. The same was plainly untrue for the Soviet Union. To support their attempts to expand their influence and retain control over the territories they had received after the Second World War, military expenditures consistently remained a high percentage of the Soviet gross national product (GNP). Western estimates placed military expenditure between 15 and 25 percent of its GNP. Soviet premier Mikhail Gorbachev estimated that in the 1980s it reached as high as 40 percent. While America's domestic economy prospered, the Soviet Union suffered shortages of the most basic consumer items and had a standard of living that lagged behind that of the West in every measurable way. The great size and efficiency of the American economy allowed it to match and ultimately to overcome the Soviet military without ever investing more than 8 percent of its vastly greater GNP in defense spending.

Comparisons of the two systems are also revealing with respect to the relative abilities of the superpowers to sustain economic growth. The economic liberty of the United States created a smoothly functioning capitalist economic system that prized innovation and rewarded efficiency. American technological development and industrial productivity led the world. The Soviet economy was based on a centrally planned system directed by bureaucrats who risked their careers if they embarked on an initiative that failed or was found not to be ideologically compatible with the dogma of Marxist Leninism. The complete absence of privately owned businesses and a consumer-oriented market economy only made the lack of initiative more chronic. The Brezhnevite principle of "stability in cadres" (for example, not changing the complexion of the bureaucracy) translated in practice into a general freezing of upward social mobility (such as it existed in a socialist society) and into the creation of a bureaucracy that steadily became older and less vital. When "high" technology became a factor later in the cold war, the Soviet government's suspicion of its own people prevented the widespread use of what in the West were such commonplace items as personal computers and photocopiers. Military and industrial high technology was so far beyond their capabilities that the Soviets made strenuous efforts to purchase it from the West outright or steal it through KGB industrial-espionage operations.

The political systems also affected the relative ability to maintain efficient military spending. The United States enjoys a stable and democratic system of checks and balances, which is enshrined in its Constitution. Different elements of the government, private interests, and social institutions are purposely kept apart to prevent any single element from gaining predominance. Military spending went up only when a broad consensus within the leadership determined that it was necessary, as it did after China was "lost" to the communist camp and when North Korea invaded South Korea. In the Soviet Union all of these elements were fused under the leadership and supervision of the Communist Party. Although Stalin solved the problem by eliminating anyone who might have posed a threat to his position, his successors had to maintain a delicate balance within the elite and cater to different interests to remain in power. The Soviet military establishment was one of several vital interests to be appeased, and pleasing it often forced policy reevaluations—as in 1960, when pressure from the military elite forced Khrushchev to abandon his plan to reduce Soviet conventional forces in order to devote more resources to building up the nuclear arsenal.

Alliance politics was another area in which the militarization of the cold war was a less important consideration for the United States than for the Soviets. Unlike the Soviets, the United States never invaded its allies. The Soviet obsession with security was so crucial that "deviations" from a strictly Leninist political system and Moscow-centered foreign policy in eastern Europe, such as those in Hungary in 1956 and Czechoslovakia in 1968, were greeted with direct military intervention to restore the status quo. Even the suspicion of disloyalty was sufficient for the Soviets to deploy one rifle division to shadow each invading East German division lest it prove unreliable in battle against troops of West Germany. Ideological similarities notwithstanding, the Soviet relationship with China was scarred by strategic differences and related Soviet assertions of leadership in the communist world, and Moscow was forced to deploy hundreds of thousands of troops along the Sino-Soviet frontier, at times in conflict situations.

In contrast the United States tolerated broad domestic political differences among its allies, weathered strategic conflicts of interest with them, and allowed them to reorient their foreign policies freely. Indeed, NATO easily embraced countries with strong socialist proclivities and the right-wing military dictatorships of Spain and Portugal. The integrity of the alliance did not suffer during or after the Suez Crisis of 1956, when the United States voted in the United Nations Security Council with the Soviet Union and against its British and French allies to further its own interests in the Middle East. There was no American-led invasion of France when that country withdrew its forces from the NATO command structure in 1966. (One of the reasons the Soviets had invaded Hungary ten years before had been its withdrawal from the Warsaw Pact.) Nor was West German chancellor Willy Brandt abducted and shot for negotiating a nonaggression pact and treaty of friendship with the Soviet Union in 1970—as the Soviets did with Hungarian premier Imre Nagy for his expressions of independence from Moscow in 1956. Compared to those of the Soviet Union, the stability and flexibility of America's alliance relationships vastly reduced its external military commitments. Washington had to worry about its principal opponent, not about its allies as well.

In terms of raw military power, the United States, even though it was provoked into developing a substantial military-industrial complex, was actually willing to enter negotiations to reduce diplomatic tension with the Soviet Union and to control the arms race. During the 1970s three separate administrations pursued détente with the Soviet Union, a relaxed relationship that had arms control as one of its leading components. Despite the best intentions of the Western proponents of this new relationship, however, the nature of the Soviet system caused Moscow to pursue domestic and foreign policies that eventually undermined American confidence in the prospects for the success of détente. The Soviets' continued harsh persecution of dissidents and minorities at home, issues on which good relations with the United States were explicitly predicated, caused several agreements on trade and arms control to fall through. During the 1970s the Soviet attempt to expand Moscow's influence worldwide reached its height. A relatively large number of Third World countries as far apart as Nicaragua, Angola, and South Vietnam fell into communist hands with the direct support of Moscow. The invasion of Afghanistan in 1979, variously described by Soviet apologists as a "necessity" for Soviet security, a justifiable continuation of Soviet influence in that country, or a response to Western aggres-

MILITARY POSTURING

Not long before George F. Kennan sent his well-known "long telegram" of February 1946, he had begun writing "The United States and Russia," a book he never completed. The following passage from that work states one of the rules Kennan devised for handling relations with the Soviet Union:

Do not be afraid to use heavy weapons for what seem to us to be minor matters.

This is likewise a very important point, and one which many Americans will receive with skepticism. In general, it may be bad practice to take a sledgehammer to swat a fly. With the Russians it is sometimes necessary. Russians will pursue a flexible policy of piecemeal presumption and encroachment on other people's interests, hoping that no single action will appear important enough to produce a strong reaction on the part of their opponents, and that in this way they may gradually bring about a major improvement in their position before the other fellow knows what's up. In this way, they have a stubborn tendency to push every question right up to what they believe to be the breaking point of the patience of those with whom they deal. If they know that their opponent means business, that the line of his patience is firmly established and that he will not hesitate to take serious measures if this line is violated even in small ways and at isolated points, they will be careful and considerate. They do not like a showdown unless they have a great preponderance of strength. But they are quick to sense and take advantage of indecision or good-natured tolerance. Whoever deals with them must therefore be sure to maintain at all times an attitude of decisiveness and alertness in the defense of his own interests.

Source: *George F. Kennan,* Memoirs: 1925–1950 *(Boston: Little, Brown, 1967), p. 563.*

sion against the Soviet Union, more or less ended the possibility of détente.

In the final phase of the cold war, each side made important realizations about military power. In the Soviet Union a faction of the post-Brezhnev leadership—encouraged in 1982–1984 by General Secretary Yuri Andropov and later led by the younger and more dynamic Mikhail Gorbachev in 1985–1991—came to realize that it could not compete militarily or economically with the United States. Under these leaders, Soviet foreign policy was once again directed at reducing tensions with the West in order to minimize Moscow's external-security requirements and benefit from improved economic relations, especially in the area of high technology. Domestically, Gorbachev attempted to move toward a social market economy that would promote initiative and material incentive even

while the Communist Party's leading role in society was to be preserved. Through reform Gorbachev hoped to make his country a viable world power again.

Under the leadership of the Reagan administration, the United States realized that its military and technological advantages were so dramatic that they could be used to win the cold war. Although critics at home and abroad charged that Reagan's defense buildup was unprecedented and destabilizing—and that he and his associates were dangerous warmongers—American defense spending still remained only a fraction of what the Soviets spent in relation to the size of their respective economies. The emphasis on high technology, expressed most prominently by the Strategic Defense Initiative (SDI), presented the Soviets with an unanswerable strategic challenge. Soviet officials candidly admitted as much in interviews with Western journalists. Indeed, in addition to the estimated $50 billion they spent in research and development to counter the prospect of an effective American ballistic-missile-defense system, until 1987 the Soviets attempted to make the elimination of SDI prerequisite to all arms-control negotiations with the United States.

In more conventional strategic terms, the Reagan administration adopted official policies to disrupt the Soviet economy, create crises within the Soviets' sphere of influence, and roll back what they had gained since the Second World War. In all of these ventures Reagan was ultimately successful. Although Gorbachev, naively heralded by many as the world's great peacemaker, increased Soviet military spending by 45 percent in the period 1986–1990, by the end of the decade the Soviet Union had lost control of its satellites in eastern Europe, watched its influence dry up further afield, and been forced to abandon its costly and futile war in Afghanistan. The Reagan administration's deliberate pursuit of economic warfare and its insurmountable military challenges to Moscow, together with entrenched domestic opposition within the ranks of the Soviet leadership, caused Gorbachev's attempts at domestic reform and modernization to founder. Political concessions related to the changes in economic and foreign policy spun out of control until he had to resign and announce the dissolution of the Soviet Union in 1991.

The most sensible conclusion that can be drawn from history is that American military power originated as a response to Soviet aggression. Whether the expansionist tendencies noted by the American leadership resulted from traditional Russian concepts of insecurity, specific Bolshevik fears of capitalist encirclement, or "misunderstandings" between wartime allies is irrelevant. The fact of the matter is that the Soviet Union pursued pretensions to hegemonic power that represented a direct challenge to American security interests, and to freedom and democracy in general. Containment and militarization were necessary steps to counter those threats. In the long run the Soviets' oppression of their own people and their omnipresent dictatorship condemned the USSR to economic, technological, and ironically enough, military inferiority. Its ability to counter Moscow without placing excessive strain on its own economy and society enabled the United States not just to keep an even balance in global affairs, but actually to precipitate the collapse of Soviet tyranny, end the decades of dangerous military and diplomatic tension it had caused, and free hundreds of millions of people from its oppressive rule. It is not unfair to say that without the militarization of containment the Soviet Union would still exist and continue to be the greatest challenge in history to international peace and human liberty.

    –PAUL DU QUENOY, GEORGE WASHINGTON UNIVERSITY

References

John Lewis Gaddis, *We Now Know: Rethinking Cold War History* (Oxford: Clarendon Press / New York: Oxford University Press, 1997);

Allen Hunter, ed., *Rethinking the Cold War* (Philadelphia: Temple University Press, 1998);

Paul A. C. Koistinen, *The Military-Industrial Complex: A Historical Perspective* (New York: Praeger, 1980);

Vojtoch Mastny, *The Cold War and Soviet Insecurity: The Stalin Years* (New York: Oxford University Press, 1996);

John Newhouse, *War and Peace in the Nuclear Age* (New York: Knopf, 1988);

Peter Schweizer, *Victory: The Reagan Administration's Secret Strategy That Hastened the Collapse of the Soviet Union* (New York: Atlantic Monthly Press, 1994);

Michael S. Sherry, *In the Shadow of War: The United States Since the 1930's* (New Haven: Yale University Press, 1995);

Vladislav Zubok and Constantine Pleshakov, *Inside the Kremlin's Cold War: From Stalin to Khrushchev* (Cambridge, Mass.: Harvard University Press, 1996).

MILITARY GAPS

Was it reasonable to believe during the cold war that there were bomber and missile gaps between the United States and the Soviet Union?

Viewpoint: Yes, given the intelligence then available, it was reasonable to believe that gaps existed.

Viewpoint: No, there were no gaps in strategic forces that put the United States at a disadvantage.

The debates in the late 1950s about the "missile gap" and "bomber gap" introduced new urgency into the assessment of Soviet intentions and military capabilities. The first shock to U.S. confidence in its technological advantage over the Soviet Union came in 1957 with the launch of Sputnik, the first man-made object to orbit the earth. Some time later, Neil H. McElroy, President Dwight D. Eisenhower's secretary of defense, offered the assessment that the Soviet Union was ahead of the United States in numbers and sophistication of ballistic missiles. "Hawkish" Democrats, such as Senator Stuart Symington (D-Missouri), criticized the administration for allowing the United States to fall dangerously behind the Soviet Union. Symington was also a strong proponent of the view that there was a "bomber gap" favoring the Soviet Union. He argued that the Soviet Union was investing more money than the Americans in military research, development, and production, allowing the Soviets to acquire a preponderance of weaponry that would enable them to "wipe out our entire manned and unmanned retaliatory force" in a single nuclear strike.

Symington echoed persistent warnings issued by two leading generals. Beginning in 1953, General Nathan Twining had warned about an increasing Soviet bomber capability that would provide them the capability to breach American defenses by 1956 or 1957, unless funds cut from the U.S. defense budget were reinstated. General Curtis LeMay, commander of the Strategic Air Command (SAC), maintained that, unless the bomber and missile gaps favoring the Soviet Union were "closed," the United States would become vulnerable to Soviet attack by mid 1959.

On 19 January 1960 Thomas Gates, Eisenhower's third secretary of defense, tried to reassure the House Defense Appropriations Committee that arguments about a gap favoring the Soviet Union were wrong and that, in fact, correct estimates showed "a clear balance in our favor." Democrats accused Gates of juggling the numbers, and the issue became a major bone of contention in the 1960 presidential election, with the Democratic candidate, John F. Kennedy, accusing the Republican candidate, Richard M. Nixon (Eisenhower's vice president), of being a member of an administration that had contributed to the erosion of America's defenses. Kennedy's secretary of defense, Robert S. McNamara, announced shortly after assuming office that there had never been any bomber or missile gaps favoring the Soviet Union.

Viewpoint:
Yes, given the intelligence then available, it was reasonable to believe that gaps existed.

The superpower nuclear-arms race was a competition to develop new types of weapons and to deploy them in significant numbers as rapidly as feasible. Each superpower monitored the other's nuclear progress closely, but such oversight was hardly an exact science. At three points during the cold war U.S. intelligence estimates projected that the strategic nuclear balance might be shifting in favor of the Soviet Union. Warnings about the "bomber gap" (1955–1958), the "missile gap" (1957–1961), and the "window of vulnerability" (1975–1982) occurred at points in the cold war when concerns about Soviet nuclear programs and objectives were most intense.

These three gaps never developed to the extent that intelligence estimates predicted, and scholars now consider them to have been largely fictitious. It is frequently asserted that the belief in the gaps arose from the overreaction of zealously anticommunist intelligence analysts and opportunistic military leaders, who used such intelligence reports in arguments for increased defense spending. Close inspection, however, reveals other factors that precipitated the warnings about gaps and help to explain why their existence seemed plausible to cold-war policymakers.

Estimating the strength of Soviet weapons programs was an inherently difficult endeavor. The closed Soviet society limited the availability of high-quality intelligence, without which any estimates become tenuous. American intelligence analysts frequently found themselves having to project what Soviet leaders would do several years into the future—in effect, forcing them to anticipate decisions the leaders themselves had not yet made. Compounding these challenges were the Soviet leadership's frequent efforts to deceive the United States about the state of its military, particularly its strategic-nuclear programs. While these measures brought some deterrent benefits, they backfired by generating inflated intelligence estimates that spurred the United States to enlarge its nuclear programs. For these reasons estimates about Soviet nuclear programs were prone to error and uncertainty. As Sherman Kent, a leading American intelligence scholar and practitioner, observed, "Estimating is what you do when you do not know."

The first perception of a gap began in spring 1955 after observers at the Soviet Union May Day parade counted twenty long-range Bison jet bombers. It was a case of deliberate Soviet deception; the same ten aircraft were flown over twice to create the impression of a larger force. Lacking any other hard data on Soviet bomber programs, American analysts were fooled into believing that the Soviet Union not only possessed an operational bomber equal to the best American bomber (the B-52) but could produce it in significant numbers. National Intelligence Estimates (NIEs) soon predicted that the Soviet Union would deploy six hundred to eight hundred Bisons by the end of the decade. These estimates also anticipated an expansion in the Soviets' long-range Bear turboprop-bomber force. Overall, the NIEs projected that within a few years the Soviet Union could have a larger bomber force than the United States. For the first time, the Soviets would be able to execute a large, potentially devastating, nuclear first strike against the United States. These estimates gave rise to fears that a bomber gap was about to emerge.

When the bomber-gap estimates were leaked, the U.S. Air Force, its supporters, and critics of President Eisenhower's New Look defense policy demanded higher defense spending and accelerated B-52 deployments. Eisenhower increased B-52 production, but his changes in defense spending were not sufficient to mollify critics such as Senator Stuart Symington (D-Missouri). As the bomber-gap debate raged throughout 1956, the Eisenhower administration initiated overflights of the Soviet Union and eastern Europe by new U-2 reconnaissance aircraft. The first set of U-2 missions convinced senior Eisenhower administration officials that there was no bomber gap. Still, the issue persisted through 1957 and into 1958 because the highly classified U-2 intelligence could not be made public or even disseminated widely within the administration. The Soviet Union never deployed the Bison, or any other long-range bomber, to the extent predicted in the bomber gap NIEs—fewer than one hundred Bison were ever built. Hyped by critics of the Eisenhower administration, the bomber gap was a fiction created by deliberate Soviet deception and inadequate intelligence.

Warnings about a missile gap followed closely on the heels of the bomber-gap predictions. In October and November 1957 the Soviet Union placed the first two man-made satellites—Sputniks I and II—in orbit around the Earth. American intelligence and defense officials realized that the rockets used to launch these satellites also could deliver nuclear warheads to the United States, and they concluded that the Soviet Union was much closer than the United States to developing an operational Intercontinental Ballistic Missile (ICBM). The

Premier Nikita
Khrushchev
examining equip-
ment retrieved from
the wreckage of the
U-2 spyplane shot
down over the Soviet
Union in May 1960

and U-2 flights over the Soviet Union were discontinued. None of these flights had detected deployments of the Soviets' first ICBM, the monstrous SS-6, but they could not rule out the possibility because the few U-2 missions covered only a fraction of Soviet territory. Furthermore, electronic intelligence revealed cycles of intensive missile testing followed by months of inactivity. This intelligence picture, combined with a sustained Soviet propaganda campaign, led American intelligence officials to conclude that the Soviet leaders were refining their ICBMs before undertaking major deployments. Consequently, NIEs consistently pushed back the date when a large Soviet missile force would appear while raising estimates of Soviet missile quality. In reality first-generation Soviet ICBMs were of such poor quality that they were never mass produced, much less deployed in significant numbers.

The missile gap, like the bomber gap before it, became a public issue when the gist of the NIEs was leaked—along with the report of the Gaither panel, formed in 1957 to determine means of defending the United States from nuclear attack. The Air Force and its advocates, particularly some Democrats in Congress, pressed Eisenhower to raise defense spending and accelerate the Atlas and Titan first-generation ICBM programs. The Eisenhower administration, however, maintained stable defense spending and emphasized development of the second-generation Minuteman ICBM. Beginning in August 1960, satellite reconaissance helped to put an end to fears of a missile gap by revealing that no Soviet ICBM deployments existed and that there would be none before the U.S. deployments. The public debate over the missile gap ended in early 1961 after dismissive statements by Eisenhower and the new secretary of defense, Robert S. McNamara.

In the aftermath of the missile-gap furor, the Kennedy and Johnson administrations deployed a large strategic-nuclear triad that created a huge strategic imbalance in favor of the United States. By the mid 1960s the Johnson administration curtailed the deployments on the grounds that no additional benefits could be accrued because destruction was "assured." At the same time the Soviet Union began massive strategic expansion to close the gap with the United States. From 1965 to 1972 the Soviet ICBM force grew from 225 to 1,547 missiles. Year after year, NIEs underestimated the magnitude of Soviet ICBM programs and the ultimate objectives behind them. Soviet ICBM activity moderated slightly after the SALT I agreement in 1972. New ICBMs, however, were still undergoing development while many missiles were being fitted with independently targeted warheads (MIRVs) in 1975. Some analysts began to argue that a "window of vulnerability" was opening, during which the Soviet leaders would be

Eisenhower administration and the American public were shocked by the Soviets' achievement and its potential consequences for the nuclear balance.

Missile-gap claims began surfacing almost immediately after the Sputnik launches. NIEs projected that the Soviet Union would be able to deploy up to ten ICBMs within a year, up to one hundred in two years, and as many as five hundred in three to five years. These estimates, like subsequent NIEs, did not claim that a missile gap existed. They predicted that one could develop several years in the future if the Soviet missile program progressed steadily. If the Eisenhower administration chose not to accelerate its own missile programs, critics claimed, strategic deterrence would be dangerously undermined because the Soviet Union might be able to execute a devastating first-strike missile attack against vulnerable American strategic bombers. For the next four years American intelligence officials watched the Soviet Union, waiting for a missile gap to appear, but one never did.

American intelligence on Soviet missile programs during the missile-gap period came from two main sources: U-2 overflights and electronic surveillance by aircraft and ground installations. The intelligence gave a puzzling, inconclusive picture for American analysts. The Eisenhower administration had authorized only five U-2 overflights before the Soviets shot down a U-2 in May 1960,

MILITARY GAPS

able to use their ICBM advantage for political gains at the expense of the United States and its allies.

The intelligence community addressed the question of Soviet strategic objectives in 1976 when George Bush, then director of the Central Intelligence Agency (CIA), commissioned competitive studies by intelligence analysts and outside experts. The report from the intelligence analysts, called Team A, rejected the idea that the Soviet leadership subscribed to the American concept of mutual assured destruction (MAD): "In our view, the Soviets are striving to achieve war-fighting and war survival capabilities which would leave the USSR in a better position than the US if war occurred. The Soviets also aim for intercontinental forces which have visible and therefore politically useful advantages over the US." The consensus within the intelligence community thus endorsed the idea that a window of vulnerability was opening. The report by the outside experts, Team B, focused as much on the intelligence-estimating process as on Soviet objectives. Team B claimed that NIEs had "substantially misperceived the motivations behind Soviet strategic programs, and thereby tended consistently to underestimate their intensity, scope, and implicit threat." Team B blamed mirror imaging, political considerations, interservice rivalry, and evaluating weapons developments in isolation for the erroneous NIEs. In the wake of the two-team exercise, the intelligence community continued to be divided over some aspects of the Soviet strategic program, but there was agreement that the Soviet leadership sought a war-winning nuclear capability.

The window of vulnerability, like the previous gaps, became an issue of intense public debate from the mid 1970s until 1983. The continued development of Soviet strategic-nuclear forces constituted one element of a more-assertive, opportunistic foreign policy after America's defeat in Vietnam. Civilian strategists such as Colin Gray and Keith Payne, for example, asserted that, if the Soviet Union possessed a clear margin of nuclear superiority, it would have a political advantage over the United States in a crisis. Soviet missile throw weight (maximum payload), MIRVed Soviet ICBMs, and Soviet beliefs about warfare led former Team B members Richard Pipes and Paul H. Nitze to argue separately that the Soviet leaders might even consider nuclear war a feasible political choice. Others rejected the window-of-vulnerability thesis, arguing that the Soviets recognized the horrors of nuclear war and accepted the logic of MAD. The Carter administration's defense budgets and the SALT II treaty (1979) intensified arguments about the window of vulnerability. The Carter administration, in its last year, and the Reagan administration developed a strategic program, including weapons such as the MX ICBM and the B-1 bomber,

designed to shut the window of vulnerability. In 1983 the Scowcroft Commission's report declared the window of vulnerability closed.

The historical verdict on these three gaps can be interpreted in several ways. The key elements have been proven fictitious. No bomber or missile gap ever developed in favor of the Soviet Union. The dangers of the window of vulnerability seemed similarly exaggerated—although this conclusion is more difficult to prove because the issue was Soviet objectives rather than just capabilities. Some scholars have explained these fictitious gaps as being the result of bureaucratic interests within the military and the intelligence community and among supporters for increased spending on national security.

Such perspectives discount the enormous difficulties of estimating Soviet military capabilities and objectives during the cold war. Intelligence on capabilities was weak, especially before spy satellites, while information on objectives was often either nonexistent or speculative. Consequently, intelligence analysts had to rely on sparse information and deal with deliberate Soviet disinformation when making estimates. While NIEs effectively monitored some Soviet weapons developments, it is unreasonable to expect that they would always be accurate. Estimations of Soviet bomber and ICBM developments included the most glaring errors. The NIE process was undermined at times by erroneous assumptions, bureaucratic rivalry, and criticism from those outside of the process. These factors, however, only magnified the basic problem of the quantity and quality of raw intelligence. The bomber-gap, missile-gap, and window-of-vulnerability warnings continue to serve as the subjects of valuable case studies for understanding the inherent difficulties and limitations of estimating an adversary's capabilities and intentions.

—PETER J. ROMAN, DUQUESNE UNIVERSITY

Viewpoint:
No, there were no gaps in strategic forces that put the United States at a disadvantage.

An important aspect of superpower relations in the early cold war hinged on mutual perceptions of strength. During the administration of President Dwight D. Eisenhower, American strategic planning focused on the possibility that strategic-weapons "gaps" between the superpowers, first in bombers and later in missiles, might put the United States at a comparative disadvantage. Since both types of weapons were inextricably tied to nuclear power, many American policymakers believed that there would be "danger zones" in which the United States and its allies would be vulnerable to possible nuclear attack and, more practically, to the geopolitically coercive power that threats of nuclear attack entailed. As intelligence reports eventually proved and as the historical record shows, however, the gaps that Washington feared never existed and even their prospective existence did little to change the Eisenhower administration's approach to strategy.

In the postwar period the United States and the Soviet Union pursued vastly different policies relating to military expenditure. While Washington demobilized and reduced its military budget to levels almost as low as before the Second World War ($10 billion in 1940 compared with $13 billion in 1950), Moscow kept millions of troops under arms and vigorously pursued new military technologies, including nuclear weapons. Even though American involvement in the Korean conflict eventuated higher and higher military spending during the Truman administration, the Eisenhower administration departed from increased expenditures and pursued a strategy of avoiding costly conventional conflicts and allowing the communist world the initiative. A major component of Eisenhower's counterstrategy was elaborated by Secretary of State John Foster Dulles in a speech before the Council on Foreign Relations on 12 January 1954. Noting the cost of overseas conventional deployments that would have to be made in reaction to communist aggression anywhere in the world, Dulles maintained that a more effective deterrent was needed. In what became known as the policy of "massive retaliation," the secretary of state announced that future Soviet aggression would be checked by a full military response, including nuclear measures.

The strategic dilemma that reliance on a massive-retaliation policy created for the Eisenhower administration was that Soviet emphasis on military spending far exceeded American military investment. Beginning in 1955 there was much speculation that a gap favoring the Soviet Union would develop in strategic bombers. There was, however, little direct evidence to support that conclusion. An alarmist report made by American spectators of the Soviet "Aviation Day" spectacle that year claimed that swarms of Soviet bombers filled the skies over Moscow, causing them to believe that Soviet airpower posed a serious challenge to American superiority in strategic weapons. What the spectators did not know, however, was that on the instructions of the Soviet leadership, a much smaller number of bombers had been ordered to fly in circles over the Soviet capital specifically to leave observers with that impression.

The desire to show that Soviet strength was growing in relation to that of the United States had roots in the ideological and strategic disputes that dominated Soviet domestic politics. The immediate post-Stalin era was characterized by great uncertainty as to which member of the leadership would emerge as his successor. It looked as though Georgy Malenkov, who succeeded Stalin as premier in 1953, would have the upper hand. His association with the New Course, a plan to reduce diplomatic tension with the West in order to have more money to invest in developing the domestic economy, left him open to attack by opponents who claimed their ideas represented continuity with Stalin. Nikita Khrushchev, who eventually emerged as the leader, launched vitriolic attacks against Malenkov that focused on his soft line toward Western Europe. After Malenkov warned publicly that nuclear war would destroy civilization, Khrushchev criticized him for not having made the ideologically correct comment that nuclear war would finally destroy capitalism and leave the way open for a socialist future. The rhetorical battle ended in Malenkov's removal from power in February 1955.

Although Khrushchev embraced some of Malenkov's diplomatic initiatives, his belligerent rhetoric began to find its way into Soviet foreign policy. During the Suez Crisis in 1956, he relied on nuclear threats against Britain, France, and Israel to pressure them into withdrawing their occupation forces from the Suez Canal zone. While the threat to use nuclear weapons was not the only factor in the decision of those countries to abandon their campaign, the coercive power of nuclear retaliation proved to Khrushchev that it could be a valuable diplomatic tool in Soviet relations with the United States.

The only problem was that, while their missiles could reach continental Europe, the Soviets had no way to launch a nuclear attack on the United States. The development of intercontinental ballistic missiles was still in its beginning stages. The Soviets first launched a test version in August 1957, and two months later their success at placing the Sputnik satellite in orbit proved to the world that the Soviets could produce a missile with a range of several thousand miles. A variety of accidents in their program and bureaucratic delays, however, did not allow for the speedy development of a fully functional intercontinental ballistic missile (ICBM) system. For the duration of his tenure as the leader of the Soviet Union, Khrushchev's nuclear diplomacy had to rely on bluff.

Intelligence reports that overestimated Soviet airpower were proven wrong in 1956, when the high-altitude U-2 spy planes began to violate Soviet airspace and monitor strategic facilities. The first flights paid careful attention to Soviet air bases and discovered that nothing like the figures in earlier intelligence estimates could be substanti-

MILITARY GAPS

x

EISENHOWER ON NATIONAL DEFENSE

In his final State of the Union Address, delivered on 12 January 1961, President Dwight D. Eisenhower reported on the state of military preparedness.

For the first time in our nation's history we have consistently maintained in peace-time military forces of a magnitude sufficient to deter and if need be to destroy predatory forces in the world.

Tremendous advances in strategic weapons systems have been made in the past eight years. Not until 1953 were expenditures on long-range missile programs even as much as a million dollars a year; today we spend ten times as much each day on these programs as was spent in all of 1952.

No guided ballistic missiles were operational at the beginning of 1953. Today many types give our armed forces unprecedented effectiveness. The explosive power of our weapons systems for all purposes is inconceivable.

Today the United States has operational Atlas missiles which can strike a target 5,000 miles away in half an hour. The Polaris weapons system became operational last fall and the Titan is scheduled to become so this year. Next year, more than a year ahead of schedule, a vastly improved ICBM, the solid propellant Minuteman, is expected to be ready.

Squadrons of accurate Intermediate Range Ballistic Missiles are now operational. The Thor and Jupiter IRBM's based in forward areas can hit targets 1,500 miles away in eighteen minutes.

Aircraft which fly at speeds faster than sound were still in a developmental stage eight years ago. Today American fighting planes can go twice the speed of sound. And either our B-58 medium range jet bomber or our B-52 long range jet bomber can carry more explosive power than was used by all combatants in World War II—Allies and Axis combined.

Eight years ago we had no nuclear-powered ships. Today forty-nine nuclear warships have been authorized. Of these, fourteen have been commissioned, including three of the revolutionary Polaris submarines. Our nuclear submarines have cruised under the North Pole and circumnavigated the earth while submerged. Sea warfare has been revolutionized, and the United States is far and away the leader. . . .

Since 1953 our defense policy has been based on the assumption that the international situation would require heavy defense expenditures for an indefinite period to come, probably for years. In this protracted struggle, good management dictates that we resist overspending as resolutely as we oppose underspending. Every dollar uselessly spent on military mechanisms decreases our total strength and, therefore, our security. We must not return to the "crash-program" psychology of the past when each new feint by the Communists was responded to in panic. The "bomber gap" of several years ago was always a fiction, and the "missile gap" shows every sign of being the same.

Source: Dwight D. Eisenhower, "State of the Union Message to Congress," Vital Speeches of the Day, 27 (15 October 1960 – 1 October 1961): 233–234.

---

ated by aerial reconnaissance. It was clear that there was no bomber gap.

It was more difficult to prove that the missile gap did not exist. For one thing, missiles required much less in terms of support facilities and were expected to be located in remote areas where difficult terrain would obscure them from the high-flying U-2. Another factor that contributed to concern about Soviet ICBMs was that none could be found at all. At least enough bombers had been seen by spy planes to calculate the true strength of Soviet airpower, but the fact that no ICBMs could be seen indicated to some that they were perhaps just well hidden. Khrushchev's unabashed bluster about the strength of his missile forces created the psychological impression that the United States faced a serious threat. Soviet propaganda often used Western journalistic speculations about Soviet strategic power to buttress their own leader's claims.

In that environment a report issued in late 1957 by a panel headed by H. Rowan Gaither predicted that the Soviets would develop a fully functional ICBM by 1959, a year before the American program was scheduled to come on line. When it became public, the administration was widely criticized, especially by Senate Democrats John Fitzgerald Kennedy of Massachusetts and Lyndon Baines Johnson of Texas, for having a weak defense policy. The "missile gap" was actually one of Kennedy's

MILITARY GAPS

MILITARY GAPS

major criticisms of Eisenhower's policies in the 1960 presidential election campaign.

The problem with the Gaither report, however, was that its projections were based largely on economic data that showed the Soviet economy was growing at twice the rate of the American economy. From these figures the panel extrapolated that Moscow was poised to overtake Washington in productive capacity, a situation that would have even broader strategic implications than the rapid development of a Soviet ICBM system. It is clear now, as it was then, however, that Soviet economic growth was extremely relative. Most of its industrialized territory had been under German occupation during the Second World War and had been the site of destructive combat. Economic growth in the Soviet Union meant restoring what had been destroyed. Reviving basic industry artificially inflated the importance of economic growth. Even though that temporary recovery increased economic growth relative to that of the United States, the Soviet economy was still only one-third the size of the American economy. Even if the ratio of economic growth remained constant, it would still take decades for the Soviet Union to approach the size of the American economy.

Eisenhower's career in the Second World War doubtlessly made him aware of what conditions in the Soviet Union were like. If he had forgotten, he would have been reminded by the Soviets' constant lament about how much they had suffered and sacrificed in the war. The strategic consequences of Soviet economic growth mentioned in the Gaither report, then, were not so much of a consideration for Eisenhower. Even though the report recommended that the administration increase the military budget by as much as 50 percent and accelerate ICBM development, the president preferred to maintain the existing budget and rely on the current U.S. missile programs.

Even though Khrushchev was able to create the diplomatic crisis over the future of West Berlin in 1958 with his rhetorical bravado about the Soviet Union's nuclear capabilities, by as early as February 1959, after almost three years of U-2 flights, no evidence of Soviet ICBMs could be found. By that time the issue was a moot point anyway, because the United States had deployed its first generation ICBM, the Atlas missile, in 1958. The only missile gap that existed was in favor of the United States.

That fact remained hidden from public knowledge until relatively recently, however. Eisenhower could hardly have wanted to expose the effectiveness of American intelligence gathering to the Soviets, nor could he have desired to create a situation in which Khrushchev had to prove himself. Although shrouding that intelligence information involved negative international publicity for the United States and permitted domestic political criticism to continue with apparent basis in fact, it was much easier to allow the Soviet leader to brag about nonexistent Soviet capabilities than to challenge him to a confrontation that Eisenhower had spent his entire time in office trying to avoid. Even in September 1960, when second- and third-generation American ICBM systems were emerging, Khrushchev made a statement before the General Assembly of the United Nations about the Soviets producing strategic missiles "like sausages, rocket after rocket."

The plain fact of the matter is that there were no "gaps" in strategic forces that left the United States at a disadvantage. The Discover satellite, deployed in 1961, found that even at that late date the Soviet Union had only a handful of ICBMs. Even though hiding the decisive intelligence information caused some loss of international prestige and opened the administration to vigorous domestic criticism, the correlation of forces was never against the United States, and the Eisenhower administration knew it.

–PAUL DU QUENOY, GEORGE WASHINGTON UNIVERSITY

References

Thomas M. Coffey, *Iron Eagle: The Turbulent Life of General Curtis LeMay* (New York: Crown, 1986);

Dwight D. Eisenhower, *Waging Peace, 1956–1961: The White House Years* (Garden City, N.Y.: Doubleday, 1965);

Lawrence Freedman, *U.S. Intelligence and the Soviet Strategic Threat,* second edition (Princeton, N.J.: Princeton University Press, 1986);

John Lewis Gaddis, *We Now Know: Rethinking Cold War History* (Oxford: Clarendon Press / New York: Oxford University Press, 1997);

Tom Gervasi, *The Myth of Soviet Military Supremacy* (New York: Harper & Row, 1986);

Townsend Hoopes, *The Devil and John Foster Dulles* (Boston: Little, Brown, 1973);

Walter LaFeber, *America, Russia, and the Cold War,* eighth edition (New York: McGraw-Hill, 1997);

John Prados, *The Soviet Estimate: U.S. Intelligence Analysis & Russian Military Strength* (New York: Dial, 1982);

Peter J. Roman, *Eisenhower and the Missile Gap* (Ithaca, N.Y.: Cornell University Press, 1995);

Donald P. Steury, ed., *Intentions and Capabilities: Estimates on Soviet Strategic Forces, 1950–1983* (Washington, D.C.: Center for the Study of Intelligence, 1996).

MISSILE DEFENSE

Was a ballistic-missile defense system a viable option?

Viewpoint: Yes, a ballistic-missile defense system would have provided protection to the United States and put military and financial pressure on the USSR.

Viewpoint: No, a ballistic-missile defense was technologically unfeasible, strategically unwise, ill-advised, prohibitively costly, and irrelevant to the threats the United States was facing.

The history of warfare is the story of the struggle between offensive and defensive military technologies. In some periods offensive technologies had supremacy, while at other times defensive measures were in ascendance. The combination of nuclear explosives and ballistic missiles appears to have made permanent the dominance of the offense. From the beginning of the nuclear age, however, there have been insistent calls for finding defensive responses to this offensive dominance. The interest in such defenses—as manifested in investment in research and development, the elaboration of military doctrines, and the public commitment of elected officials—has fluctuated in response to changes in the political climate and advances in the relevant technologies.

The discussion about how to defend against nuclear weapons and other weapons of mass destruction is largely about how to build a defense against one means to deliver them—missiles. For a long time the focus was on the protection of the continental United States from a ballistic-missile attack, as is apparent in the names given such defensive efforts—for example, BMD for Ballistic Missile Defense or NMD for National Missile Defense. More recently the defense of troops in the field against tactical missiles has gained prominence, and new acronyms have been added to the discussion—for example, TMD for Theater Missile Defense or ATBM for Anti-Tactical Ballistic Missiles.

In the last fifteen years there have been two major U.S. initiatives to promote the building of ballistic-missile defenses for the purpose of defending the U.S. population. The first was President Ronald W. Reagan's call in March 1983 for a defensive system that would make nuclear weapons "impotent and obsolete." President Reagan's plan was translated into the Strategic Defense Initiative (SDI), also known as "Star Wars." There is consensus now that Reagan's vision of a kind of leakproof astrodome over the United States is unfeasible and unattainable in the foreseeable future. Accordingly, the debate over population defense now revolves around three more-modest systems—limited defense, ground-based point defense, and scaled-down SDI.

The most recent initiative was triggered by the 1991 Persian Gulf War. Television cameras captured images of Iraqi Scud missiles cruising toward their targets in Israel and Saudi Arabia and the efforts of American Patriot antimissile systems to shoot down the Scuds. The vulnerability to missile attacks of the American soldiers in Saudi Arabia provided a renewed impetus for looking seriously at theater-missile defense. The other lesson drawn from the Gulf War, however, was more controversial. The Iraqi missile attacks on the civilian population in Israel and the seeming success of the Patriot in thwarting those attacks energized supporters of NMD. The result was enactment by the Republican-controlled Congress of the Defend America Act of 1996 (H. R. 3144, S. 1635), which called for a defensive system to protect the American population from enemy missiles.

The Gulf War changed the focus of the general debate over BMD. The emphasis of the early efforts to construct missile defenses was on stopping the Soviet arsenal and, to a lesser extent and for a shorter period of time, the nascent Chinese missile fleet. The growing emphasis in the current arguments about the desirability of missile defense involves the acquisition of ballistic missiles by Third World nations, especially "rogue" states. There are currently about thirty-five non-NATO countries with ballistic missiles. It is estimated that about eighteen of them are capable of installing nuclear, chemical, or biological warheads on the missiles. By the end of the twentieth century, six of them will likely have missiles with ranges exceeding 5,500 kilometers.

Viewpoint:
Yes, a ballistic-missile defense system would have provided protection to the United States and put military and financial pressure on the USSR.

On 23 March 1983 President Ronald Reagan announced that the United States would begin development of the Strategic Defense Initiative (SDI), a space-based ballistic-missile defense system, derided by many as "Star Wars." Domestic critics of the program charged that it would be scientifically unfeasible and absurdly expensive. Many argued that the clear strategic advantage such a system would give the United States would destabilize superpower nuclear relations and violate the spirit of previous arms-control agreements, which prohibited space-based forms of ballistic-missile defense. While all of these arguments have some merit, the exaggeration of their importance clouded the broader picture of SDI's place in American strategy and the indisputable fact of its viability.

Perhaps the best and most basic argument is that ballistic-missile defense systems are intrinsically designed to destroy missiles and not people. If such a system could be made to work, the potential threat to the lives of millions of people would be forever eliminated, to say nothing of the millions more who would almost certainly be killed in a retaliatory nuclear strike. No matter how wounded Soviet pride might have been by losing the coercive power of its nuclear arsenal, ballistic-missile defense would surely be a much more stable way to manage superpower conflict than the maintenance of two enormous nuclear stockpiles against which there was no defense.

On a more practical level the general objective of President Reagan's strategy toward the Soviet Union was simple. Early in the administration the president and his advisers drafted National Security Decision Directives 32, 66, and 75, which formulated a broad outline of pol-

icies designed to strangle the USSR economically, exacerbate its domestic tensions and those of its satellites, and "roll back" the gains of its postwar expansion. The economic aspects of Reagan's strategy were manifold and struck the Soviets at their weakest points. Trade in industrial high technology, material so desperately needed by the Soviets that they were willing to deal with capitalists to get it and even tried to steal it through KGB industrial-espionage operations, was brought to a standstill. Even the European subsidiaries of American corporations were legally prevented from selling sensitive technology to Moscow. After finding out which specific products the Soviets were interested in acquiring, the Central Intelligence Agency (CIA) actually worked with American firms to sell versions of them that would not work to Soviet agents. Agreements between the Reagan administration and Arab states to reduce the price of oil broke Soviet purchasing power in the West because oil exports produced between 60 percent and 80 percent of their hard-currency earnings.

Soviet inferiority in industrial high technology was no less dramatic than their inferiority in military technology. "Proxy" conflicts in which combatant powers fought one another with American and Soviet military hardware illustrated the technological deficiencies in Soviet conventional weaponry all too clearly. The heavy losses of Syrian-manned Soviet fighter jets in aerial combat against Israeli-operated American planes during the Israeli invasion of Lebanon in 1982 were a timely case in point, as was the effective use of Stinger missiles by the mujahidin against Soviet helicopters in Afghanistan. When the Soviets found themselves confronted with the deployment of the fast and accurate Pershing II cruise missile in Western Europe in the early 1980s, they could only respond by using KGB funds to finance antinuclear-protest movements that agitated (unsuccessfully, it turned out) for the withdrawal of the new weapons. The Soviets were so apprehensive and insecure that KGB

MISSILE DEFENSE

agents overseas were instructed to watch for warning signs of a Western nuclear attack.

In the wake of these developments, Reagan's announcement of SDI was devastating to Soviet strategic planners. If the Americans were successful in their endeavor, the enormous efforts to which Moscow had gone to become a nuclear power and expand its arsenal to reach parity with the United States would be meaningless. The tremendous drain military spending had had on the Soviet economy since the end of the Second World War made that problem all the more acute and continued to impede broader economic development until (and after) the collapse of the Soviet Union. Having to keep up with a functioning American ballistic-missile defense system made the situation worse. The Soviets simply did not have the laser and computer technology needed to construct a system of their own, and, largely because of Reagan's international economic policies, they had no means of acquiring it. During the 1980s the Soviets spent tens of billions of dollars of their ever-declining hard-currency reserves in research and development to create a strategic response should the Americans be successful.

The expense of developing a response to SDI and modernizing the Soviet military in general was already an enormous problem, but the issue was magnified in the context of changes in the Soviet leadership. A growing faction within it believed that the lag in military technology and the Soviet Union's anemic economic growth more generally necessitated a reevaluation of the more provocative elements of Soviet strategy during the Leonid Brezhnev era. Reform and modernization had to take precedence, at least for the moment, over military might. Led at first by Yuri Andropov in 1982–1984, and by Mikhail Gorbachev in 1985–1991, the reformers favored domestic programs to encourage efficiency and initiative and a foreign policy that would reduce Soviet security requirements and allow meaningful reductions in military spending. American military challenges to a leadership with this element in the ascendancy were especially devastating for the Soviet Union because generating an arms race and basing strategic competition on high technology prevented Soviet attempts to reduce existing pressures on their weakening economy and inferior military capabilities. Over the course of the decade, the Soviet military budget actually increased. Reagan knew that they were stuck between the Scylla of allowing the unchecked development of an American strategic advantage and the Charybdis of not having the ability to respond to it. Reagan realized

Dr. Edward Teller and President Ronald Reagan at a 1988 conference on the Strategic Defense Initiative

(Associated Press)

that he had to defeat his opponent's strategy before his own could succeed.

Many of Reagan's critics have argued that the Soviet decision-making process was not at all influenced by the president's talk about SDI or the fact of increased American military spending. Yet, in the early 1980s the American press was littered with interviews in which Soviet officials candidly and perceptively told Western correspondents that they believed Reagan's goal was to overcome Moscow technologically. Soviets who identified with Gorbachev's, and to a lesser extent Andropov's, attempts to revitalize détente deplored Reagan's forceful support for an increased military budget in general. All these Soviets wanted, they said, was peace.

The Soviet approach to diplomatic negotiations with the United States strongly reflected these sentiments. Under Konstantin Chernenko, who led the Soviet Union briefly in 1984–1985, between Andropov and Gorbachev, there were no meaningful talks at all. The Soviets actually intensified the development and use of their military. Through 1987, after Gorbachev tried to initiate diplomatic relaxation with the West, all negotiations to reduce strategic arms were predicated on the elimination of ballistic-missile defense from American strategic planning. The summit meetings between the Soviet leader and President Reagan in Geneva in November 1985 and Reykjavík, Iceland, in October 1986 revolved around Gorbachev's unsuccessful attempts to negotiate the cancellation of SDI, which had become his country's strategic bête noire, before anything was said about the reduction of existing nuclear forces.

Reagan had been offering a broad arms-control proposal since October 1981, when his administration proposed a comprehensive mutual reduction in intermediate-range nuclear forces (INF). The Soviet Union had scorned that proposal. In 1981, after all, there had been little action toward restoring the American military, and Reagan's SDI announcement was still eighteen months away. Only after the balance of the Soviet leadership realized the scale of the American military challenge and the fact of Soviet technological weakness did they want to discuss serious nuclear-weapons reductions at all, and then only after they had clearly identified the principal source of their anxiety.

Finally, SDI allowed Reagan to accomplish in part another of his strategic goals, the reinforcement of American alliance relationships. In the era of détente many of America's allies departed from their traditionally firm anti-Soviet postures and entered into their own diplomatic and commercial relationships with Moscow. The aggressive Soviet behavior that brought the achievements and value of détente into serious question coincided with a return to close cooperation with the United States. SDI had many characteristics that could strengthen those ties. First, the enormous amount of scientific research that was required for the program was shared among the important NATO allies and Japan over the course of the 1980s. In addition to promoting the sharing of strategic information, joint SDI research also subjected partner countries, along with the United States, to intense Soviet criticism and alienated them from maintaining good relations with the USSR. Further still, the allies who participated received lucrative contracts from American firms to develop technology and equipment. The initial British response to the Reagan administration's offer of partnership, for example, was that it would take part in SDI research only if it were guaranteed $1 billion in American contracts.

For a variety of reasons, ballistic-missile defense was a viable option for the United States. Although the details of its scientific efficacy were, and remain, disputed, at its most basic level it was the only strategic system that could shift a nuclear battlefield from people to weapons. It was of enormous strategic benefit to the United States in the superpower confrontation because it contributed mightily to spoiling Moscow's best attempts to make communism and the Soviet system viable, especially from a military perspective. Former Soviet officials attested then, and continue to attest, to its crucial role in hastening the collapse of the Soviet Union. Measured in strategic gain for the United States and in the liberty that the peoples of the former Soviet bloc enjoy today, the Strategic Defense Initiative was not only viable but essential.

–PAUL DU QUENOY, GEORGE WASHINGTON UNIVERSITY

Viewpoint:
No, a ballistic-missile defense was technologically unfeasible, strategically unwise, ill-advised, prohibitively costly, and irrelevant to the threats the United States was facing.

Life in the shadow of the atomic bomb has not been easy. The fact that tens, if not hundreds, of millions of people may be killed instantaneously—and the earth ravaged and spoiled for decades (in what is called "nuclear winter")—is unnerving indeed. From the beginning of the nuclear age, therefore, there were efforts to design a defense against nuclear weapons. As long as these weapons were carried aboard planes, it was possible to believe that there could be a defense against them: planes could be shot down whether they carried nuclear or non-nuclear munitions. In the early 1960s, when nuclear weapons were wedded to ballistic missiles, it became increasingly evident that no defense would be possible.

By the mid 1960s, American strategists had begun to suggest that mutual vulnerability to destruction created by the inability to defend against ballistic missiles was, in fact, a good thing: it would guarantee that no one in possession of nuclear weapons would use them recklessly—or at all. Because there was no escape from a devastating retaliatory punishment, states would not initiate moves that would invite certain retaliation.

In the mid and late 1960s, as these ideas about mutual vulnerability were being developed, the United States did try to build a rudimentary defensive system against ballistic missiles, but the budget for the system was denied by a one-vote margin in the Senate in 1969. Three years later, in 1972, the technical reality of defense infeasibility combined with strategic thinking favoring vulnerability in a treaty between the United States and the Soviet

Union—the Anti-Ballistic Missiles (ABM) Treaty—the centerpiece of the historic arms-control agreements negotiated by Henry Kissinger and signed by President Richard M. Nixon. The ABM Treaty allowed each country only two bases (later reduced to one) at which to employ antiballistic missiles, with no more than one hundred interceptors at each. The United States began to build such a system in Grand Forks, North Dakota, but later abandoned the effort. The Soviets built a defensive system around Moscow, but its effectiveness was questionable. For the following decade the two sides concentrated instead on building ever-more-accurate offensive weapons—within the quantitative ceilings imposed by the Strategic Arms Limitations Talks (SALT) I and II and the Strategic Arms Reduction Treaties (START).

The dream of building a defense against nuclear weapons did not die, however. It was revived with much fanfare in March 1983 when President Ronald W. Reagan announced that he would launch the Strategic Defense Initiative (SDI), whose aim would be to make nuclear weapons "impotent and obsolete." Reagan vowed to replace the existing, deterrence-by-vulnerability system, with a defensive "astrodome" over the American population: the enemy would be deterred from attacking the United States because he would not be able to do so.

Even strong advocates of defensive systems now concede that the expansive vision of a defensive "astrodome" over the United States cannot be realized. As *The New York Times* reported in May 1999, "The 'Star Wars' dream of zapping enemy warheads with orbiting lasers, which President Ronald Reagan championed, is long gone." The current level of scientific knowledge and engineering capabilities and the state of software development make it impossible to defend the United States against any attack of more than a mere handful of nuclear (or, for that matter, biological or chemical) warheads. President Reagan's dream of strategic defense has been abandoned, replaced by three more-modest defensive systems under consideration: limited population defense, a ground-based system aiming to protect the American population from an accidental or unauthorized missile launch from an adversary, or from an intentional, but small, attack by a Third World country; ground-based point defense, a system aiming to protect U.S. military installations (such as second-strike nuclear forces or command, control, and communication nodes) against a small nuclear attack; and scaled-down SDI, a reduced version of the original SDI, combining ground- and space-based components and aiming to defend the United States against a medium-size attack by a major country.

The first system complies with the 1972 ABM Treaty. The third system cannot be built without scrapping the treaty and replacing it with another agreement (or doing without one altogether). The second system, depending on its makeup, may require the renegotiation of the treaty.

All can be criticized on the grounds of technical difficulties, prohibitive cost, and the lack of strategic desirability of an anti-ballistic-missiles defensive system. Reagan's more expansive definition of defense, however, deserves special attention. If the ambitions of Reagan's defense plan are scaled down considerably—for example, defending hardened military installations rather than urban centers, defending against ten to thirty warheads as opposed to hundreds of warheads, and defending against land-based ballistic missiles rather than against submarine-launched missiles in depressed trajectory—then some of the criticism offered may be relaxed a bit. The thrust of the argument, however, remains.

On the surface, the idea of defense against ballistic missiles is appealing. Why would any people choose to live completely exposed to nuclear annihilation? In practice, however, it is a bad idea and an unattainable goal, for five reasons: it is technically impossible; it can be defeated easily; it is exorbitantly expensive; it is strategically destabilizing; and if, miraculously, it did work, an adversary of the United States would have a myriad of other ways to use nonconventional weapons to inflict grievous damage on the U.S. population.

Shooting a missile or a warhead out of the sky is like shooting a bullet with a bullet. At the current state of technology, it cannot be done. In the 1991 Gulf War, for example, U.S. Patriot antimissile missiles failed to shoot down even a single Iraqi Scud missile, even though the Scud is an ancient missile relying on old technology. Since 1976 the Pentagon has conducted sixteen tests to see whether it would be possible to destroy an incoming warhead with an interceptor, or "kill vehicle." Fourteen of the tests failed, the last one in March 1999. Two, one in June 1984 and the second in January 1991, were described by the Pentagon as successful. Subsequent congressional investigation, however, discovered that the tests were rigged. In the June 1984 test, the warhead was heated before launch to 100 degrees, then instructed to fly sideways in order to expose greater surface area to the heat-seeking kill vehicle. According to *The New York Times,* the Congressional General Accounting Office bluntly noted that the Pentagon's many claims about the success of the test failed to mention "the steps taken to enhance the target's signature." In regard to the January 1991 test, the Pentagon claimed that, not only did the kill vehi-

MISSILE DEFENSE

REAGAN ON STAR WARS

In a 23 March 1983 speech on military spending and nuclear defense, President Ronald W. Reagan made the following remarks about the need for development of the new missile-defense system that became known as "Star Wars":

If the Soviet Union will join with us in our effort to achieve major arms reduction we will have succeeded in stabilizing the nuclear balance. Nevertheless it will still be necessary to rely on the specter of retaliation—on mutual threat, and that is a sad commentary on the human condition.

Wouldn't it be better to save lives than to avenge them? Are we not capable of demonstrating our peaceful intentions by applying all our abilities and our ingenuity to achieving a truly lasting stability? I think we are—indeed, we must!

After careful consultation with my advisers, including the Joint Chiefs of Staff, I believe there is a way. Let me share with you a vision of the future which offers hope. It is that we embark on a program to counter the awesome Soviet missile threat with measures that are defensive. Let us turn to the very strengths in technology that spawned our great industrial base and that have given us the quality of life we enjoy today.

What if free people could live secure in the knowledge that their security did not rest upon the threat of instant U.S. retaliation to deter a Soviet attack: that we could intercept and destroy strategic ballistic missiles before they reached our own soil or that of our allies?

I know this is a formidable technical task, one that may not be accomplished before the end of this century. Yet, current technology has attained a level of sophistication where it is reasonable for us to begin this effort. It will take years, probably decades, of effort on many fronts. There will be failures and setbacks just as there will be successes and breakthroughs. And as we proceed we must remain constant in preserving the nuclear deterrent and maintaining a solid capability for flexible response. But isn't [it] worth every investment necessary to free the world from the threat of nuclear war. We know it is!

Source: "President's Speech on Military Spending and a New Defense," New York Times, 24 March 1983, p. A20.

cle destroy the warhead, but it also distinguished the warhead from two inflatable decoys. The Congressional General Accounting Office investigation, however, found that the decoys had been tethered on each side of the warhead and that the interceptor's computer had been programmed to pick up the middle target.

There are two additional difficulties that would further complicate the defense's already near-impossible task. First, to overwhelm this kind of defense, an adversary can simply add to his offensive capabilities—what football coaches would call "flooding the zone." It is much cheaper to augment offensive capabilities—procure more missiles and warheads—than it will ever be to build up more defenses. If shooting one bullet with a bullet is not possible, shooting several bullets simultaneously is even more impossible. Second, in addition to augmenting his offensive capabilities, an adversary would have another way to foil any defensive measures, even more cheaply than augmenting his offensive capabilities. There are many countermeasures that can disrupt and defeat any defense, such as shortening the boost phase of launched missiles, launching missiles in a depressed trajectory, launching a large number of missiles from widely dispersed launch pads, adding penetration aids and decoys to accompany the real warheads (hinted at in the description of the rigging of the January 1991 test; defensive sensors are currently unable to distinguish between the decoys and real warheads), and shortening the reentry time of warheads. An adversary may also launch a direct attack against the components of the defensive system itself.

Even if the system can somehow be built, the entire system can never be properly tested and evaluated. To measure the feasibility and true effectiveness of a defensive system we must evaluate both its individual components and the operation of the integrated system as a whole. There are four reasons why the evaluation of the technical feasibility and effectiveness of a defensive system is especially difficult. First, the integrated system as a whole, and many of its individual components, cannot be tested in a realistic fashion under any circumstances. Short of evaluating the system under conditions of an actual nuclear attack on the United States, we will never know its true effectiveness. Second, a limited number of aspects of the defensive system may be tested in a more or less realistic fashion, but such testing is mostly proscribed by the 1972 ABM Treaty. Third, the system will have to be continuously updated to cope with countermeasures that adversaries will take to overcome it. Fourth, the defensive system itself will face grave challenges to its survivability because the adversary will surely try to destroy it by attacking and disabling its components. The effectiveness of the added measures the defensive system will have to take to cope with the ever-evolving countermeasures, and the effectiveness of the measures the defensive system will have to take to ensure its own survivability will themselves not be subjected to true evaluation because of the limitations on testing under realistic conditions. This most complicated of systems will rely on tens of millions of lines of software code and on the smooth and flawless performance of a well-integrated system comprising thousands of ground-based and space-based components—and it will have to work perfectly the first time it is ever used, during an actual war.

Then there is the issue of cost. Because offense is much cheaper than defense, the race between the two is hopeless for the defense. No matter what the defense does—assuming there is anything meaningful it can do to defend against ballistic missiles—for the foreseeable future the offense will be able to defeat it by building more offense more cheaply. In this way any effort to build defenses will accelerate the arms race because countries facing a defensive build-up by a potential adversary would want to make sure that they do not lose their offensive leverage against that adversary. The quickest and cheapest way to do so is to add to one's offensive capabilities.

If defenses were technologically feasible and economically affordable, should the United States want to build such defenses? The answer is no, for two reasons. The condition of mutual vulnerability is not pleasant, but it is stable and predictable. With each of the superpowers in possession of thousands of missiles and warheads, and with Britain, France, China, and Israel in possession of a few hundred warheads each, states have powerful incentives not to launch nuclear attacks on each other. Whatever they may gain in an initial attack, they will more than lose in the punitive and inescapable retaliation that would surely follow. Thus, the size of the arsenals of the nuclear states, as well as their diversity and invulnerability to a preemptive first strike, contribute to a stable nuclear climate.

If, however, states began to compete with each other in both defensive and offensive technologies, the situation would rapidly deteriorate into a dangerous instability. If one country began to deploy defenses that its adversary viewed as likely to be effective, that adversary would have strong incentive to launch a preemptive strike in order to prevent that country from gaining an insurmountable edge. It is true that a preemptive strike might invite a nuclear retaliation, but the adversary might well believe that he has nothing to lose.

It is important to distinguish between general stability and crisis stability. General strategic stability is the condition that is obtained when the likelihood of war is low. Stability may be achieved by a robust deterrence posture or by political means (such as confidence-building measures, agreements, and treaties)—or, preferably, by both. Since the early 1960s U.S. policy has relied on deterrence and political means to lower the risk of war with the Soviet Union. Relying only on deterrence to achieve stability is dangerous, because it exposes the tensions between general stability and crisis stability.

Depending on deterrence to achieve stability naturally leads to the desire to attain military superiority over the adversary by whatever means possible. On paper, at least, the more weapons state A has, the heavier the punishment it can inflict on state B. State B, of course, is aware of this unfavorable disparity of forces. In a crisis situation, when the stakes are high, state B's inferiority might lead it to contemplate a first strike against the militarily superior state A: using a small fraction of its forces, state B may well destroy a much larger portion of state A's forces, thus leveling the strategic playing field. In what has become the classic statement of crisis instability, Thomas Schelling, a leading theoretician on nuclear strategy, wrote in 1960 that, as the crisis deepens, the initial temptation to strike first would be compounded "through a process of interacting expectations, with additional motives for attack being produced by successive cycles of 'He thinks we think . . . he'll attack; so he thinks we shall; so he will; so we must.'" The buildup by one country of militarily superior offensive and defensive capabilities, especially in the absence of arms control and monitoring agreements, may thus lead the country falling behind to take desperate measures.

What, however, if the country that is ahead in developing defensive technologies offered to share this technology with its adversary? In fact, to the consternation of his advisers, President Reagan suggested just that. This strategy looks appealing at first, but it is dangerously destabilizing in practice. Because the two major reasons for the nuclear stability of the last four decades have been the large sizes and invulnerability of nuclear arsenals of the major states and the fact that these states were utterly vulnerable to attack, the arms race between the superpowers has been less destabilizing. The addition of a few hundred warheads to either arsenal, or technological improvements to this or that segment of the arsenal, did not and could not make any difference in the relative-power position of either superpower. (Winston Churchill once said that, after an attack by a couple of hundreds of warheads, any subsequent warhead would just "make the rubble bounce.") If both superpowers (and other nuclear states) were to acquire effective defenses, the qualitative offensive-arms race would be launched in earnest, with dire consequences. If country A were to find a way to defeat the defenses of country B, then country A, with but a handful of defense-penetrating nuclear warheads, could blackmail country B. Country A, hiding behind its still-effective defense, could then threaten to inflict unacceptable damage on country B (country B's defensive systems having become permeable). Moreover, country A might not even wait to threaten country B, but might launch a devastating attack against its adversary before country B could shore up its failing defenses. A world in which defenses were shared would thus be a tense, anxious one in which the qualitative arms race would likely reach new intensity. Even minute technological breakthroughs would have exceedingly destabilizing consequences, and even small changes in the size of arsenals might have profound strategic effects. The current robust, stable balance of terror would be replaced by a delicate, fragile, even brittle—and easily disruptable—balance constantly teetering on the brink of nuclear disaster.

Any of these criticisms of SDI—that an anti-ballistic-missile defense is technologically impossible, easily defeated, prohibitively expensive, and strategically dangerous—should be sufficient to raise serious doubts about the feasibility and desirability of such a system. There is, however, an additional, even more damning criticism of the system: it is utterly irrelevant to most of the likely attack scenarios the United States is ever likely to face. A state planning to attack the American population with nuclear, biological, or chemical weapons would not have to rely on ballistic missiles to do so. It is not even clear why such a state would choose ballistic missiles—the most expensive and technologically demanding means of delivery. It would be much easier to put a nuclear bomb on a ship and sail into New York Harbor. (There would be no need, for example, to miniaturize the warhead, one of the major difficulties in bomb design.) Nonconventional weapons may also be brought into the United States aboard commercial planes, in cars, or in suitcases. The components of such weapons may be smuggled into the country individually and then assembled here. Even a state planning to use ballistic missiles to attack the U.S. population with biological weapons would find ballistic-missile defense to be no hindrance. As the *Times* has reported, such a state could load a missile with hundreds of small bomblets filled with lethal germs. These bomblets, similar to those in a cluster bomb, would be impossible to locate in the air or hit with an interceptor.

The states likely to threaten the United States with nonconventional weapons fall into two categories. The first includes states whose arsenals are large and diverse enough to overwhelm any possible defense the United States may develop by attacking with a large number of missiles or by launching them in a depressed trajectory from submarines off the U.S. shore. Advanced nuclear- and nonconventional-weapons states—such as Russia, France, and Britain—belong in this category. The second category includes nuclear- and nonconventional-weapons states with a smaller number of warheads or missiles (such as China, Israel, India, and Pakistan) and countries in various stages of developing

these weapons (such as Iran, Iraq, and North Korea). Such states would likely not use missiles to deliver nuclear and nonconventional warheads against the United States. They would choose other, cheaper means of delivery. Ballistic-missile defense will not stop an attack from countries in either category.

There is one more argument made in favor of SDI: that regardless of its technical or strategic merits, it convinced the Soviets that they could no longer compete with the United States and had to abandon communism, thus hastening the demise of the USSR. The dream behind SDI (and it was just that—a dream; it could not be built and has been abandoned) may have convinced the Soviets, if they needed any more convincing, that their system was not working and that they could not keep up with the West. The Soviets had plenty of evidence for how far behind the United States they were falling, and it is difficult to believe why they would take an unrealizable dream to persuade them further on this point. Their economic and political difficulties aside, the Soviet Union had top-rate physicists, engineers, and computer scientists, and they must surely have realized what their counterparts in the Unites States knew: it was impossible to build an impermeable astrodome over the U.S. population.

Even if SDI did hasten the demise of the Soviet Union, the question remains whether there were less expensive—and less potentially dangerous and destabilizing—ways to do so. Because the plan for SDI envisioned reliance on space-based weapons and new technologies such as the laser, it was an exceedingly expensive exercise. The Soviet Union may have realized that it was being bankrupted in the effort to keep pace in the arms race with the United States, but, as commentator Gary Wills pointed out (mindful of the huge budget deficits created during the Reagan years), Reagan should be given credit not for bankrupting one empire but for bankrupting or nearly bankrupting two empires. It should also be recalled that the Reagan administration not only launched SDI, but also engaged in a massive buildup of offensive nuclear capabilities and openly talked about "prevailing" in a nuclear war with the USSR. The effort to build strategic defenses was thus not part of a transition to a defense-dominant world that would replace the Mutual Assured Destruction (MAD)/mutual-vulnerability paradigm. SDI was perceived as an effort to enhance U.S. offensive capabilities and enable it to launch a nuclear attack from a position of safety. This effort to regain nuclear superiority against an already armed-to-the-teeth adversary was a dangerous, some would say reckless, gambit. The Americans lucked out: the Soviets blinked first. Winning in the lottery,

MISSILE DEFENSE

however, is not an argument for gambling. The United States—and the world—could have lost, with historically disastrous consequences.

One measure of maturity is the acceptance of reality for what it is. The combination of nuclear (and other nonconventional) weapons and the ease of delivering them against an adversary's population has made human societies uncomfortably, unnervingly, vulnerable to attack. There is no escape from this grim reality. Decades of test failures of various defensive schemes, and $110 billion of defense research, should have convinced U.S. leaders of this fact. Instead of dreaming up technological panaceas for this depressing situation, they should work to minimize the risk through a combination of verifiable arms-control agreements, international conventions to deny certain countries the technology to build such weapons, an active intelligence-gathering campaign, close monitoring of emerging threats, and the maintenance of a robust deterrence capability. In some cases, overt or covert action may have to be taken to reduce the risk. Whatever measure of security we may achieve in a nuclear world would be reached through these means. Dreaming an impossible defensive dream will not do the trick.

—BENJAMIN FRANKEL, SECURITY STUDIES

References

William J. Broad, "After Many Misses, The Pentagon Still Pursues Missile Defense," *New York Times,* 24 May 1999, pp. A1, 23;

Harold Brown, ed., *The Strategic Defense Initiative: Shield or Snare?* (Boulder, Colo.: Westview Press, 1987);

Dusko Doder, *Shadows and Whispers: Power Politics Inside the Kremlin from Brezhnev to Gorbachev* (New York: Random House, 1986);

Sidney D. Drell, Philip J. Farley, and David Holloway, "Preserving the ABM Treaty: A Critique of the Reagan Strategic Defense Initiative," in *The Star Wars Controversy: An International Security Reader,* edited by Steven E. Miller and Stephen Van Evera (Princeton, N.J.: Princeton University Press, 1986), pp. 57–97;

Charles L. Glaser, "Do We Want the Missile Defense We Can Build?" in *The Star Wars Controversy: An International Security Reader,* pp. 98–130;

Glaser, "Why Even Good Defense May be Bad," in *The Star Wars Controversy: An International Security Reader,* pp. 25–56;

Oleg Gordievsky and John Andrews, *KGB: The Inside Story* (New York: HarperCollins, 1990);

Stanford A. Lakoff and Herbert F. York, *A Shield in Space? Technology, Politics and the Strategic Defense Initiative: How the Reagan Administration Set Out to Make Nuclear Weapons "Impotent and Obsolete" and Succumbed to the Fallacy of the Last Move* (Berkeley: University of California Press, 1989);

Sean M. Lynn-Jones, "Offense-Defense Theory and Its Critics," *Security Studies,* 4 (Summer 1995): 660–691;

Steven E. Miller and Stephen Van Evera, eds., *The Star Wars Controversy: An International Security Reader* (Princeton, N.J.: Princeton University Press, 1986).

Theodore A. Postol, "Lessons of the Gulf War Experience with Patriot," *International Security,* 16 (Winter 1991/1992): 119–171;

The President's Strategic Defense Initiative (Washington, D.C.: The White House, 1985);

Ronald Reagan, "President's Speech on Militray Spending and a New Defense," *New York Times,* 24 March 1983, p. A20;

Thomas C. Schelling, *The Strategy of Conflict* (Cambridge, Mass.: Harvard University Press, 1960);

Peter Schweizer, *Victory: The Reagan Administration's Secret Strategy That Hastened the Collapse of the Soviet Union* (New York: Atlantic Monthly Press, 1994);

Caspar W. Weinberger, *Fighting for Peace: Seven Critical Years in the Pentagon* (New York: Warner Books, 1990).

NATO

Was Wilsonianism or realpolitik the most important reason for the creation of NATO?

Viewpoint: The most important reason for the creation of NATO was Wilsonian idealism about international security.

Viewpoint: NATO was created to counter real threats to Western democracies.

The strategic partnership shared by the United States and the Soviet Union during the Second World War collapsed within months of the end of hostilities. Disagreements about the final peace settlement in Europe and Asia and Soviet attempts to challenge the limits of what the Western Allies had conceded to the USSR during the wartime conferences exacerbated the situation. By 1948, and arguably much earlier, disputes between the superpowers had evolved into the cold war.

American strategic planners had to find a way to manage the new international order. In April 1949 the United States sponsored the creation of the North Atlantic Treaty Organization (NATO), a mutual-defensive alliance that viewed an attack against one member as an attack against all. In successive years the alliance expanded to include virtually every country in Western Europe. The fact of its existence and its highly inclusive character have maintained general peace in Europe for the past fifty years.

In the context of the cold war it is perhaps easy to see the alliance as a reaction specifically against potential Soviet aggression. While it certainly was a factor, the NATO charter does not specify any one enemy as the sole justification for its existence. An earlier defensive alliance between Britain and France, the 1948 Treaty of Dunkirk, was based on fears of aggression from a resurgent Germany. NATO has also complemented the broader development of European political and economic integration, a process that has promoted peace and stability in its own right. This development, together with the military security guaranteed by NATO, have practical applications that have outlived the cold war. Three nations entered the alliance in March 1999, ten years after the Berlin Wall came down.

Viewpoint:
The most important reason for the creation of NATO was Wilsonian idealism about international security.

Wilsonianism reflects the ongoing influence of President Woodrow Wilson's articulation of American exceptionalism in the world. One enduring legacy of Wilson's imprint on U.S. foreign policy and world politics is the North Atlantic Treaty Organization (NATO), an alliance that was created in 1949 and remains the most successful and longest-lasting in history. Other alliances throughout history have come and gone with the immediate threat that

spawned them. The Wilsonian roots of NATO help to explain its longevity and success.

At the close of the Second World War, the United States stood without peer in the world in terms of objective power capabilities and influence. As many have argued, nations that have established hegemony have the luxury of projecting their domestic values onto the world stage in a way that less-powerful states cannot afford. The heart of American conceptions about the postwar world was the Wilsonian vision, which included clear assumptions and prescriptions about how interstate relations ought to be managed.

During the second decade of the twentieth century President Wilson defined an international role for the United States that influenced generations of American policymakers. He was responding to what he perceived as the negative forces in foreign relations that had led to the First World War (1914–1918): great-power politics, or European realpolitik. Wilson located the source of the calamitous major war that involved all the great powers of the day in the European balance-of-power system, holding the view that the zealous pursuit of narrow and selfish national interests by autocratic and imperialistic governments would increasingly result in major conflicts. For Wilson the aggressive policies of imperial Germany embodied what was wrong with European balance of power. Reflecting the long-standing American aver-

sion to this system, Wilson offered an alternate vision of world order that was at once distinctly American and also a continuation of the Western-liberal tradition. At its core Wilsonian security meant transcending the logic of balance-of-power politics and replacing them with an international order that favored democratic governance at the domestic level, interdependence among states, multilateralism to manage international relations, and a collective-security system that bound member nations to each other. Through this integrative process, states would learn to cooperate and over time to identify the interests of others with their own. Crucial to the Wilsonian blueprint was the assumption that this new order needed the leadership of the United States because it was "the hope of the world" and presented "the only sufficient guarantee to the peace of the world."

While Wilsonianism failed to sustain the peace and create a new world order after the First World War, the next generation of policymakers and leaders who projected post–Second World War American power were influenced by Wilson's vision. Nowhere was this influence more clearly displayed than in U.S. policy toward Europe. As the cold-war competition between the United States and the Soviet Union emerged from the ashes of the U.S.-Soviet wartime alliance, stabilizing and democratizing Western Europe as a fortress against the Soviet threat became paramount.

President Harry S Truman (second from left) watching Secretary of State Dean Acheson sign the NATO Treaty, 4 April 1949

(CORBIS/Bettmann)

NATO

When the United States and its Western allies forged NATO in 1949, the organization assumed a role far greater than the traditional alliance goal of balancing against an external threat. NATO became the nucleus for a western community of democracies, a construct that was emphatically Wilsonian, and one that was intended to outlive the immediate threat that inspired it. The NATO treaty reveals the Wilsonian inclination to link the concept of transnational security to that of shared democratic governance. The guiding principle of the treaty is its democratic bias—the insistence on the "sovereign equality of all its members." The preamble declares that member states are "determined to safeguard the freedom, common heritage and civilization of their peoples, founded on the principles of democracy, individual liberty and the rule of law." Article 2 connects greater economic collaboration among member states to the strengthening of "free institutions." Article 10 holds open the promise of membership to other democratizing European states that were "in a position to further the principles" of the treaty. The current policy of NATO enlargement derives from this section and bears testimony to the long-term and farsighted goals established by the founders of NATO.

In short, NATO has been much more than a defensive alliance. This Western alliance was the flagship transatlantic institution entrusted with establishing and solidifying a community of equal, freely associated, interdependent, democratic states. Member nations were bound through the NATO treaty to consult, collaborate, and cooperate with each other on a regular basis in a plethora of interlocking policy areas. NATO was the child of the Wilsonian vision of world order.

Hastings Lionel Ismay, first Baron Ismay, secretary-general of NATO from 1952 to 1957, coined a phrase about NATO that has passed into common parlance. He observed that NATO had three tasks: to "keep Russia out [of Western Europe]; Germany down; and the United States in [Europe]." Indeed, an important NATO assignment was Western collective defense against the Soviet threat, as identified in article 5 of the NATO treaty. Equally critical was the central role of the United States. Having forfeited its mantle of leadership after the First World War, the United States rose to the Wilsonian call to assume leadership after the Second World War, and this role was most clearly on display in the creation of NATO. A momentous issue faced American foreign-policy makers in the wake of the total collapse and surrender of the Third Reich—what to do about the twice-defeated German nation. Echoing the concerns raised by Wilson decades earlier, American foreign-policy makers determined that Germany, at least West Germany, must be democratized and integrated into the community of Western democratic nations. While Wilson had excluded Germany

from immediate membership in the League of Nations until such time as its people "got over that dream of conquest and of oppression" and could show "that their Government really is based upon new principles and upon democratic principles," American policymakers after the Second World War eschewed this policy and set to work at once to democratize and integrate West Germany. Seen in this light, Lord Ismay's observation missed a critical aspect of Western policy regarding Germany and its entry into NATO in 1955. Post–Second World War U.S. strategy was to integrate West Germany into the community of Western democracies as soon as possible. This approach was a cornerstone of NATO policy and helped to ensure the success of the alliance. It also reflected the Wilsonian predilection to link security and democracy.

The Wilsonian blueprint for collective security was meant to be universal and was intended to establish an institution whose membership was beholden to recognize collectively held principles. The world was not meant to be divided into competing alliances, as happened with the formation of NATO and the Warsaw Pact, the alliance formed by the Soviet Union and its East European satellites in response to the admission of West Germany to NATO in 1955. Wilson's concept was one for all and all for one. In this ideal situation wayward member states would bring upon themselves the wrath of the entire community. In this regard NATO failed as a Wilsonian institution. The evidence is abundant, however, that this Western alliance embodied many of the basic principles articulated by Wilson in his pursuit of a redefined world order. NATO was the child of the cold war and of American exceptionalism. Wilson's vision of international security was the progenitor for the NATO treaty. NATO has outlived the Soviet threat and stands ready to embrace new members who have demonstrated their democratic credentials. The creation of NATO was the official birth of the transatlantic security community of democratic states.

—MARY HAMPTON, UNIVERSITY OF UTAH

Viewpoint:
NATO was created to counter real threats to Western democracies.

With the passage of time organizations change and evolve as people do. Both organizations and individuals also have more than one goal. Indeed, one definition of evolution and change would point to the reordering of priorities and the rearranging of preferences over time. The entry into the North Atlantic Treaty Organization (NATO) of

THE NORTH ATLANTIC TREATY ORGANIZATION

MEMBER	YEAR OF ACCESSION	POPULATION*	ARMED FORCES*
Belgium	1949	10,104	43.7
Canada	1949	28,959	60.6
Czech Republic	1999	10,311	59.1
Denmark	1949	5,246	32.1
France	1949	58,905	358.8
Germany	1955	81,102	333.5
Greece	1952	10,597	168.5
Hungary	1999	10,050	43.3
Iceland	1949	278	nil
Italy	1949	57,900	298.4
Luxembourg	1949	414	0.8
Netherlands	1949	15,655	57.2
Norway	1949	4,407	28.9
Poland	1999	38,569	240.6
Portugal	1949	9,873	53.6
Spain	1982	39,200	193.9
Turkey	1952	62,600	639.0
United Kingdom	1949	58,644	210.9
United States	1949	270,629	1,401.6

*Numbers in thousands as of mid 1997

Source: International Institute for Strategic Studies, The Military Balance, 1998/99 (London: Oxford University Press, 1998).

Poland, the Czech Republic, and Hungary in 1999 was accompanied by the explanation that these former Soviet-bloc countries had become democracies, entitling them to join the organization. NATO is a military alliance, but these countries did not face a direct military threat. Other applicants for admission to NATO have been given specific goals concerning reforms of their domestic political institutions and practices to ensure that they would become democratic before serious consideration of their applications took place.

These developments, highlighting as they do the domestic political characteristics of the new and prospective member states, provide support for a reading of the creation of NATO that emphasizes the "Wilsonian impulse": at its root the founding of NATO was an effort driven by idealistic aspirations to bring together democratic nations. A closer examination of the early years of the organization, however, reveals that the considerations of its architects were rooted more firmly and unambiguously in realpolitik considerations than in Wilsonian idealism. After the organization dealt with its pressing realpolitik concerns, it also indulged in addressing other, higher aspirations.

The purpose for the creation of NATO was once described as to "keep Russia out; Germany down; and the United States in." This rather undiplomatic depiction captures well the two major problems Western leaders faced in the late 1940s, and the key to any solution to these problems. The first problem was how to contain the Soviet Union and prevent it from extending its power and influence beyond its newly acquired sphere of influence in eastern and central Europe. The second problem was how to prevent a resurgence of German power. From the beginning, then, the true purpose of NATO has been not just containing the threat that the authoritarian Soviet regime posed to the Western European democracies; rather, it was the dual containment of the Soviet Union and Germany. The key element of any answer to these two problems was the continued presence of a large number of U.S. forces in Europe. The leaders of the West were preoccupied with power, balance, and strategy, all realpolitik considerations.

NATO

As Western leaders were grappling with how to construct a security structure of post–Second World War Western Europe that would be robust enough to deter a possible Soviet attack and, if need be, repel it, they were facing two issues, not one. The first was the dire economic condition of the war-ravaged continent; the second was what to do about Germany. The economic misery and social dislocation caused by the war led many to fear that a combination of communist subversion and political success of local communist parties might deliver major countries in Western Europe to the communist camp. (The communist parties of Italy and France were still powerful.) The need to improve rapidly economic and social conditions led to the launching in 1948 of the European Recovery Program (the Marshall Plan), which injected billions of dollars in aid into the economies of the western half of the continent. Economic aid was also offered to eastern and central European countries, which were under Soviet domination, but Soviet premier Joseph Stalin forced them to reject the offer.

The German problem appeared more complicated. Before NATO was created in April 1949, there were earlier efforts to bolster Western European defense. In 1947 Britain and France signed a mutual defense pact, called the Dunkirk Treaty. The following year, in what came to be called the Brussels Treaty, the pact was expanded to include the Benelux countries (Belgium, the Netherlands, and Luxembourg). The treaty committed its members to help in each other's defense for fifty years. Increased Soviet pressures in eastern and central Europe, and the growing awareness by U.S. decisionmakers that the United States would have to be more involved in ensuring European security than it had been after the First World War, led the United States to join with ten European countries (the five members of the Brussels Treaty, plus Iceland, Denmark, Italy, Norway, and Portugal) and Canada to create NATO. Germany was not part of this group of nations.

The United States initially envisioned its involvement to consist of not much more than a loose, even temporary, security pledge. Yet, after the treaty was signed and entered into force in 1949, growing tensions with the Soviet Union, and especially the North Korean invasion of South Korea in June 1950, convinced American decisionmakers that a more-permanent structure would have to be built. The issue of Germany also had to be addressed. Because of its location, size, population, and industrial resources—now devastated by war, but soon to be recovered—Germany would have to be a major element in any Western European defense system against the Soviet Union. Germany's neighbors—and victims during the Second World War—however, still carried painful memories of German occupation and abuse, and they were exceedingly leery of any scheme that would allow Germany to rearm too freely. The problem, as Europeans uneasily joked at the time, was how to make Germany powerful enough militarily to deter the Soviet Union but not so powerful as to threaten Luxembourg. These fears of German rearmament were so deep that they dominated Western European thinking even as the looming Soviet threat was increasing in scope and intensity. Western Europeans would not attend to the task of containing an increasing Soviet menace before they found a way to contain Germany.

In late October 1950, French prime minister René Pleven introduced what came to be known as the Pleven Plan. The plan called for the recruitment and training of German troops—not by the government in Bonn (there would be no national German army or German general staff), but by a supranational European authority. The German troops would serve in a European army, would not exceed one-fifth of the entire army, and would be tightly integrated into NATO, which itself will continue to consist of the national militaries of member nations.

According to Marc Trachtenberg, many believed that the French offered the Pleven Plan to prevent German rearmament. Under pressure from the NATO commander-general, Dwight D. Eisenhower, however, the Pleven Plan—which some described as an effort to "rearm the Germans without rearming Germany"—soon developed into the European Defense Community (EDC). German units were created and integrated into NATO forces at the division level. The treaties creating the EDC were signed on 27 May 1952. France did not rush to approve the treaty, however. The French were reluctant to consider the creation of armed German units, even if they were embedded into the EDC structure. In fact, the EDC structure was the problem: still trying to find ways to withdraw American forces from Europe, the United States realized that without German military resources, it would be difficult, if not impossible, to build a credible defense of its European allies. The EDC would make such buildup possible. An additional benefit of the EDC was that it showed the way for greater European integration, something the United States supported because it would make Western Europe a more formidable political, economic, and military bulwark against Soviet expansion. The French and other Europeans did not want the United States to leave Europe, however. To aid its campaign for ratification of the EDC and assuage European suspicions, the United States had to reiterate its commitment to maintain American troops in Europe. The French insisted on tangible American and British guarantees against an attack from a rearmed Germany and on the permanent presence of U.S. troops on the continent to intervene against any EDC member (that is, Germany) which violated the treaty. In December 1953 U.S. secretary of state John Foster Dulles threatened an "agonizing reappraisal" of

U.S. policies in Europe, hinting that if European countries failed to ratify the EDC, the United States and Britain might unilaterally rearm Germany. All this campaigning was to no avail. The French National Assembly rejected the EDC in a vote on 30 August 1954.

The Western Europe allies of the United States were overwhelmed by the fear of a resurgent Germany and the belief that they could not contain a rearmed Germany on their own. An alternative defense structure for the West had to be found to allay some of their concerns. The alternative was to have Germany join the Western European Union (WEU) and NATO. From the point of view of the Western European nations, both organizations had distinct advantages over the defunct EDC, which was a continental venture that did not include Britain or the United States. If Germany were allowed to rearm, even under the EDC restrictions, France would be left alone to watch Germany, and balance against it if necessary. Since Britain was a member of the WEU and both Britain and the United States were members of NATO, inviting Germany to join these organizations and then allowing it to rearm made sense. Germany would be enmeshed in the restrictions of these two organizations, whose leading members, Britain and the United States, would assume the lead role in keeping a watchful eye on Germany and containing it. The charters of the two organizations would assure the presence of hundreds of thousands of American and British troops on German soil.

Another sign that realpolitik concerns prevailed was the fact that the creators of NATO were not overly interested in whether or not a member country was a democracy. This point is clear from the membership roster of the alliance. Portugal, one of the founding members, was ruled by the authoritarian (if not outright fascist) Antonio de Oliveira Salazar, an ideological soul mate to Francisco Franco of Spain. While a member of NATO, Portugal fought bitter colonial wars in its African possessions (as did France and Britain). The only time Portugal's membership in NATO came into question was in 1974, when the military regime that replaced Salazar allowed for a transition to civilian rule that opened the possibility of communists coming to power in Lisbon. Another member with questionable democratic credentials is Turkey, whose civil-rights violations have led the European Community, on several occasions, to reject Turkey's application for membership in that body. Turkey also invaded a neighboring country, Cyprus, in 1974, creating a Turkish sector in the northern part of the island. It can be argued that if Turkey were to apply today for membership in NATO, it would be told to reform its civil-military relations and introduce other political reforms in order to qualify. Greece has also experienced problems that might have altered its NATO membership. In 1967 the military took power and remained in control until 1974. The junta's brutality caused many Western European leaders to keep their distance from Greece, but its standing in NATO was not damaged.

France and the Benelux countries are democracies; Italy and Germany became democracies after their defeat in the Second World War. All were facing a growing threat from the East. Yet, according to Josef Joffe, all shared democratic principles and the communist threat "never proved strong enough to suppress either memories of the past or apprehensions about the future among those key West European states. . . . even at a time of excruciating weakness, neither the Soviet challenge nor the destruction of the European balance during World War II were powerful enough to prompt the West Europeans to transcend their history." NATO was an organizational response to the fears and anxieties of countries that shared a common philosophy and faced a common threat, but could not escape—because no country can—realpolitik concerns such as power balances, fears of hegemony, and preoccupation with relative power. The success of NATO in assuaging such realpolitik concerns allowed it in later years to pursue the hopes and aspirations of some of its members to create an organization emphasizing the democratic principles of its members. At the beginning, however, things were different, and realpolitik concerns were paramount in the minds of NATO authors.

—BENJAMIN FRANKEL, SECURITY STUDIES

References

Edward Fursdon, *The European Defense Community: A History* (London: Macmillan, 1980);

Josef Joffe, *The Limited Partnership: Europe, the United States, and the Burdens of Alliance* (Cambridge, Mass.: Ballinger, 1987);

Frank Ninkovich, *Modernity and Power: A History of the Domino Theory in the Twentieth Century* (Chicago: University of Chicago Press, 1994);

John Ruggie, *Winning the Peace: America and World Order in the New Era* (New York: Columbia University Press, 1996);

Tony Smith, *America's Mission: The United States and the Worldwide Struggle for Democracy in the Twentieth Century* (Princeton, N.J.: Princeton University Press, 1994);

Marc Trachtenberg, *A Constructed Peace: The Making of the European Settlement, 1945–1963* (Princeton, N.J.: Princeton University Press, 1999);

Woodrow Wilson, *The Messages and Papers of Woodrow Wilson*, volumes 1 and 2 (New York: Review of Reviews Corporation, 1924).

NEW LOOK

Was the New Look an effective and prudent doctrine?

Viewpoint: Yes, during the early years of the Eisenhower administration the New Look policy allowed the United States to secure its vital interests at a relatively low cost.

Viewpoint: No, the New Look was dangerous and poorly controlled.

Few policies captured President Dwight D. Eisenhower's philosophy of government better than the New Look doctrine he introduced after assuming office in 1953. His military experience and Republican Party budgetary preferences combined in the new strategy, which replaced the national-security stance of the outgoing administration of Harry S Truman.

At the core of the New Look was a recognition of the limits of American power and a criticism of the symmetrical nature of the Truman administration's national-security policy. The symmetrical approach meant that the United States had to respond in kind, or in a symmetrical fashion, to any new Soviet military capability or initiative. Eisenhower saw five problems with Truman's approach. First, it was reactive, allowing the Soviet Union to dictate the scope, character, and content of U.S. national strategy. Second, it was economically wasteful, draining away money that could be used for productive purposes. Third, it was not clear how sustainable such a policy would be over time, since the American public might not agree for long to invest the vast sums required to meet and emulate every Soviet military capability. Fourth, there was a danger that in reaction to what would be required by a symmetrical approach, Americans would revert to dangerous isolationism. Fifth, the creation of a large standing army and the allocation of large sums of money to it might lead to a subversion of American institutions and democratic practices.

The New Look offered an asymmetrical approach to the Soviet threat, one based on emphasizing capabilities in which the United States was superior. The goal, to use the words of a senior administration official was to get "more bang for the buck." The emphasis on asymmetry led the administration to shift money from the Navy and the Army, where most of the U.S. conventional forces were concentrated, to the Air Force, the custodian of nuclear weapons. The Army budget was cut from $12.9 billion in 1954 to $8.8 billion in 1955; Navy funding was reduced from $11.2 billion in 1954 to $9.7 billion in 1955. The Air Force budget, however, was increased from $15.6 billion in 1954 to $16.4 billion in 1955. As part of the New Look, the Eisenhower administration also beefed up covert-operations capabilities.

Critics of the New Look argued that a policy relying too heavily on nuclear weapons was at the same time less credible and more dangerous. By turning to nuclear weapons in a greater number of contingencies, the administration lowered the nuclear threshold, making nuclear use more likely. At the same time, it was unlikely the United States would resort to nuclear weapons in situations short of grave emergency, thus allowing an adversary to undermine U.S. interests on the margins in a manner that would harm the United States but would still not justify nuclear employment.

Viewpoint:
Yes, during the early years of the Eisenhower administration, the New Look policy allowed the United States to secure its vital interests at a relatively low cost.

The New Look policy, designed by the Eisenhower administration to wage the cold war more cheaply and dynamically by emphasizing the threat of nuclear attack, was effective and prudent during the first three years of Eisenhower's first term. It became a dangerous policy, however, once the Soviet Union began to develop a thermonuclear arsenal of its own, a situation that forced Eisenhower and his secretary of state, John Foster Dulles, to abandon the New Look after 1956.

In early 1950 the Truman administration issued National Security Council document 68 (NSC-68). Written primarily by Paul H. Nitze, director of the State Department Policy Planning Staff, NSC-68 stated that, if the United States were to meet the threat of global communist expansion effectively, it had to increase defense spending severalfold and prepare to counter communist action anywhere around the world with immediate military response. As if on cue, the North Koreans crossed the thirty-eighth parallel in June of that year, and the Truman administration responded by sending U.S. troops to Korea, where they waged a long, limited war, quadrupling the U.S. defense budget by 1952 and at the same time launching a crash program to build a thermonuclear bomb.

Dulles, a spokesman for the Republican Party on international affairs, criticized the Truman administration's policy. To Dulles, NSC-68 seemed a blueprint for an infinite future of limited, stalemated wars, such as the conflict in Korea. By obliging the U.S. government to react everywhere, to any kind of communist aggression, NSC-68 foretold staggering defense budgets, unsatisfactory, limited military engagements in obscure locations, and a cold war in which the communist side always took the initiative and the United States always reacted. In 1952 Dulles offered an alternative in "A Policy of Boldness," an article published in *Life* magazine. Rather than reacting to communist aggressions wherever they occurred, he asked, why not threaten the Soviet Union at the place and time of America's choosing? Why not put the American advantage in atomic technology to use? This strategy, he said, would put an end to the "immoral" policy of containing Soviet expansion and put the United States on the offensive in the cold war.

This new approach appealed to Eisenhower, the Republican winner of the 1952 presidential election. Though he felt less strongly about recapturing a cold-war moral initiative than did Dulles, Eisen-

hower agreed that the endless series of limited wars that seemed to follow from NSC-68 would bankrupt the U.S. treasury and threaten American democracy. His experience as Allied commander of the European Theater of Operations during the Second World War taught him that protracted hostilities tended to destroy democratic institutions, creating instead a "garrison state" in which all is subordinated to the war effort. The military emphasis of NSC-68 worried Eisenhower because it might put the United States on the road to just such an outcome. By replacing NSC-68 with a less-expensive strategy—one that would not obligate Americans to wage war in obscure corners of the world—he hoped America could avoid the absurd outcome of losing its democratic institutions in a cold war initiated to protect them.

On taking office in early 1953, Eisenhower named Dulles his secretary of state. The two men immediately began devising the New Look, a national-security doctrine that employed three main strategies. The first was a revival of covert operations. Eisenhower set loose the Central Intelligence Agency (CIA). With other organizations the CIA intensified propaganda campaigns against the Sino-Soviet bloc, funneled clandestine support to pro-American or anticommunist political figures around the world, and on two occasions actually helped to overthrow established governments—the regimes of Jacobo Arbenz Guzmán in Guatemala and Mohammad Mossadeqh in Iran, neither of which was communist. By elevating the role of covert operations, Eisenhower hoped to win cold-war battles without using military force. In such terms these clandestine activities were successful, but they began to make a bad name for the United States in contested parts of the world.

A second element of the New Look policy was the use of "atomic diplomacy" in 1953, 1954, and 1955. By using the quiet threat of nuclear attack against China in 1953, North Vietnam in 1954, and China again in 1955, the Eisenhower administration was able to get its way in negotiations over ending the Korean War, the division of Vietnam, and status of the islands of Quemoy and Matsu off the Chinese coast. While NSC-68 would have dictated waging limited conventional wars to secure favorable outcomes in each of these crises, Eisenhower and Dulles were able to realize diplomatic victories without losing American lives or spending much money. The atomic-diplomacy aspect of the New Look policy was a tremendous success.

The final feature of the New Look was the policy of "massive retaliation." In a speech to the Council on Foreign Relations in early 1954, Dulles announced that the United States would seek in the future to confront communist aggression "vigorously at places and with means of its own choosing." The primary means with which the United States would engage in such confrontation, Dulles speci-

NEW LOOK

Secretary of State John Foster Dulles and President Dwight D. Eisenhower

fied, was "the deterrent of massive retaliatory power." Massive retaliation was the linchpin of the New Look: rather than reacting to communist aggression where it occurred, the United States would assume that the act of aggression originated in Moscow or Beijing and threaten the two communist capitals directly with nuclear attack unless they put an end to the adventurism. As Dulles had suggested in his "Policy of Boldness" article, massive retaliation would not only be cheaper and help avoid limited wars, it would also give the United States the initiative. Whenever it saw fit, it could take matters directly to the Kremlin.

The New Look was a clear success for the American cold-war effort during 1953–1955. The United States maintained the status quo in contested areas without losing a single American serviceman or spending a large amount of money. American troops were not bogged down in limited wars, such as the conflict in Korea, which made the cold war unpopular in American society and raised the specter of a garrison state.

The New Look came to a quick end, however. Even as it began in 1953, both Dulles and Eisenhower realized that its days were numbered. In the fall of that year the Soviet Union successfully tested a thermonuclear device. Unless the United States was willing to wage a preemptive war against the Soviet Union, the Soviet test meant that sooner or later Russia would in all likelihood attain a nuclear arsenal sufficient to offset its American counterpart. For the near future the United States could continue its New Look policies, because in the early 1950s American weapons were still qualitatively superior. Once the Soviets developed the capability to use thermonuclear weapons on U.S. targets, however, the U.S. policy of massive retaliation would become a policy of national suicide. Dulles and Eisenhower spent the next few years arguing about how to address this problem. By 1957 Eisenhower had won the debate.

During the 1950s the many critics of the New Look argued that it limited American options and relied too heavily on the blunt instrument of nuclear war. Indeed, many called it immoral to threaten the Chinese or Vietnamese with atomic bombs over issues that were hardly crucial to American security. They also denounced the threat to unleash massive retaliation against the Soviet Union for a minor communist aggression.

The latter criticism is an important and valid one. It raises the question of whether the Eisenhower administration genuinely intended to wage such warfare or regarded the policy essentially as a bluff. The second interpretation can never wholly be verified—only refuted. Yet, Eisenhower's comments during the early years of the New Look— including his private excoriation of advisers who urged him to use atomic weapons to aid the French against the Vietnamese at Dien Bien Phu in 1954—and his aversion to nuclear war of any kind during the last years of his administration, indicate that he may well have viewed the atomic-diplomacy and massive-retaliation components of the New Look as bluffs that would never be called. Had the Chinese or Soviets called one of them during the years 1953–1956, Eisenhower would have been forced either to back down or to unleash a nuclear war over stakes that few would have viewed as justifiable. No such challenge ever happened, however. When a poker player wins a game by intimidating everyone else into folding, it no longer matters what cards he or she actually held.

–CAMPBELL CRAIG, UNIVERSITY OF CANTERBURY, NEW ZEALAND

Viewpoint:
No, the New Look was dangerous and poorly controlled.

President Dwight D. Eisenhower designed the New Look to enable the United States to fight the cold war for "the long haul." Under the New Look, the United States expanded its military alliances around the Sino-Soviet bloc as it reduced defense spending by cutting conventional military forces. The key part of the New Look was increased emphasis on thermonuclear weapons, which provided "more bang for the buck." In the eight years of Eisenhower's presidency the American nuclear stockpile grew from 1,000 bombs to more than 18,000 weapons; the arsenal was diversified and deployed throughout the armed services. The nuclear component of the New Look became known as "massive retaliation," after Dulles stated that the West could deter communist aggression only by being "willing and able to respond vigorously at places and with means of its own choosing." The New Look—and its massive retaliation component—evolved over the course of the decade, but the central elements of the policy remained unchanged. Eisenhower's emphasis on nuclear weapons raised concerns about its prudence, which have persisted over time.

Throughout the 1950s critics of the New Look claimed that the strategy lacked credibility. William Kaufmann asserted that "the doctrine of massive retaliation as it has been formulated is neither feasible nor desirable as a policy of deterrence. . . . it can-

not be made feasible because of its lack of credibility." The extension of American nuclear deterrence beyond the United States and the members of the North Atlantic Treaty Organization (NATO) to cover other regions seemed unnecessarily dangerous. In regional crises, such as the two crises over Quemoy and Matsu the Eisenhower administration was confronted with the choice of threatening to use nuclear weapons to defend marginal interests or revealing that massive retaliation was empty posturing. Many observers believed that it was unwise to make nuclear threats when the outcomes could be so harmful to American interests.

The perceived growth in Soviet nuclear capabilities over the course of the decade raised additional questions about the credibility of massive retaliation. Initially, overwhelming U.S. nuclear superiority accorded the Eisenhower administration a degree of freedom as it practiced deterrence through the threat of massive retaliation. The fictional bomber and missile gaps, however, increased fears that the Soviets would soon be able to execute a devastating nuclear first strike. Civilian strategists such as Albert J. Wohlstetter, as well as the Gaither panel—formed in 1957 with the assignment of determining ways to defend the United States from nuclear attack— asserted that strategic deterrence was more precarious than Eisenhower administration officials recognized or were willing to admit. Furthermore, some argued that the growth of Soviet nuclear capabilities would negate American nuclear threats and enable the Soviet Union to become more aggressive, especially in the developing world. Some officials in the Eisenhower administration, particularly in the State Department, lobbied to de-emphasize nuclear weapons and retract the umbrella of extended nuclear deterrence that the United States had offered its allies, but to no avail. These debates about the declining effectiveness of deterrence through massive retaliation, were premature because they were predicated on erroneous intelligence projections. Yet, they anticipated the inevitable decay of the policy of massive retaliation.

Throughout the 1950s there were other concerns about the prudence of the New Look. The most sustained criticism was that the Eisenhower administration unwisely expanded nuclear capabilities at the expense of conventional weapons systems. The New Look formula that substituted nuclear weapons for conventional forces created a shrinkage and atrophy of nonnuclear forces. Research and development funds went for new nuclear-weapons systems, even exotic ones such as a nuclear-powered bomber, rather than conventional weapons. Nonnuclear elements of each armed service (for example, tactical fighters), received insufficient funding and were relegated to a marginal status. Successive army chiefs of staff, as well as other military leaders, protested the reductions in conventional forces, arguing that the United States would have difficulty fighting

NEW LOOK

The heart of the problem is how to deter attack. This, we believe, requires that a potential aggressor be left in no doubt that he would be certain to suffer damage outweighing any possible gains from aggression.

This result would not be assured, even by collective measures, if the free world sought to match the potential Communist forces, man for man and tank for tank, at every point where they might attack. The Soviet-Chinese bloc does not lack manpower and spends it as something that is cheap. If an aggressor knew he could always prescribe the battle conditions that suited him and engage us in struggles mainly involving manpower, aggression might be encouraged. He would be tempted to attack in places and by means where his manpower superiority was decisive and where at little cost he could impose upon us great burdens. If the free world adopted this strategy, it could bankrupt itself and not achieve security over a sustained period.

The free world must devise a better strategy for its defense, based upon its own special assets. Its assets include, especially, air and naval power and atomic weapons which are now available in a wide range, suitable not only for strategic bombing but also for extensive tactical use. The free world must make imaginative use of the deterrent capabilities of these new weapons and mobilities and exploit the full potential of collective security. Properly used, they can produce defensive power able to retaliate at once and effectively against any aggressor.

. . . The American people have repeatedly shown that they are prepared to make whatever sacrifices are really necessary to insure our national safety. They would no doubt support military expenses at the levels which their government told them were required for security, even at the cost of budget deficits, resultant inflationary pressures and tax-levels which would impair incentives. But the patriotic will to sacrifice is not something to be drawn upon needlessly. Government has the high duty to seek resourcefully and inventively the ways which will provide security without sacrificing economic and social welfare. The security policies we here describe make possible more selective and more efficient programs in terms of the composition of forces and of procurement.

Source: John Foster Dulles, "Policy for Security and Peace," Foreign Affairs, 32 (April 1954): 357–358, 362.

a war without resorting to nuclear weapons. The weakening of conventional capabilities, critics asserted, undermined the ability of the United States to project power or keep a conflict limited. President Eisenhower repeatedly opposed attempts to restore funding for conventional forces, choosing to stick to his New Look formula. By the end of the decade civilian strategists such as Robert Osgood had developed theories about the conduct and problems of limited war. President John F. Kennedy jettisoned the New Look immediately on taking office in 1961. The Kennedy administration adopted General Maxwell Taylor's Flexible Response strategy, which was rooted in the ideas of the limited-war theorists.

The opening of the Eisenhower presidential papers in the 1970s led to a school of Eisenhower "revisionists," who asserted that the New Look and massive retaliation were not as dangerous as their critics had charged. Stephen Ambrose, Richard Immerman, and other revisionists cited the avoidance of nuclear war with the Soviets, stable defense budgets, and Eisenhower's crisis management as evidence of the effectiveness of New Look policy. In some respects, what contemporary critics had seen as vices, including the New Look formula for defense posture, the revisionists saw as virtues. Their perspective, however, has not been accepted unanimously. Case studies of the Taiwan Straits crises, as well as the Berlin crisis of 1958–1959, have criticized President Eisenhower's manipulation of the threat of massive retaliation. Unlike the revisionists, Richard Betts and others believe that the Eisenhower administration's "brinkmanship" was fraught with danger and at times took unnecessary risks to protect peripheral interests. The evidence indicates that Eisenhower recognized the limitations of massive retaliation; he accepted them to accrue the benefit of deterrence and fiscal control. Massive retaliation cannot be lauded without recognizing the accompanying risks and dangers.

Declassified documents, which took decades to become available, have provided new perspectives on the risks of the New Look. Revelations about nuclear-weapons control and custody, employment policies, and organizational behavior raised new questions about the prudence of the strategy.

The New Look policy precipitated monumental changes in the American nuclear arsenal and the ways in which it was controlled. The U.S. stockpile grew by more than 17,000 nuclear weapons—ranging from smaller tactical warheads to large city-busting gravity bombs. Beginning early in his administration, President Eisenhower also relaxed the strict system of civilian control through the Atomic Energy Commission (AEC), which had been established by President Harry S Truman. Eisenhower transferred custody of a large part of the nuclear arsenal from the AEC to the armed forces. This transfer took place before the development of permissive-action links (PAL) that reduced the possibility of unauthorized use. This system of "delegative" civilian control, according to Peter Feaver, placed a greater value on always being able to use nuclear weapons, even at the risk of allowing room for an unauthorized launch, than on preventing an unauthorized or inadvertent action. Thus, Eisenhower's massive-retaliation policy placed great trust that no military personnel would violate the key principle of civilian control.

One of the most dangerous aspects of massive retaliation came in Eisenhower's changes in the policies guiding the employment of nuclear weapons. During the Truman administration, nuclear weapons could be used only if the president gave a specific order to do so. As estimates of American vulnerability grew, Eisenhower predelegated the authority to use nuclear weapons to military leaders, allowing certain military leaders to use nuclear weapons under specified conditions without receiving explicit approval from the president. A 1956 order gave the military the authority to use nuclear air-defense weapons, and a 1959 order predelegated a wider range of tactical and strategic nuclear weapons. The Eisenhower administration reasoned that many of the nuclear weapons developed under the New Look could be effective only if military officers could use them instantaneously and not have to wait for orders. While predelegation orders tried to delineate the authority carefully, nuclear predelegation raised the possibility of unanticipated and unwanted nuclear escalation in a crisis.

The changes in custody and employment policies resulting from the New Look heightened the risks of accidents or other problems. Organizational factors further increased these dangers. Technological control mechanisms, such as permissive-action links, were either primitive or nonexistent; command-and-control systems had many deficiencies. Organizational routines and practices, as Scott Sagan has shown, threatened undesired escalation in a crisis. While problems arising from organizational factors were not unique to this period, massive retaliation made them more acute.

President Eisenhower secured his most important national-security objective—affordable deterrence of the Soviet Union—through his New Look policy of massive retaliation. The effectiveness of the New Look, however, should not overshadow the risks inherent in the policy. For contemporary observers, massive retaliation was an incredible policy for a variety of reasons, while threatening nuclear war too often, even for marginal interests. Declassified documents reveal that the New Look, once it was in place, increased the risk of accidental, inadvertent, or unanticipated use of nuclear weapons. The heavy reliance on nuclear weapons in an era of uncertainty and instability was particularly dangerous.

—PETER J. ROMAN, DUQUESNE UNIVERSITY

References

Richard K. Betts, *Nuclear Blackmail and Nuclear Balance* (Washington, D.C.: Brookings Institution, 1987);

Bruce G. Blair, *The Logic of Accidental Nuclear War* (Washington, D.C.: Brookings Institution, 1993);

Campbell Craig, *Destroying the Village: Eisenhower and Thermonuclear War* (New York: Columbia University Press, 1998);

Saki Dockrill, *Eisenhower's New-Look National Security Policy, 1953–61* (New York: St. Martin's Press, 1996);

Peter Douglas Feaver, *Guarding the Guardians: Civilian Control of Nuclear Weapons in the United States* (Ithaca, N.Y.: Cornell University Press, 1992);

Lawrence Freedman, *The Evolution of Nuclear Strategy* (New York: St. Martin's Press, 1989);

John Lewis Gaddis, *Strategies of Containment: A Critical Appraisal of Postwar American National Security Policy* (New York: Oxford University Press, 1982);

Gaddis, *The United States and the End of the Cold War: Implications, Reconsiderations, Provocations* (New York: Oxford University Press, 1992);

Richard H. Immerman, *John Foster Dulles: Piety, Pragmatism, and Power in U.S. Foreign Policy* (Wilmington, Del.: Schoalarly Resources, 1999);

Immerman, ed., *John Foster Dulles and the Diplomacy of the Cold War: A Reappraisal* (Princeton, N.J.: Princeton University Press, 1989);

William W. Kaufmann, ed., *Military Policy and National Security* (Princeton, N.J.: Princeton University Press, 1956);

Henry Kissinger, *Nuclear Weapons and Foreign Policy* (New York: Harper, 1957);

Stephen G. Rabe, *Eisenhower and Latin America: The Foreign Policy of Anticommunism* (Chapel Hill: University of North Carolina Press, 1988);

Peter J. Roman, *Eisenhower and the Missile Gap* (Ithaca, N.Y.: Cornell University Press, 1996);

David Rosenberg, "The Origins of Overkill," *International Security*, 7 (Spring 1983): 3–71;

Scott D. Sagan, *The Limits of Safety: Organizations, Accidents, and Nuclear Weapons* (Princeton, N.J.: Princeton University Press, 1993).

NONPROLIFERATION

Has U.S. nuclear-nonproliferation policy been successful?

Viewpoint: Yes, U.S. nuclear-nonproliferation policy has contained the spread of nuclear weapons.

Viewpoint: No, U.S. nuclear-nonproliferation policy has not been successful because of inconsistent application and lax enforcement.

The U.S. record on preventing the proliferation of nuclear weapons is uneven and difficult to characterize. Initial efforts to curb the spread of nuclear technology—for example, the Baruch Plan in 1946—were derided by critics as barely concealed attempts to ensure continued U.S. nuclear monopoly. President Dwight D. Eisenhower's 1953 Atoms for Peace program reversed the initial U.S. reluctance to share nuclear technology, promising American assistance with nuclear-energy development to nations that abstained from acquiring nuclear weapons. U.S. policies regarding emerging nuclear-weapon states, however, remained ambivalent. As the leader of the free world in its campaign to contain the spread of Soviet power and influence, the U.S. government had many pressing goals; the prevention of the spread of nuclear weapons was only one of them, and time after time this policy was superseded by what were deemed to be more urgent objectives.

In the late 1950s and early 1960s the United States was faced with its first proliferation test, as it became clear that France and Israel were about to launch their nuclear-weapons programs. The United States looked the other way as the French tested their first nuclear weapons in the Sahara Desert, but the John F. Kennedy administration exerted considerable pressure on Israel to halt its nuclear program. In a secret letter to Israeli prime minister David Ben Gurion, President Kennedy ominously suggested that Israel's continued stonewalling with regard to its nuclear-weapons plans threatened U.S.-Israeli relations. The American pressure on Israel was short-lived. President Lyndon B. Johnson gave the impression that he was going to continue the Kennedy administration's policy of pressuring Israel, but he soon abandoned it in favor of a series of toothless inspection visits by American scientists to the Israeli nuclear site in Dimona. These inspectors, despite their earnest efforts, found no evidence that the Israelis were building nuclear weapons, just as the Israelis were doing precisely that. In 1969 the incoming administration of President Richard M. Nixon accepted without qualms the status of Israel as an undeclared nuclear-weapon state.

After some hesitation the United States joined, and then led, the effort on behalf of the 1968 Nuclear Non-Proliferation Treaty (NPT), the most important international effort to prevent the further spread of nuclear weapons. In the mid 1970s, spurred by the 1974 Indian nuclear test, the Nixon and Gerald R. Ford administrations successfully pressured Taiwan and South Korea to halt their nuclear-weapons programs. President Jimmy Carter's administration was the first U.S. administration to make the prevention of the spread of nuclear weapons a top priority. It exerted pressure on the Germans and French to cease nuclear cooperation with other countries and, in 1979, froze aid to Pakistan in response to evidence of that nation's nuclear advances. In a manner that typified the difficulty successive U.S. governments had in pursuing the goal of nonproliferation, however, the Carter administration lifted the ban on aid to Pakistan after the Soviet Union invaded Afghanistan in December 1979. The goal of assisting the mujahideen fighters in Afghanistan in their campaign against the Soviet invasion became paramount, and Pakistan's assistance in this effort was indispensable. In order to ensure continued supplies to the mujahideen as the war dragged on in the 1980s, the administrations of George H. W. Bush and Ronald W. Reagan "certified" to Congress that Pakistan was not developing nuclear weapons and that it was thus entitled to U.S. military and economic aid. (Pakistan, of course, continued energetically to pursue its nuclear-weapons program, crossing the nuclear-weapons threshold in the mid 1980s.) Such certification became necessary because Congress had passed different pieces of legislation, sponsored by Senators Stuart Symington (D-Missouri), Alan Cranston (D-California), John H. Glenn Jr. (D-Ohio), and Larry Pressler (R-South Dakota), that mandated cutting aid to countries against which there was evidence that they were pursuing nuclear weapons.

With the end of the cold war, nuclear nonproliferation became a primary goal of U.S. policy. There were three reasons for this renewed emphasis. The end of the cold war meant that the pursuit of nuclear nonproliferation had to compete with fewer other foreign-policy objectives. The 1991 Gulf War revealed that Iraq, a signatory to and a member in good standing of the NPT, was much further ahead in their nuclear program than intelligence sources in the West had estimated; and it also became clear that nuclear weapons were not the only threat—that biological and chemical weapons and ballistic missiles were a menace as well. The use of sarin nerve gas by the Japanese cult Aum Shinrikyo (Supreme Truth) in 1995 and the suspicion that the Saudi master terrorist Osama bin Laden was financing plants for the production of chemical weapons and biological agents brought about the realization that the United States and the world had to worry about the spread of weapons of mass destruction (WMD), not only to other states, but to terrorist groups as well.

These new worries notwithstanding, old fears about the spread of nuclear weapons were given added emphasis by the nuclear tests India and Pakistan conducted in spring 1998 and by the continued nuclear and ballistic-missile threat from North Korea. The persistence of old threats and the emergence of new ones help to focus the attention of the United States and other governments on a problem that has become more difficult, if not intractable, as the technologies undergirding the different WMDs and the various means to deliver them have become more readily available and less expensive to obtain.

Viewpoint:
Yes, U.S. nuclear-nonproliferation policy has contained the spread of nuclear weapons.

American nuclear-nonproliferation policy is one of the true success stories of U.S. foreign relations during the last forty years. While efforts to prevent the spread of nuclear weapons have not been perfectly effective, nonproliferation policy has succeeded resoundingly in several different ways. First, it has generated a truly global consensus against proliferation. Second, nonproliferation efforts have been remarkably effective in containing the spread of nuclear weapons. Third, even in the few instances in which nonproliferation efforts have not prevented states from building nuclear weapons, they have helped to limit the states' development of their arsenals in important ways. These successes have paid big strategic dividends.

The emphases of U.S. nuclear-nonproliferation policy evolved throughout the cold war, but the main goal has remained constant. U.S. policymakers have specifically sought to influence the global nuclear environment in a manner that maximizes American security and deterrent stability.

Washington's pre–1953 policy of nuclear denial proscribed the spread of all nuclear technology, whether military or commercial. American military planners in this period had tentatively discussed preventive strikes against nuclear facilities in the Soviet Union, but planning never got too far. Even Great Britain, which had assisted in the American atomic-bomb project, was initially denied reciprocal aid from the United States. In December 1953, however, President Dwight D. Eisenhower unveiled his Atoms for Peace plan at the United Nations, heralding a shift away from simple denial to a "carrot-and-stick" approach: states eager for nuclear technology would be given assistance in developing commercial nuclear resources provided they foreswore military applications. Atoms for Peace also

The signing of the Atomic Energy Act, 30 August 1954. Seated at the table are Senator William F. Knowland, President Dwight D. Eisenhower, Representative W. Sterling Cole, and Atomic Energy Commission Chairman Lewis L. Strauss

(DOE Archives, Signal Corps photograph)

exemplified an evolving strategy of pro-active, expressly nonmilitary means of nuclear containment. The United States would limit nonproliferation efforts to diplomatic initiatives.

This same carrot-and-stick diplomacy characterized the Nuclear Non-Proliferation Treaty (NPT) negotiations of 1968–1970. The NPT is the flagship of U.S. nonproliferation policy and the coordinating vessel for global efforts. Its structure is threefold. First, the document recognizes the status of the five nuclear-weapon states (the United States, the Soviet Union, Great Britain, France, and China), while disallowing all other nations from developing nuclear weaponry. The treaty thus legitimizes a certain discrimination. Second, in exchange for their pledges not to develop atomic weapons, nonnuclear signatories are promised assistance in developing commercial technology and given security assurances against nuclear aggression. The International Atomic Energy Agency (IAEA) polices against military application of commercial nuclear technologies among signatories. Third, the five nuclear-weapon signatories promise to work toward full nuclear disarmament. The nuclear sponsors of the NPT had a strikingly ambitious aim: to engender a manifestly discriminatory, worldwide prohibition against a singularly dominant weapon that they themselves had deployed.

Over the years U.S. policymakers strengthened their own commitment to nonproliferation through domestic legislation. The 1976

Symington Amendment (initiated by Senator Stuart Symington, D-Missouri) and the 1985 Pressler Amendment (sponsored by Senator Larry Pressler, R-South Dakota) gave U.S. presidents a legal basis for leveling sanctions against proliferators that are not signatories to the NPT.

Nonproliferation is not a discrete goal in itself, but rather an important segment of the broader U.S. security agenda. Consequently, U.S. commitment to its formal nonproliferation pledges has varied somewhat in proportion to its wider strategic concerns. For instance, President Richard M. Nixon delayed Senate ratification of the NPT for two years in response to the 1968 Soviet invasion of Czechoslovakia. Although the Symington Amendment required the president to terminate aid to governments that attempted to develop nuclear weapons, it also makes provisions for suspending these sanctions if they interfere with vital American interests. Accordingly, although President Jimmy Carter suspended aid to Pakistan in 1979 amid revelations of nuclear development in that nation, he quickly reinstated and upgraded Pakistani aid after the Soviets invaded Afghanistan. Similarly, Washington has been consistently reluctant to punish Israel for its well-known nuclear development because Israel is an important American ally in the Middle East. From the American perspective, one should measure the success of nonproliferation institutions in terms of broad U.S. security concerns.

The United States has succeeded impressively in its nuclear-related security goals. Its chief victory may be in establishing a truly global nonproliferation norm. In May 1995, as the original twenty-five-year term of the NPT was scheduled to end, 174 signatories agreed to extend the treaty indefinitely. By the summer of 1998 the NPT had 186 members, a number exceeding the formal membership of the United Nations. NPT membership transcends all global political divides, incorporating democracies, communist states, and fundamentalist regimes. Dozens of nations have nuclear reactors under IAEA safeguards. Moreover, the United States has expanded the institutional framework for nonproliferation efforts. The administration of President Gerald Ford initiated the creation of the London Suppliers' Group, an organization of advanced nuclear states committed to controlling the commercial spread of dangerous nuclear technologies. Other nonnuclear, antiproliferation organizations, such as the Missile Technology Control Regime (MTCR), owe their existence to the institutional momentum of the nuclear-nonproliferation system. The technical and political world environments have been conditioned by the thoroughness of the nonproliferation organization. For any government to defy the nonproliferation system is to suffer both material and diplomatic costs.

This international political consensus is not without practical results. The rate of nuclear proliferation around the globe has been astonishingly slow—much slower than early experts predicted. In the early 1970s Nixon and his advisers secretly believed that, despite the newly ratified NPT, it would probably be only a short time before all major and regional powers developed their own nuclear arsenals. The success of nonproliferation policies, however, has exceeded those expectations, and subsequent administrations have had more ambitious forecasts. In addition to the original five nuclear-weapon powers, there are probably around sixty states with the capacity to develop nuclear bombs; only three have done so.

Since ratification of the NPT, no major power has developed nuclear weapons. Germany and Japan, which once were seen as likely near-term proliferators, have rested contentedly under the American nuclear umbrella and thereby helped stabilize the bipolar cold-war nuclear standoff. India, Pakistan, and South Africa are the only countries to have developed nuclear weapons since the NPT was ratified. Israel, the only other proliferator, constructed its first nuclear weapons in 1967, before the treaty was signed. South Africa vol-untarily dismantled its nuclear arsenal and acceded to the NPT as a nonnuclear-weapon state in 1991. The fact that there are only three proliferators not sanctioned by the NPT is striking in relation to the number of states that have pursued bomb development—a number including Libya, Egypt, Syria, Iran, Iraq, North Korea, South Korea, Taiwan, Brazil, and Argentina. Eight of these ten countries have been thwarted by direct pressure from the United States and its nonproliferation allies. The remaining two, Brazil and Argentina, abandoned their efforts by agreement with one another, though international pressure doubtlessly played a role.

There are several security benefits to this nuclear containment. Since proliferation has been slow, limited, and diligently monitored, it has greatly reduced the dangers of nuclear transitions. First, neither the cold-war camps nor regional security situations have experienced sudden and destabilizing shifts in security balances as a result of nuclearization. Second, by preventing the spread of these weapons to hostile states, the United States has ensured the adequacy of its own nuclear deterrent for the foreseeable future. Third, insofar as nuclear weapons have not spread, America enjoys greater freedom of military action abroad.

It is worth noting that even in the cases of nonproliferation failure (Israel, India, and Pakistan), U.S. policy and the global nonproliferation system have served to curtail the dangers of the emerging nuclear arsenals. In particular, nonproliferation pressures have helped to limit the size and complexity of emerging arsenals by making technological progress more difficult and expensive than it would be otherwise. There are advantages to keeping these new arsenals small and simple. Small arsenals are less threatening to the United States, and simple arsenals are less likely to overwhelm the abilities of small states to control and manage them safely.

In addition, nonproliferation pressure has forced proliferators to adopt a pattern of proliferation known as nuclear ambiguity or opacity. In this pattern states are strongly suspected of having nuclear weapons, but they do not officially declare their arsenals, and they hide weapons production and deployment. They do so because they do not want to violate global nonproliferation norms openly and incur diplomatic and material sanctions. Since the signing of the NPT, all new nuclear-weapon states have cultivated opacity. Indeed, despite their nuclear tests in 1998, India and Pakistan still carefully deny that they have plans actually to build arsenals. Opacity is advantageous in that it augments the constraints on the size and complexity of arsenals: they are too hard to conceal if they are large and broadly dispersed. Ambiguity also has political advantages. By obscuring nonproliferation violations, opacity manages to affirm the nonproliferation system in the instance of its deficiency. Opacity also helps to reduce the regional turbulence that would otherwise attend proliferation; for instance, the fact that Israel's arsenal is opaque and somewhat "deniable" helps Arab moderates fend off hard-line agitation for reckless military responses to Israel's nuclear development.

Even when the global nonproliferation system fails to prevent nuclear proliferation from occurring, it nonetheless suppresses that proliferation in meaningful ways.

The greatest recent success of U.S. nonproliferation policy has been the rollback of de facto nuclear proliferation in the former Soviet Union. When the Soviet state collapsed, four nuclear-weapon states were suddenly created out of one. Since then, American financial and technical aid, and political mediation, have led Ukraine, Belarus, and Kazakhstan to surrender all their inherited weapons to the Russian Federation, thereby consolidating the former Soviet arsenal under a single authority and averting a legion of potential nuclear-control dangers. The existence of a global nonproliferation arrangement helped to ensure that the cash-poor, former Soviet republics did not sell their inherited weapons abroad. Thus, the momentum of cold-war nonproliferation policy helped officials in Washington navigate what was probably the first great challenge of post-cold-war nuclear security. If the system had not already been in place, a timely and effective response would have been all but impossible.

In general the success of U.S. nonproliferation policy can be discerned by asking what the world would look like were it not for Washington's efforts. U.S. nonproliferation policy has not always been perfectly effective, but its immense salutary influence is undeniable.

—JORDAN SENG, JOHN M. OLIN INSTITUTE FOR STRATEGIC STUDIES, HARVARD UNIVERSITY

Viewpoint:
No, U.S. nuclear-nonproliferation policy has not been successful because of inconsistent application and lax enforcement.

Official U.S. policy since 1945 has opposed the spread of nuclear weapons, but successive presidential administrations have displayed a wavering commitment to nuclear nonproliferation. Throughout the cold war and beyond, military and civilian nuclear technologies have spread with the direct assistance or tacit acceptance of the United States government. From the first attempts to control proliferation in 1946 to the present, American nonproliferation policy has been ineffective, at times even self-defeating, and has often been plagued by inconsistency and ignorance.

The status of the atomic bomb emerged as one of the first questions confronting American officials in the wake of the Second World War. In early 1946, after only two months of deliberation, a special State Department committee headed by Undersecretary of State Dean G. Acheson produced "A Report on the International Control of Atomic Energy" (commonly referred to as the Acheson-Lilienthal Report). The report recommended giving the authority to develop and regulate atomic technologies to an international Atomic Development Authority, which would be under United Nations Organization (UN) supervision. The new agency would construct laboratories for nuclear research throughout the world and would conduct inspections to ensure that states were not mounting clandestine efforts to produce nuclear weapons. Although on the surface it was a generous offer, the proposal would have allowed the United States to retain its atomic monopoly during an undefined transition period. Perhaps this obstacle could have been overcome during the negotiations in the UN Atomic Energy Commission, but President Harry S Truman's appointee as delegate to these meetings, Bernard M. Baruch, changed the plan to make it even more discriminatory toward other powers. Baruch placed the greatest emphasis on punishing violators of the agreement—in effect, making the UN Security Council an antiproliferation military alliance. He also insisted that the great-power veto be eliminated in nuclear matters and made it clear that the United States would not surrender its atomic monopoly until all other powers had demonstrated their compliance with American demands. The Soviet Union predictably rejected the U.S. offer and instead countered with its own, equally nonnegotiable, proposal, which would have required the United States to dismantle its nuclear program before other countries opened themselves to inspection.

Even before the Soviets blocked passage of the Baruch Plan, the U.S. Congress signaled that it had no intention of surrendering the U.S. atomic monopoly. With passage of the Atomic Energy Act of 1946, Congress created a special classification system for nuclear infor-

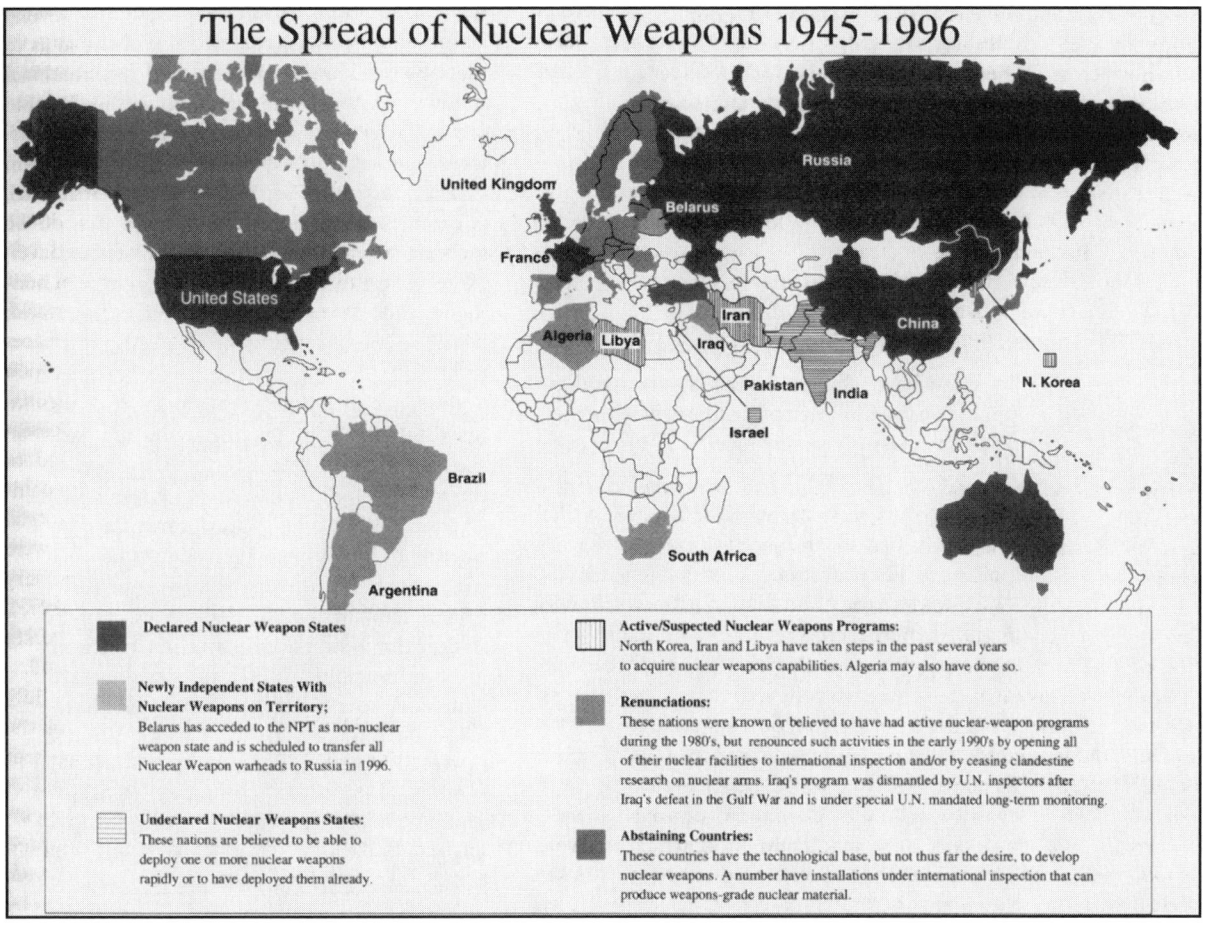

The Spread of Nuclear Weapons 1945-1996

Declared Nuclear Weapon States

Newly Independent States With Nuclear Weapons on Territory;
Belarus has acceded to the NPT as non-nuclear weapon state and is scheduled to transfer all Nuclear Weapon warheads to Russia in 1996.

Undeclared Nuclear Weapons States:
These nations are believed to be able to deploy one or more nuclear weapons rapidly or to have deployed them already.

Active/Suspected Nuclear Weapons Programs:
North Korea, Iran and Libya have taken steps in the past several years to acquire nuclear weapons capabilities. Algeria may also have done so.

Renunciations:
These nations were known or believed to have had active nuclear-weapon programs during the 1980's, but renounced such activities in the early 1990's by opening all of their nuclear facilities to international inspection and/or by ceasing clandestine research on nuclear arms. Iraq's program was dismantled by U.N. inspectors after Iraq's defeat in the Gulf War and is under special U.N. mandated long-term monitoring.

Abstaining Countries:
These countries have the technological base, but not thus far the desire, to develop nuclear weapons. A number have installations under international inspection that can produce weapons-grade nuclear material.

mation, restricted data, and denied even its wartime Manhattan Project partners, Great Britain and Canada, access to American nuclear technology. Together, the Baruch Plan and the Atomic Energy Act underlined the ignorance and arrogance of early U.S. nonproliferation policy. Prior to the Second World War, American physicists had lagged behind British, German, French, and even Soviet scientists in nuclear physics. The war had created turmoil in these countries and delayed their acquisition of nuclear weapons, but a careful scrutiny of the prewar record would have persuaded Truman and other policymakers that an American atomic monopoly could not be maintained for an extended period. Any illusions about the sanctity and duration of the American monopoly and the effectiveness of unilateral nonproliferation measures were quickly dispelled when the Soviet Union tested its first bomb in 1949 and Great Britain followed suit in 1952.

After assuming the presidency in 1953, Dwight D. Eisenhower publicly continued U.S. commitment to nonproliferation, but functionally he reversed course, especially in terms of American attitudes toward West European acquisition of nuclear weapons. Eisenhower accelerated proliferation through two sets of policies, Atoms for Peace and nuclear sharing. Atoms for Peace, put forward in 1953, pledged U.S. support for civilian nuclear-reactor research and development throughout the world. Nominally under inspection arrangements to prevent the diversion of uranium and plutonium to weapons purposes, this program actually spread nuclear technology and data to many countries, including India, Pakistan, and South Africa, which later used the information to develop military programs. Eisenhower had ignored the central principle of the Acheson–Lilienthal Report: that one could not separate the peaceful and military applications of nuclear development. Nuclear plowshares could always be recast as swords. On the military front the Eisenhower administration worked to amend the Atomic Energy Act to expand allied access to nuclear weapons. Congress resisted this effort, allowing only Great Britain to use restricted data, but Eisenhower merely modified his plans. The United States placed nuclear weapons in Europe using the "dual key" arrangement, under which host countries controlled and maintained the missiles while the United States retained ownership of the warheads. This arrangement proved more ruse than reality. According to Philip Nash, during one mis-

Since this map was prepared in 1996, India and Pakistan have tested nuclear devices

(Carnegie Endowment for International Peace)

NONPROLIFERATION

sile test in Great Britain, the U.S. officer holding the key could not be found, so a British officer substituted a screwdriver for the key and successfully launched the weapon.

A campaign for a nuclear-test-ban treaty emerged as a countervailing trend. In theory such a treaty could help to inhibit development of nuclear weapons by other powers. It needed to be comprehensive, however, and it had to be combined with other measures, such as a cutoff in fissionable-material production, to ensure its effectiveness. Eisenhower chose to emphasize the propaganda advantage of banning atmospheric tests rather than accentuating the possible nonproliferation effects of a comprehensive agreement.

Eisenhower bequeathed both his stalled test-ban proposal and NATO nuclear-sharing policy to his successor, John F. Kennedy. Nuclear sharing had failed to discourage France from developing its own nuclear-weapons capability, but for the next seven years the U.S. government believed that a multilateral nuclear force (MLF) might persuade West Germany from developing an independent nuclear capability. Given the Germans' role in both world wars, most Europeans opposed Bonn's access to nuclear weapons. The MLF proposal ultimately failed to win support within NATO or in the U.S. Congress and served only to delay conclusion of nuclear-arms-control agreements with the Soviets.

The two arms-control proposals that Kennedy and his successor, Lyndon B. Johnson, attempted to implement were a test-ban treaty and a nonproliferation agreement. Kennedy finally achieved a limited test-ban treaty in 1963, but it had little relevance for proliferation because it permitted underground nuclear testing. This loophole would allow near-nuclear, or "threshold," nations to develop limited nuclear arsenals. The Nuclear Non-Proliferation Treaty (NPT) finally came into being in 1968. Nonnuclear states criticized this agreement immediately as discriminatory because it left existing nuclear arsenals untouched while requiring nonnuclear signatories to abjure obtaining a possibly decisive class of weapons. Despite this sincere, if misguided, nonproliferation effort, during the Kennedy and Johnson administrations the Chinese acquired nuclear weapons, and Israeli and Indian nuclear programs were accelerated.

A retreat from the spirit of the nonproliferation treaty began almost immediately after Richard M. Nixon's inauguration. Both Nixon and Henry A. Kissinger, his national-security adviser, viewed the NPT as a moralistic endeavor divorced from the reality of power politics. Nations that desired and could afford nuclear weapons would produce them, they assumed. They feared that if Washington placed obstacles in their path, these countries might look to Moscow for support. Throughout its tenure, therefore, the Nixon administration ignored or downplayed proliferation threats and, instead, gave precedence to balance-of-power considerations. This dismissive attitude was reflected in the U.S. response to Israeli and South African nuclear efforts. Kissinger and Nixon went beyond tacit understanding of Israeli security needs and gave their full blessing to Tel Aviv's nuclear program. They did, however, stop short of providing direct aid. The president and his national-security adviser learned the consequences of this policy during the Yom Kippur War in October 1973, when Israel threatened to use nuclear bombs unless Washington furnished it with advanced conventional weapons to stave off an Arab offensive. In the case of South Africa, the Nixon administration continued to provide peaceful nuclear aid despite warnings from other powers that Pretoria harbored nuclear ambitions. In 1974 the United States expanded that aid, ignoring the South African government's own admission that it had achieved the capability to produce nuclear weapons. Nixon and Kissinger viewed nuclear-power production as a legitimate arena of cold-war conflict. They believed that refusing to give such aid to countries, even those harboring military ambitions, might give Moscow an advantage in the international nuclear trade. The consequences of economic maneuvering divorced from the considerations of proliferation surfaced in 1977, when American and Soviet intelligence detected a South African nuclear-test site in the Kalahari Desert. Under pressure from Washington and Moscow, the South Africans dismantled the site but continued its nuclear-weapons program. South Africa had produced six devices by the time President Nelson Mandela dismantled its program in 1993.

American inconsistency in proliferation matters was evident again in their handling of Indian efforts to obtain nuclear weapons. The Nixon administration looked at the South Asian subcontinent through the prism of the budding relationship between the United States and the People's Republic of China. Because Pakistan served as a go-between in the secret dialogue between Washington and Beijing in 1971, Kissinger and Nixon decided to "tilt" their support toward Pakistan in its ongoing rivalry with India. When war erupted in East Pakistan in 1971, Indian forces seemed on the verge of dealing the Pakistanis a crushing defeat. In the hope of preventing the complete disintegration of Pakistan, Nixon ordered the aircraft carrier USS *Enterprise* and its task force into the Bay of Bengal. The Indian government realized that the American warships could launch a nuclear assault and viewed Nixon's move as a clear insult and threat, especially given the long-standing demand by nonaligned states that the superpowers refrain from issuing nuclear threats in disputes with nonnuclear powers. Within the Indian government, a consensus grew to demonstrate the country's nuclear potential as a warning against future nuclear-gunboat diplomacy. The specter of imperialism, past and future, eventually provided the justification for an Indian "peaceful nuclear explosion" in May 1974. Pakistan, in turn, concluded that without nuclear weapons it would be vulnerable to future Indian attacks and initiated its own clandestine nuclear program in 1972.

In the 1970s several U.S. client states, including Taiwan, South Korea, and Iran, pushed forward with covert nuclear-weapons programs, concluding that they faced little, if any, opposition from Washington. U.S. attitudes, however, could change suddenly. While Nixon had not taken a clear stance on the Pakistani military nuclear program, his successors, Gerald R. Ford and Jimmy Carter, pressured Islamabad to suspend its weapons research, especially after rumors arose of a nuclear alliance between Pakistan and Libya. American officials feared the Arab nationalism and anti-Americanism of Libyan leader Mu'ammar Gadhafi, and his sponsorship of terrorism. The Pakistanis, however, resisted American efforts and grew angry that they had received such treatment while U.S.-Indian nuclear cooperation went forward undisturbed. The Carter administration realized that such an uneven approach to nonproliferation in South Asia would not work and switched from coercive tactics to seduction, hoping that generous conventional-weapons sales to Pakistan would persuade it to forego a nuclear option—a strategy that had failed when previous administrations had tried it with Israel. Even this inconsistent nonproliferation effort evaporated in the wake of the Soviet invasion of Afghanistan in 1979. Persuading the Indians and Pakistanis to support the U.S. stance became far more important to the Carter and Ronald W. Reagan administrations than did curbing regional arms races.

Amid the U.S. government's ever-shifting attitude toward various countries' nuclear programs, the United States did attempt to stem the transfer of reactor technology and nuclear fuel. Nixon and Kissinger wanted to use American dominance of the international nuclear trade as a check on nuclear programs that threatened U.S. interests. This "free-market" approach did not work, however, because French, West German, Swedish, and many European multinational corporations had eliminated the American advantage in peaceful nuclear technologies. If the United States refused to provide nuclear reactors, a rejected applicant could easily turn to a more-willing seller. The Indian nuclear explosion of 1974 delivered a clear blow to the unilateral market strategy because Canadian firms had provided the peaceful nuclear technology that the Indians later converted to military purposes. Any nonproliferation effort that used market mechanisms to curtail nuclear spread required the cooperation of all suppliers.

The need for a multilateral approach became even more apparent after West Germany sold Brazil uranium-enrichment facilities that could be adapted to either military or peaceful applications. Since the 1950s the United States had participated in and helped to organize meetings of the leading Western uranium suppliers. In light of the increasing proliferation threat, the Ford administration sought to formalize this arrangement through the creation of the London Suppliers' Group. This organization included all major nuclear exporters and worked to coordinate guidelines for technology and fuel transfers with the goal of reducing the negative effect of commercial competition on nonproliferation. The group specifically attempted to implement the strictest international safeguards for all nuclear-trade agreements. Carter strengthened this approach by codifying some of its recommendations via the passage of the domestic Nuclear Nonproliferation Act of 1978.

When Ronald W. Reagan launched a period of intensified cold-war competition with Moscow in 1981, he abandoned most American arms-control goals, including nonproliferation. Although his administration reaffirmed its commitment to export controls and the International Atomic Energy Agency (IAEA), Reagan made reestablishing the United States as a reliable supplier of nuclear technology and fuel the primary objective of the U.S. peaceful-nuclear-uses policy. In practice this new approach allowed many potential proliferators to sign bilateral-cooperation agreements with the United States. It also resulted in a Sino-American cooperation arrangement, despite Beijing's poor record in nonproliferation matters—including its aid to nuclear programs in South Africa, India, Pakistan, and Argentina. Reagan's laissez-faire approach allowed Argentina, Brazil, India, Iraq, and Pakistan to obtain large amounts of nuclear aid through covert arrangements with more advanced nuclear countries.

NONPROLIFERATION

The end of the cold war and the disintegration of the Soviet Union, however, helped give a new focus to U.S. nonproliferation policy. In the early 1990s President George H. W. Bush and Soviet premier Mikhail Gorbachev took important steps toward answering some of the near-nuclear states' demands regarding balanced nonproliferation obligations. The two leaders negotiated two Strategic Arms Reduction Treaties (START), which went beyond the earlier Strategic Arms Limitation Treaty (SALT), to commit the two superpowers to reducing their nuclear arsenals for the first time. Along with a more favorable climate for arms control, the end of the cold war also brought a greater sense of urgency to controlling proliferation threats in the Middle East and Asia. After the Persian Gulf War in 1991 the United States seemed more aware that nuclear proliferation existed even among states that had accepted the requirements of the NPT. Despite the status of Iraq as a nonnuclear-weapon state, under the leadership of Saddam Hussein it had clandestinely worked toward a nuclear-weapons program for more than a decade. As early as 1981 the Israeli government had feared such a development and bombed an Iraqi nuclear reactor at Osiraq, near Baghdad. The Reagan administration, however, had never curtailed U.S. nuclear aid to Iraq, nor had it pressured other governments to stop sending nuclear technology to Baghdad.

Instability within the former Soviet Union and the increasing potential for regional proliferation caused President William J. Clinton's administration to designate nonproliferation as "one of our nation's highest priorities." In his first term Clinton oversaw several major advances in U.S. nonproliferation policy. Important nonsignatories—including France, China, and Argentina—finally acceded to the NPT just prior to or shortly after Clinton's election. The Clinton administration also helped defuse potential proliferation crises in North Korea and the former Soviet republics. The United States led international attempts to renew the NPT indefinitely in 1995 and concluded the long-awaited Comprehensive Test Ban Treaty (CTBT) in 1996. Despite success on these fronts, however, the United States failed to win Indian or Pakistani approval of either treaty. In spring 1998 both South Asian countries decided to make their status as nuclear-weapon states official and conducted a series of underground nuclear tests. Although they promised to sign the CTBT, both nations refused to sign the NPT. The CTBT appears near death, having been ratified by only a handful of the forty-four states needed for it to

take effect. Overall, the Clinton administration has compiled a mixed record with several symbolic and substantive successes, but it has exhibited a tendency to repeat the mistakes and inconsistencies of past administrations. China and Israel have escaped criticism and sanctions, while Iran, Iraq, Pakistan, and India have not. This pattern reveals how little has changed since 1945.

–SHANE J. MADDOCK, U.S. COAST GUARD ACADEMY

References

Graham T. Allison, *Avoiding Nuclear Anarchy: Containing the Threat of Loose Russian Nuclear Weapons and Fissile Materials* (Cambridge, Mass.: MIT Press, 1996);

Avi Beker, *Disarmament without Order: The Politics of Disarmament at the United Nations* (Westport, Conn.: Greenwood Press, 1985);

Peter A. Clausen, *Nonproliferation and the National Interest* (New York: HarperCollins, 1993);

Zachary S. Davis and Benjamin Frankel, eds., *The Proliferation Puzzle: Why Nuclear Weapons Spread and What Results* (London & Portland, Ore.: Frank Cass, 1993);

Benjamin Frankel, ed., *Opaque Nuclear Proliferation: Methodological and Policy Implications* (London & Portland, Ore.: Frank Cass, 1991);

Michael T. Klare, *Rogue States and Nuclear Outlaws: America's Search for a New Foreign Policy* (New York: Hill & Wang, 1995);

Philip Nash, *The Other Missiles of October: Eisenhower, Kennedy, and the Jupiters, 1957–1963* (Chapel Hill: University of North Carolina Press, 1997);

Scott D. Sagan and Kenneth N. Waltz, *The Spread of Nuclear Weapons: A Debate* (New York: Norton, 1995);

Leonard S. Spector and Jacqueline R. Smith, *Nuclear Ambitions: The Spread of Nuclear Weapons, 1989–1990* (Boulder, Colo.: Westview Press, 1990);

Robert C. Williams and Philip L. Cantelon, eds., *The American Atom: A Documentary History of Nuclear Policies from the Discovery of Fission to the Present, 1939–1984* (Philadelphia: University of Pennsylvania Press, 1984).

NONPROLIFERATION

NUCLEAR DETERRENCE

Has nuclear-deterrence theory been a sound basis for policy?

Viewpoint: Yes, nuclear-deterrence policies have prevented major wars among the nuclear powers.

Viewpoint: No, nuclear deterrence risks nuclear holocaust.

During the first decade of the nuclear age nuclear weapons were thought of in traditional terms—as weapons that could be used effectively and decisively in war. The U.S. strategy of massive retaliation reflected this understanding. As long as the United States enjoyed nuclear monopoly, there were no reasons to consider nuclear weapons in any other way. The increasing size of the Soviet nuclear arsenal, however, and the development of ballistic missiles against which there was no defense, brought about a shift in U.S. thinking on the role of nuclear weapons. Beginning in the early 1960s, more and more civilian theorists and military planners came to believe that nuclear weapons were too destructive to be used effectively in war. Moreover, the punishment the other side would inflict on the initiator of a nuclear war would far outweigh the benefits of their use. This reality, many argued, should be enshrined in a doctrine that should govern the use of nuclear weapons: the role of nuclear weapons should be to deter war by holding out the prospect of a heavy and inescapable punishment against the initiator of a war. To bolster deterrence, the United States and the Soviet Union adopted similar policies, some as a result of mutual agreements, others on their own. The two sides built large and diverse arsenals, making most of their nuclear weapons invulnerable to a disarming first strike—thus ensuring that, regardless of who started a war, each side would have plenty of weapons with which to retaliate. The USSR and the United States also abstained from building defenses, each leaving its population vulnerable to the other's attack.

Supporters of nuclear deterrence argued that this measure was the only sane way to use nuclear weapons in support of the national interest. Critics of this "deterrence through mutual vulnerability" (or deterrence by punishment) posture did not agree. First, they argued, it was profoundly immoral to base U.S. security on the threat to annihilate hundreds of millions of innocent civilians. The task of the national leadership should be to devise ways to limit "collateral" damage and concentrate instead of attacking the military forces of the adversary. Second, it was the task of the national leadership to protect the American population, not to leave it completely exposed to enemy attacks. Third, the national leadership should, of course, try to avoid war, but, should war occur, these leaders should devise ways to prevail in the war; they should have a strategy that would leave the United States in a better position relative to the Soviet Union following a nuclear war. Critics of deterrence by punishment thus urged the adoption of "deterrence by denial," or "warfighting," nuclear strategy. This strategy called for using U.S. nuclear weapons to destroy the military capabilities of the adversary, limiting his ability to inflict damage on the United States and leaving him exposed to further punishment against his population should he refuse to back down. Supporters of warfighting strategy also supported efforts to build defenses against ballistic missiles, something to which the mutual-vulnerability school strenuously objected. There was also a fourth criticism leveled against mutual vulnerability. Critics pointed out that societal vulnerability, which helped maintain deterrence by punishment, also left these same societies utterly naked to accidental or unauthorized use of nuclear weapons. Because of their unprecedented destructiveness, these weapons bring into sharp relief questions about prudence, proportionality, effectiveness, and morality in war.

Viewpoint:
Yes, nuclear-deterrence theory has been a sound basis for policy because it has prevented major wars among the nuclear powers.

Whatever else might be said of nuclear-deterrence theory as a basis for foreign policy, it is possible to assert that it did not fail outright. The degree of its success might be contested but only within basically favorable parameters. After two world wars in the first half of the twentieth century, the advent of the atomic bomb began an era of great-power peace without precedent in modern history. There have been no shooting wars between major states since nuclear deterrence began. Nations that have relied on nuclear deterrence have avoided not only nuclear war but all war with each other. Nuclear deterrence correlates powerfully with peace, and on this observation alone one can make an exceptionally strong case that nuclear-deterrence theory has been a sound basis for policy. Nuclear-deterrence advocates could probably get away with saying little more in its defense.

Much more can be said, however. First, nuclear-deterrence policy provided the right conceptual framework for realizing the opportunity benefits of nuclear weapons. It seized on the revolution in destructive power they represented; it strengthened nuclear-war prevention over and against nuclear-war fighting; it illuminated the strategic value of mutual assured destruction (MAD), the reciprocal ability to devastate opposing societies to the point at which recovery became impossible; and it elicited cooperative stabilization of the cold war. Second, not only has nuclear-deterrence theory been a sound basis for policy, but other policy approaches would have been untenable.

Deterrence prevents war by threatening punishment that outweighs an enemy's potential gains from aggression. Deterrence theorists conceptualize this interaction using three fundamental terms. The first is a state's *capability* to inflict damage (for example, the quality of its deterrent weapons). The second is the *credibility* with which the state can make its

deterrent threat in the face of the enemy's retaliatory threat. To make one's deterrent threats credible, one wants to be perceived as caring enough about the issue at stake to run the risk of being counterattacked. The third crucial element is the amount of *benefit* the enemy thinks it will gain through its aggression. In formal terms, deterrence occurs when a state's capability to inflict punishment costs (C) is combined with a high probability that the capability will actually be used (p(C)), thereby exceeding the enemy's prospective benefits (B) and the probability with which it thinks it can win those benefits on the battlefield (p(B)). If $C \times p(C) > B \times p(B)$, then deterrence obtains. This essential deterrence model has been the basis for U.S. nuclear policy.

The use of deterrence theory as a basis for policy was the right conceptual choice for several reasons. First, nuclear-deterrence theory recognizes the potent synergy between deterrence and nuclear weapons. Nuclear bombs are inherently good deterrent weapons because they represent a quantum leap in destructive capability. Nuclear warheads create unprecedented certainty that the benefits of aggression cannot outweigh its costs—unless the nuclear deterrer chooses not to use its nuclear weapons. Thus, credibility becomes the salient issue, and warfare gets marginalized. Perhaps states can risk some wars against nuclear deterrers, but the more significant the war issues, the less likely war is to occur. If wars happen, they are restrained. To fight for total victories becomes too dangerous.

Second, given that nuclear weapons exist and will be applied somehow, deterrence theory provides the most stabilizing use framework. By embracing deterrence theory, early planners effectively chose to make nuclear weapons instruments for preventing wars rather than instruments for fighting them. It could have been different. Nuclear bombs could have been seen as nothing more than extensions of conventional forces—just especially big bombs to be used in the normal way. Some early American planners tended to think in such terms. Choosing nuclear deterrence, however, is different from choosing nuclear defense. Deterrence is based on the prospect of punishing an adversary for taking a certain action. Defense is about defeating an enemy

on the battlefield and thereby keeping it from accomplishing its goal. Deterrence prevents war by threats; defense wins wars with battles. Of course, the more horrible war figures to be, the more important it is to use deterrence to prevent it from happening. Nuclear war would be horrible. Accordingly, the choice to emphasize war prevention was powerfully important. Deterrence theory capitalized on the nuclear revolution in a way that made war less likely rather than making it more destructive. To be sure, American and Soviet planners incorporated some "defense thinking" into their nuclear postures—for example, counterforce weapons were defensive in that they were designed to limit an enemy's ability to inflict damage—but it was an addendum to their fundamentally deterrent stances. The bottom line is that nuclear-deterrence strategy made it unnecessary to fight a war for the sake of increasing security.

Third, nuclear-deterrence theory encouraged planners to *capitalize* on the inescapability of MAD in ways that reinforced stability. Once provisions for a secure second-strike capability were made, nuclear states had an impregnable basis for assured destruction.

States, however, could have reacted to MAD in different ways. A security concept centered on defense or war-fighting strategies might have driven them to find decisive tactical advantages at all costs, leading them toward desperate military gambits destined only to destroy and fail. Deterrence theory, however, is based on punishment capability rather than tactics. Recognizing mutual vulnerability as a foundation for stability, the theory led planners to make the most of it. Leaders could think in terms of security management rather than zero-sum security competition. Such thinking led to cooperative agreements, the 1972 Anti-Ballistic Missile (ABM) Treaty, and functional détente. By embracing the dynamics of inescapability, nuclear-deterrence theory encouraged helpful cooperation amid competition.

Perhaps nuclear-deterrence theory was not the only viable option. Were there policy alternatives that would have performed equally well or better over the past fifty years? Three possibilities come to mind.

First, cold-war nuclear states could have relied on a deterrence strategy that used purely conventional forces. Conventional weaponry has become increasingly destructive, and it

President John F. Kennedy, Secretary of Defense Robert S. McNamara, and General Thomas Power, head of the Strategic Air Command, watching an Atlas missile launch at Vandenberg Air Force Base in California

(CORBIS/Bettmann)

could provide impressive deterrent threats on its own. To say that nuclear states would opt for purely conventional strategies is to presume that they would have been willing to eliminate all their nuclear weapons. This possibility is impractical for several reasons, not the least of which is that former nuclear states retain their nuclear know-how and could secretly rebuild nuclear weapons to get the upper hand on conventional adversaries. In any case, conventional deterrence would not be as robust as nuclear deterrence. It would take a much larger and more perfectly delivered force to threaten massive levels of destruction with conventional warheads rather than nuclear weapons. Conventional deterrence would, therefore, have been more vulnerable to technological and tactical innovation than nuclear deterrence. Besides, history suggests that the prospect of even massive conventional devastation does not have the same deterrent effect as the prospect of nuclear holocaust. The amount of death and destruction the First World War brought to Europe was horrifying and unprecedented. It was called "the war to end all wars." Yet, twenty years later, Europe was not deterred from beginning the Second World War.

Second, nuclear states could have based their security policies around a strategy of conventional defense. For instance, America might have relied exclusively on conventional forces to protect its coastlines from invasion and to beat back Soviet armies in Europe. Again, this conventional strategy would have been difficult to execute under a nuclear shadow. Without total and robust nuclear disarmament, conventional forces would always be vulnerable to nuclear attack—unless nuclear attack were deterred by threat of nuclear reprisal. Conventional defense has played a large role in U.S. military strategy, but it could not stand alone without the backing threat of nuclear escalation.

A third alternative to reliance on nuclear weapons involves not jettisoning nuclear-deterrence theory but rather de-emphasizing it. Nuclear states might have chosen to anchor their security in conventional force, maintaining only a relative handful of nuclear weapons to reinforce their conventional capabilities. Nuclear deterrence would still have operated somewhat, but it would not have involved threats to annihilate societies completely. Nuclear deterrence theory would have been a complement to conventional strategy. In truth, it is hard to imagine that the presence of nuclear deterrence on any scale would not somehow become central to states' security thinking. It is just a matter of degrees.

This final alternative, however, underscores the most objectionable consequence of cold-war nuclear deterrence; namely, that it rested on the possibility of global holocaust. It is important to note, though, that the nuclear-deterrence model does not require the huge holocaust arsenals that the superpowers had. Damage capability merely needs to outweigh the benefits of aggression—threats to annihilate societies need not obtain. Indeed, the fact that the superpowers had such huge arsenals was more a function of their "defense thinking" (that is, their counterforce-weapons buildup) than their "deterrence thinking" (their assured-destruction requirements). It should be hoped that post-cold-war nuclear states will not find it necessary to maintain weapons in such mind-numbing numbers. Even if they do, however, nuclear-deterrence theory offers the best chance for maintaining their threat peacefully.

Though the spread of nuclear weapons has been slow, it does proceed. American efforts to prevent Iraq from getting the nuclear bomb are problematic. Iran is reportedly within a decade or less of developing its nuclear weapon. India and Pakistan have tested nuclear weapons openly after years of secretive development. Israel is an undeclared nuclear proliferator. If anything, the growing number of nuclear states means that nuclear-deterrence theory is growing in importance. Wherever nuclear weapons materialize, one would prefer planners to opt for deterrence theory: to embrace the deterrent value of nuclear weapons, to emphasize war prevention over war fighting, and to think of security management instead of zero-sum security competition. One would like to see duplication of the cold-war nuclear-deterrent success.

—JORDAN SENG, JOHN M. OLIN INSTITUTE FOR STRATEGIC STUDIES

Viewpoint:
No, nuclear deterrence risks nuclear holocaust.

To deter means to prevent an attack by making clear to one's adversary that it stands to lose more than it gains by an aggression. Until the twentieth century, deterrence required convincing an aggressor that the forces of its target could vanquish its military in battle. With the advent of long-range air power and nuclear weapons, a tempting new possibility emerged. One could base deterrence on a threat to destroy the attacker's cities without defeat-

GLOSSARY OF NUCLEAR-WEAPONS TERMS

Antiballistic missile (ABM): A weapon system designed to protect a country's population centers or military installations by knocking down incoming nuclear warheads or the delivery vehicles (intercontinental ballistic missiles [ICBMs] or sea-launched ballistic missiles [SLBMs]) that carry them. Most forms of ballistic-missile defense were prohibited by the 1972 Anti-Ballistic Missile (ABM) Treaty.

Ballistic missile: A rocket capable of carrying a single or several conventional or nonconventional warheads. Ballistic missiles may be grouped by range: intercontinental ballistic missiles (ICBMs), with a range exceeding 6,000 miles (10,000 km); intermediate-range ballistic missiles (IRBMs), with a range between 2,000 miles (3,340 km) and 6,000 miles (10,000 km); medium-range ballistic missiles (MRBMs), with a range between 1,000 miles (1,670 km) and 2,000 miles (3,340 km); and short-range ballistic missiles (SRBMs), with a range under 1,000 miles (1,670 km). They may also be grouped by method of launch (land-based ballistic missiles; sea-launched ballistic missiles [SLBMs]; or air-launched ballistic missiles [ALBMs]); by their payload capacity (light, medium, or heavy); or by their fuel type (liquid or solid). Ballistic missiles carrying more than a single warhead are called MIRVed missiles (for multiple independently targeted reentry vehicles).

Cruise missile: Initially a low-flying, pilotless, jet-propelled aircraft (such as the German Second World War V-1 and V-2 rockets) designed to deliver conventional or nuclear munitions. The first models were controlled by internal or radio-command guidance. In the mid 1970s the United States began to build cruise missiles with miniaturized jet engines capable of carrying heavy payloads with great accuracy. The air-launched cruise missile (ALCM) and the Tomahawk sea-launched cruise missile (SLCM) are now equipped with terrain comparison and matching guidance (TERCOM). The TERCOM system consists of an onboard radar that scans the terrain over which the missile cruises on its way to its target, then feeds that information to an onboard computer that compares the radar information to a digitized terrain map stored in the guidance computer's memory. The comparison is fed to the missile's inertial guidance unit, enabling the missile to achieve unparalleled accuracy. Missile accuracy is measured in CEP (circular error probable), which is the radius of a circle centered on the target, within which half of all weapons aimed at the target are expected to fall (that is, the median inaccuracy). The CEP of the Tomahawk SLCM is under ten meters.

Intermediate-range ballistic missile (IRBM): Any land-based missile with a range between 2,000 miles (3,340 km) and 6,000 miles (10,000 km). The United States and the Soviet Union have deployed such systems in Europe since the 1950s. These systems are also the mainstay of the French and Chinese nuclear arsenals. The first generation of IRBMs were liquid-fuel missiles, such as the American Thor and Jupiter. The United States largely abandoned IRBMs until the early 1980s, when it developed the Pershing II medium-range ballistic missile (MRBM) and the Tomahawk ground-launched cruise missile (GLCM). In the early 1970s the Soviet Union introduced its first solid-fuel IRBM, the SS-16, and in the late 1970s it began production of the SS-20s, which carried three 500 kt nuclear warheads each. By 1988 more than nine hundred SS-20s were built. In response, the United States and NATO deployed long-range intermediate nuclear forces (LRINF), comprising 108 Pershing IIs and 464 Tomahawks. The Intermediate Nuclear Forces (INF) Treaty of December 1987 mandates the dismantling of all LRINF systems, including the SS-20s, and prohibits the development of new American IRBMs.

Long-range intermediate nuclear forces (LRINF), also called intermediate nuclear forces (INF): Delivery systems for nuclear weapons (ballistic missiles, cruise missiles, aircraft) with a range between 500 miles (835 km) and 1,500 miles (2,505 km). According to the December 1987 Intermediate Nuclear Forces (INF) Treaty, all INF-range ballistic missiles and ground-launched cruise missiles were to be eliminated from the inventories of the United States and the Soviet Union.

Reentry vehicle: The vehicle (or encasing) that contains the warhead (nuclear or otherwise) atop a ballistic missile. The aerodynamically designed reentry vehicle shields the warhead from heat during the warhead's reentry into the atmosphere and provides for a stable and predictable trajectory to the intended target. Current warheads are designed to fall freely onto their targets after reaching their trajectory in the atmosphere; both the United States and the Soviet Union have also tested warheads with maneuvering capability. A maneuvering reentry vehicle (MaRV) is equipped with its own attitude-control thrusters or aerodynamic control surfaces, and onboard guidance, enabling it to correct targeting mistakes or evade ballistic missiles.

Strategic Defense Initiative (SDI): A proposal by President Ronald Reagan in March 1983 for the United States to develop a defensive system to make nuclear weapons "impotent and obsolete." The system, commonly referred to as "Star Wars," was envisioned to rely partly on installations in space capable of destroying incoming ICBMs and warheads by both laser beams and kinetic-energy weapons.

ing the enemy's armed forces first. That is, a nation could try to immobilize an aggressive state by holding its population hostage. Debates about the merits of "nuclear deterrence" generally refer to this idea of preserving peace by threats to punish the civilians of an aggressor state.

This debate had two historical phases during the cold war. In the first phase, nuclear deterrence seemed attractive to American presidents because of U.S. nuclear superiority. The second phase began after a Soviet nuclear buildup made clear that the Soviet Union could absorb an American "first strike" and still retain the ability to retaliate and destroy American cities. This condition of mutual deterrence, labeled "mutual assured destruction" (MAD), became—and remains—the basis for U.S.-Russian nuclear-arms control.

The arguments on behalf of nuclear deterrence have changed over time in a succession of three bad decisions: to adopt nuclear deterrence, to preserve it even after both sides had achieved the ability to destroy one another, and finally (a "nondecision") to preserve MAD capabilities long after cold-war rationales for relying on mass-destruction threats had faded into history.

After nuclear weapons were used against Hiroshima and Nagasaki in 1945, many hoped and believed that the United States would take the lead in averting a nuclear-arms race. Yet, as the cold war deepened in the late 1940s and early 1950s, U.S. decisionmakers abandoned any consideration of proposals for superpower negotiations—whether the aim was complete nuclear disarmament, limitations on testing and deployment of offensive nuclear weapons, or a bilateral agreement to emphasize homeland defense.

Contrary to claims that the United States rejected such arms-control alternatives as impractical, the real reason for the U.S. nuclear buildup was that nuclear threats seemed like a good way to prevent communist employment of conventional forces in Europe or Asia. The reasoning was that nuclear weapons were cheaper than conventional forces, and that U.S. nuclear superiority would make American threats highly credible. In a 1954 policy that came to be known as "massive retaliation," the United States essentially threatened to annihilate the Soviet people (and perhaps those of China and eastern Europe as well) in response to a range of unspecified provocations. Since then the United States has retained the option of using nuclear weapons first.

Unfortunately, the original U.S. rationale for relying on nuclear deterrence was badly flawed. Soviet leaders, facing the "ultimate weapon" in the hands of their enemy, were compelled to counter American nuclear superiority with their own nuclear buildup. In rejecting arms control, the Eisenhower administration conveniently overlooked the point made by J. Robert Oppenheimer (and many others) that, no matter how many bombs the United States was making, the "Soviet Union may fairly soon have enough to threaten the destruction of our whole society . . . beyond a certain point we cannot ward off the Soviet threat merely by 'keeping ahead of the Russians.'"

As the Soviet Union pursued its own nuclear buildup, three unintended consequences of U.S. reliance on nuclear deterrence emerged. First, as critics had predicted, the U.S. homeland soon became vulnerable to devastating attack for the first time in its history. Second, American vulnerability cast grave doubt on the original objective of the nuclear buildup: the threat of nuclear retaliation for provocations other than direct attacks on the United States. Was it really believable, asked skeptical Europeans, that the United States would be willing "to lose Washington in order to save Paris?" Finally, as a result of declining faith in the ability of nuclear threats to deter conventional aggression, the United States found itself investing more and more money in conventional forces, in addition to having to continue the ongoing competition in nuclear weapons. Despite the short-sighted optimism of their early proponents, nuclear weapons had failed to provide "more bang for the buck."

In the absence of any serious efforts at arms control the superpowers quickly developed thermonuclear weapons (which dwarfed the destructive potential of the original atomic bombs) and intercontinental ballistic missiles (ICBMs) that could reach their targets in minutes. These new developments gave American and Russian leaders the power to end human civilization at any moment, in less than an hour's time. In the midst of that terrifying arms race the 1962 Cuban Missile Crisis brought the world to the brink of nuclear war.

Undaunted by that episode—in which an apocalypse was averted only by a combination of frantic improvisation and considerable luck—the superpowers intensified their nuclear-arms competition. Making nuclear deterrence fully credible, each reasoned, required achieving an ability to wage and win a nuclear war. The superpowers poured billions of dollars into developing highly accurate missiles with multiple warheads (MIRVs) that could limit retaliatory damage by destroying the enemy's missiles before they could be launched. More billions were spent on developing antiballistic missile defenses (ABMs), despite the obvious fact that either side could overwhelm any defense by expanding its inventory of offensive nuclear missiles.

By 1967, after five more years of frantic building, Secretary of Defense Robert S. McNamara finally realized that it was impossible for either side to achieve nuclear superiority over the other. One might think that this insight would have prompted negotiations designed to end reliance on nuclear deterrence and to dismantle what had become a balance of terror. Instead, McNamara argued that the unintended result of the U.S. nuclear buildup—that is, the mutual vulnerability of both superpowers to a holocaust no matter who struck first—was in fact the perfect solution to the nuclear danger. In a 1967 speech, McNamara made his first public appeal for permanent United States and Soviet reliance on nuclear threats as a means to avert all-out war. He began by claiming that the prospective death of billions from nuclear war was not attributable to the folly of statesmen, but instead to an autonomous force known as "technology," which, he explained, "has now circumscribed us all with a horizon of horror that could dwarf any catastrophe that has befallen man in his more than a million years on earth . . . , and if man is to have any future at all, it will have to be one overshadowed with the permanent possibility of thermonuclear holocaust." To address that danger McNamara offered the theory—and policy—of nuclear deterrence: "we must be able to absorb the total weight of nuclear attack on our country . . . and still be capable of damaging the aggressor to the point that his society would be simply no longer viable in twentieth century terms. That is what deterrence of nuclear aggression means."

McNamara proposed what he called "a reasonably riskless agreement" premised on Soviet acceptance of the same doctrine. That nuclear relationship, later known as MAD, became the basis for the first superpower strategic-arms-control agreements in 1972. As the cold war fades into history, MAD capabilities remain intact, and the United States has never seriously pursued any alternative approach to nuclear danger.

Even if Americans excuse the short-sighted conclusion that the Red Army threat to Europe or Asia once justified building "assured destruction" capabilities, should they not expect their leaders to regard the disappearance of that threat as an opportunity to dismantle the cold-war doomsday machine? However strange it might seem, most politi-

cians and nuclear-policy experts do not regard MAD as a pressing problem—or in fact as a problem at all. Instead, nuclear-deterrence theory is so highly regarded that some scholars in the field deem it wise to encourage other states facing real or potential rivals (for example, Japan, Germany, India, Pakistan, and Ukraine) to build up their own capabilities for MAD. These proponents of nuclear proliferation, one should concede, at least have the courage of their convictions.

Every defense of MAD can be reduced to two words: "it works." That assertion is in part based on the fact that the world has survived the first half century of the nuclear age without a nuclear war. In response one must point out that we have no way of knowing if nuclear threats were the reason we have not had a Third World War, or whether the terror they inspired increased the intensity of the cold war. Yet, from what they regard as a successful experiment (whose subject was the entire human species), the defenders of MAD draw the conclusion that we can always expect even the most reckless leaders to exert a bare minimum of caution and refrain from any aggression that might trigger nuclear retaliation.

If this assumption were 100 percent reliable, one might indeed concede many virtues to nuclear-deterrence theory. For example, it is arguably not immoral to threaten tens of millions of innocents if no one will ever carry out the threat. "We threaten evil," says Michael Walzer in support of nuclear deterrence, "in order not to do it." Nuclear deterrence, it follows, is not only morally defensible but also highly desirable from a practical standpoint, since in the absence of any danger of failure, nuclear deterrence should provide the best possible solution to national-security planning, allowing a state to save billions on defense once it has enough nuclear weapons to assure an enemy's destruction. Best of all, nuclear deterrence, if reproduced globally, would ensure a permanent peace. "Safety," as British prime minister Winston Churchill elegantly put in 1955, would forever be "the sturdy child of terror." Nuclear war, and perhaps all war, would no longer be a cause for concern.

Unfortunately, there is no justification for the decisive level of optimism required to rely indefinitely on nuclear deterrence. Those who regard the risks as tolerable are guilty of a variety of errors: a questionable interpretation of historical experience with nuclear weapons, a simplistic understanding of human motivation, and an underestimation of the dangers of technical or human failure in highly complex systems.

Short of a catastrophe that disconfirms the benign expectations of nuclear-deterrence proponents, we have insufficient knowledge regarding the probability of nuclear use. It would be prudent to recognize that we are far from understanding why two societies spent decades feverishly building tens of thousands of nuclear weapons, all the while actively contemplating their use, despite compelling evidence that one accident or error in judgment could destroy civilization.

Case studies have challenged the deterrence-theory assumption that decision making always entails the rational calculation of prospective gains and losses. Applying experimental research in cognitive and depth psychology to analyses of conventional deterrence failures, these studies document how—particularly in stressful circumstances—assessments of prospective costs and risks may be highly distorted or even irrelevant to a decision. Attachment to goals can create wishful thinking, leading decisionmakers to dismiss or misinterpret credible warnings and generally to exaggerate their chances of success. Moreover, psychologically important values (for example, a need not to appear weak or a sense of national honor) may outweigh rational calculations of consequences. Thus, interstate wars, as well as rebellions by ethnic, religious, or national minorities, have been initiated with little or no hope of success and with a high probability of catastrophe, and violent resistance has been sustained long after total defeat was certain. These tendencies should give pause to those who assume that a mixture of prudence and fear will always prove sufficient to deter a highly motivated adversary.

There is also an organizational dimension that, in the case of nuclear weapons, further exacerbates the well-documented propensity of humans to act irrationally. Nuclear forces are embedded in highly complex systems, placing a premium on rapid and perfectly reliable detection of attack and on complex safeguards against accidental or unauthorized launch. The historical record of close calls (for example, false warnings of a nuclear attack) and the general finding that complex systems are prone to catastrophic failure suggest that faith in nuclear-weapons technologies may not be warranted. Finally, even if we assume it is possible to attain a high degree of competence in safely controlling nuclear weapons, no state can permanently guarantee its ability to prevent unauthorized, mistaken, or accidental launches. Russia, which has kept most of its cold-war nuclear arsenal intact, has the potential of becoming the first nuclear power to decline to the point of losing control over its weapons of mass destruction.

It is the ineradicable—and immeasurable—risk of deterrence failure that makes MAD immoral. Millions, even hundreds of millions, of innocent people could die as a result of the appeal of this "theory." Moreover, that real possibility has practical consequences, as military establishments and political leaders have repeatedly resisted accepting the total vulnerability of their societies called for by the doctrine of MAD. MAD theorists have consistently erred in their expectation that policymakers will resign themselves to the doctrine, especially since it promises that one can purchase national security cheaply (that is, simply by maintaining a nuclear arsenal of a few hundred weapons, rather than large standing military forces). Instead of saving money, however, following this doctrine—after a half-century of maintaining "assured destruction" capabilities against Russia and China, as well as fruitless efforts to build "damage limitation" weapons that could undermine Russia's "assured destruction" threat and thereby reestablish U.S. nuclear superiority—had cost the United States approximately 5.5 trillion dollars by 1998.

Perhaps it will one day dawn on the political leaders of nuclear states that even a minimal commitment to humanity dictates cooperation in reducing mass-destruction capabilities to as far below capacities for "assured destruction" as human ingenuity and ironclad inspection regimes permit. Such former nuclear "hawks" as Fred Iklé, deputy defense secretary in the Reagan administration and General George Lee Butler, former head of the Strategic Air Command, have agreed that nuclear disarmament is vital to the future of human civilization. These voices of responsibility give the lie to claims that MAD is either a necessary or inescapable component of national-security policy.

MAD doctrine assumes the preservation of deterrence for an eternity of rational leaders and stable societies and of freedom from accident and miscalculation. We need not dwell on case studies of psychopathic rulers, or of descents into "wars nobody wanted," to prove that nuclear deterrence is fatally flawed as theory and policy. Now that the conflict that justified reliance on nuclear threats has ended, MAD must give way to a safer arrangement for securing peace. There is no justification for insisting that a strong national defense, including deterrence against attack, requires the permanent capacity to unleash a nuclear holocaust.

—DAVID GOLDFISCHER, UNIVERSITY
OF DENVER

References

Bernard Brodie, *Strategy in the Missile Age* (Princeton, N.J.: Princeton University Press, 1959);

Freeman Dyson, *Weapons and Hope* (New York: Harper & Row, 1984);

Charles L. Glaser, *Analyzing Strategic Nuclear Policy* (Princeton, N.J.: Princeton University Press, 1990);

NUCLEAR DETERRENCE

David Goldfischer, *The Best Defense: Policy Alternatives for U.S. Nuclear Security from the 1950s to the 1990s* (Ithaca, N.Y.: Cornell University Press, 1993);

Gregory S. Kavka, *Moral Paradoxes of Nuclear Deterrence* (New York: Cambridge University Press, 1987);

James H. Lebovic, *Deadly Dilemmas: Deterrence in U.S. Nuclear Strategy* (New York: Columbia University Press, 1990);

Steven P. Lee, *Morality, Prudence, and Nuclear Weapons* (Cambridge & New York: Cambridge University Press, 1993);

Robert S. McNamara, *The Essence of Security: Reflections in Office* (New York: Harper & Row, 1968);

J. Robert Oppenheimer and others, "Report by the Panel of Consultants of the Department of State to the Secretary of State: Armaments and American Policy," January 1953, *Foreign Relations of the United States, 1952–1954,* volume 2, *National Security Affairs* (Washington, D.C.: U.S. Government Printing Office, 1984);

Edward Rhodes, *Power and Madness: the Logic of Nuclear Coercion* (New York: Columbia University Press, 1989).

Scott D. Sagan, *The Limits of Safety: Organizations, Accidents, and Nuclear Weapons* (Princeton, N.J.: Princeton University Press, 1993);

Sagan and Kenneth N. Waltz, *The Spread of Nuclear Weapons: A Debate* (New York: Norton, 1995);

Thomas C. Schelling, *Arms and Influence* (New Haven: Yale University Press, 1966);

Stephen I. Schwartz, ed., *Atomic Audit: The Costs and Consequences of U.S. Nuclear Weapons since 1940* (Washington, D.C.: Brookings Institution Press, 1998);

Glenn Snyder, *Deterrence and Defense: Toward a Theory of National Security* (Princeton, N.J.: Princeton University Press, 1961);

Paul C. Stern, and others, eds., *Perspectives on Deterrence* (New York: Oxford University Press, 1989);

Michael Walzer, *Just and Unjust Wars: A Moral Argument with Historical Illustrations,* second edition (New York: Basic Books, 1992).

NUCLEAR DETERRENCE

NUCLEAR PREEMPTION

Was the United States correct in not trying to preempt the nascent Soviet nuclear arsenal?

Viewpoint: Yes, trying to destroy the Soviet nuclear arsenal would have been imprudent and immoral.

Viewpoint: No, the United States should have attacked the Soviet nuclear arsenal to slow the Russians' nuclear-weapons development.

When the Soviet Union detonated its first atomic device in 1949, American strategic planners were surprised. They had not expected the Soviets to reach that point for several more years. In the development of their atomic-weapons program the Soviets had spurned no means to reach their aim. Documentary evidence proves that, in addition to using kidnapped German scientists and slave labor from Soviet prison camps, Moscow employed a vast spy network to obtain Western nuclear technology.

Once the Soviets had constructed a nuclear device, the United States lost its monopoly on nuclear energy and on the coercive power of atomic weapons. Despite this much-publicized event the American government did nothing to preempt the emergence of the Soviet Union as a nuclear power. U.S. intelligence operations were designed more to assess what capabilities the Soviets had than to look for ways to disrupt their strategic-weapons program.

Largely because of its espionage operations, Soviet technological advances allowed the USSR to develop the vastly more powerful hydrogen bomb before the United States. In 1957 the Soviets launched an experimental intercontinental ballistic missile, which was followed in short order by the rocket-based deployment of Sputnik, the first man-made satellite to orbit the Earth. For a time American strategic planners feared that a strategic-weapons "gap" would open between the superpowers and leave the United States at a disadvantage.

Viewpoint:
Yes, trying to destroy the Soviet nuclear arsenal would have been imprudent and immoral.

In the late 1940s and early 1950s it was well within the margins of acceptable debate to endorse an unprovoked nuclear strike against the Soviet Union or to use the threat of such an attack to compel some ver-sion of Soviet surrender in the cold war. The American nuclear monopoly, and after 1949 the decisive U.S. nuclear advantage, made the idea seem at least plausibly realistic. The day when the Soviets could retaliate and destroy American cities was quickly approaching, it was argued, after which the chance to defeat them would be gone forever. If war were inevitable, and if each passing day increased the possible damage to one's own country and people, did not both prudence and morality demand that one strike the first blow?

Fortunately, that position was rejected by the two American presidents—Harry S Truman and Dwight D. Eisenhower—who commanded American nuclear forces during the period when America's nuclear advantage made preventive war thinkable. Their self-restraint (despite occasional temptation) avoided an act that would surely have been regarded as one of history's supreme cases of madness, evil, and sheer folly.

The call for preventive war against the Soviet Union actually predated the nuclear age, as General George S. Patton proposed in 1945 to rearm the newly defeated German army and march against Russia. "We are going to have to fight them sooner or later," he reasoned, so "why not do it now?" Proposed at the moment of victory over Adolf Hitler's Germany by the U.S.-Soviet wartime alliance, Patton's argument seemed totally outlandish. Within a few short years, however, the onset of the nuclear age and the cold war had combined to popularize the idea of starting a war with Russia.

Some early advocates of preventive war gave little attention to any specific threat posed by the Soviet leadership or political system and argued instead for war as the ultimate means of preserving the U.S. nuclear monopoly—which presumably meant that any prospective nuclear power would be a candidate for attack. Manhattan Project commander General Leslie Richard Groves, chairman of the Joint Committee on Atomic Energy Senator Brien McMahon (D-Connecticut), and the philosopher Bertrand Russell each argued that a nuclear-arms race imposed intolerable dangers for the entire world. Therefore, if the Soviet Union refused an ultimatum to disarm, a war should be launched with the minimal aim of crippling Moscow's ability to develop nuclear weapons.

For most advocates of preventive war, however, it was the particular evil—and danger—represented by Soviet communism that provided the decisive justification for war. Here the envisioned attack would have to go far beyond mere destruction of the adversary's capability to develop and deploy nuclear weapons. Thus, William Christian Bullitt, the first U.S. ambassador to the Soviet Union, proposed in 1946 an ultimatum in which the Soviets would be told to give up their planned "conquest of the earth for communism." If that failed, "the United States should annihilate the U.S.S.R." It was only a short step to putting that argument in the language of morality. In a U.S. Air Force publication scholar Bret J. Cillesen found a 1947 article by the British second-in-command of the wartime Royal Air Force (RAF), Air Marshall Sir Robert Saundby, that maintained the West

The first Soviet atomic-bomb test, 29 August 1949

should "embrace the higher morality that bids us to take advantage of [atomic weapons] to abolish the new slavery and exorcise from the world the evil ideology that threatens twentieth-century humanity."

Two factors ensured that this kind of reasoning would go beyond mere loose talk and enter the inner sanctums of U.S. nuclear policy making. The first was the formation of the U.S. Air Force as an independent branch of the armed services, and the second was the mounting frustration at what appeared to be relentless Soviet challenges to Western interests. The air force came into existence imbued with the notion that strategic bombing would provide the key to victory in any future war. Particularly with the advent of nuclear weapons in the hands of the Soviet Union, applying that doctrine increasingly seemed to require striking the first blow—in a way that crippled the enemy's ability to retaliate and destroyed its capacity to wage a sustained war. From 1947 until 1953, elements in the air force lobbied for preventive war with the Soviet Union, making their case by means of classified studies (such as "Project Control"), public appeals by individuals in leadership positions, and private advice to presidents—as exemplified by air force chief of staff General Hoyt Sanford Vandenberg's 1950 effort to persuade Truman to start a war with Russia.

The inevitability of a final showdown seemed to gain credence with a series of apparent communist provocations between 1948 and 1950: the seizure of control in Czechoslovakia, the Berlin blockade, the first Soviet atomic test, the "fall" of China, and the invasion of South Korea by the North Koreans. Truman and then Eisenhower found themselves contemplating a future that seemed to include both the forceful expansion of world communism and the steady growth of the Soviet nuclear stockpile. When a 1953 air force study on "The Coming National Crisis" predicted a "militarily unmanageable" position for the United States, Eisenhower considered the implications: "if the contest to maintain this relative position should have to continue indefinitely, the cost would either drive us to war—or into some form of dictatorial government. In such circumstances we would be forced to consider whether or not our duty to future generations did not require us to initiate war at the most propitious moment we could designate."

Such speculation notwithstanding, Truman and Eisenhower both decisively rejected the option of starting a war with the Soviet Union. Given their ultimate responsibility, it was perhaps easier for them to recognize the disastrous consequences of such a reckless act. Those consequences can be divided into three related dimensions: strategic, political, and moral.

In strategic terms sober thinkers understood that using the American nuclear advantage did not necessarily translate into a desirable military outcome. First, during the years of the American nuclear monopoly (until 1949), the U.S. lacked the atomic power to launch a crippling blow. Available maps of the Soviet Union were inaccurate and incomplete, making it questionable whether bombers could find some of the most critical targets, such as military bases and oil-storage facilities. Moreover, the thirty nuclear-capable bombers the United States had by the end of 1948 would have faced heavy Soviet anti-aircraft capabilities. To increase their chances planners envisioned striking under cover of darkness and bad weather. While attacks against Soviet urban areas might have killed hundreds of thousands, it had to be assumed that the Soviet war machine would not be decisively weakened. That meant one had to anticipate a rapid Soviet invasion of Western Europe, after which the populations of such cities as Paris, Brussels, and Rome would be held hostage against further attacks by the U.S. Air Force against the Soviet population. Advocates of preventive war had nothing to say about that possibility.

By the time rapid growth of the U.S. nuclear stockpile in the early 1950s made a crippling strike more feasible, a new problem had arisen: the Soviets possessed their own nuclear weapons. Now a president contemplating a first strike had to assume nuclear retaliation, weighing what sort of victory celebration might follow the nuclear devastation of Washington, New York, and other American cities. While good luck (and limited Soviet bomber capabilities) might have averted that outcome, its plausibility made war a poor bet for any president, who after all would be held forever accountable for guessing wrong. In short, the United States went quickly from having too little nuclear firepower to prevent a long war, including the likely Soviet occupation of Western Europe, to a period of steady growth in the Soviet potential for atomic retaliation. Once thermonuclear weapons—first tested by the Soviets in August 1953—entered their arsenal, single bombs would be able to obliterate major cities. At that point, as the movie *Dr. Strangelove* (1963) evoked so effectively, calls for "preventive war" began to warrant accusations of madness.

Even if one imagined a genuine "window of opportunity" in which the United States could have defeated the Soviet Union while remaining unscathed, the strategic challenge would have remained truly daunting. Eisenhower recognized the problem, asking: "What do you do with the world after you have won victory in such a catastrophic nuclear war?" His own answer was that "the colossal job of occupying the territories of the defeated enemy would be far beyond the resources of the United States at the end of such a war."

That answer, while accurate as far as it goes, does not begin to capture the scope or scale of possible horror that could have been unleashed by a surprise nuclear attack on Russia. Here, it is worth citing the eloquent depiction by cold-war historian Louis Halle: "Perhaps the whole fabric of world order, such as it was, would have cracked and crumbled. The shock of horror at the scenes of piled-up death in the Russian cities, the collapse of the Russian state . . . the sudden vacuum of power and authority over half the world—one felt instinctively that these possible consequences, with their implications, would immediately make the situation of human civilization everywhere, not excepting the United States, desperate."

Did Halle exaggerate the likely political consequences within the United States? One must begin by noting that it is virtually unimaginable that either Truman or Eisenhower would have asked Congress for a declaration of war on Russia absent a far graver provocation than offered by any of the actual early cold-war crises. Had either done so, efforts to envision the consequences must recognize that American society was already under great stress in the early 1950s, as the anticommunist hysteria unleashed by Senator Joseph R. McCarthy (R-

Wisconsin) challenged the premise of open and peaceful political debate. Pouring fuel onto already inflamed passions on both sides of that debate with a plan for slaughtering defenseless Russian civilians in peacetime might well have torn the country apart. When asked in a 1954 Gallup poll whether America "should go to war now while we still have the advantage in atomic and hydrogen weapons," only 13 percent of Americans supported the idea. Any presidential effort to generate nuclear-war fever would have met bitter resistance.

Since any sane president would have realized in advance that Congress would surely bow to such overwhelming antiwar sentiment on so fateful a question, prospects for preventive war would have depended on a presidential decision to launch war without consulting Congress and the American people. Had a war-obsessed president decided to bypass Congress—and had his orders to attack the Soviet Union been obeyed—the rage and revulsion of the American people might well have destroyed the authority of the U.S. government. Given these daunting obstacles, it is not surprising that even the notoriously trigger-happy commander of the Strategic Air Command, General Curtis E. LeMay, conceded in 1949 that "as a democracy we are not prepared to wage preventive war."

These political implications of preventive war are inextricably rooted in the moral dimension of the debate. Those making the case for preventive war appealed to the need, as Groves put it, to be "ruthlessly realistic." It was on this premise of realism that the noted Harvard political scientist Walter Burns (a devotee of the so-called realist school of international relations) based his 1949 moral argument for preventive war: "If there is good reason to believe that a sudden massive armed blow would . . . as compared with waiting for such a blow from the enemy . . . , result in less destruction and social disintegration, give a better chance for building a workable world polity, then to strike such a blow, far from being morally wrong, is morally obligatory."

The terrible flaw in that argument flows directly from its wild and irresponsible unrealism. On what basis, one wonders, were the preventive war advocates assuming that war between the United States and the Soviet Union was inevitable? After all, once one acknowledged the uncertainty of prospects for superpower war, then the case for striking first collapses. If the Soviets, in the end, had no intention to launch a third world war, then a surprise attack, with its attendant risk of global chaos, would be nothing other than an act of mass murder.

Truman and Eisenhower, of course, were sufficiently sane and moral to understand the implications of that uncertainty and to try to resolve their doubts—not by pushing the button but by seeking policies aimed at reducing the risk of war. All alive on earth today should be thankful that U.S. Air Force hotheads and anticommunist zealots were firmly repudiated in their calls for preventive war. In retrospect, we know of course that the worse war they claimed to be averting by striking first never came. For that result we can hardly thank the "superhawks" on either side, whose bellicose rhetoric helped drive the arms race and invite dangerous games of brinksmanship during crises. Despite their misguided efforts the cold war ended peacefully, ensuring a harsh historical judgment on calls four decades earlier for preventive nuclear war.

—DAVID GOLDFISCHER, UNIVERSITY OF DENVER

Viewpoint:
No, the United States should have attacked the Soviet nuclear arsenal to slow their nuclear-weapons development.

The Soviet Union detonated its first atomic bomb in August 1949, several years ahead of the schedule predicted by American military intelligence. The ramifications of this development for American strategic policy were enormous. Washington's monopoly on atomic weapons was at an end. For the rest of the cold war, the conflict between the superpowers was to be darkly overshadowed by nuclear tension.

An important question both for the strategists of the day and for historians is what the United States could have done to counter the erosion of its strategic advantage. The fact of history is that the Truman administration accepted the Soviet acquisition of nuclear weapons as a fait accompli. No preemptive strikes were undertaken to destroy Soviet nuclear facilities, and it is apparent that no surreptitious means were adopted to sabotage the Soviet program. Perhaps the administration believed that it was too provocative a step to be taken. The blockade of West Berlin, the first situation that had a true potential for open military conflict between the superpowers, had only just ended. It may also have been the administration's belief that a tactical strike on Soviet nuclear facilities would be futile. Regardless of the damage a targeted attack would have inflicted, the technological know-how would remain. There is, however, a compelling argument that preemption of the Soviet nuclear arsenal was a viable proposition and that the United States should at least have attempted it.

The most obvious means of preempting a nuclear arsenal is a direct military assault. Even though the cold war had already developed into the dominant factor in international relations and

BULLITT ON STALIN

In a 13 April 1950 speech at Yale University, William C. Bullitt, former ambassador to the Soviet Union and an advocate of strong military action against communism, called for the United States to be prepared to confront Joseph Stalin. His speech included the following warning:

Can we stop Stalin without war? It is not impossible but it will not be easy. For Stalin will not stop unless we keep him constantly confronted by superior force and unless he knows that we will use that force against his direct and indirect aggressions. To stop Stalin without war we must, therefore, have both the superior force and the will to use it.

Do we have the superior force? In 1945 we had the atomic bomb and the world's greatest air force to carry it. Our industrial plant was intact. China, the key to all Asia, was our ally. Stalin had no atomic bomb and no long-range bombing planes. His industrial plant was, in large part, worn out or destroyed. Compared to the Soviet Union we were overwhelmingly strong. . . .

The balance of military force is swinging so rapidly to the Soviet side that some officials in Washington who have access to secret information believe that Stalin will attack us this autumn. They argue that by August 1950 he will probably have 50 A-bombs—enough to destroy our great cities and our atomic production plants, and thus prevent effective American counter-attack. But my belief is that Stalin will not launch a shooting war until he is certain that he can defeat us easily. He is a cautious and crafty leader who strikes only when he feels sure of quick victory. This autumn, his first surprise attack might not be successful. We would probably be able to strike back effectively. Therefore, it seems likely that he will not start bombing this year but will go on increasing his military strength faster than we are adding to ours, and seize more peoples, resources, and strategic areas, until he feels that his power is irresistible. We are allowing time to run on his side. And he knows it.

Source: *"Foreign Policy Based on Wishful Thinking,"* Vital Speeches of the Day, *16 (15 October 1949 – 1 October 1950): 563–564.*

Soviet military for a major war against the United States and its allies was not at all attractive.

Soviet foreign policy in the first postwar years had been directed at improving Moscow's geopolitical position vis-à-vis the West through subtlety and insinuation. By 1948 the communist parties of the liberated countries of Eastern Europe had become the dominating factors in politics and society. Although this success was achieved with indirect Soviet support, at least the legal fiction of constitutional processes and "free elections" had been maintained. It is true, furthermore, that during the war the United States had confirmed a de facto Soviet sphere of influence in the region; only mute protests could be offered.

Further afield, however, Soviet attempts to insinuate communist influence in regions not addressed in wartime Allied agreements were resisted both firmly and successfully. When Soviet premier Joseph Stalin attempted to extract base rights from Turkey in 1946, the United States made a major show of force in the eastern Mediterranean and caused the Soviet leader to back off. When Stalin seemed reluctant to withdraw his forces from Iran that same year, pressure from the West changed his mind. Research surrounding Soviet responses to the Marshall Plan illustrates that the Soviet leadership entertained the possibility that it could actually take advantage of the program without succumbing to its political conditions.

Soviet foreign minister Vyacheslav Molotov's proposal for four-power occupation of the industrial Ruhr region of Germany (located in the Western occupation zones) was rebuffed by the three Western allies, who responded with increased political and economic integration of their occupation sectors. When the economic integration, specifically the currency reform of 1948, led the Soviets to blockade West Berlin in the summer of that year, the United States responded with a massive airlift that breached the blockade and violated the airspace of the Soviet occupation zone in Germany. For more than a year the Soviet military watched thousands of tons of supplies fly over them and land in a city they had surrounded. No steps were taken to antagonize the West over their relief expedition.

Stalin wanted to expand his influence as far as possible without losing a relationship with the West that would, at a minimum, allow the USSR to recover in a peaceful international climate and possibly even assist that recovery in material terms. The Soviet race to develop the atomic bomb can be characterized as an integral part of this postwar strategy. Indeed, secret-police chief Lavrenty Beria's direction of the Soviet nuclear-weapons program spared no effort or resource. His aim was pursued with as much vigor as any other Soviet policy designed to improve Moscow's position. The pro-

its battle lines had solidified, it is questionable that a tactical strike on Soviet nuclear facilities would have led to a general war between the superpowers. Years after the Second World War the Soviet Union still lay in ruins. Twenty-seven million of its people had died in the war. Most of the Soviets' industrial and agricultural regions had been under highly exploitative German military occupation. Without a massive infusion of American financial and material assistance, it is doubtful that the Red Army would have achieved anything like its wartime successes. The prospect of mobilizing the

duction of a nuclear device years before it had been expected in the West was based on measures that would easily have provoked forceful reactions had they been applied in more conventional challenges. Most important among these was that the Soviet acquisition of nuclear-weapons technology came from wholesale espionage in the West. Even before the first successful tests of an American atomic bomb, sensitive information from the Manhattan Project already had reached Soviet hands. When President Harry S Truman mentioned to Stalin at the Potsdam Conference in July 1945 that the United States was preparing a great new weapon to end the war with Japan, Stalin did not seem too surprised or interested in the details. We now know that he was almost certainly aware of what was about to happen. Beria received his orders within days of the dropping of the atomic bombs on Hiroshima and Nagasaki.

American planners knew both from the speed of the Soviet development and from investigation over the next few years that a spy network in the United States had recruited individuals in sensitive positions to help the Soviet Union develop atomic weapons. Recent documentary evidence about nuclear spying has merely verified much of what was either suspected or proven inductively at the time. Since the Soviets created their initial device and continued to expand and develop their nuclear capabilities with American technology, retaliation was not so far-fetched.

History abounds with examples, both nuclear and conventional, where preemption was employed as a viable policy option simply because the potential for an improvement in the military power of an enemy was seen justifiably as a threat. The British had something of a tradition of preemptively destroying challenges to its naval power, as in 1807, when it raided the Danish fleet to keep it out of Napoleon's hands, and in 1940, when it attacked the North African bases of the French fleet to keep it out of Hitler's grasp. In the nuclear age Israel did not suffer from its covert sabotage and assassination campaign in 1961–1963 to prevent Egypt from acquiring nuclear and missile technology, or from its preemptive aerial assault on an Iraqi nuclear-power plant in 1981. Significantly, the incident did not touch off a general Middle Eastern war against Israel. The United States and its coalition partners went after Iraq's nuclear, chemical, and biological capabilities during the 1991 Gulf War, and in 1994 the United States was close to attacking North Korea's nuclear facilities if an agreement between the two countries were not reached. The Soviet Union itself suggested to the United States in 1964 and again in 1969 that China's emerging nuclear capability should be preempted. Despite Beijing's communist ideology, the geopolitical differences that had evolved between the two major communist powers were significant

enough for Moscow to try hard to avoid a situation in which Chinese nuclear capabilities were another factor they would have to confront. The United States and the Soviet Union were not friends in 1949.

The technological implications of a preemptive strike, moreover, were rather significant. Theoretically, as long as the Soviets kept the blueprints in a safe, the fact of their nuclear capability could be held in doubt. The actual testing and construction of nuclear weapons, however, is by no means that simple. The destruction of nuclear facilities and the killing of personnel involved in nuclear-weapons development would have gone a long way to preempt the deployment of a functional weapons system. Such attacks, however, are not sufficient in and of themselves. The Israeli attack on the nuclear reactor in Iraq in 1981 inflicted a blow to that country's program of developing a plutonium bomb, but it pushed Iraq into a clandestine effort to develop an enriched-uranium device. On the eve of the 1991 Gulf War, Saddam Hussein ordered his scientists to launch a crash program to build one or two explosive devices with the bomb-grade uranium at his disposal, but the war disrupted this effort. What is more, his uranium-enrichment facilities were destroyed, either by coalition bombing or by the United Nations Special Commission (UNSCOM) monitors. The setbacks in 1981 and 1991 made it impossible for Iraq to build a nuclear bomb, at least as long as the world's vigilance continues.

To assess the significance that a preemptive attack would have had on the Soviet nuclear-weapons program, one need look no further than the history of Moscow's strategic-weapons program in the mid and late 1950s. While the Soviets succeeded in developing a vastly more powerful hydrogen bomb before the United States and appeared to have made significant strides in rocket technology, their strategic-weapons program suffered several setbacks. A series of disastrous accidents destroyed nuclear facilities and caused the deaths of more than a few leading scientists and administrators. Although the USSR remained a nuclear power, it fell dangerously far behind its much-anticipated goal of overtaking the United States in strategic capabilities by the end of the decade. Indeed, the Soviet inability to deploy a serious intercontinental ballistic missile (ICBM) system until the late 1960s demonstrated that the accidental destruction of installations and the deaths of important individuals had a serious impact. Can one imagine how far back an intentional and targeted plan of nuclear preemption would have set them?

The fact that there was no attempt to preempt the emergence of Soviet nuclear capabilities is unfortunate. Its achievements could have been legion in the early stages of Soviet atomic-weapons development while there are good reasons to believe that the consequences (which could have been only conventional at the stage) would have been negligible. Because this step was not taken early, however, American planners were condemned for the rest of the cold war not to have the option. When the handful of Soviet installations and weapons grew into aggregate totals that ran into the thousands, nuclear preemption was no longer an option.

–PAUL DU QUENOY, GEORGE WASHINGTON UNIVERSITY

References

Russell D. Buhite and William Christopher Hamel, "War for Peace: The Question of an American Preventive War against the Soviet Union, 1945–1955," *Diplomatic History,* 14 (Summer 1990): 367–384;

Bret J. Cillesen, "Embracing the Bomb: Ethics, Morality, and Nuclear Deterrence in the US Air Force, 1945–1955," *Journal of Strategic Studies,* 21 (March 1998): 96–134;

Louis J. Halle, *The Cold War as History* (New York: Harper & Row, 1967);

David Halloway, *Stalin and the Bomb: The Soviet Union and Atomic Energy, 1939–1956* (New Haven: Yale University Press, 1994);

Peter Roman, "Curtis LeMay and the Origins of NATO Atomic Targeting," *Journal of Strategic Studies,* 16 (March 1993): 46–74;

David Allen Rosenberg, "The Origins of Overkill: Nuclear Weapons and American Strategy, 1945–1960," *International Security,* 7 (Spring 1983);

Pavel Sudoplatov and Anatoli Sudoplatov, with Jerrold L. and Leona P. Schecter, *Special Tasks: The Memoirs of an Unwanted Witness, A Soviet Spymaster,* updated edition (Boston: Little, Brown, 1995);

Marc Trachtenberg, *History and Strategy* (Princeton, N.J.: Princeton University Press, 1991);

Steven J. Zaloga, *Target America: The Soviet Union and the Strategic Arms Race, 1945–1964* (Novato, Cal.: Presidio, 1993).

NUCLEAR SPYING

How important was Soviet nuclear spying in the United States to the Soviet nuclear-weapons program?

Viewpoint: Soviet nuclear spying in the United States was vital to the Soviet nuclear-weapons program.

Viewpoint: Nuclear spying in the United States helped the Soviets, but their development of nuclear weapons was the result of domestic scientific advances as well as foreign espionage.

Viewpoint: Soviet nuclear spying in the United States was not critically important to the Soviet nuclear-weapons program.

There were few more hotly debated issues in early cold-war America than the issue of Soviet atomic spying. The intensity of the debate was reflected in the human drama of the electrocution of a husband and wife—Julius and Ethel Rosenberg—parents to young children, put to death after they were found guilty of being spies for the Soviet Union. In the midst of the controversy three issues gained special resonance. First was the concern that Soviet spying might have been made more effective—if not, at times, even facilitated—by the permissive environment created by American liberals in the government who were sympathetic to the Soviet cause. This concern led to accusations that not only communists and communist sympathizers such as Theodore Hall, Klaus Fuchs, Julius and Ethel Rosenberg, and David Greenglass spied for the Soviet Union, but that some of the leading nuclear scientists who took part in the Manhattan Project—J. Robert Oppenheimer, Enrico Fermi, and Niels Bohr—directly or indirectly passed atomic secrets to the USSR. The fear spread that the Soviet spies were merely the visible part of a larger, but mostly invisible, pro-Soviet cadre that came to Washington during the New Deal, became encouraged by U.S.-Soviet cooperation against the Nazis, and was now bent on helping the Soviet Union attain parity with the United States. This notion gave rise to a second issue, having to do with the degree to which fear of spying led to the Red Scare and communist "witch hunt" and a climate of demagoguery, suspicion, and fear that pushed the U.S. government to enact a series of measures, which, critics argue, violated the Constitutional rights of Americans. The third issue is to what extent the information gleaned by the Soviet atomic spies was helpful to the USSR in building its nuclear weapons, or developing them sooner rather than later. Were Soviet scientists on their way to developing the bomb on their own, or were the Soviet atomic spies in the United States responsible for the strategic change in the balance of power between the United States and the Soviet Union that was created by the existence of the Soviet atomic bomb? Would the United States have been able to pursue its goals more effectively during the early phases of the cold war if the USSR were slower to come by nuclear weapons?

Viewpoint:
Soviet nuclear spying in the United States was vital to the Soviet nuclear-weapons program.

Espionage played a crucial role in the early Soviet nuclear-weapons program. Although Soviet nuclear scientists eventually would have been able to build nuclear weapons without secret information from the West, the massive Soviet espionage effort reduced the time needed to develop a nuclear bomb by several years. Evidence from archives and memoirs confirms that the Soviet Union had vast spy networks in the United States and Great Britain throughout the 1930s and 1940s. In the United States alone, more than three hundred Soviet agents acquired government posts, including many high-ranking jobs. Several of these agents worked directly on the Manhattan Project, and others were affiliated with it. Newly declassified materials underscore the crucial importance of information provided by Klaus Fuchs and Theodore Hall, two of the major sources for Soviet nuclear espionage. Although there is no evidence that the leaders of the Manhattan Project—J. Robert Oppenheimer, Enrico Fermi, and Niels Bohr—spied for the Soviet Union, there is overwhelming evidence that Fuchs, Hall, and other key personnel gave invaluable help to Moscow.

The full extent of the Soviet nuclear-espionage network in the United States and Great Britain has yet to be revealed. Despite the availability of more than two thousand declassified messages from the Venona Project (the code name of the elaborate U.S. effort between 1939 and 1946 to intercept and decrypt Soviet NKVD (People's Commissariat of Internal Affairs) communications with intelligence stations abroad) and selected materials from the KGB archives, the identities of at least one major American spy and several minor British spies are still unknown. It is known, however, that a large amount of valuable information on the nuclear-weapons program came from two physicists working at Los Alamos: Fuchs and Hall.

Fuchs began supplying information on nuclear research to the Soviet intelligence services in August 1941, while he was still in Great Britain. From that point until December 1943, when he left for the United States, he gave several reports to the main intelligence directorate of the Soviet general staff describing the gaseous diffusion method of uranium-isotope separation. Fuchs passed on similar information to Soviet officials when he was in New York during the first half of 1944. Subsequently, when he was at Los Alamos from August 1944 until June 1946, he had access to virtually all information on the theory and design of the nuclear bomb. Fuchs informed his Soviet intelligence con-

tacts about theoretical issues, details of bomb construction, and political issues related to the Manhattan Project. His first report after arriving in Los Alamos, dated February 1945, revealed that the risk of spontaneous fission with plutonium (because of the presence of the isotope Pu-240) would preclude the use of the simple gun-barrel method of detonation that had been used with the enriched-uranium (U-235) bomb. The report discussed the alternative implosion method then being developed at Los Alamos, and it disclosed the critical mass of plutonium (Pu-239) and the amount that would be necessary for a bomb. The most crucial information appeared in Fuchs's next report, dated June 1945, which fully described the plutonium bomb and provided a sketch of the device and its components. The report also described the detonation mechanism, the aluminum shell of the bomb, the tamper, and the explosive-lens system. In addition, Fuchs noted the location and timing of the Trinity test of the nuclear bomb, as well as the Truman administration's plans to use the bomb against Japan.

Fuchs's final meeting with Harry Gold, Fuchs's Soviet courier while he was at Los Alamos, occurred on 19 September 1945. Fuchs handed over a report about the rate of production of U-235 and Pu-239 at the Oak Ridge and Hanford processing plants, thus enabling the Soviet government to calculate how many nuclear bombs the United States could produce. Although Fuchs remained at Los Alamos for another nine months, he was unable to pass on any further information to Soviet agents.

When Fuchs was reassigned to the Harwell nuclear-weapons laboratory in Great Britain in 1946, he initially refrained from reestablishing contact with Soviet intelligence. Within a year, however, he resumed his espionage activities. From July 1947 to April 1949, Fuchs had six meetings with Aleksandr Feklisov, his new Soviet handler, to whom he transferred information about bomb design, plutonium output at the Windscale plant in Britain, blast effects of the Hiroshima and Nagasaki explosions, and the presence of a British spy in the Soviet nuclear-weapons project. Even so, Fuchs was increasingly leery about continuing his espionage activities. These doubts led him to skip several meetings in the summer of 1949 and culminated in his confession and subsequent arrest in early 1950.

Another crucial spy for the Soviet Union was Hall, who began working for the Manhattan Project in January 1944 after distinguishing himself as a brilliant physicist during his first year at Harvard University. Hall was then only eighteen years old. After his first several months at Los Alamos, Hall decided that information about nuclear weapons should not remain a U.S. monopoly and needed to be shared with the Soviet Union. Beginning in October 1944, he regularly gave informa-

NUCLEAR SPYING

tion about the Manhattan Project to Soviet agents. The information he passed on during his first meeting included a description of Los Alamos and a list of the scientists working there. In December 1944 Hall gave Soviet officials their first information about the "implosion" method of detonation that would make a plutonium bomb possible. This disclosure came three months before a similar report was delivered by Fuchs. Hall also provided a basic description of how the bomb would work and a projected construction time line. Although the information was not as complete as that given by Fuchs, it arrived in Moscow several months earlier. In addition, Hall provided the first detailed set of plans of the plutonium bomb, dated May 1945, a month before Fuchs delivered his version to Harry Gold. A second set of technical plans, delivered by Hall in August, described the bomb used in the Trinity test.

After leaving Los Alamos in June 1946, Hall continued to spy for the Soviet Union off and on while enrolled in graduate study at the University of Chicago. Although the evidence is not definitive, it seems likely that Hall was the one who, in 1949, informed Moscow how to mass produce polonium 210, a key ingredient in the triggering mechanism of nuclear bombs. This information allowed the Soviet Union to begin mass production of nuclear weapons. Although Hall did not transfer much information after 1949, he maintained links with his Soviet handlers until 1953.

New evidence from the Venona papers and from Soviet intelligence archives confirms that the Soviet Union also benefitted from the work of Julius Rosenberg, who built up a small network of spies in the United States. In June 1945 one of the members of that network, David Greenglass, provided information to Moscow about the manufacture of high-explosive lenses used in the implosion of the plutonium bomb. Later that year, Greenglass turned over some materials used in the manufacture of the bomb, including a cartridge for the detonator. Although the information provided by the Rosenberg-Greenglass network was much less important (and, in some cases, less accurate) than the data transferred by Fuchs and Hall, the materials from Greenglass were a useful supplement.

In addition to these major and well-known agents, several other spies who provided information about the Manhattan Project have been identified. The first report about the Manhattan Project and the state of nuclear research in Britain and the United States was turned over in 1941 by John Cairncross, one of the five members of the infamous Soviet spy ring in Great Britain, which also included Harold "Kim" Philby, Guy Burgess, Donald MacLean, and Anthony Blunt. Allan Nunn May, a British physicist working at the Montreal Laboratory, handed over a report in the spring of 1945 describing what he knew about nuclear

SUDOPLATOV ON THE ROSENBERGS

Pavel Sudoplatov was the Soviet NKVD officer in charge of espionage and "special tasks," which included infiltrating the U.S. nuclear-bomb program by recruiting Americans to serve as spies. In the following passage from his memoir he discusses the Rosenbergs:

Julius and Ethel Rosenberg were recruited by Gaik Ovakimian, our resident in New York, in 1938. The irony is that the Rosenbergs are portrayed by the American counterintelligence service as the key figures in delivering atomic secrets to the Soviet Union, but actually they played a very minor role. They were absolutely separate from my major networks gathering atomic secrets. The New York rezidentura from 1943 to 1945 was run by Leonid Kvasnikov, working with Yatskov and Semyonov. In the summer of 1945, shortly before the first nuclear test explosion, a report had been prepared by David Greenglass, code name Calibar, the brother of Ethel Rosenberg. Greenglass was an army sergeant working in a Los Alamos machine shop on parts for the test. The courier scheduled to pick up his report could not make the trip, and Yatskov, eager to supply the report to Moscow, and authorized by the Center, ordered Harry Gold, Klaus Fuchs's courier, to substitute. Gold met Fuchs in Santa Fe, and then went to Albuquerque to pick up the report from Greenglass. The Center had broken the first commandment: never allow an agent or courier from one cell to have contact with or know the members of another group. When Gold, having been implicated by Fuchs, was arrested in 1950, he identified Greenglass, who incriminated the Rosenbergs.

I first learned of the arrest of Julius and Ethel Rosenberg in 1950 from a TASS report. I was not concerned about it. This might strike some as odd, but it is important to note that as well as being responsible for the thousands of fighters behind German lines during the war, we had hundreds of agents in the United States, not including illegals, sources, and informers. As the director of Department S, I was familiar with our personnel, though not with any but their most important sources; the Rosenbergs were not important or significant sources of information. It occurred to me that they might have been related to our intelligence operations, but they were not major players in my atomic intelligence networks. I considered the whole affair to be routine business.

Source: *Pavel Sudoplatov and Anatoli Sudoplatov, with Jerrold L. and Leona P. Schecter,* Special Tasks: The Memoirs of an Unwanted Witness—A Soviet Spymaster *(Boston: Little, Brown, 1995), p. 213.*

research. He followed up in August 1945 with samples of U-235 and U-233. May was arrested in March 1946 after being exposed by a Soviet embassy cipher clerk Igor Gouzenko, who defected in 1945. Clarence Hiskey, a scientist at the Metallurgical Laboratory in Chicago, provided information about early developments in the U.S. nuclear-weapons program (and possibly about the design of nuclear reactors) to a communist friend who was secretly a Soviet agent. Although Hiskey is known to have had communist sympathies, it is possible that he did not realize the information would be transferred to the Soviet Union. After arousing the suspicion of the U.S. Army, Hiskey had his security clearance revoked in April 1944 and spent the remainder of the war in Alaska.

Several Soviet spies at the Manhattan Project have remained unidentified. The most important of these appears to have been an agent whose code name was "Fogel" (later "Pers") and who worked at the Oak Ridge uranium-separation plant in Tennessee. Fogel sent plans of the facility to Moscow in June 1944, along with information about the amount of uranium that could be produced at the plant. A second agent (code name "Eric") was based in Great Britain and was one of the few sources on the nuclear-weapons project who were active in Britain before 1944. Eric provided some of the initial reports describing the role of the Uranium Commission in Britain, as well as a report on the establishment of the Manhattan Project in the United States.

Even if the identities of these and other unnamed spies are never discovered, the evidence that has emerged leaves no doubt that the Soviet Union had a massive nuclear-espionage network in the United States and Great Britain, which greatly expedited the Soviet nuclear-bomb program. If information from the United States had not been available, the Soviet Union eventually could have developed nuclear weapons on its own; but the espionage gained at least two years, and possibly as many as four, for the Soviet bomb program. The initial reports provided by John Cairncross and Klaus Fuchs in 1941 led to the initiation of a Soviet nuclear-weapons project, which at first was given only limited resources. Once the project was upgraded in 1943, information from intelligence sources convinced Soviet nuclear scientists to focus on the gaseous-diffusion method of isotope separation, which they had previously ruled out. Most crucially, Soviet scientists did not know about the implosion method of bomb detonation until they received elaborate reports about it from Hall and Fuchs. Without this information, it would have been impossible to construct a plutonium bomb. (Because of a lack of usable uranium in the USSR during the early postwar years, the Soviet bomb project had to focus on a plutonium bomb. Not until 1951 did the Soviet Union build its first uranium bomb.)

Even though Soviet nuclear scientists had made some crucial advances on their own (for example, in developing spontaneous fission), the detailed plans of the plutonium bomb provided by Hall and Fuchs gave the Soviet Union a ready-made blueprint to follow in manufacturing its first bomb.

Soviet scientists and engineers still had to do a good deal of research to confirm that the blueprint would work, but the intelligence, at a minimum, enabled Soviet scientists to avoid dead ends and to pursue the right path in the shortest possible amount of time. The extensive network of Soviet spies who infiltrated the Manhattan Project thus gave a crucial boost to the Soviet nuclear-weapons program.

–MARK KRAMER, HARVARD UNIVERSITY

Viewpoint:
Nuclear spying in the United States helped the Soviets, but their development of nuclear weapons was the result of domestic scientific advances as well as foreign espionage.

In the years immediately following the conclusion of the Second World War, the United States held a monopoly on the power of the atomic bomb. This monopoly came to an abrupt end on 29 August 1949, when the Soviet Union shocked the world with the successful test of their first atomic bomb. U.S. intelligence had predicted that the earliest date the Soviet Union would likely be able to explode an atomic bomb was mid 1953. The capability of Soviet science to produce an atomic weapon was known, but underestimated, in the West. What Western intelligence officers and political leaders did not know at the time was the extent to which Soviet espionage had supported and accelerated the Soviet atomic-weapons program. Espionage played a crucial role in the early years of the Soviet atomic program, from its inception to the successful 1949 test of an exact replica of the "Fat Man" bomb that the United States dropped on Nagasaki four years earlier.

Soviet physics was well established and world class in the 1930s. Leading Soviet scientists such as Igor Vasilyevich Kurchatov, Yuly Borisovich Khariton, Iakov Zeldovich, Konstantin A. Petrzhak, and Georgy N. Flerov had published articles and performed experiments on the nature of the atom and conditions necessary for sustaining a chain reaction in uranium. As they performed ground-breaking research in the 1930s, these scientists came to understand that atomic energy could be a source of great power. They went on to make important discoveries in the field, including proving the phenomenon of spontaneous fusion in uranium and certain principles of chain reactions. In 1940 they strenuously recommended that work begin to study and harness atomic energy.

The German invasion of the Soviet Union in June 1941 derailed scientific work on atomic energy in the Soviet Union. By necessity the staffs and scientists of the various physics labs were sent to the front or redirected their efforts to work on technologies with an immediate practical military application such as radar, armor, and demagnetizing ships. The Soviet leadership received mixed advice from their scientists regarding the benefits of continuing atomic research during the war.

Many senior scientists believed that it would be impossible to develop an atomic weapon in time to affect the outcome of the war with Germany. Others were convinced that research should continue. In one striking example, Flerov wrote a letter to Joseph Stalin from the front lines in 1942, urging the Soviet premier to direct that research commence in using atomic energy as a weapon. Flerov had been stationed near a university library that had international journals on physics, and on reading them he noted that preeminent western scientists in the field were no longer publishing papers. From that absence of articles he deduced that the United States and Britain were working on the atomic problem and realized that his country must have an atomic program of its own. While it has not been determined if Stalin actually received the letter, it eventually reached the Soviet leadership and had an impact on the decision to renew research into the atomic question.

The first information to reach Lavrenty Beria, chief of the NKVD (People's Commissariat of Internal Affairs), on the Western decision to initiate research into atomic energy came in 1941. British scientific findings describing the state of knowledge on atomic theory and proposals for continued research were presented in the Maud Report. This document was passed to the Soviets by John Cairncross, the "fifth man" of the famous British spy ring the "Cambridge Five" (which also included Harold "Kim" Philby, Guy Burgess, Donald MacLean, and Anthony Blunt). Beria also received intelligence on the status of German research into atomic energy, which appeared to be less advanced than in Britain and the United States. Based on this intelligence, Beria recommended that a scientific committee be established, if only to evaluate the feasibility of developing atomic energy. Information about atomic programs in the West was made an intelligence-gathering priority. Soviet intelligence successfully gathered detailed information, first from Britain and then from the United States, on the decisions to research and build an atomic bomb, and ultimately on the technical details of that research.

Though some atomic research began earlier, work began in earnest in 1943, shortly after the Soviet victory over the Germans at Stalingrad. With the tide of the war turning against the Ger-

mans, the Soviet leadership could start to look toward postwar issues. In early 1943 the head of the Soviet atomic program, Igor Kurchatov, had doubts as to whether the Soviet Union would be able to build an atomic bomb. At this point Politburo member Vyacheslav Molotov showed Kurchatov for the first time intelligence that the Soviet Union had gathered from its espionage in the West. Kurchatov was amazed by the wealth of information, which not only confirmed much of the Soviet work but also suggested new lines of research and the proper methods of undertaking them. The Soviet leadership had not understood the importance of the information they had gathered. According to David Holloway, when Molotov asked Kurchatov to evaluate the information, he responded, "Wonderful materials, they fill in just what we are lacking." Americans were far ahead of the Soviets in developing atomic weapons.

Soviet leaders did not grasp the full significance of the atomic bomb until the United States used it over Hiroshima and Nagasaki in 1945. Before then, Stalin distrusted his scientists' appraisals of the potential power of the weapon. Beria was especially concerned that the intelligence he was gathering was elaborate disinformation, designed to trick the Soviet Union into wasting precious rubles on researching a fantasy. Nevertheless, Beria was incredibly protective of this intelligence. Only Kurchatov, as the scientific director of the Soviet atomic project, had direct access to the intelligence materials. In turn, Kurchatov helped direct Soviet intelligence to find information the Soviet program needed to proceed.

With the help of espionage the Soviet program was able to proceed along several different lines of investigation, which was extremely important to Stalin. In a June 1946 meeting with Beria, Molotov, and Kurchatov, Stalin authorized an all-out effort to develop the bomb. Joseph Albright and Marcia Kunstel quote the Soviet leader as saying, "It is not worth dealing with small-scale works, and it is necessary to carry out works widely, with Russian-type dimensions, and the broadest possible help will be provided." After defeating the Germans, Stalin was shocked to find that the gains of the victory were jeopardized by the power imbalance the atomic bomb represented, and he directed that every scientific and intelligence resource at the Soviet Union's disposal be used to catch up with the Americans as quickly as possible.

As work progressed in the Soviet Union on the atomic-weapons project, materials from the West continued to play a major role in inspiring and guiding the Soviet scientists. One important revelation provided by Soviet espionage in 1945 was the concept of the implosion method for detonating the atomic bomb, in which a ball-shaped charge of nuclear material is sur-

Ethel and Julius Rosenberg in a prison vehicle after their conviction for conspiracy to commit espionage, 29 March 1951

(AP / Wide World Photo)

cially uranium and heavy water. Without the original ingredients to fire a nuclear reactor, the Soviets could not hope to produce the necessary fissile material for an atom bomb. The lack of uranium also made it impossible for the Soviets to develop on their own a method for purifying uranium isotopes. In surmounting these problems, and many others, the Soviet scientists proved ingenious. A great quantity of needed materials, including uranium, was recovered from Germany and occupied eastern Europe. Science and intelligence worked even more closely in one dramatic instance, when some two or three dozen Soviet scientists, including Khariton and Flerov, flew to Soviet-occupied Germany to learn about the German atomic program and to capture German uranium supplies. Dressed in the uniforms of NKVD lieutenant colonels, the scientists found the German atomic program was not advanced and had nothing to teach the Soviets. More important, they uncovered more than one hundred metric tons of uranium oxide, which provided the necessary fuel to build the Soviets' first reactor. In the end Stalin's directive to "carry out works widely" and pursue multiple paths in the atomic project was followed but only as a result of the close cooperation between Soviet science and intelligence.

Although a full list of informers in the allies' nuclear programs has not yet been—nor will likely ever be—completely revealed, three major figures have been identified. British scientist Klaus Fuchs (code name Charl'z) provided the most information, starting as early as 1942, including techniques for purifying uranium and the plans for the construction of the Fat Man atomic bomb. American physicist Theodore Hall (code name Mlad) was only eighteen when he joined the atomic-bomb project in 1944; he provided the first technical details on the implosion method of detonating the atomic bomb that so impressed Kurchatov. Finally, American machinist David Greenglass (code name Kalibr), who also worked on the detonation project, furnished information on the engineering details of the implosion mechanism. A network of Soviet agents in the United States supported these informers in passing secrets to the Soviet Union, including Julius and Ethel Rosenberg, who were executed in 1953 for espionage.

The question of which other scientists in the American nuclear program passed information or otherwise cooperated with the Soviets, and their motives for doing so, is a complicated one. The main motive of the informers that were discovered, rather than financial considerations, was the concern that no nation should possess a monopoly on the atom bomb. The same motive was ascribed to other figures in the American atomic project. First excerpted in a *Time* magazine article in 1994, the

rounded by a lens system of high explosives, somewhat resembling a soccer ball. The implosion compresses the nuclear material to critical mass and results in a high-yield explosion. Previously, Soviet scientists had thought that the best method of forcing the nuclear material to critical mass was the "gun-assembly" technique, in which two hemispheres of a uranium isotope are fired into one another at massive speeds. The United States also worked on a "gun-assembly" design and used it for the first bomb, dropped on Hiroshima. Kurchatov found the new information on the "explosion toward the inside" method (the Russian language lacked the word "implosion") to be of "great interest," his highest praise for information gathered by intelligence.

The need for speed and ideas was not the only force driving Soviet scientists' use of intelligence from the West. The most serious problem the program faced was the lack of materials, espe-

memoir of former Soviet spy Pavel Sudoplatov accused leading figures in the U.S. atomic-bomb project—Leo Szilard, Enrico Fermi, Niels Bohr, and J. Robert Oppenheimer—of providing information or placing agents for the Soviets. These accusations immediately provoked a storm of controversy. Certainly, this memoir will not be the final word in the matter, however, as there are several inconsistencies in it.

One episode described by Sudoplatov is illustrative: a 1945 meeting of Bohr with Soviet physicist Yakov Terletsky and an NKVD interpreter. According to Sudoplatov, the meeting provided valuable ideas for the Soviets and was essential to starting the Soviet reactor. In fact, according to Bohr's son, himself a physicist and a participant in the meeting, Bohr revealed no information that was not contained in Henry De Wolf Smyth's *Atomic Energy for Military Purposes* (1945), a report published by the U.S. government to explain to the world the science behind the atomic bomb. Another account of the meeting from an actual participant, Terletsky, confirmed that Bohr revealed nothing beyond what was contained in the Smyth Report.

Even if no help came from Fermi, Oppenheimer, or Bohr, the information from Fuchs, Hall, and Greenglass was certainly enough to give the Soviet nuclear program the start and support it needed in its early years. Soviet espionage provided blueprints and technical details that were crucial to the early success of the Soviet atomic-weapons program. The information was crucial, but not because Soviet scientists were incapable of producing atomic weapons on their own. Instead, the information was the catalyst that spurred Stalin to begin and support the program while the pleas of his own scientists had been ignored. The information provided essential shortcuts considering the Soviet's material position after the devastation unleashed by the German invasion. Finally, the information provided inspiration to Kurchatov in certain design elements of the bomb, such as the implosion method. Soviet scientists were directed to abandon their "gun-assembly" design, which was later proved viable by the Hiroshima bomb, in favor of following the more complete plans gathered by intelligence on the implosion design. At Stalin's insistence speed and certainty were of the essence. The successful explosion of the Soviets' first atomic bomb in 1949 was the result of the collaboration of science and espionage.

The intelligence crutch was soon stripped away from the Soviets. In the late 1940s the American Venona code-breaking project uncovered much, if not all, of the Soviet's atomic-spying network in the United States. By then, the Soviet Union was well positioned to continue research on its own. Years into the recovery after the war the command structure of the economy

enabled Stalin to funnel enormous resources to the Soviet nuclear program. The scientists were motivated by patriotism, by their successes under conditions of deprivation in the war years, and by desperation to catch up to the United States. Four years later, in August 1953, the Soviet Union successfully tested the first hydrogen bomb, a full six months before the United States.

–JOSEPH DRESEN, KENNAN INSTITUTE, WOODROW WILSON CENTER

Viewpoint:
Soviet nuclear spying in the United States was not critically important to the Soviet nuclear-weapons program.

In 1950 Klaus Fuchs confessed to giving atomic secrets to the Soviet Union and was subsequently sentenced to fourteen years in jail. Fuchs's confession led to a broad spy hunt, especially in the United States, where anticommunist furor was engulfing the popular imagination. This investigation led to the arrest of a spy ring of U.S. citizens. David Greenglass confessed and gave evidence that, in part because of the political climate of the time, sent his sister and brother-in-law, Ethel and Julius Rosenberg, to their deaths. Yet, neither the Rosenbergs nor even Fuchs had passed the "secret" that in itself had enabled the Soviets to build their atomic bomb. In fact, the Soviets already knew that secret.

Several misunderstandings have colored the received wisdom about the Soviet atomic-bomb problem. First, many people assume that the projected time line of ten to twenty years for the Soviet bomb project, which was offered by General Leslie Groves, the director of the Manhattan Project, was based on fact—or, at least, well-educated guesses. In reality his estimate was based on two serious miscalculations: that the Soviets did not have an indigenous supply of uranium (an assumption based on outdated geologic maps) and that they lacked the technical expertise for the project. In contrast the scientists involved with the Manhattan Project estimated that another country (such as the Soviet Union) could have the bomb within four or five years. Second, many people assume that since so much information about the Manhattan Project was classified for so long, there must have been an "atomic secret." The biggest secrets of the Manhattan Project, however, were revealed to the world on 6 August 1945: that an atomic bomb was possible and that the United States had built it. With the feasibility of such weapons established, the largest obstacle was overcome. The third misunderstanding stems from the first two: the Soviets were able to build their bomb so quickly only because of their spies' help. Yet, one can argue that this supposition is not true.

In 1940 the U.S. government took its first real steps toward an unprecedented collaboration between science and the military—the Manhattan Project. While the United States was trying to determine whether or not uranium fission could produce a bomb, Soviet scientists had already come to an affirmative conclusion. In October 1940 two Soviet scientists submitted a patent application describing a group of subcritical masses of uranium-235 separated by partitions, the removal of which would produce an explosion. While this design was unworkable, it shows that the Soviets were indeed capable of independent work on the bomb. Also in 1940, Soviet scientists had worked out the theoretical basis for a sustained chain reaction, including the experimental determination of secondary neutron production. Even as Enrico Fermi's "pile" was constructed under Stagg Field at the University of Chicago in 1942, he was not certain that enough neutrons would be produced to sustain the reaction. In December 1941, as the United States decided to assign responsibility for its nascent atomic-weapons program to the army, Georgy N. Flerov sent a proposal for a Little Boy–type weapon to the head of the Soviet bomb project, Igor Kurchatov. With it Flerov included some initial thoughts on a second idea, based on compressing the fissile material.

These first steps on the Soviet side illustrate that Groves grossly underestimated the capabilities of Soviet physicists. Why, if they were so advanced in this field, did they spy on the Manhattan Project? At least two factors contributed to the Soviet decision to spy on the Anglo-American atomic endeavor. First, Fuchs was a willing agent already in place. Second, and probably more important in the end, the Soviet program was slowed and disrupted by the Second World War, not only because of the drain on resources caused by the war, but also because the laboratories involved were in areas coming under German attack. Atomic espionage kept Soviet scientists apprised of the progress of their American counterparts, as well as their methods and theories. Although David Holloway attributes Kurchatov's "intuition" about which way the Soviet program should follow to these reports, Yuli Khariton asserts that Kurchatov was very cautious about the information he received this way. These two views are not necessarily mutually exclusive. Ronald Radosh and Joyce Milton argue that part of the reason David Greenglass was recruited was to confirm Fuchs's reports.

The material from Fuchs did provide the Soviets with the design used for their 1949 test, but even without that information they would have succeeded within the four or five years estimated by the Manhattan Project scientists. After the Soviets made the decision to use the proven American design for their first test, resources were diverted from the development of the Soviets' own design for about three years. In 1948 work on the Soviet version resumed. The Soviet model was tested in 1951. It weighed half as much as the American bomb they had copied; yet, it produced twice the yield. If one removes the three years during which work on the Soviet version was suspended, it becomes clear that the Soviets would probably have had an atomic weapon in 1949 even without information from the American atomic program.

Much of the data that Fuchs provided the Soviets was published by the U.S. government in Henry De Wolf Smyth's *Atomic Energy for Military Purposes* (1945). This report does not divulge technical data, but it does discuss the paths Manhattan Project scientists took toward their goal. In many ways, this report represents the military assumption that the technical data contained the "secret" to the atomic bomb. Since the Soviets had begun working on the technical problems before the American program started, the descriptions in the Smyth Report, coupled with the technical knowledge the Soviets had acquired through their own experiments, were quite sufficient to point out the right direction for further work. The Smyth Report was translated into Russian by November 1945, making those descriptions available to the scientists concerned.

The Smyth Report leads to a brief point regarding recent charges that some of the brightest lights of the Manhattan Project—including J. Robert Oppenheimer, Leo Szilard, Enrico Fermi, and Niels Bohr—were Soviet spies. The charges against Oppenheimer, Fermi, and Szilard appear in a memoir by Pavel Sudoplatov, a Soviet intelligence officer. These allegations have been investigated in the Soviet archives by several researchers and dismissed. The charges against Bohr stem from a document recording a meeting between Bohr and a Soviet agent, who represented himself as a scientist. Bohr is accused of naively transferring classified information to the Soviets during this interview. Instead, the "smoking gun" document shows that Bohr did not exceed the limits set by the Smyth Report.

How much did the Soviet atomic weapons program benefit from espionage? The intelligence certainly enabled Soviet scientists to avoid some of the dead ends and delays that the Manhattan Project encountered. Therefore, one could argue that the spies were important. Yet, the Smyth Report provided the same information, at approximately the same time.

While it is tempting to assume that Khariton is exaggerating the accomplishments of Soviet science (since he was involved with the project), his version of events fits the facts far better than claims that the Soviet program was almost completely dependent on intelligence from the West. During the cold war, the latter version was preferred, as it gave people in the West reassurance that the Soviets would never get ahead in the arms race because they lacked the technical competence to do anything but copy the West. Related to this version is the assumption that Soviet advances in missile technology owed much to the German scientists brought to the Soviet Union following the war. Until the opening of the Soviet archives, the evidence (all Western) supported this theory at least superficially.

The best guide, though, to the quality of Soviet science lies in the estimates of the Manhattan Project scientists. Based on their knowledge of the physicists likely to be involved in the Soviet program, they predicted it would take the Soviet Union four to five years to test an atomic weapon. The Soviet test came four years and three weeks after Hiroshima and Nagasaki. The scientists of the Manhattan Project knew their Soviet colleagues' capabilities better than the military or the government. Yes, spies provided American atomic data to the Soviet atomic-bomb project, but their contribution was far less significant than the West would like to believe. Without it the Soviets might have produced a better bomb by 1949 (or perhaps 1950) based solely on their own efforts and declassified U.S. sources.

—MARGOT BAUMANN, GEORGE WASHINGTON UNIVERSITY

References

Joseph Albright and Marcia Kunstel, *Bombshell: The Secret Story of America's Unknown Atomic Spy Conspiracy* (New York: Random House, 1997);

"Document II: The Interrogation of Niels Bohr," *Cold War International History Project Bulletin*, no. 4 (Fall 1994): 57–59;

G. A. Goncharov, N. I. Komov, and A. S. Stepanov, "Research Notes: The Russian Nuclear Project: Setting up the A-bomb Effort, 1946," *Cold War International History Project Bulletin*, no. 8–9 (Winter 1996–1997): 410–416;

John Earl Haynes and Harvey Klehr, *Venona: Decoding Soviet Espionage in America* (New Haven: Yale University Press, 1999);

Daniel Hirsch and William Matthews, "The H-bomb: Who Really Gave Away the Secret?" *Bulletin of the Atomic Scientists*, 46 (January/February 1990): 22–30;

"Historians, Physicists Mobilize to Refute Spy Stories," American Institute of Physics [online report] (n.d.);

David Holloway, "Sources for Stalin and the Bomb," *Cold War International History Project Bulletin*, no. 4 (Fall 1994): 1–9;

Holloway, *Stalin and the Bomb: the Soviet Union and Atomic Energy, 1939–1956* (New Haven: Yale University Press, 1994);

Yuli Khariton and Yuri Smirnov, "The Khariton Version," *Bulletin of the Atomic Scientists*, 49 (May 1993): 20–31;

Sergei Leskov, "An Unreliable Witness," *Bulletin of the Atomic Scientists*, 50 (July/August 1994): 33–36;

Priscilla McMillan, "Flimsy Memories," *Bulletin of the Atomic Scientists*, 50 (July/August 1994): 30–33;

Norman Moss, *Klaus Fuchs: The Man Who Stole the Atom Bomb* (London: Grafton Books, 1987);

Ronald Radosh and Joyce Milton, *The Rosenberg File*, revised edition (New Haven: Yale University Press, 1997);

Richard Rhodes, *The Making of the Atomic Bomb* (New York: Simon & Schuster, 1986);

Yuri Smirnov, "The KGB Mission to Niels Bohr: its Real 'Success,'" *Cold War International History Project Bulletin*, no. 4 (Fall 1994): 51, 54–57;

Pavel Sudoplatov, Anatoli Sudoplatov, and others, *Special Tasks: The Memoirs of an Unwanted Witness—A Soviet Spymaster* (Boston: Little, Brown, 1995);

Tad Szulc, "The Untold Story of How Russia 'Got the Bomb,'" *Los Angeles Times*, 26 August 1984, IV: 1, 3;

Allen Weinstein and Alexander Vassiliev, *The Haunted Wood: Soviet Espionage in America—The Stalin Era* (New York: Random House, 1999);

Nigel West and Oleg Tsarev, *The Crown Jewels: The British Secrets at the Heart of the KGB Archives* (London: HarperCollins, 1998);

Robert Chadwell Williams, *Klaus Fuchs, Atom Spy* (Cambridge, Mass.: Harvard University Press, 1987);

Vladislav Zubok, "Atomic Espionage and its Soviet 'Witnesses,'" *Cold War International History Project Bulletin*, no. 4 (Fall 1994): 50, 52–53.

NUCLEAR WEAPONS

Did the cold war remain "cold" because of the existence of nuclear weapons?

Viewpoint: Yes, the cold war remained "cold" because both sides feared nuclear devastation.

Viewpoint: No, the cold war remained "cold" because of a status quo that satisfied the basic interests of the United States and the Soviet Union.

The introduction of nuclear weapons preceded the onset of the cold war by a couple of years. Many point to nuclear weapons as the most important reason why the cold-war superpowers—the United States and the Soviet Union—did not go to war with one another despite the tensions, conflicts, and crises that characterized their relations from the late 1940s to the late 1980s. This explanation for the cold war's relative peacefulness rests on the argument that nuclear weapons, because of their destructiveness, tame even the most ambitious leaders and restrain even the most aggressive states.

Others suggest that relations—including the nuclear relationship—between the United States and the Soviet Union remained peaceful because of many other reasons. The two countries were not contiguous and had no territorial claims against one another. Their basic interests were satisfied by the post–Second World War international order. Both had strong political systems (albeit, one democratic and the other authoritarian) and stable command-and-control procedures. During the cold war the two countries were also led by cautious and pragmatic leaders. Nuclear weapons were thus introduced into a situation that had many stabilizing factors.

This debate is still relevant. Many of those who believe nuclear weapons made a major contribution to peaceful U.S.-Soviet relations during the cold war are more sanguine about the prospects of the further proliferation of nuclear weapons around the world. They argue that nuclear weapons will have the same taming, restraining effects in turbulent regions that they had in the superpowers' relationship. Critics of this view contend that, in the absence of other stabilizing elements, such as those already present in U.S.-Soviet relations, nuclear weapons and the missiles that carry them will exacerbate instability and tensions.

Viewpoint:
Yes, the cold war remained "cold" because both sides feared nuclear devastation.

Although it is impossible to say for certain why an event failed to take place, the presence of nuclear weapons, especially the large arsenals eventually deployed by the Soviet Union and the United States, can explain why the cold war never deteriorated into open hostilities between the superpowers. Nuclear weapons had a profound effect on the way politicians and soldiers on both sides of the "iron curtain" perceived the risks and benefits of any superpower confrontation that threatened to end in war. The consequences of nuclear war were so dire that the existence of nuclear weapons virtually eliminated the direct use of force between the superpowers as a way to secure national objectives. Regardless of how eager some Soviets and Americans might have been to engage in a final showdown, nuclear weapons prevented rational leaders from choosing war as a way to end quickly decades of simmering hostility.

The argument that nuclear weapons helped keep the cold war "cold" is based on the explanation of what causes war that suggests leaders will engage in war if they believe the benefits they will likely gain are greater than the costs they are likely to suffer. Geoffrey Blainey summarized this line of thinking with the observation that anything that increases expectations of a quick and cheap victory will make war more likely, while anything that reduces optimism about the likelihood of a positive outcome makes conflict less likely. Of course, exceptions to this generalization can be found. For instance, Egyptian president Anwar Sadat initiated the October 1973 war against Israel knowing that military victory was beyond Egypt's grasp. Still, both sides in a conflict generally choose to engage in war because they believe that they can advance or defend their interests at an acceptable cost.

History shows, however, that people are notoriously bad at estimating their state's prospects for success in war. Given that most conflicts produce a winner and a loser, Blainey's ideas suggest that leaders are wrong about half the time in calculating their prospects for success in war. Several factors make it difficult to estimate the outcome of war.

While a "bean count" (for example, numerical comparisons of force sizes) can be undertaken before battle, simple quantitative measures of military capability do not always provide an accurate indication of a war's outcome. A variety of qualitative factors—including leadership, morale, strategy, and training—can influence greatly the course of a war. War itself provides the only accurate test of military effectiveness, and even predictions based on past conflicts can be misleading when applied to different opponents at other moments in history. For example, North Vietnam withstood years of American military pressure, while Iraq, which on paper had far more impressive military capabilities than North Vietnam, sued for peace after just a few weeks of war against the United States. The fact that politicians, officers, and citizens are all likely to be swept up by nationalistic fervor, fear, or wishful thinking as a crisis looms on the horizon only makes it more difficult to judge accurately the prospects for success in some nascent conflict.

Nuclear weapons vastly reduce uncertainty and optimism about positive outcomes in two important ways. First, nuclear weapons are extraordinarily powerful. One can produce a blast equivalent to hundreds of thousands of tons of TNT. A couple of nuclear explosions are enough to destroy a large city. Second, because their effects are largely determined by physics and not political, strategic, or tactical dexterity, the consequences of a nuclear detonation can be calculated in advance. In other words, since Soviets and Americans shared the same physics, if not the same ideology or political agenda, they could develop a similar understanding of the effects of nuclear weapons.

Because they are so destructive and because their destructiveness is easily recognized by politicians, soldiers, and citizens alike, even a few nuclear weapons can greatly alter attitudes toward conflict. Thomas Schelling describes the effect produced by nuclear weapons as the "diplomacy of violence." Before the advent of nuclear weapons, he argues, states had first to defeat opposing armies before they could strike at what countries valued most: home territory, industry, population, or leadership. In other words, because militaries could defeat an opponent's army, people could hope to escape the worst ravages of war. In conventional war, argues Richard Harknett, the costs are contestable in the sense that states can avoid deterrent threats made by their opponents by defeating their armies on the battlefield, thereby greatly protecting their populations from the horrors of war. In contrast, because only a few nuclear weapons can inflict catastrophic damage, states can bypass opposing military forces and directly punish opposing societies. Since nuclear-weapon states, especially following the introduction of long-range ballistic missiles, could always launch attacks against targets valued highly by their opponents, the benefits provided by conventional victory in war begin to fade as nuclear war became possible. A state defeated on the battlefield could still deny the winners the benefits of victory by launching a nuclear attack against their homeland. When faced with a nuclear-armed opponent, states begin to lose the ability to contest the costs of war.

The disincentives to resort to hostilities become overwhelming, however, when both sides in a standoff are equipped with secure second-strike capabilities. Under these circumstances, a situation emerges known as mutual assured destruction, often referred to by the colorful acronym "MAD." MAD is not a policy: no state deliberately would adopt a plan that would allow an opponent to destroy it. Rather MAD exists when no matter how much damage one side does to the other by using nuclear weapons first in a crisis, the victim of the opening attack can launch a devastating retaliatory strike, destroying the state that initiated the exchange.

If states find themselves in a situation of MAD, it would become impossible to distinguish winners from losers following a full-scale nuclear war. Under these circumstances, it would be the height of folly for leaders or soldiers to become embroiled in a conflict that would virtually ensure the complete destruction of their countries. Some observers have noted that even though MAD is based on unconstrained offensive capability, it results in an unconstrained advantage for the defense. In other words, no matter what happens, if one state triggers MAD, it will still lose the war. The consequence of MAD is peace because the prospect of winning a war has been eliminated.

Evidence that MAD kept the cold war from becoming "hot" is indirect, not definitive. For instance, as MAD emerged, cold-war crises became less frequent or severe. After an early enthusiasm for nuclear weapons, if not nuclear war, by the early 1960s nuclear-war planners were beginning to reach the conclusion that nothing but devastation would be produced by a nuclear war. Academics and scientists abandoned efforts to find ways to prevail in a nuclear conflict and began pioneering work in arms control as a way to reduce the costs and risks of MAD. By the 1980s, studies of inadvertent and accidental nuclear war received increasing attention because these were considered to be a greater risk than a deliberate decision to initiate nuclear war. Ultimately, MAD might have offered its greatest service by eliminating war as an instrument for Soviet leaders to use to save their crumbling empire and by protecting the Soviet Union from outside intervention as it went through its death throes. Ironically, because nuclear weapons are so destructive, they not only helped to limit conflict during the cold war, but when the time arrived, they also demonstrated to all concerned that forty years of cold war could end peacefully.

–JAMES J. WIRTZ, U.S. NAVAL POSTGRADUATE SCHOOL

Viewpoint:
No, the cold war remained "cold" because of a status quo that satisfied the basic interests of the United States and the Soviet Union.

Between 1945 and 1989 Europe enjoyed the longest respite from war in its history. It was easy to lose sight of this achievement, however,

amid the belligerent rhetoric, arms races, and crises of this cold-war era. The cold-war system rapidly collapsed during 1989–1991. How could so fragile a system have produced so durable a peace?

Most explanations for the absence of war in Europe—for example, the one offered by John Lewis Gaddis—rest primarily on two leading characteristics of the postwar system: bipolarity and nuclear weapons. According to this explanation, bipolar international systems are more likely to remain peaceful than multipolar ones because they are less dependent on statesmanship. Multipolar systems require the formation of coalitions to restrain aspiring hegemonic powers. These efforts frequently falter because powers fail to recognize the threat until too late or do not cooperate effectively. Those who hold that nuclear weapons played a decisive role in preventing major wars during the cold war argue that the destructiveness of these weapons tames even the most reckless of leaders, imposing discipline and restraint that would otherwise be lacking.

The importance of both bipolarity and nuclear weapons has been overemphasized. In a sense the cold war was an accidental peace. Though neither superpower aimed initially at the division of Germany, and though the United States resisted the establishment of a hard Soviet sphere of influence, the unofficial territorial solution that emerged from the Yalta summit in 1945 and the diplomatic deadlock thereafter did meet minimal objectives of both the United States and the Soviet Union. Thus, the long peace rested not solely on the strength of nuclear deterrence but also on the weakness of any motive to alter the status quo.

How could this situation have been otherwise? The existence of bipolarity by no means guarantees that the basic security requirements of the leading states can be met easily. When the structure of the international system makes it difficult for one leading state to achieve safety without reducing another to great vulnerability, international politics become not merely a zero-sum game but a winner-take-all competition. Security becomes indivisible and conflict irremediable. Security for the victors of the Second World War, like the continent of Europe itself, was divisible.

Fear of Germany was a central concern of the Soviet Union. In April 1945, with the fight against the Nazi regime still raging, Soviet premier Joseph Stalin told an interviewer that the Germans "will recover, and very quickly. That is a highly developed industrial country with an extremely qualified and numerous working class and technical intelligentsia. Give them twelve to fifteen years and they'll be on their feet again."

SCIENTISTS PROTEST NUCLEAR WEAPONS

In 1955 an international group of scientists concerned about the destructive power of nuclear weapons agreed to meet periodically to discuss nuclear policy. The first of these meetings, which became known as Pugwash Conferences, was held in Pugwash, Nova Scotia, in July 1957. At the third conference, held in Kitzbühel and Vienna, Austria, in September 1958 the participants (with one abstention) voted to issue the Vienna Declaration, which included the following conclusions:

Our conclusions about the possible consequences of war have been supported by reports and papers submitted to our Conference. These documents indicate that if, in a future war, a substantial proportion of the nuclear weapons already manufactured were delivered against urban targets, most centers of civilization in the belligerent countries would be totally destroyed, and most of their populations killed. This would be true whether the bombs used derived most of their power from fusion reactions (so-called "clean" bombs) or principally from fission reactions (so-called "dirty" bombs). In addition to destroying major centers of population and industry, such bombs would also wreck the economy of the country attacked, through the destruction of vital means of distribution and communication.

Major states have already accumulated large stocks of "dirty" nuclear weapons; it appears that they are continuing to do so. From a strictly military point of view, dirty bombs have advantages in some situations; this makes likely their use in a major war.

The local fallout resulting from extensive use of "dirty" bombs would cause the death of a large part of the population in the country attacked. Following their explosion in large numbers (each explosion equivalent to that of millions of tons of ordinary chemical explosive), radioactive fallout would be distributed, not only over the territory to which they were delivered but, in varying intensity, over the rest of the earth's surface. Many millions of deaths would thus be produced, not only in belligerent but also in nonbelligerent countries, by the acute effects of radiation.

There would be, further, substantial long-term radiation damage to human and other organisms everywhere from somatic effects such as leukemia, bone cancer, and shortening of the lifespan; and from genetic damage affecting the hereditary traits transmitted to the progeny. . . .

It is sometimes suggested that in a future war, the use of nuclear weapons might be restricted to objectives such as military bases, troop concentrations, airfields, and other communication centers; and that attacks on large centers of population could thus be avoided.

Even tactical weapons now have a large radius of action; cities and towns are commonly closely associated with centers of supply and transportation. We, therefore, believe that even a "restricted" war would lead, despite attempted limitation of targets, to widespread devastation of the territory in which it took place, and to the destruction of much of its population. . . .

Source: *"The Vienna Declaration," in* The Atomic Age: Scientists in National and World Affairs, *edited by Morton Grodzins and Eugene Rabinowitch (New York: Basic Books, 1963), pp. 560–561.*

"The war shall soon be over," he continued, with strong emphasis. "We shall recover in fifteen or twenty years, and then we'll have another go at it." Domination over all Germany would have been the most effective means of forestalling another war, and Stalin continued to hope for such control in 1946. When opposition from the West made that goal unattainable, Stalin's successors came to see the unintended division of Germany—arising from the diplomatic impasse of 1945–1947 and confirmed in the Berlin crisis in 1948—as a solution that afforded them considerable protection against a resurgent Germany. The Soviet's hegemony over eastern Europe allowed them to secure the cooperation that refractory Poland had refused them in the interwar period and to deny the Germans potential allies, such as Romania. Eastern Europe also became a security buffer in the event of an attack and a conduit through which Soviet influence could flow to the West. Moscow's East German client soon became a valuable military and economic asset (accounting for 10 percent of Soviet trade and a large percentage of its industrial imports) and, more important, a staging ground for Soviet forces in central Europe. From this forward position the Red Army could not only deflect a German attack far from Soviet borders but also

NUCLEAR WEAPONS

intimate and perhaps eventually "Finlandize" the Western powers.

The United States, on the other hand, had been drawn twice into European wars when one power, Germany, had threatened to overturn the balance of power and establish hegemony over the continent. Experience had taught sophisticated Americans that premature disengagement from Europe, leaving behind an unstable power balance, was a recipe not for normalcy but for further turmoil. The best strategy for the United States, as it had been for Great Britain, was timely intervention to preserve a balance of power before hegemony had to be uprooted through war. By sponsoring the recuperation of European economies and the reintegration of the Western occupation zones of Germany into Western Europe both economically and politically, the United States could prevent the vital Ruhr industrial complex from falling into Russian hands and tipping the balance of power decisively against the Western powers. Moreover, the division of Germany also appeared to provide a satisfactory solution to the German problem. German industrial and military power could be revived and German statehood restored, but within a multilateral framework that reassured Germany's current partners and former victims (perhaps even those east of the Elbe) that its power could not be used recklessly. Even the Soviet occupation of central Europe could be seen as a blessing of sorts since it provided a convincing rationale for a permanent U.S. presence in Europe.

The division of Europe and Germany that evolved without conscious design thus met the minimal objectives of both parties. It preserved a balance of power on the continent for the United States while also affording Soviet Russia reasonable protection against a resurgent Germany. These effects, it must be emphasized, did not rest on the presence of nuclear weapons and would have provided a large measure of stability to the continent even if neither side had procured them. To be sure, both sides could have wished for more. Republicans responded in the early 1950s to public impatience with containment and called for "liberation" of eastern Europe and Asia from totalitarian domination. On the Soviet side, there is evidence that Stalin's ambitions were by no means confined to his "sphere" east of the Elbe and that he was biding his time, awaiting an opportunity to push farther west. Some cold-war analysts argue that, after the division of Europe hardened, the Soviets continued to hope that the United States could be pushed out of Europe and that West Germany could be enticed out of the North Atlantic Treaty Organization (NATO). When eastern Europeans rose in revolt against totalitarianism

in 1953 (East Germany) and 1956 (Hungary)—at a time when North America was beyond the reach of Soviet rockets—the United States quickly disclaimed any intention of intervention. Stalin, for his part, advised his compatriots in Hungary, Czechoslovakia, and France during 1945–1947 that tactical moderation would be the wisest course until the recurrence of depression and absence of any overt communist threat led the United States to withdraw from Europe. Had liberation of the East or revolution in the West been attainable at low risk, either power might have become revisionist regarding the disposition of territory, but neither was willing to challenge the Yalta system at the risk of war, even when nuclear arsenals were inadequate or nonexistent. The U.S.-Soviet balance of terror was superimposed later on a status quo that was minimally satisfactory to both states. The weapons may have reinforced this peace, but they did not make it.

The nonsettlement at Yalta, a geopolitical compromise that satisfied vital interests of the victors of the Second World War, would have provided a fundamental source of stability over the next four decades even if nuclear weapons had never been invented. The peace that division brought Europe was by no means perdurable, however, for in opposition to it ran several sources of potential instability, chief among them the German question and the shifting nuclear balance. How and why these forces were contained is an important part of the explanation for the long peace and merits close examination.

Since 1871 Germany's power and geographical situation had made her the critical issue in European security. Her central position and indefensible borders meant that Germany was not only able to bring great power to bear on many other states, but also highly vulnerable to their efforts to exercise their power against her. Lying in the heart of the continent, Germany often faced enemies on several fronts. If she were unable to defeat all of these well-dispersed antagonists simultaneously or sequentially, Germany would be highly vulnerable; but if she were capable of winning decisively on all sides, Germany was potentially mistress of Europe. Geography, industry, and, some would say, overemphasis on offensive military doctrine made it difficult for Germany and her neighbors to coexist in mutual safety. For Germany it was difficult to attain safety without hegemony. Security, in short, became indivisible from it.

The cold-war system solved this problem. As Josef Joffe contended in 1991, the problem of Germany was resolved because division brought a permanent American presence in Europe, institutionalized through NATO. The Americans pro-

NUCLEAR WEAPONS

Soviet tanks and missiles in the 1965 May Day Parade in Moscow

vided security for the Federal Republic of Germany, easing her defense burden and enabling her to pursue a more narrowly economic vocation. West Germany's military forces were also enmeshed in a joint command that reassured her allies and enemies that German power could not easily be used to challenge the status quo. The U.S. commitment and institutions of NATO eliminated the dilemma of indivisible security arising from the presence of a powerful state in the middle of Europe and provided a solution to the central problem of European security that was minimally acceptable to all sides, including the Soviet Union. For the first time in several generations, the Germans and their neighbors achieved security simultaneously.

Despite the advantages this solution held for Germany and Europe as a whole, it also imposed dreadful burdens on the German nation: at least eight million Germans from east of the Oder were uprooted and dispossessed and another sixteen million remained behind the Iron Curtain. Even the *Diktat* at the Versailles Peace Conference (1919) appears generous by comparison. Yet, the West German government acquiesced willingly in policies and decisions that made these consequences unalterable for four decades. Why, then, did the Germans cooperate in their own division?

The main reason was that the Federal Republic of Germany was permitted to regain her sovereignty and to participate as an equal partner in Western multilateral organizations and thereby to begin repairing the Nazis' damage to the national reputation of Germany. The price of this rehabilitation, however—the apparently irrevocable partition of Germany—was a price not all Germans were prepared to pay.

Integration into the West was not the only option available to the Federal Republic of Germany from 1945 to 1960; revisionism of either the pacifist left or militant right were conceivable alternatives. Postwar Germany was forced to absorb 8–10 million refugees from the eastern territories, raw material for a right-wing revanchist movement. The leader of the opposition Social Democratic Party (SPD), Kurt Schumacher, believed that the commitment of Konrad Adenauer, the first chancellor of the Federal Republic, to the West would eliminate any chance of reunification. Schumacher resisted integration into Western institutions, stridently denouncing Adenauer in one famous parliamentary exchange as "the Chancellor of the allies." In 1951 Adenauer's policy was supported by less than one-fourth of the German public. If successful, the SPD plan would have created a neutral Germany. This form of tripolarity would indisputably have presented many dangers. Had a neutral Germany not raised arms to defend itself, it would probably have fallen under Soviet influence; had it begun to reconstitute its military, the vicious security spirals of the past might have been set in motion.

NUCLEAR WEAPONS

MAD

Mutual Assured Destruction (MAD) is a term used to describe the likely consequences of an all-out nuclear war between the United States and the Soviet Union. Some also used the term to describe what appeared to be the nuclear strategy adopted by Secretary of Defense Robert S. McNamara after he appeared to have retreated from his earlier advocacy of "city-avoidance" doctrine (also called warfighting or limited nuclear war). The record shows, however, that, public statements about the mutual assured destruction notwithstanding, the United States never adopted MAD as a operational doctrine. Ever since McNamara's 1962 speech at a University of Michigan commencement address, in which he advocated that the United States move away from an all-out nuclear exchange doctrine, the United States has persistently developed weapons systems and military doctrines aimed at "fine tuning" nuclear exchanges and limiting the scope of nuclear war. There were three purposes for opting for ever more refined nuclear scenarios: to bolster the credibility of U.S. extended-deterrence posture, create "intra-war" deterrence, and limit the scope of destruction of suchwar.

These perils were averted by the tenacity and vision of Adenauer, who skillfully defused the rightist danger by coopting the refugees into the coalition led by the Christian Democratic Union (CDU) and recruited to the CDU camp Ludwig Erhard, whose bold economic liberalization as economics minister under the occupation regime laid the foundation for Germany's postwar economic miracle. Adenauer adhered doggedly to the policy of integration into Western institutions despite its unpopularity with the German public and heavy opposition in the parliament, constitutional court, and even his own coalition.

Germany thus committed herself to the West and avoided the temptations of both revanchism and neutralism. Statesmanship, as always, was constrained by structure, but the structure of the Yalta system was also shaped by statesmanship. The clarity of threat present after the destruction of the Nazi regime did, indeed, give West Germany a strong incentive to cooperate with Britain and the United States. Yet, the danger of imminent partition and territorial truncation provided a powerful countervailing inducement for Germans to pursue a more independent course. Under Social Democratic leadership West Germany would have been strongly inclined to negotiate with the East rather than amalgamate with the West, with serious con-

sequences for European security. Europe in 1948 was in a state of actual bipolarity but latent tripolarity. United and neutralized, Germany might have become either the third corner of an unstable triad or an indivisible stake too important for either superpower to yield to its adversary. The creation of the bipolar balance may, thus, be attributed to Adolf Hitler's reckless ambition; its preservation may in no small measure be credited to Adenauer's prudence. For this achievement he deserves to be remembered as one of the principal architects of the long postwar peace.

The postwar settlement was initially acceptable to the most powerful states, but it included, especially for the Soviets, serious flaws that they might have endeavored to remedy if the prospects for success had been commensurate with the dangers. Hence, motives cannot be analyzed in the abstract; the potential risks and costs of attempting to alter the status quo must also be considered. The commitment of the United States and the rehabilitation of West Germany improved the balance of conventional forces, but after 1952 NATO never made a serious effort to achieve parity with the enormous conventional forces of the Warsaw Pact. As Gregg Harken has explained, one of the principal reasons for this lack of effort is that the confidence the atomic bomb afforded to the American public left them reluctant to assume the burden of conventional defense. As a result, Western Europe came to rely on American nuclear-striking power to offset the offensive threat posed by the Red Army. The difficulty with this arrangement, as American planners recognized, was that nuclear superiority could not continue forever, and when it ended, the deterrent effect of U.S. weapons might be dangerously attenuated. When, with the launching of Sputnik in 1957, this loss of superiority appeared to be happening, the U.S.-Soviet relationship entered a period of instability and high tension that led the superpowers to the brink of nuclear war. During this period, most of the "rules of the game" that Gaddis cites as part of his explanation for the long peace were broken by the Soviets:

1. "Respect spheres of influence" (Nikita Khrushchev placed missiles ninety miles from Florida);

2. "Avoid direct military confrontation" (Soviet tanks in Berlin trained their guns across Checkpoint Charlie at American forces for twenty-four hours in mid October 1961);

3. "Use nuclear weapons only as an ultimate resort" (Khrushchev boasted repeatedly of his capacities and made horrifying threats against the United States regarding Berlin). Even if observers are convinced that the huge atomic arsenals of the late cold war precluded the outbreak of fighting, they should not forget that the transition to this condition of presumed stability was fraught with

danger and will be so again for states seeking nuclear capability.

The greatest source of stability in the postwar settlement was that it met the minimal requirements of the two states that had emerged from the Second World War as superpowers. The Soviets achieved reasonable protection against a third German invasion by claiming a territorial buffer in east-central Europe, while the Americans preserved a balance of power on the continent by holding the industrial heartland of Germany and averting revolution in France and Italy. For both sides the advantages of any alteration of this state of affairs would have been less than the costs of another major conventional war, even in the absence of nuclear weapons. In time, the atomic bomb may have reinforced this settlement by raising the costs of its revision even higher, but the balance of military forces resulting from U.S. acquisition of the bomb was potentially unstable, and the passage to this era of greater stability was therefore treacherous.

This solution was threatened by the discontent of those who lost most from it, the Germans and east Europeans, as well as by the Soviets' acquisition of nuclear power and the manifold instabilities generated by the unresolved problem of Berlin. These sources of disorder were contained by a fortunate combination of circumstances and statesmanship that was by no means inevitable under bipolar conditions. The bipolar balance of power after the Second World War presented both a clear threat (from the Soviet Union) and a clear responsibility (to the United States). Yet, clear responsibility had not elicited U.S. participation after 1919; and the clear Soviet threat encouraged but did not guarantee cooperation between Germany and the Western powers. Although the beginnings of the Yalta system may have been unintended, the successful construction of the system and management of its inherent contradictions must be credited to the wisdom and determination of postwar Western leadership; its final dismantling to the sober judgment and humanity of statesmen on both sides, including Harry S Truman, Konrad Adenauer, John F. Kennedy, and Mikhail Gorbachev. Had they failed to act, or acted differently, at crucial junctures, the long peace might never have held. It is to them, and not only to Robert Oppenheimer and the other scientists who developed the nuclear bomb at Los Alamos, that the world owes its thanks.

–JOHN ORME, OGLETHORPE UNIVERSITY

References

Geoffrey Blainey, *The Causes of War*, third edition (New York: Free Press, 1988);

A. W. DePorte, *Europe between the Superpowers: The Enduring Balance* (New Haven: Yale University Press, 1979);

Milovan Djilas, *Conversations with Stalin*, translated by Michael B. Petrovich (New York: Harcourt, Brace & World, 1962);

Laurence Freedman, *The Evolution of Nuclear Strategy*, second edition (New York: St. Martin's Press, 1989);

John Lewis Gaddis, *The Long Peace: Inquiries into the History of the Cold War* (New York: Oxford University Press, 1987);

Louis Halle, *The Cold War as History*, expanded edition (New York: HarperCollins, 1991);

Gregg Harken, *The Winning Weapon: The Atomic Bomb in the Cold War 1945–1950* (New York: Knopf, 1980);

Richard Harknett, "The Logic of Conventional Deterrence and the End of the Cold War," *Security Studies*, 4 (Autumn 1994): 86–114;

Robert Jervis, *The Meaning of Nuclear Revolution: Statecraft and the Prospect of Armageddon* (Ithaca, N.Y.: Cornell University Press, 1989);

Josef Joffe, "The End of the Postwar Order and the Future of European Security," in *Reshaping Western Security: The United States Faces a United Europe*, edited by Richard Perle (Washington: AEI Press, 1991);

Joffe, *The Limited Partnership: Europe, the United States and the Burdens of Alliance* (Cambridge, Mass.: Ballinger, 1987);

Jean Laloy, *Yalta: Yesterday, Today, Tomorrow*, translated by William R. Tyler (New York: Harper & Row, 1988);

Melvyn P. Leffler, *A Preponderance of Power: National Security, the Truman Administration, and the Cold War* (Stanford, Cal.: Stanford University Press, 1992);

Scott D. Sagan and Kenneth N. Waltz, *The Spread of Nuclear Weapons: A Debate* (New York: Norton, 1995);

Thomas C. Schelling, *Arms and Influence* (New Haven: Yale University Press, 1966);

Marc Trachtenberg, *History and Strategy* (Princeton, N.J.: Princeton University Press, 1991).

NUCLEAR WEAPONS

ORIGINS

Did the Soviet Union start the cold war?

Viewpoint: Yes, the cold war was the result of the belligerence of Joseph Stalin and the insecurity it caused in the United States and the West.

Viewpoint: No, the primary responsibility for the cold war derives from the hard-line policies of the United States.

The question of who "started" the cold war has been an issue of rancorous debate among historians and policymakers for more than four decades. Most of what was written in the 1950s and 1960s about the origins of the cold war came to be defined as "orthodox" or "traditional." In the 1960s and 1970s a new interpretation of the sources of the cold war emerged and was dubbed "revisionist" because of its challenge to the orthodox interpretation. Shortly after the first revisionist studies appeared, and at an accelerated pace during the late 1980s and early 1990s, as archives in the Soviet Union (later Russia) and Soviet-bloc countries opened to Western scholars, a "postrevisionist" reading of the origins of the cold war appeared.

Traditionalists put the blame for the cold war on the Soviet Union. They argue that the Soviets' denial of free elections in Poland and Czechoslovakia, their meddling in Greece, Turkey, and Iran, their assistance to communist forces in China, and their opposition to U.S.-sponsored postwar plans for controlling weapons and promoting economic development—such as the Baruch Plan and the Marshall Plan—caused the Truman administration to reassess its initially more conciliatory approach to the Soviet Union and adopt a harder line toward it. There are differences among traditionalists regarding the driving motivation behind Soviet conduct. Some emphasize the messianic nature of communist ideology, while others offer a combination of traditional Russian imperial impulses, and also point out that Soviet conduct was in line with historical patterns of traditional power politics.

Revisionists argue that Soviet behavior was largely defensive in nature. After the devastation of the Second World War, the Soviet leadership was interested in rebuilding its country and addressing legitimate security concerns—especially making sure that the countries of east and central Europe would no longer be used as a corridor of invasion into Russia. According to this argument, it was the United States, driven by a capitalist need for markets and raw materials, that adopted a confrontational, bullying tone toward the Soviet Union, leading to the outbreak of the cold war.

Postrevisionists reject what they regard as the dogmatic Marxism that characterized much of the revisionist reading, but they also challenge what they consider an excessive emphasis by traditionalists on the role of communist ideology in guiding Soviet foreign policy. Postrevisionist analyses emphasize geopolitical considerations and strategic realities to suggest a more balanced view of responsibility for the cold war. In their writings, however, there is a return to traditionalist themes, as they point to provocative Soviet actions and to an exceedingly bellicose Soviet rhetoric as major contributing factors in the breakdown of cooperation between the two countries and the onset of the cold war.

Viewpoint:
Yes, the cold war was the result of the belligerence of Joseph Stalin and the insecurity it caused in the United States and the West.

The cold war—the discrete, globalized confrontation between the United States and the Soviet Union that began immediately after the Second World War and came to an end with the disintegration of the Soviet Union in 1991—occurred as a result of the belligerence of Joseph Stalin and the insecurity it caused in the United States. The "revisionist" interpretation of the cold war, which stipulates that it originated in the expansionist tendencies of American capitalism, accurately explains some kinds of U.S. expansion after 1945, but it fails to account for the particular hostility of U.S.-Soviet relations during this period.

There can be no doubt that after the Second World War the United States engaged in the most lucrative and widespread economic expansion in the history of modern empires. A powerful, confident, industrial powerhouse, the United States saw every one of its major economic competitors go down to defeat or demoralization during the war. Japan and Germany were reduced to rubble; Great Britain, and, to a greater extent, France, were shorn of their colonial holdings and exposed as declining economic powers. Unscathed by the war and brimming with wartime industrial capability, the United States sought to fill the vacuum left by the reduction and retrenchment of its economic rivals. New York City replaced London as the center of world capitalism. American goods and American popular culture flooded every corner of the world. American corporations wielded immense power and leverage over dozens of foreign societies, squeezing profits from them and in so doing enriching the American population.

This imperial project had nothing essentially to do with the Soviet Union of 1946. The United States had been engaged in global economic expansion since the 1890s; its postwar policies were merely an accelerated continuation of its earlier agenda. If the Soviet Union had been taken over by the Walt Disney Company in 1946, the basic elements and direction of American economic expansion would have continued unchanged. Nations that emerge triumphant after world wars, such as the Netherlands after

the Thirty Years' War (1618–1648) or Great Britain after the Napoleonic wars (1803–1815), tend to exploit their hard-won success materially; the United States was no exception to this rule.

What pushed postwar international politics beyond simple imperial rivalry and into the volatile and militarized cold war was the growing insecurity of the United States, particularly key officials in President Harry S Truman's administration, about the belligerence and aggressiveness of the Soviet Union under its tyrannical leader Joseph Stalin. This insecurity manifested itself in late 1945 and reached a critical level in February 1946. By that point Truman administration officials had become convinced that, left unchecked, the Soviet Union would eventually threaten the security of the United States.

During the wartime Tehran Conference of late 1943, President Franklin D. Roosevelt declined to support a British proposal to revive French and German power after the war. By announcing this decision he was making it clear to Great Britain and the Soviet Union that the United States would not oppose Soviet domination of the European continent. As Roosevelt, British prime minister Winston Churchill, and Stalin all understood, with Germany and France weakened, the Soviet Union would be the only remaining great power on the Eurasian continent. Nonetheless, Roosevelt believed in 1943 that the United States could tolerate Soviet hegemony. Certainly, Germany was not then regarded as a nation to be rejuvenated, and the dismal performance of France during the war had discouraged Roosevelt from viewing it as a legitimate European postwar power.

At the Yalta Conference in 1945 Roosevelt's acquiescence to the obvious signs of Soviet domination over eastern Europe merely affirmed his earlier decision. By once again declining to bolster France and Germany and by tolerating Stalin's flagrant imposition of Soviet-style regimes in Poland and elsewhere, Roosevelt, a dying man at Yalta, gave no signal that the U.S. position on the postwar balance of power in Europe had changed. This crucial question faced Truman when he became president on the death of Roosevelt in April 1945: would he continue to regard the expansion of Soviet power in Europe as acceptable to the United States?

From the vantage point of basic American national security, this question did not have an obvious answer. Certainly the Soviet Union was in many ways a hostile regime. As Truman's more hard-line advisers and his Republican crit-

ORIGINS

Prime Minister Clement R. Attlee, President Harry S Truman, and Premier Joseph Stalin meeting at Potsdam in July 1945. Standing behind the three leaders are Admiral William D. Leahy, chief of staff to President Truman; British Foreign Secretary Ernest Bevin, U.S. Secretary of State James F. Byrnes; and Soviet Foreign Minister Vyacheslav Molotov.

ics in Congress were quick to point out, the Soviets had violated wartime agreements in eastern Europe, having ruthlessly and often brutally imposed client regimes on the long-suffering populations in that part of the continent. Moreover, the Soviet Union adhered to an ideology of global communist revolution and the destruction of capitalist regimes such as the United States, an ideology that Stalin had already used to justify the liquidation of millions of "class enemies" and political opponents in the 1920s and 1930s. On the other hand, many American officials regarded the Soviet domination of eastern Europe as an understandable, defensive act, considering that Germany had crossed the central European plain to invade Russia twice in the space of thirty years. Revelations about Stalinist atrocities and terror were widely discounted as American and British propaganda or at least regarded as internal matters. Finally, the physical devastation of the Soviet population and the Red Army, together with the American monopoly over the atomic bomb, led many to minimize the possibility of a Soviet threat to American security.

The answer to the question boiled down to a reading of Stalin's true objectives and an interpretation of those objectives in light of U.S.

national security. If the Soviet government were interested in moving beyond eastern Europe and dominating the entire continent, and if the Soviet domination of Europe could be seen as a threat to American survival, then it would make sense to abandon Roosevelt's Tehran policy and adopt a more confrontational position toward the Soviet Union. During late 1945 and early 1946 Truman and his advisers debated this problem, and in February 1946 they decided that the Soviet Union indeed sought to expand its power and therefore posed a serious long-term threat to the security of the United States.

Three events pushed Truman and his aides to adopt this position. On 9 February 1946, Stalin delivered a public address in which he revived a form of volatile communist rhetoric that had been suppressed during the war. In his speech Stalin blamed American criticism of his actions in eastern Europe on the forces of international capitalism, asserting that the Second World War was the result of capitalist rivalries and predicting that the Soviet Union would prevail over its capitalist enemies. This ill-timed speech discredited those individuals who saw Stalin as a defensive-minded Russian nationalist, and it emboldened Americans who viewed him as a messianic communist revolutionary. On 16 February the U.S. government announced the discovery of a spy ring in the United States: agents of the Soviet Union, acting as Canadian emissaries and scientists, had been caught infiltrating U.S. atomic facilities. This revelation fueled American animosities toward its erstwhile ally, as well as sparking concern of an imminent Soviet atomic arsenal. A week later George F. Kennan, an American diplomat working in Moscow, sent a telegram to Washington explaining Stalin's recent actions. The Soviets, he argued, adhered to a different view of international politics than did the United States and other western nations. He contended that the Russians were much more cynical about international agreements, considering them as pieces of paper to be discarded when convenient, rather than as binding documents. They regarded the West as an eternal adversary of Russia, always arrogant in its dealings with "backward" Russia and never to be trusted. They thought of adversaries in international relations not as rival nations but as sworn enemies to be destroyed. These Russian traditions, Kennan argued, were strengthened by Soviet ideology, which lent a sense of historical inevitability to the looming conflict with the West. Kennan's "long telegram" captivated its many readers in the Truman administration, who were receptive to a clear, historically based assessment of the Soviet threat.

Could Soviet belligerence threaten the United States? In 1946 Americans faced a world far more dangerous than any they had seen before. The Japanese attack at Pearl Harbor in 1941 had shown that nations could launch surprise attacks on America from across oceans, something that had never before been technologically possible. The rapid Nazi conquest of Europe had demonstrated that the balance of power in Europe can change in an instant—that nations will often fold in the face of seemingly inexorable power. Its geographical isolation, together with the historically stable balance of European power, had long provided the United States with free national security. Recent history had proven beyond a doubt that it had become possible for a regime to dominate the Eurasian continent quickly and attack the United States directly and devastatingly.

In 1946 the only nation even remotely capable of threatening the United States was the Soviet Union. The Soviets still had an immense army, which was certainly capable of marching through war-torn Europe and attaining inestimable geopolitical momentum and military resources. The Soviets formally

STALIN'S WORLDVIEW

On 9 February 1946 Soviet premier Joseph Stalin delivered a radio address to his nation, reviving the anticapitalist rhetoric that he had tempered during the Second World War. The following excerpts explain his view of the struggle between capitalism and communism and his faith in the strength of the Soviet state:

During the past four years the events of the struggle against the German and Japanese aggressors developed—the events of the Second World War. Doubtless the war was the main event of that period.

It would be incorrect to think that the war arose accidentally or as the result of the fault of some of the statesmen. Although these faults did exist, the war arose in reality as the inevitable result of the development of the world economic and political forces on the basis of monopoly capitalism.

Our Marxists declare that the capitalist system of the world economy conceals elements of crisis and war, that the development of world capitalism does not follow a steady and even course forward, but proceeds through crises and catastrophes. The uneven development of the capitalist countries leads in time to sharp disturbances in their relations and the group of countries which consider themselves inadequately provided with raw materials and export markets try usually to change this situation and to change the position in their favor by means of armed force.

As a result of these factors, the capitalist world is sent into two hostile camps and war follows.

Perhaps the catastrophe of war could have been avoided if the possibility of periodic redistribution of raw materials and markets between the countries existed in accordance with their economic needs, in the way of coordinated and peaceful decisions. But this is impossible under the present capitalist development of world economy. . . .

The point is that the Soviet social system has proved to be more capable of life and more stable than a non-Soviet social system, that the Soviet social system is a better form of organization of society than any non-Soviet social system. . . .

Source: *"New Five-Year Plan for Russia,"* Vital Speeches of the Day, 12 (15 Octover 1945 – 1 October 1946): 300.

adhered to an ideology that endorsed the violent overthrow of capitalist regimes such as the United States. The only question was whether the Soviet Union actually intended to embark on such a campaign. Stalin's brutal treatment of his own citizens, his cynical treaty with Nazi Germany, and his imposition of tyrannical regimes in eastern Europe confirmed the suspicions of Truman and his

ORIGINS

advisers. The events of early 1946 convinced them it would be too great a risk to assume that the Soviet Union did not intend to dominate Europe or to believe that the United States would be safe in a world where the Soviets controlled that entire region. No one could be sure that the Soviet Union would embark on such a campaign; more important, it had become impossible for Truman and his aides to believe with certainty that the Soviets would not. Erring on the side of national security, Truman therefore decided to adopt a harder line toward the Soviet Union in the many postwar negotiations of 1946 and 1947. Despite the American atomic monopoly, the Soviet Union did not back down. The cold war ensued.

–CAMPBELL CRAIG, UNIVERSITY OF CANTERBURY, NEW ZEALAND

Viewpoint:
No, the primary responsibility for the cold war derives from the hard-line policies of the United States.

Three main perspectives have dominated the debate on the origins of the cold war. For traditionalists the cold war was caused by hostile Soviet intentions rooted in communist ideology and the need to justify internal repression. Once Soviet expansionist goals became clear in 1946 and 1947, the United States was forced into a firm containment posture that it would otherwise have avoided. The revisionists turn this argument on its head, arguing that the origins of the cold war lie in hostile U.S. actions from 1945 to 1947, at a point when Soviet leaders sought peace so that they could rebuild their idevastated country. The reasons revisionists give for U.S. aggression vary, but they include American efforts to promote global capitalism and American paranoia in regard to U.S. security needs. The third perspective, postrevisionism, offers a middle-ground position. Postrevisionists hold that the cold war was, above all, the tragic result of the anarchic international system. Both superpowers were driven primarily by the quest for security; yet, each saw the other as aggressive, and thus each acted to protect its respective sphere. These actions fueled an unnecessary spiral of mistrust and hostility, one that persisted into the 1980s.

This essay, building on the seminal work of Melvyn Leffler in 1992, agrees with the postrevisionist argument but pushes it a bit further. By 1946–1947 both superpowers were indeed caught up in a tragic spiral of distrust. Primary responsibility for the cold war, however, lies with the United States because it was the first state to shift to hard-line policies after the Second World War. As early as mid 1945 President Harry S Truman began to move toward a policy that later became known as "containment," despite his awareness that this policy would likely lead to a destabilizing arms race. He took this provocative action, Leffler argues, to ensure that the United States maintained its "preponderance of power" against the rising Soviet colossus. Containment strategies in 1945 thus reflected rational geopolitics rather than greed or irrational paranoia.

Truman's adoption of hard-line policies was not based on a belief that Soviet premier Joseph Stalin had aggressive intentions. In fact, Truman liked and even respected Stalin at that time. Rather, Truman recognized that if America did not act, the Soviet Union would grow significantly, and the Soviet leaders who later replaced Stalin might not be so moderate. In short, the cold war began for systemic, realistic reasons: the fear of decline; uncertainty about the future intentions of the other nation; and the prudent realization that unless preventive action were taken at that time, it might be too late in the future.

Standard accounts of the cold war usually designate 1947 as the year in which the American containment strategy was set in place. Yet, the core foundations of this containment were actually laid by August 1945. The full extent of this policy may be seen in the following eight interlocking actions taken in 1945 to restrict Soviet economic and military growth:

1. The surrounding of the Soviet Union with U.S. air and naval bases in order to project military power into the Soviet heartland;

2. the termination of U.S. aid to the Soviets, even as aid was extended to the Chinese—an action that included resisting Soviet claims to badly needed reparations from Germany;

3. the use of the atomic bomb, which—in addition to ending the Pacific war quickly—was designed to make Moscow more accommodating in postwar relations;

4. the American effort to rebuild western Europe, which required the revitalization of the western half of Germany, a nation that had just killed more than twenty million Russians;

5. the rapid deployment of U.S. and allied troops in Korea, China, and Manchuria to prevent communist penetration of the region;

6. the U.S. refusal to give atomic secrets and materials to the Soviet Union;

7. the restricting of Soviet naval access to the Mediterranean and North Sea despite recognition of Soviet legal rights;

8. the exclusion of any Soviet role in the occupation and revitalization of Japan, a nation that had fought several wars with Russia in the first half of the twentieth century.

In implementing this policy Truman did not believe he was abandoning all chances of cooperation with the Soviet Union; a great-power modus vivendi might still be worked out. Any such arrangement, however, would be on U.S. terms. In short, the United States would do everything necessary to maintain a preponderant position. If the Soviets cooperated, so much the better. If they did not, Truman preferred a cold war—with all its attendant risks of inadvertent escalation—to a situation in which the United States cooperated at the expense of long-term power. Allowing the Soviet Union to achieve a dominant position would threaten U.S. security, should Soviet intentions prove aggressive down the road.

On 2 April 1945 a top-secret report from the Office of Strategic Services (OSS), forerunner of the Central Intelligence Agency (CIA), was forwarded to President Roosevelt; it was subsequently given to Truman. The report outlined the dilemma: Russia would emerge from the war as the strongest nation in Eurasia. Indeed, "Russia's natural resources and manpower are so great that within a relatively few years she can be much more powerful than either Germany or Japan has ever been. In the easily foreseeable future Russia may well outrank even the United States in military potential." These fears were reinforced by similar OSS intelligence reports in May. Later that month James F. Byrnes, who was soon to be secretary of state, summed up the feelings of Truman's inner circle. He argued that the best U.S. strategy would be to push ahead as quickly as possible in the development of atomic weaponry to ensure that America stayed ahead of the Soviet Union, even as the United States tried to maintain good relations.

The tragic side of U.S. policy in 1945 is that it sprang from a fear of future Soviet intentions, not present ones. During the Potsdam Conference in July–August 1945, as he crystallized his containment strategy, Truman found Stalin not entirely disagreeable. In late July he wrote in his diaries and to his wife that he liked Stalin and found him honest and straightforward. Near the end of the conference Stalin canceled a meeting because of a cold, and Truman wrote in a diary entry that he was worried about what would happen were Stalin suddenly to die. Some "demagogue on horseback" would take over the Soviet state and destroy the fragile European peace. Byrnes expressed similar concerns throughout the fall of 1945.

Maintaining the U.S. preponderance of power was thus considered necessary as protection against an uncertain future. Yet, U.S. leaders also understood that the policies required to secure this preponderance could antagonize Moscow. In discussions over the spring and summer with his old friend Joseph E. Davies, a former ambassador to the Soviet Union, Truman was warned repeatedly that, given their history, the Russians were extremely anxious about foreign attacks. In particular Davies cautioned that the demonstration of atomic weaponry over Japan and the withholding of atomic secrets would only undermine Soviet trust, causing a massive arms race that might lead to nuclear annihilation. Yet, by the fall of 1945 Truman's sense of prudence had led him to reject all atomic sharing. In October an old friend, Fyke Farmer, asked him if this policy meant that the armaments race was on. The president replied in the affirmative, but added that the United States would stay ahead.

It is now generally accepted that at least part of the reason for dropping atomic bombs on Japan was to send a signal of U.S. superiority to Moscow. In particular Byrnes and Secretary of War Henry L. Stimson believed in the summer of 1945 that demonstrating the effectiveness of the bomb would impress Russia with American military might. Byrnes thought the atomic bomb might help to keep the Soviets from overwhelming Manchuria and northern China in August. After the mid-July atomic tests revealed the true destructive power of the bomb, Truman was much more confident that it could be employed as a diplomatic tool to restrict Soviet expansion. As he told an assistant at Potsdam, the bomb "would keep the Russians straight." This conviction made him more willing to press U.S. demands at the conference, which could only have heightened growing Soviet suspicions.

Nothing in the foregoing argument implies that the Soviet Union was a "good" state; it was, as Truman realized, a brutal dictatorship that killed and oppressed its own citizens. Yet, out of simple geopolitical self-interest, Stalin wanted to maintain good relations with the West in 1945: he needed breathing space to rebuild his war-ravaged country. Loans from the United States, reparations from Germany, and relative peace in the near term were critical to this rebuilding process. It is thus not surprising that Truman found Stalin straightforward and businesslike at Potsdam. Yet, it is evident that after August, once the elements of Truman's containment policy were in place, Moscow became much less accommodating. Stalin pressed for early development of a Soviet atomic bomb, sought to prevent Soviet exclusion from the occupation of Japan, and resisted any Soviet retreat from northern Iran.

By 1946 Soviet rhetoric was predicting that a clash between the two superpowers was all but inevitable.

In the end, of course, it is difficult to say whether, even without the provocative U.S. actions in 1945, the Soviets would have shifted to a policy of confrontation. Stalin and his advisers were a highly suspicious, if not paranoid, lot. It is clear, however, that in terms of relative hostility of policy, the United States moved first in the escalation spiral. Although the Soviets did seek to consolidate their hold in eastern Europe, both Roosevelt and Truman in 1945 had resigned themselves to the division of Europe. Yet, the series of actions Truman undertook during the summer of 1945 could only have been seen by Moscow as an effort to project superior American power against the Soviet periphery and to maintain U.S. strategic preponderance.

American policy was not immoral, only tragic. It reflected the twin problems of the fear of decline and the fear of future intentions of the rising Soviet state. In such circumstances it was only prudent for the stronger state to move reluctantly to shore up its dominance across the board. Truman's understanding that his policies would likely bring on a cold-war spiral only heightens the sense of tragedy. He was forced to choose a policy that represented the lesser of two evils: preponderance and an increased risk of war in the short term over decline and a possible war later under less auspicious power conditions.

—DALE C. COPELAND, UNIVERSITY OF VIRGINIA

References

Gar Alperovitz, with assistance of Sanho Tree and others, *The Decision to Use the Atomic Bomb and the Architecture of an American Myth* (New York: Knopf, 1995);

Dale C. Copeland, *Anticipating Power: Dynamic Realism and the Origins of Major War* (Ithaca, N.Y.: Cornell University Press, forthcoming 2000);

Herbert Feis, *From Trust to Terror: The Onset of the Cold War, 1945–1950* (New York: Norton, 1970);

Robert H. Ferrell, ed., *Off the Record: The Private Papers of Harry S. Truman* (New York: Harper & Row, 1980);

Denna Frank Fleming, *The Cold War and Its Origins*, 2 volumes (Garden City, N.Y.: Doubleday, 1961);

John Lewis Gaddis, *The United States and the Origins of the Cold War, 1941–1947* (New York: Columbia University Press, 1972);

Gaddis, *We Now Know: Rethinking Cold War History* (Oxford: Clarendon Press, 1997);

Alonzo L. Hamby, *Man of the People: A Life of Harry S Truman* (New York: Oxford University Press, 1995);

Gregg Herken, *The Winning Weapon: The Atomic Bomb in the Cold War, 1945–1950* (New York: Knopf, 1980);

Michael J. Hogan, *A Cross of Iron: Harry S. Truman and the Origins of the National Security State, 1945–1954* (Cambridge & New York: Cambridge University Press, 1998);

Hogan, ed., *America in the World: The Historiography of American Foreign Relations Since 1941* (Cambridge & New York: Cambridge University Press, 1995);

Howard Jones and Randall Woods, "Origins of the Cold War in Europe and the Near East," *Diplomatic History,* 17 (Spring 1993): 251–310;

Michael Kort, ed., *The Columbia Guide to the Cold War* (New York: Columbia University Press, 1998);

Melvyn P. Leffler, *A Preponderance of Power: National Security, the Truman Administration, and the Cold War* (Stanford, Cal.: Stanford University Press, 1992);

Thomas J. McCormick, *America's Half-Century: United States Foreign Policy in the Cold War and After,* second edition (Baltimore: Johns Hopkins University Press, 1995);

David G. McCullough, *Truman* (New York: Simon & Schuster, 1992);

William Appleman Williams, *The Tragedy of American Diplomacy* (Cleveland: World, 1959).

QUEMOY AND MATSU

Were the stakes at Quemoy and Matsu high enough for the United States to risk war with communist China?

Viewpoint: Yes, preventing communist China from taking over Quemoy and Matsu was important to check communist expansion.

Viewpoint: No, Quemoy and Matsu were not strategically important enough to warrant a war between the United States and communist China.

After losing the Chinese civil war to Mao Tse-tung's communist insurgency, the Nationalist forces and their leader, Chiang Kai-shek, fled to the island of Taiwan, establishing there the Republic of China (ROC). In addition to Taiwan, the Nationalists kept under their control two small offshore island groups, named after their largest islands, Quemoy and Matsu.

The Chinese communists on the mainland were uncomfortable with Taiwanese control of these islands. The People's Republic of China (PRC) never recognized the independent existence of Taiwan, and the presence of Taiwanese military on the islands gave credence to Chiang's pledge to launch a war to "liberate" China from the communists.

In September 1954 Chinese batteries began to bombard the island of Quemoy. Taiwan responded by launching its air force against targets in China and by increasing its military presence on the islands. Coming as it did on the heels of the Korean War, the Chinese military action and subsequent buildup led U.S. and Taiwanese policymakers to fear that China was planning to seize the islands and perhaps even to invade and take over Taiwan itself. In response, on 2 December 1954 the United States and Taiwan signed a defense treaty, and on 28 January 1955 Congress passed the Formosa Doctrine, committing the United States to the defense of Taiwan's independence. In April 1955 the United States threatened to resort to nuclear weapons to achieve this end. The crisis gave way to negotiations between the United States and the PRC, and the two governments agreed to meet regularly in Geneva to resolve outstanding disputes between them.

A second crisis over the islands, however, occurred within three years. Dissatisfied with the progress made in their talks with the United States, the Chinese decided to take a firmer stand on the issue of the islands. In August 1958 they began to bombard the islands again, with U.S. and Taiwanese forces responding in kind. For a while it appeared that the United States might get involved in a war with China and perhaps even with the Soviet Union, which supported the Chinese position. Tensions again subsided, but without a formal agreement. China still maintains that it is the rightful owner of the islands and continues to claim Taiwan as an integral part of China.

Viewpoint:
Yes, preventing communist China from taking over Quemoy and Matsu was important to check communist expansion.

On two separate occasions the United States chose to confront the People's Republic of China (PRC) over the Chinese decision to attack Quemoy and Matsu. The U.S. decision to turn Chinese harassment of these islands into a cold-war crisis stemmed from an extreme version of the domino theory that is more commonly associated with the Vietnam War. Nevertheless, the American decision to oppose China over Quemoy and Matsu must be distinguished from a genuine American willingness to initiate general war to defend them.

Following the Chinese civil war in 1948 and 1949, a Nationalist, anticommunist government, led by Chiang Kai-shek, fled the Chinese mainland and settled on the offshore island of Taiwan (Formosa). President Harry S Truman's administration offered Chiang's government substantial economic and military aid and promised to defend Nationalist China from a prospective communist attack. The Truman administration's decision in 1950 to wage cold war on an intensive, global level, together with the outbreak later that year of the Korean War, naturally solidified American support for Taiwan. By 1954 Taiwan had become a staunch American ally in the Far East.

Two elements in American foreign policy pushed U.S. support for Taiwan beyond a simple military alliance. The strong China Lobby in American politics, a group with which the new secretary of state, John Foster Dulles, was in sympathy, vocally supported the policy of encouraging Chiang's regime to return to the mainland and liberate China from the communist regime. An idea also endorsed by many in the U.S. military, "liberation" became a mantra not only for supporters of Chiang in Congress but also for Chiang himself, who was eager to lead an American-financed army onto the mainland and depose his old communist adversaries. American policymakers also had become generally persuaded by an argument put forth by George F. Kennan (then a professor at Princeton), Hans J. Morgenthau (an American political scientist), and other students of international politics. Their "bandwagon" principle, or "domino theory," postulated that tremendous swings in the balance of power can result from minor concessions or defeats. As the early success of Nazi Germany during the Second World War had demonstrated, a small victory by an expansionist regime can psychologically demoralize large populations, making them vulnerable to the temptation of jumping on the expansionist's bandwagon. According to this psychological interpretation, following the conquest of a small nation, larger nations nearby could fall like dominoes as the expansionist regime's momentum builds up and populations face the inevitable. During the Korean War, Truman administration officials, and later their successors in the administration of Dwight D. Eisenhower, identified Taiwan as the first domino in East Asia. Should the United States allow Taiwan to fall, officials such as Dulles warned, Indochina, South Korea, and Japan were certain to follow, and all of East and Southeast Asia would be lost.

Aware of this intense American support for his nation, Chiang hoped to parlay it into a war to liberate the mainland. One way to achieve that goal, he believed, was to deploy a large part of his army on the barren island groups of Quemoy and Matsu, both of which are much closer to the mainland than to Taiwan. By doing so, he would provoke the communists and demonstrate his readiness to begin the liberation. American officials endorsed Chiang's decision out of deference to the China Lobby and amid the generally inflamed cold-war climate of the early 1950s.

In the fall of 1954 the PRC initiated an artillery attack on Quemoy and Matsu. The Chinese were uneasy about Chiang's forces being deployed so close to their borders, particularly given the recent decision by the United States to advance toward the Yalu River during the Korean War. Chinese leaders also wanted to humiliate Chiang and hoped that the United States would force the Nationalist leader to evacuate the tiny islands. Finally, the communist government wanted to pick a fight with the United States in order to force the Soviet Union to side with the PRC in an active cold-war confrontation. Chinese leaders such as Mao Tse-tung and Chou En-lai suspected that the Soviet Union was eager to establish better relations with the United States. Instigating a crisis in the Taiwan Strait would compel the Russians to show their true colors.

The United States had to decide how to interpret the Chinese attack, which could be classified as something between harassment and outright invasion. This ambiguity posed a dilemma for the Eisenhower administration because its New Look policy had diminished American conventional forces and replaced them with atomic weapons. Moreover, the minuscule size of the islands made them difficult, if not impossible, to defend from an actual amphibious attack. American military

QUEMOY AND MATSU

officers agreed that, if the United States were to defend Quemoy and Matsu, it would have to launch a nuclear attack against the artillery bases on the Chinese coast.

Over the winter of 1954–1955 the Eisenhower administration debated its alternatives. In March 1955 it decided to wage "atomic diplomacy." On 8 March, Dulles announced that a new and powerful weapon of precision might be used to defeat the Chinese attack; on 12 March, Eisenhower, at a press conference, compared the use of atomic weapons to that of a bullet. The administration's intention was to suggest that the United States would not be squeamish about using an atomic attack if the Chinese persisted in their bombardment of the islands. After a month of internal debate and a struggle with their Soviet allies, on 23 April the Chinese announced a desire to begin negotiations over Quemoy and Matsu. At a conference in Geneva later that year, the two sides agreed to allow Chiang to retain possession of them.

In August of 1958 the Chinese communists resumed their artillery attacks on Quemoy and Matsu. Their motivations were similar to those in 1954: an exasperation over Chiang's deployment of troops so close to the mainland shore and a desire to force the Soviet Union to side with the PRC against the United States. The correlation of military forces, however, had changed. By 1958 the Soviet Union possessed (or so the Americans suspected) a significant number of thermonuclear bombs that could be dropped on American cities by Soviet planes flying one-way missions. Threatening China with nuclear war over Quemoy and Matsu now had much graver consequences. Nevertheless, the United States did not want to force Chiang to abandon the islands. As Dulles again argued, this move would lead to the collapse of East Asia and the retrenchment of the United States back to Hawaii.

Eisenhower, who was less pessimistic than Dulles about the durability of America's Asian allies—and at the same time more eager to avoid thermonuclear war in defense of tiny islands—sought to make a quiet deal with the communist Chinese. He ordered Dulles to convey a message to the Chinese through diplomatic intermediaries: The United States would force Chiang to evacuate his troops from the islands in exchange for an agreement to stop shelling them. The islands would remain nominally in Taiwanese possession, but they would be demilitarized and hence unsuitable as staging grounds for a liberation of the mainland. Enraged by the decision, Chiang nevertheless had no choice but to accede to it.

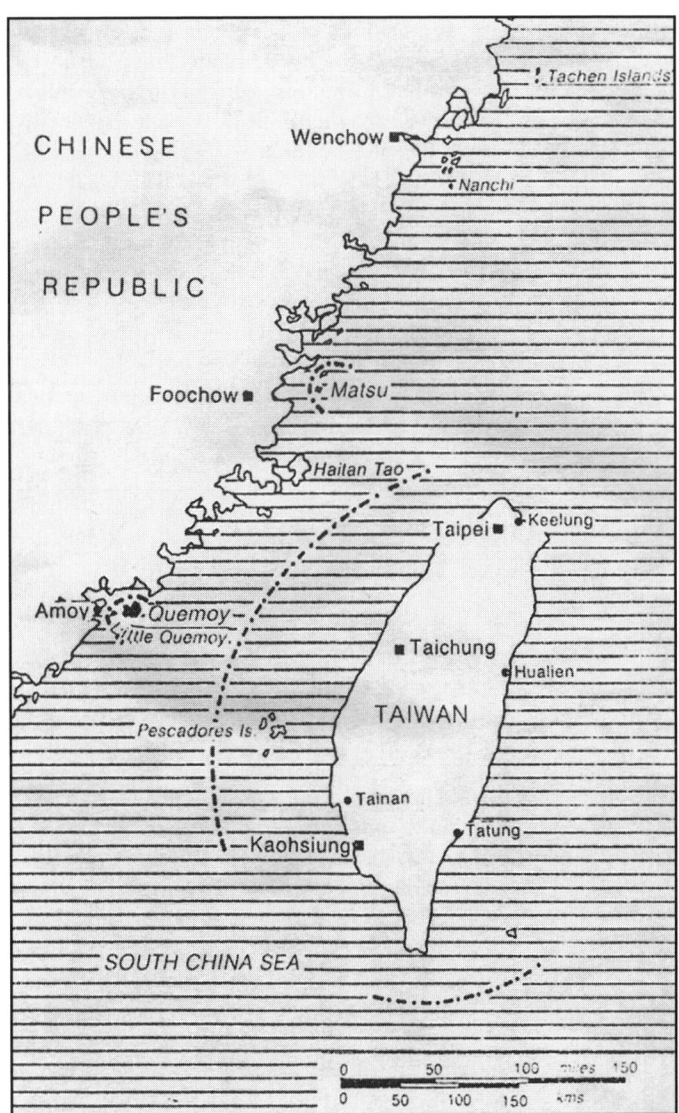

Map of the South China Sea, showing the proximity of the Quemoy and Matsu island chains to mainland China

In September the Chinese agreed in principle to this deal, and over the next month the two sides hammered out the details in Warsaw, Poland. By the end of 1958 Quemoy and Matsu were demilitarized and largely abandoned, as they remain today.

The American decision to confront communist China over the Quemoy and Matsu island chains was based on an extreme interpretation of the bandwagon, or domino, theory. No high-ranking American official argued that defending the two islands was, in an objective, geopolitical sense, obviously crucial to the security of Taiwan: the United States could have compelled Chiang to abandon them in 1954 while assuring him of America's determination to defend his nation. Nor did the United States, on the other hand, view the islands as stepping-stones to the liberation of mainland China. Eisenhower's atomic bluff in 1955 and his rapid pursuit of compromise in 1958 belie the picture of a United States eager to commence the counterrevolution against communism. Rather, Quemoy and Matsu were remnants of American cold-war policy prior to the advent of thermonuclear arsenals; worthy, perhaps, of defending with war before 1953 but manifestly not so afterward. Unable to announce this new reality publicly, Eisenhower turned to diplomacy, bluff, compromise, and, in the case of Chiang, betrayal in order to avoid the colossal folly of waging a thermonuclear war to defend the tiny island outposts of Quemoy and Matsu.

–CAMPBELL CRAIG, UNIVERSITY OF CANTERBURY, NEW ZEALAND

Viewpoint:
No, Quemoy and Matsu were not stragetically important enough to warrant a war between the United States and communist China.

The islands of Quemoy and Matsu are within a short distance of Fujian Province of mainland China. Quemoy is only two miles from the mainland port Xiamen, and Matsu is ten miles from the mainland port Fuzhou. After Chiang Kai-shek's Nationalist regime fled the mainland to Taiwan in the wake of its defeat by Mao Tse-tung's communist forces in 1949, Nationalist troops retained control of the islands, which Taiwan still controls.

In 1954 and 1955, and again in 1958, the communist People's Liberation Army (PLA) launched artillery attacks on Quemoy and Matsu, opening a new crisis not only between Taiwan and mainland China but also between China and the United States. Despite the hostile rhetoric and preemptive actions, the administration of Dwight D. Eisenhower had no plans to engage in an all-out war with China, even if the PLA continued to bombard and then attempted to take over the islands.

After air and naval clashes between the PLA and Nationalist forces, as well as Nationalist intrusions against mainland offshore areas, on 3 September 1954 the PLA launched concentrated artillery bombardments on Quemoy. Two days later, three U.S. aircraft carriers, a cruiser, and three destroyer divisions took up positions a few miles from Quemoy.

The majority of the U.S. National Security Council did not want to face a war with China, which would be essentially a continuation of the Chinese civil war. Neither President Eisenhower nor Secretary of State John Foster Dulles intended to fight an all-out war with China over

the islands, although both confirmed their support for the Nationalists. Eisenhower warned that "Quemoy is not our ship." He said that the importance of the offshore islands was trivial, "except psychologically." That is, the fall of Quemoy and Matsu would undermine Nationalist Chinese confidence that they might eventually conquer the mainland.

U.S. commitment to Quemoy and Matsu was limited in legal terms. In January 1955 the U.S. Congress passed the Formosa Doctrine (or Taiwan Resolution), giving the president authority to employ U.S. armed forces for the protection of Taiwan and related islands. Nevertheless, Eisenhower did not clarify which offshore islands he would defend and said that the United States would not intervene unless a communist attack was aimed at Taiwan itself. When Chiang Kai-shek claimed that the United States would defend Matsu and Quemoy as vital to the defense of Taiwan, Dulles responded that "the United States has no commitment and no purpose to defend the coastal islands as such." Furthermore, Dulles was unwilling to encourage the Nationalists to invade the mainland.

In December 1954 the United States and Chiang's Republic of China had signed a mutual-security treaty, which gave the United States the right to dispose its forces in Taiwan and the Pescadores. There was, however, no indication that mutual defense would be extended to cover Quemoy or Matsu. Also, when the treaty was signed, there was an unusual exchange of notes between Dulles and Nationalist foreign minister George Yeh. The notes stipulated that the Nationalist government would not resort to force against communist China, except in joint agreement with the United States and subject to the legitimate need for self-defense. During the offshore crises in the 1950s, the Eisenhower administration had been consistent in restraining the Nationalist government from using force against the mainland.

Even the U.S. atomic threat at the peak of the crisis appeared to be a passing bluff. In March 1955, as the PLA campaign against Quemoy intensified, Dulles and Eisenhower believed that the situation had seriously deteriorated. Eisenhower claimed that atomic bombs would be used to protect the island. That policy became known as the doctrine of "massive retaliation." Immediately after it made this policy public, however, the Eisenhower administration became reluctant, cautious, and self-restrained.

The administration first worried that the European security arrangement might be jeopardized by the use of atomic weapons in East Asia. British Commonwealth countries, France, and Japan all backed away from the U.S. war theme. They did not want a war over those islands. The

American public and Congress also exercised pressure on the administration. As a response, Eisenhower stated that the "United States is not going to be a party to an aggressive war," that there would be no "war talk." Then, the Eisenhower administration urged avoidance of intervention if possible. If the United States did enter a war, it would do so only with conventional weapons. Atomic weapons should be considered only as a final resort. Finally, Eisenhower confirmed the policy that the United States had no defense commitment to Quemoy and Matsu.

Despite U.S. pressure not to take aggressive actions toward the mainland, in 1958 Chiang deployed some one hundred thousand troops on Quemoy and Matsu and used the offshore islands as a base for commando raids. In turn, on 23 August 1958, the PLA shelled Quemoy and set up a naval blockade around the island.

Again, a crisis erupted. Eisenhower dispatched the Seventh Fleet to the area. The U.S. government warned the Chinese communist government about its threat to the peace of the region. In the end, however, Eisenhower made no official clarification about whether the United States would employ its armed forces to defend Quemoy.

Intentions, limited legal commitments, vocal nuclear threat, and then a swift retreat all indicate that the Eisenhower administration did not want an all-out war against mainland China. Adding to this point, the most interesting part of the crisis in the 1950s was the diplomacy that eased the anxiety and prevented a war.

When the PLA started bombardment of Quemoy in 1954, the U.S. Joint Chiefs of Staff favored defending the offshore islands and even supporting Chiang's invasion of the mainland. Dulles also believed that the United States should stand firm, but he suggested taking the case to the United Nations Security Council. Eisenhower endorsed the move. This prompt turn onto the diplomatic track illustrates that the United States did not intend to engage in a fight with communist China. As the crisis intensified in January 1955, Eisenhower once again overruled his bellicose advisers from the Joint Chiefs of Staff and stated that Taiwan's status should ultimately be decided by the United Nations.

Corresponding to U.S. diplomatic gestures, at the Afro-Asian conference in Bandung, Indonesia, Chinese premier Chou En-lai made the surprising announcement on 23 April 1955 that his government intended to open negotiations with the United States on security issues in East Asia. Although Dulles

NUCLEAR DEFENSE

On 13 August 1958 State Department Director of Policy Planning Gerard C. Smith wrote a letter to Undersecretary of State Christian A. Herter describing Joint Chiefs of Staff plans for a nuclear defense of Quemoy and Matsu and the possible results. His letter says in part:

1. It is our understanding that current JCS war plans call for the defense of Quemoy and Matsu by nuclear strikes deep into Communist China, including military targets in the Shanghai-Hangchow-Nanking and Canton complexes where population density is extremely high. . . .

3. While nuclear strikes would be with "low yield" weapons, this would include weapons having a yield comparable to 20K weapons dropped on Hiroshima and Nagasaki. It is my judgement that before such hostilities were over there would be millions of non-combatant casualties. . . .

5. The President recently directed the preparation of a National Intelligence Estimate on Sino-Soviet and Free World Reactions to US Use of Nuclear Weapons in Limited Wars in the Far East. . . . It concludes that if our present military planning was carried out Peiping and its Soviet ally would probably feel compelled to react with nuclear attacks at least on Taiwan and the Seventh Fleet. Under our present strategic concept, this would be the signal for general nuclear war between the US and the USSR.

6. I doubt that Congressional leaders are aware of the implications of exercising the authority under the resolution of January 29, 1955, by the method planned by the JCS. If a decision is taken to issue a clarifying statement, it may be desirable to consult with key Congressional leaders.

In light of the above considerations, it seems to me that the US does not have a politically feasible capability to defend Quemoy and Matsu. I question whether, in the event of an attack on Quemoy and Matsu, we should or will run the very grave risk of general nuclear war attendant on our present military planning. If the vital security interests of the US require us to defend these islands, we should, on an urgent basis, develop an alternative military capability based on a local defense of these islands which would give some hope of limiting the hostilities. Until we are within sight of such a local defense capability, I question the wisdom of any public clarification of our commitment in regard to Quemoy and Matsu.

Source: *The National Security Archive, George Washington University*

QUEMOY AND MATSU

remained suspicious of the Chinese initiative, the Quemoy-Matsu crisis soon abated.

Again, in September 1958, as the crisis escalated, Chou suggested opening Sino-U.S. ambassadorial talks on the Taiwan issue in Warsaw. The U.S. State Department promptly indicated its acceptance of this idea. Dulles hoped the talks could lead to a cease-fire.

Since an all-out war over Quemoy and Matsu was not U.S. policy, what was the bottom line for the United States during the crises? First, as events demonstrated, the Eisenhower administration essentially struck a balance between mainland China and Taiwan. On the one hand, it wanted to save the offshore islands from communist control; on the other, it did not support Chiang's invasion of the mainland or engage in an all-out war because of the islands. The U.S. government could not accept use of force by either party. Any change without resorting to armed forces, including U.S. forces, would best suit U.S. interests.

Second, because of this U.S. interest, Eisenhower adopted a strategy of brinkmanship. Dulles made this point in January 1956: "The ability to get to the verge without getting into the war is the necessary art. If you try to run away from it, you are lost." Thus, the Eisenhower administration "walked to the brink and looked it in the face. We took strong action." Brinkmanship was different from a plan for an all-out war.

Third, the Eisenhower administration also applied a range of tactics from nuclear deterrence to diplomacy. Nevertheless, there was no evidence that nuclear threat was effective. In 1958, just three years after the threat to use nuclear weapons against the mainland, the PLA launched a new round of bombardment on Quemoy. On the diplomatic front there was more clear reciprocity; both Mao's government and the Eisenhower administration showed willingness for negotiations.

—MING ZHANG, ASIA RESEARCH INSTITUTE

References

Gordon H. Chang, *Friends and Enemies: The United States, China, and the Soviet Union, 1948–1972* (Stanford, Cal.: Stanford University Press, 1990);

Thomas J. Christensen, *Useful Adversaries: Grand Strategy, Domestic Mobilization, and Sino-American Conflict, 1947–1958* (Princeton, N.J.: Princeton University Press, 1996);

O. Edmund Clubb, "Formosa and the Offshore Islands in American Policy, 1950–1955," *Political Science Quarterly,* 74 (December 1959): 517–531;

Campbell Craig, *Destroying the Village: Eisenhower and Thermonuclear War* (New York: Columbia University Press, 1998);

Foster Rhea Dulles, *American Policy Toward Communist China, 1949–1969* (New York: Crowell, 1972);

U.S. Department of State, *Foreign Relations of the United States 1952–54,* volume 14: *China* (Washington, D.C.: U.S. Government Printing Office, 1979);

U.S. Department of State, *Foreign Relations of the United States 1955–57,* volume 2: *China* (Washington, D.C.: U.S. Government Printing Office, 1986);

Shu Guang Zhang, *Deterrence and Strategic Culture: Chinese-American Confrontations, 1949–1958* (Ithaca, N.Y.: Cornell University Press, 1992).

ROLLBACK

Did the Eisenhower administration regard "rollback" as a viable policy option?

Viewpoint: Yes, the Eisenhower administration regarded "rollback" as an effective countermeasure to communist expansion.

Viewpoint: No, the Eisenhower administration decided that "rollback" was a dangerous strategy.

After initial hesitation, the United States adopted the policy of "containment" as the most suitable strategy to cope with the Soviet challenge. Containment, however, had its critics. They argued that containment implied a U.S. consent for the division of the world into spheres of influence, allowing the Soviet Union to retain and dominate countries that came under its control as a result of the Second World War or, as in China, countries in which it had supported the coming to power of communist movements. The Soviet Union, the critics argued, not only dominated those vast areas, but imposed harsh regimes on the people there.

The purpose of U.S. policy, these critics argued, should not be to "contain" the Soviet Union from expanding beyond the areas into which it had already expanded but to "roll back" Soviet domination and "liberate" people now under Soviet control. Support for rolling back Soviet domination came from two, at times overlapping, sources within the American body politic. The first was immigrant groups that came to the United States from countries such as Poland, which were now occupied by the Soviet Union. These groups and their representatives agitated for a more assertive U.S. policy vis-à-vis what they called the "captive nations" of central and eastern Europe. They were joined by the Catholic Church, which was especially critical of atheistic communism and to which many of the immigrants from eastern and central Europe belonged.

The Eisenhower administration, especially in the early period and in the person of Secretary of State John Foster Dulles, appeared to adopt some of the "liberation" rhetoric of the pro-rollback forces. In practice, however, it did not exhibit great enthusiasm to translate the rhetoric into policy. In 1953 the administration accepted the division of Korea rather than push for liberating the North. It also did not intervene to help anti-Soviet insurgencies in East Germany (1951), Poland (1953), and Hungary (1956).

**Viewpoint:
Yes, the Eisenhower administration regarded "rollback" as an effective countermeasure to communist expansion.**

The term *administration* is an abstraction. Administrations consist of the individuals who lead them, and the policies an administration "regards" as desirable and viable are the leaders in an administration regarded as desirable and viable. The key figure on foreign-policy decisions in the Eisenhower administration

Fragment of a statue of Joseph Stalin pulled down during the Hungarian uprising in 1956

was Secretary of State John Foster Dulles, who—the record shows—was more convinced than Eisenhower that rollback was a workable policy.

Dulles perceived of rollback as an important tool of psychological warfare against the Soviet Union and as a reflection of his own deeply held religious beliefs. The precise term for Dulles's view of rollback, however, is *liberation*. In summer 1953 the Eisenhower administration engaged in Operation Solarium, in which three study groups were asked to make the most compelling arguments for three foreign-policy options the administration might follow. The first option was a continuation of the Truman administration's containment policy; the second was deterrence; and the third was liberation: the use of all means (political, economic, military, and covert) to roll back Soviet influence and power. Dulles's belief in rollback was portrayed by some scholars as a political ploy to placate the right-wing of the Republican Party, led by Senators Robert A. Taft (Ohio), William F. Knowland (California), and Joseph R. McCarthy (Wisconsin). Dulles may have been looking over his shoulder at skeptical elements within the Republican Party, but his criticism of containment and support for rollback was in line with his worldview and philosophy, to which he gave consistent and clear

expression. As Ole Holsti wrote in 1975, unlike future Republican secretary of state Henry Kissinger, Dulles believed that "the ideological differences between the free world and the communist bloc were critical and defined relations between them." As Holsti correctly notes, it is not likely that Kissinger would ever analyze Soviet foreign policy in this way: "Soviet Communism starts with an atheistic, Godless premise. Everything else flows from that premise." Dulles, however, did.

It is not surprising that Dulles would place ideology—indeed, theology—at the core of his view of the world. He was "a preacher in a world of politics," said former British prime minister Anthony Eden. Other observers agree. "Three or four centuries ago . . . it was not rare to encounter men of the type of Dulles," said an associate, Sir Oliver Franks: "Like them, in vigorous and systematic reflection Dulles had come to unshakable convictions of a religious and theological order. Like them, he saw the world as an arena in which the forces of good and evil were continuously at war. Like them, he believed that this was the contest which supremely mattered."

Even before coming to prominence in 1944 as foreign-policy adviser to Republican Thomas E. Dewey (who was making the first of his two attempts to challenge an incumbent Democratic president), Dulles made a name for himself as someone who thought long and hard about the relationship of religion, morality, and international politics. He had written a book and many articles on the subject. He never attained James Madison's or Henry Kissinger's reputation as a deep thinker, but Dulles's interest in this subject was genuine, and his treatment of them able. (He studied philosophy in Paris with Henri Bergson.)

Dulles believed that the cold war was more than a strategic competition between two powers. For him it was a moral struggle between good and evil. As John Lewis Gaddis has pointed out, Dulles also saw the cold war as a zero-sum game, in which any gain for one side was, of necessity, a loss to the other. The basic division of the world, according to Dulles, was conceived in spiritual terms; thus, as Holsti noted in 1970, "It followed from this premise that fundamental cold war political issues, being at root moral ones, are rarely susceptible to negotiation or compromise." Because Dulles based his worldview on Christian morality, he tended to be optimistic about the long run: in the end good will triumph over evil. The problem was the short run, an arena susceptible to tactical gains by the bad guys owing to miscalculations, misperceptions, shortsightedness, or stupidity by the good guys. The key was to maintain dynamism and movement, rather than passivity and acceptance of the status quo: the good must keep the bad at bay, unbalanced, and on the defensive. As they engaged in active, dynamic foreign policy, policymakers had to make sure that they did not lose sight of their ultimate goals as they grappled with the noise and bustle of day-to-day issues. In Dulles's view policies had to be based on moral principles, not on fleeting expediency.

Dulles's specific policy stances stemmed from this overarching view. He denounced the Yalta Agreement as having brought about the "loss of 800,000,000 people" to communist rule. The countries of central and eastern Europe were not merely part of the Soviet sphere; they were "captive nations." He pledged to put an end to "the negative, futile and immoral policy of containment which abandons countless human beings to a despotism of Godless terrorism." Yalta and containment did not sufficiently take into account the nature of the communist threat. The Soviet Union had a "carefully prepared and superbly implemented program which, in a single generation, has brought a small Communist group into control over one-third of the world's population." Because of the moral nature of the contest, Dulles looked with jaundiced eyes at the emergence of the nonaligned movement in the mid 1950s. In Dulles's view

the leaders behind the movement–Josip Tito of Yugoslavia, Gamal Abdel Nasser of Egypt, and Sukarno of Indonesia–failed to appreciate the true measure of the East-West conflict. "Neutrality is an obsolete conception," Dulles proclaimed; "except under very exceptional circumstances . . . [it is] an immoral and short-sighted conception."

Though Dulles saw international politics as a crusade and believed that the free world was facing a fundamental moral and philosophical challenge in communism, he was willing to engage in pragmatic calculations and tactical retreats. The key was not to lose sight of the ultimate stakes in the struggle and not to elevate tactics to the level of strategy. His criticism of containment was that it accepted the status quo and settled for a long communist domination of vast numbers of people. Moreover, containment also had an air of accepting a certain equivalence between the West and the communists. That Dulles drew sharp moral and value distinctions between the free world and the socialist block and that he called for an active policy of rolling back communist sway did not mean that he entertained suicidal tendencies. He was an accomplished lawyer, trained in assessing the odds of winning a case. Grudging acceptance of a momentary gain by a morally defective adversary, however, should not lead to rapprochement or détente with that adversary. This more nuanced understanding of Dulles helps explain what critics see as inexplicable–his acceptance of Soviet moves in East Germany (1953), Hungary (1956), and Suez (1956). When workers in East Germany staged an uprising against the communist government in 1953, and when Hungarian freedom fighters took over the government in Budapest from local communists, many expected Dulles to recommend bold American action of assistance to the uprisings. Dulles, however, fully understood the Soviet military advantage in East Germany and Hungary and the dangers of U.S. intervention inside the Soviet sphere of influence. In the Suez case, Dulles was offended by the blatant display of power by two colonial countries, Britain and France, against an emerging Third World state, Egypt. When the communist foe was in a weaker position, however, Dulles was less restrained in recommending military action. Thus, he was firm with China during negotiations in 1953 over a cease-fire in the Korean War. Georges Bidault, a leading French politician and cabinet minister, said that Dulles offered the French three atomic bombs for use against the Vietnamese who were closing in on the French forces at Dien Bien Phu in 1954. Dulles talked of giving the Chinese a "hell of a licking" and said it would be a good thing to keep things "on boil" in Indochina for several years.

The Eisenhower administration did not do much to roll back communism from places to which it had expanded. The rhetoric of the administration, however—especially that of its chief foreign-policy spokesman—gave expression to the sharp distinctions between the free world and the communist bloc. Administration spokesmen used the liberation rhetoric for three reasons: to keep the Soviets off balance and guessing about the next U.S. move, to keep the U.S. alliance system intact by emphasizing the external threat members of the alliance system faced, and to placate and mobilize domestic public opinion. It is undeniable, however, that the liberation approach also accorded with Dulles's own philosophical and religious beliefs. Liberation rhetoric appealed to the Christian true believer in Dulles. Not all the parts of an individual's—or a culture's—belief system are translated into specific actions. There is a hierarchy and a competition among beliefs. Some serve to indicate higher ideals to which we aspire but which we must compromise because of the demands of daily life. Liberation rhetoric occupied this place in the hierarchy of beliefs guiding the Eisenhower administration. It was a viable instrument of psychological pressure on the Russians and a rhetorical device to galvanize domestic and allied public opinion, but less of a guide for policies in specific cases such as East Germany or Hungary. In any event, it reflected Dulles's personal beliefs. It thus had a place, a role, and an influence.

—BENJAMIN FRANKEL, SECURITY STUDIES

Viewpoint:
No, the Eisenhower administration decided that "rollback" was a dangerous strategy.

During the 1952 presidential election campaign, Republican candidate Dwight D. Eisenhower and his future secretary of state, John Foster Dulles, promised that their administration would abandon President Harry S Truman's policy of "containing" communism and seek, instead, to "roll back" the expansion of communist regimes. Such rhetoric appealed to American anticommunists dissatisfied with the current policy of "coexisting" with the Soviet client states in eastern Europe and the new communist regime in China. It also attracted American voters of eastern European descent who were eager to see their homelands liberated from the Soviet yoke. Once in office, however, Eisenhower and Dulles backed away from rollback,

primarily because the Soviet Union's attainment of thermonuclear weaponry made such a strategy excessively dangerous.

In the early years of the cold war the United States adopted what appeared to be an inconsistent approach to the Soviet Union. On the one hand, the American policy of "containment," articulated first in 1947 by Soviet expert George F. Kennan, posited a long-term strategy of confronting the Soviet Union in key areas of Europe and East Asia while, at the same time, not seeking to overthrow the Soviet Union or its established communist allies in eastern Europe and, by 1949, China. On the other hand, Truman administration officials often characterized the Soviet threat in moralistic, even Manichaean terms, comparing Soviet aggression to that of Nazi Germany and defining communism as an ideology utterly abhorrent to the United States. This latter view underlay, for example, the key Truman administration security document, National Security Council memorandum 68 (NSC-68), written by Paul H. Nitze, director of Policy Planning in the U.S. State Department. Given the recent American experience of waging total war against the Nazis, it stood to reason that the Soviet Union and its brand of communism were indeed an insufferable threat to the American way of life. Was not the crusade against Hitler's Germany a moral campaign to rid the world of an aggressive, intolerable regime? If the Soviet Union were just as bad and just as threatening, how could the United States justify a policy of coexisting with it?

These questions rose to the top of American political discourse during the Korean War. Anticommunist politicians such as Senator Joseph R. McCarthy (R-Wisconsin) scored political points by identifying the inconsistency of the Truman administration's cold-war policies: How could the Truman administration tolerate communism at home while American soldiers were dying in Korea to defend it against communist aggression? Why did the administration allow communist victories in other parts of the world to go unchallenged? McCarthy's intensive and well-publicized investigations of communist subversion—together with revelations that a group of Americans, including Julius and Ethel Rosenberg, were caught passing atomic secrets to the Russians—made moralistic anticommunism the dominant issue of the 1952 presidential campaign. To secure the Republican nomination and win the election in November, Eisenhower was quite willing to embrace Dulles's rollback policy as a conspicuous alternative to Truman's containment.

As any casual observer of American politics is aware, what is promised during a political campaign can often differ significantly from what is actually implemented once the candidate is in office. Such was the case with the policy of rollback. Despite their pledge to overturn communist successes and take the offensive in the cold war, Eisenhower and Dulles, once in office, actually adopted a careful, unprovocative approach toward the Sino-Soviet bloc. While they did successfully overthrow procommunist (or at least anti-American) leaders in peripheral areas such as Iran and Guatemala, Eisenhower and Dulles made no attempts to implement their policy of rollback in areas more central to the cold war, such as East Asia and Eastern Europe.

American politics had been divided by the Truman administration's decision to seek the restoration of the status quo ante in the Korean War rather than to try to liberate North Korea from communist control or, as General Douglas MacArthur had hoped, to use the war as a staging ground to invade mainland China and overthrow its communist government. During the 1952 campaign Eisenhower promised in vague terms that he would end the war in Korea, and many of his Republican supporters took this statement to mean that he would lead a war of conquest against North Korea and perhaps China as well.

Instead, Eisenhower rapidly moved in 1953 to end the war. Using the threat of atomic attack to bring the Chinese to the table, Eisenhower managed quickly to negotiate a cease-fire, dividing Korea at the thirty-eighth parallel. These negotiations specified that the United States would not attempt to overthrow the North Korean regime with military force. The Eisenhower administration lived up to this promise, and Korea has remained divided to the present day.

Many Republicans in Congress believed that the Eisenhower administration would help the Chinese nationalist leader, Chiang Kai-shek, recapture mainland China and liberate it from communist control. Dulles, in particular, cultivated this hope among sympathetic Republicans, and the liberation of China remained a formal objective of the Republican platform for decades.

Not only did Eisenhower refuse to consider waging a unilateral war against the Chinese communists, but he also declined on two separate occasions to use the communist attack on the Quemoy and Matsu island chains, tiny offshore islands held by Chiang's regime, as excuses to pick a fight with the mainland government. In 1954–1955, and again in 1958, China launched artillery attacks against these islands, hoping to humiliate the nationalist regime and force the United States into a confrontation. Despite Chiang's pleas for military support to avenge these attacks, pleas echoed by many American military figures, Eisenhower steadfastly refused

POLICY ON POLAND AND HUNGARY

On 31 October 1956 the National Security Council issued a document outlining strategies the Eisenhower administration should adopt in response to recent anticommunist uprisings in eastern Europe. It includes the following points:

15. In the development of economic relations with Poland encourage the Poles to devote their energies to the satisfaction of consumer demands and peaceful trade. . . .

18. In pursuing our immediate objectives . . . in Hungary . . . mobilize all appropriate pressures, including UN action, on the USSR. . . .

26. As a matter of high priority, exploit fully throughout the world propaganda opportunities afforded by recent events in Poland and Hungary.

27. The Planning Board should urgently undertake a study of policies and actions which will encourage or bring about withdrawal of Soviet forces from Eastern Germany and Eastern Europe. . . .

29. As a matter of urgency, under currently organized governmental mechanisms, undertake a study of the situation in other European satellites to determine U.S. courses of action in the event of future revolutionary actions or uprisings in those countries which indicate a movement away from control by the USSR.

Source: *"Draft Statement of Policy by the Planning Board of the National Security Council," NSC 5616: "U.S. Policy on Developments in Poland and Hungary," 31 October 1956,* Foreign Relations of the United States, *25 (1955–1957): 356–358.*

to give in to the Chinese provocations. Indeed, during the crisis of 1958, Eisenhower forced Chiang to remove his troops from Quemoy and Matsu and to agree to the permanent demilitarization of the islands. Such a step was well removed from the rollback rhetoric of the 1952 campaign.

In 1958–1959 a leftist revolutionary group led by Fidel Castro rose up and overthrew a pro-American regime in Cuba. Despite a widespread recognition by many Americans that the pro-American government, led by Fulgencio Batista, was profoundly corrupt and in need of replacement, the news that a radical regime had taken control of an island ninety miles from the coast of Florida was startling indeed. After Castro's government began to receive aid from the Soviet Union in late 1959 and 1960, many conservatives in Congress began to call for the overthrow of the new regime in Cuba.

While it is true that the Eisenhower administration instructed the Central Intelligence

ROLLBACK

Agency (CIA) to develop a covert plan to bring down Castro's regime, it nevertheless remains that Eisenhower declined to go through with it while in office. That his decision not to pursue the CIA plan was owing to ongoing negotiations with the Soviets over Berlin and then the abortive Paris Summit of 1960 only highlights the general inclination of the Eisenhower administration to prefer stable cold-war relations with the Soviet Union over the rollback of leftist regimes, even those a stone's throw from the American border. It was left to Eisenhower's successor, President John F. Kennedy, to implement the CIA scheme, which he did in early 1961 to disastrous results.

By far the most conspicuous example of the Eisenhower administration's abandonment of rollback was its decision in 1956 to do nothing to aid the Hungarian rebels. For years the administration had called on eastern Europeans to revolt against their Soviet masters, primarily through the Voice of America radio network and other media. Certainly political dissenters contemplating the dangerous step of instigating rebellion against the Soviet Union were encouraged by the implication—in surreptitious radio broadcasts and underground hearsay—that the United States would come to the aid of a genuine rebellion against the Russian tyrants. In the fall of 1956 a group of Hungarian nationalists, led by Imre Nagy, attempted to engineer a coup against the Soviet-dominated Hungarian government in Budapest.

Despite adamant dissent from his advisers, including his secretary of state, Eisenhower chose not to intervene in the Hungarian rebellion at all. As a consequence, the Soviet Union was able to crush the uprising easily by sending its army into Budapest and putting down the rebellion with tanks and machine guns. The rebel leaders were either imprisoned or executed, and the USSR reimposed a client state. While these events were occurring, the United States sided with the Soviet Union in the Suez crisis.

The dilemma faced by American policymakers during the cold war was whether to pursue basic national security, which could apparently be had by containing the Soviet Union within its own sphere of influence, or to engage in offensive war, with the hope of liberating captive peoples from Soviet domination. This dilemma was exacerbated by the lesson taken from the late 1930s, when the West's appeasement of the Nazi empire encouraged Hitler to go beyond local conquests and threaten the appeasing nations directly.

One of the many systemic effects of the thermonuclear revolution—the acquisition of nation-destroying nuclear arsenals by both cold-war superpowers—was to make the pursuit of basic national security far more preferable to policymakers on both sides than the liberation of suppressed nations. Waging an offensive war against an aggressive empire in the nuclear age raises a different set of consequences than it did during the Nazi era. By instigating a thermonuclear war, the United States puts a probable end to its own national survival, not to mention those people whom it would purport to liberate from Soviet domination. Thermonuclear war threatens national existence, and the recognition of this fact by Eisenhower and others put an end to the policy of rollback.

–CAMPBELL CRAIG, UNIVERSITY OF CANTERBURY, NEW ZEALAND

References

Stephen E. Ambrose, *Eisenhower,* volume 2 (New York: Simon & Schuster, 1984);

Robert R. Bowie and Richard H. Immerman, *Waging Peace: How Eisenhower Shaped an Enduring Cold War Strategy* (New York: Oxford University Press, 1998).

Jeff Broadwater, *Eisenhower & the Anti-Communist Crusade* (Chapel Hill: University of North Carolina Press, 1992);

Robert A. Divine, *Eisenhower and the Cold War* (New York: Oxford University Press, 1981);

Anthony Eden, *Full Circle: The Memoirs of Anthony Eden* (Boston: Houghton Mifflin, 1960);

David J. Finlay, Ole R. Holsti, and Richard R. Fagen, *Enemies in Politics* (Chicago: Rand McNally, 1967);

John Lewis Gaddis, *Strategies of Containment: A Critical Appraisal of Postwar American National Security Policy* (New York: Oxford University Press, 1982);

Michael A. Guhin, *John Foster Dulles: A Statesman and His Times* (New York: Columbia University Press, 1972);

Holsti, "The 'Operational Code' Approach to the Study of Political Leaders: John Foster Dulles' Philosophical and Instrumental Beliefs," *Canadian Journal of Political Science,* 3 (March 1970): 123–157;

Ole R. Holsti, "Will the Real Dulles Please Stand Up?" *International Journal,* 30 (Winter 1974/1975): 34–44;

Townsend Hoopes, *The Devil and John Foster Dulles* (Boston: Little, Brown, 1973);

Richard H. Immerman, ed., *John Foster Dulles and the Diplomacy of the Cold War* (Princeton, N.J.: Princeton University Press, 1990).

SUEZ WAR

Was it wise for the United States to pressure Britain, France, and Israel to withdraw their forces from Egypt during the Suez War of 1956?

Viewpoint: Yes, to maintain good relations in the Middle East, assert its anti-imperialist principles, and uphold its responsibilities as a superpower, the United States had to oppose the invasion of Egypt by British, French, and Israeli forces.

Viewpoint: No, U.S. pressure on Great Britain, France, and Israel during the 1956 Suez crisis increased tensions in the Middle East, creating the need for greater U.S. military involvement in the region and facilitating Soviet intrusion into Middle Eastern affairs.

Israel proclaimed its independence in May 1948 and was immediately attacked by its Arab neighbors. Despite the Arabs' numerical advantage, Israel won. Many Arabs blamed the defeat on the corruption and inefficiency of Arab regimes throughout the Middle East. On 22 July 1952, a group of Egyptian officers toppled King Farouk I and seized power. The leader of the Free Officers Committee was General Muhammad Neguib, who, by late 1954, had been replaced by Colonel Gamal Abdel Nasser as the supreme political authority in Egypt.

For a while Nasser was trying to find a distinct voice for Egyptian foreign policies. Two events caused him to embark on a course that was not to the West's liking. On 24 February 1955 the Baghdad Pact between Iraq and Turkey was signed. Like the North Atlantic Treaty Organization (NATO) and the Southeast Asia Treaty Organization (SEATO), the pact was part of a U.S.-led effort to surround the Soviet Union with pro-Western alliances aiming to limit Soviet influence. Nasser had to decide whether to have Egypt join in these efforts. The answer came two months later. Between 18 and 25 April 1955, Nasser joined Chou En-lai of China, Jawaharlal Nehru II of India, Josip Tito of Yugoslavia, Sukarno of Indonesia, Kwame Nkrumah of Ghana, and other leaders of Third World and nonaligned nations at a conference in Bandung, Indonesia. Nasser emerged from the conference emboldened to engage in what was called "positive neutrality," that is, a willingness to play on the rivalry between the United States and the Soviet Union to Egypt's advantage. In September 1955 Nasser announced the signing of an arms deal between Egypt and Czechoslovakia, then a Soviet satellite, signaling the entry of the Soviet Union into Middle Eastern affairs. The tensions between Egypt and Western countries continued, leading Britain and the United States to announce, on 19 July 1956, that they were withdrawing their financial support from the Aswan High Dam project, deemed essential to bolster Egypt's faltering economy. Nasser responded a week later by announcing the nationalization of the Suez Canal, then largely owned by Britain and France.

Negotiations on the future of the canal continued for four months, but to no avail. Parallel to these negotiations, Israel and France, then Israel's chief supplier of military material, began to examine the possibility of taking military action against Egypt. France had long been alarmed by Nasser's support of the Front de Libération Nationale (National Liberation Front, commonly called the FLN), the guerrilla movement fighting for the independence of Algeria from France. Toward the end of October, Britain joined in the plans. In a secret meeting in Sèvres, France, on 22–24 October 1956, Israeli prime minister David Ben-Gurion, French premier Guy Mollet, and British foreign secretary John Selwyn Lloyd agreed on a joint military attack on Egypt. The plan called for Israel to attack Egyptian positions in the Sinai Peninsula and advance toward the Suez Canal. British and French forces were to "intervene" in order to prevent the canal from being destroyed in the fighting between the Israelis and the Egyptians.

Israeli forces attacked as planned on 29 October 1956. On 6 November British and French expeditionary forces landed in the canal zone. The United States immediately began to pressure the three governments to withdraw their forces. When France and Britain used their vetoes to prevent a decision in the United Nations Security Council, the United States moved to the General Assembly, sponsoring a resolution calling for a cease-fire and withdrawal of foreign forces from the canal zone. At first Britain believed that the U.S. pressure was a mere formality, intended to give its European allies cover behind which they could keep their forces on the canal. Soon, however, it became clear that the United States meant for the three countries to leave. Britain's need for U.S. assistance in shoring up the faltering pound, joint U.S.-Soviet political pressure, and a veiled Soviet nuclear threat against Israel persuaded the three countries to leave. British and French forces sailed from Egypt on 22 December 1956. Israeli forces remained in parts of the Sinai until March 1957, when they were withdrawn as well.

Viewpoint:
Yes, to maintain good relations in the Middle East, to assert its anti-imperialist principles, and to uphold its responsibilities as a superpower, the United States had to oppose the invasion of Egypt by British, French, and Israeli forces.

U.S. leaders were wise to intervene against Britain, France, and Israel at Suez in 1956. This decision strained U.S. relations with three of its most important allies at the height of the cold war, increased the prestige and influence of Egyptian president Gamal Abdel Nasser, and failed to win friends for the United States in the developing world; yet, the intervention was necessary for a variety of reasons.

First, U.S. decisionmakers were uncomfortable with the close relationship between the United States and traditional colonial powers such as Britain and France. As a former colony itself, the United States would have been in an awkward posture if it had stood by while its allies resorted to gunboat diplomacy to regain control of the Suez Canal from Egypt, a developing nation that had been subject to European meddling since the time of Napoleon Bonaparte. U.S. anticolonial sentiments, which date back to the American colonial past, received additional impetus from the cold-war environment. Locked in a global struggle with the Soviet Union, which styled itself as an anti-imperialist power, the United States would have found itself politically hamstrung if it had not opposed the Anglo-French-Israeli invasion. After standing by while its allies pummeled Egypt, the United States

could not claim the moral high ground against the Soviets in the developing world. In the end, however, the U.S. stand did little to win friends there, but at the time President Dwight D. Eisenhower and Secretary of State John Foster Dulles could not have predicted this outcome.

Second, at the time of the Suez crisis the United States was opposing the Soviet invasion of Hungary, bemoaning the use of force against a sovereign state. Had the United States failed to intervene in the Suez, it would have been difficult, if not impossible, to differentiate between Soviet and allied aggression. In the halls of the United Nations, an organization built in part to provide collective security for its member nations and to uphold the principle of territorial integrity, American diplomats would have had trouble justifying U.S. inaction over the Suez invasion after expressing outrage about Hungary.

Third, one must consider the emergence of the United States as a superpower and the responsibilities entailed in this new role. When the term "superpower" was initially coined, it referred to three nations—the United States, the Soviet Union, and Great Britain. Not until the 1950s did it become fully apparent that the British could no longer maintain the level and scope of influence that they had had in the past. This change was partly the result of the debacle of Suez, when their ally forced them to withdraw from a military action that they had previously declared to be in their vital interest to execute. It is possible that the British misunderstood the American attitude, thinking that the United States opposed Nasser privately but could not do so publicly.

By initiating a military operation that had important cold-war implications without consulting the United States, the British deeply

SUEZ WAR

DULLES ON THE SUEZ INVASION

In response to the invasion of the Suez by British, French, and Israeli forces, the United Nations met in an emergency session on 1 November 1956 and voted to call for a cease-fire. During the debates, Secretary of State John Foster Dulles, who noted that the United States had "ties, deep friendship, admiration, and respect" for the three nations involved in the military action, nonetheless opposed it and called for an end to hostilities.

Surely, I think, we must feel that the peaceful processes which the Charter requests every member to follow had not been exhausted. Even in the case of Israel, which has a legitimate complaint due to the fact that Egypt has never complied with the 1951 resolutions of the Security Council recognizing Israel's right to use of the Canal—even there, there was a better prospect because the principles adopted by the Security Council with the concurrence of Egypt called for the passage of ships and cargoes through the Canal without discrimination, and provided that the Canal could not be used or abused for the national purposes of any nation, including Egypt.

So there seemed to be peaceful processes that were at work and which had not yet—it seemed to us at least—run their course. . . . I would be the last to say that there can never be circumstances where resort to force may not be employed, and certainly there can be resort to force for defensive purposes under Article 51. It seems to us that, under the circumstances which I have described, the resort to force, the violent armed attack by three of our members upon a fourth, cannot be treated other than as a grave error inconsistent with the principles

and purposes of the Charter, and one which, if persisted in, would gravely undermine our Charter and this Organization. The question then is: What do we do?

We do not, any of us, live in societies in which acts of disorder do not occur. But we all of us live in societies where, if those acts occur, something is done by constituted authority to deal with them. At the moment we are the constituted authority. And while we do not have under the Charter the power of action, we do have a power of recommendation—a power which, if it reflects the moral judgement of the world community, of world opinion, will I think be influential upon the present situation. It is animated by such considerations that the United States has introduced its resolution.

If we do not act, and act promptly, and if we do not act with sufficient unanimity of opinion so that our recommendations carry a real influence, there is great danger that what is started, and what has been called a police action, may develop into something far more grave. Even if that does not happen, the apparent impotence of this Organization to deal with this situation may set a precedent which will lead other nations to attempt to take in their own hands the remedying of what they believe to be their own injustices. If that happens, the future is dark indeed.

Source: Keesing's Contemporary Archives (3–10 November 1956): 15185–15186.

offended their ally and suffered the consequences. It is not difficult to understand Eisenhower's rage at being presented with the invasion as if it were a fait accompli. Lest it encourage additional freelancing from its allies, the United States had to act or risk the erosion of its position in NATO and the world as a whole. Not acting would have had an impact on perceptions of U.S. power. If it did not know about the plans of its allies, how could it hope to counter its enemies? The U.S. intervention showed its allies that they had to consult America before planning any future adventures. It also confirmed that the United States was leading the worldwide battle against communism and that it would take the primary role in leading the West against the Soviets.

The regional implications of the Suez crisis provide a fourth reason why the United States was wise to intervene. Most observers of international politics agree that the Middle East is an important region. In addition to its strategic geographic location, its oil fields supply vitally needed energy for world economies. The Suez Canal is important because it allows the oil-rich states of the Persian Gulf region to ship their oil to Europe without having to circumnavigate Africa. The United States needed to intervene over the Suez invasion to establish itself in the Middle East as the principal Western power, if not the principal foreign power. During the cold war the United States could not allow a power struggle that might result in Soviet control of the region. In addition, the United States was in the process of courting Arab states. The United States has the difficult and ticklish task of balancing its support for Israel and its friendships with Arab states. The Suez intervention helped this effort, demonstrating that the United States was not the pawn of Israel. Building support for the United States in the Arab world has been difficult. Failing to intervene at Suez might have made this task impossible.

The last justification for intervention arises for its importance as a demonstration to the American people of the need for the United States to play a role in world affairs. Throughout its history, the United States has been blessed with relatively benign neighbors to the north and south, and with wide oceans on the east and west. Unlike its continental European allies, the United States has rarely been invaded. Its relative safety contributed to a strong isolationist trend in American foreign policy. Indeed, U.S. reluctance to involve itself abroad dates back to President George Washington's famous farewell address (1796), which cautions against foreign entanglement. U.S. intervention abroad, which played an important role in ending both the First and Second World Wars, came about after long periods of unwillingness to enter the fray. Following the Second World War and the Korean War, isolationist sentiments remained strong in America.

In addition to its traditional unwillingness to do so, the structure of the U.S. government also makes it difficult to get involved in foreign affairs. American presidents command the military and the diplomatic corps, but they are beholden to Congress for funding and must allow congressional oversight of foreign policy. The executive branch is often split by policy disagreements, but these differences often pale in comparison to those between the executive and legislative branches. These splits limit the power of the president to act internationally.

The Korean War might have established the importance of U.S. involvement abroad, but the Suez crisis showed the need for the United States to play an active world role. The U.S. intervention at Suez led to the Eisenhower Doctrine, in which the president declared that he had the authority to intervene militarily to counter communism abroad. The foreign-policy struggle between the executive and legislative branches continues to this day, but the Eisenhower Doctrine, a direct result of American actions at Suez, gave other cold-war presidents the justification they needed to act assertively.

Some of the most terrifying events of the cold war occurred during the 1950s. It could not have been obvious to American policymakers at the time that intervening against three important allies at Suez was a wise choice. Nevertheless,

after surveying a range of global, regional, and domestic factors, it becomes clear that U.S. intervention in this instance was wise indeed. Sometimes it is necessary to speak up to ensure that one's voice will be heeded, and in this instance the Eisenhower administration spoke loudly and was heard throughout the world and at home.

–MICHAEL SPIRTAS, U.S. CREST

Viewpoint:
No, U.S. pressure on Great Britain, France, and Israel during the 1956 Suez crisis increased tensions in the Middle East, creating the need for greater U.S. military involvement in the region and facilitating for Soviet intrusion into Middle Eastern affairs.

A policy—any policy—should be judged by its results, not the intentions of the policymakers who fashioned it. The two criteria by which a policy decision should be evaluated are straightforward: did it advance the nation's welfare, and did it protect national interests? Measuring the 1956 U.S. decision to pressure Britain, France, and Israel to withdraw from the Suez Canal by these yardsticks leads to one inescapable conclusion: it was a bad policy decision.

The reasons that prompted Britain, France, and Israel to attack Egypt in October 1956 were not at all noble or wise. Britain was angered by Egyptian president Gamal Abdel Nasser's challenge to, and subversion of, conservative pro-British regimes in the Middle East. Nasser's nationalization of the Suez Canal was a challenge Prime Minister Anthony Eden thought he could not ignore. Eden made a name for himself in the late 1930s when, as young officer in the Foreign Office, he courageously challenged Prime Minister Neville Chamberlain's appeasement policy toward Nazi Germany. Eden did not conceal his view that Nasser was a Mussolini-like dictator, bent on expanding Egypt's influence and reach by subverting pro-Western regimes in the region. (The French prime minister, Guy Mollet, described Nasser as a new Hitler). If there were a lesson to be drawn from the painful 1930s, Eden argued, it was that ambitious dictators had to be stopped sooner rather than later, and that it would be less expensive to meet the threat they posed early on, before they accumulated power and influence. Nasser came to power in 1954. His pan-Arabic rhetoric inflamed the Arab masses; his acts of subversion destabilized friendly regimes. Beginning with the 1955 Egyptian-Czech arms deal, he allowed the Soviet Union a toehold in the Middle East, opening it for communist encroachment.

The French shared many of Britain's anxieties but were particularly concerned with Nasser's assistance to the FLN, the pro-independence guerrilla movement in Algeria. Many in France considered Algeria part of France, not a distant colony. There were more than a million French settlers in Algeria, and the guerrilla war and the harsh countermeasures by the French military soon plunged the desert province into a grim cycle of escalating brutalities. The French believed that removing or weakening Nasser would deal a blow to the FLN, and would also teach other potential supporters of the Algerian pro-independence movement that such support came at a price.

Israel had three goals in joining the British and French in the campaign, the first two strategic in nature, the third of more immediate concern. Israel's first concern was the changing military balance in the region. Israel, with its small population, was numerically inferior to its Arab neighbors. It relied on the superior training of its troops and better-quality weapons to compensate for its disadvantages. The Egyptian-Czech arms deal threatened to disrupt this tenuous balance. The quality and quantity of arms the Czechs were delivering to Egypt convinced Israeli prime minister, David Ben-Gurion, that Israel's strategic position might be dangerously harmed. Israel's second strategic concern had to do with Nasser's pan-Arabic designs. Small and vulnerable, Israel benefited from the fact that it was facing a deeply divided Arab world that, because of its internal divisions, could not bring its full weight to bear against the Jewish state. Many Arab intellectuals and theoreticians attributed the Arab defeat in the 1948 war, which gave rise to the independent state of Israel, to the divisions and corruption that plagued the Arab world. Nasser tried to change that state of affairs by launching an aggressive pan-Arab campaign aimed at creating a united Arab world under his leadership. He began a campaign of subversion against conservative, traditional Arab monarchies in Iraq, Jordan, Saudi Arabia, Yemen, Libya, and the Gulf sheikdoms, and he supported anticolonialist movements in Algeria and other places. A united Arab world was Israel's nightmare, and toppling or weakening the charismatic and energetic Nasser was one way for Israel to prevent it from materializing. The third and most immediate reason for Israel to attack Egypt was Nasser's decision to close the Strait of Tiran to Israeli shipping, blocking access to the port of Elat. Since the Suez Canal was already off limits to Israel, the blocking of the Strait of

Tiran meant that Israel was denied maritime access to Asia and Africa.

What were the U.S. motives in so harshly condemning the three countries' campaign? The United States had three goals. First, the United States had traditionally been critical of British and French colonialism. Acting almost instinctively on this anticolonial impulse, the Eisenhower administration felt compelled to resist a move by two old colonial powers against a Third World country. More than impulse was involved, however. The administration harbored hope that, by distinguishing the United States from Britain and France, it would position itself on "the side of change," strengthening its standing among the newly independent and soon-to-be-independent countries of the Third World and weakening the Soviet appeal there. Second, by rescuing Nasser from political, if not military, defeat, the administration was hoping to restrain his anti-American activities and gain respite for pro-Western regimes in the Middle East. Third, the administration was harshly critical of the Soviet invasion of Hungary, and it would have been difficult for it to criticize the Soviets' actions without at the same time condemning the British-French-Israeli campaign.

The third and least important goal was achieved; U.S. criticism of the Soviet invasion of Hungary appeared consistent with U.S. condemnation of its allies' attack on Egypt. This minor accomplishment, however, was the only achievement of the administration's policy. In every other respect the policy exacerbated the U.S. position and harmed its interests. The U.S. pressure dramatically and precipitously diminished

President Shukri al-Kuwatli of Syria, King Saud of Saudi Arabia, and President Gamal Abel Nasser displaying their unity during the Suez Crisis

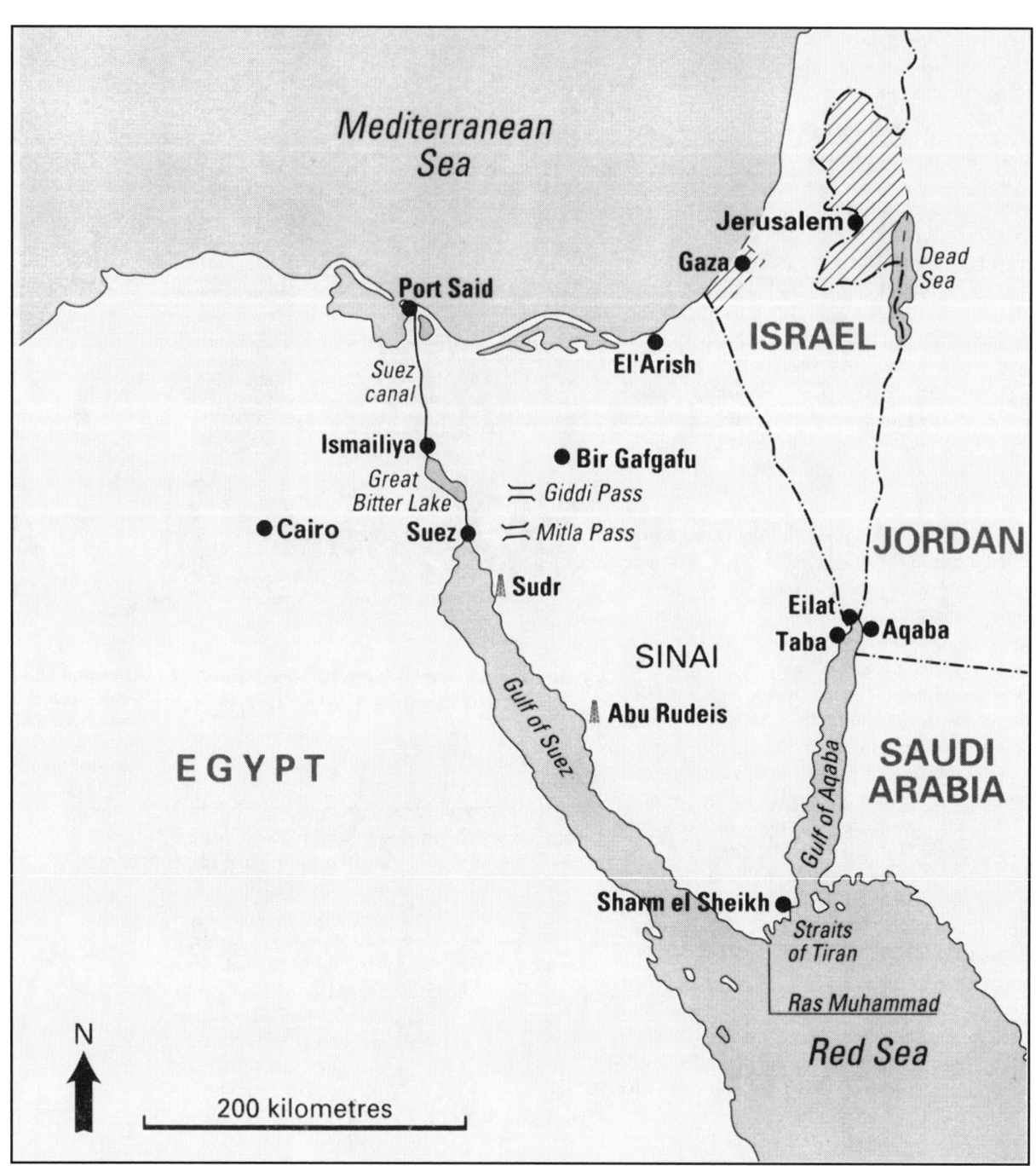

Mediterranean
Sea

Port Said

Suez canal

Jerusalem

Gaza

Dead Sea

El'Arish

ISRAEL

Ismailiya

Great Bitter Lake

● Bir Gafgafu

≋ *Giddi Pass*

● Cairo

Suez

≋ *Mitla Pass*

JORDAN

🛢 Sudr

SINAI

Eilat
Taba

Aqaba

EGYPT

🛢 Abu Rudeis

Gulf of Suez

Gulf of Aqaba

**SAUDI
ARABIA**

Sharm el Sheikh ●

Straits of Tiran

Ras Muhammad

Red Sea

N

200 kilometres

Map of the Suez Canal region showing the canal between the Mediterranean Sea and the Gulf of Suez

British influence in the Middle East. The decrease in British influence in the region did not decrease tensions there; it increased them. British retreat created a vacuum, necessitating greater U.S. involvement in the region and leading to the enunciation of the Eisenhower Doctrine. The first such involvement came in 1958 when the U.S. Marines landed in Lebanon to stave off a coup against the pro-Western regime there.

Another result of the U.S. pressure on Britain, France, and Israel was a huge surge in Nasser's popularity and prestige. His sway over the Arab masses increased considerably. If President Eisenhower and Secretary of State John Foster Dulles were hoping for a show of grati-

tude from Nasser, they were sorely disappointed. Emboldened by his political survival and by the fractures in the Western position in the region, Nasser intensified his campaign of agitation and subversion against pro-Western regimes. In 1958 he helped the Iraqi army topple the Iraqi king, Faisal II, and end the pro-British regime in Iraq; the same year Egypt and Syria formed a pro-Soviet federation called the United Arab Republic (UAR); in 1962 Egypt helped the Yemenite military kill the ruler of Yemen, Imam Ahmad, plunging that country into a five-year civil war in which the Egyptian military, fighting on the side of the Republican forces, used chemical weapons against Yemenite soldiers and civilians. These successes were accompanied by a ceaseless cam-

SUEZ WAR

paign to destabilize other pro-Western regimes in the region. The added prestige Nasser gained as a result of the Eisenhower administration's decision also helped solidify his leadership position in the anti-Western "nonaligned" movement. Led by heads of state critical of the United States and its policies—among them Sukarno of Indonesia, Fidel Castro of Cuba, and Josip Tito of Yugoslavia—this group of nations, while not affiliated with the Soviet Union, more often than not supported the Soviet Union against the United States, complicating American policies and frustrating U.S. objectives.

Another unintended, if readily foreseen, result of the Eisenhower policy was the fact that it facilitated the entry of the Soviet Union into Middle Eastern affairs. The Soviets took credit for forcing Britain, France, and Israel to withdraw, and the fact that the Soviet pressure was accompanied by a nuclear threat against France and Israel lent credence to their claim. In any event Nasser was already developing a military relationship with the Soviet Union, and the U.S. intervention on Egypt's behalf did not change that situation. Nasser's success in toppling the pro-Western regimes in Iraq and Yemen, and the rise of a leftist government in Syria, allowed the Soviet Union additional entry points into the region, which it quickly exploited.

The Eisenhower administration's misguided policy inflicted damage on other American policy objectives, chief among them the cause of nuclear-weapons nonproliferation. As a result of the fact that they were forced to retreat under joint superpower pressure, both the French and the Israelis decided to launch nuclear-weapons programs. France considered itself a great power and, following the Suez trauma, insisted on acquiring all the trappings of a great power. Fearful of the deteriorating conventional military balance between itself and its neighbors and doubtful about the willingness of Western powers to come to its aid in time of need, Israel decided to build the ultimate deterrent. The two countries cooperated closely after 1956, with France exploding its first nuclear bomb in 1960, and Israel, without atomic testing, crossing the nuclear-weapons threshold in 1967.

The American pressure also proved fatal for the French Fourth Republic. Within two years Charles de Gaulle was head of the new Fifth Republic. A few short years later he had weakened NATO by taking France out of the NATO joint military command and fractured the Western alliance by vetoing Britain's membership in the European Economic Community.

The decision by the Eisenhower administration to pressure Britain, France, and Israel to end their attack on Egypt was made with the best of intentions. None of the hopes that prompted the decision was realized, while every single thing that could go wrong with it did. Nasser did not return the U.S. favor but increased his anti-American agitation; the Soviet penetration into the Middle East was not slowed but accelerated; Third World countries did not warm up to U.S. policy goals but rejected them even more resolutely; Britain's diminished role in the region created a vacuum and increased tensions, forcing the United States to become even more involved there; France and Israel decided to go nuclear, with France weakening its ties to NATO. It is not often that a single policy has so many pernicious effects. In the pantheon of bad foreign policies, the Eisenhower administration's Suez decision occupies a prominent place.

—BENJAMIN FRANKEL, SECURITY STUDIES

References

Issac Alteras, *Eisenhower and Israel: U.S.-Israeli Relations, 1953–1960* (Gainesville: University of Florida Press, 1993);

Yaacov Bar-Siman-Tov, *Israel, the Superpowers, and the War in the Middle East* (New York: Praeger, 1987);

Sylvia K. Crosbie, *A Tacit Alliance: France and Israel from Suez to the Six-Day War* (Princeton, N.J.: Princeton University Press, 1974);

Anthony Gorst and Lewis Johnman, *The Suez Crisis* (New York: Routledge, 1997);

Peter L. Hahn, *The United States, Great Britain, and Egypt, 1945–1956: Strategy and Diplomacy in the Early Cold War* (Chapel Hill: University of North Carolina, 1991);

Cole C. Kingseed, *Eisenhower and the Suez Crisis of 1956* (Baton Rouge: Louisiana State University Press, 1995);

Diane B. Kunz, *The Economic Diplomacy of the Suez Crisis* (Chapel Hill: University of North Carolina, 1991);

Keith Kyle, *Suez* (New York: St. Martin's Press, 1991);

William Roger Louis and Roger Owen, eds., *Suez 1956: The Crisis and Its Consequences* (Oxford: Clarendon Press, 1989);

Anthony Nutting, *No End of a Lesson: The Story of Suez* (New York: Potter, 1967);

Selwyn Ilan Troen and Moshe Shemesh, eds., *The Suez-Sinai Crisis, 1956: Retrospective and Reappraisal* (London: Frank Cass, 1990).

UNIVERSALISM

Was the universalist approach to foreign affairs a viable option for U.S. policymakers in the immediate aftermath of the Second World War?

Viewpoint: Yes, the universalist approach was a reasonable policy for fostering international cooperation.

Viewpoint: No, Soviet expansionism made the universalist approach an unworkable policy option for the United States.

During the second half of the 1940s there occurred a clash between two traditional American approaches to foreign policy, which U.S. diplomat George F. Kennan defined as "universalistic" and "particularized."

Those who supported the universalist approach believed that the ordeal of the Second World War—and memories of the First World War—would persuade world leaders that there were better ways than war to conduct international politics and that competition and conflict among nations could be replaced by a more-orderly procedure of resolving disputes. According to Kennan, who was head of the U.S. State Department Policy Planning Staff in 1947–1949, this approach was based on typical American attitudes to international relations, combining idealism, optimism, and legalistic tendencies. These attitudes led American policymakers to believe that international institutions run like domestic institutions—by majority vote and agreed-on procedures—could be constructed to govern world affairs. The best way for the United States to secure its interests would thus be to "improve" international politics to resemble the domestic politics of democracies. Rather than resort to military force when conflicts arouse, states could appeal to international institutions (the League of Nations, the United Nations) for mediation and resolution. The existence of such institutions and frameworks would allow America to be actively involved in the world but would obviate the need for the United States to assume the burdensome responsibilities of a major power in a power-politics world. Writing in an unpublished, 20 August 1948 paper, Kennan stated that universalism was based on the belief "that if all countries could be induced to subscribe to certain standard rules of behavior, the ugly realities—the power aspirations, the national prejudices, the irrational hatreds and jealousies—would be forced to recede behind a protective curtain of accepted legal restraint, and . . . the problems of our foreign policy could thus be reduced to the familiar terms of parliamentary procedure and majority decision."

Kennan described such beliefs as naive, and supported a "particularized" approach to securing U.S. national interests. (Others would call it realpolitik.) This approach, he wrote in a 24 February 1948 article for *Foreign Relations of the United States* was "skeptical of any scheme for compressing international affairs into legalistic concepts. It holds that the content is more important than the form, and will force its way through any formal structure which is placed upon it. It considers that the thirst for power is still dominant among so many peoples that it cannot be assuaged or controlled by anything but counter-force."

The particularist approach emphasized not how to change and "improve" the nature of world politics, but how best to secure American interests within the existing imperfect world, which was populated by many different peoples and cultures that were unlikely to agree to uniform standards of conduct. At times war was necessary to change an unacceptable situation. The goal of U.S. foreign policy should be to achieve and maintain a balance of power so that no one nation or group of nations would achieve dominance.

Viewpoint:
Yes, the universalist approach was a reasonable policy for fostering international cooperation.

Following the Allies' victory in the Second World War, American policymakers found themselves grappling with an issue they had not had to face before: how to secure and enhance the U.S. national interest in a world transformed by war, a world in which the United States was one of the great powers. Germany and Japan were devastated by war. Although they were members of the winning coalition and still in control of their vast empires, the United Kingdom and France were exhausted and in decline; China was in the throes of a debilitating civil war. The Soviet Union, not much of a factor in international relations after its own revolution in 1917, appeared poised to become the main competitor of the United States in world affairs. Although an ally of the United States during the war against Germany, the Soviet Union was dominated by a socialist ideology and appeared dedicated to the cause of world revolution.

Even in this new world, some old tendencies remained. In the United States powerful politicians—especially Republican senators and congressmen from the Midwest, such as Senator Robert A. Taft of Ohio—called on the United States to revert to its traditional isolationist stance. They warned against entering into "entangling alliances" that would draw the United States into conflicts and wars in which it had no direct interest. Majorities in both parties, however, seemed to recognize the need for the United States to remain and active in world affairs.

Policymakers were not certain about the extent to which the American public would be willing to support a high degree of U.S. involvement in world affairs during peacetime. George F. Kennan was right in principle to argue that the universalist approach of creating international institutions to solve world problems was naive. Yet, President Franklin Delano Roosevelt believed that while the American public would be reluctant to adopt the responsibilities of being a superpower in a realpolitik world, Americans may be willing to accept a high-profile role for the United States in international institutions, which would make the world safer and more stable. He also knew that such a sentiment, alien to traditional isolationism, might not last long after the end of the war. He had the example of the League of Nations in mind. He believed that if President Woodrow Wilson had brought the Versailles Treaty, which included the League of Nations covenant, before Senate for ratification soon after he returned from Paris, the treaty probably would have been approved. Instead, Wilson waited, allowing opponents of the treaty to mobilize, rally public opinion, and organize opposition in the Senate. By the time the treaty came to a vote, it was too late. At Yalta in 1945, therefore, Roosevelt was already pushing hard for the early convening of the founding conference of the United Nations (UN), although not all of the issues concerning the organization had been resolved. One such issue was the question of how many seats in the General Assembly the Soviet Union and its allies would have. The Soviets initially insisted that all sixteen Soviet republics be admitted as full-fledged members of the UN, but the United States and Britain objected. After tense negotiations, the Soviets suggested that they would be satisfied with three additional seats—for the Ukraine, Belarus, and the Soviet Union as a whole. No agreement was reached, but, according to Robert James Maddox, Roosevelt nonetheless pressured the other leaders for an early meeting of the founding conference, saying that the unresolved issues would be addressed there—or after the organization was already in existence.

The administration of President Harry S Truman inherited many of the problems of the Roosevelt administration. In the immediate aftermath of the four exhausting years of war the American public showed little interest in foreign affairs and little inclination to assume the burdens of world leadership. The desire to attend to domestic issues found similar expressions in both Britain and the United States. In Britain, Winston Churchill was defeated in the elections of 1945, and the Labour Party came to power. In the elections of 1946 in the United States, the Republicans ran against Truman on the slogan "Had enough?"—winning fifty-five additional House seats and thirteen new Senate seats to take control of Congress for the first time since the presidency of Herbert Hoover. Both Labour

UNIVERSALISM

Chairmen of delegations
to the United Nations
Conference on
International Organization
in San Francisco standing
after their unanimous
vote to approve the
United Nations Charter,
26 June 1945

in Britain and the Republicans in the United States ran on platforms promising greater attention to the domestic issues that were neglected during the war years.

This public preoccupation with domestic questions, however, did not translate into an isolationism similar to that which occurred after the First World War. Two contrasting events from 1946 demonstrate this point. Congress overwhelmingly supported the creation of the United Nations Organization, which James A. Nathan and James K. Oliver call "one of the greatest efforts of institutionalized multilateralism and internationalism undertaken up to that time." This overwhelming approval of an international organization and U.S. participation in it was far different from the rejection two-and-a-half decades earlier of American involvement in the League of Nations. The same public that supported U.S. participation in the UN, however, was skeptical of a more active U.S. role in world affairs, if such a role was to be assumed under adverse global conditions. That is, the American public and its representatives in Congress were willing to support an active U.S. role in creating a new world order based on the management of world affairs by international institutions such as the UN; they were uncertain about supporting active involvement in a hostile global political climate, which would necessitate that the United States conduct itself like great powers of the past. Evidence for that reluctance emerged in the cool public reception to Winston Churchill's February 1946 "iron curtain" speech in Fulton, Missouri. Churchill

declared, "From Stettin in the Baltic to Triest in the Adriatic, an iron curtain has descended across the continent . . . ," challenging the notion that cooperative multilateral institutions such as the UN could be effective in replacing traditional power-politics at the core of international relations. He described the Soviet Union as not amenable to the kind of cooperation it had with the Western allies during the Second World War and called for a much tougher stance by the United States vis-à-vis the Soviets. When Churchill went to New York to deliver the same message in a speech there, demonstrators gathered outside his hotel chanting "Winnie, Winnie, go away, UNO is here to stay!" Alarmed by the public dismay with Churchill's dire prognostications, the State Department at the last minute advised Dean Acheson, who was then undersecretary of state, to absent himself from Churchill's New York speech in order to prevent creating the impression that the administration was endorsing Churchill's view.

There were, no doubt, individuals in the Roosevelt and Truman administrations who earnestly, if naively, believed that the UN could and would serve as a world government, transforming the ugly realities of a realpolitik world into a harmonious and pacific community. Such a radical departure from historical practice was not possible then, or now. One could offer support for the universalist approach for more pragmatic reasons: it was the best way to prevent the American public from reverting to isolationism, and it offered a chance to educate Americans to the reality of

UNIVERSALISM

the United States as a great power. In other words support for the U.S. leading role in international organizations provided the perfect interim steps toward a more assertive U.S. global leadership role. The early rhetoric and initial hopes of some regarding the role and importance of international institutions were unrealistic, but in 1946 support for such institutions and the U.S. role in them did serve to push the American public in the right direction, allowing the United States to assume the global leadership responsibilities its size and power necessitated.

—BENJAMIN FRANKEL, SECURITY STUDIES

Viewpoint:
No, Soviet expansionism made the universalist approach an unworkable policy option for the United States.

After the Second World War many believed that the future of world peace lay in international institutions dedicated to the peaceful resolution of international conflict. In April 1945, just as the war in Europe was coming to its conclusion, the first meeting of the United Nations Organization (UNO, or UN) was held in San Francisco. Together with several other international organizations, the UN was viewed as a means to foster a managed peace, as orchestrated by the diplomatic representatives of its member states. Unfortunately, all hopes for the success of this institutionalization of international relations were quickly dashed. This "universalist" policy proved untenable.

The United Nations in many ways reflected the wartime partnership between the Allied powers. The core of its power, the Security Council, was patterned after the wartime strategic partnership and partially after President Franklin Delano Roosevelt's concept of the "four horsemen" (the United States, the Soviet Union, Great Britain, and China). Opinion polls showed that a majority of Americans believed wartime cooperation between the United States and the Soviet Union would continue in peacetime. Many American public officials, notably former Democratic vice-president Henry A. Wallace, were outspokenly in favor of cooperation.

Such optimism had little place in the postwar world, however. The sudden death of the frail President Roosevelt in April 1945 fundamentally changed the dynamic of the wartime relationship and revealed its weaknesses. Roosevelt had long and shrewdly perceived the rise of

UNITED NATIONS

At the closing session of the founding conference for the United Nations Organization, held in June 1945 in San Francisco, delegates expressed their hopes for the future of the organization. The following passages are from remarks made by American representative Edward R. Stettinius Jr. and Soviet representative Andrey Gromyko:

Stettinius:

We came as the representatives of 50 different nations. But we came here first of all as the representatives of humanity and as the bearers of a common mandate—to write the Charter of a World Organization to maintain peace for all nations and to promote the welfare of all men.

Every nation represented here has had a part in the making of the charter. Sentence by sentence, article by article, it has been hammered out around the conference tables. We have spoken freely with each other. Often we have disagreed. When we disagreed we tried again, and then again, until we ended by reconciling the differences among us.

This is the way of friendship and peace. This is the only way that nations of freemen can make a charter for peace and the only way that they can live at peace with one another. . . .

This charter is a compact born of suffering and of war. With it now rests our hope for good and lasting peace.

The words upon its parchment chart the course by which a world in agony can be restored and peace maintained and freedoms can be advanced. It is a course which I believe to be within the will and the capacity of nations at this period of world history to follow.

Gromyko:

The peace-loving nations who suffered countless sacrifices in this war naturally rest their hopes on the establishment, by collective efforts, of an international instrument which could prevent the repetition of a new tragedy for humanity. . . .

Thus, for each member of the International Organization, for all states, great and small, there are opportunities for making contributions to the common cause of the maintenance of peace and strengthening cooperation between the United Nations in the interest of the well-being and prosperity of all peoples. . . .

In conclusion I wish to express confidence that this Conference of the United Nations will go down in the history of humanity as one of the most significant events and that our efforts will be beneficial for all peace-loving peoples of the world, who endured so many hardships and sufferings as a result of the conflagration set by Hitlerite Germany.

Source: "Speeches Delivered at the Closing Plenary Session of the San Francisco Conference," Congressional Record, 79th Congress, 1st Session, 91 (1945), part 12, A3464–A3465.

UNIVERSALISM

Adolf Hitler to power in Germany and the rise of a belligerent and authoritarian Japan as significant threats to world peace and American security interests. In 1933, the first year of his administration, Roosevelt had brought about the normalization of diplomatic relations with the USSR, ending sixteen years of diplomatic estrangement. Although relations between the two countries showed some signs of strain in the 1930s, the groundwork for future strategic cooperation had been built. Nazi Germany's invasion of the Soviet Union in June 1941 and its subsequent declaration of war on the United States in December enabled Roosevelt's idea of an anti-Hitler coalition to find its fullest expression. During the war frequent conferences between the major Allied leaders led them to form close relationships based increasingly on mutual trust, especially between Roosevelt and Soviet premier Joseph Stalin. When the two discussed plans for the postwar world at the Tehran and Yalta Conferences in 1943 and 1945, respectively, Roosevelt conceded tremendous gains to Stalin, including a security belt around the Soviet periphery, occupation and reparation rights in Germany, postwar roles in China and Japan, and the status of a great power in international affairs. There is every indication that Roosevelt sincerely believed that a managed peace based on Soviet-American understanding, buttressed by an international forum for diplomatic disputes, would be the major guarantor of stability in the postwar world.

Harry S Truman's succession to the presidency changed everything. Having once said that the best policy for America to pursue in the conflict between Germany and the USSR was to support whichever side seemed to be losing at the moment, he was hardly disposed to agree with Roosevelt's optimism. Even Roosevelt in his final days showed signs of losing faith in the Soviet commitment to a managed peace. As the spring of 1945 melted into summer, Truman watched the Soviet Union violate agreement after agreement with regard to the future of eastern Europe. Over the months that followed, he was compelled to react forcefully when the Soviets presented aggressive demands to the West over occupation policy for Germany and Japan, to Turkey for base rights, and to Iran for territorial concessions. In February 1946 American diplomat George F. Kennan's "Long Telegram" from Moscow belittled the notion that international cooperation could continue and recommended what came to be called containment.

Regardless of who led the United States, Stalin based his imperatives for foreign policy on the ideological foundation that the unity of the "imperialist" nations would founder on "contradictions" (for example, conflicts) between them,

which would in turn create opportunities for Soviet aggrandizement. It was remarkably similar to his approach to domestic political opponents in the power struggles of the 1920s. Indeed, in Stalin's mind the Second World War vindicated that approach in foreign affairs, for the Soviet Union had benefited from Germany's estrangement from the rest of the "imperialist" West. The internal Soviet policy debate after the war dwelled on whether Moscow should side with Britain or the United States when the "contradictions" between these two countries began to emerge.

The Soviet outlook did not portend well for diplomatic universalism. Once the immediate threat had been neutralized and the coincidence of mutual interests was lost, there was no reason, ideological or strategic, for the USSR to try to work with the West to preserve peace. When it became apparent to Stalin that the West would resist his attempts to expand his empire through subtlety, he promptly ended his peaceful approach and consolidated control over what he already had. In a matter of months in late 1947 and the first half of 1948, he compelled all East European countries to refuse participation in the Marshall Plan, supported the firm communist takeovers of all of their governments, instructed West European communist parties to undermine the authority of their states, and blocked the West's access to its fully legal position in West Berlin. All of these actions took place with no effective opposition within the United Nations. Despite all the hopes of the idealists who favored it, international cooperation did not work. The fact of the matter was that the Soviets had no interest in pursuing peaceful relations.

Since the postwar strategic partnership between the West and the Soviet Union had deteriorated into the antagonism of the cold war, the international organizations in which the universalists had placed so much faith became more of a liability than an asset. The Soviet Union's permanent seat on the UN Security Council gave it the opportunity and legal right to veto any measure of which it disapproved. This situation was especially dangerous in June 1950, when military action in Korea that was endorsed by the United Nations could have been blocked by the Soviet veto. This outcome was avoided only because the USSR was boycotting the UN in protest of the organization's refusal to allow the Chinese communists to take Nationalist China's seat. Had Moscow not made this diplomatic blunder, the future of South Korea might have been different.

The efficacy of United Nations decisions with regard to world peace was specious throughout the cold war and remains so today. The major instances of aggression to which it turned its attention in the cold war were not solved by its actions. The UN condemnation of Britain, France, and Israel for their 1956 invasion of Egypt during the Suez Crisis (in which the United States voted with the USSR and against its own allies) did nothing more than reveal to the leaders of those countries that their attack did not have American support. Worse still, the United Nations censure of the Soviet invasion of Afghanistan, passed in January 1980, had no discernible effect on Soviet military activity there; the Soviets escalated the conflict, which lasted for another nine years. Civilian tragedies brought about by war and revolution also eluded the well-intentioned international community—nowhere more blatantly than in Pol Pot's Cambodia, where nearly two million (a third of the population) were killed for capricious ideological reasons.

In the post-cold-war world, the universalist approach has faced serious challenges. International cooperation did nothing to save the more than one million Rwandan civilians murdered in a genocidal conflict in that country, just as pathetic UN "peacekeeping" efforts have done little to end the bloody conflict in the Balkans. International terrorism and nuclear proliferation remain problems that UN task forces have yet to solve.

Apart from giving the Soviets a platform to obstruct and criticize American foreign (and domestic) policies, the universalism that inspired the creation of the United Nations has played almost no role in the international agreements that have been reached since the Second World War. Problems between the superpowers were generally resolved through purely bilateral treaties or "understandings" with no input from the United Nations. The resolution to the Cuban Missile Crisis in 1962 and the various arms-control, human-rights, and trade agreements were all the creations of American and Soviet diplomats working in accordance with their conception of mutual interests. Many more peripheral problems that arose during and after the cold war were also settled through agreements based on mutual interests. The Middle East peace process, though still ongoing, has had only marginal UN involvement and has been based on trust, strategic consensus, and American mediation. Iraq's 1990 invasion of Kuwait was dealt with by an American-led coalition of interested nations. Although the UN has been involved in inspections of Iraq's nuclear, chemical, and biological warfare capabilities, the effectiveness of UN activities there has at times been called into serious question. In Europe, independent American mediation also supplied what seems to be an effective solution to the Bosnia crisis.

Universalism was not at all viable for the United States. Even in a post-cold-war world in which there is but one superpower, the universal approach to cooperation coordinated according to the principles of an international organization does not work effectively. When there were two superpowers, the UN's role was even less viable. The organization is probably best seen as one of many new tools in a power-politics struggle. Interests prevail over principles.

–PAUL DU QUENOY, GEORGE WASHINGTON UNIVERSITY

References

Robert Dallek, *Franklin D. Roosevelt and American Foreign Policy* (New York: Oxford University Press, 1995);

John Lewis Gaddis, *Strategies of Containment: A Critical Appraisal of Postwar National Security Policy* (New York: Oxford University Press, 1982);

Gaddis, *The United States and the Origins of the Cold War, 1941–1947* (New York: Columbia University Press, 1972);

Gaddis, *We Now Know: Rethinking Cold War History* (New York: Oxford University Press, 1997);

George F. Kennan, *American Diplomacy: 1900–1950* (Chicago: University of Chicago Press, 1951);

Kennan, *The Realities of American Foreign Policy* (Princeton, N.J.: Princeton University Press, 1954);

Paul M. Kennedy, *The Rise and Fall of the Great Powers: Economic Change and Military Conflict from 1500 to 2000* (New York: Random House, 1987);

Geir Lundestad, *The American "Empire" and other Studies of U.S. Foreign Policy in a Comparative Perspective* (New York: Oxford University Press, 1990);

Robert James Maddox, *From War to Cold War: The Education of Harry S Truman* (Boulder, Colo.: Westview Press, 1988);

Vojtech Mastny, *The Cold War and Soviet Insecurity: The Stalin Years* (New York: Oxford University Press, 1996);

David McCullough, *Truman* (New York: Simon & Schuster, 1992);

James A. Nathan and James K. Oliver, *United States Foreign Policy and World Order,* fourth edition, expanded (Glenview, Ill.: Scott, Foresman, 1989);

Richard Slotkin, *Regeneration through Violence: The Mythology of the American Frontier, 1600–1860* (Middletown, Conn.: Wesleyan University Press, 1973).

VIETNAM WAR

Was U.S. military intervention in Vietnam justified?

Viewpoint: Yes, U.S. military intervention in Vietnam was in keeping with the U.S. policy of containing communism.

Viewpoint: No, U.S. military intervention in Vietnam did not serve U.S. interests, and it violated the precepts of the Western concept of a "just" war.

U.S. involvement in the Vietnam War changed the American public's perspective on the cold war and on how much the United States should be willing to pay in money and blood to attain foreign-policy goals. It also diminished public trust in the government.

Vietnam, Laos, and Cambodia were part of the French Empire, grouped together under the name Indochina. The region was occupied by Japan during the Second World War. After Japan's defeat, Vietnamese nationalists (the Vietminh), who had fought against the Japanese occupiers, demanded independence from France. France objected, and a ten-year war ensued. In 1950 France recognized a pro-French Vietnamese government, led by Bao Dai and located in Saigon in the south. Ho Chi Minh, leader of the Vietminh, claimed that he was the legitimate representative of Vietnamese nationalists and countered by declaring the independence of the northern section of Vietnam, as the Democratic Republic of Vietnam (North Vietnam) with Hanoi as its capital city. He continued the war against French colonial forces, inflicting the final defeat on the French army on 7 May 1954 at Dien Bien Phu, located in northwest Vietnam near the border with Laos, eighty miles from the Chinese border. The battle cost five thousand French casualties, and about twice that number were taken prisoner. France appealed to the United States for military help but was turned down.

At peace talks in Geneva, Switzerland, it was decided that Vietnam would be divided along the seventeenth parallel for two years, after which a nationwide democratic election would determine who should rule the united Vietnam. The United States refused to accept the agreement (but agreed not to prevent its implementation). Bao Dai also refused to abide by the agreement, as did Ngo Dinh Diem, who succeeded Bao Dai as head of state in 1955. On 26 October 1956 Diem declared the independence of the Republic of Vietnam (South Vietnam). The United States and its Western allies quickly recognized the South Vietnamese regime.

In 1957 North Vietnam began a covert military campaign to destabilize the South Vietnamese regime. The Vietcong, manned by procommunist cadres in the South, was created, trained, and supplied by the North. By 1961 its strength was estimated at one hundred thousand. South Vietnam was already sinking into turmoil, as the Buddhist-majority population became increasingly disenchanted with the oppressive Diem regime, which relied largely on the nation's Catholic minority. By early 1963 the U.S. ambassador to South Vietnam, Henry Cabot Lodge, advised the State Department that the United States should begin to search for an alternative to Diem. On 1 November 1963 South Vietnamese military officers overthrew Diem, and he and his brother were shot to death.

American support for the South Vietnamese regime began in 1955 and escalated as the Vietcong's attacks on the Saigon regime increased. Between January 1961 and June 1962, the number of U.S. military advisers in Saigon increased from 700 to 12,000. By the time of President John F. Kennedy's assassination in 1963, that number had reached 16,200. On 2 August 1964 North Vietnamese torpedo boats reportedly attacked the USS *Maddox* in the Gulf of Tonkin. President Lyndon B. Johnson ordered the destroyer *C. Turner Joy* to join the *Maddox*, and on 4 August both destroyers reportedly came under attack. In response the administration sent Congress a resolution, which came to be called the Gulf of Tonkin Resolution, authorizing the president to use American forces in Southeast Asia to defend American allies against communist attack. The House approved this resolution unanimously, and the Senate concurred with only two dissenting votes. President Johnson was thus given the authority to increase the number of troops in Vietnam and use them in battle without asking Congress for a declaration of war.

On 7 February 1965 the Vietcong attacked a U.S. base near Pleiku, killing seven Americans and wounding more than one hundred. In retaliation Johnson ordered Operation Flaming Dart, in which a North Vietnamese military base, located sixty miles north of the border separating North from South Vietnam, was bombed. On 10 February the Vietcong attacked a hotel at Qui Nhon, eighty miles east of Pleiku, killing twenty-three members of the 140th Maintenance Detachment of a U.S. Army aircraft-repair unit. On 13 February, Johnson authorized Operation Rolling Thunder, an increasingly massive bombing campaign against targets inside North Vietnam, which continued with only a few breaks until 1968, when Johnson, as part of his peace initiative, announced a bombing moratorium.

In March 1965 two U.S. Marine battalions were sent to defend the Da Nang airfield. These Marines were the first American combat troops in Vietnam. In summer 1965 General William C. Westmoreland, commander of the American forces in Vietnam, asked for forty-four additional battalions, and by December 1965 the number of U.S. troops in the country had reached 200,000. In 1966 that number reached 400,000, and by the end of 1967 more than 500,000. By the end of 1968 the number of American soldiers in Vietnam had peaked at 540,000. Under President Richard M. Nixon's "Vietnamization" plan, which shifted more of the burdens of the fighting to the South Vietnamese military, American forces were drawn down to 280,000 at the end of 1970 and 140,000 at the end of 1971.

The Vietnamization plan was part of President Nixon's dual-track policy of "peace with honor." The aims of this strategy were to reduce and then end the U.S. military involvement in Vietnam and reach an accommodation between North and South Vietnam. Nixon's national security adviser, Henry Kissinger, met in secret with a North Vietnamese negotiator in August 1969, and in February 1970 he began talks with Le Duc Tho, the chief North Vietnamese peace representative. While the secret talks were going on in Paris and the reduction of U.S. forces continued, the United States also expanded the war to neighbors of Vietnam. In 1969 the United States began bombing Vietcong hideouts in Cambodia, and, in April 1970, Nixon ordered an invasion of Cambodia by U.S. and South Vietnamese forces.

In October 1972 Kissinger announced that the talks with the North Vietnamese were progressing and that he believed "peace [was] at hand." Last minute snags in the talks led Nixon to order the Christmas bombing of 1972, and after eleven days of massive bombardment of Hanoi and Haiphong, North Vietnam returned to the negotiations table. The peace agreement between the United States and North Vietnam was signed on 17 January 1973, over the objections of South Vietnam. The last U.S. troops left Vietnam on 29 March 1973. In January 1975 the North Vietnamese resumed their offensive against the South. On 17 April, Saigon fell to the communists and was renamed Ho Chi Minh City; Vietnam was united.

More than 56,000 Americans died in the war, and 300,000 were wounded; 1,300 soldiers were reported missing in action (MIA); 400,000 South Vietnamese and 900,000 North Vietnamese soldiers were killed. It is estimated that 750,000 Cambodian civilians and 150,000 Laotian civilians also died.

The legacy of the Vietnam War may be measured by two concepts it bequeathed the political discourse in the United States. The first is *credibility gap,* coined to express the American public's increasing doubts regarding President Johnson's announcements about the progress of the war. Indeed, scholars point to the U.S. involvement (and the manner in which it was handled domestically) as one of the two major events that led to a secular diminution in the American public's support for and belief in its government institutions and the spread of cynicism and apathy among the citizenry. (The other event was Watergate.)

The second term born out of the U.S. involvement in Vietnam was the *Vietnam syndrome*—the profound reluctance of Americans to support U.S. involvement in foreign wars if the number of U.S. casualties entailed rises above an unrealistically low (and, hence, in most cases, operationally paralyzing) bar. The heavy emphasis in post-Vietnam U.S. military tactics on high-tech weapons and precision-guided munitions is a result of the Vietnam War. Reliance on such weapons diminishes the risk to American lives, but whether or not this reliance on high-tech gadgetry is always the most effective approach militarily is a different question.

Viewpoint:
Yes, U.S. military intervention in Vietnam was in keeping with the U.S. policy of containing communism.

No other issue in post–Second World War U.S. foreign policy has been more controversial and more emotionally charged than the U.S. military involvement in the Vietnam War. The Vietnam War also contributed to the demise of two presidencies. President Lyndon B. Johnson came into office with an ambitious domestic agenda to change American society forever, righting past wrongs through his Great Society and civil-rights legislation. He was soon consumed by the deepening involvement of the United States in Vietnam, and, in 1968, defeated psychologically and by all accounts a broken man, he decided not to seek a second term. His successor, Richard M. Nixon, became convinced that the antiwar movement and perhaps even the Democratic Party were secretly funded by foreign sources—the Soviet Union or Cuba. When Richard Helms, director of the Central Intelligence Agency (CIA), and J. Edgar Hoover, director of the Federal Bureau of Investigation (FBI), refused to allow their services to engage in domestic spying on Nixon's opponents, Nixon ordered the creation of the "Plumbers," a private covert army composed of Cuban émigrés and Americans of curious backgrounds who had worked for the CIA in the early 1960s in its anti-Castro campaign. One of the first operations of the Plumbers was the June 1972 break-in at the offices of the Democratic National Committee in the Watergate building in Washington, D.C. Nixon resigned his office in August 1974 after the discovery of his illegal attempts to obstruct justice by attempting to prevent an investigation of the break-in.

The passions the Vietnam War aroused—and the fact that the United States lost the war—have always made it difficult to assess the merits of the American decision to intervene in Vietnam. In addition, what we now know about the brittleness of the international communist movement and its internal divisions also makes it hard to see the events in Southeast Asia through the eyes of decisionmakers at the time. Yet, to make sense of the U.S. decisions regarding the war, one must take their point of view. Their thinking was not unreasonable for the time and was consistent with the assumptions sustaining U.S. foreign policy as a whole. This period itself may be divided in three: 1950–1965, when efforts were made to assist the South Vietnamese Army fight more effectively; 1965–1968, when Johnson Americanized the war; and 1969–1973, when the Nixon administration inherited the war and continued it for another five years. Some of the justifications used by the Nixon administration were similar to those of the Eisenhower, Kennedy, and Johnson administrations. Other, new calculations intervened as well, however, having to do with Nixon and Kissinger's efforts to fashion new relationships with the Soviet Union and China and to create a global order in which the United States would be less of a world policeman. While the United States was trying to offer the two communist powers inducements to become more status quo oriented, it was also important to make sure that the USSR and China understood that the relatively lower profile the United States was going to assume in the new order did not mean that they could engage in continuing efforts to erode the West's position by using war-by-proxy tactics.

There are other criticisms leveled against the American involvement. One addressed the question of whether or not the U.S. military employed the right strategy for fighting the war. Not only military analysts such as Harry Summers and Andrew Krepinevich raised this issue; it was also raised by the GIs themselves, some of whom chalked the letters *UUUU* on their helmets ("The unwilling, led by the unqualified, doing the unnecessary for the ungrateful"). Indeed, the strategic policies and military tactics employed by the Johnson administration under the direction of Secretary of Defense Robert S. McNamara did little to take the necessary steps to win the war or to stabilize South Vietnam and make it fully self-sufficient. McNamara's poorly conceived ideas about how to fight the war, however, do not invalidate intervention in principle. Other critics question the morality of the American

involvement, pointing to what they see as the lack of proportionality between the level of violence the U.S. forces used and the importance of the goals being pursued and the likelihood of achieving them. Once again, however, this critical approach to tactical military policy neither addresses the strategic importance of defending South Vietnam nor means that there were no alternate policies that could have been successful.

Vietnam was divided into two countries in 1954. In the context of the cold war, this situation was not unique. Moreover, when the pro-Western half of a divided state such as Germany or Korea came under attack or threat of attack from the other, pro-Soviet half, the United States did not hesitate to act quickly and decisively to defend the pro-Western sector. Thus, in 1948, when the Truman administration concluded that the Soviet Union might be planning to take over West Berlin—which, although deep inside the Soviet zone of occupation, was an undisputed part of the combined Western occupation zones of Germany—the United States put its forces on alert and began a massive airlift of supplies, letting the Soviets know that the United States would react forcefully to any effort to interfere with the Western lifeline. Two years later, when North Korea invaded South Korea, the administration reacted quickly by sending American troops to defend the South. The decisions by

the Eisenhower, Kennedy, and Johnson administrations to resist communist encroachment from North Vietnam into South Vietnam was thus entirely in keeping with U.S. policy of containment as it was practiced at the time.

There were five other reasons that prompted the U.S. intervention. With the information available today, not all these reasons appear compelling. In fact, we now know that some of them were not all based on robust factual or logical foundations. Yet, decisionmakers at the time did not have the benefit of this knowledge.

The first argument for intervention was based on the Munich analogy. The lessons drawn from the 1938 Munich Agreement among Nazi Germany, Fascist Italy, the United Kingdom, and France were a formative influence on the generation of American leaders who made the decision to intervene in Vietnam. In that agreement, the Western powers agreed to sever the Sudetenland region from Czechoslovakia and give it to Germany. Adolf Hitler had already sent German forces to occupy the Rhineland in 1936 and Austria in March 1938. Both actions were in strict contravention of the Versailles Treaty. Hitler's argument was that he was taking full control of his country (in the case of the Rhineland) and reunifying the German-speaking people (in the case of Austria). The Sudetenland was populated by people of German stock, and

President Lyndon B. Johnson (second from right) meeting with the National Security Council—George W. Bell, Dean Rusk, and Robert S. McNamara—to discuss the Tonkin Gulf incident, 4 August 1964

(Corbis/Bettmann)

VIETNAM WAR

Hitler claimed it would be his last territorial demand. The British and the French agreed to his occupation of the region. In May 1939, however, Germany invaded the rest of Czechoslovakia, and in September it invaded Poland, triggering the outbreak of the Second World War. The lesson Dwight D. Eisenhower, John F. Kennedy, Dean Rusk, McGeorge Bundy, Robert S. McNamara, Walt W. Rostow, and all the other decisionmakers who developed the U.S. strategy in Vietnam drew from the Munich experience was straightforward: a greedy dictator cannot be appeased; the more he is given the stronger and more ambitious he becomes; and eventually, and inevitably, he will threaten vital American interests, at which point the United States will have to make a stand. It was thus better and far less costly, they believed, to tackle such a ruler and defeat him early, when he is weaker rather than stronger. The North Vietnamese encroachment followed communist victories in Poland, Czechoslovakia, Hungary, Romania, Bulgaria, Albania, Yugoslavia, and China—and also communist attempts to take over Greece, break up Iran, and meddle in Turkey. Communist expansion had to be stopped; the line had to be drawn. The successful foiling of communist designs on Greece, Turkey, and Iran were recent examples for American policymakers that taking a firm stance did pay.

The second argument for U.S. intervention in Vietnam was the recognition of the growing rift between the Soviet Union and China. Mao Tse-tung accused Nikita S. Khrushchev of becoming soft and effete, more concerned with improving the living standards of Soviet citizens than with spreading the socialist revolution. Vying for legitimacy in the communist world, China took a belligerent stance toward world affairs, calling the United States a "paper tiger" and belittling the likely cost of a global nuclear war that might result from a direct confrontation between the communist and free worlds (a cost to which Khrushchev referred when explaining his adoption of a less-confrontational attitude toward the West following the 1962 Cuban Missile Crisis). U.S. decisionmakers were convinced that China was encouraging and assisting North Vietnam to attack the South as part of a Chinese master plan to take over Asia. American policymakers perceived that China had tried such expansion before—in Korea. This radical, revolutionary China harbored dangerous ambitions. Although it was actually the pro-Soviet factions in both Korea (led by Kim Il-Sung) and North Vietnam (led by Ho Chi Minh) that had launched aggressive attacks on their respective neighbors to the south, American policymakers at the time remained convinced that what they perceived as a monolithic communist movement had to be

stopped. Vietnam was a good place to draw the line.

The third reason was the Soviet Union's support for what it called "wars of national liberation." In a secret speech delivered in late 1960 Khrushchev admitted that the Marxist notion of spreading socialism through revolutions in advanced industrial societies was no longer viable because these capitalist countries had become militarily strong. Any Soviet aid to efforts in destabilizing such societies might be exceedingly costly for Russia. The alternative was to encourage communist revolutions in Third World countries, a concept advanced by Vladimir I. Lenin in his writings on imperialism. In the 1950s and 1960s liberation movements in many of these countries were fighting the colonial powers for national independence. By siding with the nationalist forces during these revolutions, indigenous communists had a good opportunity to take over the reigns of power once independence was achieved. The Soviet Union could help its communist supporters come to power and weaken Western colonial nations such as Britain and France. The Kennedy administration became convinced that Vietnam was a test case for this new Soviet policy, one that had to be thwarted.

The fourth reason had to do with an argument voiced by many: while free markets were suitable for advanced societies, command economies and planning were more suitable for Third World countries in the early stages of economic development. MIT economist Walt Rostow challenged such views in his 1960 book, *The Five Stages of Economic Growth* (somewhat immodestly subtitled *A Non-Communist Manifesto*). Kennedy read the book before his presidential-election campaign and later appointed Rostow deputy national security adviser. Rostow's beliefs were widely shared in the Kennedy administration, many of whose decisionmakers saw Vietnam as an "on-going lab" (in the words used by General Maxwell D. Taylor testifying before a Congressional committee) for U.S. economic and social development ideas. It was thus important to make a stand in Vietnam, not only to prevent a communist takeover, but also to show the efficacy of Western-style economic and social development plans. At least until 1965, policymakers placed much emphasis on various social and economic development schemes to accompany the military effort.

The fifth reason had to do with domestic politics. The Eisenhower, Kennedy, and Johnson administrations had learned—perhaps too well—the lessons of China. In 1949 Secretary of State Dean G. Acheson wrote a White Paper to explain the Truman administration's decision not to intervene in China to prevent the communists from coming to power. "The unfortunate but inescapable fact," he wrote, "is that the ominous result of the civil war in China was beyond the control of the government of the United States. Nothing that this country did or could have done within the reasonable limits of its capabilities could have changed that result; nothing that was left undone by this country has contributed to it." This statement was true, but it did not prevent the question of "Who Lost China?" from poisoning American politics for two decades, giving rise to a rabid right-wing backlash and an undemocratic communist witch hunt led by Senator Joseph McCarthy. American decisionmakers, especially Democrats, became exceedingly reluctant to "lose" another Asian country to communism because of what would be perceived as American inaction. Domestic pressures for intervening in Vietnam against communist aggression were intense, and prudent politicians felt they could not defy such pressures without risk.

America lost nearly 60,000 soldiers in Vietnam. The number of Vietnamese killed—soldiers and civilians, Southerners and Northerners—is probably ten or twenty times greater. The United States did not save South Vietnam from communism and probably could not have done so if it continued to follow the military policies of the Johnson administration. In order to save American lives, the United States used high-tech attrition tactics that inflicted terrible damage on the people and the landscape of Vietnam, both North and South. Although the communist takeover of the South and the unification of Vietnam under communist rule did not lead to the wholesale massacres that took place in neighboring Cambodia between 1975 and 1978 under the Khmer Rouge regime, hundreds of thousands of South Vietnamese civilians were sent to brutal "reeducation" camps, and many died. Vietnam did not become a pawn of China; in fact, its leadership's strong leanings toward the USSR created a new problem for Beijing in the context of its estrangement from Moscow. Although many neighboring countries in Southeast Asia remained noncommunist, Cambodia and Laos came under communism. American resolve in Vietnam, though ultimately unsuccessful, may even have discouraged and demoralized otherwise large and powerful communist revolutionary movements in countries such as Indonesia and the Philippines. Despite this current knowledge, the U.S. intervention in Vietnam should be judged to have been a costly mistake, given the way in which it was run, especially by the Johnson administration and during the early part of the Nixon administration. For this reason, it was not a "noble cause," as Ronald Reagan described it during the 1980 presidential campaign. It was not, however, a venture verging

on criminality, as some critics suggest. It was a mistake because the goals the United States set for itself, to the extent that they were achievable, could not have been achieved with the plan successive administrations adopted and within the limitations that public opinion was willing to tolerate and the restrictions that Congress imposed. Much damage and pain were caused in the futile effort to achieve them.

—BENJAMIN FRANKEL, SECURITY STUDIES

Viewpoint:
No, U.S. military intervention in Vietnam did not serve U.S. interests, and it violated the precepts of the Western concept of a "just" war.

In deciding whether to use armed force, policymakers invariably take into account national interest and moral issues, as they see them. The extensive documentation now available on the decision-making process during the Vietnam War demonstrates that both these issues informed internal U.S. governmental debate on the war, though moral considerations were often more implicit than explicit. With a few exceptions, the highest-level American policymakers convinced themselves that the ongoing war in Vietnam was crucial to American national security and morally justified in terms of the benefits to the South Vietnamese.

The national-security argument was based on the "domino theory," which held that, even though South Vietnam had little intrinsic strategic or economic significance, its fall to communism would eventually pose the gravest threat to U.S. national security. Throughout the war it was nearly axiomatic among U.S. policymakers that a communist victory in South Vietnam would inexorably be followed by the progressive and irreversible fall of neighboring countries, the rest of Southeast Asia, Japan, all of the Pacific, and then (in some versions) the Third World, Latin America, and even western Europe. Vice-president Lyndon B. Johnson's 1961 report to President John F. Kennedy asserted this accepted wisdom: "The battle against Communism must be joined in Southeast Asia . . . or the United States, inevitably, must surrender the Pacific and take up our defenses on our own shores . . . . We must decide whether to help these countries to the best of our ability or throw in the towel in the area and pull back our defenses to San Francisco and a Fortress American concept."

Apart from the national-security issue, policymakers also believed that the Vietnam War was (in Ronald Reagan's words) "a noble cause." They had two reasons for this conviction. First,

JOHNSON'S VIETNAM

President Lyndon B. Johnson's most difficult foreign-policy problem was what the United States should do with Vietnam. Recently published transcripts of White House audio tapes include a 20 February 1964 conversation, in which Johnson made the following observations to Secretary of Defense Robert S. McNamara:

I would say that we have a commitment to Vietnamese freedom. Now we could pull out of there. The dominoes would fall, and part of the world would go to the Communists. We could send our Marines in there, and we could get tied down in a Third World War or another Korea action. The other alternative is to advise them and hope that they stand and fight. Now we think that . . . in the period of three years, we can have them trained. And we've moved some there who were guarding the establishments that didn't need to be guarded anymore. . . . We'd put in ten thousand more if they could be useful and if they needed them for training. But this thousand we didn't need, because they were guarding whatever they were guarding and that's why we pulled them out.

Now we estimate that with the fifteen thousand that we've got left, and all the rest of the year and a large part of next year, that we can just train anybody. . . . And for that reason, we've said that we can reduce that number after they'd trained. Now this nation has made no commitment to go in there to fight as yet. We're in there to train them and

advise them, and that's what we're doing. Nobody really understands what it is out there and they don't know, and they're getting to where they're confused. And they're asking questions and saying why we don't do more.

Well, I think . . . you can have more war or you can have more appeasement. But we don't want more of either. And it's their war and it's their men. And we're willing to train them. And we have found that over a period of time that we kept the Communists from spreading. We did it in Greece and Turkey with the Truman Doctrine, by sending them men. We did it in Western Europe by NATO. We've done it there by advice. We haven't done it by going out and dropping bombs and we haven't done it by going out and sending men to fight. And we have no such commitment there. But we do have a commitment to help Vietnamese defend themselves. And we're there for training and that's what we're doing. And they say that the war is not going good. Well, there are days when we win, and there are days when we lose. But our purpose is to train these people and our training is going good, and we're trying to train them.

Source: *Michael R. Beschloss, ed.,* Taking Charge: The White House Tapes, 1963–1964 *(New York: Simon & Schuster, 1997), pp. 248–249.*

---

since South Vietnam was a victim of international aggression, the United States was fighting to uphold international law and order. The conflict between the communist movement in South Vietnam and the Saigon government could not be seen as a civil war or a revolution because the National Liberation Front (NLF), or Vietcong, was a tool of the communist government of Ho Chi Minh in North Vietnam. Indeed, North Vietnam itself was considered a "proxy" of the People's Republic of China, so that the true aggressor was China, or possibly even "international communism."

Second, the United States was protecting the human rights of the South Vietnamese, fighting for the causes of freedom and democracy against communist totalitarianism. Later in the war, the emphasis shifted to the principle of self-determination: the South Vietnamese must be allowed to determine their own political system, free from the coercion of com-

munist revolution or external North Vietnamese intervention.

No part of the national-security and moral justifications was persuasive. The domino theory fails on several grounds. The theory is intended to predict the consequences of allowing international aggression to succeed, and, therefore, it was irrelevant to the situation in Vietnam. For several reasons it was quite unpersuasive that South Vietnam was the victim of international aggression—unless one means American aggression. During the 1950s the communist revolution in South Vietnam was in all essential respects an indigenous movement, receiving little or no assistance from North Vietnam. To be sure, the situation changed in the 1960s, when North Vietnam began playing an increasingly larger role, eventually eclipsing the NLF, the southern communist movement. The escalation of North Vietnamese involvement, however, was in reaction to the growing American intervention, which always preceded and was far greater than any Northern role.

In a larger sense, however, the timing and extent of Northern "intervention" in South Vietnam was irrelevant since there was never a persuasive case for regarding South Vietnam as a separate state from North Vietnam. For most of its centuries-long history, Vietnam had been one country. Even after Indochina was occupied, colonized, and broken into administrative divisions by France in the nineteenth century, the French continued to treat Vietnam as essentially a single country. The French withdrew from Vietnam in 1954 after a series of defeats inflicted by the Vietminh communist forces of Ho Chi Minh, fighting for the independence not of "North Vietnam," which did not exist, but of all Vietnam.

As a way of easing the French out of Vietnam, at Geneva in 1954 Ho agreed to postpone a complete communist victory briefly. As a face-saving device for the French, Vietnam was temporarily divided into northern communist and southern noncommunist "zones." The Geneva Accords specified that the demarcation line, the seventeenth parallel, was "not in any way to be interpreted as constituting a political or territorial boundary." On the contrary, nationwide elections under international supervision were to be held in 1956 to reunify the country.

Because the scheduled elections would almost certainly have led to an overwhelming victory for Ho and the reunification of Vietnam under communist rule, the administration of President Dwight D. Eisenhower set out to undermine the Geneva Accords and to create a permanently divided Vietnam, with the south under an anticommunist government.

Whatever its persuasiveness as an account of the consequences of allowing international aggression to succeed, the domino theory was inapplicable to the Vietnamese conflict if any one of the following propositions were true: the revolution in the South was initially an indigenous one; Northern intervention in the South was a response to prior American intervention; or North Vietnam was not a separate state from South Vietnam. In fact, all three were true.

Moreover, even if there had been international aggression by North Vietnam, one state, against South Vietnam, a different state, the domino theory would still have been inapplicable unless several further requirements were met: North Vietnam had to have both the intention and capability to engage in more widespread expansion throughout Southeast Asia; North Vietnam had to be acting as an instrument of China; and even if that were the case, China had to have both the intention and

capability of widespread expansionism throughout Asia.

None of these propositions was true. As subsequent history demonstrated, North Vietnam had neither the desire nor the capability to spread beyond Laos and Cambodia, which along with Vietnam made up the traditional Indochinese Federation. Given the long history of Vietnamese resistance to Chinese domination, there was never any reason to suppose that a communist Vietnam had any intention of acting as China's proxy. Indeed, by 1979 the two countries were at war. In any case the image of China that drove American policy—that it was a radically expansionist, fanatical, and reckless power seeking domination of Asia either by outright aggression or the "export" of revolution—had little basis in fact. Even at that time most scholars of Chinese foreign policy were arguing that China had neither the capabilities nor the inclination to follow radically expansionist policies, but rather was basically defensive, pragmatic, and cautious.

Finally, of course, the most decisive refutation of the domino theory came in 1975 in the aftermath of communist victory in Vietnam. The only subsequent spread of communism in Southeast Asia—let alone beyond—was into Laos and Cambodia. Not only were those two states special cases because of their historical links to Vietnam, but, more important, their fall was of no strategic significance for Southeast Asian, let alone U.S., security. The whole point of the domino theory was that the loss of less significant countries was important because it would inexorably lead to the loss of significant ones. The United States did not go to war in Vietnam to prevent the spread of communism to two tiny states of Indochina, but rather to prevent the fall of all Southeast Asia, the eventual undermining of much of the rest of the world, and the spread of communism to the shores of America.

In the Western system of ethics, the just-war philosophy provides a commonly accepted moral language and set of principles by which to evaluate war. This philosophy holds that war is morally allowable only when several moral criteria have been satisfied. The most important criteria are *jus ad bellum*, or just cause; proportionality; and *jus in bello*, or just methods of warfare. The Vietnam War was a moral failure in all three respects.

The just-cause principle mandates that wars be fought only for unambiguously moral purposes, such as self-defense, the maintenance of international order, or, in certain extreme cases, the upholding of basic human rights in another state. If it really had been the case that the purposes of the American intervention in

VIETNAM WAR

Vietnam had been to resist international aggression, defend freedom, develop democracy, or preserve the principle of self-determination, the Vietnam War would arguably have met the just-cause criterion—indeed, the war might even have been "a noble cause." The true purposes of the U.S. intervention, however, were revealed in the behavior of the United States, not its rhetoric.

The only state guilty of international aggression in the Vietnam War was the United States, and the American intervention had neither the intention nor the consequence of upholding freedom, democracy, or self-determination. As was the case in so many Third World states during the cold war, the real purpose of the extensive U.S. intervention in Vietnam from 1954 through 1973 was to keep in power anticommunist military dictatorships, threatened not by international aggression but at first by democracy itself and later—after the United States joined the South Vietnamese government in blocking any chance at peaceful, democratic change—by indigenous revolution.

When the discrepancy between proclaimed purposes and actual behavior became widely noted, the U.S. government shifted its emphasis from the freedom-and-democracy claim to that of the principle of self-determination: the South Vietnamese, it was said, must be allowed to determine their own political system, free from the coercion of communist revolution or "external" (North Vietnamese) intervention. The communists, however, had turned to violence and revolution only after the government of Ngo Dinh Diem, with U.S. collaboration, had aborted the political process set up by the Geneva Accords of 1954, precisely because of the fear that if the Vietnamese were allowed freely to choose their political future, they would choose Ho as their national leader.

Thereafter, the United States made it clear that the goal of self-determination was acceptable only so long as the process would not lead to neutralism or nonalignment, let alone to communism. Elections were rigged; coups were arranged against South Vietnamese governments that indicated a willingness to negotiate with the North, such as the Diem government, in 1963; and only the hardest-line military governments were supported by the Americans.

As this history suggests, true American support of the principle of self-determination could have provided the United States with the long-sought "honorable exit" from the war. Rather than seize such opportunities, Washington repeatedly squelched them. In 1965, for example, the U.S. ambassador to South Vietnam, Henry Cabot Lodge, was asked by a congressional committee what American policy would be if a South Vietnamese government asked for a U.S. withdrawal. His answer was: the United States would not depart from South Vietnam if the request came from "a left wing or even neutralist government that, in the U.S. view, did not reflect the true feelings of the South Vietnamese people or military leaders."

In short, far from serving the purposes of nonaggression, freedom, democracy, or self-determination in Vietnam, the United States made a mockery of these principles. As in so many other places during the cold war, whenever ideological anticommunism clashed with morality, there was no contest.

The principle of proportionality requires that the good that may reasonably be expected to emerge from war must outweigh the evils of war itself. An alternative formulation of the same principle holds that a war must have a reasonable chance of success at a cost commensurate with the true stakes of that war.

Perhaps a case can be made that, in the initial stage of U.S. involvement in Vietnam (1954–1964), it was at least plausible (though certainly questionable) to believe that the stakes were high in terms of the global policy of containing communist expansion and that American political, economic, and military assistance to South Vietnam would be sufficient to prevent a communist victory. Even as evidence accumulated that the stakes had been exaggerated, however—because of the Sino-Soviet split, the limited nature of Soviet or Chinese support for North Vietnam, and the growing evidence that the domino theory was implausible—the American role in Vietnam expanded; the probability of success declined; and the economic, political, and, above all, human costs mounted.

It would be hard to find a more disastrous failure of proportionality. Indeed, it is difficult even to construct a coherent account of the thinking of American policymakers. Did they truly believe in the apocalyptic predictions of the domino theory? If so, then why was overwhelming force in Vietnam not applied? Devastating as the war was, obviously far more could have been done: unlimited bombing of North Vietnam, a million (or nearly unlimited) rather than 500,000 American troops in South Vietnam, perhaps an invasion of North Vietnam, and even, if necessary, the use of tactical nuclear weapons. All these measures involved high costs and serious risks, of course, but if the future of the West and direct U.S. national security had been truly at stake, surely those costs and risks had to be accepted.

The unwillingness to escalate the American military commitment to Vietnam to the level that finally might bring victory suggests that policymakers harbored doubts about whether the stakes were really global. In that case, however, why were they willing to bear the already enormous costs of the war, as well as risk Chinese or Soviet intervention? If policymakers believed the domino theory, they should have done far more; if they did not believe it, they should have done far less. Indeed, if all that was at stake was the political complexion of the strategically and economically insignificant countries of Vietnam, Laos, and Cambodia, they should have done nothing at all.

The core principle of *jus in bello* is that war must never be made on innocent civilians or noncombatants. Perhaps the worst feature of the Vietnam War was that its conduct amounted to a massive—indeed, properly considered, a criminal—violation of this principle. The "strategy" of the American war effort was one of attrition: General William C. Westmoreland, commander of all U.S. forces in Vietnam, stated, "We'll just go on bleeding them until Hanoi wakes up to the fact that they have bled their country to the point of national disaster for generations." Because of the use of massive, inherently indiscriminate firepower, together with the fact that the enemy successfully blended into the general populace, those who "bled" inevitably included more than a million North and South Vietnamese civilians.

In addition to the massive use of firepower, it was also the deliberate policy of the American government to destroy villages and farmland in South Vietnam, so as to drive people off the land and deprive the communists a population base from which to conduct the war. Moreover, throughout the war there were extensive individual or small-unit atrocities carried out by American soldiers, whose actions, while not "policy," were nonetheless widespread, largely unchecked, and unpunished.

As the war escalated, Vietnam itself became increasingly unimportant. Rather, it became a battlefield in the global ideological crusade against "international communism," a country that—regrettably—had to be destroyed in order to be saved.

Not only was the Vietnam War a military and political disaster, but it was also an intellectual disgrace (based as it was on the vacuous premises of the domino theory) and a moral catastrophe. It was unjust in its ends, for the preservation of a dictatorial and repressive anticommunist regime in South Vietnam was insufficiently compelling in either moral or national-interest terms to justify the massive intervention in an internal revolution. It was even more unjust in the means by which it was fought. Indeed, America's conduct in the Vietnam War violated every criterion of the just-war philosophy, the centuries-old consensus of Western religious, philosophical, and moral thought on war.

–JEROME SLATER, STATE UNIVERSITY OF NEW YORK AT BUFFALO

References

Leslie H. Gelb and Richard K. Betts, *The Irony of Vietnam: The System Worked* (Washington, D.C.: Brookings Institutions, 1979);

Mike Gravel, ed., *The Pentagon Papers: The Defense Department History of United States Decisionmaking on Vietnam,* 5 volumes (Boston: Beacon, 1972);

David Halberstam, *The Best and the Brightest* (New York: Random House, 1972);

George C. Herring, *America's Longest War: The United States and Vietnam, 1950–1975* (New York: McGraw-Hill, 1979);

George McTurnin Kahin, *Intervention: How America Became Involved in Vietnam* (New York: Knopf, 1986);

Stanley Karnow, *Vietnam: A History,* revised and updated edition (New York: Penguin, 1997);

Guenter Lewy, *America in Vietnam* (New York: Oxford University Press, 1978);

Norman Podhoretz, *Why We Were in Vietnam* (New York: Simon & Schuster, 1982);

Neil Sheehan, *A Bright Shining Lie: John Paul Vann and America in Vietnam* (New York: Random House, 1988);

Michael Walzer, *Just and Unjust Wars: A Moral Argument with Historical Illustrations* (New York: Basic Books, 1977).

YALTA AGREEMENT

Was the Yalta Agreement the best the West could have negotiated?

Viewpoint: Yes, because of the presence of Soviet troops in eastern and central Europe and the Soviets' strategic interest in that region, the Yalta Agreement was the best the West could have negotiated.

Viewpoint: No, the Yalta Agreement conceded too much to the Soviets.

For some, the Yalta Agreement of 1945 has come to represent a policy of appeasement similar to that of the 1938 Munich Agreement. At Munich, Britain and France tried to appease Adolf Hitler by conceding the Sudetenland region of Czechoslovakia to Germany; at Yalta, the argument goes, the United States and Britain tried to appease Joseph Stalin by conceding central and eastern portions of Europe to the Soviet Union. For others, the Yalta Agreement stands for the art of the possible: with the Red Army occupying central and eastern Europe, it is not clear what the Western Allies could have done, short of war, to dislodge the Soviet Union from these areas.

Between 4 and 11 February 1945, U.S. president Franklin Delano Roosevelt, British prime minister Winston Churchill, and Soviet leader Joseph Stalin met at the Livadia Palace in Yalta, a Soviet resort town on the Crimean peninsula. Much of the post–Second World War European order was fashioned during that week of discussions.

There were six items for discussion on the agenda at Yalta. The first was the division of Germany. Roosevelt wanted to have Germany divided into six parts, while Churchill preferred three: Prussia in the north, Bavaria-Austria in the south, and the industrial regions of Ruhr and West-phalia in the west. It was agreed that the details of division would be worked out at a later date. The second item was the creation of the United Nations Organization. Roosevelt's idea to have a Security Council with four permanent members (the United States, the Soviet Union, the United Kingdom, and China) was accepted. (France was added later.) The Soviet demand that the sixteen Soviet republics each be given a seat at the United Nations was rejected, but the United States and the United Kingdom agreed that, in addition to the Soviet Union, Ukraine and Belorussia would have their own delegations to the organization. The third item was German war reparations. The Soviets insisted on Germany paying $20 billion, of which half would go to the Soviet Union. Churchill objected, pointing to the pernicious effects of the harsh penalties that the Versailles Treaty had imposed on German society after the First World War and their contribution to the rise of Hitler and the Nazis. The issue of reparations remained unresolved.

The fourth item was a "Declaration of Liberated Europe," proposed by U.S. secretary of war Edward Stettinius. The declaration, which was accepted largely without debate, called on the three Allied powers to ensure peace and democracy in the areas that came under their occupation. Britain and the United States later pointed to the declaration as proof that the Soviet Union violated the Yalta Agreement. The fifth issue was Soviet entry into the war against Japan. The United States did not want Britain to engage more heavily in the war against Japan, fearing Britain would want to add to its imperial possessions parts of the dismembered Japanese empire. The atomic bomb was not yet tested, and Roosevelt was afraid that the United States would pay too heavy a price for shouldering alone the final push against the Japanese home islands. He, therefore, asked Stalin for Soviet participation, and Stalin agreed that the Soviet Union would join the war against Japan within three months of the end of hostilities in Europe.

The sixth and most contentious issue discussed at the Yalta Conference was the fate of Poland. Britain and France had declared war on Germany because of the invasion of Poland. London was also the home of the Polish government in exile. Roosevelt had to contend with the pressures of a large constituency of Polish American voters. The United States and Britain insisted that the London-based Polish government in exile was the legitimate voice of the Polish people and should be installed in Poland. Stalin, whose Red Army was occupying most of Poland by then, recognized a group of Polish communists, called the Lublin Government, as the legitimate leaders of Poland. He insisted that just as the Western Allies had occupied Italy and were governing it without Soviet involvement, so the Soviet Union had a right to be the main voice in Polish affairs without Western interference. He also argued that, since Poland had been the main corridor of invasion of Russia, the Soviet Union had a strategic interest in making sure that the government in Poland was a friendly one. Under Western pressure, Stalin agreed to hold free elections in Poland to determine its government, but, like his pledge to hold free elections in other countries under Soviet occupation, this commitment was not fulfilled.

Viewpoint:
Yes, because of the presence of Soviet troops in eastern and central Europe and the Soviets' strategic interest in that region, the Yalta Agreement was the best the West could have negotiated.

Politics has been defined as the art of the possible. By this definition, Yalta was an artistic achievement—perhaps not a masterpiece, but an achievement nonetheless. Contemporaneous testimony suggests that Franklin Delano Roosevelt, Winston Churchill, and their aides considered Yalta beneficial for Western interests and were satisfied with the agreement they had reached there.

Conservative Republicans seized on the Yalta Agreement with a vengeance in order to continue their unrelenting criticism of the Roosevelt administration. That criticism had begun in the early 1930s, as Republicans viewed with increasing alarm what they perceived as a dangerous concentration of power in the hands of the executive branch, a move Roosevelt had insisted was necessary for the implementation of his New Deal policies. As the rise of Nazi Germany and the increasing threats to stability in Europe caused Roosevelt to pay more attention to, and become more active in, foreign policies, the same conservative critics found new grounds for their criticism. Attacking Roosevelt on national-security grounds helped blur the partisan nature of much of the Republicans' criticism. Questioning Roosevelt's foreign policies—such as Lend-Lease, his "shoot-on-sight" orders to the U.S. Navy, and the Atlantic Charter—provided conservatives with opportunities to criticize the role and functions of government without appearing too partisan.

For conservative critics, Yalta represented many of the failings they had ascribed to Roosevelt's liberal policies and his centralized way of governing: accumulation of power in the hands of the president, executive decisions made in secrecy, presidential assistants whose loyalty to the United States was questionable, naïveté about Soviet intentions, and reluctance to play hardball politics with Stalin. The result of all these failings, Roosevelt's critics charged, was a colossal blunder: Roosevelt "betrayed" the principles of freedom and self-determination, delivering eastern and central European countries to the Soviet Union and allowing it to impose its brutal rule on peoples just as they were liberated from Nazi occupation. Roosevelt compounded this error, they charged, by arranging for the Soviet Union to join the war against Japan, thus ensuring the expansion of Soviet influence in north Asia. From 1945 until 1954–1955, criticism of Yalta was a central theme in Republican campaigns against the Roosevelt and Truman administrations. In 1952 Dwight D. Eisenhower, the Republican nominee for president, pledged to repudiate the Yalta Agreement and expel from government service those who were among its architects. The policy of "rollback" was one manifestation of this anti-Yalta position.

Prime Minister Winston Churchill, President Franklin D. Roosevelt, and Premier Joseph Stalin during their February 1945 meeting at Yalta. Standing directly behind the three leaders are British Foreign Secretary Anthony Eden, U.S. Secretary of State Edward R. Stettinius Jr., Soviet Foreign Minister Vyacheslav Molotov, and W. Averell Harriman, U.S. ambassador to the Soviet Union.

The agreements reached at Yalta, however, were not the result of misguided naiveté, although there were naive diplomats in Roosevelt's entourage. These agreements were also not the result of an effort to appease the Soviet Union, although there were no doubt those in the administration who might have entertained the belief that appeasing the Soviets would benefit the United States. The agreements at Yalta were rather the result of Roosevelt's early strategic choice to concentrate on winning the Second World War first and think about postwar arrangements later. This decision allowed the creation of facts on the ground in east and central Europe. Roosevelt was informed by a realistic assessment of these geostrategic realities when he made his decisions at Yalta.

Critics of the Yalta Agreement reserve their harshest language for its treatment of eastern and central Europe, especially Poland. It is precisely on these issues, however, that Roosevelt's and Churchill's realism and understanding of what was possible were most manifest. After breaking the Nazi siege of Stalingrad in 1943, the Red Army began to push the Wehrmacht back toward Germany. In the process, the Soviets gained control of large

areas in east and central Europe, areas that had historically served as corridors of invasion into Russia. The Soviets had another advantage in gaining control over these territories: the Nazis targeted not only Jews and Gypsies for extermination; their war on communists and communist sympathizers was as harsh. Hitler had declared war to the end on what he described as "Judeo-Bolshevism," and his troops in the field prosecuted that war with unforgiving ferocity. It was thus not surprising that, in countries under Nazi occupation during the Second World War, many of the anti-Nazi national-liberation forces were led by communists. As the war drew to a close, these local communist partisans were joined by experienced leaders who had led the communist parties in eastern and central European countries before the war and who had escaped to Moscow when these nations were taken over by the Nazis. Returning from exile in the wake of the Red Army, these communist leaders quickly established themselves as the de facto rulers of their countries.

Well-organized communist forces moved into a vacuum left by the retreating Nazis. In most eastern and central European countries the Germans had destroyed the civil and social institutions essential for a viable civic society: political parties, trade unions, churches, youth movements, and professional associations. They had also weakened and disrupted governmental and military bureaucracies. In any event, with the possible exception of Czechoslovakia, these liberated countries were without democratic traditions and experience. The Red Army and its local communist collaborators thus found themselves without much effective, organized competition for power. Roosevelt and Churchill's acceptance of provisional governments heavily dominated by local communists (governments that soon became permanent) was thus not a result of pusillanimous policy or naive belief in Stalin's promises to allow free elections; it was the result of recognizing the reality on the ground.

Roosevelt and Churchill's acceptance of these communist-dominated provisional governments was also the result of a tacit recognition of the Soviets' demand for a defensive belt in eastern and central Europe and their need to ensure that the governments of these countries would be friendly to the Soviet Union. The Soviets had no intention of allowing these countries to be ruled by the traditional, anti-Soviet regimes that had dominated the region between the wars, and they had the Red Army troops and local communist collaborators to ensure that their will prevailed. Understanding the Soviets' legitimate security needs and recognizing the local communists' advantage on the ground, however, did not mean that the two Western leaders agreed to make Poland into a communist state, and it did not mean that they were looking for a verbal formula that would allow them to conceal such an agreement. "What Roosevelt and his chief advisers were aiming at," Marc Trachtenberg wrote in 1999, "was a Poland closely aligned with Russia on matters of foreign and military policy, but with a large measure of autonomy on domestic issues. This, in fact, was the American dream for eastern Europe as a whole, a dream which persisted throughout the entire Cold War period."

It soon became clear that the Soviets were not living up to the commitments the Americans and British believed the USSR had made. On 23 April 1945 Harry S Truman, in the first week of his presidency, confronted Soviet foreign minister Vyacheslav Molotov over the Polish issue, but despite Truman's blunt language, he, like Roosevelt before him, did not believe it was in U.S. interests to precipitate a crisis with Moscow over Poland. ("I have never been talked to like this in my life," Molotov complained; "Carry out your agreements," Truman replied, "and you won't get talked to

like that.") By May the United States had recognized the communist-dominated government, effectively marking the end of U.S. efforts to secure free elections in Poland. In December 1945 the United States recognized the communist governments in Bulgaria and Romania. The United States continued to pay lip service to the notion of free elections and self-determination in eastern and central Europe, but, in reality, it accepted the facts that the region was within the Soviet sphere of influence and that the USSR should be allowed to play a dominant role in it. In return, the United States expected the Soviets to honor the Western sphere of influence, which included Western Europe, Japan, the Mediterranean, and the Middle East.

The same realism that led Roosevelt to accept Soviet terms in east and central Europe is also reflected in the Far East portion of the Yalta Agreement. In February 1945 there was no way to predict how long the war against Japan would last and how many American casualties winning would require. The first atomic test was five months away, and no one knew whether or not an operable atomic device could be developed. Soviet participation in the war against Japan was thus deemed vital. Roosevelt and his aides believed that the deal struck with the Soviets was good for the West, since Stalin agreed to stop aid to Mao Tse-tung's communist forces, to recognize the Nationalist government of Chiang Kai-shek, and even to sign a treaty of friendship with Chiang. The Soviet demands for control of the Sakhalin and Kurile islands, joint operation of the Chinese Eastern Railroad and the South Manchurian Railroad, and lease rights to Port Arthur were considered reasonable.

The critics of Roosevelt's performance at Yalta appear to be trying to have it both ways. On the one hand, they accuse him of naiveté and "softness" toward the Soviet Union, of a fundamental lack of understanding of communism and its predatory nature. On the other hand, they accuse him of being a cynical and manipulative leader who did not hesitate to betray the Poles and other states in east and central Europe to communist ruthlessness. The record shows that Roosevelt decided early that winning the war against Germany, Italy, and Japan took precedence over discussions on the shape of the postwar world. The way the war was fought, with the main battles taking place on the eastern front between Germany and Russia, meant that the Soviet Union would expand its reach into east and central Europe. At Yalta, with the end of the war in sight, the Allied leaders met to discuss the postwar arrangements. Roosevelt and

Churchill had preferences, but the autumn 1944 agreement between Churchill and Stalin on the division of influence in the Balkans, an agreement endorsed by Roosevelt, already demonstrated the Western leaders' willingness to accept the new realities the war had created. Both understood that prewar conditions could not be re-created because the Soviet Union would not allow it. Within this new reality, marked above all by Soviet dominance of east and central Europe, the two Western leaders tried to obtain as many concessions as possible from Stalin with regard to the composition of governments in that region and the way these governments were elected. They harbored no illusions, however, about the likelihood of Stalin's adhering to his commitments. When he did not, Roosevelt, Secretary of State James F. Byrnes, and Truman protested, but that was all. There was no willingness to make Stalin's recalcitrance into a crisis in great-power relations, and there was little the West could do except continue to protest. By December 1945 the United States, in fact if not in word, had reconciled itself to the existence of a Soviet sphere of influence that the Soviets deemed vital to their security. In response the United States began to organize and solidify its own sphere of influence, from which it excluded the Soviet Union.

The Yalta Agreement thus represents the Western powers' proclamation of the Wilsonian ideals of freedom and self-determination combined with their attempt to work as best they could within a reality they felt they had to accept. With the information available in February 1945 the Yalta Agreement was probably the best compromise they could reach. The harsh campaign launched by critics of the Yalta Agreement helped create what scholars describe as the "myth" of Yalta, that is, the belief that Roosevelt could have gotten more, that he gave away too much to Stalin and secured too little for the West. A close examination reveals that this pernicious myth, which energized a paranoid streak in American politics and fueled the extravagant and destructive claims of McCarthyism, is just that—a myth.

—BENJAMIN FRANKEL, SECURITY STUDIES

Viewpoint:
No, the Yalta Agreement conceded too much to the Soviets.

When President Franklin Delano Roosevelt returned to the United States from Yalta in February 1945, he hailed the agreement reached there as one of the greatest achievements of the United States. This agreement, however, was not the best that could have been attained to serve the postwar interests of the West. Noncommunist Poles considered their homeland to have been abandoned, sacrificed to Roosevelt's efforts to establish a postwar alliance with the Soviet Union. Roosevelt and Winston Churchill had gone to Yalta with the intention of supporting the London-based Polish government in exile as the legitimate government of Poland, while Stalin backed the claims of the procommunist Lublin Government, which had taken power in Poland after the Red Army invasion. At the conference, however, the two Western leaders agreed to a provisional government composed of members of both groups in return for Stalin's promise to allow free democratic elections. Under Soviet and Polish-communist control, what began as a Polish provisional government soon became a satellite of the USSR.

The other flaw of the Yalta Agreement concerned the Far East. Roosevelt insisted on giving the Soviets a role in the war against Japan and subsequent occupation of that country. In return for agreeing to join the war, the Soviets received the contested Sakhalin and Kurile islands. Another flaw in the Pacific part of the agreement was a recognition of a Soviet sphere of influence in Outer Mongolia and a provision for Soviet cooperation in Manchuria with the Nationalist Chinese government of Chiang Kai-shek, both imposed on Chiang and his government. These concessions to the Soviet Union were made because General George C. Marshall, U.S. Army chief of staff, argued that Soviet entry into the war against Japan would shorten the war and reduce American casualties, even though it was not clear that Soviet involvement was militarily necessary to an Allied victory. Roosevelt's supporters pointed out that the Soviets promised to support Chiang's Nationalist forces against Mao Tse-tung's communist rebellion. This Soviet concession should not have been given such importance, however, because a division was already opening between the communist movements in the Soviet Union and China, and the Soviets preferred to deal with Chiang rather than Mao.

The essence of Yalta is not to be found in the joint protocols signed by the participants. Rather, it may be found in the approach that animated these leaders, who believed that it provided an opportunity to create a long-lasting peace. The problem was that each of the leaders present interpreted this objective, and the means to achieve it, differently. Churchill

CHURCHILL REMEMBERS YALTA

In February 1945 Prime Minister Winston Churchill of Great Britain met with President Franklin Delano Roosevelt and Premier Joseph Stalin at the Black Sea resort of Yalta to discuss the postwar division of Europe. A few years later Churchill recorded some of their talks in a memoir, including the following conversation on the fate of Germany:

Stalin now asked how Germany was to be dismembered. Were we to have one Government or several, or merely some form of administration? If Hitler surrendered unconditionally should we preserve his Government or refuse to treat with it? At Teheran Mr. Roosevelt had suggested dividing Germany into five parts, and he had agreed with him. I, on the other hand, had hesitated and had only wanted her to be split into two, namely, Prussia and Austria-Bavaria, with the Ruhr and Westphalia under international control. The time had now come, he said, to take a definite decision.

I said that we all agreed that Germany should be dismembered, but the actual method was much too complicated to be settled in five or six days. It would require a very searching examination of the historical, ethnographical, and economic facts, and prolonged examination by a special committee. . . .

I then speculated on the future. If Hitler or Himmler were to come forward and offer unconditional surrender it was clear that our answer should be that we would not negotiate with any of the war criminals. If they were the only people the Germans could produce we should have to go on with the war. It was more probable that Hitler and his associates would be killed or would disappear, and that another set of people would offer unconditional surrender. If this happened the three Great Powers must immediately consult and decide whether they were worth dealing with or not. . . .

At Stalin's request M. Maisky then expounded on a Russian scheme for making Germany pay reparations and for dismantling her munitions industries. I said that the experience of the last war had been very disappointing, and I did not believe it would be possible to extract from Germany anything like the amount which M. Maisky had suggested should be paid to Russia alone. Britain too had suffered greatly. . . .

At this first meeting Mr. Roosevelt had made a momentous statement. He had said that the United States would take all reasonable steps to preserve peace, but not at the expense of keeping a large army in Europe, three thousand miles from home. The American occupation would therefore be limited to two years. Formidable questions rose in my mind. If the Americans left Europe Britain would have to occupy single-handed the entire western portion of Germany. Such a task would be far beyond our strength.

At the opening of our second meeting on February 6 I accordingly pressed for French help in carrying such a burden. To give France a zone of occupation was by no means the end of the matter. Germany would surely rise again, and while the Americans could always go home the French had to live next door to her. A strong France was vital not only to Europe but to Great Britain. She alone could deny the rocket sites on her Channel coast and build up an army to contain the Germans.

Source: *Winston S. Churchill,* Triumph and Tragedy *(Boston: Houghton Mifflin, 1953), pp. 351–353.*

considered the dangers to Europe to lie in Soviet expansion. Stalin believed that, to prevent another invasion of the Soviet Union from the west, the countries of eastern Europe must come under Soviet domination in order to create a buffer between the Soviet Union and its adversaries. An independent Poland—or Hungary, or Czechoslovakia—would be a Catholic (and in Stalin's view, archaic) state, oriented toward the West and hostile to Russia. Throughout the conference, Roosevelt played the role of a broker, guarding U.S. interests and switching his support from Churchill to Stalin on different issues, even though the purposes of the two were contradictory. Roosevelt was intent on achieving great-power harmony, and to that end he sacrificed the historical Anglo-American alliance in the hope of creating instead a postwar Anglo-Soviet-American security arrangement. Roosevelt's interest in going beyond traditional alliances also explains his enthusiasm for the United Nations (UN), which he saw, in keeping with the Wilsonian tradition, as a form of collective security that would sustain the peace and relieve America from having to play power politics in the future.

YALTA AGREEMENT

The Yalta conference became the most controversial event in post–Second World War diplomacy. The myth of Yalta helped usher in the cold war and intensified it. Republicans and isolationists argued that Yalta was a liberal Democratic surrender to Soviet totalitarianism, creating the climate that allowed McCarthyism to rise and flourish. Revisionist historians, however, consider Yalta a triumph of reasonableness and argue that Stalin's expansionism stemmed from purely defensive needs and security considerations, which he had pursued since 1941. A leading revisionist, Diane Clemens, disputed the charge that Roosevelt yielded to Stalin on the issues of Poland, Germany, and the Far East, arguing that Roosevelt made no more concessions than Stalin: "Although the Great Powers differed in the initial view points, a high incidence of consensus was reached at the conference."

The challenge to the revisionist interpretation is the fact that there was no equality among the three parties at Yalta. The agreement was a U.S.-Soviet dual arrangement, in which Britain was the lesser partner. A strong case can be made that one of the main reasons for Roosevelt's insistence on having the Soviets join the war against Japan was the unwillingness of the United States to include Britain in the effort against Japan, lest Britain exploit the occasion to expand its colonial holdings—a possibility to which the United States strongly objected.

Another criticism of Yalta stems from the fact that Roosevelt was already a sick man. Some critics of the agreement have charged that he abandoned Poland and Europe out of weakness. Senator Arthur Vandenberg (R-Michigan), chairman of the Senate Foreign Relations Committee in 1946–1948, claimed that Roosevelt had abandoned the realism of his cousin, President Theodore Roosevelt, and that Roosevelt's neo- Wilsonianism was responsible for the West's "surrender" at Yalta.

The critics of the Yalta Agreement were mostly Republicans, but there were distinctions among them. Athan Theoharis divides the conservative critics into three groups. The "extremists" included Senators Robert A. Taft (R-Ohio) and John W. Bricker (R-Ohio), as well as columnists such as Westbrook Pegler and George Sokolsky. Another group of Yalta detractors was the "partisans," among them Congressmen Richard M. Nixon (R-California), Karl Mundt (R-South Dakota), and the other. Republican members of the House Un-American Activities Committee (HUAC). The third group was the "moderates," among them Senator Henry Cabot Lodge (R-Massachusetts), Senator Arthur Vandenberg (R-Michigan), and General Dwight D. Eisenhower. The moderates supported the bipartisan policy during the war but were strongly anticommunist and passionately hostile to Roosevelt and the New Deal. These groups of critics differed on some things, but all echoed a single theme: Yalta was a failure and the price paid for an understanding with the Soviet Union was too high.

Although their language, especially in hindsight, may have at times been extreme, these Yalta critics were fundamentally correct in their assessment of what could have been accomplished at Yalta, possibilities Roosevelt missed. This oversight was the result of the president's attitude toward the Soviet Union and Stalin from the beginning of the war and of his general strategic conception that military victory over Germany, Italy, and Japan must come before political considerations regarding the postwar period. Diplomats Harry Hopkins, Averell Harriman, and others concentrated only on how to make sure that the USSR could be sustained and continue its contribution to a successful end of the war. The well-being of the Soviet Union became a U.S. military war interest, and nothing was allowed to interfere with that interest.

George F. Kennan, the leading critic of the president, argued that such an approach was amateurish and showed no understanding of Stalin and the Soviet regime. Before the Soviet defeat of the Nazis at Stalingrad, for example, more concessions could have been secured from Stalin on several issues. For Kennan and other critics of the president, Stalin continued to pursue the same policy goals the Soviet Union had tried to advance by signing a nonaggression pact with Nazi Germany in 1939: Soviet domination of eastern Europe and occupation of the Baltic states. Critics of Roosevelt saw no reason why the Soviet expansion should not be challenged and why massive U.S. aid to Russia during the war should not be tied more clearly to an understanding with the Soviets on how far they would be allowed to expand.

The absence of a tradition of realpolitik to animate Roosevelt's diplomacy—a tradition that should have been pursued before Stalingrad in order to have a chance to succeed—was the hallmark of Roosevelt's approach. When coupled with Roosevelt's revulsion at British and French imperialism, the resulting diminution in his mind of the role Britain and France should play in cobbling together the postwar order led to his preference for dealing directly with the Soviet Union as the new emerging global power. Thus, Yalta was a tacit alliance between two emerging superpowers, and the

Yalta Agreement was the price Roosevelt was willing to pay to cement this alliance. In the end the alliance failed to materialize, and the United States found itself falling back on its more traditional partners, Britain and France, to form a Western alliance to contain the Soviet Union. By then, thanks to Yalta, the Soviets were in a better geostrategic position to challenge the West than they had been earlier. By the time of Yalta, Roosevelt may have had but little maneuvering room to secure better terms for Western interests. He cannot escape the criticism, however, that it was his strategy during the Second World War and his insistence on attending to the military victory first and to postwar political arrangements later that boxed him in to such an extent.

−AMOS PERLMUTTER, AMERICAN
UNIVERSITY

References

Diane Shaver Clemens, *Yalta* (New York: Oxford University Press, 1970);

Lynn E. Davis, *The Cold War Begins: Soviet-American Conflict over Eastern Europe* (Princeton, N.J.: Princeton University Press, 1974);

Foreign Relations of the United States, Diplomatic Papers: The Conferences at Malta and Yalta, 1945, 84th Cong., 1st sess., H. Doc. 154 (Washington, D.C.: U.S. Government Printing Office, 1955);

Lloyd C. Gardner, *Spheres of Influence: The Great Powers Partition Europe, from Munich to Yalta* (Chicago: Ivan R. Dee, 1993);

Hua Qingzhao, *From Yalta to Panmunjom: Truman's Diplomacy and the Four Powers, 1945–1953* (Ithaca, N.Y.: Cornell University Press, 1993);

Lisle A. Rose, *After Yalta* (New York: Scribners, 1973);

Pierre de Senarclens, *From Yalta to the Iron Curtain: The Great Powers and the Origins of the Cold War,* translated by Amanda Pingree (New York: Berg, 1995);

Athan G. Theoharis, *The Yalta Myths: An Issue in U.S. Politics, 1945–1955* (Columbia: University of Missouri Press, 1970);

Marc Trachtenberg, *A Constructed Peace: The Making of the European Settlement, 1945–1963* (Princeton, N.J.: Princeton University Press, 1999).

YOM KIPPUR WAR

Why did Syria and Egypt limit their aims in their October 1973 war with Israel?

Viewpoint: Syria and Egypt limited their 1973 war aims because Egypt knew the limitations of its troops.

Viewpoint: Syria and Egypt sought political, not military, goals in the October 1973 war, and they achieved these goals.

The 1973 Yom Kippur War in the Middle East was a transformative event. The vaunted Israeli military was surprised by Egypt and Syria and suffered considerable losses during the opening stages of the war. During the years before the war the Israeli intelligence services had developed a reputation for analysis and covert action. Much of the literature devoted to the war, therefore, examines the question of why Israel was surprised. Some attribute the surprise to a flawed conception, entertained by Defense Minister Moshe Dayan and top military commanders, that the Arabs would not dare attack Israel: Israel not only had the superior military, but since 1967 it had come to enjoy an added strategic depth as a result of the territories it had occupied in the 1967 Six Day War. This conception was so dominant that General Elli Zeira, the commander of AMAN, Israel's military intelligence, refused to accept assessments by AMAN officers who had become alarmed at Egyptian and Syrian troop movements near the Israeli border. Practically on the eve of the joint Egyptian-Syrian attack, with massive Arab troop concentrations against Israeli borders, he insisted (in language that still haunts Israeli military officers) that there was only a "low likelihood" of an Arab attack on Israel.

Others lay the blame on the arrogance of the Israeli military which, as has often been the case with military establishments, was thinking and planning in terms of the last war rather than monitoring closely the tactical innovations in the Arab militaries and planning for the future. This line of argument says that Israel's surprise had less to do with the exact timing of the attack and more with the failure of Israeli military planners to appreciate the role that two new Arab weapon systems would play in the war. The first was the shoulder-mounted antitank missile, which Egyptian soldiers used with deadly effectiveness against Israeli armor in the Sinai Peninsula; the second was the Soviet surface-to-air missile (SAM), which the Egyptians had moved close to the east bank of the Suez Canal immediately after a cease-fire ended the War of Attrition in August 1970. The Israelis relied on a doctrine that called for the use of their air force as flying artillery, but the Egyptian SAMs inflicted heavy losses on the Israeli Air Force (IAF), providing effective cover for the Egyptian soldiers crossing the Suez Canal into the Sinai.

While much has been written on these two subjects, the other intriguing question—why did the Egyptian and Syrian forces not exploit more energetically their initial success to push deeper into Israel—has not earned the same attention. The Egyptians had to cross the Sinai Peninsula to get closer to Israeli urban and industrial centers, but the Syrians, presumably, would have had an easier time getting closer to the edge of the Golan Heights to threaten Israeli settlements below. Was it the case that the two armies, having been defeated in the past, were themselves surprised by their initial success? Was there fear that getting too close to Israeli population centers might cause Israel to escalate the war by resorting to unconventional weapons? Was there fear of superpower intervention? Were the goals Egypt and Syria were pursuing such that limited military gains would suffice? Regardless, the Israelis were able to mobilize their reserves and turn the tide of war in their favor, agreeing to a cease-fire with their forces on the west bank of the Suez Canal, surrounding the Egyptian forces that had crossed to the east side, and reaching deep into Syria. The question of the efficacy of and motivation behind the Egyptian and Syrian strategy remains contested.

Viewpoint:
Syria and Egypt limited their 1973 war aims because Egypt knew the limitations of its troops.

On 6 October 1973 Egyptian troops crossed the Suez Canal as part of President Anwar Sadat's grand political-military scheme to regain the Sinai Peninsula from Israel. Cairo sent 200,000 men, 1,600 tanks, and 2,000 artillery pieces across the canal. The attack was launched on Yom Kippur, the holiest day of the Jewish calendar, when most Israelis were in their synagogues and only a battalion of reservists manned the forts of the Bar-Lev line. The Egyptians had done a masterful job of concealing the operation from the Israelis, who were taken almost completely by surprise. In addition, their vast force gave the Egyptians numerical superiority on the order of twelve to one in men, twenty to one in artillery, and five to one in tanks over the Israel Defense Force (IDF) armies in the Sinai.

In theory the Egyptian plan, called "High Minarets," consisted of three phases. In phase 1 five Egyptian infantry divisions would force crossings all along the length of the canal and then consolidate a bridgehead along the so-called artillery road, roughly fifteen kilometers beyond the canal. At this point the Egyptians would cross additional armored reserves to the east bank of the canal and launch the phase 2 offensive, which would drive to the line of mountain passes in western Sinai, approximately thirty kilometers from the canal. Finally, in phase 3 they planned an armored breakout from the passes and the reoccupation of the entire Sinai.

Egyptian forces enjoyed almost uninterrupted success from the first attack until roughly the third day of the war. They pushed forward slowly and meticulously; after advancing a kilometer or two, they stopped, dug in, and braced for an Israeli attack. The moment they beat back the inevitable Israeli counterattack, the Egyptians resumed their creeping advance. The offensive, however, soon slowed to a glacial pace and on roughly 10 October, the minister of war, Lt. General Ahmed Isma'il 'Ali, ordered the Egyptian forces to dig in permanently. He would not allow his forces to advance any farther. Many of

his most senior commanders—including Chief of the General Staff Lt. General Sa'd 'ad-Din al-Shadhi—argued vociferously that they should continue the offensive and at least launch the second phase of the operation, the armored advance to the passes. Isma'il stubbornly refused and, with Sadat's backing, he prevailed. The Egyptians halted. Many Egyptians—as well as many outside observers—contended after the war that Egypt's military defeat derived from Isma'il's decision not to press the Egyptians' advantage while the Israelis were still reeling.

After the war, Isma'il told the leading Egyptian journalist, Muhammad Hasanayan Haykal, that the reason he had halted the offensive on 10 October was because the Egyptians had not moved their surface-to-air missiles (SAMs) to the east bank and, therefore, to push any farther east would have exposed Egyptian armor to the full brunt of the Israeli Air Force. Field Marshal Mohamed 'Abd al-Ghani al-Gamasy, then deputy chief of staff for operations, notes in his 1993 account of the war that Isma'il raised this point in arguments with his staff at the time. However, this argument was an excuse—a useful debating point—rather than Isma'il's actual reason for halting the offensive. Isma'il did not go beyond the bridgeheads because he believed (correctly, as the course of the later fighting demonstrated) that to do so would have jeopardized the whole purpose of the war.

Before the war it was well known among senior Egyptian officers that Isma'il never intended to move beyond the bridgeheads. Memoirs and recollections of the highest-ranking Egyptian political and military leaders—including generals Gamasy and Shadhi, as well as Sadat and National Security Adviser Hafiz Isma'il—all recount quite matter-of-factly that General Isma'il was opposed to any offensive beyond the bridgeheads and had purposely made no plans for the execution of phase 2, only occasionally paying lip service to the idea. Indeed, when Isma'il had taken over the War Ministry in October 1972 he had scrapped the three-phase High Minarets plan in favor of his own "Granite" plan, which consisted only of the phase 1 canal crossing and seizure of the bridgeheads.

Isma'il did everything he could to make sure that Egypt could not execute the envisioned second and third phase offensives of the High Min-

EGYPT PREPARES FOR WAR

On 1 October 1973, as President Anwar Sadat prepared to send Egyptian troops into battle against Israel, he issued the following directive to his generals, detailing his reasons for the attack:

1. More than six years have passed since the Israeli enemy occupied parts of our Arab land.

2. Israel enjoys American backing, particularly with regard to supply of arms. . . . It has tried and continues to try to impose its will on us and to end the Middle East crisis in such a way as to ensure almost complete domination of the Arab region, its security, and its fate.

3. Since the UN Security Council resolution for a ceasefire on 8 June 1967, Egypt has tried in every way to find a solution to the crisis. To this end it has explored various alternatives, from accepting the Security Council resolution of 26 November 1967, the efforts of Ambassador Jarring, the efforts of all the great powers, followed by those of the two superpowers, the initiative presented by the US Secretary of State William Rogers, and the direct offer of an initiative for a solution in which the opening of the Suez Canal would be the beginning of a phased total withdrawal in implementation of the Security Council resolution. All these efforts failed to reach a solution. They were either blocked or frustrated by our enemies.

4. Egypt has initiated limited military operations in 1968, 1969, and 1970. It has also provided powerful support for the activities of the Palestinian resistance on the borders or in the occupied territories. . . . None of the operations, although effective to some extent, has produced the desired pressure on the enemy.

5. Egypt has been aware throughout this period that the time would come when it would have to take its responsibilities in hand and that the most important task was to be ready for that day . . . when it was in our power to defend our land and honor.

6. The Egyptian people have endured beyond what can be imagined by friend and foe alike, both materially and psychologically—an oppressive burden which no people could have borne except those believing in freedom and willing to sacrifice for it.

7. Significant improvements have occurred in the Arab political situation in general, and this increases the chances of effective action. . . . With a growing energy crisis and international financial problems, under the appropriate conditions Arab pressure could become a valuable factor. . . .

Source: *"Directives to the Commander of the Armed Forces and Minister of War, General Ahmad Isma'il 'Ali, 5 Ramadan 1393, 1 October 1973," in Mohamed Abdel Ghani El-Gamasy,* The October War: Memoirs of Field Marshal El-Gamasy of Egypt, *translated by Gillian Potter, Nadra Morcos, and Rosette Frances (Cairo: American University in Cairo Press, 1993), p. 188.*

arets plan. Every piece of equipment needed for the phase 1 Granite offensive was procured. Every problem that Egyptian troops would face was considered, deliberated, and solved—often by novel solutions. Every possible need was addressed. For phases 2 and 3, however, nothing was done. No specialized equipment was procured. Indeed, the Egyptian General Staff had not even considered what equipment might be needed for these operations, or what problems they might encounter, or what other eventualities would have to be addressed. Under Isma'il's firm guiding hand, the General Staff did not pay any attention to phases 2 and 3 at all, devoting every ounce of their energies toward phase 1.

The most important manifestation of this divergent emphasis was in the planning of the operations orders. Phase 1 operations were planned down to the last detail. Isma'il and Shadhi decreed that every Egyptian soldier should have only one mission for phase 1 and that he should learn to perform that mission by heart. Full-scale mock-ups of the Israeli fortifications, the terrain on the east bank of the Suez, and the canal itself were constructed and used by the Egyptian units to learn their assignments. Operations were rehearsed repeatedly, until each member of every unit knew exactly what he was supposed to do at every step of the operation. The entire offensive was rehearsed as a whole thirty-five times before the actual attack. Egyptian soldiers and officers were encouraged to memorize a series of programmed steps, and during the actual canal-crossing operation, junior officers were expressly forbidden from taking actions that were not specifically ordered by the plan.

By contrast, the General Staff did not plan the second or third phases at all. No mock-ups were built. No detailed orders were issued. No operations were rehearsed. According to Egyptian brigade and division commanders, they were given a massive operations order for phase 1, while their phase 2 instructions essentially consisted of a single sentence: they were to proceed to the line of the passes in western Sinai.

Additional evidence is furnished by the handling of Egyptian logistics. Egyptian logistical depots remained on the west bank of the canal, where they could not support an offensive beyond the initial bridgeheads. During the initial crossing, Egyptian forces transferred across the canal only those supplies needed to execute the phase 1 offensive and allow the Egyptian divisions to dig in and defend themselves against the expected Israeli counterattacks. By 10 October the Egyptians still had not moved the supplies needed for a phase 2 offensive across the canal. Had Isma'il ever wanted to conduct a phase 2 offensive he would have needed the necessary logistical stockpiles in place by 10 October. An armored offensive of four to five divisions (as envisioned in the High Minarets plan) would have required tremendous logistical stocks, and hauling these supplies across the canal would have been an awkward and time-consuming process. Thus, if Isma'il had wanted to preserve the option of making such an attack he almost certainly would have begun shifting supplies to the east bank immediately after the combat units were across, starting around 8 October. This part of the plan could not be improvised.

The SAM-umbrella argument is unconvincing because the Egyptians never moved significant numbers of SAM units across the canal, even though they were all fully mobile. Egypt had a vast arsenal of air-defense systems at the time: 135 batteries of SA-2 and SA-3 missiles, 30 to 40 batteries of the new SA-6 missiles (which had never before been used in combat), 2,100 anti-aircraft guns, and 5,000 shoulder-launched SA-7 missiles. Companies equipped with SA-7 missiles were attached to the combat divisions, and Cairo moved a few SA-6 batteries—along with mobile anti-aircraft artillery (AAA) units—to the east bank, but most of the SA-6, and all of the SA-2 and SA-3 units remained on the west bank. The SA-6 is fully mobile, designed to set up and fire straight from the march. The SA-2 and SA-3 missiles are designed to be fired from static sites, but these sites can be moved and set up with relative ease. Soviet doctrine called for batteries of SA-2 and SA-3 missiles to accompany their armies on the move, displacing forward as necessary. The four days from 6 to 10 October were more than adequate to have moved forward many batteries of SA-2, SA-3, and SA-6 missiles

to the east bank of the canal, if this operation had been part of the plan.

If Isma'il had even been considering an offensive to the passes he would have begun moving those SAM units immediately, again probably around 8 October. If he had ever intended to execute the rest of the High Minarets plan—or had even wanted to preserve the option of doing so depending on the success of the phase 1 operations—there is just no reason for him not to have done so.

Further evidence is provided by Sadat's adviser Sayyid Mar'i, whom Sadat dispatched on a diplomatic mission to Saudi Arabia and the other Gulf states on 10 October to ensure their support for Egypt's war effort. Mar'i was accompanied by Major General Sa'd al-Qadi of the Egyptian General Staff, whose role was to brief the Gulf leaders on the military situation. As Mar'i wrote in a 1980 article, al-Qadi assured King Faisal of Saudi Arabia that Egyptian forces could keep moving eastward under cover of their SAM umbrella by moving their SAM batteries forward so that "Egyptian forces will be constantly and effectively protected from attacks by the Israeli Air Force." Thus, it is clear that the General Staff was fully aware of the necessity of moving the SAM batteries forward, and capable of doing so, if they were to continue driving beyond the initial ten- to fifteen-kilometer bridgehead—yet another indication that Isma'il simply did not want to move beyond the bridgehead.

In short, all of the available evidence indicates that General Isma'il purposely structured the canal-crossing operation so that it could not go beyond the artillery road. He did not plan or prepare the army for operations beyond the bridgeheads. He did not move the logistical or air-defense assets across the canal as part of the initial "master plan" that would have enabled a phase 2 offensive should he have wanted to conduct one. He did everything he could to make sure that it was not possible for Egypt to realistically launch an offensive beyond the bridgeheads. It may well be that Isma'il expected to face heavy pressure for an offensive to the passes if the initial canal crossing went well. Egyptian military and political leaders had been pressing for it even before the October War began. Isma'il's plans may have been deliberately designed to help him head off such pressure with the convenient excuse that logistic support was lacking. Of course, it is possible that Isma'il hoped that at some point he would be able to conduct another set-piece offensive to the passes. The evidence, however, is compelling that he never intended this operation to follow close on the heels of the canal crossing, that in his mind it was at least weeks if not months or years. The

General Sa'd 'ad-Din
al-Shadhi, President
Anwar Sadat, and General
Ahmed Isma'il Ali
discussing strategy
during the Yom
Kippur War

(AP)

SAM excuse was just that—an excuse, not a reason.

The most obvious reason for Isma'il's abbreviated Granite plan was that Sadat's political objective did not require it. Sadat did not believe that he needed to retake all the Sinai Peninsula, just a small piece, enough to show Israel that Egypt was not impotent and to demonstrate to the United States that, if Washington did not find a political solution, Cairo would continue to pursue a military one. Sadat made clear to his generals that he needed to be able to conquer some territory—any territory—in the Israeli-held Sinai. Until Isma'il's accession to head of the War Ministry, the Egyptian high command had consistently told Sadat that an offensive into the Sinai was impossible. They could think only in terms of a Soviet-style breakthrough and occupation of the entire canal. Sadat gave the War Minister's job to Isma'il specifically because Isma'il said he thought he could get the Egyptians across the canal (although he warned that he could not get them any farther and expressed the belief that attempting to do so would result in catastrophic defeat). Sadat is reported to have replied that he needed only "one square meter of Sinai."

Isma'il's caution derived from his own insights into the capabilities and limitations of the Egyptian armed forces. After the Six Day War of 1967, Egypt attempted an objective assessment of Israeli and Egyptian strengths and weaknesses. Egyptian intelligence prepared detailed studies of Israeli strategy; the geography, topography, and meteorology of the Sinai; the Israeli "psychological temperament"; the Israeli order of battle; and the Bar-Lev fortifications. Cairo concluded that the IDF's greatest advantages were its tremendous flexibility and its ability to maneuver in battle, which contributed to "outstanding" capabilities in armored warfare and air combat. At the same time, the Egyptians recognized Israel's extreme aversion to casualties, its inability to remain mobilized for more than a few weeks, and its overconfidence resulting from the victory of 1967.

Cairo also performed the same sort of analysis on its own forces and capabilities. According to Gamasy, Isma'il "had developed the conviction that the human element—the quality of the fighter—and not the weapon was what counted in victory." The Egyptians concluded that their troops performed poorly in mobile warfare, in combined arms operations, in dogfights, and in any situation where they were outflanked or encircled. They admitted that their forces did poorly in maneuver battles because this form of warfare required initiative, improvisation, and flexibility—all of which their junior officers lacked. They also recognized, however, that their troops were relatively successful when fighting from fixed defenses and that, ultimately, Egypt could keep a far larger army in the field longer than the Israelis.

Isma'il and Gamasy then used these assessments to develop an operational concept for an offensive across the Suez, tailoring their plans to the actual capabilities of their forces. The offensive had to have limited goals. It would begin with a surprise attack. Because Israel relied heavily on reservists, striking before they were mobilized meant that the Egyptians would face only a small IDF force in Sinai. Moreover, by surprising Tel Aviv, Isma'il hoped to be able to seize and hold the initiative and thus dictate the terms of battle to the Israelis. By forcing the Israelis onto the defensive, Isma'il would be able to shape operations in the direction of greatest Egyptian strength and avoid those areas of greatest weakness.

The offensive would rely on attrition rather than maneuver to defeat the IDF. The Egyptians would employ a strategic offensive coupled with a tactical defensive: they would surprise the Israelis, cross the canal, push five to ten miles into Sinai and then dig in. They would then let the Israeli armor crash against their defensive lines, wearing the Israeli forces down in bloody attacks against entrenched infantry rather than attempting decisive maneuvers of their own, which Isma'il concluded the Israelis would quickly defeat and then exploit. To neutralize Israel's two great advantages in armored warfare and airpower the Egyptians would deploy enormous numbers of early-generation Soviet antitank guided missiles (ATGMs), rocket-propelled grenades (RPGs), mobile AAA systems, and SAMs. Most important, the operation would rely on elaborately scripted set-piece operations to compensate for the weakness of Egyptian tactical leadership.

The care and creativity of Egyptian planning made possible the victories of the first four days of the war. The limitations of this approach, however, also quickly manifested themselves. Egypt owed its initial success to four crucial factors—surprise, the dramatic imbalance of forces on the first day of battle, Israeli unpreparedness for Egyptian antitank and anti-air tactics, and the brilliant, all-encompassing script of the Egyptian General Staff. By 9 October, all four of these advantages were slipping away: the Israelis had recovered from their surprise; they were con-

centrating forces in the Sinai; they were figuring out ways to defeat the Egyptian defensive tactics; and the course of operations was diverging further and further from the plan, forcing local commanders to shoulder more of the burden of command. Isma'il recognized this decisive shift, and—despite the pleas of Shadhi, Gamasy, and others—refused to order a new, large-scale offensive, instead ordering his troops to consolidate their positions and brace for counterattack.

The wisdom of Isma'il's decision was illustrated four days later when Syrian pleas prompted Sadat to order a new offensive toward the passes to try to force Israel to relieve the pressure on Damascus. Against Isma'il's advice, Cairo launched an assault boasting roughly two-and-a-half divisions and 800 to 1000 tanks against the Israeli forces. Without the meticulous, well-rehearsed plans of the General Staff, Egyptian forces proved just as hapless as in 1967. Their tactical leaders were unaggressive, inflexible, unimaginative, and unable to handle maneuver warfare. In a series of short, sharp tank battles, the IDF destroyed 265 Egyptian tanks while losing only 40 of their own—all but 6 of which were quickly repaired and returned to battle. The Egyptians were beaten by the shortcomings of their tactical leadership—not by deficiencies in air defense or logistics. This defeat paved the way for the Israeli counteroffensive. The Israelis crossed the canal, defeated Egypt's reserves on the west bank, and encircled the entire Egyptian Third Army. Thus, in the end, Isma'il's determination to make it impossible for Cairo to order a phase 2 offensive was proven correct.

–KENNETH M. POLLACK, NATIONAL DEFENSE UNIVERSITY

Viewpoint:
Syria and Egypt sought political, not military, goals in the October 1973 war, and they achieved these goals.

War is the continuation of politics by other means, as Carl von Clausewitz so aptly wrote. At times states go to war not because of pressing military concerns or in order to achieve impressive military gains, but in order to advance specific political goals after they have exhausted other diplomatic options. Different war aims thus lead states to adopt different strategies. In 1990 Iraq invaded Kuwait with the aim of annexing it; in the 1982 Falkland War Argentina tried to reclaim islands it believed were rightfully hers; and from 1955 to 1975, North Vietnam fought the government of South Vietnam in an effort to unify Vietnam under one rule. The countries that initiated each of these wars had different aims, and, as a result, each pursued a different military strategy. Initiated by Egypt and Syria in pursuit of specific political, rather than purely military, goals, the October 1973 war in the Middle East is an example of a limited-aims war.

This conflict was called the Ramadan War by the Arabs and the Yom Kippur War by the Israelis. Its origins go back to the war of 1948, which the Israelis call their War of Independence. For the Palestinian Arabs the conflict resulted in a catastrophic uprooting of hundreds of thousands of people, who became refugees. Other wars followed: in 1956, after Egyptian president Gamal Abdel Nasser nationalized the Suez Canal, a joint Franco-British-Israeli attack resulted in the destruction of the Egyptian military in the Sinai Peninsula, followed by an Israeli occupation of the area. The Israelis withdrew in 1957, after pressure from the United States and the Soviet Union.

The war that proved most disastrous for the Arabs was the Six Day War of June 1967. Israel defeated its Arab neighbors and expanded its territory to include the Golan Heights in the north (taken from Syria), the Sinai Peninsula and the Gaza Strip in the south (taken from Egypt), and the West Bank of the Jordan River, including Jerusalem, in the east (taken from Jordan). This war destroyed Arab confidence and inflated the Israelis' sense of military superiority, if not arrogance, to the point that their leaders thought Arab societies too weak and inferior to challenge Israel's military might. The defeat in 1967 divided the Arab world. Some leaders—such as Mu'ammar Gadhafi of Libya, who came to power in 1969 and Hafiz al-Assad, who came to power in Syria three years after the war—were hardened in their resolve to defeat Israel in war. Other Arab leaders—for example, Habib Bourguiba of Tunisia and King Hussein of Jordan—became convinced that Israel could not be defeated at a cost that was acceptable to the Arabs and that they should, therefore, seek to settle their differences with the Jewish state peacefully. This second group began, tentatively and hesitantly, to search for a way out of the cycle of conflict and war, but they found Israel less than accommodating. The Israelis, led by Prime Minister Golda Meir and Defense Minister Moshe Dayan, felt secure behind the buffer that the new territories provided and were not in a hurry to negotiate a settlement of the Arab-Israeli conflict that would require relinquishing this land. Moreover, some of the newly

acquired territories, especially the West Bank of the Jordan River and Jerusalem, held deep religious and historical significance to many Israelis, and the victory in 1967 brought about a revival of nationalist religious sentiment in Israel that complicated the domestic political landscape and made territorial compromise with the Arabs more difficult to pursue.

After 1967 there were many failed attempts to bring peace to the Middle East. Among them was the one made by Gunnar V. Jarring, a Swedish diplomat appointed by UN secretary-general U Thant on 22 November 1967. Jarring engaged in "shuttle diplomacy," traveling back and forth among Jerusalem and Arab capitals and trying to convince the various sides to start peace talks. His efforts failed. The Arabs refused to talk to the Israelis from a position of weakness, demanding complete Israeli withdrawal from the occupied territories prior to any negotiations. Israel continued to insist on direct, face-to-face talks with the Arabs as a precondition to any movement on the territories.

U.S. secretary of state William P. Rogers launched another peace initiative on 28 October 1969, when he called on the Israelis to withdraw from the occupied Arab territories in exchange for a lasting peace with the Arabs. Rogers proposed that the city of Jerusalem be united under an administration sympathetic to the interests of the three faiths and their holy places and that Jordan should play a role in the economic and social affairs of the city. Rogers's plan also called for the demilitarization of the Sinai Peninsula. The Israelis, the Arabs, and subsequently the Soviets all rejected this peace plan.

These and other peace initiatives led nowhere. In an interview with William Attwood that appeared in the 19 March 1968 issue of the American magazine *Look,* Nasser charged, "Israelis are reluctant to settle things, and they will be willing only when they feel we have an effective fighting force." A year later, in March 1969, Egypt launched what became known as the War of Attrition along the Suez Canal. The war consisted of daily artillery exchanges between the two sides, accompanied by Israeli aerial bombardments deep into Egypt and forays by Israeli commando units. Nasser thought that in order to make Israel give up land, the Israelis must realize that keeping that land was not a cost-free proposition. He could only do so by force; a call for peace was merely rhetorical. In his book *Road to Ramadan* Muhammad Hassaneyn Heykal, editor of the authoritative *Al-Ahram* newspaper and close adviser to both Nasser and his successor, Anwar Sadat, quoted Nasser as telling senior Egyptian army commanders: "Please remember what I have said before—what has been taken by force can only

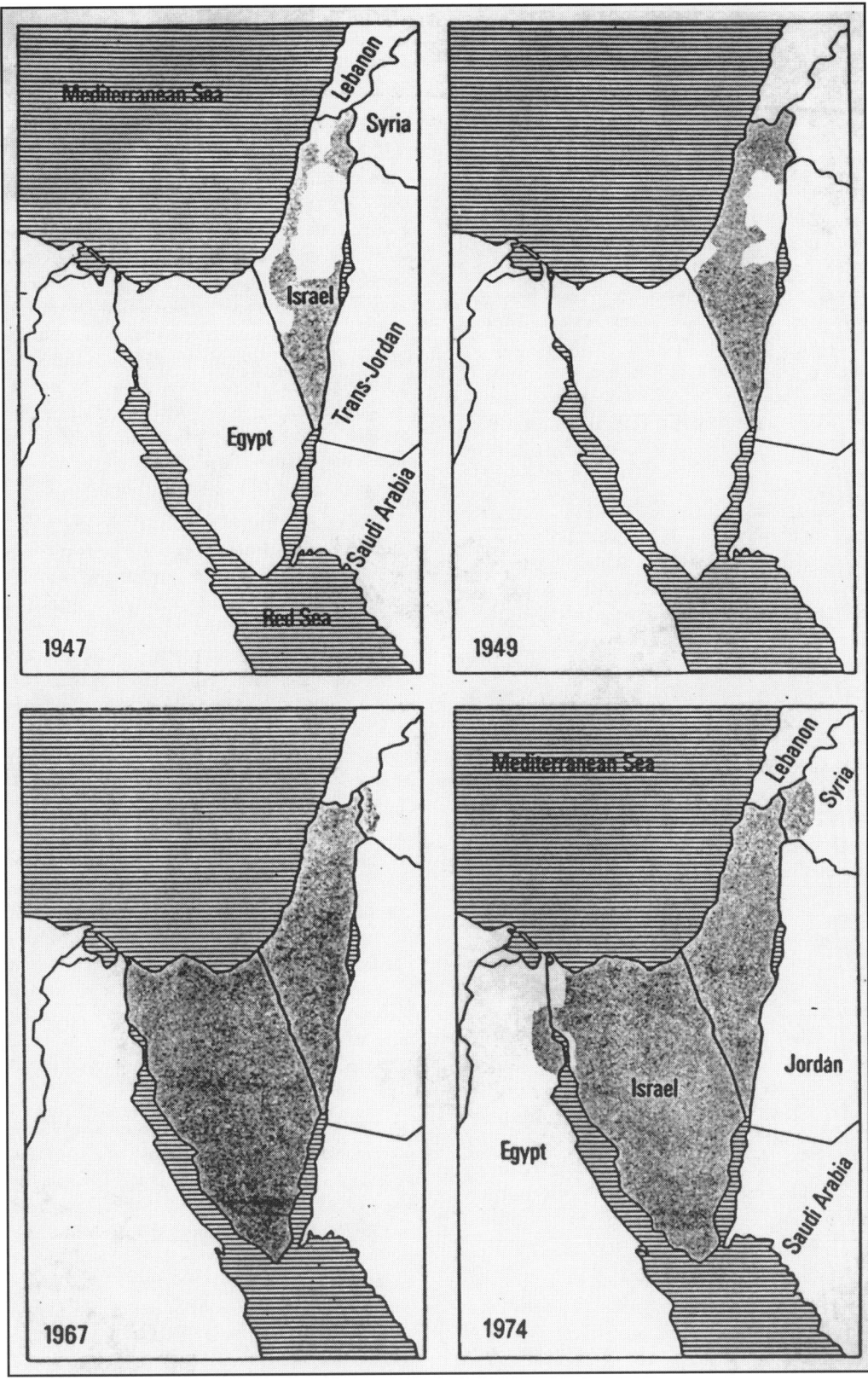

The boundaries of Israel in 1947, after David Ben-Gurion accepted the British plan to partition Palestine; 1949, after the first Israeli-Palestinian conflict; 1967, after the Six Day War; and 1974, after the Yom Kippur War

be recovered by force." General Dayan called Nasser's War of Attrition a "half war." Because he understood that Egypt was trying to weaken Israel's position along the canal in preparation for an actual war, he referred to the War of Attrition as "the battle for the battle." In retaliation for the constant Egyptian shelling of Israeli positions, Israel considered the whole of Egypt as a battlefield. Bombing and raids continued on both sides of the canal until August 1970, when both Egypt and Israel accepted a ninety-day cease-fire proposed by Secretary of State Rogers. Though such a move was forbidden by this agreement, the Egyptians used the ninety-day lull to move a large number of Soviet-made anti-aircraft missiles to the west bank of the Suez Canal. Israel protested to the United States but to no avail.

Israel was satisfied with the political stalemate that continued during the "no peace, no war" period that followed. After all, the Israelis controlled the land and with it a strategic military superiority. Referring to the strategically important fortifications at the southern tip of the Sinai Peninsula, General Dayan gave explicit expression to Israel's position when he declared that Israel "would rather have Sharam El-Sheikh without peace than peace without Sharam El-Sheikh." Dayan also said that Israeli security had "never been so good." In the Arab capitals the mood was different. Arab leaders were losing support among their populations because they were unable to correct the defeat of 1967. On 28 September of 1970 Nasser died, and Sadat, his vice-president, came to power.

As with Nasser, Sadat's main objective was to regain Arab territories lost to Israel in 1967. Realizing that he might have to resort to military means to achieve this goal, he talked of peace but continued to upgrade the Egyptian military and equip it with Soviet weapons. Sadat's "year of decision" was 1971: he promised a solution with the Israelis, by war or by peace. The year ended, however, without any action taken, and the state of "no peace, no war" continued.

Sadat's reputation, like that of other Arab leaders, was beginning to suffer. His pro-Soviet vice president Ali Sabri, and others conspired to overthrow Sadat; on 26 November 1972 it was reported that one hundred officers were arrested for plotting a coup against him. In Syria, President Hafid Al-Assad ascended to power in turbulent times; on 10 June 1973 there was a coup attempt against him, and about three hundred officers were arrested. Both Assad and Sadat needed a policy that would calm an increasingly restive population

and bring the Israelis to the negotiating table. They decided, in light of the many failed peace initiatives and Israeli complacency, that policy should be a war against Israel.

In the days leading up to the October 1973 war, Egypt waged a misinformation campaign to mislead the world about its preparations. The Egyptians and the Syrians engaged in large-scale military exercises near the Israeli borders, convincing the Israelis that the military buildup was not meant for war. On 6 October 1973 the campaign, code-named Operation Badr, began. Egyptian forces crossed the thinly defended Suez Canal and pushed into the Sinai Peninsula; the Syrians struck from the north, attacking the Golan Heights. Israel, taken by surprise, suffered major losses during the initial phases of the war, as Arab armies from both sides penetrated Israeli defense lines.

Then, after their initial success, the Egyptian and Syrian armies stopped. The two countries appeared unwilling to exploit their gains—Egypt by penetrating deeper into the Sinai, the Syrians by occupying the whole of the Golan Heights and moving down the slopes toward eastern Galilee. It is not clear why the two armies stopped. Some point out that the Egyptians did not want to come from under the protective umbrella provided by the surface-to-air missiles (SAMs) on the east bank of the canal, which kept the Israeli Air Force away. (The single Egyptian armored foray beyond the protective umbrella ended in disaster.) It is more reasonable to assume that the Syrians and the Egyptians had no intentions of going beyond the strips of land they regained. They knew well that Israel possessed nuclear weapons, and that the Israelis would not hesitate to use them if Arab armies began to approach major Israeli population centers. There was also no reason to go farther: for political reasons even limited gains were sufficient.

The Israelis used the time to mobilize their reserves, which constituted most of the Israeli army, and began to push the Egyptians and the Syrians back. Israel forced the Syrian forces off the Golan Heights and pushed deep into Syria, stopping with Damascus almost within the range of Israeli artillery. In the Sinai, General Ariel Sharon, in a brilliant move, found a seam between the Egyptian Third and Second Armies—both stationed on the eastern bank of the Suez Canal—and exploited the opening to move Israeli armored divisions (on barges and over pontoon bridges) to the western bank of the canal. There, Israeli forces moved north and south, destroying the Egyptian anti-aircraft missile batteries that had been moved there in violation of the August 1970 cease-fire agreement, and isolating the Egyptian Third Army, cutting it off from its sources of supply. No longer hobbled by the anti-aircraft missiles on the west bank of the canal, the Israeli air force pounded the Egyptian forces without mercy. Israeli forces also pushed west, and for a while some speculated that they might occupy undefended Cairo. To prevent the Egyptian military collapse from becoming a political disaster for Sadat, the Soviet Union placed some of its airborne forces on alert and moved ships toward Egypt. There were speculations in Washington that these ships were carrying nuclear weapons, and, as a result, President Richard M. Nixon placed U.S. forces on global nuclear alert. The war increasingly had the potential of getting the two superpowers involved. To avert this danger the Nixon administration exerted considerable pressure on Israel to stop its military activities in Syria and Egypt. National Security Adviser Henry Kissinger also made it clear that the Israelis would have to allow supplies to reach the besieged Third Army, or the administation would order American helicopters to do the job. Kissinger believed that the war had to end in a way that did not seem like a total Arab defeat or Sadat would not be able to continue his push for a peaceful settlement with Israel. Sadat could not appear to be pursuing peace as a result of military defeat.

Thus, although the war ended in a military defeat for Egypt and Syria, with Israeli forces deep in Syrian and Egyptian territory (a defeat all the more remarkable, in military terms, because Israel was caught unprepared), and although it took a concerted intervention by the United States to force the Israelis from doing even more damage to the routed Arab forces, the war could still be portrayed as having salvaged Arab honor: there was the audacity of attacking Israel, a militarily superior state, and there were some initial Egyptian and Syrian successes. More important, the war achieved psychological and political goals for the Arabs. Israel was no longer perceived—by itself and its neighbors—as invincible. The war was also costly to Israel, in blood and treasure. The Arabs proved even a war that they lost and Israel won might be too costly for Israel. As a result, Israel became more flexible on the issue of peace negotiations with the Arabs, especially about the key tenet: giving up occupied territory for peace. In the years that followed the war, Kissinger (who had become secretary of state) mounted a diplomatic campaign to bring the two sides together. In 1974 and 1975 he was able to negotiate troop-separation agreements between Israel and Egypt and between Israel and Syria. In November 1977 Sadat, in a historic and dramatic move, visited Israel and spoke to the Israeli parliament, the Knesset.

In 1978, with Jimmy Carter as president, the United States pressured Israel and Egypt to translate the initial contacts into a peace treaty. That treaty was signed in 1978, after intense negotiations at Camp David, the presidential retreat. In 1982 Israel handed the Sinai Peninsula back to Egypt in accordance with the Camp David peace accord. There is little doubt that the peace agreement between Israel and Egypt—which, in time, led to the peace agreements between Israel and Jordan and Israel and the Palestinians—would not have been achieved without the October 1973 war. The war forced a realization on the part of Israel that, contrary to General Dayan's beliefs, the Arabs could extract an increasingly higher price for Israel's occupation of Arab land. Advancements in weapons technology made it easier, not more difficult, for the Arabs to extract that cost. The war also salvaged Arab honor and confidence, allowing leaders such as Sadat and King Hussein to make peace with Israel without being delegitimized in the eyes of the majority of the Arabs.

Different wars have different aims, and the aims of the October 1973 war were clearly political and psychological, not purely military. Even in defeat, the Egyptians and Syrians achieved their goals—puncturing Israel's overconfidence and arrogance, restarting the peace process, convincing Israel to be more conciliatory, and getting the United States more involved in pressuring Israel to make concessions to accompany and reflect those of the Arabs. Sadat went further toward seeking peace than Assad, and, as a result, paid with his life on 9 October 1981, when he was assassinated by a group of Muslim fanatics. His successor, Hosni Mubarak, however, unflinchingly continued in Sadat's footsteps. The October war can thus be judged a success from the Arab perspective. It had limited aims, and its authors pursued a strategy that allowed them to achieve those aims.

—TALAL BELRHITI, GEORGE MASON
UNIVERSITY

References

Haytham al-Ayoubi, "The Strategies of the Fourth Campaign," translated by Edmund Ghareeb, in *Middle East Crucible: Studies on the Arab-Israeli War of October 1973,* edited by Naseer H. Aruri (Wilmette, Ill.: Medina University Press International, 1975);

William Attwood, "Nasser Talks," *Look* (19 March 1968): 61–67;

Eliot A. Cohen, Michael J. Eisenstadt, and Andrew J. Bacevich, *Knives, Tanks, and Mis-*

siles: *Israel's Security Revolution* (Washington, D.C.: Washington Institute for Near East Policy, 1998);

Mohamed Abdel Ghani El-Gamasy, *The October War: Memoirs of Field Marshal El-Gamasy of Egypt,* translated by Gillian Potter, Nadra Marcos, and Rosette Frances, (Cairo: American University in Cairo Press, 1993);

Muhammad Hassanayan Heykal, *The Road to Ramadan* (New York: Quadrangle, 1975);

Efraim Inbar, "Israeli Strategic Thinking after 1973," *Journal of Strategic Studies,* 6 (March 1983): 36–59;

Sayyid Mar'i, "A Mission to Saudi Arabia and the Gulf States in the Midst of Battle," *Akhir Sa'ah* (Cairo), 8 October 1980, pp. 16–19;

Ze'ev Schiff, *October Earthquake: Yom Kippur 1973,* translated by Louis Williams (Tel Aviv: University Publishing Projects, 1974).

REFERENCES

1. Memoirs, Biographies, and Evaluations of Major Participants in the Cold War

Acheson, Dean G. *Power and Diplomacy.* Cambridge, Mass.: Harvard University Press, 1958.

Acheson. *Present at the Creation: My Years in the State Department.* New York: Norton, 1969.

Acheson. *Sketches from Life of Men I Have Known.* New York: Harper & Row, 1961.

Adams, Sherman. *Firsthand Report: The Story of the Eisenhower Administration.* New York: Harper & Row, 1961.

Adenauer, Konrad. *Memoirs, 1945–1953,* translated by Beate Ruhm von Oppen. Chicago: Regnery, 1966.

Ambrose, Stephen E. *Eisenhower,* 2 volumes. New York: Simon & Schuster, 1984.

Ambrose. *Nixon,* 3 volumes. New York: Simon & Schuster, 1987–1991.

Ambrose. *Nixon: The Triumph of a Politician, 1962–1972.* New York: Simon & Schuster, 1989.

Anderson, Jon Lee. *Che Guevara: A Revolutionary Life.* New York: Grove, 1997.

Attlee, Clement R. *As It Happened.* New York: Viking, 1954.

Attlee. *Twilight of Empire: Memoirs of Prime Minister Clement Attlee.* New York: Barnes, 1962.

Barclay, Sir Roderick. *Ernest Bevin and the Foreign Office, 1932–1969.* London: Latimer, 1975.

Binder, David. *The Other German: Willy Brandt's Life and Times.* Washington, D.C.: New Republic, 1975.

Bohlen, Charles E. *Witness to History, 1929–1969.* New York: Norton, 1973.

Brandt, Willy. *People and Politics: The Years 1960–1975.* Boston: Little, Brown, 1978.

Brendon, Piers. *Ike: His Life and Times.* New York: Harper & Row, 1986.

Broadwater, Jeff. *Eisenhower & the Anti-Communist Crusade.* Chapel Hill: University of North Carolina Press, 1992.

Brodie, Fawn. *Richard Nixon: The Shaping of His Character.* New York: Norton, 1981.

Brzezinski, Zbigniew. *Power and Principle: Memoirs of the National Security Adviser, 1977–1981.* New York: Farrar, Straus & Giroux, 1983.

Bullock, Alan. *Ernest Bevin: Foreign Secretary, 1945–1951.* New York: Norton, 1983.

Burridge, Trevor. *Clement Attlee, a Political Biography.* London: Cape, 1985.

Caldwell, Dan, ed. *Henry Kissinger: His Personality and Policies.* Durham, N.C.: Duke University Press, 1983.

Callahan, David. *Dangerous Capabilities: Paul Nitze and the Cold War.* New York: HarperCollins, 1990.

Carlton, David. *Anthony Eden: A Biography.* London: Allen Lane, 1981.

Carr, Jonathan. *Helmut Schmidt: Helmsman of Germany.* London: Weidenfeld & Nicolson, 1985; New York: St. Martin's Press, 1985.

Carter, Jimmy. *Keeping Faith: Memoirs of a President.* New York: Bantam, 1982.

Castañeda, Jorge G. Compañero. *The Life and Death of Che Guevara,* translated by Marina Castañeda. New York: Knopf, 1997.

Churchill, Randolph S. *The Rise and Fall of Sir Anthony Eden.* London: MacGibbon & Kee, 1959; New York: Putnam, 1959.

Clay, Lucius D. *The Papers of General Lucius D. Clay: Germany, 1945–1949,* 2 volumes, edited by Jean E. Smith. Bloomington: Indiana University Press, 1974.

Coffey, Thomas M. *Iron Eagle: The Turbulent Life of General Curtis LeMay.* New York: Crown, 1986.

Dalton, Hugh. *High Tide and After: Memoirs, 1945–1960.* London: Muller, 1962.

Dickson, Peter. *Kissinger and the Meaning of History.* New York: Cambridge University Press, 1978.

Divine, Robert A. *Eisenhower and the Cold War.* New York: Oxford University Press, 1981.

Dobney, Frederick J., Jr., ed. *Selected Papers of Will Clayton.* Baltimore: Johns Hopkins University Press, 1971.

Eden, Anthony. *Full Circle: The Memoirs of Anthony Eden.* Boston: Houghton Mifflin, 1960.

Edinger, Lewis J. *Kurt Schumacher: A Study in Personality and Political Behavior.* Stanford, Cal.: Stanford University Press, 1965.

Eisenhower, Dwight D. *The White House Years,* 2 volumes. Garden City, N.Y.: Doubleday, 1963.

El-Gamasy, Mohamed Abdel Ghani. *The October War: Memoirs of Field Marshal El-Gamasy of Egypt,* translated by Gillian Potter, Nadra Marcos, and Rosette Frances. Cairo: American University in Cairo Press, 1993.

Evans, Harold. *Downing Street Diary: The Macmillan Years, 1957–63.* London: Hodder & Stoughton, 1981.

Ferrell, Robert H., ed. *The Autobiography of Harry S. Truman.* Boulder, Colo.: Associated University Press, 1980.

Ferrell, ed. *Off the Record: The Private Papers of Harry S. Truman*. New York: Harper & Row, 1980.

Finlay, David J., Ole R. Holsti, and Richard R. Fagen. *Enemies in Politics*. Chicago: Rand McNally, 1967.

Fisher, Nigel. *Harold Macmillan: A Biography*. London: Weidenfeld & Nicolson, 1982; New York: St. Martin's Press, 1982.

Fisher. *Ian Macleod*. London: Deutsch, 1973.

Foot, Michael. *Aneurin Bevan: A Biography*. New York: Atheneum, 1974.

Forrestal, James. *The Forrestal Diaries: The Inner History of the Cold War*, edited by Walter Millis and E. S. Duffield. New York: Viking, 1951.

Gaitskell, Hugh. *The Diary of Hugh Gaitskell, 1945–1956*, edited by Philip M. Williams. London: Cape, 1983.

Gardiner, George. *Margaret Thatcher: From Childhood to Leadership*. London: Kimber, 1975.

Gardner, Lloyd. *Architects of Illusion: Men and Ideas in American Foreign Policy, 1941–1949*. Chicago: Quadrangle, 1970.

Graubard, Stephen. *Kissinger: Portrait of a Mind*. New York: Norton, 1973.

Guhin, Michael A. *John Foster Dulles: A Statesman and His Times*. New York: Columbia University Press, 1972.

Haig, Alexander M. *Caveat: Realism, Reagan, and Foreign Policy*. New York: Macmillan, 1984.

Hamby, Alonzo L. *Beyond the New Deal: Harry S. Truman and American Liberalism*. New York: Columbia University Press, 1973.

Harriman, W. Averell. *America and Russia in a Changing World: A Half Century of Personal Observation*. Garden City, N.Y.: Doubleday, 1971.

Harris, Kenneth. *Attlee*. London: Weidenfeld & Nicolson, 1982.

Hersh, Seymour M. *The Price of Power: Kissinger in the Nixon White House*. New York: Summit Books, 1983.

Hershberg, James G. *James B. Conant: Harvard to Hiroshima and the Making of the Nuclear Age*. New York: Knopf, 1993.

Hixson, Walter L. *George F. Kennan, Cold War Iconoclast*. New York: Columbia University Press, 1989.

Holsti, Ole R. "The 'Operational Code' Approach to the Study of Political Leaders: John Foster Dulles' Philosophical and Instrumental Beliefs." *Canadian Journal of Political Science*, 3 (March 1970): 123–157.

Holsti. "Will the Real Dulles Please Stand Up?" *International Journal*, 30 (Winter 1974/1975): 34–44.

Hoopes, Townsend. *The Devil and John Foster Dulles*. Boston: Little, Brown, 1973.

Hoopes, and Douglas Brinkley. *Driven Patriot: The Life and Times of James Forrestal*. New York: Knopf, 1992.

Howard, Anthony. *RAB: The Life of R. A. Butler*. London: Cape, 1987.

Immerman, Richard H. *John Foster Dulles: Piety, Pragmatism, and Power in U.S. Foreign Policy*. Wilmington, Del.: Scholarly Resources, 1999.

Immerman, ed. *John Foster Dulles and the Diplomacy of the Cold War: A Reappraisal*. Princeton, N.J.: Princeton University Press, 1989.

Isaacson, Walter, and Evan Thomas. *The Wise Men: Six Friends and the World They Made: Acheson, Bohlen, Harriman, Kennan, Lovett, McCloy*. New York: Simon & Schuster, 1986.

Kalb, Marvin, and Bernard Kalb. *Kissinger*. Boston: Little, Brown, 1974.

Kearns, Doris. *Lyndon Johnson and the American Dream*. New York: Harper & Row, 1976.

Kennan, George F. *Memoirs: 1925–1950*. Boston: Little, Brown, 1967.

Kennan. *Memoirs, 1950–1963*. Boston: Little, Brown, 1972.

Kissinger, Henry. *White House Years*. Boston: Little, Brown, 1979.

Kissinger. *Years of Upheaval*. Boston: Little, Brown, 1982.

Landau, David. *Kissinger: The Uses of Power*. Boston: Houghton Mifflin, 1972.

Lyon, Peter. *Eisenhower: Portrait of the Hero*. Boston: Little, Brown, 1974.

Macmillan, Harold. *Pointing the Way*. London: Macmillan, 1972; New York: Harper & Row, 1972.

Macmillan. *Riding the Storm, 1956–1959*. London: Macmillan, 1971; New York: Harper & Row, 1971.

Macmillan. *Tides of Fortune, 1945–1955*. London: Macmillan, 1969; New York: Harper & Row, 1969.

Manchester, William. *American Caesar: Douglas MacArthur, 1880–1964*. Boston: Little, Brown, 1978.

Mankiewicz, Frank. *Perfectly Clear: Nixon from Whittier to Watergate*. New York: Quadrangle, 1973.

Markowitz, Norman. *The Rise and Fall of the People's Century: Henry A. Wallace and American Liberalism, 1941–1948*. New York: Free Press, 1973.

Martin, John Bartlow. *Adlai Stevenson and the World: The Life of Adlai E. Stevenson*. Garden City, N.Y.: Doubleday, 1977.

Martin. *Adlai Stevenson of Illinois: The Life of Adlai E. Stevenson*. Garden City, N.Y.: Doubleday, 1976.

Mayers, David. *George Kennan and the Dilemmas of US Foreign Policy*. New York: Oxford University Press, 1988.

Mazlish, Bruce. *In Search of Nixon: A Psychohistorical Inquiry*. New York: Basic Books, 1972.

Mazlish. *Kissinger: The European Mind in American Policy*. New York: Basic Books, 1976.

Mazo, Earl. *Richard Nixon: A Political and Personal Portrait*. New York: Harper, 1959.

Mazo, and Stephen Hess. *Nixon: A Political Portrait*. New York: Harper & Row, 1968.

McCullough, David. *Truman*. New York: Simon & Schuster, 1992.

McLellan, David S. *Dean Acheson: The State Department Years*. New York: Dodd, Mead, 1976.

McNamara, Robert S. *The Essence of Security: Reflections in Office*. New York: Harper & Row, 1968.

Melanson, Richard, and David Mayers, eds. *Reevaluating Eisenhower: American Foreign Policy in the 1950s*. Urbana: University of Illinois Press, 1986.

Miller, Merle. *Plain Speaking: An Oral Biography of Harry S. Truman*. New York: Berkeley, 1974.

Miscamble, Wilson. *George F. Kennan and the Making of American Foreign Policy, 1947–1950*. Princeton, N.J.: Princeton University Press, 1992.

Monnet, Jean. *Memoirs*, translated by Richard Mayne. Garden City, N.Y.: Doubleday, 1978.

Morris, Roger. *Haig: The General's Progress*. New York: Playboy Press, 1982.

Morris. *Richard Milhouse Nixon: The Rise of an American Politician*. New York: Holt, 1990.

Morris. *Uncertain Greatness: Henry Kissinger and American Foreign Policy*. New York: Harper & Row, 1977.

Nitze, Paul H., Ann M. Smith, and Steven L. Rearden. *From Hiroshima to Glasnost: At the Center of Decision—A Memoir*. New York: Grove Weidenfeld, 1989.

REFERENCES

Nixon, Richard M. *In the Arena: A Memoir of Victory, Defeat and Renewal.* New York: Simon & Schuster, 1990.

Nixon. *RN: The Memoirs of Richard Nixon.* New York: Grosset & Dunlap, 1978.

Nixon. *Six Crises.* Garden City, N.Y.: Doubleday, 1962.

Owen, David. *David Owen: Personally Speaking to Kenneth Harris.* London: Weidenfeld & Nicolson, 1987.

Owen. *Face the Future.* London: Cape, 1981.

Parmet, Herbert S. *Eisenhower and the American Crusades.* New York: Macmillan, 1972.

Parmet. *Richard Nixon and His America.* Boston: Little, Brown, 1990.

Patterson, James T. *Mr. Republican: A Biography of Robert A. Taft.* Boston: Houghton Mifflin, 1972.

Pimlott, Ben. *Hugh Dalton.* London: Cape, 1985.

Prittie, Terrence. *Willy Brandt: Portrait of a Statesman.* New York: Schocken, 1974.

Pruessen, Ronald W. *John Foster Dulles: The Road to Power.* New York: Free Press, 1982.

Reeves, Thomas C. *The Life and Times of Joe McCarthy.* New York: Stein & Day, 1982.

Reeves. *A Question of Character: JFK, Image and Reality.* New York: Free Press, 1991.

Rhodes James, Robert. *Anthony Eden.* New York: McGraw-Hill, 1987.

Sampson, Anthony. *Macmillan: A Study in Ambiguity.* London: Allen Lane, 1967; New York: Simon & Schuster, 1967.

Schandler, Herbert. *The Unmaking of a President: Lyndon Johnson and Vietnam.* Princeton, N.J.: Princeton University Press, 1977.

Spaak, Paul Henri Charles. *The Continuing Battle: Memoirs of a European, 1936–1966,* translated by Henry Fox. Boston: Little, Brown, 1971.

Starr, Harvey. *Henry Kissinger: Perceptions of International Politics.* Lexington: University Press of Kentucky, 1984.

Steel, Ronald. *Walter Lippmann and the American Century.* Boston: Little, Brown, 1980.

Stephanson, Anders. *Kennan and the Art of Foreign Policy.* Cambridge, Mass.: Harvard University Press, 1989.

Stettinius, Edward R. *Roosevelt and the Russians: The Yalta Conference.* Garden City, N.Y.: Doubleday, 1949.

Stoessinger, John G. *Crusaders and Pragmatists: Movers of Modern American Foreign Policy.* New York: Norton, 1979.

Stoessinger. *Henry Kissinger: The Anguish of Power.* New York: Norton, 1976.

Talbott, Strobe. *The Master of the Game: Paul Nitze and the Nuclear Peace.* New York: Knopf, 1988.

Thatcher, Margaret. *In Defense of Freedom: Speeches on Britain's Relations with the World 1976-1986.* London: Aurum Press, 1986; Buffalo, N.Y.: Prometheus, 1987.

Truman, Harry S. *Memoirs,* 2 volumes. Garden City, N.Y.: Doubleday, 1955, 1956.

Vance, Cyrus R. *Hard Choices: Critical Years in America's Foreign Policy.* New York: Simon & Schuster, 1983.

Vandenberg, Arthur H. *The Private Papers of Senator Vandenberg.* Boston: Houghton Mifflin, 1952.

Walters, Vernon. *Silent Missions.* Garden City, N.Y.: Doubleday, 1978.

Weinberger, Caspar W. *Fighting For Peace: Seven Critical Years in the Pentagon.* New York: Warner, 1990.

Wicker, Tom. *One of Us: Richard Nixon and the American Dream.* New York: Random House, 1991.

Williams, Edward Francis. *A Prime Minister Remembers: The War and Postwar Memoirs of the Rt. Hon. Earl Attlee Based on His Private Papers and on a Series of Recorded Conversations.* London: Heinemann, 1961.

Williams, Philip M. *Hugh Gaitskell: A Political Biography.* London: Cape, 1979.

Wills, Garry. *Nixon Agonistes: The Crisis of the Self-made Man.* Boston: Houghton Mifflin, 1970.

Witcover, Jules. *The Resurrection of Richard Nixon.* New York: Putnam, 1970.

Young, Kenneth. *Sir Alec Douglas Home.* London: Dent, 1970.

2. Histories of the Cold War

Alperovitz, Gar. *Atomic Diplomacy: Hiroshima and Potsdam; The Use of the Atomic Bomb and the American Confrontation with Soviet Power.* New York: Simon & Schuster, 1965.

Alperovitz, with the assistance of Sanho Tree and others. *The Decision to Use the Atomic Bomb and the Architecture of an American Myth.* New York: Knopf, 1995.

Arkes, Hadley. *Bureaucracy, the Marshall Plan, and the National Interest.* Princeton, N.J.: Princeton University Press, 1972.

Aronsen, Lawrence, and Martin Kitchen. *The Origins of the Cold War in Comparative Perspective: American, British, and Canadian Relations with the Soviet Union, 1941-1948.* New York: St. Martin's Press, 1988.

Backer, John H. *The Decision to Divide Germany: American Foreign Policy in Transition.* Durham, N.C.: Duke University Press, 1978.

Backer. *Priming the German Economy: American Occupational Policies, 1945-1948.* Durham, N.C.: Duke University Press, 1971.

Backer. *Winds of History: The German Years of Lucius DuBignon Clay.* New York: Van Nostrand Reinhold, 1983.

Bernstein, Barton, ed. *Politics and Policies of the Truman Administration.* Chicago: Quadrangle, 1970.

Bernstein, and Allen Matusow, eds. *The Truman Administration: A Documentary History.* New York: Harper & Row, 1966.

Cairncross, Alec. *Years of Recovery: British Economic Policy, 1945-1951.* London: Methuen, 1985.

Clarke, Sir Richard William Barnes. *Anglo-American Economic Collaboration in War and Peace, 1942-1949,* edited by Sir Alec Cairncross. Oxford: Clarendon Press, 1982; New York: Oxford University Press, 1982.

Clemens, Diane Shaver. *Yalta.* New York: Oxford University Press, 1970.

Cronin, Audrey. *Great Power Politics and the Struggle over Austria, 1945-1955.* Ithaca, N.Y.: Cornell University Press, 1986.

Davis, Lynn E. *The Cold War Begins: Soviet-American Conflict over Eastern Europe.* Princeton, N.J.: Princeton University Press, 1974.

Deibel, Terry, and John Lewis Gaddis, eds. *Containment: Concept and Policy.* Washington, D.C.: National Defense University Press, 1986.

Deighton, Anne. *The Impossible Peace: Britain, the Division of Germany, and the Origins of the Cold War.* New York: Oxford University Press, 1990.

Donnelly, Desmond. *Struggle for the World: The Cold War, 1917-1965.* New York: St. Martin's Press, 1965.

Donovan, Robert J. *Conflict and Crisis: The Presidency of Harry S. Truman, 1945-1948.* New York: Norton, 1977.

Donovan. *Tumultuous Years: The Presidency of Harry S. Truman, 1949–1953*. New York: Norton, 1982.

Douglas, Roy. *From War to Cold War, 1942–1948*. New York: St. Martin's Press, 1981.

Dunbabin, J. P. D. *International Relations since 1945: A History in Two Volumes*, volume 2: *The Post-Imperial Age: The Great Powers and the Wider World*. New York: Longman, 1994.

Etzold, Thomas H., and John Lewis Gaddis, eds. *Containment: Documents on American Policy and Strategy, 1945–1950*. New York: Columbia University Press, 1978.

Feis, Herbert. *Churchill, Roosevelt, Stalin: The War They Waged and the Peace They Sought*. Princeton, N.J.: Princeton University Press, 1957.

Feis. *From Trust to Terror: The Onset of the Cold War, 1945–1950*. New York: Norton, 1970.

Fleming, Denna Frank. *The Cold War and Its Origins, 1917–1960*. Garden City, N.Y.: Doubleday, 1961.

Fontaine, André. *History of the Cold War: From the October Revolution to the Korean War*, translated by D. D. Paige. New York: Pantheon, 1968.

Fontaine, *History of the Cold War: From the Korean War to the Present*, translated by R. Bruce. New York: Pantheon, 1969.

Foreign Relations of the United States [1933–1957]. Washington, D.C.: Government Printing Office, 1952–1986.

Foreign Relations of the United States, Diplomatic Papers: The Conferences at Malta and Yalta, 1945, 84th Congress, 1st Session, House Document no. 154. Washington, D.C.: U.S. Government Printing Office, 1955.

Friedrich, Carl J., and Zbigniew K. Brzezinski. *Totalitarian Dictatorship and Autocracy*. Cambridge, Mass.: Harvard University Press, 1956; revised, 1965.

Gaddis, John Lewis. *The Long Peace: Inquiries into the History of the Cold War*. New York: Oxford University Press, 1987.

Gaddis. *Strategies of Containment: A Critical Appraisal of Postwar American National Security Policy*. New York: Oxford University Press, 1982.

Gaddis. *The United States and the End of the Cold War: Implications, Reconsiderations, Provocations*. New York: Oxford University Press, 1992.

Gaddis. *The United States and the Origins of the Cold War, 1941–1947*. New York: Columbia University Press, 1972.

Gaddis. *We Now Know: Rethinking Cold War History*. Oxford: Clarendon Press / New York: Oxford University Press, 1997.

Gleason, Abbott. *Totalitarianism: The Inner History of the Cold War*. New York: Oxford University Press, 1995.

Halle, Louis J. *The Cold War as History*, revised edition. New York: HarperPerennial, 1991.

Halliday, Fred. *The Making of the Second Cold War*. London: Verso, 1983.

Herz, Martin F. *Beginnings of the Cold War*. Bloomington: Indiana University Press, 1966.

Herz, ed. *Decline of the West? George Kennan and His Critics*. Washington, D.C.: Ethics and Public Policy Center, Georgetown University, 1978.

Hoffmann, Paul G. *Peace Can Be Won*. Garden City, N.Y.: Doubleday, 1951.

Hoffmann, Stanley. *Primacy or World Order: American Foreign Policy Since The Cold War*. New York: McGraw-Hill, 1978.

Hoopes, Townsend. *The Limits of Intervention; (An Inside Account of How the Johnson Policy of Escalation in Vietnam Was Reversed)*, revised and updated edition. New York: McKay, 1973.

Hoopes, and Douglas Brinkley. *FDR and the creation of the U.N.* New Haven: Yale University Press, 1997.

Horowitz, David. *Containment and Revolution*. Boston: Beacon, 1967.

Hunter, Allen, ed. *Rethinking the Cold War*. Philadelphia: Temple University Press, 1998.

Jones, Joseph M. *The Fifteen Weeks (February 21–June 5, 1947)*. New York: Viking, 1955.

Kolko, Joyce, and Gabriel Kolko. *The Limits of Power: The World and the United States Foreign Policy, 1945–1954*. New York: Harper & Row, 1972.

Laloy, Jean. *Yalta: Yesterday, Today, Tomorrow*, translated by William R. Tyler. New York: Harper & Row, 1988.

Larson, Deborah Welch. *Anatomy of Mistrust: U.S.-Soviet Relations during the Cold War*. Ithaca, N.Y.: Cornell University Press, 1997.

Larson. *Origins of Containment: A Psychological Explanation*. Princeton, N.J.: Princeton University Press, 1985.

Lukacs, John A. *The Great Powers and Eastern Europe*. New York: American Book Company, 1953.

May, Ernest R., ed. *American Cold War Strategy: Interpreting NSC 68*. Boston: Bedford Books of St. Martin's, 1993.

Messer, Robert. *The End of an Alliance: James F. Byrnes, Roosevelt, Truman, and the Origins of the Cold War*. Chapel Hill: University of North Carolina Press, 1982.

Ovendale, Ritchie. *The English-Speaking Alliance: Britain, the United States, the Dominions and the Cold War, 1945–1951*. London & Boston: Allen & Unwin, 1985.

Paterson, Thomas G. *Meeting the Communist Threat: Truman to Reagan*. New York: Oxford University Press, 1988.

Paterson. *Soviet-American Confrontation: Postwar Reconstruction and the Origins of the Cold War*. Baltimore: Johns Hopkins University Press, 1973.

Paterson, ed. *Cold War Critics: Alternatives to American Foreign Policy in the Truman Years*. Chicago: Quadrangle, 1971.

Paterson, ed. *Containment and the Cold War*. Reading, Mass.: Addison, 1973.

Paterson, ed. *Major Problems in American Foreign Policy: Documents and Essays*, volume 2 (since 1914). Lexington, Mass.: Heath, 1978.

Paterson, ed. *On Every Front: The Making of the Cold War*. New York: Norton, 1979.

The Pentagon Papers: As Published by the New York Times. New York: Quadrangle, 1971.

Perlmutter, Amos. *FDR & Stalin: Not So Grand Alliance, 1943–1945*. Columbia: University of Missouri Press, 1993.

Perlmutter. *Making the World Safe for Democracy: A Century of Wilsonianism and its Totalitarian Challengers*. Chapel Hill: University of North Carolina Press, 1997.

Pollard, Robert A. *Economic Security and the Origins of the Cold War, 1945–1950*. New York: Columbia University Press, 1985.

Raucher, Alan R. *Paul G. Hoffman: Architect of Foreign Aid*. Lexington: University Press of Kentucky, 1986.

Rees, David. *The Age of Containment: The Cold War, 1945–1965*. New York: St. Martin's Press, 1967.

Senarclens, Pierre de. *From Yalta to the Iron Curtain: The Great Powers and the Origins of the Cold War*, translated by Amanda Pingree. New York: Berg, 1995.

REFERENCES

Thomas, Hugh. *Armed Truce: The Beginnings of the Cold War, 1945–1946.* New York: Atheneum, 1987.

Trachtenberg, Marc. *History and Strategy.* Princeton, N.J.: Princeton University Press, 1991.

Trefousse, H. L., ed. *The Cold War: A Book of Documents.* New York: Putnam, 1965.

Yergin, Daniel. *Shattered Peace: The Origins of the Cold War and the National Security State.* Boston: Houghton Mifflin, 1977.

3. The Cold War in Europe

Bark, Dennis L., and David R. Gress. *A History of West Germany,* 2 volumes. Oxford & New York: Blackwell, 1989.

Barnet, Richard J., and Marcus G. Raskin. *After Twenty Years: Alternatives to the Cold War in Europe.* New York: Random House, 1965.

Buchan, Alastair. *The End of the Postwar Era: A New Balance of World Power.* London: Weidenfeld & Nicolson, 1974.

Buchan. *Europe's Futures, Europe's Choices: Models of Western Europe in the 1970s.* New York: Columbia University Press, 1969.

Buchan. *Power and Equilibrium in the 1970s.* New York: Praeger, 1973.

Cioc, Mark. *Pax Atomica: The Nuclear Defense Debate in West Germany During the Adenauer Era.* New York: Columbia University Press, 1988.

DePorte, Anton W. *Europe between the Superpowers: The Enduring Balance.* New Haven: Yale University Press, 1979.

Dockrill, Michael L. *British Defence Since 1945.* Oxford & New York: Blackwell, 1989.

Dockrill, and John W. Young, eds. *British Foreign Policy, 1945–56.* London: Macmillan, 1989; New York: St. Martin's Press, 1989.

Donoughue, Bernard. *Prime Minister: The Conduct of Policy under Harold Wilson and James Callaghan, 1974–1979.* London: Cape, 1987.

Drummond, Gordon D. *The German Social Democrats in Opposition, 1949–1960: The Case Against Rearmament.* Norman: University of Oklahoma Press, 1982.

Fitzsimons, Matthew A. *The Foreign Policy of the British Labour Government, 1945–1951.* Notre Dame, Ind.: University of Notre Dame Press, 1953.

Frankel, Joseph. *British Foreign Policy, 1945–1973.* New York: Oxford University Press, 1975.

Fursdon, Edward. *The European Defense Community: A History.* London: Macmillan/New York: St. Martin's Press, 1980.

Gardner, Lloyd C. *Spheres of Influence: The Great Powers Partition Europe, from Munich to Yalta.* Chicago: Ivan R. Dee, 1993.

Gearson, John P. S. *Harold Macmillan and the Berlin Wall Crisis, 1958–62: The Limits of Interests and Force.* New York: St. Martin's Press, 1998.

Gimbel, John. *The American Occupation of Germany: Politics and the Military, 1945–1949.* Stanford, Cal.: Stanford University Press, 1968.

Gimbel. *The Origins of the Marshall Plan.* Stanford, Cal.: Stanford University Press, 1976.

Hall, Stuart, and Martin Jacques, eds. *The Politics of Thatcherism.* London: Lawrence & Wishart, 1983.

Hampton, Mary N., and Christian Soe, eds., *Between Bonn and Berlin: German Politics Adrift?* Lanham, Md.: Rowman & Littlefield, 1999.

Hathaway, Robert M. *Ambiguous Partnership: Britain and America, 1944–1947.* New York: Columbia University Press, 1981.

Henderson, Nicholas. *The Birth of NATO.* London: Weidenfeld & Nicolson, 1982.

Heuser, Beatrice. *Western "Containment" Policies in the Cold War: The Yugoslav Case, 1948–53.* London & New York: Routledge, 1989.

Hoffmann, Stanley, and Charles S. Maier, eds. *The Marshall Plan: A Retrospective.* Boulder, Colo.: Westview Press, 1984.

Hogan, Michael J. *The Marshall Plan: America, Britain and the Reconstruction of Western Europe, 1947–1952.* New York: Cambridge University Press, 1987.

Holmes, Martin. *The First Thatcher Government, 1979–1983.* London: Wheatsheaf Books, 1985.

Ireland, Timothy P. *Creating the Entangling Alliance: The Origins of the North Atlantic Treaty Organization.* Westport, Conn.: Greenwood Press, 1981.

Stent, Angela. *From Embargo to Ostpolitik: The Political Economy of West German-Soviet Relations, 1955–1980.* Cambridge & New York: Cambridge University Press, 1981.

Trachtenberg, Marc. *A Constructed Peace: The Making of the European Settlement, 1945–1963.* Princeton, N.J.: Princeton University Press, 1999.

Tusa, Ann. *The Last Division: A History of Berlin, 1945–1989.* Reading, Mass.: Addison-Wesley, 1997.

Willis, Frank Roy. *France, Germany and the New Europe, 1945–1963.* London: Oxford University Press, 1968.

Wolfe, Thomas W. *Soviet Power and Europe, 1945–1970.* Baltimore: Johns Hopkins University Press, 1970.

Wolffsohn, Michael. *West Germany's Foreign Policy in the Era of Brandt and Schmidt, 1969–1982: An Introduction.* Frankfurt am Main: Lang, 1986.

Young, John W. *Britain, France and the Unity of Europe, 1945–1951.* Leicester: Leicester University Press, 1984.

Young, ed. *The Foreign Policy of Churchill's Peacetime Administration, 1951–1955.* Leicester: Leicester University Press, 1988.

Zametica, John, ed. *British Officials and British Foreign Policy, 1945–1950.* Leicester: Leicester University Press, 1990.

4. The Cold War in the Middle East, Asia, and Africa

Alroy, Gil Carl. *The Kissinger Experience: American Policy in the Middle East.* New York: Horizon, 1975.

Alteras, Isaac. *Eisenhower and Israel: U.S.-Israeli Relations, 1953–1960.* Gainesville: University Press of Florida, 1993.

Appleman, Roy E. *South to the Naktong, North to the Yalu: June–November 1950.* Washington, D.C.: Office of the Chief of Military History, 1960.

Baldwin, Frank, ed. *Without Parallel: The American-Korean Relationship Since 1945.* New York: Pantheon, 1974.

Barnds, William. *China and America: The Search for a New Relationship.* New York: New York University Press, 1977.

Bar-Siman-Tov, Yaacov. *Israel, the Superpowers, and the War in the Middle East.* New York: Praeger, 1987.

Ben-Zvi, Abraham. *Decade of Transition: Eisenhower, Kennedy, and the Origins of the American-Israeli Alliance.* New York: Columbia University Press, 1998.

Berman, Larry. *Planning a Tragedy: The Americanization of the War in Vietnam.* New York: Norton, 1982.

Bill, James. *The Eagle and the Lion: The Tragedy of American-Iranian Relations.* New Haven: Yale University Press, 1988.

Blair, Clay. *The Forgotten War: America in Korea, 1950–1953.* New York: Times Books, 1987.

References

Borg, Dorothy, and Waldo Heinrichs, eds. *Uncertain Years: Chinese-American Relations, 1947–1950.* New York: Columbia University Press, 1980.

Buhite, Russell D. *Soviet-American Relations in Asia, 1945–1954.* Norman: University of Oklahoma Press, 1981.

Chang, Gordon H. *Friends and Enemies: The United States, China, and the Soviet Union, 1948–1972.* Stanford, Cal.: Stanford University Press, 1990.

Christensen, Thomas J. *Useful Adversaries: Grand Strategy, Domestic Mobilization, and Sino-American Conflict, 1947–1958.* Princeton, N.J.: Princeton University Press, 1996.

Clubb, O. Edmund. "Formosa and the Offshore Islands in American Policy, 1950–1955." *Political Science Quarterly,* 74 (December 1959): 517–531.

Cottam, Richard W. *Iran and the United States: A Cold War Case Study.* Pittsburgh: University of Pittsburgh Press, 1988.

Crosbie, Sylvia K. *A Tacit Alliance: France and Israel from Suez to the Six-Day War.* Princeton, N.J.: Princeton University Press, 1974.

Cumings, Bruce. *The Origins of the Korean War: Liberation and the Emergence of Separate Regimes, 1945–1947.* Princeton, N.J.: Princeton University Press, 1981.

Cumings, ed. *Child of Conflict: The Korean-American Relationship, 1943–1953.* Seattle: University of Washington Press, 1983.

Dobbs, Charles M. *American Foreign Policy, the Cold War, and Korea, 1945–1950.* Kent, Ohio: Kent State University Press, 1981.

Dowty, Alan. *Middle East Crisis: U.S. Decisionmaking in 1958, 1970, and 1973.* Berkeley: University of California Press, 1984.

Dulles, Foster Rhea. *American Policy Toward Communist China, 1949–1969.* New York: Crowell, 1972.

Fairbank, John K. *The United States and China,* fourth edition. Cambridge, Mass.: Harvard University Press, 1979.

Fishlow, Albert. *The Mature Neighbor Policy: A New United States Economic Policy for Latin America.* Berkeley: Institute of International Studies, University of California, 1977.

Fitzgerald, Francis. *Fire in the Lake: The Vietnamese and the Americans in Vietnam.* Boston: Little, Brown, 1972.

Foot, Rosemary. *A Substitute for Victory: The Politics of Peacemaking at the Korean Armistice Talks.* Ithaca, N.Y.: Cornell University Press, 1990.

Foot. *The Wrong War: American Policy and the Dimensions of the Korean Conflict, 1950–1953.* Ithaca, N.Y.: Cornell University Press, 1985.

Foreign Relations of the United States 1952–5, volume 14: *China.* Washington, D.C.: U.S. Government Printing Office, 1979.

Foreign Relations of the United States 1955–7, volume 2: *China.* Washington, D.C.: U.S. Government Printing Office, 1986.

Gelb, Leslie H., and Richard K. Betts. *The Irony of Vietnam: The System Worked.* Washington, D.C.: Brookings Institution, 1979.

Glassman, Jon D. *Arms for the Arabs: The Soviet Union and War in the Middle East.* Baltimore: Johns Hopkins University Press, 1975.

Golan, Galia. *Yom Kippur and After: The Soviet Union and the Middle East Crisis.* Cambridge & New York: Cambridge University Press, 1977.

Gorst, Anthony, and Lewis Johnman. *The Suez Crisis.* New York: Routledge, 1997.

Gravel, Mike, ed. *The Pentagon Papers: The Defense Department History of United States Decision-making on Vietnam,* 5 volumes. Boston: Beacon, 1972.

Hahn, Peter L. *The United States, Great Britain, and Egypt, 1945–1956: Strategy and Diplomacy in the Early Cold War.* Chapel Hill: University of North Carolina Press, 1991.

Havens, Thomas. *Fire across the Sea: The Vietnam War and Japan.* Princeton, N.J.: Princeton University Press, 1987.

Heikal, Mohamed. *The Road to Ramadan.* New York: Quadrangle/New York Times Book Co., 1975.

Herring, George C. *America's Longest War: The United States and Vietnam, 1950–1975.* New York: McGraw-Hill, 1979.

Herring, ed. *The Secret Diplomacy of the Vietnam War: The Negotiating Volumes of the Pentagon Papers.* Austin: University of Texas Press, 1983.

Hess, Gary R. *The United States' Emergence as a Southeast Asian Power, 1940–1950.* New York: Columbia University Press, 1987.

Isaacs, Arnold R. *Without Honor: Defeat in Vietnam and Cambodia.* Baltimore: Johns Hopkins University Press, 1983.

Jiang, Arnold Xiangze. *The United States and China.* Chicago: University of Chicago Press, 1988.

Kahin, George McTurnin. *Intervention: How America Became Involved in Vietnam.* New York: Knopf, 1986.

Karnow, Stanley. *Vietnam: A History,* revised and updated edition. New York: Penguin, 1997.

Kattenburg, Paul. *The Vietnam Trauma in American Foreign Policy, 1945–75.* New Brunswick: Transaction Books, 1980.

Kaufman, Burton I. *The Korean War: Challenges in Crisis, Credibility, and Command.* Philadelphia: Temple University Press, 1986.

Kelly, John B. *Arabia, the Gulf and the West.* New York: Basic Books, 1980.

Kim, Young Hum, ed. *Twenty Years of Crises: The Cold War Era.* Englewood Cliffs, N.J.: Prentice-Hall, 1968.

Kingseed, Cole C. *Eisenhower and the Suez Crisis of 1956.* Baton Rouge: Louisiana State University Press, 1995.

Kuniholm, Bruce. *The Origins of the Cold War in the Near East: Great Power Conflict and Diplomacy in Iran, Turkey, and Greece.* Princeton, N.J.: Princeton University Press, 1980.

Kunz, Diane B. *The Economic Diplomacy of the Suez Crisis.* Chapel Hill: University of North Carolina Press, 1991.

Kyle, Keith. *Suez.* New York: St. Martin's Press, 1991.

Levine, Steven I. *Anvil of Victory: The Communist Revolution in Manchuria, 1945–1948.* New York: Columbia University Press, 1987.

Lewy, Guenter. *America in Vietnam.* New York: Oxford University Press, 1978.

Lloyd, Selwyn. *Suez 1956: A Personal Account.* London: Cape, 1978.

Louis, William Roger. *The British Empire in the Middle East, 1945–1951: Arab Nationalism, the United States, and Postwar Imperialism.* New York: Oxford University Press, 1984.

Louis. *Imperialism at Bay 1941–1945: The United States and the Decolonization of the British Empire.* Oxford: Clarendon Press, 1977; New York: Oxford University Press, 1978.

Louis, and Roger Owen, eds. *Suez 1956: The Crisis and Its Consequences.* Oxford: Clarendon Press, 1989.

MacDonald, C. A. *Korea: The War Before Vietnam*. New York: Free Press, 1986.

Matray, James. *The Reluctant Crusade: American Foreign Policy in Korea, 1941-1950*. Honolulu: University of Hawaii Press, 1985.

Nagai, Yonosuke, and Akira Iriye, eds. *The Origins of the Cold War in Asia*. New York: Columbia University Press, 1977.

Nutting, Anthony. *No End of a Lesson: The Story of Suez*. New York: Potter, 1967.

Organski, A. F. K. *The $36 Billion Bargain: Strategy and Politics in U.S. Assistance to Israel*. New York: Columbia University Press, 1990.

Paige, Glenn D. *The Korean Decision, June 24-30, 1950*. New York: Free Press, 1968.

Parker, F. Charles. *Vietnam, Strategy for a Stalemate*. New York: Paragon House, 1989.

Perlmutter, Amos. *Egypt, The Praetorian State*. New Brunswick, N.J.: Transaction Books, 1974.

Podhoretz, Norman. *Why We Were in Vietnam*. New York: Simon & Schuster, 1982.

Porter, Gareth. *A Peace Denied: The United States, Vietnam and the Paris Agreements*. Bloomington: Indiana University Press, 1975.

Quandt, William B. *Decade of Decisions: American Policy toward the Arab-Israeli Conflict, 1967-1976*. Berkeley: University of California Press, 1977.

Quandt. *Peace Process: American Diplomacy and the Arab-Israeli Conflict Since 1967*. Washington, D.C.: Brookings Institution / Berkeley: University of California Press, 1993.

Rothwell, Victor. *Britain and the Cold War, 1941-1947*. London: Cape, 1982.

Rubenberg, Cheryl A. *Israel and the American National Interest: A Critical Examination*. Urbana: University of Illinois Press, 1986.

Rubinstein, Alvin Z. *Red Star on the Nile*. Princeton, N.J.: Princeton University Press, 1977.

Safran, Nadav. *Israel, The Embattled Ally*. Cambridge, Mass.: Belknap Press, 1978.

Schoenbaum, David. *The United States and the State of Israel*. New York: Oxford University Press, 1993.

Sewell, John W., Richard E. Feinberg, and Valeriana Kallab, eds. *U.S. Foreign Policy and the Third World: Agenda, 1985-86*. New Brunswick, N.J.: Transaction Books, 1985.

Shawcross, William. *The Quality of Mercy: Cambodia, Holocaust, and Modern Conscience*. New York: Simon & Schuster, 1984.

Shawcross. *Sideshow: Kissinger, Nixon and the Destruction of Cambodia*. New York: Simon & Schuster, 1979.

Sheehan, Edward. *The Arabs, Israelis and Kissinger: A Secret History of American Diplomacy in the Middle East*. New York: Reader's Digest Press, 1976.

Sheehan, Neil. *A Bright Shining Lie: John Paul Vann and America in Vietnam*. New York: Random House, 1988.

Shlaim, Avi. *The United States and the Berlin Blockade, 1948-1949: A Study in Crisis Decision-making*. Berkeley: University of California Press, 1983.

Shuckburgh, Evelyn. *Descent to Suez*. London: Weidenfeld & Nicolson, 1986.

Sick, Gary. *All Fall Down: America's Tragic Encounter with Iran*. New York: Random House, 1985.

Simmons, Robert R. *The Strained Alliance: Peking, P'yongyang, Moscow, and the Politics of the Korean War*. New York: Free Press, 1975.

Snepp, Frank. *Decent Interval: An Insider's Account of Saigon's Indecent End*. New York: Random House, 1977.

Spanier, John. *The Truman-MacArthur Controversy and the Korean War*. Cambridge, Mass.: Harvard University Press, 1959.

Spiegel, Steven. *The Other Arab-Israeli Conflict: Making America's Middle East Policy from Truman to Reagan*. Chicago: University of Chicago Press, 1985.

Taylor, Alan R. *The Superpowers and the Middle East*. Syracuse, N.Y.: Syracuse University Press, 1991.

Thomas, Hugh. *The Suez Affair*. London: Weidenfeld & Nicolson, 1967.

Tillman, Seth P. *The United States in the Middle East, Interests and Obstacles*. Bloomington: Indiana University Press, 1982.

Troen, Selwyn, and Moshe Shemesh, eds. *The Suez-Sinai Crisis, 1956: Retrospective and Reappraisal*. New York: Columbia University Press, 1990.

Tucker, Nancy Bernkopf. *Patterns in the Dust: Chinese-American Relations and the Recognition Controversy, 1949-1950*. New York: Columbia University Press, 1983.

Whetten, Lawrence L. *The Canal War: Four-Power Conflict in the Middle East*. Cambridge, Mass.: MIT Press, 1974.

Wirtz, James J. *The Tet Offensive*. Ithaca, N.Y.: Cornell University Press, 1991.

Wyden, Peter S. *Bay of Pigs: The Untold Story*. New York: Simon & Schuster, 1979.

5. The Cold War in Latin America

Benjamin, Jules R. *The United States and the Origins of the Cuban Revolution: An Empire of Liberty in an Age of National Liberation*. Princeton, N.J.: Princeton University Press, 1990.

Davis, Nathaniel. *The Last Two Years of Salvador Allende*. Ithaca, N.Y.: Cornell University Press, 1985.

Del Aguila, Juan M. *Cuba, Dilemmas of a Revolution*, third edition. Boulder, Colo.: Westview Press, 1994.

Desch, Michael C. *When the Third World Matters: Latin America and United States Grand Strategy*. Baltimore: Johns Hopkins University Press, 1993.

Domínguez, Jorge. *To Make the World Safe for Revolution: Cuba's Foreign Policy*. Cambridge, Mass.: Harvard University Press, 1989.

Geyer, Georgie Anne. *Guerrilla Prince: The Untold Story of Fidel Castro*. Boston: Little, Brown, 1991.

Immerman, Richard H. *The CIA in Guatemala: The Foreign Policy of Intervention*. Austin: University of Texas Press, 1982.

Levinson, Jerome, and Juan de Onís. *The Alliance That Lost Its Way: A Critical Report on the Alliance for Progress*. Chicago: University of Chicago Press, 1970.

Loveman, Brian. *Chile: The Legacy of Hispanic Capitalism*, second edition. New York: Oxford University Press, 1988.

Musicant, Ivan. *The Banana Wars: A History of United States Military Intervention in Latin America from the Spanish-American War to the Invasion of Panama*. New York: Macmillan, 1990.

Oppenheimer, Andres. *Castro's Final Hour: The Secret Story Behind the Coming Downfall of Communist Cuba*. New York: Simon & Schuster, 1992.

Paterson, Thomas G. *Contesting Castro: The United States and the Triumph of the Cuban Revolution*. New York: Oxford University Press, 1994.

Pérez, Louis A., Jr. *Cuba and the United States: Ties of Singular Intimacy*, second edition, revised. Athens: University of Georgia Press, 1997.

Rabe, Stephen G. *Eisenhower and Latin America: The Foreign Policy of Anticommunism.* Chapel Hill: University of North Carolina Press, 1988.

Scheman, L. Ronald, ed. *The Alliance for Progress: A Retrospective.* New York: Praeger, 1988.

Schlesinger, Stephen, and Stephen Kinzer. *Bitter Fruit: The Untold Story of the American Coup in Guatemala,* second edition. Garden City, N.Y.: Doubleday, 1983.

Sheahan, Joseph. *Patterns of Development in Latin America: Poverty, Repression, and Economic Strategy.* Princeton, N.J.: Princeton University Press, 1987.

Sigmund, Paul E. *The Overthrow of Allende and the Politics of Chile, 1964-1976.* Pittsburgh: University of Pittsburgh Press, 1977.

Sigmund. *The United States and Democracy in Chile.* Baltimore: Johns Hopkins University Press, 1993.

Simons, Geoff. *Cuba: From Conquistador to Castro.* New York: St. Martin's Press, 1996.

Slater, Jerome. *Intervention and Negotiation: The United States and the Dominican Revolution.* New York: Harper & Row, 1970.

Slater. *The OAS and United States Foreign Policy.* Columbus: Ohio State University Press, 1967.

Smith, Earl E. T. *The Fourth Floor: An Account of the Castro Communist Revolution.* New York: Random House, 1962.

Suchlicki, Jaime. *Cuba: From Columbus to Castro and Beyond,* fourth edition, revised and updated. Washington, D.C.: Brassey's, 1997.

6. U.S. Foreign and National-Security Policy During the Cold War

Ambrose, Stephen E. *Rise to Globalism: American Foreign Policy Since 1938,* revised edition. New York: Penguin, 1976.

Aron, Raymond. *The Imperial Republic: The United States and the World, 1945-1963.* Englewood Cliffs, N.J.: Prentice-Hall, 1974.

Ashton, S. R. *In Search of Détente: The Politics of East-West Relations Since 1945.* New York: St. Martin's Press, 1989.

Baehr, Peter R. *The Role of Human Rights in Foreign Policy.* New York: St. Martin's Press, 1994.

Ball, George W. *The Discipline of Power: Essentials of a Modern World Structure.* Boston: Little, Brown, 1968.

Barber, Stephen. *America in Retreat.* Galeshead, U.K.: Northumberland Press, 1970.

Bell, Coral. *The Diplomacy of Detente: The Kissinger Era.* New York: St. Martin's Press, 1977.

Beschloss, Michael R. *The Crisis Years: Kennedy and Khrushchev, 1960-1963.* New York: Edward Burlingame, 1991.

Bohlen, Charles E. *The Transformation of American Foreign Policy.* New York: Norton, 1969.

Bowie, Robert R., and Richard H. Immerman. *Waging Peace: How Eisenhower Shaped an Enduring Cold War Strategy.* New York: Oxford University Press, 1998.

Bowker, Mike, and Phil Williams. *Superpower Détente: A Reappraisal.* London: Royal Institute of International Affairs / Newbury Park, Cal.: SAGE Publications, 1988.

Brandon, Henry. *The Retreat of American Power.* Garden City, N.Y.: Doubleday, 1973.

Caldwell, Dan. *American-Soviet Relations: From 1947 to the Nixon-Kissinger Grand Design.* Westport, Conn.: Greenwood Press, 1981.

Chace, James. *A World Elsewhere: The New American Foreign Policy.* New York: Scribners, 1973.

Copeland, Dale C. *Anticipation Power: Dynamic Realism and the Origins of Major War.* Ithaca, N.Y.: Cornell University Press, forthcoming 2000.

Cox, Arthur. *The Dynamics of Detente.* New York: Norton, 1976.

De Santis, Hugh. *The Diplomacy of Silence: The American Foreign Service, the Soviet Union and the Cold War, 1933-1947.* Chicago: University of Chicago Press, 1980.

Destler, I. M. *Presidents, Bureaucrats, and Foreign Policy: The Politics of Organizational Reform.* Princeton, N.J.: Princeton University Press, 1972.

Donnelly, Jack. *International Human Rights,* second edition. Boulder, Colo.: Westview Press, 1993.

Fried, Jonathan L., ed. *Guatemala in Rebellion: Unfinished History.* New York: Grove, 1983.

Froman, Michael B. *The Development of the Idea of Détente: Coming to Terms.* New York: St. Martin's Press, 1991.

Fursenko, Aleksandr A., and Timothy Naftali. *One Hell of a Gamble: Khrushchev, Castro, and Kennedy, 1958-1964.* New York: Norton, 1997.

Gardner, Lloyd C., comp. *The Great Nixon Turn-around: America's New Foreign Policy in the Post-Liberal Era (How a Cold Warrior Climbed Clean Out of His Skin); Essays and Articles with an Introductory Statement.* New York: New Viewpoints, 1973.

Garthoff, Raymond L. *Détente and Confrontation: American-Soviet Relations from Nixon to Reagan,* revised edition. Washington, D.C.: Brookings Institution, 1994.

Garthoff. *The Great Transition: American-Soviet Relations and the End of the Cold War.* Washington, D.C.: Brookings Institution Press, 1994.

Garthoff. *Reflections on the Cuban Missile Crisis.* Washington, D.C.: Brookings Institution, 1989.

Gellman, Barton. *Contending with Kennan: Toward a Philosophy of American Power.* New York: Praeger, 1984.

Goldman, Eric F. *The Crucial Decade–and After: America, 1945-1960.* New York: Knopf, 1960.

Goldmann, Kjell. *Change and Stability in Foreign Policy: The Problems and Possibilities of Détente.* Princeton, N.J.: Princeton University Press, 1988.

Graebner, Norman A. *Cold War Diplomacy: American Foreign Policy, 1945-1960.* Princeton, N.J.: Van Nostrand, 1962.

Halberstam, David. *The Best and the Brightest.* New York: Random House, 1972.

Hampton, Mary N. *The Wilsonian Impulse: U.S. Foreign Policy, the Alliance, and German Unification.* Westport, Conn.: Praeger, 1996.

Hartley, Anthony. *American Foreign Policy in the Nixon Era,* Adelphi Papers, no. 110. London: International Institute for Strategic Studies, Winter 1974-1975.

Hixson, Walter L. *Parting the Curtain: Propaganda, Culture, and the Cold War.* New York: St. Martin's Press, 1996.

Hood, Donald. "'Lessons' of the Vietnam War: Henry Kissinger, George F. Kennan, Richard Falk and the Debate over Containment, 1965-1980." Dissertation, University of Washington, 1982.

Hopf, Ted. *Peripheral Visions: Deterrence Theory and American Foreign Policy in the Third World, 1965-1990.* Ann Arbor: University of Michigan Press, 1994.

REFERENCES

Horowitz, David. *The Free World Colossus: A Critique of American Foreign Policy in the Cold War.* New York: Hill & Wang, 1965.

Hughes, Emmet John. *The Ordeal of Power.* New York: Atheneum, 1963.

Hunt, Michael H. *Ideology and U.S. Foreign Policy.* New Haven: Yale University Press, 1987.

Hyland, William. *Mortal Rivals: Superpower Relations from Nixon to Reagan.* New York: Random House, 1987.

Jones, Alan M., Jr., ed. *U.S. Foreign Policy in a Changing World: The Nixon Administration, 1969–1973.* New York: McKay, 1973.

Kennan, George F. *American Diplomacy,* revised and expanded edition. Chicago: University of Chicago Press, 1984.

Kennan. *The Realities of American Foreign Policy.* Princeton, N.J.: Princeton University Press, 1954.

Kennan. *Russia and the West under Lenin and Stalin.* Boston: Little, Brown, 1961.

Kort, Michael, ed. *The Columbia Guide to the Cold War.* New York: Columbia University Press, 1998.

LaFeber, Walter. *America, Russia, and the Cold War, 1945–1992,* seventh edition. New York: McGraw-Hill, 1993.

LaFeber, comp. *America in the Cold War: Twenty Years of Revolutions and Response, 1947–1967.* New York: Wiley, 1969.

Lebow, Richard Ned, and Janice Gross Stein. *We All Lost the Cold War.* Princeton, N.J.: Princeton University Press, 1994.

Leffler, Melvyn P. *A Preponderance of Power: National Security, the Truman Administration, and the Cold War.* Stanford, Cal.: Stanford University Press, 1992.

Litwak, Robert S. *Détente and the Nixon Doctrine: American Foreign Policy and the Pursuit of Stability, 1969–1976.* New York: Cambridge University Press, 1984.

Lundestad, Geir. *The American "Empire" and other Studies of U.S. Foreign Policy in a Comparative Perspective.* New York: Oxford University Press, 1990.

Maddox, Robert J. *From War to Cold War: The Education of Harry S. Truman.* Boulder, Colo.: Westview Press, 1988.

Melanson, Richard. *Writing History and Making Policy: The Cold War, Vietnam, and Revisionism.* Lanham, Md.: University Press of America, 1983.

Mower, A. Glenn, Jr. *Human Rights and American Foreign Policy: The Carter and Reagan Experiences.* New York: Greenwood Press, 1987.

Nash, Philip. *The Other Missiles of October: Eisenhower, Kennedy, and the Jupiters, 1957–1963.* Chapel Hill: University of North Carolina Press, 1997.

Nathan, James A., and James K. Oliver. *United States Foreign Policy and World Order,* fourth edition, expanded. Glenview, Ill.: Scott, Foresman, 1989.

Nelson, Anna, ed. *The State Department Policy Planning Staff Papers, 1947–1949.* New York: Garland, 1983.

Nelson, Keith L. *The Making of Détente: Soviet-American Relations in the Shadow of Vietnam.* Baltimore: Johns Hopkins University Press, 1995.

Newhouse, John. *Cold Dawn: The Story of SALT.* New York: Holt, Rinehart & Winston, 1973.

Newhouse. *War and Peace in the Nuclear Age.* New York: Knopf, 1988.

Nincic, Miroslav. *Democracy and Foreign Policy: The Fallacy of Political Realism.* New York: Columbia University Press, 1992.

Ninkovich, Frank. *Modernity and Power: A History of the Domino Theory in the Twentieth Century.* Chicago: University of Chicago Press, 1994.

Nye, Joseph S., Jr., ed. *The Making of America's Soviet Policy.* New Haven: Yale University Press, 1984.

Orme, John David. *Political Instability and American Foreign Policy: The Middle Options.* New York: St. Martin's Press, 1989.

Osgood, Robert, and others. *Retreat from Empire? The First Nixon Administration.* Baltimore: Johns Hopkins University Press, 1973.

Oye, Kenneth, Robert Lieber, and Donald Rothchild, eds. *Eagle Resurgent?: The Reagan Era in American Foreign Policy.* Boston: Little, Brown, 1987.

Packenham, Robert A. *Liberal America and the Third World: Political Development Ideas in Foreign Aid and Social Science.* Princeton, N.J.: Princeton University Press, 1973.

Pessen, Edward. *Losing Our Souls: The American Experience in the Cold War.* Chicago: Ivan R. Dee, 1993.

Qingzhao, Hua. *From Yalta to Panmunjom: Truman's Diplomacy and the Four Powers, 1945–1953.* Ithaca, N.Y.: Cornell University Press, 1993.

Rearden, Steven L. *The Evolution of American Strategic Doctrine: Paul H. Nitze and the Soviet Challenge,* SAIS Papers in International Affairs, no. 4. Boulder, Colo.: Westview Press / Washington, D.C.: Foreign Policy Institute, School of Advanced International Studies, Johns Hopkins University, 1984.

Rearden. *History of the Office of the Secretary of Defense,* volume 1: *The Formative Years, 1947–1950.* Washington, D.C.: U.S. Government Printing Office, 1984.

Reinhart, Robert, ed. *Finland and the United States: Diplomatic Relations through Seventy Years.* Washington, D.C.: Institute for the Study of Diplomacy, Georgetown University, 1993.

Rose, Lisle A. *After Yalta: America and the Origins of the Cold War.* New York: Scribners, 1973.

Rosecrance, Richard, ed. *America as an Ordinary Country: U.S. Foreign Policy and the Future.* Ithaca, N.Y.: Cornell University Press, 1976.

Ruff, R. M. "Orthodox, Realist, and Revisionist Interpretations of the Origins of the Cold War, 1962–1972." Dissertation, University of Georgia, 1973.

Ruggie, John. *Winning the Peace: America and World Order in the New Era.* New York: Columbia University Press, 1996.

Schulzinger, Robert D. *The Wise Men of Foreign Affairs: The History of the Council on Foreign Relations.* New York: Columbia University Press, 1984.

Schurmann, Franz. *The Logic of World Power: An Inquiry into the Origins, Currents, and Contradictions of World Politics.* New York: Pantheon, 1974.

Schwartz, Thomas A. "From Occupation to Alliance: John J. McCloy and the Allied High Commission in the Federal Republic of Germany, 1949–1952." Dissertation, Harvard University, 1985.

Schweizer, Peter. *Victory: The Reagan Administration's Secret Strategy that Hastened the Collapse of the Soviet Union.* New York: Atlantic Monthly Press, 1994.

Scott, James M. *Deciding to Intervene: The Reagan Doctrine and American Foreign Policy.* Durham, N.C.: Duke University Press, 1996.

Sherry, Michael S. *In the Shadow of War: The United States Since the 1930's.* New Haven: Yale University Press, 1995.

Small, Melvin. *Johnson, Nixon, and the Doves.* New Brunswick: Rutgers University Press, 1988.

Smith, Gaddis. *Morality, Reason, and Power: American Diplomacy in the Carter Years.* New York: Hill & Wang, 1986.

Smith, Gerard. *Doubletalk: The Story of the First Strategic Arms Limitation Talks.* Garden City, N.Y.: Doubleday, 1980.

Smith, Michael Joseph. *Realist Thought from Weber to Kissinger.* Baton Rouge: Louisiana State University Press, 1986.

Smith, Tony. *America's Mission: The United States and the Worldwide Struggle for Democracy in the Twentieth Century.* Princeton, N.J.: Princeton University Press, 1994.

Sobel, Lester, ed. *Kissinger & Detente.* New York: Facts on File, 1975.

The State Department Policy Planning Staff Papers, 1947–1949. New York: Garland, 1983.

Stevenson, Richard. *The Rise and Fall of Detente: Relaxations of Tension in US-Soviet Relations, 1953-84.* Urbana: University of Illinois Press, 1985.

Sulzberger, C. L. *The World and Richard Nixon.* New York: Prentice-Hall, 1987.

Szulc, Tad. *The Illusion of Peace: Foreign Policy in the Nixon Years.* New York: Viking, 1978.

Tucker, Robert W. *Nation or Empire? The Debate over American Foreign Policy.* Baltimore: Johns Hopkins University Press, 1968.

Wells, Samuel F., Jr. "Sounding the Tocsin: NSC-68 and the Soviet Threat." *International Security,* 4 (Fall 1979): 116-158.

Williams, William Appleman. *The Tragedy of American Diplomacy.* Cleveland: World, 1959.

Wohlforth, William C. *The Elusive Balance: Power and Perceptions During the Cold War.* Ithaca, N.Y.: Cornell University Press, 1993.

7. U.S. Domestic Aspects of the Cold War

Bayley, Edwin R. *Joe McCarthy and the Press.* Madison: University of Wisconsin Press, 1981.

Belknap, Michael R. *Cold War Political Justice: The Smith Act, the Communist Party, and American Civil Liberties.* Westport, Conn.: Greenwood Press, 1977.

Bell, Daniel, ed. *The Radical Right: The New American Right Expanded and Updated.* Garden City, N.Y.: Doubleday, 1963.

Bennett, David H. *The Party of Fear: From Nativist Movements to the New Right in American History.* Chapel Hill: University of North Carolina Press, 1988.

Biddle, Francis. *Fear of Freedom: A Discussion of the Contemporary Obsession of Anxiety and Fear in the United States, Its Historical Background and Present Expression, and Its Effect on National Security and on Free American Institutions.* Garden City, N.Y.: Doubleday, 1951.

Boyer, Paul S. *By the Bomb's Early Light: American Thought and Culture at the Dawn of the Atomic Age.* New York: Pantheon, 1985.

Caridi, Ronald J. *The Korean War and American Politics: The Republican Party as a Case Study,* second edition. Philadelphia: University of Pennsylvania Press, 1969.

Divine, Robert A. *Foreign Policy and U.S. Presidential Elections, 1952-1960.* New York: Franklin Watts, 1974.

Freeland, Richard M. *The Truman Doctrine and the Origins of McCarthyism: Foreign Policy, Domestic Politics and Internal Security 1946-1948.* New York: Knopf, 1972.

Fried, Richard M. *Men Against McCarthy.* New York: Columbia University Press, 1976.

Fried. *Nightmare in Red: The McCarthy Era in Perspective.* New York: Oxford University Press, 1990.

Griffith, Robert, and Athan G. Theoharis, eds. *The Specter: Original Essays on the Cold War and the Origins of McCarthyism.* New York: New Viewpoints, 1974.

Harper, Alan D. *The Politics of Loyalty: The White House and the Communist Issue, 1946-1952.* Westport, Conn.: Greenwood Press, 1969.

Haynes, John Earl. *Red Scare or Red Menace? American Communism and Anti-Communism in the Cold War Era.* Chicago: Ivan R. Dee, 1996.

Heale, M. J. *American Anticommunism: Combating the Enemy Within, 1830-1970.* Baltimore: Johns Hopkins University Press, 1990.

Hofstadter, Richard. *The Paranoid Style in American Politics, and Other Essays.* New York: Knopf, 1965.

Hogan, Michael J. *A Cross of Iron: Harry S. Truman and the Origins of the National Security State 1945-1954.* New York: Cambridge University Press, 1998.

Kutler, Stanley I. *The American Inquisition: Justice and Injustice in the Cold War.* New York: Hill & Wang, 1982.

Latham, Earl. *The Communist Controversy in Washington: From the New Deal to McCarthy.* Cambridge, Mass.: Harvard University Press, 1966.

May, Gary. *China Scapegoat: The Diplomatic Ordeal of John Carter Vincent.* Washington, D.C.: New Republic Books, 1979.

O'Brien, Michael. *McCarthy and McCarthyism in Wisconsin.* Columbia: University of Missouri Press, 1980.

O'Reilly, Kenneth. *Hoover and the Un-Americans: The FBI, HUAC, and the Red Menace.* Philadelphia: Temple University Press, 1983.

Oshinsky, David M. *A Conspiracy so Immense: The World of Joe McCarthy.* New York: Free Press, 1983.

Pells, Richard H. *The Liberal Mind in a Conservative Age: American Intellectuals in the 1940s and 1950s.* New York: Harper & Row, 1985.

Powers, Richard Gid. *Not Without Honor: The History of American Anti-Communism.* New York: Free Press, 1995.

Rogin, Michael Paul. *The Intellectuals and McCarthy: The Radical Specter.* Cambridge, Mass.: MIT Press, 1967.

Rovere, Richard. *Senator Joe McCarthy.* New York: Harcourt, Brace, 1959.

Schneir, Walter, and Miriam Schneir. *Invitation to an Inquest.* Garden City, N.Y.: Doubleday, 1965.

Stern, Paula. *Water's Edge: Domestic Politics and the Making of American Foreign Policy.* Westport, Conn.: Greenwood Press, 1979.

Theoharis, Athan G. *Seeds of Repression: Harry S Truman and the Origins of McCarthyism.* Chicago: Quadrangle, 1971.

Theoharis. *The Yalta Myths: An Issue in U.S. Politics, 1945-1955.* Columbia: University of Missouri Press, 1970.

Whitfield, Stephen J. *The Culture of the Cold War.* Baltimore: Johns Hopkins University Press, 1991.

8. The Soviet Union

Bialer, Seweryn. *The Soviet Paradox: External Expansion, Internal Decline.* New York: Knopf, 1986.

Courtois, Stéphane, and others. *Le livre noir du communisme: crimes, terreurs, et et répression.* Paris: Laffont, 1997. Translated by Jonathan Murphy as *The Black Book of Communism.* Cambridge, Mass.: Harvard University Press, 1999.

REFERENCES

Djilas, Milovan. *Conversations with Stalin,* translated by Michael B. Petrovich. New York: Harcourt, Brace & World, 1962.

Doder, Dusko. *Shadows and Whispers: Power Politics Inside the Kremlin from Brezhnev to Gorbachev.* New York: Random House, 1986.

Fischer, Louis. *Russia's Road from Peace to War: Soviet Foreign Relations, 1917–1941.* New York: Harper & Row, 1969.

Gati, Charles. *The Bloc That Failed: Soviet-East European Relations in Transition.* Bloomington: Indiana University Press, 1990.

Gelman, Harry. *The Brezhnev Politburo and the Decline of Détente.* Ithaca, N.Y.: Cornell University Press, 1984.

Hahn, Werner G. *Postwar Soviet Politics: The Fall of Zhdanov and the Defeat of Moderation, 1946–1953.* Ithaca, N.Y.: Cornell University Press, 1982.

Halloway, David. *Stalin and the Bomb: The Soviet Union and Atomic Energy, 1939–1956.* New Haven: Yale University Press, 1994.

Kennan, George F. "The Sources of Soviet Conduct," as "X." *Foreign Affairs,* 25 (July 1947): 566–582.

Kershaw, Ian, and Moshe Lewin. *Stalinism and Nazism: Dictatorships in Comparison.* New York: Cambridge University Press, 1997.

Laqueur, Walter. *Stalin: The Glasnost Revelations.* New York: Scribners, 1990.

Mastny, Vojtech. *The Cold War and Soviet Insecurity: The Stalin Years.* New York: Oxford University Press, 1996.

Mastny. *Russia's Road to the Cold War.* New York: Columbia University Press, 1979.

Ra'anan, Gavriel D. *International Policy Formation in the USSR: Factional "Debates" During the Zhdanovschina.* Hamden, Conn.: Archon, 1983.

Shulman, Marshall. *Stalin's Foreign Policy Reappraised.* Cambridge, Mass.: Harvard University Press, 1963.

Taubman, William. *Stalin's American Policy: From Entente to Detente to Cold War.* New York: Norton, 1982.

Tucker, Robert C. *Stalin in Power: The Revolution from Above, 1928–1941.* New York: Norton, 1990.

Ulam, Adam B. *Dangerous Relations: The Soviet Union in World Politics, 1970–1982.* New York: Oxford University Press, 1983.

Ulam. *Expansion and Coexistence: The History of Soviet Foreign Policy, 1917–1967.* New York: Praeger, 1968.

Ulam. *Expansion and Coexistence: Soviet Foreign Policy, 1917–1973,* second edition. New York: Praeger, 1974.

Ulam. *The Rivals: America and Russia Since World War II.* New York: Viking, 1971.

Uldrick, Teddy. *Diplomacy and Ideology: The Origins of Soviet Foreign Relations: 1917–1930.* London & Beverly Hills: Sage, 1979.

Zaloga, Steven J. *Target America: The Soviet Union and the Strategic Arms Race, 1945–1964.* Novato, Cal.: Presidio, 1993.

Zubok, Vladislav, and Constantine Pleshakov. *Inside the Kremlin's Cold War: From Stalin to Khrushchev.* Cambridge, Mass.: Harvard University Press, 1996.

9. Military Aspects of the Cold War

Allison, Graham T. *Essence of Decision: Explaining the Cuban Missile Crisis.* Boston: Little, Brown, 1971.

Ball, Desmond. *Politics and Force Levels: The Strategic Missile Program of the Kennedy Administration.* Berkeley: University of California Press, 1980.

Ball, and Jeffrey Richelson, eds. *Strategic Nuclear Targeting.* Ithaca, N.Y.: Cornell University Press, 1986.

Behead, Russell D., and William Christopher Hamel. "War for Peace: The Question of an American Preventive War against the Soviet Union, 1945–1955." *Diplomatic History,* 14 (Summer 1990): 367–384.

Beker, Avi. *Disarmament without Order: The Politics of Disarmament at the United Nations.* Westport, Conn.: Greenwood Press, 1985.

Betts, Richard K. *Nuclear Blackmail and Nuclear Balance.* Washington, D.C.: Brookings Institution, 1987.

Blight, James, and David Welch. *On the Brink: Americans and Soviets Reexamine the Cuban Missile Crisis.* New York: Hill & Wang, 1989.

Borowski, Harry R. *A Hollow Threat: Strategic Air Power and Containment before Korea.* Westport, Conn.: Greenwood Press, 1982.

Brodie, Bernard. *Strategy in the Missile Age,* revised edition. Princeton, N.J.: Princeton University Press, 1965.

Brodie, ed. *Absolute Weapon: Atomic Power and World Order.* New York: Harcourt, Brace, 1946.

Brown, Harold, ed. *The Strategic Defense Initiative: Shield or Snare?* Boulder, Colo.: Westview Press, 1987.

Brugioni, Dino. *Eyeball to Eyeball: The Inside Story of the Cuban Missile Crisis,* edited by Robert F. McCort. New York: Random House, 1991.

Bundy, McGeorge. *Danger and Survival.* New York: Random House, 1988.

Cillesen, Bret J. "Embracing the Bomb: Ethics, Morality, and Nuclear Deterrence in the US Air Force, 1945–1955." *Journal of Strategic Studies,* 21 (March 1998): 96–134.

Clausen, Peter A. *Nonproliferation and the National Interest.* New York: HarperCollins, 1993.

Craig, Campbell. *Destroying the Village: Eisenhower and Thermonuclear War.* New York: Columbia University Press, 1998.

Davis, Zachary S., and Benjamin Frankel, eds. *The Proliferation Puzzle: Why Nuclear Weapons Spread and What Results.* London & Portland, Ore.: Frank Cass, 1993.

Dockrill, Saki. *Eisenhower's New-Look National Security Policy, 1953–61.* New York: St. Martin's Press, 1996.

Dyson, Freeman. *Weapons and Hope.* New York: Harper & Row, 1984.

Feaver, Peter Douglas. *Guarding the Guardians: Civilian Control of Nuclear Weapons in the United States.* Ithaca, N.Y.: Cornell University Press, 1992.

Frankel, Benjamin, ed. *Opaque Nuclear Proliferation: Methodological and Policy Implications.* Portland, Ore.: Frank Cass, 1991.

Freedman, Lawrence. *The Evolution of Nuclear Strategy,* revised edition. New York: St. Martin's Press, 1989.

Freedman. *U.S. Intelligence and the Soviet Strategic Threat,* second edition. Princeton, N.J.: Princeton University Press, 1986.

Gervasi, Tom. *The Myth of Soviet Military Supremacy.* New York: Harper & Row, 1986.

Glaser, Charles L. *Analyzing Strategic Nuclear Policy.* Princeton, N.J.: Princeton University Press, 1990.

Goldfischer, David. *The Best Defense: Policy Alternatives for U.S. Nuclear Security from the 1950s to the 1990s.* Ithaca, N.Y.: Cornell University Press, 1993.

Gowing, Margaret M. *Britain and Atomic Energy, 1939–1945.* New York: St. Martin's Press, 1964.

Gowing, and Lorna Arnold. *Independence and Deterrence: Britain and Atomic Energy, 1945–1952.* 2 volumes. New York: St. Martin's Press, 1974.

Halperin, Morton H. *Limited War in the Nuclear Age.* New York: Wiley, 1963.

Herken, Gregg. *Counsels of War.* New York: Knopf, 1985.

Herken. *The Winning Weapon: The Atomic Bomb in the Cold War 1945–1950.* New York: Knopf, 1980.

Jervis, Robert. *The Illogic of American Nuclear Strategy.* Ithaca, N.Y.: Cornell University Press, 1984.

Jervis. *The Meaning of the Nuclear Revolution: Statecraft and the Prospect of Armageddon.* Ithaca, N.Y.: Cornell University Press, 1989.

Jervis, Richard Ned Lebow, and Janice Gross Stein, with contributions by Patrick M. Morgan and Jack L. Snyder. *Psychology and Deterrence.* Baltimore: Johns Hopkins University Press, 1985.

Kahn, Herman. *On Thermonuclear War.* Princeton, N.J.: Princeton University Press, 1960.

Kaufmann, William W., ed. *Military Policy and National Security.* Princeton, N.J.: Princeton University Press, 1956.

Kissinger, Henry. *Nuclear Weapons and Foreign Policy.* New York: Published for the Council on Foreign Relations by Harper, 1957.

Klare, Michael T. *Rogue States and Nuclear Outlaws: America's Search for a New Foreign Policy.* New York: Hill & Wang, 1995.

Koistinen, Paul A. C. *The Military-Industrial Complex: A Historical Perspective.* New York: Praeger, 1980.

Lakoff, Stanford A., and Herbert F. York. *A Shield in Space? Technology, Politics and the Strategic Defense Initiative: How the Reagan Administration Set Out to Make Nuclear Weapons "Impotent and Obsolete" and Succumbed to the Fallacy of the Last Move.* Berkeley: University of California Press, 1989.

Miller, Steven E., and Stephen Van Evera, eds. *The Star Wars Controversy: An International Security Reader.* Princeton, N.J.: Princeton University Press, 1986.

Orme, John David. *Deterrence, Reputation and Cold-War Cycles.* Houndmills, U.K.: Macmillan, 1992.

Postol, Theodore A. "Lessons of the Gulf War Experience with the Patriot." *International Security,* 16 (Winter 1991/1992): 119–171.

Quester, George H. *Nuclear Diplomacy: The First Twenty-five Years.* New York: Dunellen, 1970.

Roman, Peter J. "Curtis LeMay and the Origins of NATO Atomic Targeting." *Journal of Strategic Studies,* 16 (March 1993): 46–74.

Roman. *Eisenhower and the Missile Gap.* Ithaca, N.Y.: Cornell University Press, 1995.

Rosenberg, David Allen. "The Origins of Overkill: Nuclear Weapons and American Strategy, 1945–1960." *International Security,* 7 (Spring 1983): 3–71.

Sagan, Scott D. *The Limits of Safety: Organizations, Accidents, and Nuclear Weapons.* Princeton, N.J.: Princeton University Press, 1993.

Sagan. *Moving Targets: Nuclear Strategy and National Security.* Princeton, N.J.: Princeton University Press, 1989.

Sagan, and Kenneth N. Waltz. *The Spread of Nuclear Weapons: A Debate.* New York: Norton, 1995.

Schelling, Thomas C. *Arms and Influence.* New Haven: Yale University Press, 1966.

Schelling. *The Strategy of Conflict,* revised edition. Cambridge, Mass.: Harvard University Press, 1980.

Schwartz, Stephen I., ed. *Atomic Audit: The Costs and Consequences of U.S. Nuclear Weapons since 1940.* Washington, D.C.: Brookings Institution Press, 1998.

Sherwin, Martin. *A World Destroyed: The Atomic Bomb and the Grand Alliance.* New York: Knopf, 1975.

Snyder, Glenn. *Deterrence and Defense: Toward a Theory of National Security.* Princeton, N.J.: Princeton University Press, 1961.

Spector, Leonard S., and Jacqueline R. Smith. *Nuclear Ambitions: The Spread of Nuclear Weapons, 1989–1990.* Boulder, Colo.: Westview Press, 1990.

Stern, Paul C., and others, eds. *Perspectives on Deterrence.* New York: Oxford University Press, 1989.

Taylor, Maxwell D. *Swords and Plowshares.* New York: Norton, 1972.

Wenger, Andreas. *Living With Peril: Eisenhower, Kennedy, and Nuclear Weapons.* Lanham, Md.: Rowman & Littlefield, 1997.

Williams, Robert C., and Philip L. Cantelon, eds. *The American Atom: A Documentary History of Nuclear Policies from the Discovery of Fission to the Present, 1939–1984.* Philadelphia: University of Pennsylvania Press, 1984.

Zhang, Shu Guang. *Deterrence and Strategic Culture: Chinese-American Confrontations, 1949–1958.* Ithaca, N.Y.: Cornell University Press, 1992.

10. Intelligence, Spying, and Covert Action

Andrew, Christopher. *Secret Service: The Making of the British Intelligence Community.* London: Heinemann, 1985.

Borovik, Genrikh. *The Philby Files: The Secret Life of Master Spy Kim Philby,* edited by Phillip Knightley. Boston: Little, Brown, 1994.

Boyle, Andrew. *The Climate of Treason: Five Who Spied for Russia.* London: Hutchinson, 1979.

Cecil, Robert. *A Divided Life: A Personal Portrait of The Spy Donald Maclean.* New York: Morrow, 1989.

Colby, William. *Honorable Men: My Life in the CIA.* New York: Simon & Schuster, 1978.

Costello, John. *Mask of Treachery.* New York: Morrow, 1988.

Glees, Anthony. *The Secrets of the Service.* London: Cape, 1987; New York: Carroll & Graf, 1987.

Gordievsky, Oleg, and John Andrews. *KGB: The Inside Story.* New York: HarperCollins, 1990.

Grose, Peter. *Gentleman Spy: The Life of Allen Dulles.* Boston: Houghton Mifflin, 1994.

Hersh, Burton. *The Old Boys: The American Elite and the Origins of the CIA.* New York: Scribners, 1992.

Jeffreys-Jones, Rhodri. *The C.I.A. and American Democracy.* New Haven: Yale University Press, 1989.

Johnson, Loch K. *Secret Agencies: U.S. Intelligence in a Hostile World.* New Haven: Yale University Press, 1996.

Mangold, Tom. *Cold Warrior: James Jesus Angleton: The CIA's Master Spy Hunter.* New York: Simon & Schuster, 1991.

Page, Bruce, David Leitch, and Phillip Knightly. *Philby: The Spy Who Betrayed a Generation.* London: Deutsch, 1968. Republished as *The Philby Conspiracy.* Garden City, N.Y.: Doubleday, 1968.

Perry, Mark. *Eclipse: The Last Days of the CIA.* New York: Morrow, 1992.

Powers, Thomas. *The Man Who Kept the Secrets: Richard Helms and the CIA.* New York: Knopf, 1979.

Prados, John. *Presidents' Secret Wars: CIA and Pentagon Covert Operations from World War II Through the*

REFERENCES

Persian Gulf, revised and expanded edition. Chicago: Dee, 1996.

Prados. *The Soviet Estimate: U.S. Intelligence Analysis & Russian Military Strength.* New York: Dial, 1982.

Radosh, Ronald, and Joyce Milton. *The Rosenberg File: A Search for the Truth.* New York: Holt, Rinehart & Winston, 1983.

Seale, Patrick, and Maureen McConville. *Philby: The Long Road to Moscow.* London: Hamilton, 1973.

Steury, Donald P., ed. *Intentions and Capabilities: Estimates on Soviet Strategic Forces, 1950–1983.* Washington, D.C.: Center for the Study of Intelligence, 1996.

Sudoplatov, Pavel, and Anatoli Sudoplatov, with Jerrold L. and Leona P. Schecter. *Special Tasks: The Memoirs of an Unwanted Witness, A Soviet Spymaster,* updated edition. Boston: Little, Brown, 1995.

Treverton, Gregory F. *Covert Action: The Limits of Intervention in the Postwar World.* New York: Basic Books, 1987.

United States Senate, Select Committee to Study Governmental Operations with Respect to Intelligence Activities, *Alleged Assassination Plots Involving Foreign Leaders: an Interim Report of the Select Committee to Study Governmental Operations with Respect to Intelligence Activities, United States Senate: Together with Additional, Supplemental, and Separate Views,* foreword by Clark R. Mollenhoff, introduction by Senator Frank Church. Washington, D.C.: Government Printing Office, 1975.

United States Senate, Select Committee to Study Governmental Operations with Respect to Intelligence Activities. *Covert Action in Chile, 1963–1973: Staff Report of the Select Committee to Study Governmental Operations with Respect to Intelligence Activities, United States Senate.* Washington, D.C.: U.S. Government Printing Office, 1975.

Weinstein, Allen. *Perjury: The Hiss-Chambers Case,* updated edition. New York: Random House, 1997.

Weinstein, and Alexander Vassiliev. *The Haunted Wood: Soviet Espionage in America–the Stalin Era.* New York: Random House, 1999.

Williams, Robert Chadwell. *Klaus Fuchs, Atom Spy.* Cambridge, Mass.: Harvard University Press, 1987.

Wise, David, and Thomas B. Ross. *The Invisible Government.* New York: Random House, 1964.

Woodward, Bob. *Veil: The Secret Wars of the CIA, 1981–1987.* New York: Simon & Schuster, 1987.

References

REFERENCES

CONTRIBUTOR NOTES

BAUMAN, Margot: Doctoral candidate in history at George Washington University.

BELRHITI, Talal: Editorial assistant, *Security Studies*.

CHAFETZ, Glenn R.: Policy planner in the Bureau of Political-Military Affairs at the Department of State; author of *Gorbachev, Reform, and the Brezhnev Doctrine: Soviet Policy Toward Eastern Europe, 1985–1990* (1993); co-editor, with Michael Spirtas and Benjamin Frankel, of *The Origins of National Interests* (1999).

COHEN, Barak: Independent scholar.

COPELAND, Dale C.: Assistant professor in the Department of Government and Foreign Affairs, University of Virginia; author of *Anticipating Power: Dynamic Realism and the Origins of Major War* (forthcoming, 2000).

CRAIG, Campbell: Lecturer in American history and foreign policy at the University of Canterbury, New Zealand; author of *Destroying the Village: Eisenhower and Thermonuclear War* (1998).

DRESEN, Joseph: Program assistant at the Kennan Institute, Woodrow Wilson Center, Washington, D.C.

DUECK, Colin: Doctoral candidate in political science at Princeton University.

FRANKEL, Benjamin: Founder and editor of *Security Studies;* editor of *Roots of Realism* (1998); *Realism: Restatements and Renewal* (1996); and co-editor of *The Origins of National Interests: Identity and State's Foreign Policies.*

GARTHOFF, Raymond L.: Senior fellow, retired, at the Brookings Institution; his books include *The Great Transition: American-Soviet Relations and the End of the Cold War* (1994), *Détente and Confrontation: American-Soviet Relations from Nixon to Reagan,* revised edition (1994), and *Reflections on the Cuban Missile Crisis* (1989).

GOLDFISCHER, David: Associate professor of international relations at the University of Denver; author of *The Best Defense: Policy Alternatives for U.S. Nuclear Security from the 1950s to the 1990s* (1993).

HAMPTON, Mary: Associate professor of political science at the University of Utah; author of *The Wilsonian Impulse: U.S. Foreign Policy, the Alliance, and German Unification* (1996); and co-editor, with Christian Soe, of *Between Bonn and Berlin: German Politics Adrift?* (forthcoming, 1999).

HIXSON, Walter L.: Professor of history and chair of the Department of History, University of Akron; author of *Parting the Curtain: Propaganda, Culture, and the Cold War* (1996); and *George F. Kennan, Cold War Iconoclast* (1989).

JOHNSON, Loch K.: Regents Professor of political science at the University of Georgia; author of *Secret Agencies: U.S. Intelligence in a Hostile World* (1996).

KASSAYE, Jomo Z.: Research assistant at the Henry L. Stimson Center, Washington, D.C.

KRAMER, Mark: Director of the Harvard Project on Cold War Studies; senior associate at the Davis Center for Russian Studies, Harvard University; and editor of the *Journal of Cold War Studies.*

LALLY, Grant M.: Attorney with Lally & Lally, Mineola, New York.

MADDOCK, Shane J.: Professor in the Department of Humanities at the U.S. Coast Guard Academy.

ORME, John D.: Professor of politics at Oglethorpe University; author of *Deterrence, Reputation, and Cold War Cycles* (1992) and *Political Instability and American Foreign Policy: The Middle Options* (1989).

PERLMUTTER, Amos: Professor of government at American University, Washington D.C.; his books include *Making the World Safe for Democracy: A Century of Wilsonianism and Its Totalitarian Challengers* (1997), *FDR & Stalin: A Not So Grand Alliance, 1943–1945* (1993), and *Egypt: The Praetorian State* (1974).

POLLACK, Kenneth M.: Senior Research Professor at the National Defense University and Director for Iran-Iraq Affairs for the National Security Council; co-author, with Daniel Byman and Gideon Rose, of "The Rollback Fantasy," *Foreign Affairs* (January-February 1999).

QUENOY, Paul du: Doctoral candidate in history at George Washington University.

RESENDE-SANTOS, João: Lecturer in political science at the University of Pennsylvania; author of "Anarchy and the Emulation of Military Systems: Military Organization and Technology in South America, 1870–1914," in *Realism: Restatements and Renewal* (1996), edited by Benjamin Frankel.

REYNOLDS, James: Independent scholar.

ROMAN, Peter J.: Associate professor of political science at Duquesne University; author of *Eisenhower and the Missile Gap* (1995).

SENG, Jordan: Postdoctoral fellow at the John M. Olin Institute for Strategic Studies, Harvard University; author of "Peeking Behind the Veil: Studying the Opaque History of Israel's Nuclear Command and Control," *Security Studies* 9 (forthcoming, Winter 2000); and "Less is More: Command and Control Advantages of Minor Nuclear States," *Security Studies* 6 (Summer 1997).

SLATER, Jerome: Professor of political science at the State University of New York, Buffalo; author of *Intervention and Negotiation: The United States and the Dominican Republic* (1970); author of "The Domino Theory and International Politics: The Case of Vietnam," *Security Studies* 3 (Winter 1993–1994); and "McNamara's Failures—and Ours: Vietnam's Unlearned Lessons," *Security Studies* 6 (Autumn 1996).

SOARES, John A., Jr.: Doctoral candidate in history at George Washington University.

SPIRTAS, Michael: Research fellow at The Center for National Policy and fellow at U.S. CREST; co-editor, with Glenn Chafetz and Benjamin Frankel, *The Origins of National Interests* (1999).

TRACHTENBERG, Marc: Professor of history at the University of Pennsylvania; his books include *A Constructed Peace: The Making of the European Settlement, 1945–1963* (1999); and *History and Strategy* (1991).

VALENTINO, Benjamin A.: Doctoral candidate in political science at the Massachusetts Institute of Technology; author of "Final Solutions: The Causes of Mass Killing and Genocide," *Security Studies* 8 (Summer 1999).

WILLIAMS, Robert E.: Professor of political science at Pepperdine University.

WIRTZ, James J.: Associate professor in the Department of National Security Affairs, Naval Postgraduate School; author of *The Tet Offensive* (1991); and co-editor, with T.V. Paul and Richard J. Harknett, *The Absolute Weapon Revisited: Nuclear Arms and the Emerging International Order* (1998).

ZHANG, Ming: Director of the Asia Research Institute (ARI); his books include *A Triad of Another Kind: The United States, China, and Japan* (1999); and *China's Changing Nuclear Posture* (1999).

INDEX

Bevin, Ernest 175
Bidault, Georges 175, 273
Bin Laden, Osama 16, 163, 217
Bishop, Maurice 54
Bison jet bombers 189
Blainey, Geoffrey 251
Blunt, Anthony 243, 245
Bogan, Gerald F. 8
Bohlen, Charles E. 160, 175
Bohr, Niels 241–242, 247–248
Boland Amendments 54
Bolivia 95
    communist guerrilla uprising of 1967 126
    in Chaco War 125
    land reform 21, 126
    nationalization of American property 126
    workers' uprising of 1952 125
Bolshevik Revolution (1917) 73
Bomber gap 188–194
Bonaparte, Napoleon 167, 239
Bonsal, Philip 94
Bosch Gavíño, Juan 24, 71
Bourguiba, Habib 314
Bradley, Omar N. 6
Brandt, Willy 35, 185
Brazil 20, 52
    communist guerilla movements 125
    coup of 1964 15, 25
    human rights record 143
    in War of the Triple Alliance 125
    influenc of Alliance for Progress 25
    nuclear proliferation 223
    nuclear–weapons development 219, 223
    reformist government of the 1950s 20
    U.S. intervention in 1964 15
Brezhnev, Leonid I. 104, 151, 153, 197
Brezhnev Doctrine 10–11
Bricker, John W. 306
British Guiana
    border dispute with Venezuela (1895) 125
    CIA operations in 24
    U.S. interventions (1953–1964) 15
Brodie, Bernard 165
Brown, Harold 166
Brown, Seyom 45
Brussels Treaty (1948) 208
Brzezinski, Zbigniew 135, 143, 146
Bukovsky, Vladimir 146
Bulgaria 107, 110, 294, 303
Bullitt, William C. 235, 238
Bundy, McGeorge 29, 120, 171, 294
Burgess, Guy 243, 245
Burke, Arleigh A. 6
Burma 15
Burnham, Forbes 24
Burns, Walter 237
Bush, George H. W., 29, 101, 104, 191
Bush administration
    nuclear-nonproliferation policy 217, 224
    policy on Afghanistan 14–16
    policy on Pakistan 15
Bush, Vannevar 28
Butler, George Lee 232
Byrnes, James F. 28, 31, 263, 304

C

Cairncross, John 243–245
Cambodia 40–42, 44–47, 145, 289, 299
    as a colony of France 290
    Khmer Rouge movement 15
    spread of communism 297
    U.S. bombing of 45, 183, 291
    U.S. invasion of 40–47, 291
Camp David agreement (1978) 159, 317
Canada 30–31
    charter member of NATO 208
    criticism of Libertad Act 98

Cuban investment 97
    nuclear weapons 28
Carter, Jimmy 48–49, 51–52, 101,106, 141, 317
    human rights as foreign policy 141
    mediator between Egypt and Israel 159
    policy toward Pakistani nuclear program 223
    response to Soviet invasion of Afghanistan 11
    suspends aid to Pakistan 218
    withdrawal of SALT II Treaty 10, 12
Carter administration 50
    Central America policy 54
    containment policy 13
    détente 102
    foreign policy 52, 57
    human rights policy 52, 140–143, 145–146
    limited-nuclear-war doctrine 171
    nuclear-nonproliferation policy 216
    policy on Afgahnistan 10, 12, 15–16
    policy on Pakistan 15
    Presidential Directive (PD) 59 171
Casey, William J. 50–51, 54
Castelo Branco, Humberto de Alencar 25
Castillo Armas, Carlos 123, 126
Castro Ruz, Fidel 49, 89, 91–94, 96, 121, 125, 283
    alliance with Soviet Union 121
    Cuban revolution 17, 275
    dispatches troops to Third World countries 142
    Kennedy administration attempts against 24
    relations with Chile 124
    support for communist uprising in Bolivia 126
Castro Ruz, Raúl 93
Catholic Church 271, 305
Ceausescu, Nicolae 110
Central America 48–57
Central Intelligence Agency (CIA) 49, 66–69, 92, 94,
      119, 191, 196, 211, 263, 292
    alleged reliance on drug traffickers 56
    anti-Sandanista forces 54
    Covert Action Staff 68
    covert operations 24, 26, 64–72, 131
    creation 64, 74
    Elimination by Illumination 68
    moles 65
    Operation CHAOS 66
    Operations Directorate 66
    plots to overthrow Castro 275
    role in Chilean presidential elections 124
    role in Guatemala coup of 1954 123
    spying on the Soviet Union 190–192
Chaco War (1932–1935) 125
Chernenko, Konstantin 14, 197
Chiang Kai-shek 58–59, 61, 86, 265–268, 275, 303–
      304
Chile 52, 127, 140, 152
    access to Import-Export Bank 53
    Christian Democrats 127
    coup of 1973 124, 127–128
    economy in1972–1973 124
    elections of 1970 123
    elections of 1973 124, 128
    human-rights record 143
    land reform 127
    nationalization of businesses 127
    relations with Cuba 124, 128
    relations with North Korea 124
    relations with North Vietnam 124
    strikes in 1972 and 1973 124, 127
    U.S. intervention (1973) 15, 123–133
China 41, 44, 54, 59, 86–87, 89, 91, 141, 145, 266–267,
      277, 287–288, 292
    attacks on Quemoy and Matsu 265–270, 275
    civil war 110, 285
    communist revolution (1949) 83, 182, 184, 294
    development pf nuclear weapons 201–202, 224,
      239
    human-rights record 143
    nuclear proliferation 222–224
    relations with Soviet Union 73, 141, 184–185,

274
    revolt (1953) 254
    strategic importance 109
ECLA. *See* Economic Commission for Latin America
Economic Commission for Latin America (ECLA) 20,
    22
Ecuador
    military coups 24
    U.S. intervention (1960-1963) 15
Eden, Anthony 272, 280
Egypt 273
    conflict with Israel 156, 159, 277-283, 308-318
    Czech arms deal 281
    in the Suez War 277-283
    fundamentalist movements 163
    in the nonaligned movement 110
    in the Yom Kippur War 308-318
    weapons development 219, 239
    revolution 158
    relations with Soviet Union 161-162
    surface-to-air missiles (SAMs) 309, 311
    violation of the 1970 cease-fire agreement 316
Eisenhower, Dwight D. 35, 64, 71, 92, 102, 169, 193,
    210-215, 274, 292, 297, 306
    as NATO supreme commander 208
    1952 presidential campaign 274
    U.S. military capabilities 188
    views on Guatemala 123, 129
    views on the arms race 182
    views on the use of nuclear weapons 168, 235-
    237
    views on the Yalta Agreement 301
Eisenhower administration 49, 66, 94, 110, 117, 151,
    194, 281, 294
    atomic diplomacy 211, 213, 267
    Atoms for Peace policy 216-217, 221
    brinkmanship strategy 270
    Central America policies 20, 49, 126
    China policy 267-268, 275
    civil liberties violations 80
    containment policy 184
    East Germany policy 271
    Hungary policy 271, 275-276
    Israel policy 162
    Korea policy 271, 275
    massive retaliationpolicy 192, 211, 213, 215, 268
    Middle East policy 161, 283
    military capabilities 188, 191
    military spending 69, 192
    New Look defense policy 115, 189, 210-215, 266
    nuclear weapons buildup 213, 215
    nuclear weapons nonproliferation 283
    Operation Solarium 272
    Operation Success 126
    Poland policy 271, 275
    rejection of arms control 230
    reliance on CIA 64
    rollback policy 271-276
    Taiwan policy 266, 268, 270
    U-2 flights 190
    Vietnam policy 293, 297
Eisenhower Doctrine 280, 282
El Salvador 48-56, 94, 141
    CIA covert operations 26
    relations with Nicaragua 50, 54
    U.S. role in 15
Elimination by Illumination 68
Erhard, Ludwig 256
Escalation dominance 118
Estonia 107
Ethiopia 95-96, 151
European Community (EC) 108
European Defense Community (EDC) 208-209
European Economic Community (EEC) 283
European Free Trade Association (EFTA) 108
European Recovery Plan. *See* Marshall Plan.
European Union 98, 209
Export-Import Bank 59

F

Faisal II 282
Falkland Islands War 56
Farabundo Martí National Liberation Front
    (FMLN) 50-51
Farmer, Fyke 263
Farouk I 277
FBI. *See* Federal Bureau of Investigation.
Feaver, Peter 215
Federal Bureau of Investigation (FBI) 62, 76-77, 292
Federal Republic of Germany. *See* West Germany.
Feklisov, Aleksandr 242
Fermi, Enrico 241-242, 247-248
Finland 107, 110, 112, 151
Finlandization 107-113
First-strike theory 234-240
First World War 88, 112, 149, 205, 284, 286
Fishlow, Albert 25
Flerov, Georgy N. 244-248
Flexible Response 115-122
FLN. *See* Front de Libération Nationale.
FMLN. *See* Farabundo Martí National Liberation
    Front.
Ford, Gerald R. 52, 101, 141
Ford administration
    and détente 102, 106
    nuclear nonproliferation policy 216, 223
    policy toward Pakistani nuclear program 223
Formosa Doctrine 265, 268
Forrestal, James V. 4, 5, 159
France 34, 151, 202, 278, 280, 283, 289, 293, 300-301,
    305
    as a colonial power 259, 297
    communist party 112, 208, 174, 176, 254
    Fifth Republic 283
    Fourth Republic 283
    in the aftermath of Second World War 173, 177,
    285
    involvement with Indochina 213, 273, 290
    nuclear deterrence 201
    nuclear nonproliferation 224
    nuclear weapons program 202, 216, 222
    rejection of European Defense Community 209
    Suez Crisis 192, 277
    UN Security Council membership 300
    U.S. encouragement to support Israel 162
    withdrawal of troops from NATO command 185
Franco, Francisco 209
Franks, Oliver 272
Free Officers Committee 277
Frei Montalva, Eduardo 124, 127
Frei Ruiz-Tagle, Edwardo 128
Friedrich, Carl 135
Fromm, Erich 171
Front de Libération Nationale (FLN) 277, 281, 296
Fuchs, Klaus, 241-249

G

Gaddis, John Lewis 83, 154, 252, 256, 273
Gadhafi, Mu'ammar 159, 223, 314
Gaither report 190, 193, 194, 213
Galtieri, Leopoldo 56
Galvin, John 119
Gamasy, 'Abd al-Ghani al- 309, 313
Gates, Thomas 188
Gati, Charles 108, 110
Gaulle, Charles de 283
Gaza Strip 156
Geneva Accords of 1954 41, 290, 297-298
Geneva Convention 170
German Democratic Republic. *See* East Germany.
Germany 85-86, 89, 110, 112-113, 135-137, 149, 154,
    176, 245, 252, 263, 285, 288, 293, 300, 305
    aftermath of Second World War 173, 206
    atomic research 245-246
    discussion of postwar status at Tehran
    Conference 259

INDEX

INDEX